Ecology and Conservation of Forest Birds

D1548519

Ecology and Conservation of Forest Birds is a unique review of the current understanding of the relationships between forest birds and their changing environments. Large ecological changes are being driven by forest management, climate change, introduced pests and pathogens, abiotic disturbances, and overbrowsing. Many forest bird species have suffered population declines, with the situation being particularly severe for birds dependent on attributes such as dead wood, old trees and structurally complex forests. With a focus on the non-tropical parts of the northern hemisphere, the text addresses the fundamental evolutionary and ecological aspects of forest birds using original data analyses and synthesising reviews. The characteristics of bird assemblages and their habitats in different European forest types are explored, together with the macroecological patterns of bird diversity and conservation issues. The book provides a valuable reference for ecologists, ornithologists, conservation professionals, forest industry employees, and those interested in birds and nature.

Grzegorz Mikusiński is an ecologist affiliated with the Forest Faculty of the Swedish University of Agricultural Sciences (SLU) where he also teaches ecology at the School for Forest Management. His research interests centre on conservation and management of forest biodiversity, with a particular focus on forest birds and their habitat.

Jean-Michel Roberge is a conservation specialist at the Swedish Forest Agency and adjunct lecturer at the Swedish University of Agricultural Sciences. He has a special interest in avian ecology and biodiversity studies in northern forests.

Robert J. Fuller is an emeritus Research Fellow at the British Trust for Ornithology and an Honorary Professor at the University of East Anglia. His central interests focus on temperate forest biodiversity, especially birds. The effects of forest management, the impacts of deer browsing and conservation strategies form the core of his work. He is author of *Bird Life of Woodland and Forest* (1995) and editor of *Birds and Habitat: Relationships in Changing Landscapes* (2012), both published by Cambridge University Press.

ECOLOGY, BIODIVERSITY AND CONSERVATION

The world's biological diversity faces unprecedented threats. The urgent challenge facing the concerned biologist is to understand ecological processes well enough to maintain their functioning in the face of the pressures resulting from human population growth. Those concerned with the conservation of biodiversity and with restoration also need to be acquainted with the political, social, historical, economic and legal frameworks within which ecological and conservation practice must be developed. The new Ecology, Biodiversity and Conservation series will present balanced, comprehensive, up-to-date and critical reviews of selected topics within the sciences of ecology and conservation biology, both botanical and zoological, and both 'pure' and 'applied'. It is aimed at advanced final-year undergraduates, graduate students, researchers and university teachers, as well as ecologists and conservationists in industry, government and the voluntary sector. The series encompasses a wide range of approaches and scales (spatial, temporal and taxonomic), including quantitative, theoretical, population, community, ecosystem, landscape, historical, experimental, behavioural and evolutionary studies. The emphasis is on science related to the real world of plants and animals rather than on purely theoretical abstractions and mathematical models. Books in this series will, wherever possible, consider issues from a broad perspective. Some books will challenge existing paradigms and present new ecological concepts, empirical or theoretical models, and testable hypotheses. Other books will explore new approaches and present syntheses on topics of ecological importance.

Ecology and Control of Introduced Plants
Judith H. Myers and Dawn Bazely

Invertebrate Conservation and Agricultural Ecosystems
T. R. New

Risks and Decisions for Conservation and Environmental Management
Mark Burgman

Ecology and Conservation of Forest Birds

Edited by

GRZEGORZ MIKUSIŃSKI
Swedish University of Agricultural Sciences

JEAN-MICHEL ROBERGE
Swedish University of Agricultural Sciences and Swedish Forest Agency

ROBERT J. FULLER
British Trust for Ornithology

CAMBRIDGE
UNIVERSITY PRESS

CAMBRIDGE
UNIVERSITY PRESS

University Printing House, Cambridge CB2 8BS, United Kingdom

One Liberty Plaza, 20th Floor, New York, NY 10006, USA

477 Williamstown Road, Port Melbourne, VIC 3207, Australia

314–321, 3rd Floor, Plot 3, Splendor Forum, Jasola District Centre, New Delhi – 110025, India

79 Anson Road, #06–04/06, Singapore 079906

Cambridge University Press is part of the University of Cambridge.

It furthers the University's mission by disseminating knowledge in the pursuit of
education, learning, and research at the highest international levels of excellence.

www.cambridge.org
Information on this title: www.cambridge.org/9781107072138
DOI: 10.1017/9781139680363

First published 2018

Printed in the United Kingdom by TJ International Ltd. Padstow Cornwall

A catalogue record for this publication is available from the British Library.

Library of Congress Cataloging-in-Publication Data
Names: Mikusiński, Grzegorz, editor. | Roberge, Jean-Michel, editor. | Fuller, Robert J., editor.
Title: Ecology and conservation of forest birds / edited by Grzegorz Mikusiński, Swedish University
    of Agricultural Sciences, Jean-Michel Roberge, Swedish University of Agricultural Sciences and
    Swedish Forest Agency, Robert J. Fuller, British Trust for Ornithology.
Description: New York, NY : Cambridge University Press, 2017. | Includes bibliographical
    references and index.
Identifiers: LCCN 2017042297 | ISBN 9781107072138 (Hardback : alk. paper)
Subjects: LCSH: Forest birds–Ecology. | Forest birds–Conservation.
Classification: LCC QL677.79.F67 E26 2017 | DDC 333.95/816–dc23 LC record available
    at https://lccn.loc.gov/2017042297

ISBN 978-1-107-07213-8 Hardback
ISBN 978-1-107-42072-4 Paperback

Contents

Acknowledgements

Many people and several organisations have participated in various ways in the preparation of this book. First, we would like to thank all the authors for their outstanding contributions and for their patience. We are also grateful to all the reviewers who helped us improve the quality of the book; at least two independent reviews were received for each chapter. Michael Usher, Dominic Lewis, Jade Scard, Natasha Wheelan and Renee Duncan-Mestel at Cambridge University Press gave continuous encouragement and support. Kathy Martin very kindly took editorial responsibility for the final chapter.

We are very grateful to Sabita Gurung for drawing the bird vignettes located at the end of each chapter. We also thank Adam Wajrak for allowing us to use his beautiful picture of the three-toed woodpecker on the front cover of the book.

GM thanks students of forest management at the Swedish University of Agricultural Sciences (SLU) for asking him in 2009 to recommend an informative book on the ecology and conservation of forest birds – the question generated the initial idea for this book. He is very grateful to the other editors for their unceasing support, knowledge, enthusiasm, friendship and hard work. Several people and organisations generously provided him with inspiring working environments: Katrin Böhning-Gaese at the Biodiversity and Climate Research Centre (BiK-F), Zenon Rodhe at the Ornithological Station of the Polish Academy of Sciences and Lluís Brotons at the CTFC Forest Sciences Centre of Catalonia. He expresses his gratitude to the heads of the Department of Ecology and the School for Forest Management at SLU (Åsa Berggren, Anna Lundhagen, Sönke Eggers, Torgny Söderman and Staffan Stenhag) for their support. He is also grateful to Per Angelstam for introducing him to forest bird ecology in the 1990s. Finally, he thanks his wife, Ela, family and friends for their encouragement.

JMR is thankful to GM for his excellent editorial leadership, RJF for sharing his valuable insights about avian ecology and his wife, Cornelia, for support and encouragement during the work with this book. He is also grateful to the Kempe Foundation for financial support.

RJF greatly appreciates the invitation from the other editors to join them in a most enjoyable partnership and for giving him the opportunity to learn so much more about forest birds. He thanks Angela for her patience and understanding.

Contributors

RAPHAËL ARLETTAZ
Division of Conservation Biology, Institute of Ecology and Evolution, University of Bern, Switzerland and Swiss Ornithological Institute, Valais Field Station, Sion, Switzerland

JACQUES BLONDEL
Centre for Functional and Evolutionary Ecology CEFE-CNRS, UMR 5175, Montpellier, France

KURT BOLLMANN
Swiss Federal Institute for Forest, Snow and Landscape Research WSL, Birmensdorf, Switzerland

VERONIKA BRAUNISCH
Forest Research Institute of Baden-Wurttemberg (FVA), Freiburg, Germany and Conservation Biology, Institute of Ecology and Evolution, University of Bern, Switzerland

LLUÍS BROTONS
InForest JRU (CTFC-CREAF), Solsona, Spain and CSIC and CREAF, Cerdanyola del Vallès, Spain

JOHN CALLADINE
British Trust for Ornithology, University of Stirling, Scotland

MARIO DÍAZ
Department of Biogeography and Global Change, National Museum of Natural Sciences (BGC-MNCN-CSIC), Madrid, Spain

MARTIN FLADE
Department of Large Protected Areas and Regional Development, Brandenburg State Agency for Environment, Eberswalde, Germany

RUUD FOPPEN
Sovon, Dutch Centre for Field Ornithology, Nijmegen, Netherlands and Radboud University, Department of Animal Ecology and Physiology, Nijmegen, Netherlands

ROBERT J. FULLER
British Trust for Ornithology, Thetford, United Kingdom and School of Environmental Sciences, University of East Anglia, Norwich, United Kingdom

SERGI HERRANDO
Catalan Ornithological Institute/European Bird Census Council, Natural History Museum of Barcelona, Spain and CREAF, Cerdanyola del Vallès, Spain

DAVID JARDINE
Forestry Commission Scotland, Whitegates, Lochgilphead, Argyll, Scotland

VASSILIKI KATI
Department of Biological Applications and Technology, University of Ioannina, Greece

ALEKSI LEHIKOINEN
The Helsinki Lab of Ornithology, Finnish Museum of Natural History, University of Helsinki, Finland

KATHY MARTIN
Department of Forest and Conservation Sciences, University of British Columbia, Vancouver, Canada

GRZEGORZ MIKUSIŃSKI
Grimsö Wildlife Research Station, Department of Ecology, Swedish University of Agricultural Sciences (SLU), Riddarhyttan, Sweden and School for Forest Management, Swedish University of Agricultural Sciences (SLU), Skinnkatteberg, Sweden

PIERRE MOLLET
Swiss Ornithological Institute, Sempach, Switzerland

MIKKO MÖNKKÖNEN
Department of Biological and Environmental Sciences, University of Jyvaskyla, Finland

LUÍS REINO
CIBIO/InBIO - Research Centre in Biodiversity and Genetic Resources, University of Porto, Vairão, Portugal

JEAN-MICHEL ROBERGE
Department of Wildlife, Fish and Environmental Studies, Swedish University of Agricultural Sciences (SLU), Umeå, Sweden and Swedish Forest Agency (Skogsstyrelsen), Umeå, Sweden

HUGO ROBLES
Evolutionary Biology Group (GIBE), Faculty of Sciences, University of A Coruña, Spain and Evolutionary Ecology Group (EVECO), Department of Biology, University of Antwerp, Wilrijk, Belgium

CLÉLIA SIRAMI
Dynafor, Université de Toulouse, INRA, INPT, INPT – EI PURPAN, Castanet-Tolosan, France

ILSE STORCH
Chair of Wildlife Ecology and Management, University of Freiburg, Germany

MARC-ANDRÉ VILLARD
Université du Québec à Rimouski, Quebec, Canada

DANI VILLERO
InForest JRU (CTFC-CREAF), Solsona, Spain

RAIMO VIRKKALA
Biodiversity Centre, Finnish Environment Institute (SYKE), Helsinki, Finland

TOMASZ WESOŁOWSKI
Laboratory of Forest Biology, Wrocław University, Poland

MARK WILSON
British Trust for Ornithology, University of Stirling, Scotland

1 · *Introduction*

GRZEGORZ MIKUSIŃSKI, JEAN-MICHEL
ROBERGE AND ROBERT J. FULLER

1.1 Birds and Forests

Throughout the world, in most habitats, birds are highly noticeable animals manifesting diverse colorations, sounds, shapes and motions. With more than 10,000 species and more than 240 families, these conspicuous creatures have fascinated people for centuries and have a distinctive cultural position in many human societies (Collar *et al.* 2007; Cocker & Tipping 2013; del Hoyo & Collar 2014, 2016; Winkler *et al.* 2015). Scientifically, especially over the last 50 years, studies on birds have played an important part in improving our understanding of environmental processes, including some with implications for human safety, such as issues linked to the unimpeded use of certain pesticides (Newton 1995). But why write a book specifically about birds that inhabit forests?

The diversity of bird life found within forests is of incalculable value from cultural, aesthetic and scientific perspectives. Yet these environments, and the bird life they support, have frequently been shaped by human activities and are vulnerable to shifts in forest management, a changed climate and other pressures, such as introduced pathogens. Changes are to be expected in the future, with consequences for biodiversity and humans (Rudel *et al.* 2005). At the same time, there are many positive messages and opportunities for protecting and enhancing wildlife within forests. This book aims to explore these interactions between humans, forests and birds from diverse, but essentially scientific, standpoints.

Globally, forests cover about 30% of the terrestrial surface, but account for some 75% of the gross primary production of the biosphere and contain 80% of the plant biomass (Kindermann *et al.* 2008; Beer *et al.* 2010; Pan *et al.* 2013). Over large tracts of the planet, forests are the dominant ecosystem. They harbour the majority of terrestrial species on Earth. Forests deliver valuable ecosystem goods and services to humanity, including food, timber, fibre, medicine, clean water and aesthetic and spiritual values, and play a crucial role in climate moderation (Millennium Ecosystem Assessment 2005; McKinley *et al.* 2011). Forests have also been crucial for the development of human societies in general (Perlin 2005).

The majority of all bird species (77%) use forest as their habitat, but not necessarily as their main habitat (BirdLife International 2017). Due to their structural and compositional diversity and complexity, forest ecosystems support particularly rich bird communities. Many forest birds are intimately linked to trees that may serve as nesting sites and foraging substrates and provide shelter. Due to forest loss, fragmentation and changes to internal forest ecosystem attributes, many specialised forest bird species have become threatened or have suffered population declines. The negative effects have been particularly severe for birds dependent on attributes such as dead wood, old trees and structurally complex forests (e.g., Imbeau *et al.* 2001; Mikusiński *et al.* 2001; Fuller *et al.* 2007; Roberge *et al.* 2008; Holt *et al.* 2011; Chollet & Martin 2013).

Research efforts to unravel relationships between human actions and forest birds have been impressive during recent decades, resulting in large numbers of research papers from around the world. These encompass global, regional, landscape and forest stand scales (e.g., Sallabanks *et al.* 2000; Schieck & Song 2006; Forsman *et al.* 2010; Hewson *et al.* 2011). The huge body of knowledge on forest birds has inspired and informed many different conservation actions. The book edited by Allen Keast (1990), *Biogeography and Ecology of Forest Bird Communities*, was a landmark ecological review with a global scope. A semi-popular book was produced a few years later, but with a much narrower western European outlook (Fuller 1995). Since 1996, more than 3,000 scientific papers containing the words 'bird' and 'forest' in their titles have been published (Web of Science, accessed 23 May 2017). Despite much fresh research and conservation effort since the mid-1990s, no book of continental or multicontinental scope devoted mainly to forest birds has been published recently. Therefore, the time seems right for a synthesis of knowledge in the fields of forest bird ecology and conservation.

It has become increasingly evident that knowledge of birds does not derive solely from professional ornithologists and ecologists. Much important information currently available, especially concerning bird distributions and population trends, has been contributed by large numbers of skilled birdwatchers (Hagemeijer & Blair 1997;

Greenwood 2007; Gregory *et al.* 2007; Sullivan *et al.* 2009; Jiguet *et al.* 2012). A citizen-based bird observation network linked to academic research is therefore a unique interface where science interacts with broader society, offering huge potential for reciprocal learning. Scientists in ornithology and avian ecology therefore have a responsibility to create feedback systems that inform conservation practitioners, land managers and the interested public about key research findings.

1.2 Contents and Structure of the Book

As a whole, this book is limited to birds and forests of the non-tropical parts of the Northern Hemisphere. Its main geographic focus is Europe: most chapters concentrate on this continent, while being informed by relevant research from North America and Asia. However, some chapters pertaining to general ecological and evolutionary issues build equally upon European and North American research.

The book consists of 13 thematic chapters organised in three parts.

The first part contains three chapters covering some fundamental evolutionary and ecological aspects. Chapter 2 sets the scene by providing a major overview of the evolutionary background of forest birds in the Northern Hemisphere. Chapters 3 and 4 deal with ecological adaptations of forest birds in Europe and North America, one of them exclusively devoted to hole-nesting birds, which form a distinctive component of forest bird assemblages.

Part II starts with Chapter 5, which documents the large-scale patterns in the richness and composition of forest birds across Europe. Chapters 6–9 are concerned with the characteristics of bird assemblages and their habitats in different European forest types, including the factors influencing finer-scale variation, together with the various pressures they face. The different biogeographical zones of Europe differ strikingly in terms of biophysical conditions that influence forests and bird communities. Hence, these topics are addressed in four chapters that take a broad 'ecoregional' approach. We recognise that any classification of forests will have its limitations; there are many gradients and 'grey areas', making it difficult to adopt an approach that will be universally acceptable. Variations in bird communities do not match comfortably with strict botanical classifications of forest types, partly because successional stage and vegetation structure are more important than exact plant composition in determining habitat quality for many birds. Therefore, we feel it appropriate to review forest bird assemblages within a broader ecoregional framework. Chapter 10 is slightly different, in that it considers birds in man-made plantations predominantly composed of non-native trees; these form a distinctive but relatively novel set of habitats for forest birds, though in many cases their bird communities show considerable similarity with those in semi-natural forest stands.

While the chapters in Part II consider conservation topics that are relevant to specific regions or types of forest, Chapters 11–14 in Part III broaden the discussion of conservation and management. Knowledge of population trends is vital in order to understand temporal community dynamics and identify which species are in greatest need of research and conservation attention. Levels of exploitation and persecution of forest birds may be lower now than in historic times, but the topic remains highly relevant to the conservation of some forest bird species. Much recent research and conservation effort has gone into working out how to mitigate the effects of forestry on biodiversity and how to best manage habitat in different forest contexts; this is the subject of Chapter 13. Finally, we, the editors, conclude with some general observations about the future of forest bird populations of the Northern Hemisphere and critical issues that will deserve increased consideration in the coming years and decades.

We do not pretend to fully cover all subjects pertaining to forest birds within our focal geographic area. For the more fundamental aspects of the population, community and behavioural ecology of forest birds, the reader will have to consult other sources. The effects of climate change on birds have been recently extensively reviewed by Pearce-Higgins and Green (2014), and therefore we cover this topic collectively with other issues concerning the future of forest birds in the concluding chapter. The same applies to forest birds in relation to urban environments, which have been addressed comprehensively by Murgui and Hedblom (2017). Also, a recently published book concerning bird habitat provides deeper insights into some of the ecological issues relevant to forest birds (Fuller 2012).

Forests and forest birds can be defined in several ways. In Part II of the book, we used the Food and Agricultural Organization of the United Nations (FAO) definition of forests (FAO 2010), which considers the minimum patch area (0.5 ha), tree height (5 m or existing potential to reach that height) and canopy cover (>10%). However, when needed, we extended our definition to include 'other wooded land'. Moreover, for simplicity, we considered 'forest' and 'woodland' as synonyms. Having this as a starting point, we defined a forest bird as a species that more than incidentally breeds or forages in (1) forest, according to the official FAO definition, or (2) other types of environments that fulfil the basic quantitative criteria of the FAO definition of forest but are predominantly under agricultural or urban use (e.g., some gardens, city parks and agroforestry systems). For more details about the adopted definitions of forests and forest birds, see Chapter 5. However, some authors of particular chapters occasionally had to deviate from these general definitions. This was the case, for example, when they presented results from previous studies where the focal bird assemblages included additional species not captured by our definition.

Many different forest bird species from Europe, North America and Asia are mentioned in the book. The naming of species has become slightly problematic with so many recent changes to both English and scientific names. In general, we have adopted the shortened (vernacular) English names in the text to assist with readability. But for formal lists of species in tables and appendices, full international English names are generally given. We have attempted to follow the International Ornithological Congress (IOC) list of bird names (BirdLife International 2017).

In total, 28 scientists participated in writing the chapters in this book. All 13 chapters following this introduction have been peer-reviewed by at least two referees. In editing this volume, we have sought to achieve a reasonably balanced treatment of the main applied aspects of forest ornithology within the geographical scope defined above. We hope that the book will provide a valuable reference not only for scientists and students, but also for conservation professionals, people working within the forest industry and a broader public interested in birds and nature. The book is largely a series of contributions that synthesise reviews and original data analyses, and, as such, we believe it has original value for ecological and ornithological science. On the other hand, an equally important goal has been to make the current breadth of knowledge concerning this important group of organisms available for broader audiences.

We deliver this book to your hands hoping that you will enjoy reading it and even learn some new, exciting things about forest birds. We also hope that the ideas and information it contains will be helpful in your professional or personal interests, and will help in some small way to ensure the continuing enjoyment of forest birds by future generations of people.

References

Beer, C., Reichstein, M., Tomelleri, E. *et al.* (2010) Terrestrial gross carbon dioxide uptake: Global distribution and covariation with climate. *Science*, **329**, 834–838.

BirdLife International (2017) Data zone. http://datazone.birdlife.org/species/search.

Chollet, S. & Martin, J.-L. (2013) Declining woodland birds in North America: Should we blame Bambi? *Diversity and Distributions*, **19**, 481–483.

Cocker, M. & Tipping, D. (2013) *Birds and People*. London: Jonathan Cape.

Collar, N.J., Long, A.J., Robles Gil, P. & Rojo, J. (2007) *Birds and People: Bonds in a Timeless Journey*. Mexico City: CEMEX–Agrupación Sierra Madre–BirdLife International.

del Hoyo, J. & Collar, N.J. (2014) *The HBW–BirdLife International Illustrated Checklist of the Birds of the World, 1: Non-passerines*. Barcelona: Lynx Edicions.

del Hoyo, J. & Collar, N.J. (2016) *The HBW–BirdLife International Illustrated Checklist of the Birds of the World, 2: Passerines*. Barcelona: Lynx Edicions.

FAO (2010) *Global Forest Resources Assessment 2010. Terms and Definitions*. Food and Agriculture Organization of the United Nations, Forestry Department. www .fao.org/docrep/014/am665e/am665e00.pdf.

Forsman, J.T., Reunanen, P., Jokimäki, J. & Mönkkönen, M. (2010) The effects of small-scale disturbance on forest birds: A meta-analysis. *Canadian Journal of Forest Research*, **40**, 1833–1842.

Fuller, R.J. (1995) *Bird Life of Woodland and Forest*. Cambridge: Cambridge University Press.

Fuller, R.J. (ed.) (2012) *Birds and Habitat: Relationships in Changing Landscapes*. Cambridge: Cambridge University Press.

Fuller, R.J., Smith, K.W., Grice, P.V., Currie, F.A. & Quine, C.P. (2007) Habitat change and woodland birds in Britain: Implications for management and future research. *Ibis*, **149** (Suppl. 2), 261–268.

Greenwood, J.J.D. (2007) Citizens, science and bird conservation. *Journal of Ornithology*, **148**, S77–S124.

Gregory, R.D., Vorisek, P. & van Strien, A. (2007) Population trends of widespread woodland birds in Europe. *Ibis*, **149** (Suppl. 2), 78–97.

Hagemeijer, J.M. & Blair, M.J. (1997) *The EBCC Atlas of European Breeding Birds: Their Distribution and Abundance.* London: T. and A.D. Poyser.

Hewson, C.M., Austin, G.E., Gough, S.J. & Fuller, R.J. (2011) Species-specific responses of woodland birds to stand-level habitat characteristics: The dual importance of forest structure and floristics. *Forest Ecology and Management*, **261**, 1224–1240.

Holt, C., Fuller, R.J. & Dolman, P. (2011) Breeding and post-breeding responses of woodland birds to modification of habitat structure by deer. *Biological Conservation*, **144**, 2151–2162.

Imbeau, L., Mönkkönen, M. & Desrochers, A. (2001) Long-term effects of forestry on birds of the eastern Canadian boreal forests: A comparison with Fennoscandia. *Conservation Biology*, **15**, 1151–1162.

Jiguet, F., Devictor, V., Julliard, R. & Couvet, D. (2012) French citizens monitoring ordinary birds provide tools for conservation and ecological sciences. *Acta Oecologica*, **44**, 58–66.

Keast, A. (1990) *Biogeography and Ecology of Forest Bird Communities.* The Hague: SPB Academic Publishing.

Kindermann, G.E., McCallum, I., Fritz, S. & Obersteiner, M. (2008) A global forest growing stock, biomass and carbon map based on FAO statistics. *Silva Fennica*, **42**, 387–396.

McKinley, D.C., Ryan, M.G., Birdsey, R.A. *et al.* (2011) A synthesis of current knowledge on forests and carbon storage in the United States. *Ecological Applications*, **21**, 1902–1924.

Mikusiński, G., Gromadzki, M. & Chylarecki, P. (2001) Woodpeckers as indicators of forest bird diversity. *Conservation Biology*, **15**, 208–217.

Millennium Ecosystem Assessment (2005) *Ecosystems and Human Well-being: Synthesis.* Washington, DC: Island Press.

Murgui, E. & Hedblom, M. (eds.) (2017) *Ecology and Conservation of Birds in Urban Environments.* Cham, Switzerland: Springer International Publishing.

Newton, I. (1995) The contribution of some recent research on birds to ecological understanding. *Journal of Animal Ecology*, **64**, 675–696.

Pan, Y., Birdsey, R.A., Phillips, O.L. & Jackson, R.B. (2013) The structure, distribution, and biomass of the world's forests. *Annual Review of Ecology, Evolution, and Systematics*, **44**, 593–622.

Pearce-Higgins, J.W. & Green, R.E. (2014) *Birds and Climate Change: Impacts and Conservation Responses.* Cambridge: Cambridge University Press.

Perlin, J. (2005) *A Forest Journey: The Story of Wood and Civilization.* Woodstock, VT: Countryman Press.

Roberge, J.-M., Angelstam, P. & Villard, M.-A. (2008) Specialised woodpeckers and naturalness in hemiboreal forests: Deriving quantitative targets for conservation planning. *Biological Conservation*, **141**, 997–1012.

Rudel, T.K., Coomes, O.T., Moran, E. *et al.* (2005) Forest transitions: Towards a global understanding of land use change. *Global Environmental Change*, **15** (1), 23–31.

Sallabanks, R., Arnett, E.B. & Marzluff, J.M. (2000) An evaluation of research on the effects of timber harvest on bird populations. *Wildlife Society Bulletin*, **28**, 1144–1155.

Schieck, J. & Song, S.J. (2006) Changes in bird communities throughout succession following fire and harvest in boreal forests of western North America:

Literature review and meta-analyses. *Canadian Journal of Forest Research*, **36**, 1299–1318.

Sullivan, B.L., Wood, C.L., Iliff, M.J., Bonney, R.E., Fink, D. & Kelling, S. (2009) eBird: A citizen-based bird observation network in the biological sciences. *Biological Conservation*, **142**, 2282–2292.

Winkler, D.W., Billerman, S.M. & Lovette, I.J. (2015) *Bird Families of the World*. Barcelona: Lynx Edicions.

Part I

Forest Birds and Their Adaptations

2 · Origins and Dynamics of Forest Birds of the Northern Hemisphere

JACQUES BLONDEL

2.1 The Evolutionary History of Forest Birds

Just as tropical latitudes encompass three huge blocks of tropical evergreen forests in South America, tropical Africa and south-east Asia–Australasia, the Northern Hemisphere is also characterised in mid and high latitudes by four forest blocks of warm-temperate, temperate-nemoral and boreal climate biomes. Excluding the much smaller temperate forest zone of North America's Pacific slope, these forest regions cover large areas in eastern North America (1.8×10^6 km^2), Europe (1.2×10^6 km^2) and eastern Asia (1.2×10^6 km^2) (Fig. 2.1). The history and composition of the bird faunas of these huge forest blocks cannot be understood without considering the three flyways that connect them to tropical forest blocks: North America/ Central and South America, Western Europe/Africa and eastern Asia/ south-eastern Asia. For a long time during the Mesozoic era, the major land masses of the Northern Hemisphere were connected. Past relationships between North America and the Palearctic left their imprint before they split during the Jurassic, 100 million years ago (Mya), separating the formerly continuous Holarctic biotas into two blocks that evolved under conditions of increasing continental isolation. Similarly, a long-standing and wide connection of the same habitat in the boreal forest biome between Europe and East Asia explains many similarities between the two realms.

During the Paleogene period (the first part of the Tertiary), tropical and subtropical forests dominated by oaks, laurels and palms covered the low-mid latitudes of Eurasia and North America as far north as 50°N. The homogeneity of ecological conditions in these regions made vegetation systems and their associated faunas quite similar (Latham & Ricklefs 1993). Continents were more or less flat, without ice caps and large cordilleras; Eurasia and North America were connected by Beringia, allowing exchanges between the two land masses. The gradual cooling of the earth,

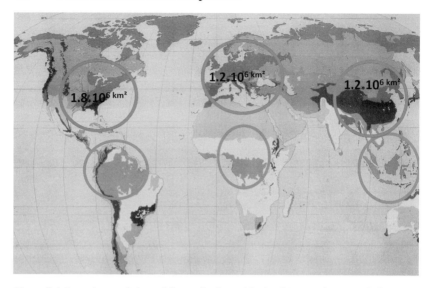

Figure 2.1 Location and size of the main forest blocks (biomes showing different shades of grey) in eastern North America, Europe and Eastern Asia (China and Manchuria). These forest blocks are the counterparts of the three blocks of tropical forests with which many forest birds are historically closely linked (the map of biomes is redrawn from Walter 1979).

which started in the mid-Oligocene (ca. 30 Mya), resulted in the appearance of seasonal climates at mid latitudes and the contraction of tropical ecosystems towards the equator (Martin 1984). Many bird families now restricted to the tropics, such as parrots (Psittacidae), trogons (Trogonidae), barbets (Lybiidae), mousebirds (Coliidae), hornbills (Bucerotidae) and others, disappeared from Europe (Mourer-Chauviré 1995). Combined with an increasing isolation of Eurasia from North America, these climatic changes favoured diversification and continental specialisation of the bird fauna, which increased when the zonal differentiation of the main vegetation belts began to develop by the late Oligocene–Early Miocene. The development of new types of vegetation, such as boreal forests, temperate forests, grasslands and steppes, provided opportunities for differentiation and specialisation into new niches. The modern bird faunas were established in this epoch (Blondel & Mourer-Chauviré 1998), with extensive radiation of passerines. From the mid-Miocene onwards, evolution of birds mostly involved differentiation at the genus and species levels within already established families, so the bird faunas of the Pliocene were largely similar to those of today. Essentially descriptive and inferential, the fossil record of the Paleogene provides an oversimplified picture of avian diversification in this time window, but it sets a framework for understanding the history of birds. Recent technological and methodological advances in the field of paleornithology will undoubtedly provide new insights into the histories of birds (Wood & De Pietri 2015).

2.1.1 The Origin of Modern Forest Birds

The spatiotemporal context in which extant bird species evolved has been a subject of long-standing controversy. Wetmore's (1959) contention that most modern species date from the Pliocene was challenged by Selander (1971), among others, who argued, mostly on paleontological grounds, that Pleistocene glacial cycles were conducive to a burst of speciation in most groups of birds. However, a wealth of studies using molecular systematics, and especially mitochondrial DNA (cytochrome b) and DNA gene sequencing, have shown that most species coalesced in a much deeper past (Bermingham *et al.* 1992; Zink & Slowinski 1995; Avise 2004), with the majority of modern species of songbirds having a Pliocene origin. This does not mean, however, that substantial Pleistocene speciation did not occur, as shown later in this chapter (Johnson & Cicero 2004; Weir & Schluter 2004; Lovette 2005; but see Zink *et al.* 2004). Some examples will illustrate the differentiation times of several clades of forest birds from both the Palearctic and the Nearctic.

A first example is that of the nuthatches of the genus *Sitta* (24–28 species), whose history has been reconstructed combining biogeographic analysis and phylogenetic systematics using two mitochondrial genes and one nuclear gene (Pasquet *et al.* 2014, Fig. 2.2). A well-resolved phylogeny of the genus reveals several clades with a first split ca. 20 Mya giving rise to the Przewalskii's nuthatch *Sitta przewalskii*, which is sister to all other species. The clade *S. carolinensis* – *S. magna* split ca. 17 Mya and is sister to the two other clades, which encompass all the other extant species. The basal nodes of the tree indicate that the genus originated in south-eastern Asia, from where several clades dispersed in North America (four species) and in the western Palearctic (Europe, six species) 17 Mya and 5 Mya, respectively. Unexpectedly, but firmly established in the topology of the tree, the three endemic 'mesogean' nuthatches which occur in coniferous forests in the Mediterranean Basin – the Corsican nuthatch *S. whiteheadi* in Corsica, the Algerian nuthatch *S. ledanti* in Algeria and the Kruper's nuthatch *S. kruperi* in Turkey – belong not to a monophyletic group, but to two separate lineages that diverged at the

(a)

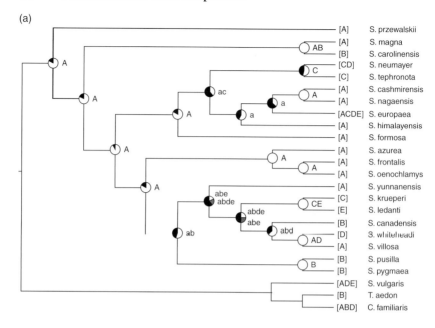

[A]	S. przewalskii
[A]	S. magna
[B]	S. carolinensis
[CD]	S. neumayer
[C]	S. tephronota
[A]	S. cashmirensis
[A]	S. nagaensis
[ACDE]	S. europaea
[A]	S. himalayensis
[A]	S. formosa
[A]	S. azurea
[A]	S. frontalis
[A]	S. oenochlamys
[A]	S. yunnanensis
[C]	S. krueperi
[E]	S. ledanti
[B]	S. canadensis
[D]	S. whiteheadi
[A]	S. villosa
[B]	S. pusilla
[B]	S. pygmaea
[ADE]	S. vulgaris
[B]	T. aedon
[ABD]	C. familiaris

(b)

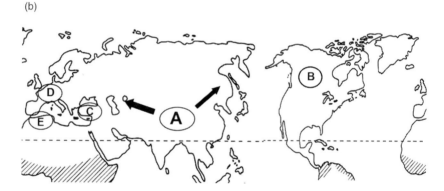

Figure 2.2 (a) Phylogenetic tree of the Sittidae family (with *Sturnus vulgaris*, *Troglodytes aedon* and *Certhia familiaris* as outgroups), based on the cyt*b*, COI and RAG-1 sequence data and extant distributional areas. Pie charts indicate relative probabilities of the most likely ancestral ranges for each node, with the proportion of white indicating the probability of the best reconstruction and grey the second best. Ancestral ranges are indicated in capitals for a probability >70% and in lowercase for a probability <70%. (b) A, Asia; B, North America; C, Middle East; D, Western Europe; E, North Africa (after Pasquet *et al.* 2014).

beginning of the Pliocene, ca. 5 Mya, with the Corsican nuthatch being a sister species of the North American *S. villosa* that diverged ca. 1 Mya.

As a second example, a comprehensive analysis of the phylogenetic relationships of the New World warblers of the family Parulidae has been provided by Lovette *et al.* (2010) from mitochondrial DNA (cytochrome b) and nuclear DNA nucleotide characters. This huge family, which includes 112–115 species distributed among 24–26 genera, is particularly interesting because the breeding distributions of species span from the Arctic to temperate South America, with centres of diversity in the tropics as well as in temperate forested blocks of eastern North America (Lovette *et al.* 2010). Moreover, the family includes both resident and tropical migratory species. There is strong molecular phylogenetic support for a monophyletic 'core Parulidae' group having differentiated in North America ca. 5–7 Mya and including all the typical wood-warbler genera (Klein *et al.* 2004; Barker *et al.* 2015; see also Parulidae in Fig. 2.3).

Among the Parulines, the Nearctic genus *Dendroica* (27 species) has been hypothesised to be ecologically equivalent to the Palearctic genus *Phylloscopus* (49 species). These two groups are dominant components of their respective communities, and they have been hypothesised to be functionally equivalent as a result of ecological convergence in similar habitats (Price *et al.* 2000). Most species are migratory and overwinter in the tropics (*Dendroica* in the Americas and *Phylloscopus* in the Old World). Molecular phylogeny (mtDNA cytochrome b) showed that the *Phylloscopus* group started to differentiate more than 12 Mya, much earlier than the *Dendroica* genus, which originated in the Pliocene. Price *et al.* (2000) have shown from ecomorphological and behavioural comparisons of *Dendroica* and *Phylloscopus* communities in New Hampshire (North America) and Kashmir (Asia), respectively, that the history of the species' radiations differs so much between the two groups that their communities are unlikely to be really convergent even when placed in similar environments. Species in the two regions differ greatly in foraging behaviour and in relationships between morphology and ecological variables. *Dendroica* species are ecologically more similar than are *Phylloscopus* species, which results in a much closer species packing in the former, with no equivalent in the Old World. Indeed, the *Dendroica* warblers offer a classic example of fine-scale niche partitioning (MacArthur 1958). Lack (1971, p. 132) pointed out that these warblers 'present a more complex case of ecological interdigitation than any found in European passerine species', which is mirrored by narrow habitat-bird associations (see below). According to Price *et al.* (2000), the unusual similarity among the *Dendroica* warblers is due to a burst of speciation driven by sexual selection, resulting in a 'species flock' of ecologically similar coexisting species.

A third example is the *Sylvia* complex (25 species), which includes many species specialised in Mediterranean-type vegetation, such as matorrals (a generic name for all kinds of Mediterranean-type bushy or scrubby habitats). From mitochondrial DNA sequencing, Böhning-Gaese *et al.* (2003) have shown that the basal split of *Sylvia* (the *atricapilla-borin-abyssinica* lineages versus all others) occurred ca. 13–16 Mya. The whitethroat *S. communis* forms the sister group (with only one species) of the species group whose breeding range is restricted to Mediterranean matorrals. The radiation of the two main clades, the *curruca-hortensis* group and the Mediterranean species group, including *S. communis*, is estimated to have occurred ca. 5.5–8.5 Mya. Although the region of origin of the common ancestor of the genus remains unknown, it presumably evolved around the Mediterranean Basin during the Pliocene, with the three major clades of Mediterranean *Sylvia* warblers presumably having evolved in the three large Mediterranean peninsulas (see Table 10.5 in Newton, 2003, p. 303). During this period, the so-called Messinian crisis (5.9–5.3 Mya), the Mediterranean Basin was very arid and *Sylvia* habitats must have been restricted to isolated pockets. Many episodes of sea level change, climatic upheaval and associated vegetation changes provided opportunities for repeated isolation of populations in refugia (Blondel *et al.* 1996; Shirihai *et al.* 2001).

Summing up, there is now much evidence that the origination of modern species started much earlier than the Pleistocene, with many extant lineages having a long history spanning from nearly 50 million to 5 million years ago (Jetz *et al.* 2012), even if substantial differentiation occurred during the Pleistocene (Weir & Schluter 2004; Wallis *et al.* 2016; and later in this chapter). Actually, the distribution of mtDNA divergence estimates of various phylogroups shows that the 'pace of speciation' is a long-lasting process which probably extended through time from Pliocene origins to Pleistocene completion, rather than a point event in time (Klicka & Zink 1997, 1999; Avise & Walker 1998).

2.1.2 Did Northern Hemisphere Forest Birds Originate in the Tropics?

A question of great biogeographic interest is concerned with the areas of origin of forest birds. In the framework of the 'faunal types' concept (Stegmann 1938), which follows the Darwinian 'dispersal-biogeography' paradigm that prevailed before the advent of vicariance biogeography, a long-standing tenet is that birds evolved within the temperate regions and only a small fraction of them originated in the tropics. However, this paradigm has been challenged by phylogenetic biogeography and the evolutionary history of long-distance tropical migrants. Historical biogeography (e.g., Voelker 1999) has discounted the notion that the centre of diversity reveals the centre of origin of lineages, so current ranges of species cannot be considered as proxies for their ranges at the time of speciation (Webster & Purvis 2002). Insight into the biogeographic origin of birds is provided by the biology of long-distance migrants and the origin of the migratory behaviour in light of phylogenetic trees of lineages, including both migrant and resident species. Of the 338 and 340 species of migratory birds breeding in the Nearctic and Eastern Asia, respectively, 162 (48%) and 106 (31%) have conspecifics in tropical regions of Central/South America and south-eastern Asia, respectively. In North America, 78% of forest-dwelling species have congeners breeding in the Neotropics, whereas in Europe, no more than 23% of the species (42 of 185) have conspecific populations in the Afrotropics (Rappole & Jones 2002). The question to be addressed is where all these long-distance tropical migrants evolved.

Two theories have been proposed to explain the area of origin of tropical migrants (Salewski & Bruderer 2007). The first theory, the 'southern home' theory, hypothesises that long-distance migrants originated in the tropics, where they exploited stable resources and subsequently evolved a migratory habit allowing them to extend their breeding range at higher latitudes to capitalise on seasonally abundant resources in regions they left for wintering in their area of origin. Berthold (2001) and Rappole (1995) argue that the presence in the tropics of close sedentary relatives of these migratory species strongly supports sedentary behaviour as ancestral in those lineages. The rationale is that population pressures in the area of origin force exploration and exploitation of seasonally abundant resources away from the ancestral home, followed by a return to the tropics upon seasonal decline of these resources (Zink 2002). This theory has been proposed for both the Palearctic-Afrotropical and Nearctic-Neotropical systems (Rappole 1995; Rappole & Jones 2002). The second theory, the 'northern home' theory, hypothesises that birds originated in the Northern Hemisphere, where they bred and were pushed southward annually to avoid deteriorating seasonal conditions in winter (Bell 2005; Salewski & Bruderer 2007). Testing these theories requires a phylogenetic framework (Zink

2002; Outlaw *et al.* 2003), because (i) having tropical sedentary relatives says nothing on the ancestral area of origin, and (ii) within a given lineage, migration may be ancestral, with extant residency being a derived condition through loss of migratory behaviour.

Clades that include both migrant and resident species are good candidates for testing these hypotheses, assuming that the phylogenetic signal of migration within bird lineages indicates whether the extant migratory behaviour has evolved *in situ* or has arisen once or several times from sedentary ancestors (Winger *et al.* 2012). Many studies that reconstructed the ancestral state of migration in an explicit phylogenetic context support a sedentary ancestor (e.g., Outlaw *et al.* 2003; Outlaw & Voelker 2006). They concluded that migration among extant birds has evolved relatively recently compared with the total age of the lineages from which migratory species derived. For example, addressing the evolution of long-distance migration and the historical biogeography of the five migrant and seven resident species of *Catharus* thrushes from a molecular phylogeny (cytochrome b and ND2 genes), Outlaw *et al.* (2003) demonstrated the non-monophyly of the migratory species. The topology of the cladogram indicates that resident behaviour is ancestral and that the most likely ancestral geographic area for the entire genus is the Neotropics. Migratory species are sister species of resident species whose ranges are restricted in tropical Central America. A general conclusion drawn from these studies and several others is that long-distance migrants breeding in temperate regions of the Northern Hemisphere evolved from historically tropical sedentary ancestors (Rappole 1995), a conclusion echoed by Berthold (2001) and Zink (2002).

However, another picture emerges from other studies. One example is a recent near-complete species-level phylogeny (832 species) of a widespread lineage, the Emberizoidea, a large group of songbirds encompassing the blackbirds (Icteridae), cardinals (Cardinalidae), American sparrows (Passerellidae), tanagers (Thraupidae) and wood warblers (Parulidae) (Barker *et al.* 2015). The phylogenetic analysis of this clade (from protein-coding genes CYTB and/or ND2 of mtDNA and four nuclear genes) has been used to generate a quantitative probabilistic analysis of Emberizoid biogeographic origins and dispersal history. A maximum likelihood analysis of Emberizoid distributional data as a discrete character strongly supports a North American origin for the group (Fig. 2.3). This is a robust result, with all replicates yielding ≥ 0.95 probability for North America as the root. With an estimated

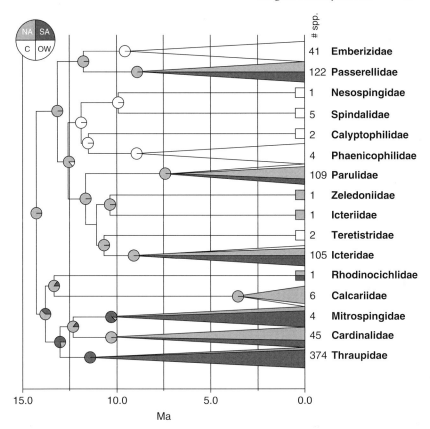

Figure 2.3 Biogeographical reconstruction of the Emberizoidea from a species-level time-scaled phylogeny of the group. Pie graphs at each node indicate the relative likelihood of each state (NA = North America, SA = South America, C = Caribbean, OW = Old World). Width of fill in terminal triangles indicates the percentage of species in each group currently found in each region. Squares = lineages with only one species sampled (Barker *et al.* 2015).

stem age of ca. 20 Mya for the Emberizoidea group of Passerida (Barker *et al.* 2004), which appears to have arisen in Sahul (the continental Australasian mass), the presence of this group of oscine passerines in the New World is likely the result of dispersal over a Beringian land bridge, in agreement with the previous judgements of Mayr (1946, 1964). The earliest history of this group was dominated by differentiation within North America, with four of the five major clades being ancestrally North American (Fig. 2.3). These are the Passerellidae (122 species), the Parulidae (109 species), the Icteridae (105 species) and the Cardinalidae (45 species). After dispersal across Beringia, one family, the Emberizidae (41 species), back-dispersed to Eurasia ca. 9.8 Mya (Fig. 2.3).

Within the Emberizoidea, the New World Parulidae are interesting for testing the evolution of migratory behaviour. This huge monophyletic group, encompassing 112–115 species distributed in 24–26 genera (Lovette *et al.* 2010), spans a wide spectrum of migratory behaviours, from mostly sedentary tropical genera to some champions of long-distance migration. Using a variety of models, Winger *et al.* (2012) demonstrated that, contrary to the *Catharus* thrushes discussed above, the migratory character of this group is ancestral, and that migratory behaviour has been lost and regained many times during the radiation of the group, which started ca. 7.5 Mya. An important point made by Winger *et al.* (2012), however, is that their results neither support nor contradict the unifying prediction of the 'southern home' theory. They only imply that the ancestral parulid was probably a Nearctic–Neotropical migrant, and that extant sedentary taxa represent a derived condition within the family. Clearly, as more comprehensive species-level phylogenies are published with detailed taxon- and area-cladograms, ancestral state reconstructions of migratory behaviour will increase our understanding of general patterns of change in migratory behaviour across the avian tree of life.

Other examples support the 'northern home' theory. A group that most probably originated and differentiated in the Northern Hemisphere is the subfamily Tetraoninae, which is a monophyletic clade (21 species) widely distributed in the Northern Hemisphere. The hypothesis of a northern origin of these birds has been strongly supported by a complete molecular phylogeny combined with paleontological data used to calibrate a molecular clock (Drovetski 2003). Estimates of divergence rates suggest that radiation of the group coincided with global cooling and climatic oscillations of the Pliocene-Pleistocene. The grouse phylogeny started in the Pliocene, 6.3 Mya, with diversification beginning ca. 3.2 Mya. Historical biogeographical reconstructions show that the western Nearctic played a major role in radiation of the group and that Eurasia has been colonised independently three times, presumably via the Beringian land bridge, and the Nearctic from Eurasia only once.

Finally, many species may arise from various mechanisms that are more or less idiosyncratic. One of them is produced by multiple invasions of the same species on islands. For example, phylogenetic analyses from mtDNA have shown that the common chaffinch *Fringilla coelebs* colonised the Canary Islands from North Africa twice: the first colonists, about 1 Mya, differentiated as the blue chaffinch *F. teydea*, and the second colonisation event from Africa gave rise to additional forms classified as subspecies in various islands of Macaronesia (Marshall & Baker 1999). Another distribution which seems odd is that of the blue-winged magpie *Cyanopica cyanus*, with populations living today at the two extremities of the Palearctic, one in south Iberia and the other in eastern Asia. A demonstration that the bird is native to Iberia (i.e., was not introduced by sailors, as is sometimes argued) has been provided by the discovery of 44,000-year-old bone remains (Cooper 2000) and then by a molecular phylogenetic analysis (Fok *et al.* 2002), which shows that a basal divergence between the two populations dates back to ca. 1.2 Mya. Actually, similar distribution patterns can be seen in a wide range of taxa that exhibit east and west pairs of species or semi-species. Examples are the western capercaillie *Tetrao urogallus* and the eastern black-billed capercaillie *T. parvirostris*, the turtle dove *Streptopelia turtur* and the eastern turtle dove *S. orientalis*, and the tree pipit *Anthus trivialis* and the Pechora pipit *A. gustavi*, among many others. Deciphering the tempo and mode of differentiation of these taxa from phylogenetic analyses would shed light on the past relationships between the western and eastern parts of the Palearctic.

2.1.3 A Legacy of History

Because more than two-thirds of the forested blocks of the Northern Hemisphere discussed in this chapter are (or have been) forested, wood-land birds represent the most important part of their terrestrial bird fauna. At the scale of Eurasia, as many as 39 families, 126 genera and several billion individual birds are more or less specialised to forest habitats. From an evolutionary viewpoint, they are a legacy of the common history of birds and plants, with close interactions between them since the Eocene (Regal 1977). Functional interactions include plant pollination (e.g., Grant 1994; Cronk & Ojeda 2008), and especially seed dispersal (e.g., Jordano 2014), with emblematic examples such as the jay-oak and nutcracker-pine associations. A point which deserves an entire chapter is that habitat diversity and species diversity have coevolved so that a high diversity of pollinating and seed-dispersing animal species promotes specialisation and differentiation among trees, which in turn offers greater habitat diversity for animals (e.g., Rosenzweig 1995). Such tight correl-ations between bird species diversity and floristic diversity as those documented in tropical forests for nectar eaters and fruit eaters by Snow (1976) hardly occur in temperate forests. Nonetheless, narrow relationships between the tree flora and the bird fauna are emphasised by Folke *et al.* (1996), who estimated that a 50–70% decline in Neotropical migrants would probably result in major changes to the tree species composition of North American temperate forests.

As a result of the common history of the main vegetation belts, the extant bird fauna of European forests is remarkably homogeneous over the whole continent, with a low faunal turnover when scaling species richness in space (Gregory *et al.* 1998). As in eastern North America (Mönkkönen 1994), the highest values of species richness are found in mid latitudes rather than in the extreme south of Europe, which departs from the classical north-south gradient of species richness (Gregory *et al.* 1998). A slight but significant west-east gradient of increasing species richness can be explained by two non-mutually exclusive causes: (i) a peninsula effect (Mönkkönen 1994), whereby, in both eastern North America and Europe, species richness increases from the edge of the continent to its centre; and (ii) presumably more severe anthropogenic pressures, which hit the forest-associated faunas harder in the west than in the east of Europe (Tomiałojć 2000; see maps in Chapter 5).

As explained later in this chapter, the repeated back-and-forth shifts of biotas across the western Palearctic during the Neogene epoch, and especially the Pleistocene, resulted in their repeated mixings. This explains the homogeneity and low rate of regional endemism of the forest avifauna across Europe today, including the Mediterranean zone and North Africa (Blondel & Vigne 1993; Hewitt 2000). The large differences in overall species richness among the main forest blocks of the Northern Hemisphere have been hypothesised to result from Pleistocene glaciations impacting more severely on the European bird fauna than on that of the other forest blocks. But phylogenetic analyses led Zink and Slowinski (1995) to estimate that less than 10% of the passerine bird species known from the Pleistocene epoch are extinct, a figure echoed by the fossil record, which shows very low extinction rates during the glacial-interglacial cycles (Willis & MacDonald 2011).

Whatever the degree of resilience of the bird fauna over millions of years, one may hypothesise that increased environmental instability caused by the Neogene-Quaternary pejoration of climatic conditions influenced rates of diversification (speciation rates minus extinction rates). In the near absence of fossil data, especially from small passerine birds, testing this hypothesis must be done from phylogenetic reconstructions (Nee *et al.* 1994; Ricklefs 2006; Jetz *et al.* 2012), because evolutionary trees of different lineages based on mtDNA provide an estimate of combined speciation and extinction rates over time. Tests of Pleistocene diversification of 11 passerine bird lineages suggest a consistent decline in net diversification rates across the Pleistocene (Zink & Slowinski 1995; McPeek 2008, but see Jetz *et al.* 2012). The question is whether the cause of this decline is reduced speciation or increased extinction. Two non-mutually exclusive hypotheses have been offered to answer this question. First, European biotas being prevented from dispersing to tropical refugia during pleniglacial times by barriers to dispersal (see below), combined with the geographic displacement and reduction in size of many habitats, could have caused extinction events. This hypothesis is supported by neither phylogenetic analyses nor fossil data. Second, a slowing down of speciation rates rather than accelerated extinction rates may have resulted from ecological limitations, such as competition for limited resources, adaptive radiation or niche filling within clades through evolutionary time (Nee *et al.* 1992; but see Moen and Morlon 2014 for alternative hypotheses). Demonstrating a slowdown of diversification rates in temperate regions requires testing the null hypothesis that diversification rates do not differ between temperate and tropical regions. Tests of this hypothesis have been done by comparing the diversity of clades of passerine birds in large tropical and temperate regions in order to determine the effects of the environment (tropical *vs* temperate) and the size of the region on rates of diversification. One conclusion, strongly supported by data including 14 clades of passerines restricted to South America and 23 clades restricted to North America, is that net rates of diversification are higher in tropical regions and decrease with the age of clades, which supports the hypothesis that the filling of ecological space constrains further differentiation (Ricklefs 2006). To sum up, the long-standing tenet regarding increased avian speciation rates in the Pleistocene is not supported by current phylogenetically based investigations on diversification rates and might have been based on an exaggerated focus on extant species. Clearly, future studies from a phylogenetic approach should shed light on the tempo and mode of speciation/extinction events of European species during the Neogene. Whatever the variation of diversification rates, Pleistocene upheavals had many evolutionary and ecological consequences on forest birds, as shown below.

2.2 The Forest Avifauna of the Different Regions of the Northern Hemisphere

2.2.1 A Common Heritage Shaped and Reshaped by Geography and History

As mentioned above, the temperate and boreal forested regions of the Northern Hemisphere consist of four main blocks which are either deciduous or mixed deciduous and coniferous, namely the western North American block (which will not be discussed further in this chapter), the eastern North American block (part of the North American continent north of the US-Mexican border and east of the 95th western longitude) and two blocks in Eurasia which are separated by large areas of steppe, deserts and massive mountain ranges, except in the far north, where the belt of boreal forests is uninterrupted. These two Eurasian blocks are the western Palearctic block (hereafter named Europe, i.e., the part of the Eurasian land mass west of the Ural mountain range) and the eastern Palearctic block (China and Manchuria; see Fig. 2.1). The sizes of these forest blocks are ca. 1.2, 1.2 and 1.8 x 10^6 km^2 for Europe, eastern Asia and eastern North America, respectively (Latham & Ricklefs 1993), and their bird fauna experienced the same early evolutionary history before they split as a result of plate tectonics. According to the species-area relationship, the bird diversity of these three regions of roughly similar size should be of a similar order of magnitude, which is not the case, because extant bird faunas include ca. 732 species in North America, ca. 513 species in Europe and ca. 1,000 species in eastern Asia. Other differences between these bird faunas include: (i) a lower taxonomic diversity in Europe compared to the other regions (Mönkkönen & Viro 1997); (ii) a larger proportion of the continental-wide bird fauna being associated with forests in eastern North American and eastern Asia (about two-thirds of the terrestrial avifauna) than in Europe (about half); and (iii) a much higher proportion of long-distance tropical migrants (i.e., birds that breed in temperate forests and overwinter in tropical regions) in eastern North America and eastern Asia than in Europe. The percentage of tropical migrants, which amounts to 68% in North America (Terborgh 1989), is much lower in Europe, for example, 21% in the oak-hornbeam-lime forest of Białowieża, Poland (Wesołowski et al. 2002). The overall numbers of species in the Palearctic-Asian and New World migration systems are quite similar, with ca. 340 species each, while the Palearctic-tropical African system is much smaller, with only 185 species (Rappole & Jones 2002). Only 48 species of tropical migrants breed in

Palearctic forests, compared to 112 species in Nearctic forests and 107 in eastern Asian forests (Rappole 1995). Similar patterns of species impoverishment have been found in tree-species richness, with three times as many tree species in mesic forests of eastern Asia (729 species) as in eastern North America (253 species) and six times more than in European forests (124 species) (Latham & Ricklefs 1993). Similar variation in bird and tree-species richness does not mean a common variation of tree-bird associations, but suggests that the speciation-extinction-dispersal processes have basically, but independently, been driven by the same factors in the two groups. Explaining these large-scale diversity patterns requires testing hypotheses addressed at temporal and spatial scales that match the scale of the processes involved.

2.2.2 Why Are There Fewer Species in European Forests Than in Northern American and Eastern Asian Ones?

Two main hypotheses can be offered to explain why the three regions of the Northern Hemisphere differ so much in species richness. The first hypothesis states that extinction and dispersal rates associated with climatic Pleistocene cycles depended on differences in geographical configuration of land masses and barriers to dispersal on the two continents (Huntley 1993). The second hypothesis proposes that the extant bird faunas result from differential dispersal-colonisation rates from tropical regions and subsequent diversification in temperate regions (e.g., Böhning-Gaese et al. 1998).

Arguments supporting the first hypothesis refer to the absence of massive east-west barriers to dispersal between temperate and tropical areas in North America, where barriers are north-south oriented (Rocky Mountains), and eastern Asia, where there are no mountainous barriers at all. In these two regions, as ecological conditions deteriorated during glacial times, temperate biotas were permanently connected with tropical biotas where they could find refuge during glacial periods. In addition, climate cooling during Quaternary ice ages was much less severe in eastern Asia, where continental ice sheets never reached the mid-latitudes. The rationale of this hypothesis is that in both North America and Eastern Asia, birds remained connected to the tropics over the whole Tertiary-Quaternary, allowing a continuous interchange between tropical and temperate bird faunas (Webb & Bartlein 1992). The successive waves of Pleistocene glaciations resulted in a back-and-forth north-south movement of forest belts and their associate faunas, which always remained in close contact with tropical forests to the south (CLIMAP 1976). This explains why extant bird faunas include representatives of tropical Indo-Malayan families such as Zosteropidae, Pycnonotidae, Timaliidae and Campephagidae and of Neotropical families such as Trogonidae and Cracidae in temperate regions of eastern Asia and eastern North America, respectively.

In contrast, massive east-west–oriented barriers (mountain ranges, seas and large desert belts) always separated the temperate European avifauna from the tropics, preventing them from finding refuge in tropical regions farther south. Although the Sahara and desert regions of south-west Asia had more vegetation during glacial times than today, this so-called eremian belt was never forested enough to provide a dispersal link for forest birds between the Afrotropics and Eurasia (CLIMAP 1976). In addition, warming effects of the Gulf Stream current result in a $10°$ north shift in vegetation belts in Europe, making the distance between the breeding grounds and the tropics much longer than in the two other regions. Tropical winter quarters are also more northern, hence closer to breeding grounds, for Nearctic migrants – Mexico, Central America, the Caribbean and even the southern parts of North America – than for Palearctic migrants. This difference between Europe and the other regions of the northern hemisphere could explain why Europe has far fewer forest plant species and why many of the extant Asian and eastern North American tree genera are represented in Europe only by pre-Pleistocene fossils (Latham & Ricklefs 1993). However, the hypothesis of high extinction rates resulting from the bird faunas having been trapped in southern Europe during glacial times contradicts the tenet of high resilience and few extinction events in the European faunas, as discussed above.

The second hypothesis to explain bird richness anomalies is differences in diversity patterns among the bird faunas of the three temperate regions of the Northern Hemisphere reflecting the history of colonisation of temperate biomes from the tropics. If, as explained above, most extant species of temperate forests or their ancestors originated in the tropics, the permanent connections between tropical and temperate regions allowed clades of tropical origin to disperse and differentiate farther north. Intense radiation probably occurred in temperate regions *after* ancestral taxa colonised them from the tropics (secondary radiation), which may explain why continental interchange has been more marked within the New World (Mönkkönen *et al.* 1992), with large groups such as Tyrannidae and Parulidae being more widespread in South America and North

America, than is the case in Europe, where the northward spread of Afrotropical species has been prevented by barriers to dispersal. One argument supporting the importance of tropical *vs* temperate regions for bird diversification is that tropical environments dominated the early Tertiary of the earth, providing deeper roots for tropical diversity compared to temperate and boreal regions (Wiens & Donoghue 2004).

One additional hypothesis is that patterns of habitat diversity and habitat selection differ between the different forest blocks. For example, many species of the Palearctic leaf warblers of the genus *Phylloscopus* exhibit clear patterns of Rapoport's rule, whereby species that live farther north have larger ranges (Price *et al.* 1997), with the consequence that fewer species can accumulate in any given habitat. In contrast, in eastern North America, close tree-bird associations and fine-grained habitat selection by Parulids result in much higher niche packing, hence higher local species diversity (Price *et al.* 2000), than in Europe.

2.2.3 Similarities and Dissimilarities of the Forest Bird Faunas of North America and Europe

The long common history experienced by Eurasia and North America before the opening of the Atlantic Ocean and the disappearance of the Beringian land bridge (last connection 10,000 years ago) explains why bird faunas of the two continents have many similarities. Three main features summarise much of the story. First, many taxa have a wide Holarctic distribution in the boreal zone (coniferous and mixed forests), with 45% and 67% of the resident genera of North America and Europe, respectively, occurring on the two continents (Helle & Mönkkönnen 1990), e.g., among the families Paridae, Sittidae, Regulidae, Bombycillidae and Certhiidae (Table 2.1). The two bird faunas increasingly differ southwards.

Second, with 48 species, or 19% of breeding species (Moreau 1972), the contribution of tropical migrants is much lower in European forests than in North American forests (112 species, more than 50%) (Rappole 1995; Holmes & Sherry 2001). In the deciduous forests of eastern North America, the typical component of mature forests is migratory species (Mönkkönen & Helle 1989), whereas in deciduous forests of Europe, most bird species of mature forests are resident, with many migratory species being short-distance migrants (Wesołowski & Tomiałojć 1997). In addition, taxonomic affinities between Europe and North America are

Table 2.1 *Examples of closely related species that occur in Eurasia and North America (compiled from Newton 2003).*

Eurasia	North America
Hazel grouse *Tetrastes bonasia*	Ruffed grouse *Bonasa umbellus*
Eurasian woodcock *Scolopax rusticola*	American woodcock *Scolopax minor*
Common buzzard *Buteo buteo*	Red-tailed hawk *Buteo jamaicensis*
Common kestrel *Falco tinnunculus*	American kestrel *Falco sparverius*
Eurasian eagle owl *Bubo bubo*	Great horned owl *Bubo virginianus*
Eurasian pygmy owl *Glaucidium passerinum*	Mountain pygmy owl *Glaucidium gnoma*
Willow tit *Poecile montanus*	Black-capped chickadee *Poecile atricapillus*
Eurasian treecreeper *Certhia familiaris*	Brown treecreeper *Certhia americana*
Goldcrest *Regulus regulus*	Ruby-crowned kinglet *Regulus calendula*
Eurasian siskin *Carduelis spinus*	Pine siskin *Carduelis pinus*
Siberian jay *Perisoreus infaustus*	Grey jay *Perisoreus canadensis*
Nutcracker *Nucifraga caryocatactes*	Clark's nutcracker *Nucifraga columbiana*

much less pronounced in long-distance migrants than in residents, with, for example, *Empidonax, Catharus, Vireo, Dendroica* and *Icterus* in North America and *Phylloscopus, Sylvia, Oenanthe, Saxicola* and *Ficedula* in Europe (Mönkkönen & Welsh 1994). Tropical affinities of the North American avifauna are a typical feature, with as many as 76% of passerine species of eastern North America having either conspecific populations or congeneric species breeding in the neotropics (Mönkkönen 1994). Prominent families of neotropical origin in North America are Parulidae, Vireonidae, Tyrannidae and Icteridae. In contrast, Afrotropical influence in the European bird fauna is negligible.

Long-distance migrants are interesting, because they help to shed light on explaining the differences between bird faunas of the different regions of the Northern Hemisphere. The long-distance migrant component of breeding communities is dominant in late-seral stages in North America, whereas it is dominant in early-seral stages in Europe, in both boreal and mixed forests farther south. In addition, contrary to Palearctic migrants, which heavily use African savannah and bushy habitats in winter, with few species wintering in closed evergreen tropical forest (Salewski & Jones 2006), North American tropical migrants depend to a much larger extent on tropical forest, where most species are site faithful throughout the winter (Rappole 1995). One explanation for these differences is that birds tend to use similar habitats in different seasons as a result of physical and physiological adaptations to them (Bilcke 1984). The fact that tropical forests are smaller in overall size and more difficult to reach by migrants in Africa than in South America could contribute to the observed differences between the two migration systems (see Rappole & Jones 2002 for a discussion). Future studies are needed to clarify this point.

Third, the diversity of European bird assemblages differs from that of North America when subjected to scale-dependent analyses (Mönkkönen 1994). This feature results from the explosive radiation of several clades, notably of the Parulidae in North America. At a continental scale, species richness of forest birds is higher in the Nearctic (95 species) than in the Palearctic (78 species). At a regional scale of 200 x 200 km², a so-called *gamma* diversity, there are on average 10 species more in the eastern Nearctic than in the western Palearctic region (mean numbers are 53.8 and 43.6, respectively, P < 0.0001), and regional species pools are also structurally and taxonomically more varied in the former region. The between-habitat component of diversity (PD in Table 2.2, a proxy for *beta* diversity) is greater in North American than in European forest bird assemblages because, on average, two-thirds of species pairs change with forest type in the Nearctic, while the turnover between the two forest types in the western Palearctic amounts to only 35.5–43.2%. This means that habitat selection patterns by birds is finer in North American

Table 2.2 *Average pairwise percentage dissimilarity (PD) of bird communities between two different forest types within a region (<100km), and average expected number of species (ES) in samples of 80 pairs of communities in eastern North America and Europe. PD varies from 0 (all species in common with equal abundances) to 100 (no species in common). N = number of comparisons in each region. Differences in PD are not significant at the between-region scale, but are highly significant at the between-continent scale. ES values do not differ statistically at the between-region scale or at the between-continent scale. See Mönkkönen (1994) for methodological details.*

	N	PD (%)	N	ES
Eastern North America:				
Boreal	6	66.2	12	20.8
Sub-boreal	13	69.1	26	19.8
Europe:				
Boreal	9	35.5	15	17.6
Sub-boreal	10	43.2	29	20.0

forests, with closer niche-packing, than it is for their European counter-parts, a typical feature for wood warblers (Lovette *et al.* 2010). Mönkkö-nen *et al.* (1992) also showed that North American long-distance migrants tend to prefer a relatively narrow range of habitats in relation to forest succession. At the local scale of bird communities (*alpha* diversity), with 18-21 expected species in samples of 80 pairs of commu-nities, average values did not differ between the two continents. In contrast to birds of North America, European birds are less specialised, as shown by the relatively low turnover rate (*beta* diversity) of local communities. These differences between the two continents presumably result from Nearctic forest–associated bird species having experienced higher radiation rates, combined with permanent contact between tropical and temperate regions. The hypothesis that there are more opportunities for bird specialisation in the floristically richer North American forests would be worth testing. It would also be interesting to make similar comparisons of diversity and habitat selec-tion patterns between eastern Asian forest birds and those of the two other forest blocks.

2.2.4 Patterns of Bird Faunas in the Latitudinal Zonation of European Forest Belts

The boreal zone, or taiga (mean winter temperature $-3°C$ and summer mean above $15°C$), is one of the most extensive biogeographic forma-tions on earth, covering 26% of the world's total forested area and extending nearly 7,000 km from end to end (Imbeau *et al.* 2001; Williams 2003). This recent vegetation formation differs greatly from all the vegetation types that were present on earth before the Pleistocene (Haila & Järvinen 1990; Niemi *et al.* 1998; Williams 2003). Dominant species are needle-leaved trees (Norway spruce *Picea abies*, fir *Abies alba*, Scots pine *Pinus sylvestris*, larch *Larix decidua*) more or less intermingled with deciduous trees such as birch *Betula* spp., aspen *Populus tremula*, willow *Salix* spp. and grey alder *Alnus incana*, which usually characterise young successional stages. Although it looks uniform and monotonous over huge areas, the taiga is by no means homogeneous, because large-scale disturbance events such as wildfires and insect outbreaks introduce heterogeneity to the structure and floristic composition of habitats. Large parts of the areas now occupied by taiga between 55°N and 70°N were under ice during glacial times, so the bird fauna of this biome includes a relatively small number of species belonging to the 'Siberian' faunal type (*sensu* Stegman 1938), most of them widespread over huge areas, often straddling Eurasia and North America. The number of species declines from east to west, from 40–42 in parts of eastern Siberia to 32 in Europe (Haila & Järvinen 1990). Typical species are the Ural owl *Strix uralensis*, three-toed woodpecker *Picoides tridactylus*, Siberian jay *Perisoreus infaustus*, Siberian tit *Poecile cinctus*, pine grosbeak *Pinicola enucleator* and rustic bunting *Emberiza rustica*. About 30% of the land birds breeding in Fennoscandia winter in the tropics, 45% are short-distance migrants and only 5–15% are permanent residents (Niemi *et al.* 1998). As in other forest formations, European bird assemblages are taxonomically less diverse than their North American counterparts (see Chapter 6).

The most important and richest vegetation formation of Europe is broadleaved deciduous forests and mixed forests, the so-called temperate-nemoral forest belt, defined by Peterken (1996) and Vera (2000) as lying below 700 m altitude and between 45°N–58°N, and 5°W–25°E (mean winter temperature above −3°C and summer mean below 21°C). In Europe, broadleaved deciduous forests extend about 10 degrees of latitude farther north (ca. 60°N) than in eastern Asia and North America because of the warming effects of the Gulf Stream. However, they do not extend as far south as in eastern Asia and North America, because of a drier summer in southern Europe, which supports a rapid transition to Mediterranean-type woodland. In the near absence of true virgin forest remaining in the lowland temperate zone of Europe, the composition and structure of primeval forests have been inferred from existing old stands that are thought to have received minimal human impact, notably in the eastern part of Europe (e.g., Peterken 1996; Tomiałojć & Wesołowski 2004). Dominant tree species include oak *Quercus* spp., beech *Fagus sylvatica*, elm *Ulmus* spp., lime *Tilia* spp., hornbeam *Carpinus betulus*, aspen, ash *Fraxinus excelsior*, alder *Alnus* spp. and *Norway* spruce, with a more or less dense understorey of hazel *Corylus avellana* and a number of shrubs. Besides their multilayer vertical structure, a major feature which conditions their bird faunas is their horizontal diversity at various spatial scales. Resulting from various causes (discussed below), openings, glades and forest interior edges are important drivers of bird species diversity. The bird species pool of deciduous forests of Europe includes 150–170 species, with passerines amounting to ca. 60% of the species and up to 95% of breeding pairs in local communities (e.g., Wesołowski & Tomiałojć 1997). About half the species are short-distance migrants and 15–20% tropical migrants, with the remaining species being resident (see Chapter 8).

The warm-temperate zone of Europe (mean winter temperature above 4°C and summer mean 21–27°C) is characterised by Mediterranean-type forests, which have no equivalent in the other forest blocks of the Northern Hemisphere except in the south-west part of North America, in California. Compared to the more homogeneous tree species assemblages of temperate Europe, Mediterranean forests are taxonomically much more diverse, with many species of oaks, both evergreen and deciduous, firs, pines *Pinus* spp. and cedars *Cedrus* spp. The bird fauna mostly consists of cold boreal and temperate species, but the diversity of tree species is not mirrored by a similar diversity of Mediterranean-specific bird species. A striking feature of the Mediterranean forest bird fauna is the very low level of endemism in forest-dwelling species, with only seven species now confined to the region: the sombre tit *Poecile lugubris*, the three mesogean nuthatches (Corsican, *Sitta whiteheadi*; Algerian, *S. ledanti*; and Kruper's, *S. krupperi*), two pigeons in the Canary Islands (*Columba bollii, C. junionae*) and the blue chaffinch *F. teydea* in Tenerife and Gran Canaria (Canary Islands). Actually, most of the Mediterranean endemic bird species that diversified in or around the Mediterranean Basin occur in the various kinds of matorrals rather than in forests (Blondel *et al.* 2010). Hence a paradox: the more the forest is mature and dominated by endemic Mediterranean tree species such as holm oak *Quercus ilex* or cork oak *Q. suber*, the less the associated bird assemblages include species of Mediterranean character. One hypothesis to explain this paradox is that Mediterranean-type forests and their associated faunas were never isolated from mid-European forests during the Neogene, because they moved *en bloc* across the western Palearctic in response to environmental upheavals, preventing allopatric speciation events from occurring. This hypothesis has been tested using an analysis of the dynamics of bird assemblages along five habitat gradients located in five localities, three in Mediterranean Europe (Provence, Corsica, Algeria) and two in temperate Europe (Burgundy, Poland). Habitat gradients have been conventionally organised into six habitat types, ranging from open bushy habitats (stage 1 in Fig. 2.4) to mature forests (stage 6) (Blondel *et al.* 2010; Pavoine *et al.* 2013). The prediction was that the between-gradient taxonomic diversity of bird assemblages should decrease from the open scrub stage (stage 1), which should include many region-specific species specialised to young successional stages, to the old mature forest stage (stage 6), where assemblages should become very similar, with many shared species. Figure 2.4, built from a combined correspondence analysis of community structure

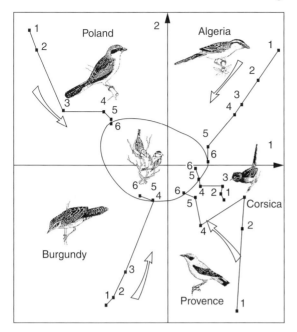

Figure 2.4 Display on the two first axes of a correspondence analysis of the ecological convergence of bird community trajectories along five successional gradients in the western Palearctic. Numbers on the black lines (1–6) correspond to habitats of increasing complexity of vegetation, ranging from habitat 1 (open shrubby habitat) to habitat 6 (old mature forest). Two gradients are non-Mediterranean (Poland and Burgundy) and three are located in the Mediterranean Basin (Algeria, Corsica, Provence). Open arrows show the increasing similarity of communities as the successional turnover proceeds (Blondel *et al.* 2010, p. 47).

in the six habitats of each gradient, strongly supports this prediction, since most region-specific species do occur in the first stages, whereas the six habitats of mature forest share the same species, hence a remarkable trend of ecological convergence in the taxonomic composition of species assemblages in the old mature forest, as shown by the converging direction of arrows in the figure. Interestingly, using a double principal coordinate analysis (DPCoA) to investigate the effects of phylogenetic diversity on bird community structure, Pavoine *et al.* (2013) found much higher phylogenetic similarities of avian assemblages in the forested habitats of these distant locations, including North Africa, compared to communities of open young successional stages (see Chapter 9).

2.3 Pleistocene Climatic Instability and the Bird Faunas of Europe

2.3.1 A Predictable Alternation of Glacial and Interglacial Cycles

The climatic instability of the Neogene peaked in the Pliocene-Pleistocene and the extant European bird fauna is a legacy of this epoch, which was characterised by wet-dry and cool-warm oscillations. The first ice ages began about 2.4 Mya, and recent studies have demonstrated that there have been 21 glacials or near-glacials with extreme climatic fluctuations. On a time scale of 10^3-10^5 years, the distribution and composition of biotas have changed continuously over the whole Northern Hemisphere, so biodiversity patterns have been repeatedly reshaped at a continental scale.

During glacial times, ice sheets covered more than one-third of all land in the Northern Hemisphere and European forests may have occupied no more than 5% of the area (Newton 2003). At the height of full glacial periods, virtually no arboreal vegetation, except scattered populations of birch and pine, persisted north of the large Eurasian mountain ranges (Pyrenees, Alps, Carpathians, Himalayas), so all the forest belts and their associated faunas of the western Palearctic had to find refugia somewhere in the south and the south-east of Europe. Using fossil pollen data to draw 'isopoll maps' (maps with lines of equal relative fossil pollen abundance for a taxon), paleobotanists have mapped the range extensions and contractions in the distribution of several dominant tree species and their presumed associated plant and animal assemblages since the last glacial maximum (LGM; 18,000 BP) (e.g., Huntley & Birks 1983; Huntley & Webb 1989). If species retain their climatic niche as climatic conditions change, which is supported by large-scale tests of niche conservatism (Guisan et al. 2014), then birds followed the north-south (and east-west) migration of their habitats as climatic conditions changed. Fossil remains in many sites dating back to the LGM provide evidence of large-scale migrations as a response to climate change, with forest belts occupying the same relative positions north to south (Mlikovsky 1996). The Mediterranean region, which was larger than today during pleniglacials, because the sea level was 100–150 m lower, acted for most biotas of Europe as the main refuge from which species spread again to the north at each climatic improvement. The large Mediterranean peninsulas – Iberia, Italy and the Balkans – were the most important refugia, but evidence from paleoecology suggests that to these areas should be added small pockets of vegetation which occupied 'cryptic' microrefugia that persisted outside the Mediterranean Basin in central and northern Europe (Hannah *et al.* 2014). Whether or not they functioned as refugia for birds, as they did for plants, remains unknown.

Paleontological and paleobotanical records have shown that the huge diversity of both geography and climatic conditions within the Mediterranean, during both glacial and interglacial periods, allowed the coexistence on a regional scale of all the vegetation belts of Europe and their associated faunas (Blondel 1998). For example, in a deposit dating back to Würm II (70,000 BP), fossil remains of disparate bird assemblages, including such species as lesser kestrel *Falco naumanni*, ptarmigan *Lagopus muta* and snowy owl *Nyctea scandiaca*, have been found together with several forest species, such as turdids and corvids (Mourer-Chauviré 1975). Such assemblages suggest that local landscapes in the Mediterranean during glacial times might have been mosaics of habitats as diverse as tundra, steppe and both coniferous and broadleaved forests, hence a striking compression and presumably dramatic reduction in the size of populations of the European faunas within the Mediterranean Basin. Changes in vegetation and bird assemblages following the retreat of glaciers appear to have been highly individualistic (Hampe & Petit 2005), giving rise to communities with no equivalent in today's biotas, which explains the unexpected composition of species assemblages that are sometimes found in fossil deposits. If movements of species across landscapes are mostly species-specific, forest ecosystems and their animal communities are constantly changing. This is a message for being cautious when modelling future communities in the face of ongoing climate change.

At the end of each glacial cycle, forest belts re-expanded northward. Birds, especially corvids, presumably played a crucial role as seed dispersers. In the early Holocene, dominant tree species with heavy seeds, such as oaks and beech, moved from southern Europe to southern Scandinavia within less than 3,000 years, at a rate of ca. 500 m–1 km per year (Huntley & Birks 1983; Petit *et al.* 1997). The Pleistocene repetition of glacial cycles implies that bird migration, as we see it, is a flexible behaviour periodically allowing migratory species to respond to fluctuations in seasonality and recurrent glacial cycles; indeed, this has been shown to occur on observable time scales (Helbig 2003). One may hypothesise that species with very large extant distribution ranges expanded to the north from southern refugia during interglacial intervals without leaving them. They alternated between reduced and often fragmented populations during glacial periods and large, extensive populations during interglacial periods. This periodic ebb and flow across the continent explains the fact that most European forest-dwelling bird species now have large distributional ranges, including Mediterranean islands and the forested parts of North Africa. Few studies, however, have examined patterns of range variation in this distant past, a topic that could be addressed by future phylogeographic studies.

2.3.2 Evolutionary Consequences of Pleistocene Climatic Instability

As discussed in Section 2.1.3, A Legacy of History, diversification rates tended to decrease across the Pleistocene epoch. However, low rates of diversification do not mean that Pleistocene climatic upheavals did not produce evolutionary signatures and differentiation events (Klicka & Zink 1997; Avise & Walker 1998). There has recently been new insight into the controversial role of recent ice ages in bird speciation. Dates of origin of passerine bird lineages were estimated by Weir and Schluter (2004) from mitochondrial sequence divergence and a molecular clock for the members of a series of superspecies complexes in boreal, sub-boreal and Neotropical forest vegetation belts. Comparing the coalescence times of pairs of species along this latitudinal gradient, these authors convincingly showed that speciation was commonly initiated during recent glacial periods, with all coalescence events in boreal superspecies dating to the late Pleistocene. In North America, patterns of differentiation and endemism of boreal superspecies are consistent with the fragmentation of the boreal forest by ice sheets during the Middle and Late Pleistocene, from 0.7 Mya onwards, giving support to the explicit hypothesis proposed a long time ago by Mengel (1964), which linked geographical patterns of distribution of sister species of wood warblers to successive glacial advances having produced western species from an eastern ancestor. Weir and Schluter (2004) showed that vicariance events caused by glacial advances had the largest impact on the most northerly breeding species of extensive boreal forest; the extreme northern forests were more repeatedly subdivided in isolated refuges than forests farther south. Consistent with these findings, 100% of boreal superspecies coalesced in the Late Pleistocene, compared with just 56% of sub-boreal and 46% of tropical superspecies, suggesting that avifaunas directly fragmented by ice sheets experienced rapid rates of diversification, whereas those distributed farther south were affected to a lesser extent. These findings support the Late Pleistocene speciation model and are consistent with patterns of distribution of many genera of both European and North American birds, which include closely related taxa that are represented by eastern and western forms. In a similar vein, differentiation occurring in mountain ranges as a result of genetic isolation during glaciations has recently been demonstrated by Wallis *et al.* (2016) from molecular studies for a wide range of taxa, including birds. Recent genomic studies show that speciation is a dynamic and complex process in which the incipient species continue to exchange genes long before they reach complete reproductive isolation (Mallet *et al.* 2016). In fact, when considered together, the seemingly contradictory data on the tempo of speciation between the Late Pleistocene speciation model and many phylogenetic studies provide a robust and complementary picture of avian diversification in the Northern Hemisphere. The Pleistocene speciation model is a matter of degree (Lovette 2005) rather than an alternative to models that root differentiation processes in a deeper past. Broad comparisons based on phylogenies of entire avian genera reveal that Pleistocene-era nodes account for only a small proportion of the total species diversity, something like the tail of the distribution of speciation times (e.g., Lovette & Bermingham 1999; Outlaw *et al.* 2003; Johnson & Cicero 2004).

At the subspecific level, much microevolutionary differentiation occurred as a result of genetic drift or changes in selection regimes in small populations that were isolated in refugia during glacial periods (Hewitt 2000, 2004). Many taxa exhibit clear east-west replacement patterns of two sister taxa, with range overlap, hybridisation or parapatry of sister populations, semi-species or allo-species when they spread again and eventually come into contact. Lines isolating different pairs of taxa are often clustered in areas that lie between former refugia, forming 'suture zones'. The most obvious of them, running north-east to south-west across central Europe, coincide with populations spreading from the Iberian refuge meeting those spreading from the Balkans. Differentiation of haplotypes in glacial refugia revealed by mtDNA, followed by subsequent range expansions of two or several phylogeographic units, has been documented in several groups of plants and animals (Petit *et al.* 1997; Taberlet *et al.* 1998). Examples of sister taxa that presumably split from a common ancestor and differentiated during the Plio-Pleistocene include the common nightingale *Luscinia megarhynchos* and the thrush nightingale *L. luscinia*, the short-toed treecreeper *C. brachydactyla* and the Eurasian treecreeper *C. familiaris* (Newton 2003). Helbig *et al.* (1996) concluded from molecular phylogenetics that the chiffchaff *Phylloscopus collybita* complex is a superspecies consisting of two allo-species (*P. canariensis, sindianus*) and two parapatric semi-species (*P. brehmii, collybita*) which evolved in isolated refuges during Pleistocene glaciations.

2.4 Forest Dynamics and Bird Diversity

Before being heavily deforested by humans in most of the Northern Hemisphere, forest belts were more or less continuously distributed over 80% or so of the area at low and mid altitudes (Peterken 1996; Williams 2003). They were far from homogeneous, however, because forests are dynamic structures with a complex interweaving of scales, both spatial and temporal. Forest dynamics are driven by processes that are also scale-dependent (Delcourt *et al.* 1983) and make forests complex habitat mosaics resulting from a combination of disturbance events and tree-specific biological processes: birth, growth, senescence, death and decomposition. Each region is characterised by its own specific regime of natural disturbance (Pickett & White 1985), which is a scale-dependent forest attribute. Disturbance events are produced by external factors, both biotic and abiotic. These can be ordered from large-scale events, such as vast wildfires in the boreal region that modify landscapes over areas covering tens to hundreds or thousands of square kilometres, to medium-scale events, such as windstorms, wildfires and parasitic diseases in temperate forests (e.g., Röhrig 1991), and then to small-scale events, especially tree falls, in all forest types. Several authors (e.g., Vera 2000; Bradshaw *et al.* 2003) argue that before the human extirpation of large herbivorous mammals such as auroch *Bos primigenius* and wild horse *Equus ferus*, and reduction of others, including bison *Bison bonasus*, red deer *Cervus elaphus* and elk *Alces alces*, forests were mosaics of grassland, regenerating scrub and forest groves. This structure was largely generated by the grazing pressure of these animals, the so-called wood-pasture hypothesis (Birks 2005), as opposed to the high forest or closed-canopy forest. Although this hypothesis is still in debate, large herbivores presumably influenced forest composition and structure to some degree (Mitchell 2005). A key point is the return rate of disturbance events, which is a region-specific attribute of disturbance regimes. Disturbance events are a starting point of ecological successions which make forest landscapes dynamic or 'shifting' mosaics (Bormann & Likens 1979) of changing patches between the start of the succession and the stage when the forest becomes, so to say, a facsimile of its state before the disturbance. Whatever their extent and magnitude, disturbance events have two main scale-dependent effects.

First, assuming that responses of species to landscape structure are taxon-specific according to their niche attributes, bird assemblages are composed of species that may be edge-sensitive, fine-grain dependent, area-sensitive, interior-sensitive, etc. (see Dolman 2012). Many wide-ranging species depend on habitat mosaics because they obtain their resources from different parts of the landscape, such as species which nest and forage in different habitat patches. To give but one example of an 'edge' bird, the raven *Corvus corax* in the Białowieża forest forages over large areas for carrion (Mueller *et al.* 2009) and nests in tall pines in poor foraging habitats. Other species that are considered 'edge' species or 'clearing' species in western Europe but breed within forest blocks in primeval-like forest are the common buzzard *Buteo buteo*, wood pigeon *Columba palumbus*, starling *Sturnus vulgaris* and many others (Wesołowski & Fuller 2012). On the other hand, examples of birds which are particularly sensitive to the loss or shrinkage of late-seral stages and habitat fragmentation are the treecreeper *Certhia familiaris* (Suorsa *et al.* 2004) and the Siberian jay *Perisoreus infaustus* in boreal forests (Schmiegelow & Mönkkönen 2002).

Second, the various habitat types that replace each other along the successional turnover are colonised by different sets of species with, as examples, buntings in the very early successional stages, warblers at intermediate stages and woodpeckers when the forest is nearly fully recovered. For example, Sierro and Posse (2014) reported that three to five years after a big wildfire which opened 310 ha of a mixed forest of pine, spruce and larch in Switzerland, new colonists included species such as nightjar *Caprimulgus europaeus*, woodlark *Lullula arborea*, ring ouzel *Turdus torquatus*, tree pipit and whitethroat. Then, as the vegetation became taller and thicker, these species were replaced by wren *Troglodytes troglodytes*, dunnock *Prunella modularis*, bullfinch *Pyrrhula pyrrhula*, mistle thrush *Turdus viscivorus* and several species of tits. All these species should globally be considered as belonging to a forest bird fauna if the term 'forest' encompasses all the habitats of the shifting mosaic of Borman and Likens (1979). Any change in the mosaic structure of forest potentially has detrimental effects on bird communities. For example, intensive forest management in Nordic European countries where wildfires are efficiently controlled likely explains severe regional declines of birds that are either specialists of the deciduous succession phase (e.g., the white-backed woodpecker *Dendrocopos leucotos*) or of old stands of deep forest (Helle & Järvinen 1986).

Ecological successions can be considered diachronically when scaled though time or synchronically when scaled through space. In either case, a forest landscape is a statistical average of the mosaic of patches, with each patch being a non-equilibrium subsystem which is unpredictable in space and time. As the landscape becomes larger and includes an increasing number of patches and ultimately all the patches of the different successional ages, it becomes predictable, making the system in quasi-equilibrium. Each of the non-equilibrium local patches includes a fraction of the regional pool of bird species, i.e., local diversity (*alpha* diversity). But the quasi-equilibrium system, which embraces all the habitat patches from across the successional gradient as a whole, includes all the bird species at the regional scale (*gamma* diversity), that is to say the legacy of the history of the bird fauna that evolved within any given regional disturbance regime.

Summing up, a key point for understanding the history of forest birds is that disturbance events are unpredictable at small scales of time and space, leading to non-equilibrium local systems, but they are predictable in a statistical sense at larger scales. Each bird species of the regional bird fauna, whatever its habitat requirements, must find at least one suitable habitat patch within the limits of its dispersal range. This is a non-trivial consideration, because habitat fragmentation and forest management often make forest ecosystems too small in size to allow the disturbance regime to be fully expressed at appropriate scales.

2.5 Effects of Habitat Loss and Fragmentation during the Holocene

Even if distributional changes of biotas are not as important within climatic stases as between them (i.e., the alternation of glacials-interglacials), the combination of climatic and anthropogenic pressures on forest ecosystems makes the Holocene an epoch of tremendous environmental instability for birds. The longest lasting and most intensive landscape transformations occurred in temperate western Europe and in the Mediterranean Basin (Thirgood 1981; Blondel *et al.* 2010; Fuller 2012), where clearing of predominantly forested landscapes started as early as 10,000–8,000 years ago in the Mediterranean and about 5,000 years ago in western and central Europe (Thirgood 1981; Williams 2003). In Europe, forests were at their minimum in the nineteenth century, and nowadays barely one-third of the once forested landscapes (ca. 6 million km^2) is covered with forests (Williams 2003). In North America, large-scale forest destruction began much later, ca. 300 years ago, and even if approximately two-thirds of the forested area of eastern North America was cleared during the 1800s, many components of human impact had supposedly less severe effects there than in Europe (Mönkkönen & Welsh 1994). Yet assemblages of passerine birds in eastern North America contain many species whose breeding populations have, at least locally, dramatically declined coincidentally with the fragmentation of habitats (Whitcomb *et al.* 1981; Terborgh 1989). Species that evolved and specialised in the structurally diverse and spatially extensive deciduous forests of the Nearctic, such as the wood thrush *Hylocichla mustelina*, the yellow-throated vireo *Vireo flavifrons*, the cerulean warbler *Dendroica cerulean* or the nearly extinct Bachman's warbler *Vermivora bachmanii*, among others, are particularly sensitive to human impact, because these specialised long-distance tropical migrants belong to taxa that evolved in and experienced only unfragmented conditions during the Pleistocene and Holocene (Terborgh 1989; Mönkkönen & Welsh 1994). This explains why they have dramatically declined wherever forests have been reduced in size and fragmented. In contrast, the global population levels of most European forest birds did not drastically change, provided that large forest tracts were left somewhere within their ranges. The European avifauna which experienced a long history of human-caused fragmentation is rather well adapted to fragmented landscapes (see Opdam *et al.* 1985; McLellan *et al.* 1986).

This is not to say, however, that human-induced changes in forest environments had little impact on forest birds in Europe. Many species went locally extinct if they did not adapt to new landscapes (Mikusiński & Angelstam 1997). From archaeozoological data and ancient records, Tomiałojć (2000) reported that more than 30 species that were widespread in the whole of Europe until one century or so ago experienced serious range contraction as a result of human pressure, with small isolated populations scattered in western Europe. Examples are the capercaillie, lesser grey shrike *Lanius minor*, white-backed woodpecker and collared flycatcher *Ficedula collaris*, which today occur in small disjunct areas. In the boreal zone, populations of species highly specialised to old forests, such as the Siberian jay, Siberian tit and three-toed woodpecker, decreased dramatically during the second half of the twentieth century as a consequence of forest habitat loss and fragmentation due to intensive forestry (Helle 1985). On the other hand, many common species experienced a general trend of northward expansion (Järvinen & Ulfstrand 1980) and increased population, including species formerly restricted to the deep primeval forest which are nowadays widespread in anthropogenic habitats (Wesołowski 2007; Wesołowski & Fuller 2012).

Getting a clear picture of the balance between natural and anthropogenic changes is a difficult endeavour. Nevertheless, it is clearly important to make the best of our knowledge about the pros and cons of forest management practices for the benefit of birds and other wildlife (see Chapter 13). Many changes in the distribution and abundance of species are natural processes, some of them perhaps as a consequence of climate changes. Here again, it is often difficult to make a distinction between human and natural drivers of change, although the latter are usually slow and apparently inconspicuous when compared with the tremendous changes due to human impact. These matters are discussed elsewhere in this book.

Acknowledgements

I warmly thank the editors of the book, Peter Ferns and an anonymous reviewer for their useful comments and suggestions, which greatly improved this chapter.

References

Avise, J.C. (2004) *Molecular Markers, Natural History, and Evolution*. Sunderland, MA: Sinauer Associates.

Avise, J.C. & Walker, D. (1998) Pleistocene phylogeographic effects on avian populations and the speciation process. *Proceedings of the Royal Society B*, **265**, 457–463.

Barker, F.K., Burns, K.J., Klicka, J., Lanyon, S.M. & Lovette, I.J. (2015) New insights into New World biogeography: An integrated view from the phylogeny of blackbirds, cardinals, sparrows, tanagers, warblers, and allies. *The Auk: Ornithological Advances*, **132**, 333–348.

Barker, F.K., Cibois, A., Schikler, P., Feinstein, J. & Cracraft, J. (2004) Phylogeny and diversification of the largest avian radiation. *Proceedings of the National Academy of Sciences*, **101**, 11040–11045.

Bell, C. (2005) The origin and development of bird migration: Comments on Rappole and Jones, and an alternative evolutionary model. *Ardea*, **93**, 115–123.

Bermingham, E., Rohwer, S., Freeman, S. & Wood, C. (1992) Vicariance biogeography in the Pleistocene and speciation in North American wood warblers: A test of Mengel's model. *Proceedings of the National Academy of Sciences*, **89**, 6624–6628.

Berthold, P. (2001) *Bird Migration: A General Survey*, 2nd ed. Oxford: Oxford University Press.

Bilcke, G. (1984) Residence and non-residence in passerines: Dependence on the vegetation structure. *Ardea*, **72**, 223–227.

Birks, H.J.B. (2005) Mind the gap: How open were European primeval forests? *Trends in Ecology and Evolution*, **20**, 154–156.

Blondel, J. (1998) History and evolution of the European Bird fauna. *Biologia e Conservazion della Fauna*, **102**, 28–37.

Blondel, J., Aronson, J., Bodiou, J.-Y. & Boeuf, G. (2010) *The Mediterranean Region: Biodiversity in Space and Time*. Oxford: Oxford University Press.

Blondel, J., Catzeflis, F. & Perret, P. (1996) Molecular phylogeny and the historical biogeography of the warblers of the genus *Sylvia* (Aves). *Journal of Evolutionary Biology*, **9**, 871–891.

Blondel, J. & Mourer-Chauviré, C. (1998) Evolution and history of the western Palaearctic avifauna. *Trends in Ecology and Evolution*, **13**, 488–492.

Blondel, J. & Vigne, J.-D. (1993) Space, time, and man as determinants of diversity of birds and mammals in the Mediterranean region. In *Species Diversity in Ecological Communities*. Ricklefs, R.E. & Schluter, D. (eds.). Chicago: Chicago University Press, pp. 135–146.

Böhning-Gaese, K., Gonzalez-Guzman, L.I. & Brown, J.H. (1998) Constraints on dispersal and the evolution of the avifauna of the Northern Hemisphere. *Evolutionary Ecology*, **12**, 767–783.

Böhning-Gaese, K., Schuda, M.D. & Helbig, A.J. (2003) Weak phylogenetic effects on ecological niches of *Sylvia* warblers. *Journal of Evolutionary Biology*, **16**, 956–965.

Bormann, F.H. & Likens, G.E. (1979) Catastrophic disturbance and the steady state in northern hardwood forests. *American Scientist*, **67**, 660–669.

Bradshaw, R.H.W., Hannon, G.E. & Lister, A.M. (2003) A long-term perspective on ungulate-vegetation interactions. *Forest Ecology and Management*, **181**, 267–280.

CLIMAP (1976) The surface of the Ice-age Earth. *Science*, **191**, 1131–1137.

Cooper, J.H. (2000) First fossil record of azure-winged magpie *Cyanopica cyanus* in Europe. *Ibis*, **142**, 150–151.

Cronk, Q.C.B. & Ojeda, I. (2008) Bird pollinated flowers in an evolutionary and molecular context. *Journal of Experimental Botany*, **59**, 715–727.

Delcourt, H.R., Delcourt, P.A. & Webb, T. (1983) Dynamic plant ecology: The spectrum of vegetational change in space and time. *Quaternary Science Reviews*, **1**, 153–175.

Dolman, P.M. (2012) Mechanisms and processes underlying landscape structure effects on bird populations. In *Birds and Habitat: Relationships in Changing Landscapes*. Fuller, R.J. (ed.). Cambridge: Cambridge University Press, pp. 93–124.

Drovetski, S.V. (2003) Plio-Pleistocene climatic oscillations, Holarctic biogeography and speciation in an avian subfamily. *Journal of Biogeography*, **30**, 1173–1181.

Fok, K.W., Wade, C.M. & Parkin, D.T. (2002) Inferring the phylogeny of disjunct populations of the Azure-winged Magpie *Cyanopica cyanus* from mitochondrial control region sequences. *Proceedings of the Royal Society B*, **269**, 1671–1679.

Folke, C., Holling, C.S. & Perrings, C. (1996) Biological diversity, ecosystems, and the human scale. *Ecological Applications*, **6**, 1018–1024.

Fuller, R.J. (ed.). (2012) *Birds and Habitat: Relationships in Changing Landscapes*. Cambridge: Cambridge University Press.

Grant, V. (1994) Historical development of ornithophily in the western North American flora. *Proceedings of the National Academy of Sciences*, **91**, 10407–10411.

Gregory, R.D., Greenwood, J.J.D. & Hagemeijer, E.J.M. (1998) The EBCC Atlas of European Breeding Birds: A contribution to science and conservation. *Biologia e Conservazione della Fauna*, **102**, 38–49.

Guisan, A., Petitpierre, B., Broennimann, O., Daehler, C. & Kueffer, C. (2014) Unifying niche shift studies: Insights from biological invasions. *Trends in Ecology and Evolution*, **29**, 260–269.

Haila, Y. & Järvinen, O. (1990) Northern conifer forests and their bird species assemblages. In *Biogeography and Ecology of Forest Bird Communities*. Keast, A. (ed.). The Hague: SPB Academic Publishing, pp. 61–85.

Hampe, A. & Petit, R.J. (2005) Conserving biodiversity under climate change. *Ecology Letters*, **8**, 461–467.

Hannah, L., Flint, L., Syphard, A.D. *et al.* (2014) Fine-grain modeling of species' response to climate change: Holdouts, stepping-stones, and microrefugia. *Trends in Ecology and Evolution*, **29**, 390–397.

Helbig, A.J. (2003) Evolution of migration: A phylogenetic and biogeographic perspective. In *Avian Migration*. Berthold, P., Gwinner, E. & Sonnenschein, E. (eds.). Heidelberg: Springer Verlag, pp. 3–20.

Helbig, A.J., Martens, J., Seibold, F., Henning, F., Schottler, B. & Wink, M. (1996) Phylogeny and species limits in the Palaearctic chiffchaff *Phylloscopous collybita* complex: Mitochondrial genetic differentiation and bioacoustic evidence. *Ibis*, **138**, 650–666.

Helle, P. (1985) Effects of forest regeneration on the structure of bird communities in northern Finland. *Holarctic Ecology*, **8**, 120–132.

Helle, P. & Järvinen, O. (1986) Population trends of north Finnish land birds in relation to their habitat selection and changes in forest structure. *Oikos*, **46**, 107–115.

Helle, P. & Mönkkönen, M. (1990) Forest succession and bird communities: Theoretical aspects and practical implications. In *Biogeography and Ecology of Forest Bird Communities*. Keast, A. (ed.). The Hague: SPB Academic Publishing, pp. 299–318.

Hewitt, G.M. (2000) The genetic legacy of Quaternary ice ages. *Nature*, **405**, 907–913.

Hewitt, G.M. (2004) Genetic consequences of climatic oscillations in the Quaternary. *Philosophical Transactions of the Royal Society B*, **359**, 183–195.

Holmes, R.T. & Sherry, T.W. (2001) Thirty-year bird population trends in an unfragmented temperate deciduous forest: Importance of habitat change. *Auk*, **118**, 589–609.

Huntley, B. (1993) Species-richness in north-temperate zone forests. *Journal of Biogeography*, **20**, 163–180.

Huntley, B. & Birks, H.J.B. (1983) *An Atlas of Past and Present Pollen Maps for Europe: 0–13000 Years Ago*. Cambridge: Cambridge University Press.

Huntley, B. & Webb III, T. (1989) Migration: Species' response to climatic variations caused by changes in the earth's orbit. *Journal of Biogeography*, **16**, 5–19.

Imbeau, L., Mönkkönen, M. & Desrochers, A. (2001) Long-term effects of forestry on birds of the eastern Canadian boreal forests: A comparison with Fennoscandia. *Conservation Biology*, **15**, 1151–1162.

Järvinen, O. & Ulfstrand, S. (1980) Species turnover of a continental bird fauna: Northern Europe, 1850–1970. *Oecologia*, **46**, 186–195.

Jetz, W., Thomas, G.H., Joy, J.B., Hartmann, K. & Mooers, A.O. (2012) The global diversity of birds in space and time. *Nature*, **491**, 444–448.

Johnson, N.K. & Cicero, C. (2004) New mitochondrial DNA data affirm the importance of Pleistocene speciation in North American birds. *Evolution*, **58**, 1122–1130.

Jordano, P. (2014) Fruits and frugivory. In *Seeds: The Ecology of Regeneration of Plant Communities*, 3rd ed. Gallagher, R.S. (ed.). Wallingford, UK: CABI, pp. 18–61.

Klein, N.K., Burns, K.J., Hackett, S.J. & Griffiths, C.S. (2004) Molecular phylogenetic relationships among the wood warblers (Parulidae) and historical biogeography in the Caribbean basin. *Journal of Caribbean Ornithology*, **17**, 3-17.

Klicka, J. & Zink, R.M. (1997) The importance of recent ice ages in speciation: A failed paradigm. *Science*, **277**, 1666–1669.

Klicka, J. & Zink, R.M. (1999) Pleistocene effects on North American songbird evolution. *Proceedings of the Royal Society B*, **266**, 695–700.

Lack, D. (1971) *Ecological Isolation in Birds*. Oxford: Blackwell.

Latham, R.E. & Ricklefs, R.E. (1993) Continental comparisons of temperate-zone tree species diversity. In *Species Diversity in Ecological Communities: Historical and Geographical Perspectives*. Ricklefs, R.E. & Schluter, D. (eds.). Chicago: Chicago University Press, pp. 294–314.

Lovette, I.J. (2005) Glacial cycles and the tempo of avian speciation. *Trends in Ecology and Evolution*, **20**, 57–59.

Lovette, I.J. & Bermingham, E. (1999) Explosive speciation in the New World *Dendroica* warblers. *Proceedings of the Royal Society B*, **266**, 1629–1636.

Lovette, I.J., Pérez-Emán, J.L., Sullivan, J.P. *et al.* (2010) A comprehensive multilocus phylogeny for the wood-warblers and a revised classification of the Parulidae (Aves). *Molecular Phylogenetics and Evolution*, **57**, 753–770.

MacArthur, R.H. (1958) Population ecology of some warblers of northeastern coniferous forests. *Ecology*, **39**, 599–619.

Mallet, J., Besansky, N. & Hahn, M.W. (2016) How reticulated are species? *BioEssays*, **38**, 140–149.

Marshall, H.D. & Baker, A.J. (1999) Colonisation history of Atlantic Islands chaffinches (*Fringilla coelebs*) revealed by mitochondrial DNA. *Molecular Phylogenetics and Evolution*, **11**, 201–212.

Martin, L.D. (1984) The origin and early radiation of birds. In *Perspectives in Ornithology*, Brush, A.H. & Clark, G.A. (eds.). Cambridge: Cambridge University Press, pp. 291–344.

Mayr, E. (1946) The history of the North American bird fauna. *Wilson Bulletin*, **58**, 1–68.

Mayr, E. (1964) Inferences concerning the Tertiary American bird faunas. *Proceedings of the National Academy of Sciences*, **51**, 280–288.

McLellan, C.H., Dobson, A.P., Wilcove, D.S. & Lynch, J.F. (1986) Effects of forest fragmentation on new- and old-world bird communities: Empirical observations and theoretical implications. In *Wildlife 2000. Modelling Habitat Relationships of Terrestrial Vertebrates*. Verner, J., Morrison, M. & Ralph, C.J. (eds.). Madison: University of Wisconsin Press, pp. 305–313.

McPeek, M.A. (2008) The ecological dynamics of clade diversification and community assembly. *American Naturalist*, **172**, E270–E284.

Mengel, R.M. (1964) The probable history of species formation in some northern Wood warblers (Parulidae). *Living Bird*, **3**, 9–43.

Mikusiński, G. & Angelstam, P. (1997) Economic geography, forest distribution, and woodpecker diversity in Central Europe. *Conservation Biology*, **12**, 200–208.

Mitchell, F.J.G. (2005) How open were European primeval forests? Hypothesis testing using palaeoecological data. *Journal of Ecology*, **93**, 168–177.

Mlikovsky, J. (1996) Tertiary avian localities of Europe. *Acta Universitatis Carolinae*, **39**, 519–852.

Moen, D. & Morlon, H. (2014) Why does diversification slow down? *Trends in Ecology and Evolution*, **29**, 190–197.

Mönkkönen, M. (1994) Diversity patterns in Palaearctic and Nearctic forest bird assemblages. *Journal of Biogeography*, **21**, 183–195.

Mönkkönen, M. & Helle, P. (1989) Migratory habits of birds breeding in different phases of forest succession: A comparison between the Palaearctic and the Nearctic. *Annales Zoologici Fennici*, **26**, 323–330.

Mönkkönen, M., Helle, P. & Welsh, D.A. (1992) Perspectives on Palearctic and Nearctic bird migration: Comparisons and overview of life-history and ecology of migrant passerines. *Ibis*, **134** (suppl.), 7–13.

Mönkkönen, M. & Viro, P. (1997) Taxonomic diversity of the terrestrial bird and mammal fauna in temperate and boreal biomes of the Northern Hemisphere. *Journal of Biogeography*, **24**, 603–612.

Mönkkönen, M. & Welsh, D.A. (1994) A biogeographical hypothesis on the effects of human caused landscape changes on the forest bird communities of Europe and North America. *Annales Zoologici Fennici*, **31**, 61–70.

Moreau, R.E. (1972) *The Palearctic-African Bird Migration Systems*. New York: Academic Press.

Mourer-Chauviré, C. (1975) Les oiseaux du Pléistocène moyen et supérieur de France. *Documents du. Laboratoire de la. Faculté des Sciences de Lyon*, **64**, 1–624.

Mourer-Chauviré, C. (1995) Dynamics of the avifauna during the Paleogene and the Early Neogene of France. Settling of the recent fauna. *Acta Zoologica Cracoviensa*, **38**, 325–342.

Mueller, T., Selva, N., Pugacewicz, E. & Prins, E. (2009) Scale-sensitive landscape complementation determines habitat suitability for a territorial generalist. *Ecography*, **32**, 345–353.

Nee, S., Holmes, E.C., May, R.M. & Harvey, P.H. (1994) Extinction rates can be estimated from molecular phylogenies. *Philosophical Transactions of the Royal Society B*, **344**, 77–82.

Nee, S., Mooers, A.O. & Harvey, P.H. (1992) Tempo and mode of evolution revealed from molecular phylogenies. *Proceedings of the National Academy of Sciences*, **89**, 8322–8326.

Newton, I. (2003) *Speciation and Biogeography of Birds*. London: Academic Press.

Niemi, G.J., Hanowski, J., Helle, P. *et al.* (1998) Ecological sustainability of birds in boreal forests. *Conservation Ecology*, **2**, 1–17.

Opdam, P., Rijsdijk, G. & Hustings, F. (1985) Bird communities in small woods in an agricultural landscape: Effects of area and isolation. *Biological Conservation*, **34**, 333–352.

Outlaw, D. & Voelker, G. (2006) Phylogenetic tests of hypotheses for the evolution of avian migration: A case study using the Motacillidae. *Auk*, **123**, 455–488.

Outlaw, D.C., Voelker, G., Mila, B. & Girman, D.J. (2003) Evolution of long-distance migration in and historical biogeography of *Catharus* thrushes: A molecular phylogenetic approach. *Auk*, **120**, 299–310.

Pasquet, E., Barker, F.K., Martens, J., Tillier, A., Cruaud, C. & Cibois, A. (2014) Evolution within the nuthatches (Sittidae: Aves, Passeriformes): Molecular phylogeny, biogeography and ecological perspectives. *Journal of Ornithology*, **155**, 755–765.

Pavoine, S., Blondel, J., Dufour, A.B., Gasc, A. & Bonsall, M.B. (2013) A new technique for analysing interacting factors affecting biodiversity patterns: Crossed-DPCoA. *PLoS One*, **8**, e54530.

Peterken, G.F. (1996) *Natural Woodland: Ecology and Conservation in Northern Temperate Regions*. Cambridge: Cambridge University Press.

Petit, R.J., Pineau, E., Demesure, B. *et al.* (1997) Chloroplast DNA footprints of postglacial recolonization by oaks. *Proceedings of the National Academy of Sciences*, **94**, 9996-10001.

Pickett, S.T.A. & White, P.S. (1985) *The Ecology of Natural Disturbance and Patch Dynamics*. New York: Academic Press.

Price, T., Helbig, A.J. & Richman, A.D. (1997) Evolution of breeding distributions in the Old World leaf warblers (genus *Phylloscopus*). *Evolution*, **51**, 552–561.

Price, T., Lovette, I.J., Bermingham, E., Gibbs, H.L. & Richman, A.D. (2000) The imprint of history on communities of North American and Asian warblers. *American Naturalist*, **156**, 354–367.

Rappole, J.H. (1995) *The Ecology of Migrant Birds: A Neotropical Perspective*. Washington, DC: Smithsonian Institute Press.

Rappole, J.H. & Jones, P. (2002). Evolution of Old and New World migration systems. *Ardea*, **90**, 525–537.

Regal, P.J. (1977) Ecology and evolution of flowering plant dominance. *Science*, **196**, 622–662.

Ricklefs, R.E. (2006) Global variation in the diversification rate of passerine birds. *Ecology*, **87**, 2468–2478.

Röhrig, E. (1991) Vegetation structure and forest succession. In *Temperate Deciduous Forests: Ecosystems of the World*, Vol. 7. Röhrig, E. & Ulrich, B. (eds.). Amsterdam: Elsevier, pp. 35–49.

Rosenzweig, M.L. (1995) *Species Diversity in Space and Time*. Cambridge: Cambridge University Press.

Salewski, V. & Bruderer, B. (2007) The evolution of bird migration: A synthesis. *Naturwissenschaften*, **94**, 268–279.

Salewski, V. & Jones, P. (2006) Palearctic passerines in Afrotropical environments: A review. *Journal of Ornithology*, **147**, 192–201.

Schmiegelow, F.K.A. & Mönkkönen, M. (2002) Habitat loss and fragmentation in dynamic landscapes: Avian perspectives from the boreal forests. *Ecological Applications*, **12**, 375–389.

Selander, R.K. (1971) Systematics and speciation in birds. In *Avian Biology*, Vol. I. Farner, D.S. & King, J.R. (eds.). New York, London: Academic Press, pp. 57–147.

Shirihai, H., Gargallo, G. & Helbig, A.J. (2001) *Sylvia Warblers*. London: Helm.

Sierro, A. & Posse, B. (2014) Evolution de l'avifaune de la forêt incendiée de Loèche. *Nos Oiseaux*, **61**, 110–112.

Snow, D.W. (1976) *The Web of Adaptation*. London: Collins.

Stegmann, B. (1938) *Grundzüge der ornithogeographischen Gliederung des paläarktischen Gebietes*. Moscow: Zoological Institute of the Russian Academy of Sciences.

Suorsa, P., Helle, H., Koivunen, V., Huhta, E. & Hakkarainen, H. (2004) Effects of forest patch size on physiological stress and immunocompetence in an area-sensitive passerine, the Eurasian treecreeper (*Certhia familiaris*): An experiment. *Proceedings of the Royal Society B*, **271**, 435–440.

Taberlet, P., Fumagali, L., Wust-Saucy, A.-G. & Cosson, J.-F. (1998) Comparative phylogeography and postglacial colonization routes in Europe. *Molecular Ecology*, **6**, 289–301.

Terborgh, J.W. (1989) *Where Have All the Birds Gone?* Princeton, NJ: Princeton University Press.

Thirgood, J.V. (1981) *Man and the Mediterranean Forest: A History of Resource Depletion*. New York: Academic Press.

Tomiałojć, L. (2000) An East-West gradient in the breeding distribution and species richness of the European woodland avifauna. *Acta Ornithologica*, **35**, 3–17.

Tomiałojć, L. & Wesołowski, T. (2004) Diversity of the Białowieża forest avifauna in space and time. *Journal of Ornithology*, **145**, 81–92.

Vera, F.W.M. (2000) *Grazing Ecology and Forest History*. Wallingford, UK: CABI Publishing.

Voelker, G. (1999) Dispersal, vicariance, and clocks: Historical biogeography and speciation in a cosmopolitan passerine genus (*Anthus*: motacillidae). *Evolution*, **53**, 1536–1552.

Wallis, G.P., Waters, J.M., Upton, P. & Craw, D. (2016) Transverse alpine speciation driven by glaciation. *Trends in Ecology and Evolution*, **31**, 916–926.

Walter, H. (1979) *Vegetation of the Earth*. New York: Springer-Verlag.

Webb, T. III & Bartlein, P.J. (1992) Global changes during the last 3 million years: Climatic controls and biotic responses. *Annual Review of Ecology, Evolution, and Systematics*, **23**, 141–173.

Webster, A. J. & Purvis, A. (2002) Testing the accuracy of methods for reconstructing ancestral states of continuous characters. *Proceedings of the Royal Society B*, **269**, 143–159.

Weir, J. & Schluter, D. (2004) Ice sheets promote speciation in boreal birds. *Proceedings of the Royal Society B*, **271**, 1881–1887.

Wesołowski, T. (2007) Primeval conditions: What can we learn from them? *Ibis*, **149** (Suppl. 2), 64–77.

Wesołowski, T. & Fuller, R.J. (2012) Spatial variation and temporal shifts in habitat use by birds at the European scale. In *Birds and Habitat: Relationships in Changing Landscapes*. Fuller, R.J. (ed.). Cambridge: Cambridge University Press, pp. 63–92.

Wesołowski, T. & Tomiałojć, L. (1997) Breeding bird dynamics in a primaeval temperate forest: Long-term trends in Białowieża National Park (Poland). *Ecography*, **20**, 432–453.

Wesołowski, T., Tomiałojć, L., Mitrus, C., Rowiński, P. & Czeszczewik, D. (2002) The breeding bird community of a primaeval temperate forest (Białowieża National Park, Poland) at the end of the 20th century. *Acta Ornithologica*, **37**, 27–45.

Wetmore, A. (1959) Birds of the Pleistocene in North America. *Smithsonian Miscellaneous Collections*, **138**, 1–24.

Whitcomb, R.F., Robbins, C.S., Lynch, J.F. *et al.* (1981) Effects of forest fragmentation on avifauna of the eastern deciduous forest. In *Forest Island Dynamics in Man-Dominated Landscapes*. Burgess, R.L. & Sharpe, D.M. (eds.). Berlin, Heidelberg, New York: Springer Verlag, pp. 125–205.

Wiens, J.A. & Donoghue, M.J. (2004) Historical biogeography, ecology and species richness. *Trends in Ecology and Evolution*, **19**, 639–644.

Williams, M. (2003) *Deforesting the Earth: From Prehistory to Global Crisis*. Chicago: University of Chicago Press.

Willis, K.J. & MacDonald, G.M. (2011) Long-term ecological records and their relevance to climate change predictions for a warmer world. *Annual Review of Ecology, Evolution, and Systematics*, **42**, 267–287.

Winger, B.M., Lovette, I.J. & Winkler, D.W. (2012) Ancestry and evolution of seasonal migration in the Parulidae. *Proceedings of the Royal Society B*, **279**, 610–618.

Wood, J.R. & De Pietri, V.L. (2015) Next-generation paleornithology: Technological and methodological advances allow new insights into the evolutionary and ecological histories of living birds. *The Auk: Ornithological Advances*, **132**, 486–506.

Zink, R.M. (2002) Towards a framework for understanding the evolution of avian migration. *Journal of Avian Biology*, **33**, 433–437.

Zink, R.M., Klicka, J. & Barber, B.R. (2004) The tempo of avian diversification during the Quaternary. *Philosophical Transactions of the Royal Society B*, **359**, 215–220.

Zink, R.M. & Slowinski, J.B. (1995) Evidence from molecular systematics for decreased avian diversification in the Pleistocene Epoch. *Proceedings of the National Academy of Sciences*, **92**, 5832–5835.

3 · Ecological Adaptations of Birds to Forest Environments

MARC-ANDRÉ VILLARD AND
RUUD FOPPEN

3.1 Introduction

When *Archaeopteryx* and other ancestors of modern birds appeared in the late Jurassic, forests dominated by gymnosperms were already well developed. Neornithes (modern birds) were first recorded in the late Cretaceous, a period during which angiosperms flourished. Hence, it is fair to say that in the north temperate zone, the lineage that led to contemporary birds evolved in the presence of forests. The floristic diversity of the world's forests and their associated structural complexity paved the way for diversification of bird form and function by offering a wide variety of ecological niches. Naturalists and avian ecologists have spent considerable effort documenting the associations between bird species and features of their habitats, yet they also recognise that bird-habitat relationships can vary according to spatial scale (Wiens *et al.* 1987) and geographic location (Betts & Villard 2009), and that they can evolve over a relatively short time. For example, Wesołowski and Fuller (2012) document many instances of rapid changes in the biotopes (habitat types) used by individual species within Europe.

In this chapter, we compare the avifaunas of temperate forest ecoregions of Europe and North America as a basis for discussing ecological adaptations, which we define as structural, behavioural or physiological traits that positively influence the relationship between an organism and its environment and that evolved through natural selection (Table 3.1). We focus on adaptations for nesting, foraging or facing challenges imposed by winter conditions, as well as on the resilience of forest birds to anthropogenic activities. For information on temperate forests of eastern Asia and their avifauna, see Askins (2014) and Chapter 2.

European and North American forests have had very different histories since the last glaciation, especially when considering the intensity and extent of the human footprint. In addition, the forest avifaunas of

Table 3.1 *Examples of ecological adaptations observed in some temperate and tropical forest birds.*

Types of adaptation	Examples
Structural	Intraspecific variability in black-throated green warbler *Setophaga virens* morphology as a function of foraging substrates and tactics (Parrish 1995)
Behavioural	Use of crevices or semi-detached pieces of bark as a nesting substrate by treecreeper *Certhia* spp.; ability to locate and extract insects from curled leaves in worm-eating warbler (Greenberg 1987); maintenance of granaries by the cooperatively breeding acorn woodpecker *Melanerpes formicivorus* (Koenig *et al.* 1995)
Physiological	Ability to digest foliage in hoatzin *Opistochomus hoazin* (Grajal 1995)

North America and Europe show profound taxonomic differences, which may, to some degree, affect their responses to both natural and anthropogenic disturbances. In Chapter 2, Jacques Blondel adopts an evolutionary perspective to examine long-term changes in forest avifaunas of the Northern Hemisphere. Here, we focus our attention on the contemporary avifaunas of temperate forests of the two continents to identify and, as far as possible, interpret differences in the structure of species assemblages.

We are aware of striking differences that exist in habitat associations of a number of species across their ranges, and therefore we chose to focus on two biogeographical regions of Europe, Atlantic and Continental (European Environment Agency 2002), and on the northern hardwood forest of North America. According to the American Ornithologists' Union Checklist of North and Middle American Birds, approximately 112 bird species occur in the northern hardwood forest of North America and 64 in the Atlantic and Continental ecoregions of Europe (Tucker & Evans 1997). These numbers include only species that are both nesting and foraging under closed canopies. Hereafter, comparisons between North America and Europe will be made between the northern hardwood forest and the two European ecoregions.

Relative to open biotopes such as prairies or marshes, the well-developed 'third dimension' of forest stands offers a multitude of potential ecological niches. Indeed, the vertical structure of the vegetation has been considered for a long time as a key predictor of bird species richness, irrespective of

tree species composition. MacArthur and MacArthur (1961) first introduced this notion, and this relationship was shown to hold when
analysing the forest avifaunas of North America and Australia (MacArthur
et al. 1966; Recher 1969). There are exceptions to this relationship: in the
southern temperate zone (Patagonia and Central Chile), plant species
composition appears to have played a stronger role than indices of vertical
structure in explaining patterns in bird diversity (Ralph 1985; Estades
1997). Both authors observed that bird species diversity was higher in scrub
than in grassland or forest. When restricting the analysis to forest habitats,
Estades (1997) did observe a positive correlation between foliage height
diversity and bird species richness. When excluding grasslands, Ralph
(1985) still observed higher bird species diversity in low scrub than in
the more structurally complex forests. He argued that this paradoxical
observation may reflect, in part, the geographical isolation of *Nothofagus*
forests.

3.2 Forest vs Open-Land Bird Assemblages: The Third Dimension

Because most species are diurnal, vocal and therefore relatively easy to
observe, birds have played a major role in the development of community ecology (Wiens 1989). The factors influencing the structure of forest
bird species assemblages include forest stand age, tree species composition
and history of disturbance, whether natural or anthropogenic. The
particular relationships linking these factors to bird diversity have
received considerable attention. One way to investigate patterns of forest
bird species diversity is to compare species assemblages of forests and
'open' biotopes. Although it is hard to control for sampling effort,
we performed a qualitative comparison to identify major differences.

Solely on the basis of their vertical structure, most forests would be
expected to host more species than open biotopes, and possibly
be characterised by higher taxonomic diversity. For example, if we
compare the species assemblage of grasslands in Maine, United States,
to that of mature deciduous forests across the Canadian border, in New
Brunswick, the latter comprises many more species than the former
(40 vs 16) and families (19 vs 10), even though the area surveyed is much
smaller (250 ha vs ca. 735 ha; Table 3.2). Relative to its species richness,
the forest bird assemblage also comprises more species per family (2.1)
than the grasslands bird assemblage (1.8). When comparing German
surveys based on standardised sampling effort, species richness was much

Table 3.2 *List of species detected in bird surveys conducted in grasslands of Maine, United States (Vickery* et al. *1994), and mature deciduous forest of New Brunswick, Canada (Villard* et al. *unpublished data; see Haché and Villard 2010 for methods).*

Grasslands	Mature deciduous forest
16 species, 10 families (n = 235 fragments; 100 m radius point counts)	40 species, 19 families (n = 10 plots; total 250 ha)
Circus cyaneus (Accipitridae)	*Accipiter gentilis* (Accipitridae)
Charadrius vociferous (Charadriidae)	*Buteo platypterus* (Accipitridae)
Bartramia longicauda (Scolopacidae)	*Bonasa umbellus* (Phasianidae)
Empidonax alnorum (Tyrannidae)	*Scolopax minor* (Scolopacidae)
Eremophila alpestris (Alaudidae)	*Strix varia* (Strigidae)
Toxostoma rufum (Mimidae)	*Archilocus colubris* (Trochilidae)
Geothlypis trichas (Parulidae)	*Dryocopus pileatus* (Picidae)
Passerina cyanea (Cardinalidae)	*Picoides pubescens* (Picidae)
Spizella pusilla (Emberizidae)	*Picoides villosus* (Picidae)
Pooecetes gramineus (Emberizidae)	*Sphyrapicus varius* (Picidae)
Passerculus sandwichensis (Emberizidae)	*Empidonax minimus* (Tyrannidae)
Ammodramus savannarum (Emberizidae)	*Contopus virens* (Tyrannidae)
Melospiza melodia (Emberizidae)	*Cyanocitta cristata* (Corvidae)
Melospiza lincolnii (Emberizidae)	*Certhia americana* (Certhiidae)
Dolichonyx oryzivorus (Icteridae)	*Sitta carolinensis* (Sittidae)
Sturnella magna (Icteridae)	*Sitta canadensis* (Sittidae)
	Poecile atricapillus (Paridae)
	Troglodytes hiemalis (Troglodytidae)
	Turdus migratorius (Turdidae)
	Catharus ustulatus (Turdidae)
	Catharus guttatus (Turdidae)
	Catharus fuscescens (Turdidae)
	Regulus satrapa (Regulidae)
	Vireo solitarius (Vireonidae)
	Vireo philadelphicus (Vireonidae)
	Vireo olivaceus (Vireonidae)
	Seiurus aurocapilla (Parulidae)
	Setophaga ruticilla (Parulidae)
	Parula americana (Parulidae)
	Setophaga caerulescens (Parulidae)
	Setophaga virens (Parulidae)
	Setophaga magnolia (Parulidae)
	Setophaga fusca (Parulidae)
	Setophaga pensylvanica (Parulidae)
	Mniotilta varia (Parulidae)
	Geothlypis philadelphia (Parulidae)
	Zonotrichia albicollis (Emberizidae)
	Pheucticus ludovicianus (Cardinalidae)
	Piranga olivacea (Cardinalidae)
	Haemorhous purpureus (Fringillidae)

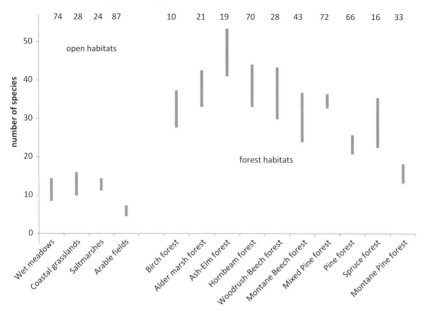

Figure 3.1 Predicted species richness of sites of 30 ha (lower limit) and 100 ha (upper limit) based on species-area regressions of plots within Atlantic and Continental ecoregions of Germany (Flade 1994). Survey effort was standardised. The numbers at the top of the graph indicate the sample size (number of surveys) used to estimate the species-area relationship.

greater in forest than in open biotopes (Fig. 3.1). Hence, it appears that forest bird assemblages are indeed richer than those of open biotopes. Further analyses would be required to determine whether they exhibit more adaptive radiation.

In the conterminous United States, Culbert *et al.* (2013) compared the relative influence of vertical and horizontal habitat structures as predictors of bird species richness at the scale of Breeding Bird Survey routes. In the Eastern Broadleaf forest region, parameters of vertical structure represented more than half of the independent contributions of explanatory variables. Although three-dimensional partitioning of space among different species of forest birds was reported long ago, early workers (e.g., Robinson 1981) mapped horizontal and vertical distributions separately. Cooper *et al.* (2014) mapped the three-dimensional positions occupied by American redstarts *Setophaga ruticilla* in mangroves and scrub on the wintering grounds. When comparing territory overlap using 2D and 3D mapping, the former overestimated overlap by as much as 30%, suggesting that individuals actually partitioned space in all three dimensions. Species can be ground, shrub or canopy specialists. They can forage preferentially on tree trunks, limbs or tiny branches. Or they can occupy the same strata but use different foraging techniques. Species that forage on tree trunks or branches have also been shown to partition bark surface as a function of their frequency of use of different portions of a tree (Török 1990), or through depth of excavation for different insect prey (Murphy & Lenhausen 1998).

The third dimension offered by trees influences several other components of avian morphology, ecology and behaviour. In the Neotropics, the antwren *Myrmotherula* complex (Thamnophilidae) was shown to exhibit both convergent evolution in body size and divergent evolution in body shape (Bravo *et al.* 2014). The latter trend is interpreted as an outcome of specialisation for different habitat and foraging strata, as well as degree of mixed-species flocking behaviour. Shady conditions and high levels of humidity in forests compared to most open biotopes are beneficial to a wide range of invertebrate taxa (e.g., Savilaakso *et al.* 2009; Merckx *et al.* 2012). Favourable microclimatic conditions combined with high foliage density explains why forests host such a high diversity of insectivorous birds.

Depending on their structure and management history, forest stands influence both the physical and biological components of the environment. In addition to offering a variety of foraging opportunities (see below), trees and understorey vegetation protect birds against high winds, which is especially critical during winter. Trees also provide roosting cavities, whether excavated by the birds themselves or created through wood decay. Such cavities provide protection against the wind, but in the case of holes resulting from wood decay, humidity may be high (Maziarz & Wesołowski 2013). Roosting cavities can be used all year round, including during migration, as shown by Gow *et al.* (2014) for a woodpecker, the Northern Flicker *Colaptes auratus*, and they can represent a limiting resource, as shown for wintering species like great tit *Parus major* and Eurasian blue tit *Cyanistes caeruleus* (Dhondt *et al.* 1991).

Forest structure can also influence predation risk on birds themselves. For example, tree diameter can influence the vulnerability of bark-foraging birds through visual obstruction, whereas dense understorey vegetation can either increase predation risk from avian predators, such as forest-living hawks (e.g., *Accipiter* spp.), which use it to approach unsuspecting prey (Whelan & Maina 2005), or alternatively provide cover from predators that are unwilling to enter dense vegetation

(Nilsson 1979). Trees and understorey vegetation can also influence bird morphology. Birds of mature forest have more pointed wings than their young forest and open-land counterparts (Desrochers 2010), probably as a result of contrasting foraging substrates and techniques. However, wing shape also, to some extent, reflects migratory behaviour (Dawideit *et al.* 2009). For example, wing pointedness is thought to offer more energy-efficient, sustained flight (Bowlin & Wikelski 2008). Finally, forest structure influences sound attenuation and, in turn, bird communication. According to the acoustic adaptation hypothesis (Morton 1975), birds should adjust their vocalisations to maximise transmission. Hence, acoustic parameters of songs should reflect vegetation structure. Consistent with this hypothesis, Wiley (1991) showed that, when controlling for body size, forest birds sing at lower maximal frequencies than birds of open biotopes. There is also evidence that birds use a 'sound window' (Morton 1975) associated with the so-called ground effect, which strongly attenuates lower frequencies (e.g., Cosens & Falls 1984). Differences in frequency of vocalisations among habitat types have been reported both among and within species. For instance, satin bowerbird *Ptilonorhynchus violaceus*, a species inhabiting a variety of forest types, produces lower sound frequencies and lower frequency modulation (i.e., few or no trills) in denser vegetation, irrespective of the geographical proximity of populations (Nicholls & Goldizen 2006).

3.3 Niche Partitioning in North American and European Forest Bird Species Assemblages

3.3.1 Foraging Strata

Korňan *et al.* (2013) compared the structure of forest bird assemblages on three continents (North America, Europe and Australia) to test the hypothesis that these assemblages should have similar foraging guild patterns (assuming similar environmental resources). They identified three foraging guilds shared across the three continents: ground and litter foragers, foliage gleaners and trunk foragers. Those guilds responded significantly to two habitat gradients: vertical distribution of resources and tree morphology. The authors also point out that their results are consistent with MacArthur and MacArthur's (1961) observation that bird species diversity is correlated with foliage height diversity. The fact that guild structure could largely be characterised by only two relatively simple habitat gradients suggests that, across such widely separated forest

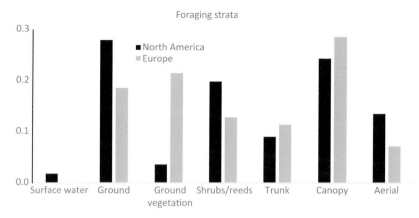

Figure 3.2 Proportion of forest bird species foraging in different strata in the northern hardwood forests of North America (n = 111) and temperate deciduous forests of Atlantic and Continental ecoregions of Europe (n = 70). Classification of North American species follows Ehrlich *et al.* (1988) and *The Birds of North America* online, whereas European birds are classified following Tucker and Evans (1997).

environments, converging patterns in adaptive evolution can be observed. Beyond these broad similarities, however, important differences exist between European and North American bird species assemblages. We will examine these differences below.

When comparing the distribution of species among foraging strata between the northern hardwood forests of North America and the temperate forests of Europe (Fig. 3.2), proportions of species assigned to the different foraging strata are surprisingly similar. The main difference pertains to species foraging in ground vegetation, such as birds of prey and some seed-eaters, which are more prominent in temperate forests of Europe. In Europe, no forest species forage mainly in surface waters like North American waterthrushes *Parkesia* spp. Note that we did not apply statistical tests, owing to potential differences in the interpretation of foraging strata between continents.

3.3.2 Nesting Substrates

Nest predation risk is thought to be largely responsible for nesting substrate selection, fecundity and a variety of behaviours associated with breeding (Martin 1993, 1995; Zanette *et al.* 2011). Using a database of life-history traits for 123 species of woodpeckers and passerines,

Martin (1995) observed a stronger relationship between fecundity, adult survival and nest sites, whereas foraging sites explained little variation in fecundity or survival, even when correcting for phylogenetic relationships. Nesting success is higher among cavity nesters than open nesters (Martin & Li 1992; Wesołowski & Tomiałojć 2005). Secondary cavity nesters (non-excavating species that use cavities) tend to have intermediate nesting success relative to primary cavity nesters and open nesters (Martin & Li 1992).

Although nest predation may have less influence on cavity nesting guilds, the availability of suitable cavities may profoundly affect the presence and density of hole-nesting species. Nest site limitation has been frequently investigated through nest box provisioning (e.g., Enemar & Sjöstrand 1972; Mänd et al. 2005; Aitken & Martin 2012), manipulation of natural substrates (Lohr et al. 2002) or, rarely, setting up artificial open-cup nests (Cancellieri & Murphy 2013). Densities of secondary cavity nesters do not appear to be limited by cavity availability in temperate primeval forests, such as the Białowieża National Park (Wesołowski 2007; Chapter 4). Evidence from managed forests, however, suggests severe limitation (Newton 1994). In eastern Canada, where conifer plantations are interspersed with naturally regenerated stands, even relatively old plantations host fewer species of cavity nesters (MacKay et al. 2014). In regions where primary forests have long been replaced by managed stands, it is difficult to run proper nest-limitation experiments, because natural rates of cavity creation and loss have been altered, both locally and regionally. Yet, it is important to address shortages of suitable nest sites from a conservation perspective, because cavity nesters may represent an important biodiversity component, not only in terms of species richness, but also because of the keystone role played by primary excavators (Martin et al. 2004; Cockle et al. 2011).

Although open-nesting species are more sensitive to nest predation than cavity-nesting ones, the variation in substrate selection or nest height exhibited by many of them indicates that they have the potential to respond adaptively to predation risk. Such variability can be seen in the black-throated blue warbler Setophaga caerulescens, which builds its open nests in a variety of shrub species (both conifer and deciduous), or sometimes in the root pads of uprooted trees. However, this species is essentially restricted to low (<2 m) nest heights (Holmes et al. 2005). In contrast, species such as the red-eyed vireo Vireo olivaceus build their nests in stereotypical situations, i.e., hanging from terminal or subterminal forks of deciduous tree branches, but at variable heights (Cimprich *et al.* 2000). Long-term studies on Siberian jay *Perisoreus infaustus* provide clear evidence that anthropogenic activities such as forest thinning and partial cutting may induce changes in territory occupancy (Griesser *et al.* 2007) and nest-provisioning behaviour (Eggers *et al.* 2008) in response to lower nest concealment and greater predation risk. Wesołowski and Fuller (2012) present many examples of shifts in habitat use, including nesting microhabitats, between a primeval forest (Białowieża) and Britain. Species that make extensive use of human structures as nesting substrates (e.g., many swallows and swifts) formerly used tree cavities (Zanchetta *et al.* 2014). Those species represent an extreme example of the degree of flexibility of bird species in their nesting habits.

In spite of the general trend towards the selection of safe nest sites (or microhabitats) by birds, a departure from a perfect match between site safety and selection is still observed in some systems. For example, blackcap *Sylvia atricapilla* has been shown to settle preferentially in a novel environment created by the planting of exotic trees, even though its reproductive success is lower than in nearby stands of native trees (Remeš 2003). This phenomenon is called an ecological trap (Battin 2004). Preference for a given habitat type over others can be challenging to determine. Some authors have used site saturation rate (Remeš 2003; Thériault *et al.* 2012) or the actual territory settlement sequence (Arlt & Pärt 2007), whereas others (e.g., Weldon & Haddad 2005) have inferred site preference on the basis of age structure, assuming despotic behaviour. To our knowledge, few well-documented ecological traps have been reported in forest birds. Robertson and Hutto (2007) reported a preference by olive-sided flycatcher *Contopus cooperi* for selectively harvested stands over its naturally occurring habitat (burns), even though it appeared to have lower reproductive success there. However, that conclusion was based on a limited sample size (n = 18) in each of two study plots. Latif *et al.* (2012) observed weak and inconsistent relationships between nesting microhabitat use and predation rate when monitoring natural nests of yellow warblers *Setophaga petechia*. They hypothesised that the population had reached an adaptive peak, which was supported by predation patterns on artificial nests placed within and outside the range of concealment corresponding to natural nests.

A comparison of species distributions among nesting strata in North American and European temperate forest ecoregions (Fig. 3.3) indicates a greater proportion of ground nesters in the northern hardwood forest of

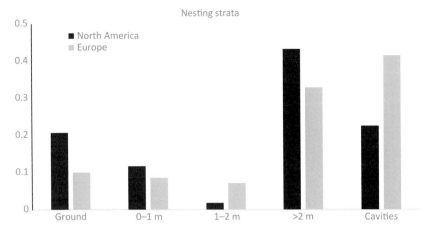

Figure 3.3 Proportion of forest bird species nesting in different strata in the northern hardwood forest of North America (n = 111) and in the temperate deciduous forests of Atlantic and Continental ecoregions of Europe (n = 70). Classification of North American species follows Ehrlich *et al.* (1988) and *The Birds of North America* online, whereas that of European birds follows van Turnhout *et al.* (2010).

North America and a lower proportion of cavity nesters than in the European ecoregions considered. On the basis of nest predation risk, this could be taken as an illustration of greater nest predation risk in Europe, but of course any interpretation must take into account phylogenetic differences between the two continents. When compiling numbers of species in our focal ecoregions, temperate forests of North America and Europe had the same number of woodpecker species, potentially creating cavities for a similar assemblage of secondary cavity nesters. Yet, temperate forests of Europe host secondary cavity nesters from a family (Muscicapidae) that is absent in North American forests, whereas the opposite is not true, except for a single cavity nester among Parulidae (prothonotary warbler *Protonotaria citrea*). On both continents, Paridae are an important group of forest birds that use cavities for nesting.

3.3.3 Migratory Strategies

European and North American avifaunas include large proportions of migratory species. In the temperate forests on which we focused, proportions of resident species were 27% and 56% in North America and Europe, respectively. The sharp difference in these proportions corresponds to the

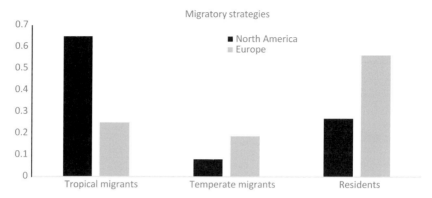

Figure 3.4 Proportion of forest bird species that use different migratory strategies in the northern hardwood forest of North America (n = 111) and in temperate deciduous forests of Atlantic and Continental ecoregions of Europe (n − 70). Classification of North American species follows Ehrlich *et al.* (1988) and *The Birds of North America* online, whereas that of European birds follows van Turnhout *et al.* (2010).

much larger contingent of Neotropical than Paleotropical migrants in these avifaunas (Fig. 3.4; see also Chapter 2; Mönkkönen & Welsh 1994). Similar patterns can be seen when comparing proportions of Nearctic and Palearctic resident and migrant species in the boreal forest (Niemi *et al.* 1998; Imbeau *et al.* 2001).

Current thinking about the evolution of migration in the Northern Hemisphere is summarised in Chapter 2. According to the southern origin hypothesis, differences between North America and Europe reflect the tropical origin of long-distance migrants and the taxonomically richer Neotropical (compared to Paleotropical) forest ecosystems. Species that breed in the Northern Hemisphere spend most of the year at tropical latitudes.

Irrespective of their geographic origin, tropical migrants have evolved to benefit from the spring peak in food resources while avoiding long periods with low food abundance (Newton 2007). However, long-distance migrants are vulnerable to climate change–induced trophic mismatches, whereby hatching dates no longer coincide with food peaks. Migratory birds that breed in forests are also more vulnerable to such mismatches than are those that breed in marshes, because food peaks last much longer in the latter habitat type (Both 2010 and references therein). Further research is needed to uncover these relationships, since solid data on food peaks are relatively sparse.

Food shortages and low winter temperatures have imposed a strong selection for adaptive behavioural and physiological traits on both continents, although Nearctic winters are more severe. For example, mean January temperature is −12°C in southern Québec, compared to −3°C in eastern Poland. Snowfall is also much greater in the former region. Climatic differences may, at least in part, explain the contrasting proportions of residents and migrants shown in Figure 3.4. In temperate Europe, milder winters are correlated with a greater abundance of residents the following spring, though not all species show significant correlations (Wesołowski & Tomiałojć 1997; Pearce-Higgins *et al.* 2015). Given the greater severity of Nearctic winters, fewer species would be expected to maintain resident populations there.

Although forests provide cover against cold winter temperatures and high winds, successful foraging during winter requires specific adaptations, as well as the cognitive ability to adopt new foraging behaviours (Sol *et al.* 2005). Among resident species, food caching has evolved in several taxa, especially corvids and parids. The latter also show several adaptations to survive intense cold. These include roosting in cavities (Pitts 1976; Lahti *et al.* 1997), burying themselves in deep snow (J.-F. Gobeil and C. Cassady-St. Clair, pers. comm.) and using facultative hypothermia (Lewden *et al.* 2014). The black-capped chickadee *Poecile atricapillus* also exhibits an uncoupling of basal metabolic rate and maximum thermogenic capacity, the latter allowing individuals to face sudden stochastic shifts in temperature (Petit *et al.* 2013). Some species, for example gnatcatchers *Polioptila* spp., treecreepers *Certhia* spp., goldcrests *Regulus* spp. and long-tailed tit *Aegithalos caudatus*, have also developed close communal roosting, probably as a behavioural adaptation to acquire a higher temperature during cold nights (see, e.g., Walsberg 1990).

3.4 Response to Landscape Structure

Until the 17th century, North American forests were mainly subjected to natural disturbance regimes, although fire-assisted agriculture and hunting by Native Americans may have influenced larger areas than previously thought (Williams 2008). By contrast, large-scale deforestation in the temperate zone of Europe can be traced back to the Neolithic, ca. 6,000 years ago (Williams 2003). Martin *et al.* (2012) reviewed the literature on the response of European and North American forest birds to anthropogenic landscape change and asked whether differences in researchers' focus reflected contrasting land use histories or distinct research traditions and human perceptions. With respect to temperate forest landscapes and their avifaunas, they concluded that there are major differences in human perception: North American researchers tend to focus on habitat loss and fragmentation as negative effects of agriculture and other agents of landscape change, whereas Europeans view cultural landscape mosaics as worthy of conservation in their own right. Interestingly, Terraube *et al.* (2016) recently stressed the conservation value of forest edges, whereas North American researchers (e.g., Whitcomb *et al.* 1981) have warned against edge creation as conservation policy, largely because such a practice contrasts with natural disturbance regimes observed in temperate forests of North America (e.g., Fraver *et al.* 2009; Drapeau *et al.* 2016).

Beyond perceptual differences between and within continents, is there evidence for adaptation to anthropogenic landscape structure in North American and European birds of the temperate forest? We hypothesised that bird species associated with European temperate forests would exhibit a greater tolerance to habitat loss, fragmentation and degradation, owing to longer exposure to anthropogenic land use and selection for adaptive traits. Comparisons between the avifauna of Białowieża National Park and Great Britain are insightful in this respect (see Wesołowski & Fuller 2012): several species show vastly different habitat associations and nesting habits, indicating far-reaching adaptation to cultural landscapes in Great Britain.

To compare European and North American forest avifaunas, we will first consider specific examples. The recent 'urbanisation' of the goshawk *Accipiter gentilis* in many regions of Europe, including Germany (Rutz 2008) and Finland (Solonen 2008), contrasts with the absence of such a tendency in North American goshawk populations. As a matter of fact, Bosakowski and Smith (1997) reported the opposite trend in a study area of the eastern United States, where some raptor species that colonised North American cities, such as the merlin *Falco columbarius*, have yet to show this tendency in Europe (Warkentin *et al.* 2005). Another comparison suggests similar tendencies between the two continents: the black woodpecker *Dryocopus martius* has been shown to respond to fragmentation of its mature forest habitat in Europe by combining resources from multiple habitat fragments (Tjernberg *et al.* 1993), a phenomenon comparable to the unexpected degree of tolerance of the pileated woodpecker *D. pileatus* to fragmentation of mature forest in eastern North America (e.g., Cadman *et al.* 1987, 2007). Hence, these examples provide equivocal evidence for a greater tolerance of European forest birds to anthropogenic land use.

Other species that exhibit high degrees of adaptation to urban environments are Eurasian blackbird *Turdus merula* and American robin *T. migratorius*. Both appear to be more successful in urban and suburban environments than in rural or forested landscapes, at least in terms of density (Snow 1958; Morneau *et al.* 1995 and references therein). Urbanised landscapes might act as demographic sinks, but research on the Eurasian blackbird by Jesko Partecke and his collaborators suggests otherwise. They hand-reared individuals from urban and forest populations and found strong selection for sedentarity among urban individuals (Partecke & Gwinner 2007). Individuals from urban populations also showed an attenuated stress response relative to their forest conspecifics in spring (males only) and winter (Partecke *et al.* 2006). Although we are not aware of similar studies on the American robin, it is known as an indicator of exurban (low-density) development (Suarez-Rubio *et al.* 2011) and appears to thrive in suburban areas (Morneau *et al.* 1995), but has yet to adapt to urban cores.

There is evidence that urbanisation influences the composition of bird species assemblages, even in protected areas (Marzluff 2005). Wood *et al.* (2014) examined the effects of housing development within and near protected areas throughout the United States. They observed an increase in proportional abundance and richness of synanthropic species (e.g., mourning dove *Zenaida macroura*) with housing density within protected areas, and the inverse relationship for species of conservation concern (e.g., American three-toed woodpecker *Picoides dorsalis*). Housing density outside protected areas had the same, but weaker, effects.

Forest birds have also been shown to adapt to various non-forest biotopes, in addition to urban landscapes. For example, many Neotropical migrant songbirds use a variety of semi-open biotopes, such as shade coffee plantations, on their wintering grounds, sometimes reaching higher densities there than in primary forest (Greenberg *et al.* 1997; Bakermans *et al.* 2009). Many Palearctic forest birds that winter in sub-Saharan Africa occur in sparsely vegetated savanna habitats, exhibiting a preference for a small number of specific tree species (Zwarts *et al.* 2015). However, there are several cases of species originally considered as forest birds that have evolved to nest in virtually bare biotopes (e.g., raven *Corvus corax*) or scrub and hedgerows (dunnock *Prunella modularis*, bullfinch *Pyrrhula pyrrhula*) in cultural landscapes (Wesołowski & Fuller 2012).

Forest bird response to habitat loss and fragmentation is a much debated area, mainly because the effects of those two processes are so intimately linked as to be nearly inseparable, statistically. Yet, some researchers stress the importance of separating the effects of these processes, because they have contrasting implications for land-use planning and conservation (Fahrig 2003; Betts *et al.* 2014). Nonetheless, the fact must be recognised that habitat loss and fragmentation covary over a broad portion of the landscape change continuum (Didham *et al.* 2012). To identify optimal habitat configurations for species persistence for a given amount of habitat, it is important that research focuses on this portion of the landscape change continuum (Villard & Metzger 2014). At any point in time, habitat loss and fragmentation produce specific landscape configurations, which can, in turn, influence processes such as edge effects, matrix effects or functional connectivity. We discuss evidence for those processes below (see also Chapter 13).

Much has been written about edge effects on forest birds of North America (e.g., Gates & Gysel 1978; Whitcomb *et al.* 1981; Flaspohler *et al.* 2001; Falk *et al.* 2011) and, to a lesser extent, Europe (e.g., Andrén & Angelstam 1988; Andrén 1995; McCollin 1998; Terraube *et al.* 2016). A critical issue is the distinction between actual responses to edges between biotopes and species responses to forest stand structure or other environmental conditions associated with proximity to an edge. Many species appear to respond to the latter rather than to the edge per se (Villard 1998; Imbeau *et al.* 2003). Studies that investigated species preferences for forest edges or 'forest interior' habitat (sensu Whitcomb *et al.* 1981) have reported little evidence (e.g., Fuller 2000; Villard *et al.* 2007). Similarly, Vatka *et al.* (2014) compared nest site selection in willow tits *Poecile montanus* at various scales (1–34 ha) and found their top model at the finest scale. Tits avoid open areas and select moist forest with a high density of potential nest sites. However, there is evidence that individuals nesting closer to edges may experience lower reproductive success (Flaspohler *et al.* 2001; Poulin & Villard 2011), though responses may vary widely with the nature of the matrix. For example, Rodewald *et al.* (2011) suggested that there may be a decoupling between predators and prey when anthropogenic activities in the matrix provide major food subsidies to generalist predators. They compared patterns in the predation of natural nests in forest fragments surrounded by agriculture versus urban areas and found that nest survival declined with an index of nest predator abundance in rural landscapes, whereas they were unrelated in urban landscapes.

Hence, it appears that edge effects on both bird occurrence and nest survival are much more complex than previously thought, because they may be influenced by the nature of the landscape matrix and its effects on the composition of the nest predator community (Andrén 1992) and by alternative sources of food. Comparisons between North America and Europe are further complicated by the fact that, especially in Europe, forest species sensitive to habitat loss and fragmentation may have been lost long ago. In the context of the 'single large or several small' (SLOSS) reserves debate, Ford (1987) found little difference in the occurrence of forest birds in small fragments (<20 ha) versus plots within larger fragments in England, and concluded that there was little evidence for contemporary effects of fragmentation. In Spain, Robles and Ciudad (2012) observed a stronger effect of habitat quality than forest patch size or connectivity on patch occupancy dynamics in the middle spotted woodpecker *Leiopicus medius*.

Another approach to investigate species response to landscape change is to examine the movement patterns of species across more or less fragmented landscapes, with varying matrix compositions. Technological developments have made it possible to track small birds, such as passerines, using satellite transmitters. However, the limiting factor remains the very short life of batteries that can be carried by smaller species. Still, radio transmitters have been used successfully to track the movements of territorial birds during their breeding season, with surprising results. Some species (hooded warbler *Wilsonia citrina*, Norris & Stutchbury 2001; wood thrush *Hylocichla mustelina*, MacIntosh *et al.* 2011) were found to perform extensive off-territory forays, whereas others (scarlet tanager *Piranga olivacea*) appeared to combine several forest patches into a single territory (Fraser & Stutchbury 2004). These studies revealed surprising movement ability, even in species that were thought to be relatively sensitive to fragmentation based on occurrence patterns (e.g., scarlet tanager, Villard *et al.* 1999). Yet no one, to our knowledge, has successfully tracked small passerines during the dispersal phase, owing to technological limitations preventing long-term satellite tracking.

In response to this, clever experiments have been used to examine the gap-crossing ability of different species in experimental situations, using playbacks of conspecific or sometimes heterospecific vocalisations (e.g., Bélisle & Desrochers 2002). Such experiments allow testing the relative ability (or reluctance) of different species to cross non-habitat (e.g., recently clearcut forest). However, they are restricted to relatively fine spatial scales and can be used to fine-tune our knowledge on species response to specific habitat configurations. To examine responses to landscape structure (including matrix composition) over larger scales, several studies have used experimental translocations, whereby individuals (usually males) are captured on their territory and released a specific distance away, in pre-selected situations. This allows comparing the probability of return or return speed as a function of landscape structure. Although the motivation of individuals to return to their territory once displaced may not be equivalent to that of dispersing individuals, such translocations facilitate movement tracking while controlling for the landscape features which individuals experience. For example, Bélisle *et al.* (2001) and Gobeil and Villard (2002) observed that return speed increased in forest birds with the proportion of mature forest in the intervening landscape. Villard and Haché (2012) found that individuals from a species nesting in deciduous and mixed forest were half as likely to return to their territory when the matrix was dominated by spruce plantations than when it comprised fragments of deciduous forest. In European forests, we are aware of few studies addressing landscape permeability at the level of individuals. Lens and Dhondt (1994) observed delayed natal dispersal in young crested tits *Lophophanes cristatus* born in forest fragments relative to those born in a large pine forest. However, their results suggest that habitat quality may explain at least part of this delay, as young born in fragments had a lower body mass. Matthysen and Currie (1996) studied nuthatches *Sitta europaea* and also observed that juvenile dispersal was apparently altered by forest fragmentation. In fragments, settlers arrived at a slower rate and often remained unpaired.

Given the technical difficulty involved in tracking the movements of small passerines, even when conducting experimental translocations, researchers are increasingly making use of numerical approaches, such as circuit theory (e.g., St-Louis *et al.* 2014) and stochastic movement simulators (e.g., Aben *et al.* 2014) to identify landscape features/structures that have the greatest influence on landscape resistance to movements, and thus homing speed. Connectivity analyses derived from graph theory can also be used to identify habitat patches critical to the persistence of a habitat network (Keitt *et al.* 1997) and have been applied to model range expansion and identify habitat patches acting as critical stepping stones (Saura *et al.* 2014). However, when Laita *et al.* (2011) compared the performance of graph-theoretic connectivity metrics, they observed large variations in their sensitivity to patch network properties. Some of the metrics assume that animals will use the shortest (or least costly) link or the shortest path, when in reality several alternative links between nodes (patches) increase connectivity. There is also evidence that including perceptual range, or an estimate thereof, and non-random movement paths (e.g., 'directional persistence') can improve model performance (e.g., Coulon *et al.* 2015).

3.5 Conclusion

Forest birds show a wide range of adaptations to their dynamic habitat and to human-driven changes in forest stands and forest landscapes. On the basis of current knowledge, we cannot test the hypothesis that European forest birds show more evidence for adaptation to anthropogenic landscapes than their North American counterparts. On both continents, species exhibit a surprising ability to cope with matrix and edge effects, as well as open gaps among forest fragments. In Europe, we may be facing a shifting baseline, as forests have been extensively altered for millennia. In North America, several lines of evidence suggest that fragmented forest avifaunas are actually impoverished by intensive anthropogenic activities (Whitcomb *et al.* 1981; Robinson *et al.* 1995), yet there is reason for hope when we consider the status of species such as the pileated woodpecker, whose occurrence has increased in certain portions of its range in spite of fairly extensive loss and fragmentation of its habitat (Cadman *et al.* 2007). This careful optimism must be tempered by the combined threats posed by climate change, land-use intensification and the spread of invasive species, which could severely test the adaptive capacity of forest birds across the world.

The investigation of life-history traits or behavioural repertoire that make species more or less adaptable to anthropogenic landscape change is an active research area. In spite of their tremendous mobility, some forest songbirds have been shown to be reluctant to move across fairly narrow gaps in forest cover (e.g., Bélisle & Desrochers 2002; Volpe *et al.* 2014), and such reluctance may, in turn, influence ecosystem function, for example through reduced pollination efficiency (Hadley *et al.* 2014), seed dispersal (Escribano-Avila *et al.* 2014) and possibly insect control (Bereczki *et al.* 2014). Forest birds are increasingly confronted with new invasive species that may alter habitat structure or phenology, sometimes creating ecological traps (e.g., Remeš 2003), and they face rapid climate change, with all the challenges this entails (Wormworth & Sekercioglu 2011; Pearce-Higgins & Green 2014). The greatest challenge to researchers is to consider these simultaneous, multiscale factors of environmental change while accounting for phenotypic plasticity and the pace of avian adaptation. Our success will not only promote functional ecosystems, but also protect the incomparable source of awe that wild species represent.

Acknowledgements

We are grateful to Tom Sherry and Sönke Eggers for their reviews of earlier versions of the manuscript. We also thank the editors for their invitation and insightful comments on the manuscript, as well as Chris van Turnhout, who gave us access to a database on traits of forest bird species.

References

Aben, J., Strubbe, D., Adriaensen, F. *et al.* (2014) Simple individual-based models effectively represent Afrotropical forest bird movement in complex landscapes. *Journal of Applied Ecology*, **51**, 693–702.

Aitken, K.E.H. & Martin, K. (2012) Experimental test of nest-site limitation in mature mixed forests of central British Columbia, Canada. *Journal of Wildlife Management*, **76**, 557–565.

Andrén, H. (1992) Corvid density and nest predation in relation to forest fragmentation: A landscape perspective. *Ecology*, **73**, 794–804.

Andrén, H. (1995) Effects of landscape composition on predation rates at habitat edges. In *Mosaic Landscapes and Ecological Processes*. Hansson, L., Fahrig, L. & Merriam, H.G. (eds.). London: Chapman and Hall, pp. 225–255.

Andrén, H. & Angelstam, P. (1988) Elevated predation rates as an edge effect in habitat islands: Experimental evidence. *Ecology*, **69**, 544–547.

Arlt, D. & Pärt, T. (2007) Nonideal breeding habitat selection: A mismatch between preference and fitness. *Ecology*, **88**, 792–801.

Askins, R.A. (2014) *Saving the World's Deciduous Forests*. New Haven: Yale University Press.

Bakermans, M.H., Vitz, A.C., Rodewald, A.D. & Rengifo, C.G. (2009) Migratory songbird use of shade-coffee in the Venezuelan Andes with implications for conservation of cerulean warbler. *Biological Conservation*, **142**, 2476–2483.

Battin, J. (2004) When good animals love bad habitats: Ecological traps and the conservation of animal populations. *Conservation Biology*, **18**, 1482–1491.

Bélisle, M. & Desrochers, A. (2002) Gap-crossing decisions by forest birds: An empirical basis for parameterizing spatially-explicit, individual-based models. *Landscape Ecology*, **17**, 219–231.

Bélisle, M., Desrochers, A. & Fortin, M.-J. (2001) Influence of forest cover on the movements of forest birds: A homing experiment. *Ecology*, **82**, 1893–1904.

Bereczki, K., Odor, P., Czoka, G., Zsuzsa, M. & Baldi, A. (2014) Effects of forest heterogeneity on the efficiency of caterpillar control service provided by birds in temperate oak forests. *Forest Ecology and Management*, **327**, 96–105.

Betts, M.G., Fahrig, L., Hadley, A.S. *et al.* (2014) A species-centered approach for uncovering generalities in organism responses to habitat loss and fragmentation. *Ecography*, **37**, 1–11.

Betts, M.G. & Villard, M.-A. (2009) Landscape thresholds in species occurrence as quantitative targets in forest management: Generality in space and time? In *Setting Conservation Targets for Managed Forest Landscapes*. Villard, M.-A. & Jonsson, B.G. (eds.). Cambridge: Cambridge University Press, pp. 185–206.

Bosakowski, T. & Smith, D.G. (1997) Distribution and species richness of a forest raptor community in relation to urbanization. *Journal of Raptor Research*, **31**, 26–33.

Both, C. (2010) Food availability, mistiming, and climatic change. In *Effects of Climate Change on Birds*. Møller, A.P., Fiedler, W. & Berthold, P. (eds.). Oxford: Oxford University Press, pp. 129–147.

Bowlin, M.S. & Wikelski, M. (2008) Pointed wings, low wingloading and calm air reduce migratory flight costs in songbirds. *PLoS ONE*, **3**, e2154.

Bravo, G.A., Remsen Jr., J.V. & Brumfield, R.T. (2014) Adaptive processes drive ecomorphological convergent evolution in antwrens (Thamnophilidae). *Evolution*, **68**, 2757–2774.

Cadman, M.D., Eagles, P.F.J. & Helleiner, F. (eds.) (1987) *Atlas of the Breeding Birds of Ontario*. Waterloo, ON: University of Waterloo Press.

Cadman, M.D., Sutherland, D.A., Beck, G.G., Lepage, D. & Couturier, A.R. (eds.) (2007) *Atlas of the Breeding Birds of Ontario 2001–2005*. Toronto: Bird Studies Canada, Environment Canada, Ontario Field Naturalists, Ontario Ministry of Natural Resources and Ontario Nature.

Cancellieri, S. & Murphy, M.T. (2013) Experimental examination of nest reuse by an open-cup-nesting passerine: Time/energy savings or nest site shortage? *Animal Behaviour*, **85**, 1287–1294.

Cimprich, D.A., Moore, F.R. & Guilfoyle, M.P. (2000) Red-eyed Vireo (*Vireo olivaceus*). In *The Birds of North America* online. Poole, A. (ed.). Ithaca: Cornell Lab of Ornithology.

Cockle, C., Martin, K. & Wesołowski, T. (2011) Woodpeckers, decay, and the future of cavity-nesting vertebrate communities worldwide. *Frontiers in Ecology and the Environment*, **9**, 377–382.

Cooper, N.W., Sherry, T.W. & Marra, P.P. (2014) Modeling three-dimensional space use and overlap in birds. *Auk*, **131**, 681–693.

Cosens, S.E. & Falls, J.B. (1984) A comparison of sound propagation and song frequency in temperate marsh and grassland habitats. *Behavioral Ecology and Sociobiology*, **15**, 161–170.

Coulon, A., Aben, J., Palmer, S.C.F. *et al.* (2015) A stochastic movement simulator improves estimates of landscape connectivity. *Ecology*, **96**, 2203–2213.

Culbert, P.D., Radeloff, V.C., Flather, C.H., Kellndorfer, J.M., Rittenhouse, C.D. & Pidgeon, A.M. (2013) The influence of vertical and horizontal habitat structure on nationwide patterns of avian biodiversity. *Auk*, **130**, 656–665.

Dawideit, B.A., Phillimore, A.B., Laube, I., Leisler, B. & Böhning-Gaese, K. (2009) Ecomorphological predictors of natal dispersal distances in birds. *Journal of Animal Ecology*, **78**, 388–395.

Desrochers, A. (2010) Morphological response of songbirds to 100 years of landscape change in North America. *Ecology*, **91**, 1577–1582.

Dhondt, A.A., Kempenaers, B. & DeLaet, J. (1991) Protected winter roosting sites as a limiting resource for blue tits. *Acta Congressus Internationalis Ornithologici*, **20**, 1436–1443.

Didham, R.K., Kapos, V. & Ewers, R.M. (2012) Rethinking the conceptual foundations of habitat fragmentation research. *Oikos*, **121**, 161–170.

Drapeau P., Villard M.-A., Leduc A. & Hannon S.J. (2016) Natural disturbance regimes as templates for the response of bird species assemblages to contemporary forest management. *Diversity and Distributions*, **22**, 385–399.

Eggers, S., Griesser, M. & Ekman, J. (2008) Predator-induced reductions in nest visitation rates are modified by forest cover and food availability. *Behavioral Ecology*, **19**, 1056–1062.

Ehrlich, P.R., Dobkin, D.S. & Wheye, D. (1988) *The Birder's Handbook*. New York: Simon and Schuster.

Enemar, A. & Sjöstrand, B. (1972) Effects of the introduction of Pied Flycatchers on the composition of a passerine bird community. *Ornis Scandinavica*, **3**, 79–89.

Escribano-Avila, G., Calvino-Cancela, M., Pias, B., Virgos, E., Valladares, F. & Escudero, A. (2014) Diverse guilds provide complementary dispersal services in a woodland expansion process after land abandonment. *Journal of Applied Ecology*, **51**, 1701–1711.

Estades, C.F. (1997) Bird-habitat relationships in a vegetational gradient in the Andes of central Chile. *Condor*, **99**, 719–727.

European Environment Agency (2002) *The Biogeographical Regions Map of Europe*. Copenhagen: European Environment Agency.

Fahrig, L. (2003) Effects of habitat fragmentation on biodiversity. *Annual Review of Ecology, Evolution and Systematics*, **34**, 487–515.

Falk, K.J., Nol, E. & Burke, D. (2011) Weak effect of edges on avian nesting success in fragmented and forested landscapes. *Landscape Ecology*, **26**, 239–251.

Flade, M. (1994) *Die Brutvogelgemeinschaften Mittel- und Norddeutschlands: Grundlagen für den Gebrauch vogelkundlicher Daten in der Landschaftsplanung*. Berlin: IHW-Verlag.

Flaspohler, D.J., Temple, S.A. & Rosenfield, R.N. (2001) Species-specific edge effects on nest success and breeding bird density in a forested landscape. *Ecological Applications*, **11**, 32–46.

Ford, H.A. (1987) Bird communities on habitat islands in England. *Bird Study*, **34**, 205–218.

Fraser, G.S. & Stutchbury, B.J.M. (2004) Area-sensitive birds move extensively among forest patches. *Biological Conservation*, **118**, 377–387.

Fraver, S. White, A.S. & Seymour, R.S. (2009) Natural disturbance in an old-growth landscape of northern Maine, USA. *Journal of Ecology*, **97**, 289–298.

Fuller, R.J. (2000) Influence of treefall gaps on distributions of breeding birds within interior old-growth stands in Białowieża Forest, Poland. *Condor*, **102**, 267–274.

Gates, J.E. & Gysel, L.W. (1978) Avian nest dispersion and fledging success in field-forest ecotones. *Ecology*, **59**, 871–883.

Gobeil, J.-F. & Villard, M.-A. (2002) Permeability of three boreal forest landscape types to bird movements as determined from experimental translocations. *Oikos*, **98**, 447–458.

Gow, E.A., Wiebe, K.L. & Fox, J.W. (2014) Cavity use throughout the annual cycle of a migratory woodpecker revealed by geolocators. *Ibis*, **157**, 167–170.

Grajal, A. (1995) Structure and function of the digestive tract of the hoatzin (*Opistochomus hoazin*), a folivorous bird with foregut fermentation. *Auk*, **112**, 20–28.

Greenberg, R. (1987) Seasonal foraging specialization in the Worm-eating Warbler. *Condor*, **89**,158–168.

Greenberg, R., Bichier, P. & Sterling, J. (1997) Bird populations in rustic and planted shade coffee plantations of eastern Chiapas. *Biotropica*, **29**, 501–514.

Griesser, M., Nystrand, M., Eggers, S. & Ekman, J. (2007) Impact of forestry practices on fitness correlates and population productivity in an open-nesting bird species. *Conservation Biology*, **21**, 767–774.

Haché, S. & Villard, M.-A. (2010) Age-specific response of a migratory bird to an experimental alteration of its habitat. *Journal of Animal Ecology*, **79**, 897–905.

Hadley, A.S., Frey, S.J.K., Robinson, W.D., Kress, W.J. & Betts, M.G. (2014) Tropical forest fragmentation limits pollination of a keystone understory herb. *Ecology*, **95**, 2202–2212.

Holmes, R.T., Rodenhouse, N.L. & Sillett, S.C. (2005) Black-throated Blue Warbler (*Setophaga caerulescens*). In *The Birds of North America* online. Poole, A. (ed.). Ithaca: Cornell Lab of Ornithology.

Imbeau, L., Desrochers, A. & Mönkkönen, M. (2001) Long-term effects of forestry on birds of the eastern Canadian boreal forests: A comparison with Fennoscandia. *Conservation Biology*, **15**, 1151–1162.

Imbeau, L., Drapeau, P. & Mönkkönen, M. (2003) Are forest birds categorised as 'edge species' strictly associated with edges? *Ecography*, **26**, 514–520.

Keitt, T., Urban, D. & Milne, B.T. (1997) Detecting critical scales in fragmented landscapes. *Conservation Ecology* 1:4. www.consecol.org/vol1/iss1/art4/.

Koenig, W.D., Stacey, P.B., Stanback, M.T. & Mumme, R.L. (1995) Acorn Woodpecker (*Melanerpes formicivorus*). In *The Birds of North America*. Rodewald, P.G. (ed.). Ithaca: Cornell Lab of Ornithology. Retrieved from *Birds of North America*: https://birdsna-org.bnaproxy.birds.cornell.edu/Species-Account/bna/species/acowoo.

Korňan, M., Holmes, R.T., Recher, H.F., Adamík, P. & Kropil, R. (2013) Convergence in foraging guild structure of forest bird assemblages across three continents is related to habitat structure and foraging opportunities. *Community Ecology*, **14**, 89-100.

Lahti, K., Koivula, K. & Orell, M. (1997) Daily activity and winter survival in willow tits: Detrimental cost of long working hours? *Behaviour*, **134**, 921–939.

Laita, A., Kotiaho, J.S. & Mönkkönen, M. (2011) Graph-theoretic connectivity measures: What do they tell us about connectivity? *Landscape Ecology*, **26**, 951–967.

Latif, Q., Heath, S.K. & Rotenberry, J.T. (2012) How avian nest site selection responds to predation risk: Testing an 'adaptive peak' hypothesis. *Journal of Animal Ecology*, **81**, 127–138.

Lens, L. & Dhondt, A.A. (1994) Effects of habitat fragmentation on the timing of Crested Tit *Parus cristatus* natal dispersal. *Ibis*, **136**, 147–152.

Lewden, A., Petit, M., Milbergue, M., Orio, S. & Vézina, F. (2014) Evidence of facultative daytime hypothermia in a small passerine wintering at northern latitudes. *Ibis*, **156**, 321–329.

Lohr, S.M., Gauthreaux, S.A. & Kilgo, J.C. (2002) Importance of coarse woody debris to avian communities in loblolly pine forests. *Conservation Biology*, **16**, 767–777.

MacArthur, R.H. & MacArthur, J.W. (1961) On bird species diversity. *Ecology*, **42**, 594–598.

MacArthur, R.H., Recher, H.F. & Cody, M. (1966) On the relation between habitat selection and species diversity. *American Naturalist*, **100**, 319–332.

MacKay, A., Allard, M. & Villard, M.-A. (2014) Capacity of older plantations to host bird assemblages of naturally-regenerated conifer forests: A test at stand and landscape levels. *Biological Conservation*, **170**, 110–119.

MacIntosh, T., Stutchbury, B.J.M. & Evans, M.L. (2011) Gap-crossing by Wood Thrushes (*Hylocichla mustelina*) in fragmented landscapes. *Canadian Journal of Zoology*, **89**, 1091–1097.

Mänd, R., Tilgar V., Lõhmus, A. & Leivits, A. (2005) Providing nest boxes for hole-nesting birds: Does habitat matter? *Biodiversity and Conservation*, **14**, 1823–1840.

Martin, J.-L., Drapeau, P., Fahrig, L. *et al.* (2012) Birds in cultural landscapes: Actual and perceived differences between northeastern North America and western Europe. In *Birds and Habitat: Relationships in Changing Landscapes*. Fuller, R.J. (ed.). Cambridge: Cambridge University Press, pp. 481–515.

Martin, K., Aitken, K.E.H. & Wiebe, K.L. (2004) Nest sites and nest webs for cavity-nesting communities in interior British Columbia, Canada: Nest characteristics and niche partitioning. *Condor*, **106**, 5-19.

Martin, T.E. (1993) Nest predation among vegetation layers and habitat types: Revising the dogmas. *American Naturalist*, **141**, 897–913.

Martin, T.E. (1995). Life-history evolution in relation to nest sites, nest predation, and food. *Ecological Monographs*, **65**, 101–127.

Martin, T.E. & Li, P. (1992) Life-history traits of open- vs cavity-nesting birds. *Ecology*, **73**, 579–592.

Maziarz, M. & Wesołowski, T. (2013) Microclimate of tree cavities used by Great Tits *Parus major* in a primeval forest. *Avian Biology Research*, **6**, 47–56.

Marzluff, J.M. (2005) Island biogeography for an urbanizing world: How extinction and colonization may determine biological diversity in human-dominated landscapes. *Urban Ecosystems*, **8**, 157–177.

Matthysen, E. & Currie, D. (1996) Habitat fragmentation reduces disperser success in juvenile nuthatches *Sitta europaea*: Evidence from patterns of territory establishment. *Ecography*, **19**, 67–72.

McCollin, D. (1998) Forest edges and habitat selection in birds: A functional approach. *Ecography*, **21**, 247–260.

Merckx, T., Feber, R.E., Hoare, D.J. *et al.* (2012) Conserving threatened Lepidoptera: Towards an effective woodland management policy in landscapes under intense human land-use. *Biological Conservation*, **149**, 32–39.

Mönkkönen, M. & Welsh, D.A. (1994) A biogeographical hypothesis on the effects of human caused landscape changes on the forest bird communities of Europe and North America. *Annales Zoologici Fennici*, **31**, 61–70.

Morneau, F., Lépine, C., Décarie, R., Villard, M.-A. & DesGranges, J.-L. (1995) Reproduction of American Robin (*Turdus migratorius*) in a suburban environment. *Landscape and Urban Planning*, **32**, 55–62.

Morton, E.S. (1975) Ecological sources of selection on avian sounds. *American Naturalist*, **109**, 17–34.

Murphy, E.C. & Lehnhausen, W.A. (1998) Density and foraging ecology of woodpeckers following a stand-replacement fire. *Journal of Wildlife Management*, **62**, 1359–1372.

Newton, I. (1994) The role of nest sites in limiting the number of hole-nesting birds: A review. *Biological Conservation*, **70**, 265–276.

Newton, I. (2007) *The Migration Ecology of Birds*. London: Academic Press.

Nicholls, J.A. & Goldizen, A.W. (2006) Habitat type and density influence vocal signal design in satin bowerbirds. *Journal of Animal Ecology*, **75**, 549–558.

Niemi, G.J., Hanowski, J., Helle, P. *et al.* (1998) Ecological sustainability of birds in boreal forests. *Conservation Ecology* **2** (2), 17.

Nilsson, S.G. (1979) Seed density, cover, predation and the distribution of birds in a beech wood in southern Sweden. *Ibis*, **121**, 177–185.

Norris, D.R. & Stutchbury, B.J.M. (2001) Extraterritorial movements of a forest songbird in a fragmented landscape. *Conservation Biology*, **15**, 729–736.

Parrish, J.D. (1995) Experimental evidence for intrinsic microhabitat preferences in the Black-throated Green Warbler. *Condor*, **97**, 935–943.

Partecke, J. & Gwinner, E. (2007) Increased sedentariness in European Blackbirds following urbanization: A consequence of local adaptation? *Ecology*, **88**, 882–890.

Partecke, J., Schwabl, I. & Gwinner, E. (2006) Stress and the city: Urbanization and its effects on the stress physiology in European Blackbirds. *Ecology*, **87**, 1945–1952.

Petit, M., Lewden, A. & Vézina, F. (2013) Intra-seasonal flexibility in avian metabolic performance highlights the uncoupling of basal metabolic rate and thermogenic capacity. *PLoS One*, **8** (6), e68292.

Pearce-Higgins, J.W., Eglington, S.M., Martay, B. & Chamberlain, D.E. (2015) Drivers of climate change impacts on bird communities. *Journal of Animal Ecology*, **84**, 943–954.

Pearce-Higgins, J.W. & Green, R.E. (2014) *Birds and Climate Change: Impacts and Conservation Responses*. Cambridge: Cambridge University Press.

Pitts, T.D. (1976) Fall and winter roosting habits of Carolina Chickadees. *Wilson Bulletin*, **88**, 603–610.

Poulin, J.-F. & Villard, M.-A. (2011) Edge effect and matrix influence on the nest survival of an old forest specialist, the Brown Creeper (*Certhia americana*). *Landscape Ecology*, **26**, 911–922.

Ralph, C.J. (1985) Habitat association patterns of forest and steppe birds of northern Patagonia, Argentina. *Condor*, **87**, 471–483.

Recher, H.F. (1969) Bird species diversity and habitat diversity in Australia and North America. *American Naturalist*, **103**, 75–80.

Remeš, V. (2003) Effects of exotic habitat on nesting success, territory density, and settlement patterns in the Blackcap (*Sylvia atricapilla*). *Conservation Biology*, **17**, 1127–1133.

Robertson, B.A. & Hutto, R.L. (2007) Is selectively harvested forest an ecological trap for Olive-sided Flycatchers? *Condor*, **109**, 109–121.

Robinson, S.K. (1981) Ecological relations and social interactions of Philadelphia and Red-eyed Vireos. *Condor*, **83**, 16–26.

Robinson, S.K., Thompson, F.R., Donovan, T.M., Whitehead, D.R. & Faaborg, J. (1995) Regional forest fragmentation and the nesting success of migratory birds. *Science*, **267**, 1987–1990.

Robles, H. & Ciudad, C. (2012) Influence of habitat connectivity, population size, patch size, and connectivity on patch-occupancy dynamics of the Middle Spotted Woodpecker. *Conservation Biology*, **26**, 284–293.

Rodewald, A.D., Kearns, L.J. & Shustack, D.P. (2011) Anthropogenic resource subsidies decouple predator-prey relationships. *Ecological Applications*, **21**, 936–943.

Rutz, C. (2008) The establishment of an urban bird population. *Journal of Animal Ecology*, **77**, 1008–1019.

Saura, S., Bodin, O. & Fortin, M.-J. (2014) Stepping stones are crucial for species' long-distance dispersal and range expansion through habitat networks. *Journal of Applied Ecology*, **51**, 171–182.

Savilaakso, S., Koivisto, J., Veteli, T.O. & Roininen, H. (2009) Microclimate and tree community linked to differences in lepidopteran larval communities between forest fragments and continuous forest. *Diversity and Distributions*, **15**, 356–365.

Snow, D.W. (1958) The breeding of the blackbird Turdus merula at Oxford. *Ibis*, **100**, 1–30.

Sol, D., Lefebvre, L. & Rodriguez-Teijeiro, J.D. (2005) Brain size, innovative propensity and migratory behaviour in Palaearctic birds. *Proceedings of the Royal Society B*, **272**, 1433–1441.

Solonen, T. (2008) Larger broods in the Northern Goshawk *Accipiter gentilis* near urban areas in southern Finland. *Ornis Fennica*, **85**, 118–125.

St-Louis, V., Forester, J.D., Pelletier, D. *et al.* (2014) Circuit theory emphasizes the importance of edge-crossing decisions in dispersal scale movements of a forest passerine. *Landscape Ecology*, **29**, 831–841.

Suarez-Rubio, M., Leimgruber, P. & Renner, S.C. (2011) Influence of exurban development on bird species richness and diversity. *Journal of Ornithology*, **152**, 461–471.

Terraube, J., Archaux, F., Deconchat, M., van Halder, I., Jactel, H. & Barbaro, L. (2016) Forest edges have high conservation value for bird communities in mosaic landscapes. *Ecology and Evolution*, **6**, 5178–5189.

Thériault, S., Villard, M.-A. & Haché, S. (2012) Habitat selection in site-faithful Ovenbirds and recruits in the absence of experimental attraction. *Behavioral Ecology*, **23**, 1289–1295.

Tjernberg, M., Jonsson, K. & Nilsson, S.G. (1993) Density variation and breeding success of the black woodpecker, *Dryocopus martius*, in relation to forest fragmentation. *Ornis Fennica*, **70**, 155–162.

Török, J. (1990) Resource partitioning among three woodpecker species *Dendrocopos* spp. during the breeding season. *Holarctic Ecology*, **13**, 257–264.

Tucker, G.M. & Evans, M.I. (1997) *Habitats for Birds in Europe: A Conservation Strategy for the Wider Environment*. Cambridge: BirdLife International. BirdLife Conservation Series No. 6.

Van Turnhout, C.A.M., Foppen, R.P.B., Leuven, R.S.E.W., van Strien, A. & Siepel, H. (2010) Life-history and ecological correlates of population change in Dutch breeding birds. *Biological Conservation*, **143**, 173–181.

Vatka, E., Kangas, K., Orell, M., Lampila, S. & Nivala, V. (2014) Nest site selection of a primary hole-nesting passerine reveals means to developing sustainable forestry. *Journal of Avian Biology*, **45**, 187–196.

Vickery, P.D., Hunter, M.L. & Melvin, S.M. (1994) Effects of habitat area on the distribution of grassland birds in Maine. *Conservation Biology*, **8**, 1087–1097.

Villard, M.-A. (1998) On forest-interior species, edge avoidance, area sensitivity, and dogmas in avian conservation. *Auk*, **115**, 801–805.

Villard, M.-A. & Haché, S. (2012) Forest plantations consistently act as barriers to movement in a deciduous forest songbird: A translocation experiment. *Biological Conservation*, **155**, 33–37.

Villard, M.-A. & Metzger, J.P. (2014) Beyond the fragmentation debate: A conceptual model to predict when habitat configuration really matters. *Journal of Applied Ecology*, **51**, 309–318.

Villard, M.-A., Schmiegelow, F.K.A. & Trzcinski, M.K. (2007) Short-term response of forest birds to experimental clearcut edges. *Auk*, **124**, 828–840.

Villard, M.-A., Trzcinski, M.K. & Merriam, G. (1999) Fragmentation effects on forest birds: Relative influence of woodland cover and configuration on landscape occupancy. *Conservation Biology*, **13**, 774–783.

Volpe, N.L., Hadley, A.S., Robinson, W.D. & Betts, M.G. (2014) Functional connectivity experiments reflect routine movement behavior of a tropical hummingbird species. *Ecological Applications*, **24**, 2122–2131.

Walsberg, G.E. (1990) Communal roosting in a very small bird: Consequences for the thermal and respiratory gas environments. *Condor*, **92**, 795–798.

Warkentin, I.G., Sodhi, N.S., Espie, R.H.M., Poole, A.F., Oliphant, L.W. & James, P.C. (2005) Merlin (*Falco columbarius*). In *The Birds of North America* online. Poole, A. (ed.). Ithaca: Cornell Lab of Ornithology.

Weldon, A.J. & Haddad, N.M. (2005) The effects of patch shape on indigo buntings: Evidence for an ecological trap. *Ecology*, **86**, 1422–1431.

Wesołowski, T. (2007) Lessons from long-term hole-nester studies in a primeval forest. *Journal of Ornithology*, **148**, S395-S405.

Wesołowski, T. & Fuller, R.J. (2012) Spatial variation and temporal shifts in habitat use by birds at the European scale. In *Birds and Habitat: Relationships in Changing Landscapes*. Fuller, R.J. (ed.). Cambridge: Cambridge University Press, pp. 63–92.

Wesołowski, T. & Tomiałojć, L. (1997) Breeding bird dynamics in a primaeval temperate forest: Long term trends in Białowieża National Park (Poland). *Ecography*, **20**, 432–453.

Wesołowski, T. & Tomiałojć, L. (2005) Nest sites, nest predation, and productivity of avian broods in a primeval temperate forest: Do the generalizations hold? *Journal of Avian Biology*, **36**, 361–367.

Whelan, C.J. & Maina, G.G. (2005) Effects of season, understory vegetation density, habitat edge, and tree diameter on patch-use by bark-foraging birds. *Functional Ecology*, **19**, 529–536.

Whitcomb, R.F., Robbins, C.S., Lynch, J.F., Whitcomb, B.L., Klimkiewicz, M.K. & Bystrak, D. (1981) Effects of forest fragmentation on avifauna on Eastern deciduous forest. In *Forest Island Dynamics in Man-dominated Landscapes*. Burgess, R.L. & Sharpe, D.M. (eds.). New York: Springer-Verlag, pp. 125–206.

Wiens, J.A. (1989) *The Ecology of Bird Communities. Vol. 1. Foundations and Patterns*. Cambridge: Cambridge University Press.

Wiens, J.A., Rotenberry, J.T. & van Horne, B. (1987) Habitat occupancy patterns of North American shrubsteppe birds: The effects of spatial scale. *Oikos*, **48**, 132–147.

Wiley, R.H. (1991) Associations of song properties with habitats for territorial oscine birds of eastern North America. *American Naturalist*, **138**, 973–993.

Williams, M. (2003) *Deforesting the Earth: From Prehistory to Global Crisis*. Chicago: University of Chicago Press.

Williams, M. (2008) A new look at global forest histories of land clearing. *Annual Review of Environment and Resources*, **33**, 345–367.

Wood, E.M., Pidgeon, A.M., Radeloff, V.C. *et al.* (2014) Housing development erodes avian community structure in U.S. protected areas. *Ecological Applications*, **26**, 1445–1462.

Wormworth, J. & Sekercioglu, C. (2011) *Winged Sentinels: Birds and Climate Change*. Melbourne: Cambridge University Press.

Zanchetta, C., Tozer, D.C., Fitzgerald, T.M., Robinson, K. & Badzinski, D. (2014) Tree cavity use by Chimney Swifts: Implications for forestry and population recovery. *Avian Conservation and Ecology* **9**(2), 1. http://dx.doi.org/10.5751/ACE-00677–090201.

Zanette, L.Y., White, A.F., Allen, M.C. & Clinchy, M. (2011) Perceived predation risk reduces the number of offspring songbirds produce per year. *Science*, **334**, 1398–1401.

Zwarts L., Bijlsma R.G., van der Kamp J., Sikkema M. & Wymenga E. (2015) Moreau's Paradox reversed, or why insectivorous birds reach high densities in savanna trees. *Ardea*, **103**, 123–144.

4 · Tree Holes and Hole-Nesting Birds in European and North American Forests

TOMASZ WESOŁOWSKI AND
KATHY MARTIN

4.1 Introduction

The formation of tree holes consists of the destruction and loss of wood, a result that can be achieved with a multitude of physical, chemical or biological agents. Given enough time, holes will develop in most trees. Thus, in natural conditions, forests worldwide contain tree holes, although their types differ enormously (Gibbons & Lindenmayer 2002; Wesołowski 2007a; Cockle *et al.* 2011). The appearance of tree holes created an evolutionary opportunity, widely utilised by numerous groups of forest-dwelling organisms, including birds (reviews in Gibbons & Lindenmayer 2002; Hansell 2002). The hole-nesting habit arose independently in almost every large taxonomic group of forest birds and is found on all continents except Antarctica (Von Haartman 1957; Newton 1998). Globally, 18% of all bird species, representing at least 68 families, are known to nest in tree holes (van der Hoek *et al.* 2017).

Hole-nesting birds have been studied intensively in Europe and North America. Work in Europe has been dominated by studies of a few species easily attracted to breeding in nest boxes, with only a few studies dealing with hole-nesters breeding in their ancestral tree hole sites. Work in North America has been less concentrated on species breeding in nest boxes, and there has been relatively more interest in studying the ecology of entire hole-nester assemblages, their hole resources and the forest conditions that promote their persistence (e.g., Martin & Eadie 1999; Martin 2014; Fig. 4.1). Studies in Europe and North America were carried out largely independently, generally pursuing different sets of research questions (see Dhondt 2007 for a review of work on Paridae).

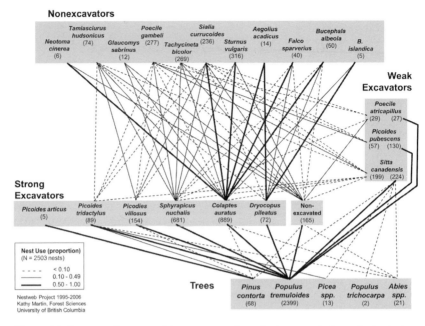

Figure 4.1 A nest web summarising resource flow (hole or tree) through the hole-nesting vertebrate assemblage in interior British Columbia. Resource use in the nest web is organised by nidic levels and shows links between species using nests (e.g., non-excavators and excavators) and the excavator or tree species below that provided the resource. For example, bufflehead *Bucephala albeola* (n = 50 nests) primarily used flicker (*Colaptes*) holes, but regularly (10–49% of cases) occupied holes excavated by pileated woodpecker *Dryocopus pileatus* and occasionally (<10%) used sapsucker *Sphyrapicus* holes and also decay-formed holes. The number under each species indicates the number of occupied nests for which there was information on the excavator or tree species used. Nidic links for species with fewer than 15 occupied nests are considered preliminary relationships. Updated with additional data from Fig. 5 in Martin *et al.* (2004).

In the only global meta-analysis of tree hole supply, Remm & Lõhmus (2011) found that the mean density of cavities was highest in the Austral-asian realm and lowest in the Palearctic regions, with the Nearctic regions of North America having significantly higher hole densities than the Palearctic. Besides their review, no systematic attempts have been made to contrast tree hole supply in the forests of Europe and North America, nor their use by species in hole-nesting vertebrate communities.

Due to historical reasons, the current forest tree flora in Europe is less speciose than that in North America (see Chapter 2). Species differ between the continents, but the European trees largely belong to the same genera as the North American ones (Latham & Ricklefs 1993; Askins 2014). The number of bird species breeding in tree holes in North America is about 20% higher than in Europe (Nearctic, 128 species; Palearctic, 100 species; van der Hoek *et al.* 2017); they are mostly different species, but several genera are common to the two continents (Keast 1990; Newton 1998). By comparing hole-nesting communities in Europe and North America, we can observe the results of two independent evolutionary 'experiments' and see whether tree hole–nesting birds converged or diverged in their patterns of tree hole use.

Here we present a systematic comparison of tree hole supply and hole-nesting bird communities in the forests of Europe and North America (north of Mexico). We restrict our analyses to tree holes used for breeding (roosting holes may have different qualities). We do not attempt to provide an exhaustive review of the literature. Instead, we present representative examples from intensively studied systems on both continents. We focus attention on studies done in natural or semi-natural old-growth forests, as these could serve as key benchmarks offering the birds a diverse range of holes from which to select.

We draw heavily on our own long-term research in Europe (TW) and North America (KM). Studies in Europe were carried out in Białowieża National Park, Poland (52°29′–52°57′N and 23°31′–24°21′E), where strictly protected patches of primeval lowland temperate forests, both broadleaved and coniferous, have been preserved (Wesołowski 1989; 2007a, b; 2011a; detailed description in Chapter 8). In this forest, all agents and processes responsible for the production, quality and persistence of holes still operate naturally, and the diversity and number of holes remain largely unaffected by human activities. Hole-nesting birds can choose among diverse hole types and must cope with a diverse assemblage of predators and competitors. Studies in North America were undertaken in central British Columbia, Canada (Martin & Eadie 1999; Martin *et al.* 2004; Aitken & Martin 2007; Cockle & Martin 2015). These forests are mostly mature temperate, dry, mixed coniferous and broadleaved forests embedded in a matrix of grasslands and shallow ponds (51°52′N, 122°21′W; Martin & Eadie 1999; Aitken & Martin 2007) in a region that lies within the warm and dry interior Douglas fir *Pseudotsuga menziesii* and sub-boreal pine-spruce biogeoclimatic zones (Meidinger & Pojar 1991). These forests are dominated by lodgepole pine *Pinus contorta var. latifolia* (41% of standing trees), Douglas fir (29%), trembling aspen *Populus tremuloides* (15%) and hybrid white spruce *Picea glauca engelmannii* (15%) (Martin *et al.* 2004; Cockle & Martin 2015).

In reviewing data from both continents with an emphasis on selected intensive studies, we seek to compare the processes of hole production and patterns of tree hole use by breeding birds. We also examine whether and how hole diversity differs between mostly broadleaved temperate forests and conifer-dominated boreal forests on both continents. Additionally, we identify questions requiring future study, and conclude by underlining some key points emerging from these intercontinental comparisons.

4.2 Defining Tree Holes

Despite enormous interest in tree holes and hole-nesters, there is not a single, generally agreed definition of a tree hole, making comparisons across studies difficult. Studies of availability versus use of holes are especially affected, as the number of potentially useable holes available in the system depends on the definition. It is straightforward to classify a freshly excavated breeding hole of a woodpecker as a tree hole, but there are large challenges in classifying and counting the many types of non-excavated holes, as most of these openings form gradually over time, and some of them eventually become useable holes. Studies vary in whether broken trunks or limbs with open tops ('chimneys') are included (e.g., Wesołowski 1996, 2007a; Vaillancourt *et al.* 2009) or not (e.g., Robles *et al.* 2011), or if holes at the bases of trees qualify as useable holes (Camprodon *et al.* 2008). Similar disagreement concerns the internal depth at which holes count as holes (van Balen *et al.* 1982; Aitken & Martin 2007; Walankiewicz *et al.* 2014) and if they include 'bottomless' hollow trunks ('pipes', e.g., Wesołowski 2011a). Depending on the criteria used, some birds are classified as hole-nesters in some studies but not in others. For example, treecreepers are either treated as hole-nesters (*Certhia familiaris*; Wesołowski 2007a; Wesołowski *et al.* 2015; Fig. 4.2), classified as 'bark-nesters' (*C. americana*; Aitken & Martin, 2007; Poulin *et al.* 2013) or excluded from this group altogether (*Certhia brachydactyla*; van Balen *et al.* 1982). In the majority of studies conducted in Białowieża Forest (e.g., Wesołowski 1989, 2007a; Maziarz *et al.* 2015a) as well as in Sweden (Carlson *et al.* 1998), British Columbia (Aitken & Martin 2007) and Arizona (Martin 2015), researchers let the hole-nesting birds define suitable holes; any type of hole used for breeding by an obligate hole-nesting species was considered to be a suitable tree hole.

Intensive searches aimed at locating all nesting attempts, repeated over multiple seasons and across species, enable a realistic characterisation of the full range of nest sites used in any hole-nesting bird assemblage.

A combination of this approach (i.e., finding the range of holes used by the local avifauna to set the minimum requirements for potentially suitable breeding holes) with later assessment of the number of

(a)   (b)

Figure 4.2 Diversity of hole formation and transformation processes: (a) Excavation, mostly by woodpeckers (red-naped sapsucker *Sphyrapicus nuchalis* in freshly excavated hole in live aspen, a trial hole above; photo A. Norris); (b) Decay-formed slit holes, used by smaller species (here, blue tit *Cyanistes caeruleus*; photo J. Fabijański); (c) 'Knotholes' in trunks and limbs of living trees, where branches become detached and heartwood is exposed (photo T. Wesołowski); (d) Wind- or frost-made cracks (here, used by treecreeper *Certhia familiaris*; photo T. Wesołowski); (e) Living trees strive to occlude wounds, and birds can prevent occlusion by removing callus and renovating the interior (older hole of northern flicker *Colaptes auratus* with trial excavation hole above to the left; photo K. Martin); (f) As long as holes remain surrounded by sound wood, they are immune to larger intruders, but woodpeckers (notably great spotted woodpecker *Dendrocopos major*) can reach interiors of holes with decayed walls by excavating a new entrance at the nest level (photo T. Wesołowski). Hole sizes are not to scale.

(c)
(d)
(e)
(f)

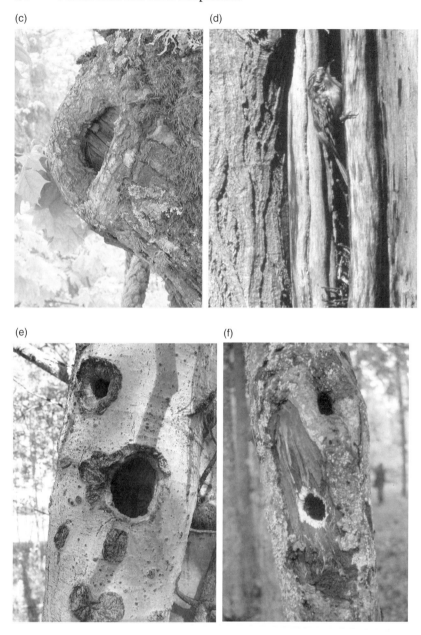

Figure 4.2 (cont.)

potentially useable holes present (Carlson *et al.* 1998; Aitken & Martin 2007) constitutes an excellent solution for comparing the number of suitable versus occupied holes within an area. To provide reliable results, inventories of useable holes must involve visual checks of their interiors, as it is often impossible to determine from ground-based checks whether detected openings are suitable breeding holes (Cockle *et al.* 2010; Ouellet-Lapointe *et al.* 2012).

The range of holes available varies for each species in the hole-nesting assemblage, as the holes available for passerines vary from those available for ducks. Patterns of hole use can also vary temporally and spatially, as there may be hole types that are never used in one area that are readily occupied in other areas.

4.3 Diversity of Hole-Producing Processes and Hole Types

For a tree hole to form, woody tissue must be removed via decay or other means. These processes produce a wide variety of hole types (Figs. 4.2, 4.3). The excavated holes on both continents are largely of the same shape (a rounded or oblong entrance leading to a horizontal or slightly ascending corridor, which reaches a pear-shaped vertical chamber), and they differ in size (internal diameter 5–21 cm) and firmness of walls (sound to completely rotten wood) (Glutz von Blotzheim & Bauer 1980; Martin *et al.* 2004). Non-excavated holes are much more diverse (Fig. 4.3), and in addition to the variations in the firmness of walls and size of the interior, their entrances can have vastly different shapes and varying horizontal orientation – the chamber can be anywhere between a pipe and a dome. The majority of excavated nest holes are suitable for nesting as soon as they are formed, although most birds require wood softened by decomposition (see below). In contrast, the majority of non-excavated holes often take many decades to centuries to develop into useable nest holes. Tree-decay processes provide the basis for the formation of both excavated and decay-formed holes (Cockle *et al.* 2011).

Tree size and age strongly influence the probability of development of nest holes. To harbour even the smallest useable hole, a tree in Białowieża Forest must be at least 11 cm in diameter at breast height (DBH) (used by marsh tit *Poecile palustris*; Wesołowski 1996) or, in North America, 11–12 cm (used by black-capped chickadee *Poecile atricapillus* and downy woodpecker *Picoides pubescens*; Jackson & Jackson 2004;

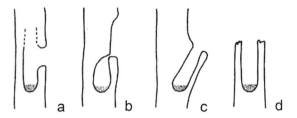

Poecile palustris Marsh Tit

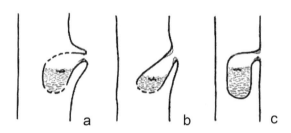

Sitta europaea European Nuthatch

Figure 4.3 Longitudinal section through different types of holes used by marsh tits *Poecile palustris* and nuthatches *Sitta europaea* in Białowieża Forest. Slightly simplified drawings of the actual holes but with their original proportions maintained. Marsh tit: (a) trunk hole in rotten sapwood, slit-like opening, entrance in the vertical plane; (b) as the former, entrance in horizontal plane; (c) knothole (formed at the site of a previous limb break); (d) 'chimney', entrance facing diagonally upwards. Nuthatch: (a) knothole (formed at the site of a previous limb break) in a conical bulge; (b) knothole, entrance facing diagonally upwards, its size reduced by plastering; (c) woodpecker-made hole, entrance size reduced by plastering. From Wesołowski (1996) and Wesołowski and Rowiński (2004).

K. Martin unpubl.). The largest species require much larger trees; black woodpecker *Dryocopus martius* excavates holes in trees with DBH that usually exceeds 38 cm (reviewed in Glutz von Blotzheim & Bauer 1980) and pileated woodpecker *Dryocopus pileatus* in trees with 45–50 cm DBH (Martin *et al.* 2004; Bull & Jackson 2011). Mean DBH of snags harbouring Ural owl *Strix uralensis* holes can be up to 50 cm (Lõhmus 2003). Non-excavated holes suitable for breeding first appear in Białowieża Forest in 70 to 80 year-old small-leaved lime *Tilia cordata*, but most of them are in larger and older trees, which could be ca. 130

years old (ash *Fraxinus excelsior*), ca. 200 years old (oak *Quercus robur*) or more than 200 years old (hornbeam *Carpinus betulus*) (references in Wesołowski 2012).

The probability that decay-formed holes will develop usually increases with tree age, as the cumulative number of wounds susceptible to fungal infection and the subsequent decomposition of wood by fungi increase with time, and the defence mechanisms of senescing individuals become less efficient (Schwarze *et al.* 2000; Jackson & Jackson 2004; Jusino *et al.* 2015; Worrall 2015). Due to these factors, more holes occur in larger and older trees of any given tree species (Remm & Lõhmus 2011). The biological traits of trees often affect hole formation. Decay holes form more easily in living broadleaved trees than in conifers, as resin released by conifers impregnates their heartwood, protecting it against decay better than gum-filled cells formed in the living sapwood of broadleaved trees (Schmidt 2006). Additionally, the branches of most coniferous trees are thinner than those of many broadleaved trees, so compartmentalisation of the heartwood exposed by branch detachment is easier in conifers.

Broadleaved species differ in their ability to occlude wounds: hornbeam, oak, lime and beech *Fagus sylvatica* seal off wounds much more efficiently than birches *Betula* spp., willows *Salix* spp. or aspens *Populus* spp. (Schmidt 2006; Worrall 2015). The latter genera are fast-growing, short-lived, pioneer species which attain dimensions sufficient to form holes relatively quickly. Additionally, *Populus* and *Salix* wood has relatively low density (Kiełbaska 1991), workable by the strongest excavators when intact or only slightly decayed. If aspen *Populus tremula* (Europe) or *P. tremuloides* (N. America) are present, they are usually the most important hole-providing trees (review in Remm & Lõhmus 2011). In the most exceptional cases, more than 96–98% of holes are situated in these tree species, despite aspen forming only 12–50% of those tree stands (British Columbia: Martin *et al.* 2004, Edworthy *et al.* 2012; Québec: Drapeau *et al.* 2009, Cadieux 2011; Arizona: Martin 2015).

4.3.1 Decay-Formed Holes

Decay fungi causing chemical digestion of wood are the most important agent involved in producing holes or facilitating their creation by other factors. Live trees with intact bark can only be infected by fungal spores when their woody tissue becomes exposed and they become vulnerable to fungal inoculation (Jackson & Jackson 2004; Schmidt 2006; Worrall

2015; Jusino *et al.* 2016). If the sapwood of inoculated trees remains alive, it is capable of active chemical response that can suppress the growth of fungus, for example through resin production in many conifers. On the other hand, heartwood shows no active metabolic resistance to fungi (Schmidt 2006). Hence any factor that causes injuries deep enough to expose the heartwood – snow, frost, fire, lightning, insects, foraging birds or loss of dead branches – enables wood-decaying fungi to invade. If a tree dies, its sapwood becomes accessible to fungi as well, in which case it becomes more prone to fungal decay than the heartwood. Thus the pattern of decay in living and dead trees differs (Jackson & Jackson 2004; Schmidt 2006; Edworthy *et al.* 2012; Jusino *et al.* 2015; Worrall 2015).

To form a hole useable by wildlife, trees have to grow large enough to contain a sufficient amount of heartwood for the decay process to form a sizeable hole. Heartwood decay can progress vertically at a rate of 6–10 cm per year in living trees (Leisne 1991; Worrall 2015). The time between initial infection and the appearance of decay holes in living trees can range from several to many decades (Gibbons & Lindenmayer 2002). While heartwood decay is necessary to make a tree hole, an entrance to the hole must be created to make it accessible. This can be done by the birds themselves (Fig. 4.2), or by the natural breaking of hollow trunks/ limbs, creating 'chimneys' (Fig. 4.3). Such chimneys can be common in some forests, for example, ca. 40 trees/10 ha in old-growth beech forests in Germany (Winter *et al.* 2015). Some species, such as Ural owl, may be critically dependent on large chimneys (Lõhmus 2003), but non-excavators in Białowieża Forest use this type of hole infrequently (such holes constitute <5% of non-excavator nests; Wesołowski 1996).

A useable hole for breeding usually requires the presence of a solid bottom. Bottomless 'pipes' can be used for breeding by only a few species, such as jackdaw *Coloeus monedula* and stock dove *Columba oenas*, which build nest platforms of sticks (Glutz von Blotzheim & Bauer 1993), or occasionally by tits in Europe that make moss 'hammocks' (T. Wesołowski, unpubl.), or *Chaetura* swifts in North America that glue their stick nests to hole walls.

Slitholes and knotholes are the most common types of decay-formed holes used by non-excavating passerines in Białowieża Forest (Wesołowski 2007a; Wesołowski & Rowiński 2014; Maziarz *et al.* 2015a), and these are also regularly used in other places in Europe (van Balen *et al.* 1982). Slit-like openings (Fig. 4.2) can be formed quickly by large mechanical injuries or develop gradually. North American publications do not mention slitholes, but other types of non-excavated holes occur there: knotholes, crevices behind loose bark and chimneys are the most common types of non-excavated holes used in British Columbia (Aitken & Martin 2007), and knotholes are regularly used in riverine forests dominated by plains cottonwood *Populus sargentii* in Colorado (Sedgwick & Knopf 1990). Knotholes form in places where branches are detached and wounded but unsuccessfully occluded (Fig. 4.2); such places are immediately accessible to wood-decaying fungi.

Sometimes holes can be 'formed' instantly in sound wood by strong mechanical forces (wind, heavy snowfall, freezing, fire) splitting trunks and/or breaking trunks or limbs. Such holes occur at low frequency in Białowieża Forest (Fig. 4.2), in British Columbia (Aitken & Martin 2007) and in other areas (Camprodon *et al.* 2008). Finally, holes that appear among roots at the tree base, variably created by decay or soil erosion, may be relevant in places where forests grow on steep slopes (Camprodon *et al.* 2008).

4.3.2 Excavator-Formed Holes

Excavation by birds, mostly woodpeckers, is an important source of tree holes in both Europe and North America (Fig. 4.2). In Białowieża Forest, eight species of excavating woodpeckers (Wesołowski 2007a), with body masses ranging from 30 g (lesser spotted woodpecker *Dryobates minor*) to 260–340 g (black woodpecker), and two species of excavating tits (body mass 10–11 g) produce a wide array of holes that differ vastly in their locations and characteristics (Wesołowski & Tomiałojć 1986; Wesołowski 1989, 2011a). In central interior British Columbia, ten species of woodpeckers and three species of excavating passerines with body masses ranging from 10 g (black-capped chickadee, red-breasted nuthatch *Sitta canadensis*) to 305–350 g (pileated woodpecker) produce a wide array of holes (Martin *et al.* 2004; Bull & Jackson 2011; Cockle *et al.* 2011).

The majority of excavated holes are formed in dead trees in Białowieża Forest, or in dead fragments of living ones, in places where sapwood has been already softened by fungal digestion. The weakest (usually smallest) species are able to excavate only in very soft decayed wood. The strongest woodpeckers can excavate holes in apparently sound (bearing no visible signs of wood decay) parts of living trees. In Europe, these are mostly the great spotted woodpecker *Dendrocopos major* and black woodpecker (Mazgajski 1997; Pasinelli 2007; Wesołowski 2011a; Zahner *et al.* 2012; Zawadzka *et al.* 2016). In North America, the large and medium-sized woodpeckers, such as hairy woodpecker *Picoides villosus*, black-backed woodpecker *P. arcticus,* pileated woodpecker, red-naped sapsucker *Sphyrapicus nuchalis* and yellow-bellied sapsucker *S. varius,* excavate in live trees with some fungal decay, while the smaller woodpeckers excavate in dead trees (Conner *et al.* 1994; Martin & Eadie 1999; Jackson & Jackson 2004; Straus *et al.* 2011; Tozer *et al.* 2011; Blanc & Martin 2012). Some larger woodpeckers, such as northern flicker *Colaptes auratus* and American three-toed woodpecker *Picoides dorsalis,* create a large proportion of their holes in dead trees or fragments of trees that have recently died. Some excavated cavities occur in trees with no external signs of decay; nevertheless, the birds detect tree sections with some internal decay (hard trees with soft spots of decay; Blanc & Martin 2012; Tozer *et al.* 2012).

4.3.3 Variable Role of Excavators as Hole Providers

Dependence of non-excavators on excavated holes varies from 0% to 100% globally (Cockle *et al.* 2011). In Europe, no excavators occurred in Ireland until recently (Mcdevitt *et al.* 2011), yet non-excavating hole-nesters were widespread there (Hagemeijer & Blair 1997). At the other extreme, the excavated holes constitute 99.3% of nesting holes used by non-excavating hole-nesters in longleaf pine *Pinus palustris*–dominated forests in Florida (Blanc & Walters 2008a).

Cockle *et al.* (2011) showed that non-excavators were much more likely to use excavated holes than decay-formed holes in North America than in Europe or other continents. In this review, we suggest that forest habitat types may partly explain this correlation, as the proportion of excavated holes available or used by non-excavators tends to vary with habitat type within geographical locations (Table 4.1). On both continents, excavated holes constitute >75% of those used in mixed coniferous/broadleaved forests, with most holes excavated in aspens where these species occur (review in Remm & Lõhmus 2011). Most study areas covered in that review were affected by past management to some extent, which probably reduced the availability of large dead coniferous trees providing alternative excavation sites – in Białowieża Forest, 80% of excavated holes were located in Scots pine *Pinus sylvestris* snags (Walankiewicz *et al.* 2014). Before large-scale man-made transformations began in Europe, coniferous forests occurred mostly in the boreal zone and in

Table 4.1 *Proportion of excavated holes among those available in the forest (A) or used by local non-excavator birds (U) in Europe and North America.*

Area	Available or Used	Excavated (%)	Habitat Type	Source
Europe				
N Sweden	A	95	Boreal, coniferous, *Picea*, *P. tremula*, past management	Michon (2014)
S Sweden	A	24	Broadleaved, *Quercus,*	Carlson *et al.*
	U	22	*Acer, Tilia*	(1998)
Estonia	A	88	Mixed coniferous, *P. tremula,*	Remm *et al.* (2006)
Białowieża Forest	A	<31	Broadleaved, lowland, primeval *Carpinus,* *Acer, Tilia, Quercus*	Wesołowski (2007a), Cockle *et al.* (2011)
	U	16		
Białowieża Forest	A	80	Mixed coniferous, lowland, primeval	Walankiewicz *et al.* (2014), D. Czeszczewik (pers. comm.)
Spain	A	35	Broadleaved, *Fagus,* mature	Camprodon *et al.* (2008), recalculated
	U	7		
North America				
Québec	A	88	Boreal, mixed coniferous, with *P. tremuloides*	Ouelett-Lapointe *et al.* (2012)
British Columbia	A	91	Temperate, mixed coniferous, with *P. tremuloides*	Cockle *et al.* (2011)
	U	90		
Southern Ontario	A	33	Carolinian broadleaved, with *Acer, Quercus, Fagus, Betula, Fraxinus, Carya*	Bavrlic (2008)
	U	50		
Central Ontario	A	89	Broadleaved, Great Lakes St. Lawrence, with *Acer, Fagus, Betula*	Tozer *et al.* (2011), D. Tozer (pers. comm.)
	A	85	Broadleaved, Great Lakes St. Lawrence, with *Populus*	Tozer *et al.* (2011), D. Tozer (pers. comm.)
Iowa	U	75	Broadleaved, riparian, second growth	Stauffer & Best (1982)

Table 4.1 (*cont.*)

Area	Available or Used	Excavated (%)	Habitat Type	Source
			(*Ulmus, Fraxinus. Salix, Tilia, Fagus, Quercus*)	
Virginia	A	35	Broadleaved, Appalachians *Quercus, Acer, Prunus* (90–188 yr)	Kahler & Anderson (2006)
California	U	73	Coniferous, mountains, second-growth	Raphael & White (1984)
Florida	U	>99	Coniferous, lowland, *Pinus palustris* dominated, mature	Blanc & Walters (2008a)

the mountains of the temperate zone (Chapter 7). More field studies, especially from boreal forests in Europe and broadleaved forests in North America, are needed to refine our predictions about continental level variation in the relative reliance on excavated holes by non-excavating bird communities.

In broadleaved forests composed of long-lived hardwood trees such as oak, hornbeam, lime and maple, birds use excavated holes much less often than decay-formed holes, despite the high availability of excavated holes. For example, the supply of woodpecker-made holes in Białowieża Forest (45–50 holes/10 ha; Wesołowski 2007a) would suffice to cover the breeding requirements of all non-excavators there, even when populations are at high density (Fig. 4.4). In southern and central Europe generally, most of the non-excavators avoid using woodpecker-made holes (Günther & Hellmann 2001; Wesołowski 2007a; Maziarz *et al.* 2015a).

There are not enough studies of hole-nester communities from broadleaved habitats in North America to evaluate whether the habitat-specific patterns of variation in excavator importance found in Europe also occur in North America. One study in West Virginia and another in Ontario recorded that excavated holes provided one-third of the holes available in broadleaved forests (Table 4.1). The Ontario study found that non-excavators preferred excavated holes, with 50% of the used holes being

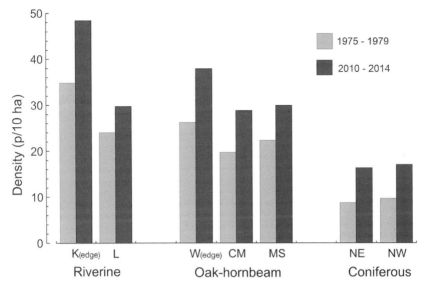

Figure 4.4 Densities of 33 hole-nesting species, including excavators (10 species) and non-excavators (23 species) in different types of primeval habitats of Białowieża National Park and their long-term variation. Mean five-year values are given for seven individual plots (24–33 ha) sampled in 1975–1979 (Tomiałojć *et al.* 1984) and in 2010–2014 (Wesołowski *et al.* 2015). Species composition of the hole-nester assemblage remained stable. No extinctions or colonisations were observed over this period (Wesołowski *et al.* 2014). Higher densities in the edge plots (K and W) were in both periods due to high abundance of breeding starlings *Sturnus vulgaris* (Wesołowski *et al.* 2015).

excavated ones, whereas these contributed an estimated 33% of all holes available (Bavrlic 2008).

It appears that in undisturbed coniferous or mixed coniferous–broadleaved forests, excavators (mostly woodpeckers, and in North America also nuthatches) are the keystone hole providers on both continents (Johnsson *et al.* 1990; Martin & Eadie, 1999; Cockle *et al.* 2011; Andersson *et al.* 2017). However, decay-formed holes are more important in old-growth broadleaved habitats in Europe. Due to the large-scale replacement of broadleaved forests by conifer plantations (Chapter 10) and the generally short rotations adopted in many managed tree stands, excavators may eventually emerge as the major hole providers in the lowlands of the temperate zone in Europe (Chapter 8).

4.4 Dynamics of Tree Hole Resources

4.4.1 Hole Formation

The number of holes present in the forest depends on rates of formation and persistence (Cockle *et al.* 2011). It is problematic to calculate rates of 'production' of new decay-formed holes/unit area annually, given the extended time period for their formation, but it is relatively straightforward to estimate the number of freshly excavated holes created annually. Generally, excavators, especially resident ones, excavate one or several new holes annually, and their reuse and renovation of breeding holes from previous years is low, except for flickers *Colaptes* spp. (Hansen 1989; Martin 1993; Meyer & Meyer 2001; Harding & Walters 2002; Wiebe *et al.* 2007; Blanc & Martin 2012; Wiebe 2017) and black woodpeckers in managed woods (e.g., Rolstad *et al.* 2000; Meyer & Meyer 2001). Assuming that each pair creates at least one new hole, we can use the density of excavators as a proxy of the minimum number of new holes added annually. At the densities found in Białowieża Forest, these could be 3–5 new holes/10 ha. The annual number of new holes added may be higher, as some excavated roosting holes can be used for nesting (Bonar 2000; Wesołowski 2007a).

4.4.2 Hole Persistence

In Białowieża Forest, holes can last for at least 31 (excavated) or 36 (non-excavated) years, but some holes may be destroyed before the first breeding season is completed (Wesołowski 2011a, 2012, unpubl. data). Non-excavated holes persisted longer, with a median life of 12 years, compared with 7 years for excavated holes (Table 4.2; Wesołowski 2011a). This difference is probably even more pronounced in reality, as only the minimum age of non-excavated holes is recorded (age of first known use). The longevity of holes varies across habitats (Wesołowski 2011a; Wesołowski 2012). Excavated holes persisted longer in coniferous trees (median 10 years) than deciduous trees (6–7 years; Wesołowski 2011a), whereas non-excavated holes in coniferous trees had a shorter lifespan (median 4.4 years) than those in broadleaved trees (11–13 years). In contrast, both excavated and non-excavated holes in aspen trees in British Columbia can persist for up to 21 years (K. Martin, unpubl. data). Persistence times are longer for holes in living than dead trees, and also for holes excavated by stronger excavators than weak excavators (Edworthy *et al.* 2012). Variation in

Table 4.2 *Median persistence time of non-excavated holes in Europe and North America.*

Area	Number of Study Years	Median Persistence (years)	Source
Białowieża Forest	30	12	Wesołowski (2012)
Estonia	5	18[a]	Remm et al. (2006)
British Columbia	15	14	Cockle et al. (2011); Edworthy et al. (2012)
Illinois, US	10	14[a]	*Aix sponsa* holes; Nielsen et al. (2007)
Colorado, US	5	6[a]	Sedgwick & Knopf (1990, 1991)

[a] Extrapolated from data provided in the paper.

persistence of holes made by different excavator species is related to the decay stage of their substrates, with holes of species excavating in strongly decomposed wood being shortest-lived (Bonar 2000; Meyer & Meyer 2001; Wesołowski 2011a; Blanc & Martin 2012; Edworthy et al. 2012).

4.4.3 Changes of Hole Properties over Time

Tree holes are dynamic structures, the characteristics of which change during their lifespan. As individual members of the hole-nesting assemblages show clear preferences for different hole properties, changes in hole characteristics may make them suitable for different species at different times. Some changes are unidirectional – a living tree with a hole may die, then gradually decompose, moving through more advanced stages of decay (e.g., Edworthy & Martin 2014). Other hole features can change bidirectionally – entrances can either get smaller (become grown over) or be enlarged by wood decay or renovating excavators (e.g., Günther & Hellmann 1995; Blanc & Walters 2008b). Holes can deepen due to decay (Meyer & Meyer 2001; Edworthy & Martin 2014) or get shallower with accumulation of debris. Their diameter can also increase through decay (Günther et al. 2004) or shrink by tissue growth. The net effect of these opposing processes differs with tree species, tree health and ecosystem type. Dimensions of holes excavated by great spotted woodpeckers in living oak trees in Germany changed slowly: over a 10-year period, the size of entrances remained the same, and average hole diameter increased by 7% and average hole depth by 16% (Günther & Hellmann 1995). Edworthy & Martin (2014) analysed temporal changes of dimensions of holes excavated in aspen in British Columbia. While hole entrance diameter increased by 0.6 cm/decade and horizontal depth by 0.9 cm/decade, the depth of holes increased by 8.4 cm/decade in live trees and only 1.4 cm/decade in dead trees. Hole depth changed most dramatically when excavators renovated holes formed by other excavators or by decay. In British Columbia, hole renovations by most excavators are rare, except by northern flickers, which renovated 13.5% of holes they used, increasing hole depth by an average of 16.5 cm in one year (Edworthy & Martin 2014). In other areas, especially where suitable substrates for excavation are limited, enlargement of small holes is a prevalent behaviour. Larger woodpeckers have been reported to renovate or destroy the majority of lesser spotted woodpecker holes located in rotten deciduous wood (Höntsch 2001) and of red-cockaded woodpecker *Picoides borealis* holes in living pines (Harding & Walters 2002).

4.4.4 Hole Destruction

Blow-down of nesting trees or sections of trees supporting holes appears to be the major cause of hole destruction (Table 4.3). It accounted for 90% of hole loss in British Columbia (Edworthy *et al.* 2012) and for the majority of destruction in other areas. Wind, facilitated by tree decay, is thus the most influential destructive agent. Its impact is greatest in exposed locations, such as forest edges (Edworthy & Martin 2013), and on tree species most susceptible to uprooting or trunk failure (Wesołowski 2011a, 2012).

Overgrowth of injured tissue was the most frequent cause of hole loss in living lime trees in Białowieża Forest (Wesołowski 2012, Table 4.3). Similarly, tissue growth was responsible for 50% of the loss of great spotted woodpecker holes excavated in living oaks in Germany (Table 4.3) and up to 12% of holes destroyed in living plains cottonwood trees in Colorado (Table 4.3; Sedgwick & Knopf 1991). In British Columbia, despite the fact that 55% of holes used were in living trees, only 3% of holes were lost due to closure of their entrances

Table 4.3 *Causes of hole failure (%) in relation to hole formation type and tree decay state in different areas. Blow-down = tree fall, or breaking of the tree section supporting the hole; vertebrate damage = tearing apart walls, including making a new entrance by a woodpecker; decay of substrate = disappearance of walls or bottom due to wood decomposition; growing over = reducing entrance size by growing tissues below minimum passable.*

Area & origin	N	Blow-down	Vertebrate Damage	Decay of Substrate	Growing Over	Source
Białowieża Forest						
Excavated	465	79	11	8	2	Wesołowski (2011b)
Non-excavated – dead	96	67	7	26	0	Wesołowski (2012)
Non-excavated – living	780	35	8	24	33	Wesołowski (2012)
Germany						
Excavated – living	14	50	0	0	50	Günther & Hellmann (1995)
British Columbia						
Excavated	402	90	Not reported	7	3	Edworthy et al. (2012)
Illinois						
Non-excavated – living	23	52	Not reported	35	13	Nielsen et al. (2007)
Colorado						
Excavated	38	78	0	10	12	Sedgwick & Knopf (1992)

Cause of Failure (%)

(Table 4.3; Martin *et al.* 2004; Edworthy *et al.* 2012). Overall, hole loss due to healing wounds seems to be most frequent in fast-growing softwood tree species (Wesołowski 1995a). Degradation of holes due to wood decomposition was a moderately frequent cause of loss of non-excavated holes in Białowieża Forest and in Illinois. The destruction of walls by woodpeckers or mammals was occasionally recorded in Białowieża Forest (Table 4.3).

4.4.5 Transient Inactivation

In addition to permanent hole loss, some holes become temporarily unusable because the hole's entrance may be blocked, its bottom lost or its chamber filled with debris or water. Visual checks of 1,131 hole interiors over eight years in Białowieża Forest revealed that about 12% of non-excavated holes were rendered unusable annually due to the chamber filling with rotten wood, flooding, damage to the bottom or accumulation of old material (Wesołowski 2001).

4.4.6 Hole Availability in Relation to Stand Age and Management

Mature and old-growth forests should contain the highest numbers of holes, as the chance of a tree supporting a hole increases with its age, size and declining health. The highest estimated hole densities are in old unmanaged patches (Remm & Lõhmus 2011). In Białowieża Forest, surveys recorded an available hole density of 125/10 ha in coniferous forest (Walankiewicz *et al.* 2014) and >160/10 ha in deciduous forest (Wesołowski 2007a). Similarly, a hole density of 123/10 ha was recorded in mature forests in British Columbia (Aitken & Martin 2007; Cockle *et al.* 2011). Values within this range are found in other mature forests on both continents (reviewed in Remm & Lõhmus 2011).

Finally, the overall proportion of young to mature tree patches influences hole availability at the forest landscape level. In unmanaged forests, old-growth stands cover most of the area (ca. 70% of Białowieża Forest; Jędrzejewska & Jędrzejewski 1998). Similarly, late-seral stages dominate unmanaged forest landscapes in Québec (Drapeau *et al.* 2009). This was also originally the case in most European temperate forests (Chapter 8). Under natural conditions, younger tree patches are less hole-poor than those in managed forests. Even after severe disturbance (e.g., fire, storm), existing holes in unmanaged forests are partially retained and new holes can be excavated in snags created by the disturbance (Saab *et al.* 2004; Edworthy *et al.* 2011; Wiebe 2014).

4.5 Hole–nesting Birds and Other Hole–dependent Taxa

4.5.1 Composition of Hole–nesting Assemblages

Hole-nesters constitute an important component of breeding bird communities in all forest types on both continents. While the diversity of hole-nesting assemblages is greater in the Palearctic (n = 229 species) than in the Nearctic (n = 137) zoogeographic region, North America (Canada and the continental United States) supports more species in fewer families (85 species in 17 families) than Europe (71 species in 19 families) (Scott *et al.* 1977; van der Hoek *et al.* 2017). In Białowieża Forest, ca. 36% of breeding species and up to 45% of breeding pairs nest in holes (Wesołowski 2007a). Apart from obligate hole-nesters, there are also facultative hole-breeders that use holes and other nest site types (Table 4.4). One finds similar patterns in other old-growth forests in Europe, where up to 60% of breeding pairs can use tree holes (cf. Chapter 8). In interior British Columbia, about 25% of 171 forest breeding species are hole-nesting birds; the majority of these species are obligate hole-nesters (Martin *et al.* 2004; Table 4.4).

Hole-nesting species range in mass from the 6 g Lucy's warbler *Oreothlypis luciae* (North America) and the 10 g wren *Troglodytes troglodytes* (Europe) to the 2 kg goosander *Mergus merganser* (both continents). They encompass species that are year-round residents and those that have short- and long-distance migratory habits (Table 4.4). About one-third of hole-nesters are able to excavate their own holes (Table 4.4). Species differ somewhat in their dependence on holes, as there are more facultative hole-nesting passerines in Białowieża Forest and more facultative hole-nesting owls in British Columbia. The species richness of the hole-nester avifauna in Białowieża Forest is high, possibly among the highest found in Europe (Wesołowski 2007a). The richness of the assemblage in British Columbia is higher than in Białowieża Forest, as it supports several waterfowl and raptor species. Barring a few exceptions (a non-excavating woodpecker in Europe, no hole-using pigeons in British Columbia), many species have ecological counterparts on each continent (Table 4.4). These similarities are partially due to the widespread distribution of waterfowl species (e.g., goldeneye *Bucephala clangula*,

Table 4.4 *Composition of hole-nesting avifauna in Białowieża Forest (after Tomiałojć et al. 1984; Tomiałojć 1995; Wesołowski et al. 2003, 2010, 2014) and in central British Columbia, Canada (after Martin et al. 2004; Aitken & Martin 2007; Cockle & Martin 2015). Migratory (Migr.) habits of individual species: long-distance (LD) migrants wintering south of the Sahara/tropical Asia (European birds) or in Central/South America (North American birds); short-distance (SD), mainly in south-west Europe and the Mediterranean basin or within North America, respectively; residents (R) wintering outside of the forest itself but still within the same geographic and climatic region, also including nomadic species. A subcategory of resident forest (RF) birds, which stay the whole year in their breeding habitats, is additionally given for Białowieża.*

	Białowieża Forest		Interior British Columbia	
Category/Order	Species	Migr.	Species	Migr.
Excavators				
Piciformes	*Dryobates minor*	RF	*Melanerpes lewis*[d]	SD
	Leiopicus medius	RF	*Sphyrapicus nuchalis*[e]	R
	Dendrocopos leucotos	RF	*Sphyrapicus ruber*[e]	SD
	Dendrocopos major	R	*Sphyrapicus varius*[e]	LD
	Picoides tridactylus	RF	*Picoides pubescens*	R
	Dryocopus martius	RF	*Picoides villosus*	R
	Picus viridis	R	*Picoides arcticus*	R
	Picus canus	R	*Picoides dorsalis*	R
			Colaptes auratus	R
			Dryocopus pileatus	R
Passeriformes	*Lophophanes cristatus*	RF	*Poecile atricapillus*	R
	Poecile montanus	RF	*Poecile hudsonicus*	R
			Sitta canadensis	R
Non-excavators				
Anseriformes	—[a]		*Aix sponsa*	SD
			Bucephala albeola	SD
			Bucephala clangula	SD
			Bucephala islandica	SD
			Lophodytes cucculatus	SD
Columbiformes	*Columba oenas*	SD	—	
Apodiformes	*Apus apus*	LD	*Chaetura vauxii*	LD
Strigiformes	*Strix aluco*	RF	*Otus flameolus*	LD
	Glaucidium passerinum	RF	*Glaucidium gnoma*	R

Table 4.4 (*cont.*)

Category/Order	Białowieża Forest		Interior British Columbia	
	Species	Migr.	Species	Migr.
	Aegolius funereus	RF	*Aegolius acadicus*	R
			Surnia ulula	R
Piciformes	*Jynx torquilla*	LD	–	
Falconiformes	*Falco tinnunculus*[b]	SD	*Falco sparverius*	SD
Passeriformes	*Periparus ater*	R	*Tachycineta bicolor*	LD
	Poecile palustris	RF	*Tachycineta thalassima*	LD
	Cyanistes caeruleus	R	*Poecile gambeli*	R
	Parus major	R	*Certhia americana*[f]	R
	Ficedula hypoleuca	LD	*Troglodytes aedon*[d]	SD
	Ficedula albicollis	LD	*Sialia currucoides*	SD/LD
	Certhia familiaris[c]	RF	*Sturnus vulgaris*	R
	Sitta europaea	RF		
	Sturnus vulgaris	SD		
	Phoenicurus phoenicurus	LD		
Facultative (all non-excavators)				
Anseriformes	–		*Mergus serrator*	SD
Strigiformes	–		*Bubo virginianus*	R
			Strix varia	R
			Strix nebulosa	R
Passeriformes	*Prunella modularis*	SD	*Empidonax difficilis*	LD
	Ficedula parva	LD		
	Troglodytes troglodytes	SD		
	Erithacus rubecula	SD		
	Turdus merula	SD		
	Turdus philomelos	SD		

[a] No large water bodies in Białowieża Forest, but *Bucephala clangula* breeds in other forests of the region (Tomiałojć 1995).
[b] *Falco tinnunculus* breeds in Białowieża Forest outside Białowieża National Park (Tomiałojć 1995).
[c] Most often breeds under loose tree bark.
[d] Not found on the study sites, but breeds in the region.
[e] *Sphyrapicus* woodpeckers breeding in the region are interspecific hybrids.
[f] Nests exclusively under loose tree bark.

goosander) and partially due to common ancestry – closely related species (e.g., *Poecile*, *Certhia*, *Troglodytes*), which replace each other geographically.

4.5.2 Non-avian Hole-users

In almost all forest wildlife communities, birds must share holes with a range of non-avian taxa, notably insects, mammals and reptiles. Mammals regularly use tree holes for breeding or roosting, and can be predators of bird eggs and nestlings as well as adults. These are small (*Mustela*) to medium-sized (*Martes*) mustelids, squirrels (*Sciurus*, Europe and North America; *Tamiasciurus*, North America), flying squirrels (*Pteromys*, Europe, boreal forests; *Glaucomys*, North America) and smaller rodents such as yellow-necked mouse *Apodemus flavicollis*, bank vole *Myodes glareolus* and dormice (Gliridae) in Europe and members of *Tamias*, *Neotoma* and *Peromyscus* genera in North America. Bats usually roost in holes located higher in trees than birds do, and typically prefer larger trees (Ruczyński & Bogdanowicz 2005). Social Hymenoptera occupy holes in Białowieża Forest at a low frequency (Wesołowski 2001), which may be generally the case in European forests (review in Broughton *et al.* 2015). Non-avian animals collectively occupy <10% of non-excavated holes in living trees per year (Wesołowski 2001; Czeszczewik *et al.* 2008). In North America, a range of mammals similar to that in Europe regularly competes for and uses the same holes as excavators and non-excavators. In British Columbia, 4.5% of our 4,867 nesting records of hole-nesting vertebrates are mammals (e.g., American red squirrel *Tamiasciurus hudsonicus*, northern flying squirrel *Glaucomys sabrinus*; K. Martin unpubl. data). The use of holes by non-avian taxa is often underestimated, given the difficulty in estimating their presence using the standard techniques for bird studies. To obtain accurate estimates of all vertebrates using holes, one needs to conduct regular visual checks of hole interiors or use automatic recording devices such as photo traps.

4.5.3 Structure and Function of Hole-nester Assemblages

Hole-nesting species in forest ecosystems constitute a structured assemblage where species interact through the creation of, and competition for, nest sites. Avian species can be classified into three guilds according to their mode of cavity acquisition. Strong excavators create holes in trees for nesting and roosting. Non-excavating hole-nesters include a variety of passerines, ducks, birds of prey and small mammals that require, but cannot excavate, cavities. Thus, they rely on those shelters created by excavators or naturally occurring non-excavated holes. A third guild, weak hole excavators (e.g., chickadees, nuthatches), excavate their own cavities in decayed wood, or use existing non-excavated or excavated holes. The interdependence among the three groups with respect to the creation and use of nest hole resources was termed a 'nest web' by Martin and Eadie (1999). They proposed that hole-nesting vertebrate assemblages exist within nest webs (Fig. 4.1) directly analogous to food webs, whereby some species depend partly or entirely on excavators to produce a critical resource (holes). Thus, hole-nesting assemblages exhibit a hierarchical structure with potentially strong interdependencies among assemblage members. These ecological dependencies can vary with habitat features such as forest type, condition and stage of succession. Application of the nest web concept was first demonstrated in an assemblage of hole-nesting vertebrates in British Columbia, Canada, where the nest web structure showed that most hole resource use flowed up the assemblage through aspen trees and holes excavated by northern flickers (Fig. 4.1; Martin & Eadie 1999; Martin et al. 2004). Nest webs have been generated for hole-nester assemblages elsewhere in North America, for example, boreal forest in Québec and Alberta (Cadieux 2011; Cooke & Hannon 2011), Carolinian broadleaved forest in Ontario (Bavrlic 2008) and southern pine forests in Florida (Blanc & Walters 2008a), as well as globally (Cockle et al. 2011). No formal nest web has been constructed for European hole-nesting assemblages.

4.6 Hole Availability and Inter- and Intra-specific Competition in Limiting Breeding Density

It is a commonly held view that breeding numbers of non-excavating birds are generally limited by a shortage of holes and that hole-nesters must compete to acquire and retain holes (Newton 1994, 1998; Wesołowski 2007a, 2011b; Wiebe 2011). Interspecific competition for holes in highly simplified environments (natural holes absent, only one type of nest box available, high density of birds) may be acute (Newton 1998). In such circumstances, killing of prospecting birds by box owners frequently occurs (refs in Walankiewicz & Mitrus 1997). Thus, interspecific competition for nesting sites appears to be an important proximate factor influencing numbers and species of hole-nesters, as well as the major selective force shaping hole use patterns (Newton 1994). However, if the holes are not in short supply, there is not much reason to compete for them, unless the quality of the hole strongly influences their fitness (Lõhmus & Remm 2005). We review the evidence for and against nest site limitation for this group of birds in managed and old-forest ecosystems.

The introduction of nest boxes has often resulted in strong increases in the number of non-excavating birds (reviews in Graczyk 1973; Newton 1994, 1998; Wesołowski 2011a; Wiebe 2011). Individual species can reach unusually high densities; for example, in Europe: up to 70 collared flycatcher *Ficedula albicollis* nests/10 ha (L. Gustafsson, pers. comm.), 40 pied flycatcher *Ficedula hypoleuca* pairs/10 ha (Tiainen *et al.* 1984) and 37 blue tit *Cyanistes caeruleus* pairs/10 ha (East & Perrins 1988). Holt and Martin (1997) allowed passerine hole-nesters to initiate breeding, and then added nest boxes that were occupied immediately by mountain bluebirds *Sialia currucoides* and tree swallows *Tachycineta bicolor*, thus demonstrating a surplus of non-breeding birds. These nest box addition 'experiments' were often carried out in managed forests in which the availability of holes was reduced by human activities, often in conjunction with predator control programmes, and their results have been generalised to all non-excavator assemblages.

In contrast, studies in Białowieża Forest do not provide much support for an important role of nest site competition (Walankiewicz 1991; Wesołowski 2003, 2007a). Although hole usurpation occurs (Tomiałojć *et al.* 1984; Wesołowski 1995b), it is infrequent (Wesołowski 2003), and no killing of birds prospecting for holes has been recorded (Walankiewicz & Mitrus 1997). Holes used by various non-excavator species in Białowieża Forest differ in many respects. For example, the area of hole bottoms ranges from a median 64 cm^2 for the marsh tit (Wesołowski 2003) to 290 cm^2 for the nuthatch *Sitta europaea* (Wesołowski & Rowiński 2004), and the distance from the hole entrance to the top of the nest cup ranges from 9 cm for the nuthatch to 19 cm for the great tit *Parus major* (Maziarz *et al.* 2015a). Despite these differences, there is substantial interspecific overlap in the range of acceptable holes that could potentially lead to interspecific competition for holes. Birds mostly use holes occupied earlier by their own species, but up to five other non-excavator species could breed in holes previously used by collared flycatcher (Wesołowski 1989). In British Columbia, some holes are used almost every year by a wide range of species, while other holes are only used for one or two years. Over their lifetimes, some holes were used up to 20 times in 17 years by up to 6 different species, with individual holes used by raptors, waterfowl, mammals and small passerines (K. Martin unpubl.).

Studies in old natural forest stands in Europe do not support the notion that hole-nesting birds are limited by a shortage of holes. Observations in old-growth deciduous forests suggest that holes are superabundant there (Wesołowski 2007a). The densities of hole-nesters recorded in Białowieża Forest (up to 47 pairs/10 ha; Wesołowski *et al.* 2006) are at least three times lower than the number of holes available, and numerous useable holes remain unused in most years, both in deciduous (Wesołowski 2007a) and coniferous (Walankiewicz *et al.* 2014) habitats. Similar situations were found in semi-natural forests in Sweden (Sandström 1992; Carlson *et al.* 1998). Even in areas where non-excavator densities are very high, they are largely not limited by the shortage of holes. In Moscow, Russia, Morozov (2009) blocked all breeding holes in trees used by blue tits in a semi-natural oak wood containing no nest boxes. He repeated this procedure after each breeding season, so that by the end of the experiment, all holes used by this species in the previous five years were made inaccessible for the birds. A threefold reduction in hole supply did not lower the breeding numbers of blue tits, which remained very high (25–30 pairs/10 ha) throughout the whole experiment. Interspecific conflicts over holes remained rare, and the proportion of unpaired males did not increase.

Using an experimental approach at the community level can reveal other insights about nest site limitation. In mature forests of British Columbia, hole abundance was high: 112 holes/10 ha in the aspen forest groves and 11 holes/10 ha in the continuous mixed-forest, and in both forest types most holes remained unoccupied (occupancy rates were 44% and 9%, respectively). This suggests that holes were not in limited supply in this system (Aitken *et al.* 2002; Aitken & Martin 2004, 2007). However, a multi-year BACI (before and after control/hole blocking) experiment with high-use holes was implemented in high-nesting-density aspen groves (Aitken & Martin 2008). A 50% decline in nesting density occurred at the community level during the blocking of holes, and a recovery of nesting density was observed after the blocking was removed. This finding indicated strong preferences for these high-quality holes that appeared to be limited at these sites, despite the abundance of unused holes. In the continuous mixed-forest sites with lower densities of holes and nesting birds, nesting densities tripled when the number of nest holes was tripled using a nest box addition treatment (Aitken & Martin 2012). Since birds were not banded in this study, it was unknown whether they had to forgo breeding in the cavity-blocking experiment or whether birds moved from adjacent areas to breed in the cavity-addition experiment, but nesting densities did not change significantly in control areas. These nest hole manipulation experiments taken together suggest that, despite there being many unused nest holes, some species show strong nest site preferences, and high-quality nest holes can be limited both in high-nesting-density aspen groves and in low-nesting-density coniferous–broadleaved forest stands.

Wiebe (2011) reviewed the evidence that nest site availability limited the number of breeding pairs of hole-nesting birds in mature forests at the population or landscape scale. She concluded that no studies have been conducted that provided strong confirmation of nest site limitation (i.e., studies using replicated control and experimental sites and marked birds at relevant spatial scales so it could be shown that birds colonising the boxes did not move in from elsewhere). However, data were available from 15 studies on 21 hole-nesting bird species in mature forests where hole availability was changed (increased via nest box addition, or decreased via hole blocking), and in 21 of 31 species-site cases, the authors failed to detect significant changes in breeding density. In most of the 10 cases showing an effect, no surveys were done to demonstrate that the number of breeding pairs was limited by the availability of nest sites at the population scale (Wiebe 2011).

The starling *Sturnus vulgaris,* a non-excavator species native to Europe but introduced to North America more than 100 years ago, is a strong nest site competitor worthy of mention because it has the potential to impact the structure and function of hole-nesting assemblages. It often breeds at high densities (semi-colonially) and is able to aggressively evict many other users from holes (Glutz von Blotzheim & Bauer 1993; Koenig 2003; Wiebe 2003; Páclik *et al.* 2009). Starlings present a novel challenge for North American hole-nesters, while hole-nesting birds in Europe have a longer history of interactions with the species. A strong depressing effect on the numbers of other hole-nesters was found in several studies on both continents (van Balen *et al.* 1982; Ingold 1989; Frei *et al.* 2015). However, contrary to expectations, their presence did not affect the densities of other hole-nesters in Białowieża Forest (Tomiałojć *et al.* 1984; Wesołowski *et al.* 2010, 2015) or in North America at the continental level (correlative study based on breeding bird survey data; Koenig 2003). When starlings were present in habitat patches in British Columbia, native passerine hole-nesters selected other nest hole types or delayed breeding until starlings selected their holes, with no reduction in their breeding success in those sites (Koch *et al.* 2012). However, in the same study area, it was not a favourable strategy for northern flickers to delay breeding to avoid usurpation by starlings (7% usurpation rate for northern flickers, Wiebe 2003). In general, most negative impacts on native hole-nesters attributed to starlings have been found for woodpeckers rather than non-excavators. As starlings require open areas for foraging, they breed mostly along forest edges, thus they would affect mostly birds in fragmented forests with high edge/interior ratios, whereas they would generally not pose a threat for birds breeding inside extensive continuous forests.

In summary, it seems that under ancestral conditions (large extensive forests, high abundance of excavated and decay-formed holes), the availability of nest holes is sufficient to enable the coexistence of diverse hole-nester assemblages on both continents. However, much of the forested area on both continents has been converted to younger forest or non-forest habitats, with consequent reductions in the supply, diversity and quality of holes.

4.7 Advantages and Disadvantages of Breeding in Holes

4.7.1 Holes – Safe Harbours?

Tree holes are considered to be successful breeding places for forest birds. In Białowieża Forest, the nesting success of hole-nesters (51–74%) was the highest among all types of nesters, including open-cup and ground nesters (Wesołowski & Tomiałojć 2005). In Arizona, nesting success of non-excavators (58%) was higher than for open-cup nesters (43%), but much lower than for excavators (88%; Li & Martin 1991; Martin & Li 1992). Excavating woodpeckers, as a group, have higher nesting success rates than many other forest bird groups. More than 50% of their breeding attempts succeed in fledging offspring. Seven species in Europe experienced average nesting success of 76–82% (annual averages range from 42–97%). In North America, average nesting success for 14 woodpecker species ranged from 60–91% (annual averages from 47–100%; Paclík *et al.* 2009).

Despite the relative safety of hole-nesting, nest predation is still the major cause of nesting failure in holes. Up to 35% of woodpecker broods can be lost due to predation (Paclík *et al.* 2009). It also accounts for 64–91% of the total loss among eight species studied in Białowieża Forest (Wesołowski 2007a; Wesołowski & Rowiński 2012; Maziarz *et al.* 2015b). In some cases, nest predators also kill incubating adults. For example, in Białowieża Forest, adult remains were found in >3% of depredated collared flycatcher nests (Czeszczewik *et al.* 2008), and in ca. 23% of destroyed blue and great tit nests (Wesołowski & Rowiński 2012; Maziarz *et al.* 2015b).

What makes a hole predator-proof? A predator could enter a hole, insert its paw or beak through the entrance, or even remove a part of the hole wall to gain access to the eggs, nestlings or adults. To reduce potential attacks, a hole should simultaneously have: (a) an entrance just large enough to admit the hole occupant, (b) walls made of hard wood and (c) sufficient depth for the nest contents to be placed beyond the predator's reach (Wesołowski 2002). Additionally, a nest placed high above the ground can be advantageous, as this can make its detection more difficult and access more risky for generalist predators approaching from the ground (Nilsson 1984).

A narrow entrance can prevent larger predators from entering the hole, but it does not constitute a barrier for smaller predators able to pass through it (Fig. 4.5). Because of small predators, the minimum entrance diameter of holes with depredated and fledged broods of three tit species and pied flycatcher *Ficedula hypoleuca* in Białowieża

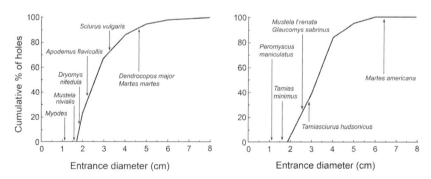

Figure 4.5 Distribution of minimum entrance diameters of 343 holes used for nesting by marsh tit *Poecile palustris* in, left, Białowieża Forest (after Wesołowski 2002, modified) and for 321 holes used by mountain chickadee *P. gambeli* in, right, British Columbia (K. Martin, unpubl.). The minimum sizes of openings passable by different predator species are shown by arrows.

Forest did not differ (Wesołowski 2002; Czeszczewik & Walankiewicz 2003; Wesołowski & Rowiński 2012; Maziarz *et al.* 2015b). However, holes with smaller entrances were less frequently depredated for collared flycatcher (Walankiewicz 1991), nuthatch (Wesołowski & Rowiński 2004) and mountain chickadee *Poecile gambeli* (Norris 2012). Rates of predation on woodpecker broods tend to increase with the size of their hole entrance (Paclík *et al.* 2009).

Small entrances are efficient as an antipredator defence as long as they are combined with walls of living or only slightly decomposed sapwood that cannot be destroyed by larger predators. Non-excavators in Białowieża Forest strongly avoid holes in dead wood, as such holes are more frequently depredated (Wesołowski 2002, 2007a; Maziarz *et al.* 2015b). Nuthatches use holes in living substrates, with entrances narrowed by a plaster they make of dried mud. If it is dry, the plaster makes an impenetrable barrier, but in a very rainy season, the plaster can soften, and in several cases predators were able to remove the plaster (Wesołowski & Rowiński 2004). The importance of strong hole walls was also confirmed in studies of non-excavators elsewhere (Ludescher 1973; Alatalo *et al.* 1990; Albano 1992; Christman & Dhondt 1997). Large predators often fail to reach woodpecker broods in tree holes with sound wood, but can destroy tree holes in dead wood (Paclík *et al.* 2009; Tozer *et al.* 2012). Birds could save much time and energy by excavating holes in mechanically weaker (softer) substrates, yet they excavate in what is likely the hardest wood they can manage (Cockle *et al.* 2011; Wesołowski 2011a; Blanc & Martin 2012).

Nests situated closer to the entrance were more frequently depredated in several species studied (Czeszczewik & Walankiewicz 2003; Wesołowski & Rowiński 2012; Maziarz *et al.* 2015b). In Białowieża Forest, nest contents could be pulled through the entrance if hole depth was less than ca. 17 cm from the entrance (Wesołowski 2002). Raccoons *Procyon lotor,* introduced to Europe, can reach down to 33 cm (Günther & Hellmann 2002). Woodpecker holes are usually deep enough and sometimes have a recessed chamber, so they can avoid being accessed from the entrance by mammalian predators.

In contrast to the above-described defences, placing or using holes higher on trees does not appear to be a generally beneficial means of predator avoidance. This effect was found in some studies (Nilsson 1984; Rendell & Robertson 1989; Fisher & Wiebe 2006; Robles & Martin 2013), but not in others (Wesołowski 2002; Czeszczewik & Walankiewicz 2003). Sometimes lower nest holes were actually more successful

(Wesołowski & Rowiński 2004, 2012; Maziarz *et al.* 2015b). The most secure nesting height may vary locally. Where ground-restricted predators are the main threat, nesting high could be beneficial, while in areas such as Białowieża Forest, where crown-operating predators are more prevalent (Walankiewcz 2002b; Wesołowski 2007a), lower holes are more secure. In North America, some generalist meso-predators such as squirrels and chipmunks also need to avoid their predators, and thus tend to avoid visiting higher nest holes in more open sites (Fisher & Wiebe 2006).

Beyond these general methods, several groups of birds on both continents have evolved additional specific behaviours that could serve as means of predator avoidance. These include covering eggs with nest material by tits during the laying stage (Haftorn & Slagsvold 1995; Wesołowski 2013) and by nuthatches throughout the laying and incubation periods (Matthysen 1998; Wesołowski & Rowiński 2004), and possibly smearing resin around the hole entrance by red-breasted nuthatches (Matthysen 1998). To avoid predation by pine marten *Martes martes*, black woodpeckers excavate new holes each season (Nilsson *et al.* 1991) and red-cockaded woodpeckers *Picoides borealis* select nest trees in open areas with no vegetation touching the nest tree to prevent snakes from accessing the nest (Harding & Walters 2002), while northern flickers experience lower predation if there is more vegetation concealing the nest hole (Fisher & Wiebe 2006).

4.7.2 Comparing Risk of Predation for Hole-nesters between the Continents

Here we address the relative safety of breeding in tree holes in Europe and North America. Are hole-nesters exposed to their respective predators using equivalent detection and attack techniques in both regions?

Birds and mammals are the most important nest predators in Białowieża Forest (Tomiałojć *et al.* 1984; Walankiewicz, 2002a; Wesołowski 2007a), while mammals are the most important predators in British Columbia and in boreal and temperate forests generally (Mahon & Martin 2006; Paclík *et al.* 2009). Rodents (*Tamiasciurus, Eutamias* and *Glaucomys*), several mustelid species (American marten *Martes americana*, least weasel *Mustela nivalis* and fisher *Martes pennanti*) and bears are the most common predators of hole-nesters in Canada (Evans *et al.* 2002; Fisher & Wiebe 2006; Tozer *et al.* 2012). Most of these mammalian predators on both continents are generalists, for which neither hole-nesting birds nor their nest contents constitute the main source of food. Predation rates on hole-nesters can vary across time and space, depending on the availability of alternative food sources (Evans *et al.* 2002; Walankiewcz 2002b; Mahon & Martin 2006; Tozer et al. 2009, 2012)

Predation by snakes becomes relevant mainly in the southern parts of both continents. The impact of snakes as predators of nests in holes is probably modest in southern Europe (Sorace *et al.* 2000). Snakes that climb trees are regular predators of many hole-nesters in southern Canada and the United States. As possible adaptations against snake predation in North America, red-cockaded woodpeckers make resin wells around the hole entrances of live trees (Rudolph *et al.* 1990; Kappes & Sieving 2011), and acorn woodpeckers *Melanerpes formicivorus* select nesting trees with smooth bark (Hooge *et al.* 1999).

Most mammalian and avian predators have geographical counterparts in Europe and North America, but there are some relevant continental differences. There are two types of predators that seem to be particular to Europe. One is a predatory woodpecker. The other is small rodents, which are able to kill adult birds in holes and are active in the tree crowns, making nesting high above the ground ineffectual.

Great spotted woodpecker is the most widespread and abundant European woodpecker (Glutz von Blotzheim & Bauer 1980) excavating the majority of holes in forests. It is a serious predator of non-excavator broods everywhere within its range (Ludescher 1973; Nilsson, 1984; Alatalo *et al.* 1990; Kuitunen & Aleknonis 1992; Walankiewicz 2002a; Morozov 2009; Paclík *et al.* 2009). Thus, having the choice, non-excavator species should avoid woodpecker-made holes, which is indeed the case in Europe (Fig. 4.6; see also Günther & Hellmann 1997, 2001; Wesołowski 2007a; Cockle *et al.* 2011). However, where the supply of non-excavated holes is more limited, such as in coniferous habitats (Carlson *et al.*1998; Czeszczewik & Walankiewicz 2003; Wesołowski & Rowiński 2004; Walankiewicz *et al.* 2014; Andersson *et al.* 2017) or in young forest patches (Remm & Lõhmus 2011), excavated holes could become more important to non-excavators. There are very few records of woodpeckers in North America destroying hole-nesting broods (Paclík *et al.* 2009), and no species appears to do so on a regular basis. Thus, woodpecker-made holes, as well as holes in decayed wood, are presumably less secure in Europe than in North America.

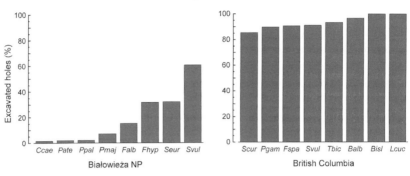

Figure 4.6 Frequency of use of excavated holes by non-excavator species in Białowieża Forest and British Columbia. Species in Białowieża are, from left to right: blue tit *Cyanistes caeruleus*, coal tit *Periparus ater*, marsh tit *Poecile palustris*, great tit *Parus major*, collared flycatcher *Ficedula albicollis,* pied flycatcher *F. hypoleuca*, nuthatch *Sitta europaea* and starling *Sturnus vulgaris*. After Wesołowski (1996, 2007a); Czeszczewik & Walankiewicz (2003); Wesołowski & Rowiński (2004, 2012); Maziarz (2012). Species in BC are, from left to right, mountain bluebird *Sialia currucoides*, mountain chickadee *Poecile gambeli*, American kestrel *Falco sparverius*, starling *Sturnus vulgaris*, tree swallow *Tachycineta bicolor*, bufflehead *Bucephala albeola*, Barrow's goldeneye *Bucephala islandica* and hooded merganser *Lophodytes cucculatus*; data updated from Aitken & Martin (2007).

Species of dormice (Gliridae), especially forest dormouse *Dryomys nitedula*, which live in tree canopies in central, eastern and southern Europe, are small enough to enter any hole used by hole-nesting birds (Fig. 4.5). They regularly kill adult birds in holes and constitute a serious and almost unavoidable threat to all smaller hole-nesters. The only means to reduce the risk of predation by dormice is to breed in lower holes and/ or earlier in the spring, when the forest dormouse is hibernating (Juškaitis 2006; Adamík & Král 2008; Maziarz *et al.* 2015b). Most of the North American hole-using rodents and mustelids could play a similar role, as they are small enough to enter the majority of holes as predators or competitors, but they do not appear to kill young or adults regularly. Some small mammals in North America, such as the deermouse *Peromyscus maniculatus*, prey infrequently on hole-nester eggs, nestlings and adults (Wiebe & Moore 2008; Paclík *et al.* 2009).

Some types of nest predators are specific to North America. The American black bear *Ursus americanus* regularly preys upon woodpecker and hole-nesting duck broods (Wiebe & Moore 2008; Nappi &

Drapeau 2009; Paclík *et al.* 2009; Tozer *et al.* 2009, 2011), while the European brown bear *Ursus arctos* is usually too heavy to climb trees. Raccoons are widespread generalist predators in North America, but they are not important hole-nester predators, as birds comprise a very minor part of their diet. However, there are occasional reports of them preying on eggs, nestlings and adult sapsuckers and flickers (Kilham 1971), and introduced racoons could locally become a serious threat (Germany; Günther & Hellmann 2002).

The house wren *Troglodytes aedon* is small enough to enter active nest-holes and has been recorded destroying eggs and nestlings of several hole-nesting passerines early in the breeding season (before laying) in some locations (Belles-Isles & Picman 1986). House wrens can cause nest failure of the nests of Bewick's wren *Thryomanes bewickii*, prothonotary warbler *Protonotaria citrea* and several other hole-nesting passerines, but whether this destruction behaviour negatively impacts populations remains unclear (Kennedy & White 1997; Johnson 2014). Studies using infrared cameras placed near hole entrances are needed to determine how hole-nesting birds deal with the risk of cohabiting in sites with mammals or bird species that are both nest-site predators and competitors.

4.7.3 Other Challenges of Breeding in Tree Holes

To capitalise on the advantages of the safety offered by nesting in holes, hole-nesting birds must be able to cope with the challenges of breeding in this environment. These involve being able to operate in very dim light (Wesołowski & Maziarz 2012; Maziarz & Wesołowski 2014), avoiding microbial and fungal infections in constantly humid conditions, especially in non-excavated holes (West *et al.* 2015; Maziarz *et al.* 2017), and dealing with potentially insufficient aeration (Howe *et al.* 1987) and waterlogging of nest contents. Nest loss due to soaking has been observed in most groups of hole-nesters and is the second most important cause of nest failure in Białowieża Forest (Wesołowski *et al.* 2002; Wesołowski 2007a). Nests in decay-formed holes can be flooded by rainwater flowing down the trunk and also by sap draining into holes in live trees. Holes in living trees are permanently humid (Maziarz & Wesołowski 2013). To avoid nest soaking, hole-nesting birds should use holes in dead wood, in limbs and high above the ground (Wesołowski 2002). Hole-nesting passerines (mostly non-excavators) tend to

(a)　　　　　　　　　　　　　　(b)

(c)　　　　　　　　　　　　　　(d)

(e)　　　　　　　　　　　　　　(f)

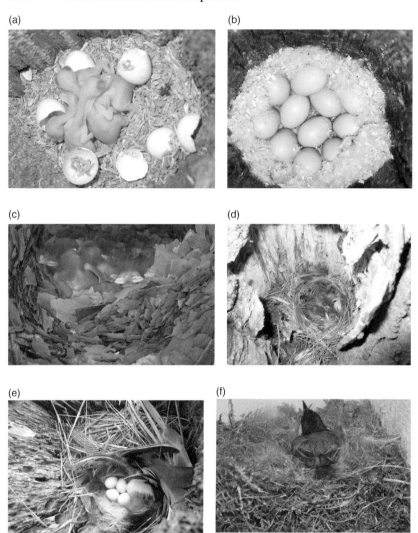

Figure 4.7 Diversity of nests of the hole-nesting birds in Europe and North America. (a) Woodpeckers, owls and birds of prey do not build any nests (*Picoides arcticus* with hatching eggs; photo Y. Rochepault). (b) Anseriformes use their own body feathers (*Bucephala clangula*; photo H. Blümel). (c) Some birds make them of bark flakes (e.g., *Sitta europaea*; photo G. Hebda). (d) Several groups of passerines use fine, bendable plant material (*Sialia currucoides*; photo A. Norris). (e) Some line them with feathers as well (*Tachycineta bicolor*; photo A. Fouillet). (f) Parids make a foundation from moss and line the cup with mammalian hair (*Parus major*; photo G. Hebda). Sizes of nests not to scale.

cope with the flood risk by building bulky nests (Fig. 4.7) that raise nest cups above hole bottoms (e.g., by an average of 11 cm for great tits) (Maziarz et al. 2015a), as well as separating nest cups from moist hole walls. Species vary in their use of materials to absorb water (moss, dry leaves, rootlets, grasses, bark flakes). Owls use no nest material, thus flooding could be an important threat for them; >20% of Tengmalm's owl *Aegolius funereus* nests have been reported to have flooded, with some nestlings surviving by resting on the backs of their drowned siblings (Rudat et al. 1979).

In contrast, woodpecker nests are soaked rather infrequently (Wesołowski et al. 2002). By excavating holes preferentially in dead wood or decaying wood, often in snags or broken limbs of living trees, they can avoid sap drain, and nesting near the top of a snag also strongly reduces the chance of flooding by stem flow. A few woodpecker species – black woodpecker and red-cockaded woodpecker – that habitually excavate holes in living trees have apparently solved the problem of keeping their nests dry by providing their hole entrances with water-protecting eaves and sills or excavating immediately under a bracket fungus (Meyer & Meyer 2001; Jackson & Jackson 2004). If their holes get flooded, the larger young of black woodpeckers can survive by clinging to the walls above the water surface (Rudat et al. 1979). Excavating holes from the undersides of sloping limbs/trunks could also reduce the chance of flooding (Kilham 1971; Stauffer & Best 1982; Wesołowski 1989; Hooge et al. 1999; Hebda et al. 2016). Flooding and soaking rarely occur in aspen tree holes in North America, because the majority of holes used are excavated in the trunks and most entrances do not face upwards.

4.7.4 Trade-offs in Hole Use

To breed successfully in tree holes, birds have to deal with all the problems listed above. Although avoiding nest predation remains the most important issue, birds may not be able to maximise nest site security, because they are constrained by other things essential for the development and growth of young (nest site competition, nest predators in proximity, proximity to foraging sites, protection against nest soaking, microclimate, etc.). The few studies that have considered multiple factors in nest site selection all show that the solutions differ across species, and often spatially and temporally (Wesołowski 2002; Harding & Walters

2002; Wiebe & Moore 2008; Tozer *et al.* 2011; Maziarz & Wesołowski 2013; Maziarz *et al.* 2015b).

4.8 Conservation of Hole-nester Assemblages and Tree Hole Resources

The distribution and density of hole-nesters might be influenced or limited by a number of factors, which could act outside the breeding season and, in the case of migrants, away from the breeding grounds (Newton 1998). For example, the distribution of species that require access to open foraging grounds, such as the starling, may be limited by the presence of edges. The distribution of northern flickers on migratory stopover habitats in spring and fall may be limited by the availability of nightly roosting holes (Gow *et al.* 2015), and the breeding numbers of several woodpecker species in southern Finland may be limited by severe winters (Saari & Mikusiński 1996) and of wryneck *Jynx torquilla* by wintering conditions in the Sahel (Zwarts *et al.* 2009). For woodpeckers and bark-foraging species generally, the availability of dead trees on which to forage can be a limiting factor (Walankiewicz *et al.* 2002; Roberge *et al.* 2008; Czeszczewik *et al.* 2013; Tremblay *et al.* 2014; Nappi *et al.* 2015). Successful conservation of hole-nesters requires taking all critical factors into account. As this chapter is focused on relationships between hole-nesters and their nesting tree holes, we concentrate here on conservation of this resource.

To preserve entire hole-nesting assemblages in functioning nest webs (*sensu* Martin & Eadie 1999), a full range and density of hole types should be available to enable the coexistence of a full complement of avian and non-avian hole users in the forest landscape. Hole formation and persistence processes need to be sufficiently functional to produce adequate supplies of high-quality nesting and roosting sites (Aitken & Martin 2004; Martin *et al.* 2004; Drapeau *et al.* 2009; Cockle *et al.* 2011; Wesołowski 2011a, 2012; Bunnell 2013). To maintain diversity and continuity of these processes, it is essential to leave some forest stands free of human management, allowing these patches to undergo natural processes of growth and decay (Gustafsson *et al.* 2012; Lindenmayer *et al.* 2012; Bunnell 2013). As a priority, these should be tracts of old growth, because large decaying trees occur at the highest concentrations in such places, and these structures are the most difficult to replace when lost.

Allowing healthy trees to remain in the forest past the commercial harvest age is crucial. Currently, trees are harvested in European forests at such a young age that few opportunities exist for the formation and retention of non-excavated holes (Wesołowski 2012). This is particularly important in European broadleaved forests, where hole-nesters depend primarily on decay rather than excavators to provide holes. Widespread application of the 'retention forestry' approach (Oliver *et al.* 1994; Gustafsson *et al.* 2012; Lindenmayer *et al.* 2012; see also Chapter 13) should be recommended in timber-managed forests. Under this management system, portions of original stands are left unaffected in all forestry operations, to provide continuity in structure, function and composition across forest generations. The structures to be retained could be anything from single trees to groups of trees. Retention forestry is not a substitute for large non-intervention reserves, but rather a partial measure to preserve portions of the hole-nester diversity in timber-production landscapes (Gustafsson *et al.* 2012; Lindenmayer *et al.* 2012). Modelling has indicated that retaining 30% of forest stands of the Pacific Northwest in North America would likely preserve only about two-thirds of the avian hole-nester assemblage (Bunnell 2013). Specialist species and certain functional groups would probably be lost in this reduction of vertebrate biota (Ibarra *et al.* 2017).

Hole-bearing live and dead trees, as well as wounded and decayed trees, should be retained as 'biological legacies', to assure conditions for future hole formation. Retaining such trees that have little to no commercial value would not substantially decrease profits from forestry operations. Large-scale disturbances – wildfires, hurricanes, insect outbreaks – can kill many trees simultaneously (Lindenmayer *et al.* 2008). Such areas provide attractive foraging and nesting conditions for several excavators (e.g., black-backed woodpecker and American three-toed woodpecker in North American post-fire areas; Nappi & Drapeau 2009, 2011; Nappi *et al.* 2010; Tremblay *et al.* 2015). Post-disturbance 'salvage/sanitary' logging destroys these biological legacies and also can hinder tree regeneration, while providing only small gains from removed timber (Lindenmayer *et al.* 2008; Chapters 8 and 13). Reductions in salvage operations and other forms of post-harvest intervention would result in substantial conservation gains without causing meaningful economical loss.

As discussed above, it takes many decades for non-excavated holes to form (Wesołowski 2012). In Białowieża Forest, non excavated holes are formed mostly in larger trees older than 130–200 years (Wesołowski 2012). Small-leaved lime is the only tree species in Białowieża Forest in which non-excavated holes are formed in small trees, but they have to be at least 70–80 years old to acquire sufficient levels of decay for natural hole formation (Wesołowski 2012). Despite the fact that holes in such trees are relatively short-lived and the trees harbour holes suitable only for smaller hole-nester species, lime provides the first non-excavated holes in regenerating forest patches. As this tree species is widespread in deciduous and mixed-forest zones in Europe and can grow in a variety of soils, adding lime trees to newly established plantations and retaining them during harvesting should become standard forestry procedure in managed woods, as this would result in more non-excavated holes in forests (Wesołowski 2012).

In many younger or mature forests of Europe and North America, woodpeckers are able to excavate holes quickly in relatively healthy trees and thus can produce high-quality holes in younger trees, and at a faster rate, than in systems that rely on decay hole-making processes. Great spotted woodpecker and middle spotted woodpecker *Leiopicus medius* are able to excavate holes in trees with a minimum diameter at breast height of 20 cm (Günther 1993; Mazgajski 1997; Smith 1997; Fauvel *et al.* 2001; Kosiński & Winiecki 2004). Birch can achieve this size in about 30 years in England (Smith 1997), but, as woodpeckers strongly prefer to nest in dead birches there (Smith 1997, 2007), additional time is probably needed before trees become suitable. Great spotted woodpeckers can excavate holes in ca. 70-year-old pedunculate oak (Smith 1997), and in <60-year-old aspen (Lõhmus & Remm 2005), while black woodpeckers can create holes in beech trees that are 90 years old (Johansen 1989). Strong excavators can excavate in aspens that are 60–80 years old. As the excavated holes in coniferous forests are found predominantly in aspen, retaining or promoting mature aspen trees in all conifer-dominated forestry operations should be a major conservation goal. Retaining mixed conifer and aspen patches of 0.5–2 ha is an effective means of protecting key nesting trees from blow-down. Such retention patches provide other critical habitat requirements, such as foraging areas, perches and cover for hole-nesting fauna in close proximity to nesting trees (Drever & Martin 2010; Ouellet-Lapointe *et al.* 2012; Tremblay *et al.* 2015).

In North American temperate forests, managed landscapes can be very productive for hole-nesters in terms of diversity and density

(Drever *et al.* 2008; Drever & Martin 2010; Bunnell 2013). Some solutions, such as retaining snags or some hole-bearing trees in clear-cuts, have been incorporated into forestry practices in individual regions, with a positive response in terms of maintaining the species richness of hole-nesting communities (Drapeau *et al.* 2009). In the boreal mixed coniferous stands of North America, moderate harvest levels may have few detrimental effects in the short term, or even lead to increases in excavator and non-excavator densities (Drever & Martin 2010; Cooke & Hannon 2011, 2012). Woodpeckers that are keystone excavators, such as northern flickers, increase in density when primary forest is opened up, as this species feeds on ants in open areas (Drever & Martin 2010). However, after 15–20 years, when plantations start to fill in with young trees, the densities of excavators decrease, and hole density also decreases, with the loss of existing aspen nesting trees and a reduction in the rate of hole creation. Therefore, in these situations, retaining old-growth habitat attributes in wildlife tree patches is critical to maintaining a diverse supply of hole-nesters until the young forest matures. In some cases, excavators can accelerate hole production and increase the diversity of hole-nester assemblages in medium- to mature-aged forests once aspen or other nesting trees reach a size and decay condition suitable for hole excavation.

Providing nest boxes as artificial holes can be considered an alternative management approach to restore the loss of holes when mature trees are removed. This approach is generally ineffective in maintaining complete nest web communities. Excavating woodpeckers will not use nest boxes, and only a minority of non-excavating species use them in Europe; the main beneficiaries are already common species such as blue tit, great tit and pied flycatcher. However, well-designed species-oriented programmes of nest-box provisioning can sometimes be successful in population augmentation (Evans *et al.* 2002). On both continents, such programmes have resulted in the restoration of several species, including waterfowl, owls, birds of prey and passerines (Newton 1998). In some instances, providing nest boxes can be useful in augmenting local populations as a short-term emergency measure to rescue declining species that lack nest holes in proximity to foraging areas (Wiebe 2011; Wesołowski 2012; Martin *et al.* 2015).

Providing nest boxes is neither a long-term solution nor a feasible substitute for preserving hole-bearing trees and natural hole-'making' processes on either continent. The cost of establishing and maintaining nest box programmes in managed forests is prohibitive on a regional or landscape scale, even for commercially important hunted species such as hole-nesting ducks. Another problem with relying on nest boxes in predator-rich systems is that the nest box plots often become deadly traps for the birds that breed in them (Graczyk 1973; Czeszczewik *et al.* 1999). Several meso-predators and American black bears rapidly cue in to occupied nest boxes, and they can prey on an entire set of nest boxes in an area within a few days (Evans *et al.* 2002). Predator guards can be used, but most nest boxes are not sufficiently secure to deter the effects of these predators.

In summary, it is crucially important to preserve old trees with decay within all protected forest areas. In managed forests, the key message is: retain a sufficient number of suitable trees with holes in all forest management operations, and maintain a range of tree species and conditions that can provide a continuous supply of holes at the forest landscape scale. In broadleaved forests, there should be a focus on maintaining older forest stands where natural holes can be formed, but also a sufficient supply of trees that are suitable for excavation. This is especially important in Europe, where the ranges of several wood-pecker species are restricted due to a lack of suitable trees for excavation and foraging (Mikusiński & Angelstam 1997). In the conifer-dominated areas, it is possible to focus first on the habitat requirements of excav-ators (woodpeckers and passerines), as these species provide the major-ity of holes that are used by the entire assemblage of hole-dependent vertebrates (Martin *et al.* 2004). However, it is also important to maintain old trees that will generate decay-formed holes, particularly for the larger hole-dependent wildlife species. Despite the differences in processes and patterns that we describe here between North America and Europe, it is important to stress that tree decay is at the basis of all types of hole formation and is a keystone structuring process for hole-dependent bird assemblages globally (Cockle *et al.* 2011). Maintaining tree-decay dynamics in our forest systems is critical to maintaining diverse hole-nesting communities.

Acknowledgements

We are grateful to Pierre Drapeau and Asko Lõhmus for many helpful comments and suggestions that have greatly improved the chapter. We also thank Karen Wiebe for discussions on nest site limitation.

References

Adamík, P. & Král, M. (2008) Nest losses of cavity nesting birds caused by dormice (Gliridae, Rodentia). *Acta Theriologica*, **53**, 185–192.

Aitken, K.E.H. & Martin, K. (2004) Nest cavity availability and selection in aspen-conifer groves in a grassland landscape. *Canadian Journal of Forest Research*, **34**, 2099–2109.

Aitken, K.E.H. & Martin, K. (2007) The importance of excavators in hole-nesting communities: Availability and use of natural tree holes in old mixed forests of western Canada. *Journal of Ornithology*, **148** (Suppl. 2), 425–434.

Aitken, K.E.H. & Martin, K. (2008) Resource selection plasticity and community responses to experimental reduction of a critical resource. *Ecology*, **89**, 971–980.

Aitken, K.E.H. & Martin, K. (2012) Experimental test of nest-site limitation in mature mixed forests of central British Columbia. *Journal of Wildlife Management*, **76**, 557–565.

Aitken, K.E.H., Wiebe, K.L. & Martin, K. (2002) Nest-site reuse patterns for a cavity-nesting bird community in interior British Columbia. *Auk*, **119**, 391–402.

Alatalo, R., Carlson, A. & Lundberg, A. (1990) Polygyny and breeding success of Pied Flycatchers nesting in natural cavities. In *Population Biology of Passerine Birds*. Blondel, J., Gosler, A., Lebreton, J.D. & McCleery, R. (eds.). Berlin: Springer Verlag, pp. 323–330.

Albano, D.J. (1992) Nesting mortality of Carolina Chickadees breeding in natural cavities. *Condor*, **94**, 371–382.

Andersson, J., Domingo Gómez, E., Michon, S. & Roberge, J.-M. (2017) Tree cavity densities and characteristics in managed and unmanaged Swedish boreal forest. *Scandinavian Journal of Forest Research*. DOI: 10.1080/02827581.2017.1360389.

Askins, R.A. (2014) *Saving the World's Deciduous Forests*. New Haven: Yale University Press.

Bavrlic, K. (2008) *The effects of partial harvesting on cavity-nesting birds in the Carolinian forests of southwestern Ontario: Habitat responses and species interactions*. MSc Thesis, Trent University, Ontario. 222 pp.

Belles-Isles, J.C. & Picman, J. (1986) House Wren nest-destroying behaviour. *Condor*, **88**, 190–193.

Blanc, L. & Martin, K. (2012) Identifying suitable woodpecker nest trees using decay selection profiles in trembling aspen (*Populus tremuloides*). *Forest Ecology and Management*, **286**, 192–202.

Blanc, L.A. & Walters, J.R. (2008a) Cavity-nest webs in a longleaf pine ecosystem. *Condor*, **110**, 80–92.

Blanc, L.A. & Walters, J.R. (2008b) Cavity excavation and enlargement as mechanisms for indirect interactions in an avian community. *Ecology*, **89**, 506–514.

Bonar, R.L. (2000) Availability of pileated woodpecker cavities and use by other species. *Journal of Wildlife Management*, **64**, 52–59.

Broughton, R.K., Hebda, G., Maziarz, M., Smith, K.W., Smith, L. & Hinsley, S.A. (2015) Nest-site competition between bumblebees (Bombidae), social wasps (Vespidae) and cavity-nesting birds in Britain and the Western Palearctic. *Bird Study*, **62**, 427–437.

Bull, E.L. & Jackson, J.A. (2011) Pileated Woodpecker (*Dryocopus pileatus*). In *The Birds of North America* online. Poole, A. (ed.). Ithaca: Cornell Lab of Ornithology; Retrieved from Birds of North America online: http://bna .birds.cornell.edu/bna/species/148 doi:10.2173/bna.148.

Bunnell, F.L. (2013) Sustaining cavity-using species: Patterns of cavity use and implications to forest management. *ISRN Forestry*, 2013, 1–33.

Cadieux, P. (2011) *Dynamics of cavity nesters along a forest age gradient in Boreal mixed wood or eastern North America*. MSc Thesis, Université du Québec à Montréal, Québec.

Camprodon, J., Salvanyá, J. & Soler-Zurita, J. (2008) The abundance and suitability of tree cavities and their impact on hole-nesting bird populations in beech forests of NE Iberian Peninsula. *Acta Ornithologica*, **43**, 17–31.

Carlson, A., Sandström, U. & Olsson, K. (1998) Availability and use of natural tree holes by cavity nesting birds in a Swedish deciduous forest. *Ardea*, **86**, 109–119.

Christman, B.J. & Dhondt, A.A. (1997) Nest predation in Black-capped Chickadees: How safe are cavity nests? *Auk*, **114**, 769–773.

Cockle, K.L. & Martin, K. (2015) Temporal dynamics of a commensal network of cavity-nesting vertebrates: Increased diversity during an insect outbreak. *Ecology*, **96**, 1093–1104.

Cockle, K.L., Martin, K. & Drever, M.C. (2010) Supply of tree-holes limits nest density of cavity-nesting birds in primary and logged subtropical Atlantic forest. *Biological Conservation*, **143**, 2851–2857.

Cockle, K.L., Martin, K. & Wesołowski, T. (2011) Woodpeckers, decay, and the future of cavity-nesting vertebrate communities worldwide. *Frontiers in Ecology and the Environment*, **9**, 377–382.

Conner, R.N., Rudolph, D.C., Saenz, D. & Schaefer, R.R. (1994) Heartwood, sapwood, and fungal decay associated with Red-cockaded Woodpecker cavity trees. *Journal of Wildlife Management*, **58**, 728–734.

Cooke, H.A. & Hannon, S.J. (2011) Do aggregated harvests with structural retention conserve the cavity web of old upland forest in the boreal plains? *Forest Ecology and Management*, **261**, 662–674.

Cooke, H.A. & Hannon, S.J. (2012) Nest site selection by old boreal forest cavity excavators as a basis for structural retention guidelines in spatially-aggregated harvests. *Forest Ecology and Management*, **269**, 37–51.

Czeszczewik, D. & Walankiewicz, W. (2003) Natural nest sites of the Pied Flycatcher *Ficedula hypoleuca* in a primeval forest. *Ardea*, **91**, 221–230.

Czeszczewik, D., Walankiewicz, W., Mitrus, C. & Nowakowski, W. (1999) Nest-box data of Pied Flycatcher *Ficedula hypoleuca* may lead to erroneous generalizations. *Vogelwelt*, **120**, 361–365.

Czeszczewik, D., Walankiewicz, W., Mitrus, C. *et al.* (2013) Importance of dead wood resources for woodpeckers in coniferous stands of the Białowieża Forest. *Bird Conservation International*, **23**, 414–425.

Czeszczewik, D., Walankiewicz, W. & Stańska, M. (2008) Small mammals in nests of cavity-nesting birds: Why should ornithologists study rodents? *Canadian Journal of Zoology*, **86**, 286–293.

Dhondt, A.A. (2007) What drives differences between North American and Eurasian tit studies? In *The Ecology and Behavior of Chickadees and Titmice*. Otter, K. (ed.). Oxford: Oxford University Press, pp. 299–310.

Drapeau, P., Nappi, A., Imbeau, L. & Saint-Germain, M. (2009) Standing dead-wood for keystone bird species in the eastern boreal forest: Managing for snag dynamics. *Forestry Chronicle*, **85**, 227–234.

Drever, M.C., Aitken, K.E.H., Norris, A.R. & Martin, K. (2008) Woodpeckers as reliable indicators of bird richness, forest health and harvest. *Biological Conservation*, **141**, 624–634.

Drever, M.C. & Martin, K. (2010) Response of woodpeckers to changes in forest health and harvest: Implications for conservation of avian biodiversity. *Forest Ecology and Management*, **259**, 958–966.

East, M.L. & Perrins, C.M. (1988) The effect of nestboxes on breeding populations of birds in broadleaved temperate woodlands. *Ibis*, **130**, 393–401.

Edworthy, A., Drever, M.C. & Martin, K. (2011) Woodpeckers increase in abundance but maintain fecundity in response to an outbreak of mountain pine bark beetles. *Forest Ecology and Management*, **261**, 203–210.

Edworthy, A.B. & Martin, K. (2013) Persistence of tree cavities used by cavity-nesting vertebrates declines in harvested forests. *Journal of Wildlife Management*, **77**, 770–776.

Edworthy, A.B. & Martin, K. (2014) Long-term dynamics of the characteristics of tree cavities used for nesting by vertebrates. *Forest Ecology and Management*, **334**, 122–128.

Edworthy, A.B., Wiebe, K.L. & Martin, K. (2012) Survival analysis of a critical resource for cavity-nesting communities: Patterns of tree cavity longevity. *Ecological Applications*, **22**, 1733–1742.

Evans, M.R., Lank, D.B., Boyd, W.S. & Cooke, F. (2002) A comparison of the characteristics and fate of Barrow's Goldeneye and Bufflehead nests in nest boxes and natural cavities. *Condor*, **104**, 610–619.

Fauvel, B., Carré, F. & Lallement, H. (2001) Middle Spotted Woodpecker *Dendrocopos medius* ecology in the Champagne Region (East France). *Alauda*, **69**, 87–101 [in French, English summary].

Fisher, R.J. & Wiebe, K.L. (2006) Nest site attributes and temporal patterns of northern flicker nest loss: Effects of predation and competition. *Oecologia*, **147**, 744–753.

Frei, B., Nocera, J.J. & Fyles, J.W. (2015) Interspecific competition and nest survival of the threatened Red-headed Woodpecker. *Journal of Ornithology*, **156**, 743–753.

Gibbons, P. & Lindenmayer, D. (2002) *Tree Hollows and Wildlife Conservation in Australia.* Collingwood: CSIRO Publishing.

Glutz von Blotzheim, U.N. & Bauer, K.M. (eds.) (1980) *Handbuch der Vögel Mitteleuropas*, Vol. 9. Wiesbaden: AULA-Verlag.

Glutz von Blotzheim, U.N. & Bauer, K.M. (1993) *Handbuch der Vögel Mitteleuropas*, Vol. 13. Wiesbaden: AULA-Verlag.

Gow, E.A., Wiebe, K.L. & Fox, J.W. (2015) Cavity use throughout the annual cycle of a migratory woodpecker as revealed by geolocators. *Ibis*, **157**, 167–170.

Graczyk, R. (1973) Höhlenbrütende Vögel und biologische Bekämpfung von Insekten. *Angewandte Ornithologie*, **4**, 71–94.

Gustafsson, L., Baker, S.C., Bauhus, J. *et al.* (2012) Retention forestry to maintain multifunctional forests: A world perspective. *BioScience*, **62**, 633–645.

Günther, E. (1993) Selection of location of holes of Great Spotted Woodpecker and Middle Spotted Woodpecker (*Dendrocopos major* and *D. medius*) in the northeastern Harz Mountains (Sachsen-Anhalt). *Ornithologische Mitteilungen des Museum Heineanum*, **11**, 67–73. [in German, English summary]

Günther, E. & Hellmann, M. (1995) Development of holes of spotted woodpeckers (*Picoides*) in nature-near deciduous forest in the northeastern Harz Mountains (Sachen-Anhalt) – Results of more than ten years of investigations of the use of natural tree holes. *Ornithologische Mitteilungen des Museum Heineanum*, **13**, 27–52. [in German, English summary]

Günther, E. & Hellmann, M. (1997) Die Höhlen des Buntspechts – haben wir ihre Bedeutung für die Nachnutzer überschätzt? *Naturschutz im Land Sachsen-Anhalt*, **34**, 15–24. [in German, English summary]

Günther, E. & Hellmann, M. (2001) Woodpeckers are seen as 'key species' – A key for whom? *Abhandlungen und Berichte am dem Museum Heineanum*, **5**, 7–22. [in German, English summary]

Günther, E. & Hellmann, M. (2002) Strong decrease of population of tree-breeding Swift *Apus apus* in the northeastern Harz Mountains (Sachsen-Anhalt) – Was it the Racoon *Procyon lotor*? *Ornithologische Mitteilungen des Museum Heineanum*, **20**, 81–98. [in German, English summary]

Günther, E., Hellmann, M. & Nicolai, B. (2004) Tree-breeding Common Swifts *Apus apus* – Relicts of ancient forest features? *Vogelwelt*, **125**, 309–318. [in German, English summary]

Haftorn, S. & Slagsvold, T. (1995) Egg covering in birds: Description of the behaviour in tits (*Parus* spp.) and a test of hypotheses of its function. *Cinclus*, **18**, 85-106.

Hagemeijer, E.J.M. & Blair, M.J. (1997) *The EBCC Atlas of European Breeding Birds*. London: Poyser.

Hansell, M. (2002) *Animal Architecture*. Oxford: Oxford University Press.

Hansen, F. (1989) Nest hole excavation and reuse of nest holes by the Black Woodpecker on Bornholm, Denmark. *Dansk Ornitologisk Forenings Tidsskrift*, **83**, 125–129. [in Danish, English summary]

Harding, S.R. & Walters, J.R. (2002) Processes regulating the population dynamics of red-cockaded woodpecker cavities. *Journal of Wildlife Management*, **66**, 1083–1095.

Hebda, G., Wesołowski, T. & Rowiński, P. (2016) Nest sites of Middle Spotted Woodpeckers *Leiopicus medius* in a primeval forest. *Ardea*, **104**, 119–128.

Holt, R.F. & Martin, K. (1997) Landscape modification and patch selection: The demography of two secondary cavity nesters colonizing clearcuts. *Auk*, **114**, 443–455.

Höntsch, K. (2001) Nesting and roosting holes of Lesser Spotted Woodpecker *Picoides minor*. *Abhandlungen und Berichte am dem Museum Heineanum*, **5**, 107–120. [in German]

Hooge, P.N., Stanback, M.T. & Koenig, W.D. (1999) Nest-site selection in the Acorn Woodpecker. *Auk*, **116**, 45–54.

Howe, S., Kilgore, D.L. & Colby, C. (1987) Respiratory gas concentrations and temperatures within nest cavities of the northern flicker (*Colaptes auratus*). *Canadian Journal of Zoology*, **65**, 1541–1547.

Ibarra, J.T., Martin, M., Cockle, K.L. & Martin, K. (2017) Maintaining ecosystem resilience: functional responses of tree cavity nesters to logging in temperate forests of the Americas. *Scientific Reports*, **7**, 4467.

Ingold, D.J. (1989) Nesting phenology and competition for nest sites among red-headed and red-bellied woodpeckers and European starlings. *Auk*, **106**, 209–217.

Jackson, J.A. & Jackson, B.J.S. (2004) Ecological relationships between fungi and woodpecker cavity sites. *Condor*, **106**, 37–49.

Jędrzejewska, B. & Jędrzejewski, W. (1998). *Predation in Vertebrate Communities. The Białowieża Primeval Forest as a Case Study*. Berlin: Springer Verlag.

Johansen, B.T. (1989) Nest trees and nest holes of Black Woodpeckers in North Zealand, 1977–1986 *Dansk Ornitologisk Forenings Tidsskrift*, **83**, 119–124. [in Danish, English summary]

Johnson, L.S. (2014) House Wren (*Troglodytes aedon*). In *The Birds of North America* online. Poole, A. (ed.). Ithaca: Cornell Lab of Ornithology; Retrieved from Birds of North America online: http://bna.birds.cornell.edu/bna/species/380 doi:10.2173/bna.380.

Johnsson, K., Nilsson S.G. & Tjernberg, M. (1990) The black woodpecker – A key-species in European forests. In *Conservation and Management of Woodpecker Populations*. Carlson, A. & Aulén, G. (eds.). Uppsala: Swedish University of Agricultural Sciences, pp. 99–103.

Jusino, M.A., Lindner, D.L., Banik, M.T., Rose, K.R. & Walters, J.R. (2016) Experimental evidence of a symbiosis between red-cockaded woodpeckers and fungi. *Proceedings of the Royal Society B*, **283**, 20160106.

Jusino, M.A., Lindner, D.L., Banik, M.T. & Walters, J.R. (2015) Heart rot hotel: Fungal communities in red-cockaded woodpecker excavations. *Fungal Ecology*, **14**, 33–44.

Juškaitis, R. (2006) Interactions between dormice (Gliridae) and hole-nesting birds in nestboxes. *Folia Zoologica*, **55**, 225–236.

Kahler, H.A. & Anderson, J.T. (2006) Tree cavity resources for dependent cavity-using wildlife in West Virginia forests. *Northern Journal of Applied Forestry*, **23**, 114–121.

Kappes, J.J. & Sieving, K.E. (2011) Resin-barrier maintenance as a mechanism of differential predation among occupants of red-cockaded woodpecker cavities. *Condor*, **113**, 362–371.

Keast, A. (1990) Distribution and origin of forest birds. In *Biogeography and Ecology of Forest Bird Communities*. Keast, A. (ed.). The Hague: SPB Academic Publishing, pp. 49–59.

Kennedy, E.D. & White, D.W. (1997) Bewick's Wren (*Thryomanes bewickii*). In *The Birds of North America*, no. 315. Poole, A. & Gill, F. (eds.). Philadelphia & Washington, DC: Academy of Natural Sciences of Philadelphia and American Ornithologists' Union.

Kiełbaska, M. (ed.) (1991) *Mała encyklopedia leśna*. Warszawa: PWN. [in Polish]

Kilham, L. (1971) Reproductive behavior of Yellow-bellied Sapsuckers. I. Preference for nesting in fomes-infected aspens and nest hole interrelations with flying squirrels, raccoons, and other animals. *Wilson Bulletin*, **83**, 159–171.

Koch, A., Martin, K. & Aitken, K.E.H. (2012) The relationship between introduced European Starlings and the reproductive activity of Mountain Bluebirds and Tree Swallows in British Columbia. *Ibis*, **154**, 590–600.

Koenig, W.D. (2003) European starlings and their effect on native cavity-nesting birds. *Conservation Biology*, **17**, 1134–1140.

Kosiński, Z. & Winiecki, A. (2004) Nest-site selection and niche partitioning among the Great Spotted Woodpecker *Dendrocopos major* and Middle Spotted Woodpecker *Dendrocopos medius* in riverine forest of Central Europe. *Ornis Fennica*, **81**, 145–156.

Kuitunen, M. & Aleknonis, A. (1992) Nest predation and breeding success in Common Treecreepers nesting in boxes and natural cavities. *Ornis Fennica*, **69**, 7–12.

Latham, R.E. & Ricklefs, R.E. (1993) Continental comparisons of temperate-zone tree species diversity. In *Species Diversity in Ecological Communities*. Ricklefs, R.E. & Schluter, D. (eds.). Chicago: University of Chicago Press, pp. 294–314.

Leisne, C. (1991) *Untersuchungen zur Frage der nutzunstechnischenfolgen nach Fäll- und Rückeschäden bei Fichte*. Freiburg: Mitteilungen der Forstlichen Versuchs und Forschungsanstalt Baden-Württemberg.

Li, P. & Martin, T.E. (1991) Nest-site selection and nesting success of cavity-nesting birds in high elevation forest drainages. *Auk*, **108**, 405–418.

Lindenmayer, D.B., Burton, P.J. & Franklin, J.F. (2008) *Salvage Logging and Its Ecological Consequences*. Washington, DC: Island Press.

Lindenmayer, D.B., Franklin, J.F., Lõhmus, A. *et al.* (2012) A major shift to the retention approach for forestry can help resolve some global forest sustainability issues. *Conservation Letters*, **5**, 421–431.

Lõhmus, A. (2003) Do Ural owls (*Strix uralensis*) suffer from the lack of nests in managed forests? *Biological Conservation*, **110**, 1–9.

Lõhmus, A & Remm, J. (2005) Nest quality limits the number of hole-nesting passerines in their natural cavity-rich habitat. *Acta Oecologica*, **27**, 125–128.

Ludescher, F.B. (1973) Sumpfmeise (*Parus p. palustris* L.) und Weidenmeise (*P. montanus salicarius* Br.) als sympatrische Zwillingsarten. *Journal of Ornithology*, **114**, 3–56.

Mahon, C.L. & Martin, K. (2006) Nest survival of chickadees in managed forests: Habitat, predator, and year effects. *Journal of Wildlife Management*, **70**, 1257–1265.

Martin, K., Aitken, K.E.H. & Wiebe, K.L. (2004) Nest sites and nest webs for cavity-nesting communities in interior British Columbia, Canada: Nest characteristics and niche partitioning. *Condor*, **106**, 5–19.

Martin, K. & Eadie, J. M. (1999) Nest webs: A community-wide approach to the management and conservation of cavity-nesting forest birds. *Forest Ecology and Management*, **115**, 243–257.

Martin, K., Ibarra, J.T. & Drever, M. (2015) Avian surrogates in terrestrial ecosystems: Theory and practice. In *Indicators and Surrogates in Ecology, Biodiversity and Environmental Management*. Lindenmayer, D., Barton, P. & Pierson, J. (eds.). London: CSIRO Publishing, CRC Press, pp. 33–44.

Martin, T.E. (1993) Evolutionary determinants of clutch size in cavity-nesting birds: Nest predation or limited breeding opportunities? *American Naturalist*, **142**, 937–946.

Martin, T.E. (2015) Consequences of habitat change and resource selection specialization for population limitation in cavity-nesting birds. *Journal of Applied Ecology*, **52**, 475–485.

Martin, T.E. & Li, P. (1992) Life history traits of open- vs. cavity-nesting birds. *Ecology*, **73**, 579–592.

Matthysen, E. (1998) *The Nuthatches*. London: Poyser.

Mazgajski, T.D. (1997) Changes in the numbers and nest sites of the Great Spotted Woodpecker *Dendrocopos major* and the Middle Spotted Woodpecker *D. medius* in the Las Bielański Reserve in Warsaw. *Ochrona Przyrody*, **54**, 155–160. [in Polish, English summary]

Maziarz, M., Broughton, R.K. & Wesołowski, T. (2017) Microclimate in tree cavities and nest-boxes: Implications for hole-nesting birds. *Forest Ecology and Management*, **389**, 306–313.

Maziarz, M. & Wesołowski, T. (2013) Microclimate of tree cavities used by Great Tits (*Parus major*) in a primeval forest. *Avian Biology Research*, **6**, 47–56.

Maziarz, M. & Wesołowski, T. (2014) Darkness can limit the use of tree cavities for nesting by birds. *Journal of Ornithology*, **155**, 793–799.

Maziarz, M., Wesołowski, T., Hebda, G. & Cholewa, M. (2015a) Natural nest-sites of Great Tits (*Parus major*) in a primeval temperate forest (Białowieża National Park, Poland). *Journal of Ornithology*, **156**, 613–623.

Maziarz, M., Wesołowski, T., Hebda, G., Cholewa, M. & Broughton, R.K. (2015b) Breeding success of Great Tits *Parus major* in relation to attributes of natural nest-cavities in a primeval forest. *Journal of Ornithology*, **157**, 343–354.

Mcdevitt, A.D., Kajtoch, Ł., Mazgajski, T.D., Carden, R.F. & Coscia, I. (2011) The origins of Great Spotted Woodpeckers *Dendrocopos major* colonizing Ireland revealed by mitochondrial DNA. *Bird Study*, **58**, 361–364.

Meidinger, D. & Pojar, J. (eds.) (1991) *Ecosystems of British Columbia*. Victoria: British Columbia Ministry of Forests Special Report Series No. 6.

Meyer, W. & Meyer, B. (2001) Construction and use of Black Woodpecker *Dryocopus martius* holes in Thuringia/Germany. *Abhandlungen und Berichte am dem Museum Heineanum*, **5**, 121–131. [in German, English summary]

Michon, S. (2014) *Comparison of tree cavity abundance and characteristics in managed and unmanaged Swedish boreal forest*. MSc Thesis. Swedish University of Agricultural Sciences, Umeå.

Mikusiński, G. & Angelstam, P. (1997) European woodpeckers and anthropogenic habitat change: A review. *Vogelwelt*, **118**, 277–283.

Morozov, N.S. (2009) A city as an object for synecological studies: A search for density compensation among birds breeding in urban woodlands. In *Species and Communities in Extreme Environments*. Golovatch, S.I., Makarova, O.L., Babenko, A.B. & Penev, L.D. (eds.). Sofia: Pensoft Publishers & KMK Scientific Press, pp. 459–520.

Nappi, A. & Drapeau, P. (2009) Reproductive success of the black-backed woodpecker (*Picoides arcticus*) in burned boreal forests: Are burns source habitats? *Biological Conservation*, **142**, 1381–1391.

Nappi, A. & Drapeau, P. (2011) Pre-fire forest conditions and fire severity as determinants of the quality of burned forests for deadwood-dependent species: The case of the black-backed woodpecker *Canadian Journal of Forest Research*, **41**, 994–1003.

Nappi, A., Drapeau, P., Angers, V.A. & Saint-Germain, M. (2010) Effect of fire severity on long-term occupancy of saproxylic beetles and bark-foraging birds in burned boreal conifer forests. *International Journal of Wildland Fire*, **19**, 500–511.

Nappi, A., Drapeau, P. & Leduc, A. (2015) How important is dead wood for woodpeckers foraging in eastern North American boreal forests? *Forest Ecology and Management*, **346**, 10–21.

Newton, I. (1994) The role of nest sites in limiting the numbers of hole-nesting birds: A review. *Biological Conservation*, **70**, 265–276.

Newton, I. (1998) *Population Limitation in Birds*. San Diego: Academic Press.

Nielsen, C.L.R., Gates, R.J. & Zwicker, E.H. (2007) Projected availability of natural cavities for wood ducks in Southern Illinois. *Journal of Wildlife Management*, **71**, 875–883.

Nilsson, S.G. (1984) The evolution of nest-site selection among hole-nesting birds: The importance of nest predation and competition. *Ornis Scandinavica*, **15**, 167–175.

Nilsson, S.G., Johnsson, K. & Tjernberg, M. (1991) Is avoidance by Black Woodpeckers of old nest holes due to predators? *Animal Behaviour*, **41**, 439–441.

Norris, A. (2012) *Mechanisms regulating ecological responses to resource pulses within cavity-nesting bird communities.* PhD thesis. University of British Columbia, Vancouver.

Oliver, C.D., Harrington, C. & Bickford, M. (1994) Maintaining and creating old grown structural features in previously disturbed stands typical of eastern Washington Cascades. *Journal of Sustainable Forestry*, **2**, 353–387.

Ouellet-Lapointe, U., Drapeau, P., Cadieux, P. & Imbeau, L. (2012) Woodpecker excavations suitability for and occupancy by cavity users in the boreal mixed-wood forest of eastern Canada. *Écoscience*, **19**, 391–397.

Paclík, M., Misík, J. & Weidinger, K. (2009) Nest predation and nest defence in European and North American woodpeckers: A review. *Annales Zoologici Fennici*, **46**, 361–379.

Pasinelli, G. (2007) Nest site selection in middle and great spotted woodpeckers *Dendrocopos medius* & *D. major*: Implications for forest management and conservation. *Biodiversity and Conservation*, **16**, 1283–1298.

Poulin, J-F., D'Astous, E., Villard, M-A. *et al.* (2013) Brown Creeper (*Certhia americana*). *The Birds of North America* online. Poole, A. (ed.). Ithaca: Cornell Lab of Ornithology. Retrieved from Birds of North America online: http://bna.birds.cornell.edu/bna/species/669 doi:10.2173/bna.669.

Raphael, M.G. & White, M. (1984) Use of snags by cavity-nesting birds in the Sierra Nevada. *Wildlife Monographs*, **86**, 1–66.

Remm, J. & Lõhmus, A. (2011) Tree cavities in forest – The broad distribution pattern of a keystone structure for biodiversity. *Forest Ecology and Management*, **262**, 579–585.

Remm, J., Lõhmus A. & Remm, K. (2006) Tree cavities in riverine forests: What determines their occurrence and use by hole-nesting passerines? *Forest Ecology and Management*, **221**, 267–277.

Rendell, W.B. & Robertson, R.J. (1989) Nest-site characteristics, reproductive success and cavity availability for tree swallows breeding in natural cavities. *Condor*, **91**, 875–885.

Roberge, J.-M., Angelstam, P. & Villard, M.-A. (2008) Specialised woodpeckers and naturalness in hemiboreal forests – Deriving quantitative targets for conservation planning. *Biological Conservation*, **141**, 997–1012.

Robles, H. & Martin, K. (2013) Resource quantity and quality determine the interspecific associations between ecosystem engineers and resource users in a cavity-nest web. *PLoS ONE*, 8(9): e74694.

Robles, H., Ciudad, C. & Matthysen, E. (2011) Tree-cavity occurrence, cavity occupation and reproductive performance of secondary cavity-nesting birds in oak forests: The role of traditional management practices. *Forest Ecology and Management*, **261**, 1428–1435.

Rolstad, J., Rolstad, E. & Sæteren, Y. (2000) Black woodpecker nest sites: Characteristics, selection, and reproductive success. *Journal of Wildlife Management*, **64**, 1053–1066.

Ruczyński, I. & Bogdanowicz, W. (2005) Roost cavity selection by *Nyctalus noctula* and *N. leisleri* (Vespertilionidae, Chiroptera) in Białowieża Primeval Forest, Eastern Poland. *Journal of Mammalogy*, **86**, 921–930.

Rudat, V., Kühlke, D., Meyer, W. & Wiesner, J. (1979) On the nest-site ecology of Black Woodpecker (*Dryocopus martius* [L.]), Tengmalm's Owl (*Aegolius funereus* [L.]) and Stock-Dove (*Columba oenas* [L.]) *Zoologische Jahrbücher Systematik*, **106**, 295–310. [in German, English summary]

Rudolph, D.C., Kyle, H. & Conner, R.N. (1990) Red-cockaded Woodpeckers vs rat snakes: The effectiveness of the resin barrier. *Wilson Bulletin*, **102**, 14–22.

Saab, V.A., Dudley, J. & Thompson, W.L. (2004) Factors influencing occupancy of nest cavities in recently burned forests. *Condor*, **106**, 20–36.

Saari, L. & Mikusiński, G. (1996) Population fluctuations of woodpecker species on the Baltic Island of Aasla, SW Finland. *Ornis Fennica*, **73**, 168–178.

Sandström, U. (1992) Cavities in trees: Their occurrence, formation and importance for hole-nesting birds in relation to silvicultural practice. Report 23. Swedish University of Agricultural Sciences, Uppsala.

Schmidt, O. (2006) *Wood and Tree Fungi*. Berlin: Springer.

Schwarze, F.W., Engels, M.R., Engels, J. & Mattheck, C. (2000) *Fungal Strategies of Wood Decay in Trees*. Berlin: Springer.

Scott, V.E., Evans, K.E., Patton, D.R. & Stone, C.P. (1977) *Cavity-nesting Birds of North American Forests*. US Department of Agriculture Handbook No. 511.

Sedgwick, J.A. & Knopf, F.L. (1990) Habitat relationships and nest site characteristics of cavity-nesting birds in cottonwood floodplains. *Journal of Wildlife Management*, **54**, 112–124.

Sedgwick, J.A. & Knopf, F.L. (1991) The loss of avian cavities by injury compartmentalization. *Condor*, **93**, 781–783.

Sedgwick, J.A. & Knopf, F.L. (1992) Cavity turnover and equilibrium cavity densities in a cottonwood bottomland. *Journal of Wildlife Management*, **56**, 477–484.

Smith, K.W. (1997) Nest site selection of the Great Spotted Woodpecker *Dendrocopos major* in two oak woods in Southern England and its implications for woodland management. *Biological Conservation*, **80**, 283–288.

Smith, K.W. (2007) The utilization of dead wood resources by woodpeckers in Britain. *Ibis*, **149** (Suppl. 2), 183–192.

Sorace, A., Consiglio, C., Tanda, F., Lanzuisi, E., Cattaneo, A. & Iavicoli, D. (2000) Predation by snakes on eggs and nestlings of Great Tit *Parus major* and Blue Tit *P. caeruleus*. *Ibis*, **142**, 328–330.

Stauffer, D.F. & Best, L.B. (1982) Nest-site selection by cavity-nesting birds of riparian habitats in Iowa. *Wilson Bulletin*, **94**, 329–337.

Straus, M.A., Bavrlic, K., Nol, E., Burke, D.M. & Elliott, K.A. (2011) Reproductive success of cavity-nesting birds in partially harvested woodlots. *Canadian Journal of Forest Research*, **41**, 1004–1017.

Tiainen, J., Saurola, P. & Solonen, T. (1984) Nest distribution of the Pied Flycatcher *Ficedula hypoleuca* in an area saturated with nestboxes. *Annales Zoologici Fennici*, **21**, 199–204.

Tomiałojć, L. (1995) The birds of the Białowieża Forest – Additional data and summary. *Acta Zoologica Cracoviensia*, **38**, 363–397.

Tomiałojć, L., Wesołowski, T. & Walankiewicz, W. (1984) Breeding bird community of a primaeval temperate forest (Białowieża National Park, Poland). *Acta Ornithologica*, **20**, 241–310.

Tozer, D.C., Burke, D.M. & Nol, E. (2011) Quality of mature aspen and maple forests for breeding yellow-bellied sapsuckers (*Sphyrapicus varius*). *Canadian Journal of Zoology*, **89**, 148–160.

Tozer, D.C., Burke, D.M., Nol, E. & Elliott, K.A. (2012) Managing ecological traps: Logging and sapsucker nest predation by bears. *Journal of Wildlife Management*, **76**, 887–898.

Tozer, D.C., Nol, E., Burke, D.M., Elliott, K.A. & Falk, K.J. (2009) Predation by bears on woodpecker nests: Are nestling begging and habitat choice risky business? *Auk*, **126**, 300–309.

Tremblay, J.A., Ibarzabal, J., Savard, J.-P.L. & Wilson, S. (2014) Influence of old coniferous habitat on nestling growth of Black-backed Woodpeckers *Picoides arcticus*. *Acta Ornithologica*, **49**, 273–279.

Tremblay, J.A., Savard, J.-P. & Ibarzabal, J. (2015) Structural retention requirements for a key ecosystem engineer in conifer-dominated stands of a boreal managed landscape in eastern Canada. *Forest Ecology and Management*, **357**, 220–227.

Vaillancourt, M., Drapeau, P., Robert, M. & Gauthier, T. (2009) Origin and availability of large cavities for Barrow's Goldeneye (*Bucephala islandica*), a species at risk inhabiting the eastern Canadian boreal forest. *Avian Conservation and Ecology*, **4**(1), 6. www.ace-eco.org/vol4/iss1/art6/.

van Balen, J.H., Booy, C.J.H., van Franeker, J.A. & Osieck, E.R. (1982) Studies on hole-nesting birds in natural nest sites. 1. Availability and occupation of natural nest sites. *Ardea*, **70**, 1–24.

van der Hoek, Y., Gaona, G.V. & Martin, K. (2017) The diversity, distribution and conservation status of the tree-cavity nesting birds of the world. *Diversity and Distributions*, **23**, 1120–1131.

Von Haartman, L. (1957) Adaptation in hole-nesting birds. *Evolution*, **11**, 339–347.

Walankiewicz, W. (1991) Do secondary cavity-nesting birds suffer more from competition for cavities or from predation in a primeval deciduous forest? *Natural Areas Journal*, **11**, 203–212.

Walankiewicz, W. (2002a) Nest predation as a limiting factor to the breeding population size of the Collared Flycatcher *Ficedula albicollis* in the Białowieża National Park (NE Poland). *Acta Ornithologica*, **37**, 91–106.

Walankiewicz, W. (2002b) Breeding losses in the Collared Flycatcher *Ficedula albicollis* caused by nest predators in the Białowieża National Park (Poland). *Acta Ornithologica*, **37**, 21–26.

Walankiewicz, W., Czeszczewik, D., Mitrus, C. & Bida, E. (2002) Snag importance for woodpeckers in deciduous stands of the Białowieża Forest. *Notatki Ornitologiczne*, **43**, 61–71. [in Polish, English summary]

Walankiewicz, W., Czeszczewik, D., Stański, T., Sahel, M. & Ruczyński, I. (2014) Tree cavity resources in spruce-pine managed and protected stands of the Białowieża Forest, Poland. *Natural Areas Journal*, **34**, 423–428.

Walankiewicz, W. & Mitrus, C. (1997) How nest-box data have led to erroneous generalizations: The case of the competition between Great Tit *Parus major* and *Ficedula* flycatchers. *Acta Ornithologica*, **32**, 209–212.

Wesołowski, T. (1989) Nest-sites of hole-nesters in a primaeval temperate forest (Białowieża National Park, Poland). *Acta Ornithologica*, **25**, 321–351.

Wesołowski, T. (1995a) The loss of avian cavities by injury compartmentalization in a primeval European forest. *Condor*, **97**, 256–257.

Wesołowski, T. (1995b) Ecology and behaviour of White-backed Woodpecker (*Dendrocopos leucotos*) in a primaeval temperate forest (Białowieża National Park, Poland). *Vogelwarte*, **38**, 61–75.

Wesołowski, T. (1996) Natural nest sites of Marsh Tits *Parus palustris* in a primaeval forest (Białowieża National Park, Poland). *Vogelwarte*, **38**, 235–249.

Wesołowski, T. (2001) Ground checks – An efficient and reliable method to monitor holes' fate. *Ornis Fennica*, **78**, 193–197.

Wesołowski, T. (2002) Antipredator adaptations in nesting marsh tits *Parus palustris* – The role of nest site security. *Ibis*, **144**, 593–601.

Wesołowski, T. (2003) Bird community dynamics in a primaeval forest – Is interspecific competition important? *Ornis Hungarica*, **12**, 51–62.

Wesołowski, T. (2007a) Lessons from long-term hole-nester studies in a primeval temperate forest. *Journal of Ornithology*, **148** (Suppl. 2), 395S–405S.

Wesołowski, T. (2007b) Primeval conditions – What can we learn from them? *Ibis*, **149** (Suppl. 2), 64S–77S.

Wesołowski, T. (2011a) "Lifespan" of woodpecker-made holes in a primeval temperate forest: A thirty year study. *Forest Ecology and Management*, **262**,1846–1852.

Wesołowski, T. (2011b) Reports from nestbox studies: A review of inadequacies. *Acta Ornithologica*, **46**, 13–17.

Wesołowski, T. (2012) "Lifespan" of non-excavated holes in a primeval temperate forest: A 30 year study. *Biological Conservation*, **153**, 118–126.

Wesołowski, T. (2013) Timing and stages of nest building by Marsh Tits *Poecile palustris* in a primaeval forest. *Avian Biology Research*, **6**, 31–38.

Wesołowski, T., Czeszczewik, D., Hebda, G., Maziarz, M., Mitrus, C. & Rowiński, P. (2015) 40 years of breeding bird community dynamics in a primeval temperate forest (Białowieża National Park, Poland). *Acta Ornithologica*, **50**, 95-120.

Wesołowski, T., Czeszczewik, D., Mitrus, C. & Rowiński, P. (2003) Birds of the Białowieża National Park. *Notatki Ornitologiczne*, **44**, 1–31. [in Polish, English summary]

Wesołowski, T., Czeszczewik, D., Rowiński, P. & Walankiewicz, W. (2002) Nest soaking in natural holes – A serious cause of breeding failure? *Ornis Fennica*, **79**, 132–138.

Wesołowski, T. & Maziarz, M. (2012) Dark tree cavities – A challenge for hole nesting birds? *Journal of Avian Biology*, **43**, 454–460.

Wesołowski, T., Mitrus, C., Czeszczewik, D. & Rowiński, P. (2010) Breeding bird dynamics in a primeval temperate forest over 35 years: Variation and stability in a changing world. *Acta Ornithologica*, **45**, 209–232.

Wesołowski, T. & Rowiński, P. (2004) The breeding behaviour of the Nuthatch *Sitta europaea* in relation to natural hole attributes in a primeval forest. *Bird Study*, **51**, 143–155.

Wesołowski, T. & Rowiński, P. (2012) The breeding performance of Blue Tits *Cyanistes caeruleus* in relation to the attributes of natural holes in a primeval forest. *Bird Study*, **59**, 437–448.

Wesołowski, T. & Rowiński, P. (2014) Do Blue Tits *Cyanistes caeruleus* synchronise reproduction with caterpillar peaks in a primeval forest? *Bird Study*, **61**, 235–245.

Wesołowski, T., Rowiński, P., Mitrus, C. & Czeszczewik, D. (2006) Breeding bird community of a primeval temperate forest (Białowieża National Park, Poland) at the beginning of the 21st century. *Acta Ornithologica*, **41**, 55–70.

Wesołowski, T. & Tomiałojć, L. (1986) The breeding ecology of woodpeckers in a temperate primaeval forest – Preliminary data. *Acta Ornithologica*, **22**, 1–21.

Wesołowski, T. & Tomiałojć, L. (2005) Nest sites, nest predation, and productivity of avian broods in a primeval temperate forest: Do the generalisations hold? *Journal of Avian Biology*, **36**, 361–367.

West, A., Cassey, P. & Thomas, C.M. (2015) Microbiology of nests and eggs. In *Nests, Eggs and Incubation*. Deeming, D.C. & Reynolds, S.J. (eds.). Oxford: Oxford University Press, pp. 75–81.

Wiebe, K.L. (2003) Delayed timing as a strategy to avoid nest-site competition: Testing a model using data from starlings and flickers. *Oikos*, **100**, 291–298.

Wiebe, K.L. (2011) Nest sites as limiting resources for cavity-nesting birds in mature forest ecosystems: A review of the evidence. *Journal of Field Ornithology*, **82**, 239–248.

Wiebe, K.L. (2014) Responses of cavity-nesting birds to fire: Testing a general model with data from the Northern Flicker. *Ecology*, **95**, 2537–2547.

Wiebe, K.L. (2017) Northern flickers only work when they have to: How individual traits, population size and landscape disturbances affect excavation rates of an ecosystem engineer. *Journal of Avian Biology*, **48**, 431–438.

Wiebe, K.L., Koenig, W. D. & Martin, K. (2007) Costs and benefits of nest reuse versus excavation in cavity-nesting birds. *Annales Zoologici Fennici*, **44**, 209–217.

Wiebe, K.L. & Moore, W.S. (2008) Northern Flicker (*Colaptes auratus*). In *The Birds of North America* online. Poole, A. (ed.). Ithaca: Cornell Lab of Ornithology. Retrieved from Birds of North America online: http://bna.birds.cornell.edu/bna/species/166a.

Winter, S., Begehold, H., Herrmann, M. *et al.* (2015) *Praxishandbuch – Naturschutz im Buchenwald*. Naturschutzziele und Bewirtschaftungsempfehlungen für reife Buchenwälder Nordostdeutschlands. Potsdam: Ministerium für Ländliche Entwicklung, Umwelt und Landwirtschaft Brandenburg.

Worrall, J.J. (2015) Forest & Shade Tree Pathology. www.forestpathology.org/. Accessed 6 December 2015.

Zahner, V., Sikora, L. & Pasinelli, G. (2012) Heart rot as a key factor for cavity tree selection in the black woodpecker. *Forest Ecology and Management*, **271**, 98–103.

Zawadzka, D., Drozdowski, S., Zawadzki, G. & Zawadzki, J. (2016) The availability of cavity trees along an age gradient in fresh pine forests. *Silva Fennica,* **50**, 3, id 1441.

Zwarts, L., Bijlsma, R.G., van den Kamp, J. & Wymenga, E. (2009) *Living on the Edge: Wetlands and Birds in a Changing Sahel.* Zeist: KNNV Publishing.

Part II
European Forests and Their Bird Communities

5 · *Macroecological Patterns in Forest Bird Diversity in Europe*

GRZEGORZ MIKUSIŃSKI, DANI VILLERO,
SERGI HERRANDO AND LLUÍS BROTONS

5.1 Introduction

Large-scale patterns of species distributions result mainly from geographic, historic, climatic and ecological constraints (Peterson *et al.* 2011), but they are also strongly influenced by direct and indirect effects of human activity (Di Marco & Santini 2015). In the case of forest birds, the past and current spatial distributions of different forest types are also of crucial importance in determining large-scale patterns in community structure at the continental scale. Biogeographically, European forests can be classified into four major types (ecoregions) that reflect the climate and ecological factors acting on these systems: boreal in the north, Mediterranean in the south, temperate in mid latitudes and subalpine forests on major mountain ranges of the continent (Fig. 5.1). As elsewhere in the Northern Hemisphere, we can also observe a strong signal derived from the history of species extinctions and colonisations after the latest glaciation that is apparent in the pattern of current species distributions and richness across Europe (Chapter 2).

Moreover, local factors produce a range of finer forest categories associated with microhabitat conditions and relief (e.g., riverine forests, swamp forests, coniferous, mixed and deciduous, evergreen broadleaved stands, etc.) or human activities (e.g., forest plantations). In addition, all forests are subject to different forms of natural disturbance and human management, causing different compositional and structural diversity, age distribution or degree of fragmentation or complexity of particular stands or forest blocks (Bengtsson *et al.* 2000). So even if European forests are not particularly species rich in terms of tree diversity (Latham & Ricklefs 1993), the combination of factors that have shaped them has led to other forms of diversity. In Chapters 5–10, which comprise Part II of this book,

Forest ecoregions

Alpine and subalpine zone
Temperate
Boreal
Mediterranean

Other ecoregions

Steppe and wooded steppe
Arctic

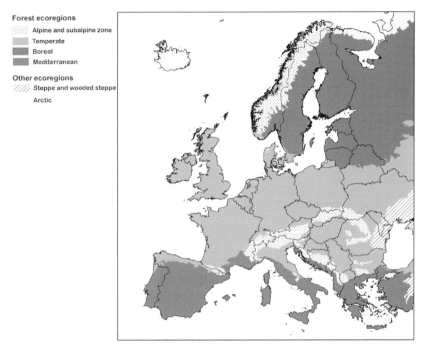

Figure 5.1 Forest ecoregions of Europe. This map is an adaptation of the delineations used in the EU Habitats Directive (biogeographical regions).

the authors describe and analyse this variation within the four main types of forests mentioned above and, in addition, take a closer look at plantations of non-native tree species.

5.2 Defining Forests and Forest Birds

Analysis of forest bird communities, at whatever spatial scale, requires unambiguous definitions of forests and forest birds. The general characterisation of forest birds was discussed in Chapter 1. For the purpose of Part II of the book, we adopted the official definition of forest provided by the Food and Agricultural Association of the United Nations (FAO) (FAO 2010), which builds on minimum patch area (0.5 ha), tree height (5 m or existing potential to reach that height) and canopy cover (>10%). This definition formally excludes 'other wooded land', which encompasses areas with shrubs but without trees. However, in the present book, the concept is extended to other wooded land when necessary (see Chapter 9). Moreover, for simplicity, we consider 'forest' and 'woodland' as synonyms. This is largely consistent with the British use of the term 'woodland' (which includes a range of different tree-covered land types) but different from some definitions of 'woodland' implying widely spaced trees forming an open canopy.

Following the above, we define a forest bird as a species that more than incidentally breeds or forages in (1) forest according to the official FAO definition or (2) other types of environments that fulfil the basic quantitative criteria of the FAO definition of forest (minimum area, tree height, tree cover) but are predominantly under agricultural or urban use (e.g., some gardens, city parks and agroforestry systems).

For clarification, this definition includes:

- Species that forage mostly in farmland, grassland or wetlands, and on water or in the air, but more than incidentally breed in forest (e.g., jackdaw *Coloeus monedula*, goldeneye *Bucephala clangula*, grey heron *Ardea cinerea*, starling *Sturnus vulgaris*, stock dove *Columba oenas*, woodpigeon *C. palumbus*, greenshank *Tringa nebularia*, kestrel *Falco tinnunculus*, swift *Apus apus*).
- Typical farmland, grassland or wetland species that can breed or forage on clearcuts, burned forest or very young forest (e.g., ortolan bunting *Emberiza hortulana*, yellowhammer *E. citrinella*, yellow wagtail *Motacilla flava*, white wagtail *M. alba*, whinchat *Saxicola rubetra*, red-backed shrike *Lanius collurio*, short-eared owl *Asio flammeus*).
- Species that forage by flying over clearcuts and the forest canopy (e.g., house martin *Delichon urbica*, barn swallow *Hirundo rustica,* nightjar *Caprimulgus europaeus*).

This definition excludes:

- Typical farmland or grassland birds that never or only incidentally use clearcuts or burned forests (e.g., skylark *Alauda arvensis*, lapwing *Vanellus vanellus*, curlew *Numenius arquata*, grey partridge *Perdix perdix*).
- Typical high-alpine or tundra species that only incidentally use clearcuts or burns (e.g., red-throated pipit *Anthus cervinus*).
- Species that breed or forage on/near water or on mires in the forest landscape without (more than incidentally) using the forest itself for breeding or foraging (e.g., whooper swan *Cygnus cygnus*, common sandpiper *Actitis hypoleucos*, red-throated diver *Gavia stellata*).

Some species can be defined as either forest birds or non-forest birds, depending on variations in local conditions or local behaviour within the geographic range of the species. Still, based on the guidelines above, we have compiled a list of European forest birds to be used in analyses and discussions in this chapter, as well as in other chapters in Part II of the book. This list includes all species that fulfil the definition of 'forest bird' in a substantial part of their European distribution range.

We have further divided all forest species into obligate forest specialists and facultative forest birds. Forest specialists are species that do not frequently breed elsewhere other than in (1) forest according to the FAO definition or (2) other types of environments that fulfil the basic criteria of the FAO definition but are often included as agricultural or urban categories on common land-use maps (e.g., some gardens, city parks and agroforestry systems). Examples of forest specialists include capercaillie *Tetrao urogallus*, three-toed woodpecker *Picoides tridactylus*, Siberian jay *Perisoreus infaustus*, treecreeper *Certhia familiaris*, hazel grouse *Tetrastes bonasia*, goshawk *Accipiter gentilis*, wood warbler *Phylloscopus sibilatrix* and crested tit *Lophophanes cristatus*. This definition of a forest specialist excludes species that require trees for nesting but can use single dispersed trees outside forest habitats for that purpose (e.g., green woodpecker *Picus viridis*, buzzard *Buteo buteo*). Facultative forest birds are any forest species which are not forest specialists.

By applying these criteria, we ended up with a list encompassing 241 forest species, of which 52 could be counted as forest specialists (see Appendix 5.1). We used this list for our analyses of macroecological patterns in forest species diversity.

5.3 From Local Bird Communities to Macroecological Patterns in Species Diversity

European forests have a relatively homogeneous and species-poor bird fauna compared to their counterparts in North America and Asia (Newton 2003; Greenberg & Marra 2005). Possible explanations for these differences are discussed in more detail in Chapter 2, but repeated shifts of biotas during the Neogene (Pleistocene glaciations and interglacial periods in particular), along with somewhat limited geographical connectivity with richer faunas in the tropical forest to the south, have been suggested as the main factors underlying current species richness patterns. European forest birds have also a relatively low level of endemism and include a relatively low proportion of tropical migrants (Newton 2003; Greenberg & Marra 2005). Interestingly, a gradient of forest bird species richness increasing from west to east has been repeatedly reported in Europe. Two hypotheses have been put forward to explain these patterns. The first is a large-scale peninsular effect involving a decrease in species diversity from the base to the tip of a peninsula (Cook 1969) (earlier described for mammals in Europe; Baquero & Telleria 2001), and the second is a large-scale gradient in anthropogenic impact decreasing from west to east (Tomiałojć 2000; Chapter 8). Nonetheless, local bird communities show substantial variability within a given region and are often strongly influenced by the intensity of local land use. For example, the natural forest stands of Białowieża Forest, on the Polish-Belarussian border, have an almost complete set of temperate forest species encompassing all ecological guilds (Chapter 8), whereas structurally and compositionally impoverished forest plantations nearby may have only a fraction of that community, with forest specialists being almost absent (e.g., Angelstam *et al.* 2002). Similar situations occur elsewhere in Europe where local landscapes encompass a broad range of forest environments ranging from areas of protected old growth to areas that are very intensively managed, including tree plantations (e.g., Martínez-Jauregui *et al.* 2016).

Dominant land-use practices over large regions may have led to large-scale impoverishment of forest bird communities (e.g., forests in Denmark and Ireland). In Ireland, the natural isolation of the island additionally reduces the richness of its forest bird communities. Mikusiński and Angelstam (1997, 1998) found a clear link between the species richness of woodpeckers and the degree of anthropogenic impact on European landscapes: the higher the impact, the lower the richness of this group of specialist forest birds. Such macroecological patterns in species richness may have serious consequences for conservation strategies, particularly since many conservation efforts are undertaken at the national level (e.g., red-listing of species, implementation of action plans for endangered species or creation of protected areas). Knowledge of macroecological patterns in species occurrence and diversity could provide crucial scientific guidance for the development of a more coherent and integrated conservation policy encompassing a large part of the European continent. Forests are central to European biodiversity because they constitute a large component of the Natura 2000 network (50% of the total area of the network; European Comission 2015) and are considered as the main natural vegetation over most of the continent. In this context, understanding the macroecological patterns of forest birds, a species group of high cultural interest, is strongly relevant to conservation at both regional and continental scales within Europe.

In this chapter, we describe macroecological patterns of richness of breeding season forest bird communities in Europe based on published atlas data with a spatial resolution of 50 × 50 km (Hagemeijer & Blair 1997). This coarse spatial resolution does not allow comparison of particular forest blocks or landscapes, but it enables examination of continent-wide patterns and their underlying factors, leading to testable hypotheses. For example, Mikusiński and Angelstam (2004) used these data to relate occurrence patterns of several species to forest cover and found different species-specific responses depending on the degree of specialisation to forest environments. Due to constraints in data availability, our exploration is largely limited to the western part of the continent and omits most of the Russian Federation and eastern Ukraine. For practical reasons, we use the term 'eastern Europe' for the easternmost parts of our study area (Baltic countries, eastern parts of Poland and Slovakia, Belarus, Ukraine), whereas areas located in most of Poland and Slovakia, Hungary, the Czech Republic, Austria and eastern Germany are called 'central Europe'.

Due to the presence of the so-called third, vertical dimension of forest environments linked to the height of trees and the resulting foliage height diversity (*sensu* MacArthur & MacArthur 1961), forest bird communities are particularly rich in different ecological guilds adapted to the structural diversity of forests (Chapter 3). Therefore, patterns in species richness can be examined not only at the level of obligate and facultative forest birds, but also at the guild level. Migratory habits, nesting preferences, food types and foraging modes can all be examined separately in terms of species richness and related to patterns in environmental variables. Here, we provide a description of geographic patterns in forest bird species diversity across Europe and discuss possible causal factors. We also examine the proportions of forest specialist species and of species with different migratory habits among the total number of forest species occurring in different parts of Europe. Habitat specialists are usually considered the most threatened by the human-induced changes taking place in their environments (e.g., Mikusiński *et al.* 2001; Angelstam *et al.* 2004; Roberge & Angelstam 2006). Therefore, a high proportion of habitat specialists in forest bird communities may be indicative of their vulnerability. Similarly, forest birds with different migratory habits have been found to respond to habitat transformations in different ways. In Finland, for example, many resident forest birds declined strongly (in terms of both local abundance and distribution) with the introduction of intensive forestry, while some long-distance migrants profited from these changes (e.g., Helle & Järvinen 1986; Chapter 11). In contrast, in Britain, long-distance migrants have disproportionately declined in recent decades, probably mainly due to factors operating outside the breeding season (Hewson & Noble 2009). Therefore, the relative proportions of resident and migratory birds in space can potentially offer useful information for forest conservation assessments. Finally, considering the importance of spatial turnover in the composition of species assemblages in the context of climate change and conservation planning (Gaston *et al.* 2007), we also quantified local dissimilarity in species composition (beta diversity) across the continent.

5.4 Materials and Methods

Data on the spatial distribution of forest bird species were extracted from the EBCC Atlas of European Breeding Birds, describing the occurrence of bird species in the 50 × 50 km Universal Transverse Mercator grid cell system (Hagemeijer & Blair 1997). We used species classified as forest birds according to the definition provided above (see also Appendix 5.1), distinguishing forest specialists and facultative forest species. We also assigned each species to the different guilds described in Table 5.1 based on the information available in *The Birds of the Western Palaearctic* (Snow & Perrins 1998; Cramp *et al.* 1977–1994). Most species could be placed into more than one guild. The resulting table with 241 forest bird species (see Appendix 5.2) was then linked to the database of the EBCC Atlas, allowing for the spatial mapping of species diversity patterns for the different groups. Maps showing the percentages of some groups among all forest birds or forest specialists were also produced.

We present results only for plots where the 'completeness of coverage' was considered 'high' according to the EBCC Atlas (Hagemeijer & Blair 1997). As a result, these results are essentially restricted to the European Union plus Switzerland and Norway. This situation will improve in the future, since the New European Breeding Bird Atlas 2013–2017 is making extraordinary progress in countries such as Russia and Ukraine (Herrando *et al.* 2014), which will facilitate the analysis of breeding bird community patterns in this region.

We quantified dissimilarity in species composition (beta diversity) using the Sørensen index (Koleff *et al.* 2003). Beta diversity for each cell was quantified as the average of beta diversity values between the focal cell and adjacent cells. Hence, it represents local-scale turnover in species composition, i.e., how much the species composition changes from one atlas square to the adjacent squares. Only focal cells with more than one adjacent cell were taken into account in the computations. Map units are expressed as percentages, and the scale shows values from 0 to 20%.

5.5 Species Diversity of Forest Birds in Europe – Macroecological Patterns

Out of our global set of 241 forest bird species, 52 species (21.6%) were classified as forest specialists. Species foraging on invertebrates were most common (79.7%), followed by the seed-/nut-eating species (36.9%) and frugivorous species (32.0%). Over half of the species were assigned as residents (53.5%), while long-distant migrants and short-distance migrants were less numerous (40.7% and 31.5%, respectively). Ground foragers were the most common foraging guild among forest birds (71.4%), followed by arboreal foragers (44.4%) and species that forage in the understorey (39.0%). Fifty species of forest birds (20.7%) were categorised as cavity-nesting species. Note that the above percentages do not add up to 100% for each variable, because one species can occur in more than one category for a given variable. For a full account of the results and interrelations among different groups, see Table 5.1. The classification key for species that belong to different guilds is presented in Appendix 5.2.

All 'top 20' facultative forest birds (defined based on their percentage of occurrence across all atlas squares) are clearly more widespread than the 'top 20' forest specialists (Table 5.2). Also, the relative drop in the level of spatial occurrence from the first to the twentieth place was much more pronounced among forest specialists (from 92.7% to 80.9% and from 78.5% to 28.4% in facultative and specialised forest species, respectively).

The general species richness pattern for all forest birds (Fig. 5.2) shows a clear west-east gradient of increasing richness (particularly noticeable in the temperate forest region), as well as a visible pattern of decreasing numbers of forest species towards the Mediterranean and large Atlantic islands (Great Britain and Ireland) and northern Fennoscandia.

The species richness pattern for forest specialists (Fig. 5.3) also follows the patterns of decreasing species richness towards the west and the Mediterranean region. The most important species richness hotspots for this group are found in highly forested areas of eastern and northern

Table 3.1 Numbers of European forest bird species that belong to different guilds.

	Forest birds	Forest specialists	Facultative forest species	Carnivorous species	Piscivorous species	Insectivorous species	Frugivorous species	Seed-/nut-eating species	Other plant food–eating species	Resident/sedentary species	Short-distance migrants	Long-distance migrants	Aerial foragers	Arboreal/canopy foragers	Understorey foragers	Ground foragers	Wetland species	Cavity nesters
Forest birds	241																	
Forest specialisation																		
Forest specialists	52																	
Facultative forest species	189																	
Food type																		
Carnivorous species	54	12	42															
Piscivorous species	15	1	14	10														
Insectivorous species	192	44	150	28	8													
Frugivorous species	77	19	60	6	1	68												
Seed-/nut-eating species	89	18	71	7	1	75	42											
Other plant food–eating species	46	9	37	3	1	35	29	35										
Migratory habits																		
Resident/sedentary species	129	37	93	31	5	92	48	68	35									
Short-distance migrants	76	8	68	18	8	59	25	33	19	53								
Long-distance migrants	98	16	82	17	7	90	29	14	6	5	9							
Foraging habits																		
Aerial foragers	43	7	36	17	2	36	8	2	2	13	10	29						
Arboreal/canopy foragers	107	38	69	13	1	92	48	48	22	66	27	37	15					
Understorey foragers	94	23	71	8	0	84	46	38	18	55	28	37	12	72				
Ground foragers	172	32	140	44	6	132	59	78	42	103	63	59	29	72	69			
Wetland species	28	1	27	11	15	19	1	3	2	10	13	13	3	1	0	14		
Cavity nesters	50	19	31	8	3	42	14	23	6	39	8	10	8	32	24	35	5	
Introduced species	12	3	9	0	0	7	6	8	8	12	0	0	0	2	1	9	2	3

Table 5.2 *The most widespread European forest birds. Based on data from 2,601 squares (50 × 50 km) with 'high' survey completeness in the EBCC atlas (Hagemeijer & Blair 1997).*

Facultative forest birds	Percentage occurrence	Forest specialists	Percentage occurrence
White wagtail *Motacilla alba*	92.7	Eurasian sparrowhawk *Accipiter nisus*	78.5
Barn swallow *Hirundo rustica*	91.5	Chiffchaff *Phylloscopus collybita*	76.7
Great tit *Parus major*	91.4	Northern goshawk *Accipiter gentilis*	70.3
Hooded/carrion crow *Corvus corone*	91.3	Lesser spotted woodpecker *Dryobates minor*	64.4
Chaffinch *Fringilla coelebs*	90.5	Goldcrest *Regulus regulus*	62.9
House martin *Delichon urbicum*	90.3	Wood warbler *Phylloscopus sibilatrix*	60.8
Common cuckoo *Cuculus canorus*	89.6	Honey buzzard *Pernis apivorus*	56.1
Common kestrel *Falco tinnunculus*	89.3	European crested tit *Lophophanes cristatus*	56.0
Blackbird *Turdus merula*	88.6	Willow tit *Poecile montanus*	54.4
Greenfinch *Chloris chloris*	87.9	Marsh tit *Poecile palustris*	53.7
Magpie *Pica pica*	87.5	Black woodpecker *Dryocopus martius*	52.9
Wood pigeon *Columba palumbus*	85.6	Eurasian siskin *Carduelis spinus*	49.9
European robin *Erithacus rubecula*	85.2	Common crossbill *Loxia curvirostra*	47.9
Spotted flycatcher *Muscicapa striata*	84.5	Firecrest *Regulus ignicapillus*	35.7
Common swift *Apus apus*	84.4	Grey-headed woodpecker *Picus canus*	33.4
Blue tit *Cyanistes caeruleus*	83.6	Green sandpiper *Tringa ochropus*	32.3
Blackcap *Sylvia atricapilla*	83.1	Hazel grouse *Tetrastes bonasia*	31.3
Eurasian jay *Garrulus glandarius*	82.7	Tengmalm's owl *Aegolius funereus*	31.1
Eurasian wren *Troglodytes troglodytes*	81.2	Middle spotted woodpecker *Leiopicus medius*	30.3
Common buzzard *Buteo buteo*	80.9	Capercaillie *Tetrao urogallus*	28.4

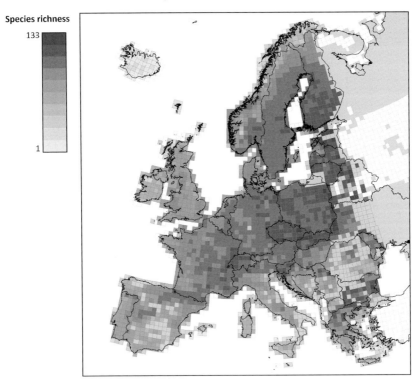

Figure 5.2 Species richness of forest birds.

Europe (Fennoscandia and Baltic countries) and in the mountain ranges of central and eastern Europe. In contrast to the pattern for total forest bird species richness (Fig. 5.2), the number of forest specialists is relatively low in northern Germany, eastern France and north-western Poland.

While most guilds (aerial, ground, understorey and arboreal foragers, frugivorous and insectivorous species, seed-/nut-eating species, cavity nesters) follow the overall pattern of species richness, some display more idiosyncratic patterns. For example, among carnivorous forest birds (dominated by birds of prey, including owls), high species richness is observed in eastern Europe, the Balkans, Iberia and southern France (Fig. 5.4).

The most important species richness hotspots for wetland forest birds are located where most of the water bodies and non-coastal wetlands occur, which happens to be the heavily forested north-eastern part of the study region, especially Fennoscandia (Fig. 5.5).

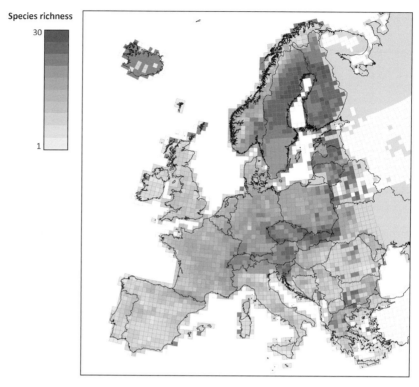

Figure 5.3 Species richness of forest specialists.

The species richness pattern of cavity-nesting birds (Fig. 5.6) largely resembles that of forest specialists, with a striking west-to-east increase and an elevated number of species in some mountain ranges. The main difference is relatively fewer cavity-nesters in northern Fennoscandia.

High proportions of forest specialists are clearly linked to the areas with high forest cover in the boreal region and the mountain ranges of Central Europe and the Balkans (Fig. 5.7). This pattern of specialist proportion is similar to that for the absolute number of specialists (Fig. 5.3).

The proportion of long-distance migrants among forest birds is highest in southern (Mediterranean) and eastern Europe (Fig. 5.8a). This pattern is even more pronounced among forest specialists, showing a clear north-south gradient (Fig. 5.8b).

On the other hand, the share of resident birds in the total number of forest species is quite uniform across the whole of Europe (map not shown).

Species richness

42

1

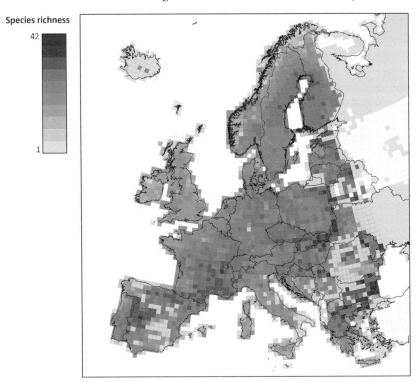

Figure 5.4 Species richness of carnivorous forest birds.

However, among forest specialists, this share is very high in boreal Europe, Britain and Ireland, and in the central part of the temperate forest region (Fig. 5.9).

The highest rates of spatial change in community composition in forest bird species measured by the Sørensen index were found in the Scandinavian, Iberian and Italian peninsulas (Fig. 5.10). Also, part of south-central Europe (e.g., Hungary) showed relatively high beta diversity values.

5.6 What Factors Drive the Macroecological Patterns?

According to classical niche-assembly models, the composition of biotic communities is determined chiefly by the autecology of species, interspecific competition and the diversity of resources and habitats available (Graves & Rahbek 2005). Moreover, the historical factors

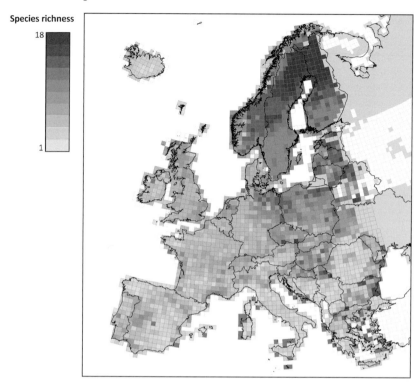

Species richness

18

1

Figure 5.5 Species richness of wetland forest birds.

behind changes in forest extent and typology are also important, even for birds that generally disperse well (e.g., Chapter 2). However, the relative contribution of these different factors to determining the composition of biotic communities is a subject of intense debate that encompasses both deterministic and stochastic factors in shaping species distribution patterns and affects macroecological patterns of species diversity, including species richness (Vellend 2010). At global and continental scales, the availability of energy and water (or the water-energy balance) seems to be the main variable explaining species richness of most taxa including birds (Hawkins *et al.* 2003). Van Rensburg *et al.* (2002) demonstrated that avifaunal richness in South Africa is driven both by climatic factors influencing productivity and by habitat heterogeneity. The latitudinal and altitudinal gradients in productivity appear to be directly linked to species richness in birds (e.g., Stevens 1992), but in the case of altitudinal gradients, this relationship may

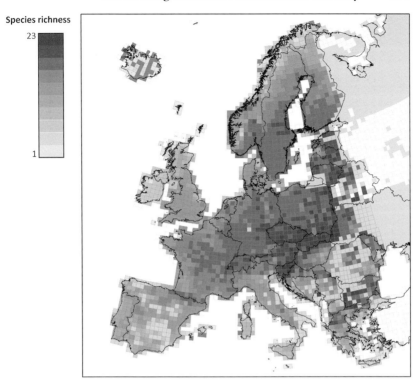

Figure 5.6 Species richness of cavity-nesting forest birds.

be largely a consequence of area effects (e.g., Rahbek 1997). Moreover, within large areas of land, so-called geometric constraints can cause species richness to peak in the middle of a 'bounded one-dimensional domain' (Jetz & Rahbek 2001). In his global analysis, McCain (2009) established that birds in the mountains actually display four diversity patterns in nearly equal frequency: decreasing diversity, low-elevation plateaus, low-elevation plateaus with mid peaks and unimodal mid-elevational peaks. Landscape heterogeneity, both natural and anthropogenic, appears to be the most important factor explaining regional avian species richness in Spain (Atauri & De Lucio 2001). In North America, Carnicer and Diaz-Delgado (2008) found that the large-scale patterns of bird species richness result from several divergent, group-specific processes and claimed that understanding diversity gradients requires identifying the functional ecological groups involved (see also Carnicer *et al.* 2012). In boreal Europe, the local species richness of

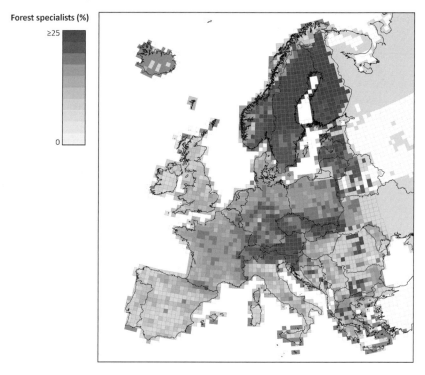

Figure 5.7 Forest specialists as a percentage of the total number of forest species.

forest birds has been shown to be largely determined by energy density (i.e., the amount of potential energy per unit area) and its variation linked to spatial habitat heterogeneity (Honkanen *et al.* 2010; Elo *et al.* 2012; Chapter 6).

Our results show that the species richness of forest birds in Europe does not follow a clear north-south (latitudinal) gradient. This is in contrast to the latitudinal gradient described for tree species richness in Europe (Svenning & Skov 2007). This difference is interesting, as trees constitute the main structural biotic structures in forest environments. We actually found a reverse north-south gradient of declining species richness in several functional ecological groups of forest birds, e.g., forest specialists and wetland species (Figs. 5.3 and 5.5, respectively). Telleria *et al.* (2003) established that latitudinal distribution of regional richness in European forest birds displayed a convex form, with the highest values in central Europe. This is in general agreement with the pattern observed in our study for all forest species at the scale of

(a)

Long-distance migrants (%)

≥50

0

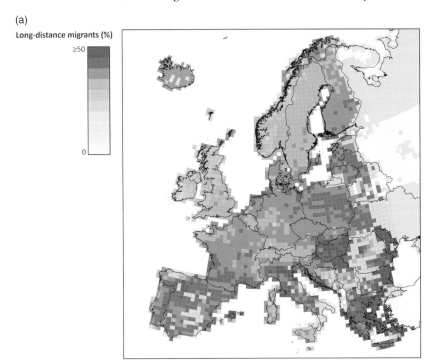

Figure 5.8 Long-distance migrants as a percentage of (a) the total number of forest species and (b) the number of forest specialists.

50 × 50 km squares (Fig. 5.2). These authors suggest that in the very fragmented forests of the Mediterranean, forests birds have a depressed ability to prevent regional extinction. On the other hand, according to Mönkkönen (1994), the largest regional species pools of forest birds (in both Europe and North America) coincide with the areas where coniferous (boreal) forests meet deciduous forests (i.e., the hemiboreal zone and regions with high altitudinal variation). However, as pointed out by other studies (e.g., Korpimäki & Marti 1995; Gregory & Blackburn 1998; Clergeau *et al.* 2006; Whittaker *et al.* 2007), there are many factors acting at different scales that affect the macroecological patterns of bird species diversity in Europe.

The pattern of total species richness among forest birds in Europe (Fig. 5.2) appears to show evidence of a peninsula effect (particularly visible on the Iberian and Italian peninsulas) and of large-scale spatial isolation (few species on the islands), possibly strengthened by the

(b)

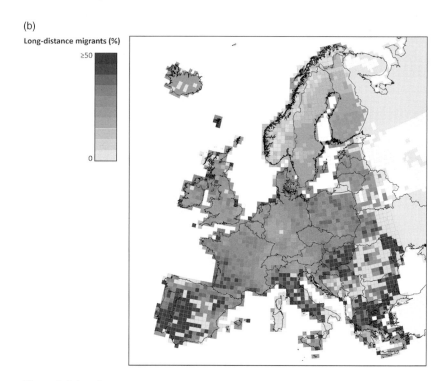

Figure 5.8 (cont.)

effects of human change, particularly the loss of forest cover (both in the Mediterranean region and on large islands). All of these areas have a relatively impoverished forest bird fauna. One can also assume that lower species richness of forest birds in the areas close to the Atlantic Ocean (e.g., western France) is at least partially an effect of geometric constraints on species distributions (Fig. 5.2). The contiguous boreal forests appear to be most homogeneous, whereas most other regions show high spatial variability in the number of occurring forest bird species, possibly linked to variations in both natural conditions (e.g., productivity, topography and natural habitat diversity) and the degree of human impact expressed by land use. The hemiboreal zone of eastern Europe shows the richest forest bird assemblages, which may be explained by the fact that two major vegetation zones (boreal and temperate) and their corresponding diversities meet there (Mönkkönen 1994; Nilsson 1997). Moreover, the hemiboreal zone in eastern Europe

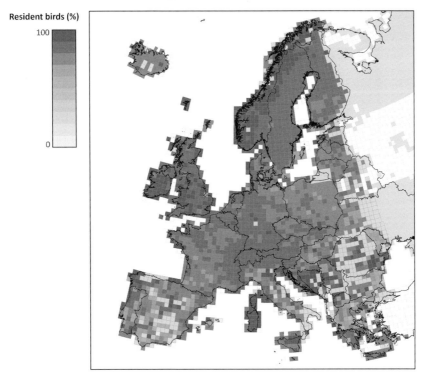

Resident birds (%)

100

0

Figure 5.9 Resident forest specialists as a percentage of the total number of forest specialists.

has relatively high forest cover and low human density and is less affected by human action compared to more central parts of Europe (Angelstam *et al.* 1997).

The west–east gradient of increasing species richness is particularly obvious among forest specialists and cavity nesters (Figs. 5.3 and 5.6, respectively), for which a positive effect of larger mountain ranges (e.g., Alps or Carpathians) is also apparent. Tomiałojć (2000), using a different dataset, found a similar west–east gradient in species richness in forest birds and strongly argued for anthropogenic impact as the main driver of this gradient. The greater deviation of forests in the west from their natural state is thought to be a key driver (see Chapter 8). Mikusiński and Angelstam (1997, 1998) described a similar gradient for woodpeckers in Europe and related it to a number of socio-economic indices, maintaining that urban-economic development along with landscape degradation and homogenisation were the main underlying factors. Fuller *et al.*

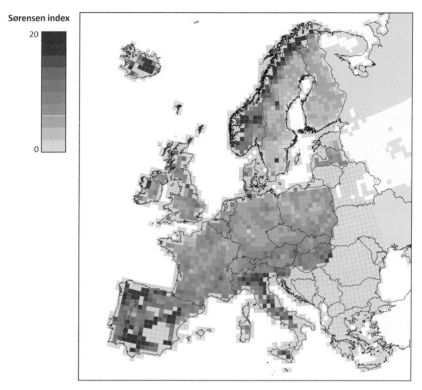

Figure 5.10 Beta diversity in forests birds as measured by the Sørensen index.

(2007) confirmed a west–east gradient of increasing species richness in Europe for all studied guilds of forest birds and concluded that in Britain and Ireland, the distributions and abundances of several species may be particularly affected by the position of these islands at the edge of species' geographical ranges.

In the case of mountain ranges, the high species richness among forest specialists is caused by both the reduced disturbance of mountain forests (resulting from more difficult working conditions and the risk of soil erosion) and mountains encompassing series of climatically different life zones over short elevational distances (Mönkkönen 1994; Körner 2004). The presence of regionally rare forest specialists such as capercaillie, hazel grouse, three-toed woodpecker, white-backed woodpecker *Dendrocopos leucotos*, Tengmalm's owl *Aegolius funereus* and citril finch *Serinus citrinella* in the European mountains gives rise to locally elevated species richness in this group. The high species richness in Fennoscandia appears to be associated with the natural occurrence of typically boreal species (e.g.,

Siberian jay, Siberian tit *Poecile cinctus*, parrot crossbill *Loxia pytyopsittacus*, pine grosbeak *Pinicola enucleator*, rustic bunting *Emberiza rustica* and hawk owl *Surnia ulula*) and generally very high forest cover that might explain the occurrence of such species as capercaillie and hazel grouse (Miku-siński & Angelstam 2004).

Species richness of carnivorous forest birds (mostly birds of prey, including owls) is strongly constrained by high human population density. Possibly both direct persecution and indirect disturbance from human activities affect the observed patterns. The most interesting appear to be a very clear belt of higher species richness of this guild along the eastern border of the European Union (Fig. 5.4). For wetland birds, quite different species richness patterns are observed, with north-ern Europe having more species than other parts of the continent (Fig. 5.5). The occurrence of four different breeding species of *Tringa* and some other waders largely restricted to this highly forested part of the continent explains this pattern. The map showing the share of all forest specialists in the total number of forest species (Fig. 5.7) resembles the pattern of richness for wetland species (Fig. 5.5). Also here is a similar west-east gradient, with relatively high values in the boreal region and a high share of forest specialists in the mountain ranges, all of which can be explained in a similar way as for the absolute number of forest specialists.

An interesting pattern emerges on maps illustrating the share of forest species with different migratory habits within forest species. The propor-tion of long-distance forest birds, particularly forest specialists, shows a clear north–south gradient, with an increasing share of those species in the south and also partially to the east (Fig. 5.8b). This pattern is mostly caused by a decrease in overall forest species richness in Mediterranean habitats affecting residents (Fig. 5.9) to a larger degree (Chapter 9; Santos *et al.* 2002). Long-distance migrants spend a substantial part of their lives in the tropics, and the Mediterranean provides a home for many species in the warm season. In addition, we observed an intriguing difference between Scandinavia and Finland among forest-living long-distance migrants (Fig. 5.8a). This difference is based on the fact that several species in this group occur in Finland but are rare or absent in Scandinavia. The species with more eastern distribution ranges include Blyth's reed warbler *Acrocephalus dumetorum*, arctic warbler *Phylloscopus borealis,* river warbler *Locustella fluviatilis*, yellow-breasted bunting *Emberiza aureola*, little bunting *E. pusilla*, golden oriole *Oriolus oriolus* and turtle dove *Streptopelia turtur* (see Chapter 6 for further discussion of the east-west gradient of species richness in boreal Europe).

Patterns in species spatial turnover are central to macroecological phenomena. Species turnover is a consequence of the gain and loss of species in space and is related to the local gradients in species composition, the species-area relationship and spatial autocorrelation (Harrison *et al.* 1992). The beta diversity gradients that we found for forest birds of Europe (Fig. 5.10) result from the presence of sharp environmental gradients across space. In particular, areas with strong environmental gradients over short distances translate into high beta diversity values. In the case of Europe, such gradients are observed mainly in mountain regions (Keil *et al.* 2012): for example, transitions between subalpine/alpine vegetation zones and boreal forest in Scandinavia and montane vs Mediterranean forests in Italy. Our results emphasise the fundamental role of habitat heterogeneity gradients in the Mediterranean peninsulas and the mountain ranges in determining patterns of forest species turnover.

5.7 Conservation Implications

Macroecological patterns in species richness have often been used to assess spatial prioritisation of conservation measures, such as creating nature reserves or delineating areas of particular significance for biodiversity (Bonn & Gaston 2005). Areas of high species diversity (e.g., for particular taxonomic groups or endemic species) are treated as biodiversity hotspots that deserve special conservation attention (Myers *et al.* 2000). Bird species richness has often been used as a surrogate for broader diversity (Cavalcanti 1999; Hurlbert & Jetz 2007; John & Kabigumila 2011), but analyses of their usefulness in predicting species richness of other taxa give mixed results (Eglington *et al.* 2011). In Europe, the transcontinental network of conservation areas Natura 2000 is based on the EU Birds and Habitats Directives (Evans 2012), with birds being a critical taxon in the former, and therefore a cornerstone of the overall strategy of the conservation network. Annex 1 to the EU Birds Directive lists species which 'shall be the subject of special conservation measures concerning their habitat in order to ensure their survival and reproduction in their area of distribution'. This annex includes 71 forest bird species, according to the definition adopted in this chapter.

Eastern Europe has the highest richness of such species (Fig. 5.11), thus indicating that many areas of particular conservation value for the forest avifauna are located at the periphery of the European Union. Large parts of western and southern Europe have very few forest species listed in Annex I. However, it should be recognised that, due to the fact that

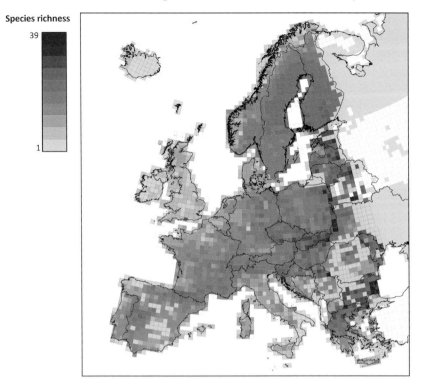

Figure 5.11 Species richness of forest birds listed in Annex 1 of the EU Birds Directive.

the list includes many raptors, mountain areas in southern France and Spain have a relatively large number of threatened forest species. These patterns, together with the high species richness of forest specialists and cavity-nesters found in northern and central (eastern) Europe and in the mountains (see Figs. 5.3 and 5.6), suggest that conservation priorities should encompass these regions. There is also a case for giving high conservation priority to regions with high beta diversity, because these represent areas with high environmental heterogeneity (Fig. 5.10).

The forest cover of Europe is steadily increasing (Alix-Garcia *et al.* 2016). This trend will probably continue in the future, due to both abandonment of former agricultural land and climate change mitigation processes (Galos *et al.* 2013). The 'new forests of Europe' encompass intensively managed tree plantations (see Chapter 10), often of rather limited value for forest bird communities; naturally regenerated forests growing on abandoned agricultural land with areas of potentially valuable avian habitat; and forests of intermediate quality, for example in urban and amenity areas (see Chapter 14). In the longer term, these new forests should be allowed to develop in ways that provide new opportunities for forest biodiversity, including birds (e.g., Gil-Tena *et al.* 2009; Rey Benayas *et al.* 2009). The patterns in bird species richness and diversity described above can inform conservation restoration efforts, in both new and existing forests, about the guilds and assemblages that are likely to benefit in different geographical contexts.

Acknowledgements

We are grateful to Ian Newton and Sören Svensson for providing valuable comments and suggestions on an earlier draft of the manuscript.

References

Alix-Garcia, J., Munteanu, C., Zhao, N. *et al.* (2016) Drivers of forest cover change in Eastern Europe and European Russia, 1985–2012. *Land Use Policy*, **59**, 284–297.

Angelstam, P., Anufriev, V., Balciauskas, L. *et al.* (1997) Biodiversity and sustainable forestry in European forests – how West and East can learn from each other. *Wildlife Society Bulletin*, **25**, 38–48.

Angelstam, P., Breuss, M., Mikusiński, G., Stenström, M., Stighäll, K. & Thorell, M. (2002) Effects of forest structure on the presence of woodpeckers with different specialisation in a landscape history gradient in NE Poland. In *Avian Landscape Ecology*. Chamberlain, D. & Wilson, D. (eds.). Proceedings of the 2002 Annual IALE (UK) Conference, University of East Anglia, pp. 25–38.

Angelstam, P., Roberge, J.-M., Lõhmus, A. *et al.* (2004) Habitat modelling as a tool for landscape-scale conservation – A review of parameters for focal forest birds. *Ecological Bulletins*, **51**, 427–453.

Atauri, J.A. & De Lucio, J.V. (2001) The role of landscape structure in species richness distribution of birds, amphibians, reptiles and lepidopterans in Mediterranean landscapes. *Landscape Ecology*, **16**, 147–159.

Baquero, R.A. & Telleria, J.L. (2001) Species richness, rarity and endemicity of European mammals: A biogeographical approach. *Biodiversity and Conservation*, **10**, 29–44.

Bengtsson, J., Nilsson, S.G., Franc, A. & Menozzi P. (2000) Biodiversity, disturbances, ecosystem function and management of European forests. *Forest Ecology and Management*, **132**, 39–50.

Bonn, A. & Gaston, K.J. (2005) Capturing biodiversity: Selecting priority areas for conservation using different criteria. *Biodiversity and Conservation*, **14**, 1083–1100.

Carnicer, J., Brotons, L., Stefanescu, C. & Penuelas, J. (2012) Biogeography of species richness gradients: Linking adaptive traits, demography and diversification. *Biological Reviews*, **87**, 457–479.

Carnicer, J. & Diaz-Delgado, R. (2008) Geographic differences between functional groups in patterns of bird species richness in North America. *Acta Oecologica*, **33**, 253–264.

Cavalcanti, R.B. (1999) Bird species richness and conservation in the Cerrado region of central Brazil. *Studies in Avian Biology*, **19**, 244–249.

Clergeau, P., Croci, S., Jokimäki, J., Kaisanlahti-Jokimäki, M.-L. & Dinetti, M. (2006) Avifauna homogenisation by urbanisation: Analysis at different European latitudes. *Biological Conservation*, **127**, 336–344.

Cook, R.E. (1969) Variation in species density of North American birds. *Systematic Zoology*, **18**, 63–84.

Cramp, S., Simmons, K.E.L. & Perrins, C.M. (eds.). (1977–1994) *The Birds of Western Palaearctic*. Vols I–IX. Oxford: Oxford University Press.

Di Marco, M. & Santini, L. (2015) Human pressures predict species' geographic range size better than biological traits. *Global Change Biology*, **21**, 2169–2178.

Eglington, S.M., Noble, D.G. & Fuller, R.J. (2012) A meta-analysis of spatial relationships in species richness across taxa: Birds as indicators of wider biodiversity in temperate regions. *Journal for Nature Conservation*, **20**, 301–309.

Elo, M., Roberge J.-M., Rajasärkkä, A. & Mönkkönen, M. (2012) Energy density and its variation in space limit species richness of boreal forest birds. *Journal of Biogeography*, **39**, 1462–1472.

European Commission (2015) *Natura 2000 and Forests: Technical Report 2015-088, Directorate-General for the Environment*. Luxembourg: Office for Official Publications of the European Communities, p. 108.

Evans, D. (2012) Building the European Union's Natura 2000 network. *Nature Conservation*, **1**, 11–26.

FAO (2010) *Global Forest Resources Assessment 2010: Terms and Definitions*. Food and Agriculture Organization of the United Nations, Forestry Department. www.fao.org/docrep/014/am665e/am665e00.pdf.

Fuller, R.J., Gaston, K.J. & Quine, C.P. (2007) Living on the edge: British and Irish woodland birds in a European context. *Ibis*, **149** (Suppl. 2), 53–63.

Galos, B., Hagemann, S., Hansler, A. *et al.* (2013) Case study for the assessment of the biogeophysical effects of a potential afforestation in Europe. *Carbon Balance and Management*, **8**, part 3.

Gaston, K.J., Davies, R.G., Orme, C.D.L. *et al.* (2007) Spatial turnover in the global avifauna. *Proceedings of the Royal Society B*, **274**, 1567–1574.

Gil-Tena, A., Brotons, L. & Saura, S. (2009) Mediterranean forest dynamics and forest bird distribution changes in the late 20th century. *Global Change Biology*, **15**, 474–485.

Graves, G.R. & Rahbek, C. (2005) Source pool geometry and the assembly of continental avifaunas. *Proceedings of the National Academy*, **102**, 7871–7876.

Greenberg, R. & Marra, P.P. (2005) *Birds of Two Worlds: The Ecology and Evolution of Migration*. Baltimore: John Hopkins University Press.

Gregory, R.D. & Blackburn, T.M. (1998) Macroecological patterns in British breeding birds: Covariation of species' geographical range sizes at differing spatial scales. *Ecography*, **21**, 527–534.

Hagemeijer, J.M. & Blair, M.J. (1997) *The EBCC Atlas of European Breeding Birds: Their Distribution and Abundance*. London: T. and A.D. Poyser.

Harrison, S., Ross, S.J. & Lawton, J.H. (1992) Beta diversity on geographic gradients in Britain. *Journal of Animal Ecology*, **62**, 151–158.

Hawkins, B.A., Field, R., Cornell, H.V. *et al.* (2003) Energy, water, and broad scale geographic patterns of species richness. *Ecology*, **84**, 3105–3117.

Helle, P. & Järvinen, O. (1986) Population trends of North Finnish land birds in relation to their habitat selection and changes in forest structure. *Oikos*, **46**, 107–115.

Herrando, S., Voříšek, P., Kupka, M., Anton, M. & Keller, V. (2014) Ongoing EBBA2: A first pilot data provision of 50×50 km data. *Bird Census News*, **27**, 1–2; *European Atlas News*, 27–35.

Hewson, C. M. & Noble, D. G. (2009) Population trends of breeding birds in British woodlands over a 32-year period: Relationships with food, habitat use and migratory behaviour. *Ibis*, **151**, 464–486.

Honkanen, M., Roberge, J.-M., Rajasärkkä, A. & Mönkkönen, M. (2010) Disentangling the effects of area, energy and habitat heterogeneity on boreal forest bird species richness in protected areas. *Global Ecology and Biogeography*, **19**, 61–71.

Hurlbert, A.H. & Jetz, W. (2007) Species richness, hotspots, and the scale dependence of range maps in ecology and conservation. *Proceedings of the National Academy of Sciences*, **104**, 13384–13389.

Jetz, W. & Rahbek, C. (2001) Geometric constraints explain much of the species richness pattern in African birds. *Proceedings of the National Academy of Sciences*, **98**, 5661–5666.

John, J.R.M. & Kabigumila, J.D.L. (2011) The use of bird species richness and abundance indices to assess the conservation value of exotic Eucalyptus plantations. *Ostrich*, **82**, 27–37.

Keil, P., Schweiger, O., Kühn, I. *et al.* (2012) Patterns of beta diversity in Europe: The role of climate, land cover and distance across scales. *Journal of Biogeography*, **39**, 1473–1486.

Koleff, P., Lennon, J.J. & Gaston, K.J. (2003) Are there latitudinal gradients in species turnover? *Global Ecology and Biogeography*, **12**, 483–498.

Korpimäki, E. & Marti C.D. (1995) Geographical trends in trophic characteristics of mammal-eating and bird-eating raptors in Europe and North America. *Auk*, **112**, 1004–1023.

Körner, C. (2004) Mountain biodiversity, its causes and function. *Ambio*, **33**, special issue 13, 11–17.

Latham, R.E. & Ricklefs, R.E. (1993) Continental comparisons of temperate-zone tree species diversity. In *Species Diversity in Ecological Communities: Historical and Geographical Perspectives*. Ricklefs, R.E., Schluter, D. (eds.), Chicago: University of Chicago Press, pp. 294–314.

MacArthur, R.H. & MacArthur, J. (1961) On bird species diversity. *Ecology*, **42**, 594–598.

Martínez-Jauregui, M., Díaz, M., Sánchez de Ron, D. & Soliño, M. (2016) Plantation or natural recovery? Relative contribution of planted and natural pine forests to the maintenance of regional bird diversity along ecological gradients in Southern Europe. *Forest Ecology and Management*, **376**, 183–192.

McCain, C.M. (2009) Global analysis of bird elevational diversity. *Global Ecology and Biogeography*, **18**, 346–360.

Mikusiński, G. & Angelstam, P. (1997) European woodpeckers and anthropogenic habitat change: A review. *Die Vogelwelt*, **118**, 277–283.

Mikusiński, G. & Angelstam, P. (1998) Economic geography, forest distribution and woodpecker diversity in central Europe. *Conservation Biology*, **12**, 200–208.

Mikusiński, G. & Angelstam P. (2004) Occurrence of mammals and birds with different ecological characteristics in relation to forest cover in Europe: Do macroecological data make sense? *Ecological Bulletines*, **51**, 265–275.

Mikusiński, G., Gromadzki, M. & Chylarecki, P. (2001) Woodpeckers as indicators of forest bird diversity. *Conservation Biology*, **15**, 208–217.

Mönkkönen, M. (1994) Diversity patterns in Palaearctic and Nearctic forest bird assemblages. *Journal of Biogeography*, **21**, 183–195.

Myers, N., Mittermeler, R.A., Mittermeler, C.G., Da Fonseca, G.A.B. & Kent, J. (2000) Biodiversity hotspots for conservation priorities. *Nature*, **403**, 853–858.

Newton, I. (2003). *The Speciation and Biogeography of Birds*. London: Academic Press.

Nilsson, S.G. (1997) Forests in the temperate-boreal transition: Natural and man-made features. *Ecological Bulletins*, **46**, 61–71.

Peterson, A.T., Soberón, J., Pearson, R.G. *et al.* (2011) *Ecological Niches and Geographic Distributions*. Princeton University Press. New Jersey.

Rahbek, G. (1997) The relationship among area, elevation, and regional species richness in neotropical birds. *American Naturalist*, **149**, 875–902.

Rey Benayas, J. M., Newton, A. C., Diaz, A. & Bullock, J.M. (2009) Enhancement of biodiversity and ecosystem services by ecological restoration: A meta-analysis. *Science*, **325**, 1121–1124.

Roberge, J.-M. & Angelstam, P. (2006) Indicator species among resident forest birds: A cross-regional evaluation in northern Europe. *Biological Conservation*, **130**, 134–147.

Santos, T., Tellería, J. L. & Carbonell, R. (2002) Bird conservation in fragmented Mediterranean forests of Spain: Effects of geographical location, habitat and landscape degradation. *Biological Conservation*, **105**, 113–125.

Snow, D.W. & Perrins, C.M. (1998) *The Birds of the Western Palearctic* (Concise Edition). Oxford: Oxford University Press.

Stevens, G.C. (1992) The elevational gradient in altitudinal range: An extension of Rapoport's latitudinal rule to altitude. *American Naturalist*, **140**, 893–911.

Svenning, J.-C. & Skov, F. (2007) Could the tree diversity pattern in Europe be generated by postglacial dispersal limitation? *Ecology Letters*, **10**, 453–460.

Telleria, J.L., Baquero, R. & Santos, T. (2003) Effects of forest fragmentation on European birds: Implications of regional differences in species richness. *Journal of Biogeography*, **30**, 621–628.

Tomiałojć, L. (2000) An East-West gradient in the breeding distribution and species richness of the European woodland avifauna. *Acta Ornithologica*, **35**, 3–17.

Van Rensburg, B.J., Chown S.L. & Gaston K.J. (2002) Species richness, environmental correlates, and spatial scale: A test using South African birds. *American Naturalist*, **159**, 566–577.

Vellend, M. (2010) Conceptual synthesis in community ecology. *Quarterly Review of Biology*, **85**, 183–206.

Whittaker, R.J., Nogues-Bravo, D. & Araujo, M.B. (2007) Geographical gradients of species richness: A test of the water-energy conjecture of Hawkins et al. (2003) using European data for five taxa. *Global Ecology and Biogeography*, **16**, 76–89.

Appendix 5.1

Species list with ecological characteristics. Only behaviours marked with '1' were used in producing the diversity maps. The asterisks indicate that a given species may, on rare occasions, exhibit other behaviours.

SCIENTIFIC	ENGLISH	Forest birds	Forest specialists	Carnivorous species	Piscivorous species	Insectivorous species	Frugivorous species	Seed-/nut-eating species	Other plant food–eating species	Resident/sedentary species	Short-distance migrants	Long-distance migrants	Aerial foragers	Arboreal/canopy foragers	Understorey foragers	Ground foragers	Wetland species	Cavity-nesting species	Introduced species
Accipiter brevipes	Levant sparrowhawk	1		1								1	★	★	★	1			
Accipiter gentilis	Northern goshawk	1	1	1						1	★		1	1	1	1			
Accipiter nisus	Eurasian sparrowhawk	1	1	1		★				1	1		1	1	1	1			
Acrocephalus dumetorum	Blyth's reed warbler	1				1						1		1	1				
Acrocephalus palustris	Marsh warbler	1				1	★					1		★	1				
Actitis hypoleucos	Common sandpiper	1				1				1	★	1				1			
Aegithalos caudatus	Long-tailed tit	1				1	★	★	★	1	★		1	1	1	★			
Aegolius funereus	Tengmalm's owl	1	1	1						1								1	
Aix galericulata	Mandarin duck	1				1				1							1	1	1
Aix sponsa	Wood duck	1								1							1	1	1
Alectoris barbara	Barbary partridge	1				★	1	1	1	1									
Alectoris chukar	Chukar	1				★	1	1	1	1									
Alectoris graeca	Rock partridge	1				1	1	1	1	1									
Alopochen aegyptiaca	Egyptian goose	1						1	1	1							★	1	1

Scientific name	Common name												
Anser fabalis	Bean goose	1						1			1		★
Anthus hodgsoni	Olive-backed pipit	1		1	1			1			1		
Anthus pratensis	Meadow pipit	1		1	1			1				1	
Anthus trivialis	Tree pipit	1					★	1					
Apus apus	Common swift	1		1			1						1
Aquila adalberti	Spanish imperial eagle	1	1										
Aquila chrysaetos	Golden eagle	1	★	★	1	★					1		
Aquila clanga	Greater spotted eagle	1	1	1	1								
Aquila fasciata	Bonelli's eagle	1		1	1	1	★	1	★	★	1		
Aquila heliaca	Eastern imperial eagle	1		★	1	★	★			★	1		★
Aquila pennata	Booted eagle	1	★	1	1	1	1	1					
Aquila pomarina	Lesser spotted eagle	1	★	★			★						
Ardea cinerea	Grey heron	1	1	1	1		1	1	1				
Ardeola ralloides	Squacco heron	1	1	1	1			1			1		
Asio flammeus	Short-eared owl	1			1			1					
Asio otus	Long-eared owl	1			1			1					
Athene noctua	Little owl	1		1	1		★	1	1	★	1	★	1
Bombycilla garrulus	Bohemian waxwing	1		1	1		1	1	1				
Bubo bubo	Eurasian eagle owl	1		1			1	1		1			
Bubulcus ibis	Cattle egret	1		1							1	1	
Bucephala clangula	Common goldeneye	1		1							1	1	1
Buteo buteo	Common buzzard	1		1	1		1				1	★	
Buteo lagopus	Rough-legged buzzard	1		1	1		1				1	1	1

(cont.)

(cont.)

SCIENTIFIC	ENGLISH	Forest birds	Forest specialists	Carnivorous species	Piscivorous species	Insectivorous species	Frugivorous species	Seed-/nut-eating species	Other plant food–eating species	Resident/sedentary species	Short-distance migrants	Long-distance migrants	Aerial foragers	Arboreal/canopy foragers	Understorey foragers	Ground foragers	Wetland species	Cavity-nesting species	Introduced species
Caprimulgus europaeus	European nightjar	1				1						1	1			*			
Carduelis cannabina	Common linnet	1				*		1		1	1			1	*	1			
Carduelis carduelis	European goldfinch	1				1		1		1	1			1	1	1			
Carduelis flammea	Common redpoll	1				1		1		1	1			1	*	1			
Carduelis hornemanni	Arctic redpoll	1				1		1		1	1			1	*	1			
Carduelis spinus	Eurasian siskin	1	1			1	1	1		1	1		*	1	1	1			
Carpodacus erythrinus	Common rosefinch	1				1	1	1	1			1		1	1	1			
Certhia brachydactyla	Short-toed treecreeper	1				1				1				1				1	
Certhia familiaris	Eurasian treecreeper	1				1				1	*			1	1			1	

Scientific name	Common name															
Chloris chloris	European greenfinch	1		★		1			1		1	1		1	1	1
Chrysolophus amherstiae	Lady Amherst's pheasant	1	1	1	1	1	1		1			1		1	1	
Chrysolophus pictus	Golden pheasant	1		1	1	1	1		1							1
Ciconia nigra	Black stork	1	1	1	1	1	★		1						1	
Circaetus gallicus	Short-toed eagle	1	1	1	1				1			1	1			
Circus pygargus	Montagu's harrier	1	1	★	1	1			1		★	1	1			
Clamator glandarius	Great spotted cuckoo	1	1	1	1	1		★	1		1	1	1			
Coccothraustes coccothraustes	Hawfinch	1	1	1	1	1			1		1	1	1			
Colinus virginianus	Northern bobwhite	1	1	1	1	1			1							1
Coloeus monedula	Western jackdaw	1	★	1	1	1		1	1		★					1
Columba oenas	Stock dove	1		★	1	1	1	1	1		★			★		1
Columba palumbus	Common wood pigeon	1		★	1	1	1	1	1		1					
Columba trocaz	Trocaz pigeon	1		1	★	1	1		1		1					
Coracias garrulus	European roller	1		1	1	1		1	1							1
Corvus corax	Common raven	1	1	1	1	1	★		1		1					
Corvus corone	Carrion crow	1	1	1	1	1			1							
Corvus frugilegus	Rook	1	1	1	1	1	1		1		★					
Cuculus canorus	Common cuckoo	1		1	1	1		1	1		1		1		1	
Cuculus saturatus	Himalayan cuckoo	1	1	1	1	1		1	1		1		1		1	
Cyanistes caeruleus	Eurasian blue tit	1	1	1	1	1		1	1		1	1	1		1	1

(cont.)

(cont.)

SCIENTIFIC	ENGLISH	Forest birds	Forest specialists	Carnivorous species	Piscivorous species	Insectivorous species	Frugivorous species	Seed-/nut-eating species	Other plant food–eating species	Resident/sedentary species	Short-distance migrants	Long-distance migrants	Aerial foragers	Arboreal/canopy foragers	Understorey foragers	Ground foragers	Wetland species	Cavity-nesting species	Introduced species
Cyanistes cyanus	Azure tit	1				1	1	1		1				1	1	1		1	
Cyanopica cyanus	Azure-winged magpie	1		1		1	1	1		1				1	1	1			
Delichon urbicum	Common house martin	1				1						1	1	★		★			
Dendrocopos leucotos	White-backed woodpecker	1	1			1	1	1		1				1	1			1	
Dendrocopos major	Great spotted woodpecker	1		1		1	1	1		1				1	1			1	
Dendrocopos syriacus	Syrian woodpecker	1				1	1	1	1	1				1	1			1	
Dryobates minor	Lesser spotted woodpecker	1	1			1	★			1			★	1	1	★		1	
Dryocopus martius	Black woodpecker	1	1			1									1			1	
Egretta garzetta	Little egret	1		1	1							1					1		
Elanus caeruleus	Black-winged kite	1		1						1			1				1		

Scientific name	Common name												
Emberiza aureola	Yellow-breasted bunting	1		1						1			
Emberiza calandra	Corn bunting	1		1	1					1			
Emberiza cirlus	Cirl bunting	1		1	1					1			
Emberiza citrinella	Yellowhammer	1		1	1					1			
Emberiza hortulana	Ortolan bunting	1		1					1	1			
Emberiza leucocephalos	Pine bunting	1		1						1	1		
Emberiza melanocephala	Black-headed bunting	1		1						1	1		
Emberiza pusilla	Little bunting	1								1	1		
Emberiza rustica	Rustic bunting	1	1							1	1		
Emberiza schoeniclus	Common reed bunting	1		1						1	1	★	
Erithacus rubecula	European robin	★		1	1					1	1		
Estrilda astrild	Common waxbill	★		1	1					1	1		1
Falco columbarius	Merlin	1		1	★	1		1					
Falco peregrinus	Peregrine falcon	1		1	1	1		1					
Falco rusticolus	Gyr falcon	1		1	1	★		1					
Falco subbuteo	Eurasian hobby	1		1		1		1					
Falco tinnunculus	Common kestrel	1		1		1		1					
Falco vespertinus	Red-footed falcon	1		1		1		1					
Ficedula albicollis	Collared flycatcher	1	1	1		1		1		1	1		
Ficedula hypoleuca	European pied flycatcher	1	1	1		1		1		1	1		

(cont.)

SCIENTIFIC	ENGLISH	Forest birds	Forest specialists	Carnivorous species	Piscivorous species	Insectivorous species	Frugivorous species	Seed-/nut-eating species	Other plant food–eating species	Resident/sedentary species	Short-distance migrants	Long-distance migrants	Aerial foragers	Arboreal/canopy foragers	Understorey foragers	Ground foragers	Wetland species	Cavity-nesting species	Introduced species
Ficedula parva	Red-breasted flycatcher	1	1			1	*					1	*	1	1	*		1	
Ficedula semitorquata	Semicollared flycatcher	1	1			1						1	1	*	1	*		1	
Fringilla coelebs	Common chaffinch	1				1	1	1	1	1	1			1	1	1			
Fringilla montifringilla	Brambling	1				1	1	1			1			1	1	1			
Gallinago gallinago	Common snipe	1				1				1	1					1	1		
Garrulus glandarius	Eurasian jay	1		*		1		1		1	*			1	1	1			
Glaucidium passerinum	Eurasian pygmy owl	1	1	1						1			1	1	1	1		1	
Grus grus	Common crane	1		1	1	1	1	1	1	*	1					1	1		
Haliaeetus albicilla	White-tailed eagle	1		1	1		1			1	*		*	1	1	1	1		
Hippolais icterina	Icterine warbler	1				1	1					1		1	1	1	1		

Species	Common name	1	2	3	4	5	6	7	8	9	10	11
Hippolais olivetorum	Olive-tree warbler	1		★			1		1	1	1	
Hippolais polyglotta	Melodious warbler	1		★			1		1	1	1	
Hirundo rustica	Barn swallow	1			★	1	1	★	1	1	★	
Iduna caligata	Booted warbler	1				1	1	1	1	1	1	
Jynx torquilla	Eurasian wryneck	1		★	★	1	1	★	1	1	1	1
Lagopus lagopus	Willow grouse	1		1		★			1		1	
Lanius collurio	Red-backed shrike	1	1		1	1	1		1	1	1	
Lanius excubitor	Great grey shrike	1	1		1	1	1	1	1	1	1	
Lanius nubicus	Masked shrike	1	1			1	1	1				
Lanius senator	Woodchat shrike	1	★			1	1	1	1			
Leiopicus medius	Middle spotted woodpecker	1		★	1	1	1	1	1			1
Locustella fluviatilis	River warbler	1				1			1			
Locustella lanceolata	Lanceolated warbler	1				1		1	1		1	
Locustella naevia	Common grasshopper warbler	1				1	★	1	1		1	
Lophophanes cristatus	Crested tit	1		★	1	1			1		1	1
Loxia curvirostra	Common crossbill	1	1	1	1	1			1		1	
Loxia leucoptera	Two-barred crossbill	1	1	1	1	1			1		1	
Loxia pytyopsittacus	Parrot crossbill	1		1	1	1			1		1	
Loxia scotica	Scottish crossbill	1			1	1			1		1	

(cont.)

(cont.)

SCIENTIFIC	ENGLISH	Forest birds	Forest specialists	Carnivorous species	Piscivorous species	Insectivorous species	Frugivorous species	Seed-/nut-eating species	Other plant food–eating species	Resident/sedentary species	Short-distance migrants	Long-distance migrants	Aerial foragers	Arboreal/canopy foragers	Understorey foragers	Ground foragers	Wetland species	Cavity-nesting species	Introduced species
Lullula arborea	Wood lark	1				1	1	1		1	1		★	★		1			
Luscinia luscinia	Thrush nightingale	1				1	1					1			1	1			
Luscinia megarhynchos	Common nightingale	1				1	1					1	★		1	1			
Luscinia svecica	Bluethroat	1				★	1	1			1	1	★			1			
Lyrurus mlokosiewiczi	Caucasian grouse	1					1	1	1	1				1	★	1			
Lyrurus tetrix	Black grouse	1				★	1		1	1	1			1	1	1			
Meleagris gallopavo	Wild turkey	1							1	1	1			1	1	1			1
Mergellus albellus	Smew	1			1	1					1						1	1	
Mergus merganser	Goosander	1			1						1						1	1	
Merops apiaster	European bee-eater	1				1						1	1						
Milvus migrans	Black kite	1		1	1						1	1	1				1		
Milvus milvus	Red kite	1		1	1					★	1	1	1	★					
Motacilla alba	White wagtail	1				1					1	1	1	1	1	1	1		
Motacilla flava	Yellow wagtail	1				1					1	1	1		1	1	★		

Scientific name	Common name													
Muscicapa striata	Spotted flycatcher	1	1	1	1	1	1	1	1	1	1			
Myicpsitta monachus	Monk parakeet	1	1	1	1	1	1	1	1	1	1	1	1	1
Nucifraga caryocatactes	Spotted nutcracker	1	★	1	1	1	1	★						
Numenius phaeopus	Whimbrel	1	1	1	1	1	★	1	1					
Nycticorax nycticorax	Black-crowned night heron	1	★	1	1	1	★	1	1	1				
Oenanthe hispanica	Black-eared wheatear	1	★	1	1	1	1							
Oenanthe oenanthe	Northern wheatear	1	1	1	1	1	1	1						
Oenanthe pleschanka	Pied wheatear	1	1	1	★	1	1	★	1					
Oriolus oriolus	Eurasian golden oriole	1	1	1	1	1	1	★						
Otus scops	European scops owl	1	★	1	★	★	1	★	1	★	1			
Pandion haliaetus	Osprey	1	1	★	1	1								
Parus major	Great tit	1	1	1	1	1	1	1						
Passer hispaniolensis	Spanish sparrow	1	1	1	1	1	1	1	1					
Passer montanus	Eurasian tree sparrow	1	1	1	1	1	1							
Periparus ater	Coal tit	1	1	1	1	1	1	1	1					
Perisoreus infaustus	Siberian jay	1	1	★	★	1	1	1	★	1	1	1		

(cont.)

(cont.)

SCIENTIFIC	ENGLISH	Forest birds	Forest specialists	Carnivorous species	Piscivorous species	Insectivorous species	Frugivorous species	Seed-/nut-eating species	Other plant food-eating species	Resident/sedentary species	Short-distance migrants	Long-distance migrants	Aerial foragers	Arboreal/canopy foragers	Understorey foragers	Ground foragers	Wetland species	Cavity-nesting species	Introduced species
Pernis apivorus	European honey buzzard	1	1	1		1	★					1				1			
Phalacrocorax carbo	Great cormorant	1		1	1					1	1						1		
Phalacrocorax pygmeus	Pygmy cormorant	1		1	1	★				1	1						1		
Phasianus colchicus	Common pheasant	1		★		1	1	1	1	1				★	★				1
Phoenicurus phoenicurus	Common redstart	1				1	1					1		1	1			1	
Phylloscopus bonelli	Western Bonelli's warbler	1	1			1						1		1	1				
Phylloscopus borealis	Arctic warbler	1				1	1			★		1	★	1	1	★			
Phylloscopus collybita	Chiffchaff	1	1			1	1		★	1		1		1	1				

Genus/species	Common name											
Phylloscopus inornatus	Yellow-browed warbler		1				1		1	1	1	1
Phyllcscopus lorenzii	Caucasian mountain chiffchaff		1				1		1	1	1	1
Phyllcscopus nitidus	Green warbler		1				1				1	
Phyllcscopus orientalis	Eastern Bonelli's warbler		1				1		1	1	1	
Phylloscopus sibiatrix	Wood warbler		1				1	1	1	1	1	
Phylloscopus trocailoides	Greenish warbler		1				1		1	1	1	
Phylloscopus trochilus	Willow warbler		1				1		1	1	1	
Pica pica	Common magpie	1	1	1			1		1		1	
Picoides tridactylus	Three-toed woodpecker	1	1	★			1		1		1	1
Picus canus	Grey-headed woodpecker	★	1			★	1		1		1	1
Picus viridis	European green woodpecker	1	★			1	1		1		1	1
Pinicola enucleator	Pine grosbeak	1	1	1	★	1	1		1		1	1
Platalea leucorodia	Eurasian spoonbill	1	1	1	★	★	1		1		1	
Plegadis falcinellus	Glossy ibis	★	1	★		1	1		1		★	1
Poecile cinctus	Siberian tit	1	1			1	1		1		1	1
Poecile lugubris	Sombre tit	1	1			1	1		1		1	1
Poecile montanus	Willow tit	1	1			1	1		1		1	1
Poecile palustris	Marsh tit	1	1			1	1		1		1	1 *(cont.)*

(cont.)

SCIENTIFIC	ENGLISH	Forest birds	Forest specialists	Carnivorous species	Piscivorous species	Insectivorous species	Frugivorous species	Seed-/nut-eating species	Other plant food–eating species	Resident/sedentary species	Short-distance migrants	Long-distance migrants	Aerial foragers	Arboreal/canopy foragers	Understorey foragers	Ground foragers	Wetland species	Cavity-nesting species	Introduced species
Prunella atrogularis	Black-throated accentor	1				1		★				1				1			
Prunella modularis	Dunnock	1				1		1		1	1				1	1			
Prunella montanella	Siberian accentor	1				1		1		1				1		1			
Psittacula krameri	Rose-ringed parakeet	1					1	1	1	1				1		1		1	1
Pryonoprogne rupestris	Eurasian crag martin	1				1				1	1	★	1			★			
Pyrrhula murina	Azores bullfinch	1				1	1	1	1	1				1	1				
Pyrrhula pyrrhula	Eurasian bullfinch	1				1	1	1	1	1	1			1	1				
Regulus ignicapilla	Firecrest	1	1			1				1	1			1		★			
Regulus regulus	Goldcrest	1	1			1				1				1	1				
Riparia riparia	Sand martin	1				1						1	1			★			
Saxicola maurus	Eastern stonechat	1				1				1	1	1		1	1	1			

Scientific name	Common name												
Saxicola rubetra	Whinchat	1	1			★		1		1		1	1	1
Scolopax rusticola	Eurasian woodcock	1	1		1		1	1		1		1	1	1
Serinus canaria	Atlantic canary	1	★	1			1	1		★		1	1	1
Serinus citrinella	Citril finch	1	1	★	1		1	1	1	1		1	★	1
Serinus serinus	European serin	1	★	1	1		1	1	1	1		1	1	1
Sitta europaea	Eurasian nuthatch	1	1	1	1	★	1	1		1		1	1	1
Sitta krueperi	Krüper's nuthatch	1	1	1	1	★	1	1		1	1	1	1	1
Sitta whiteheadi	Corsican nuthatch	1	1	1	1	★	1	1		1	1	1	1	1
Streptopelia decaocto	Eurasian collared dove	★	1	1	★		1	1		1		★	1	1
Streptopelia turtur	European turtle dove	1	1	1	1		1	1		★		★	1	1
Strix aluco	Tawny owl	1	1		1		1	1		1	1	★		1
Strix nebulosa	Great grey owl		1	1	1		1	1		★	★	★	★	1
Strix uralensis	Ural owl		1	1	1		1	1						1
Sturnus unicolor	Spotless starling	1	1		1	★	1	1		1		1	1	1
Sturnus vulgaris	Common starling	1	1		1	1	1	1	★	★		1	1	1
Surnia ulula	Northern hawk owl	1	1	1	1	★	1	1	1	1	1	★	1	1
Sylvia atricapilla	Blackcap	1	1		1		1	1		1		1	1	1
Sylvia borin	Garden warbler	1	1		1		1	1		1		1	1	1
Sylvia cantillans	Subalpine warbler	1	1		1		1	1		1		1	★	
Sylvia communis	Common whitethroat	1	1		1		1	1		1		1	1	
Sylvia conspicillata	Spectacled warbler	1	1		1		1	1		1		1	1	1
Sylvia crassirostris	Eastern Orphean warbler	1	1				1	1		1		1	1	
Sylvia curruca	Lesser whitethroat	1			★		1	1		1		1	1	1

(cont.)

(cont.)

SCIENTIFIC	ENGLISH	Forest birds	Forest specialists	Carnivorous species	Piscivorous species	Insectivorous species	Frugivorous species	Seed-/nut-eating species	Other plant food–eating species	Resident/sedentary species	Short-distance migrants	Long-distance migrants	Aerial foragers	Arboreal/canopy foragers	Understorey foragers	Ground foragers	Wetland species	Cavity-nesting species	Introduced species
Sylvia hortensis	Western Orphean warbler	1				1	1					1		1	1				
Sylvia melanocephala	Sardinian warbler	1				1	1			1	1			1	1	1			
Sylvia mystacea	Ménétries's warbler	1	1			1	1	1				1		1	1	★			
Sylvia nisoria	Barred warbler	1	1			1	1					1		1	1				
Sylvia ruppeli	Rüppell's warbler	1				1	★					1		1	1				
Sylvia undata	Dartford warbler	1				1	★			1	1			1	1				
Symaticus reevesii	Reeves's pheasant	1	1			1	1	1	1	1				★	1	1			
Tarsiger cyanurus	Red-flanked bluetail	1	1			1	1	1	1	1	1	1		★	1	1			
Tetrao urogallus	Western capercaillie	1	1			1	1	1	1	1	★			1	1	1			
Tetrastes bonasia	Hazel grouse	1	1			1	1	1	★	1				1	1	1			1
Tringa erythropus	Spotted redshank	1				1		1	★		★	1					1		
Tringa glareola	Wood sandpiper	1				1		1			★	1	1				1		
Tringa nebularia	Common greenshank	1			1						★	1	1			1	1		

Species	Common name								
Tringa ochropus	Green sandpiper	1	1		1		1	1	1
Troglodytes troglodytes	Eurasian wren	1		1	1		1	1	1
Turdus atrogularis	Black-throated thrush	1	1	1	★		1	1	1
Turdus iliacus	Redwing	1	1	1	★	1	1	1	
Turdus merula	Common blackbird	1	★	1	1	1	★	1	1
Turdus philomelos	Song thrush	1	1	1	1	1	1	1	
Turdus pilaris	Fieldfare	1	★	1	1	★	1	1	
Turdus torquatus	Ring ouzel	1	1	1	1	1	1	1	
Turdus viscivorus	Mistle thrush	1	1	1	1	★	1	1	
Turnix sylvaticus	Small button-quail	1	1				1	1	1
Upupa epops	Eurasian hoopoe	1	1	1	1	1	1		
Xenus cinereus	Terek sandpiper	1	1	1			1	1	
Zoothera dauma	Scaly thrush	1	1	1			1	1	

Appendix 5.2

Classification of species by different ecological guilds. To qualify for a guild, a species must show relevant regular or seasonal behaviour.

Ecological guild	Classification base
Carnivorous species	Species that eat vertebrates
Piscivorous species	Fish-eating species
Insectivorous species	Species with invertebrates in their diet
Frugivorous species	Species that eat fruits
Seed-/nut-eating species	Species that eat seeds and/or nuts
Other plant food–eating species	Species that eat other types of food originating from plants (leaves, roots, catkins, buds, flowers, sap)
Resident/sedentary species	Species resident in the majority of their European range
Short-distance migrants	Species that in the majority of their European breeding range undertake seasonal migrations within the continent (including all Mediterranean regions)
Long-distance migrants	Species that in the majority of their European breeding range undertake long-distance seasonal migrations to wintering grounds outside of Europe or Mediterranean (tropical migrants)
Aerial foragers	Species that regularly forage in the air
Arboreal/canopy foragers	Species that regularly forage in the tree canopies or other parts of the trees above the ground
Understorey foragers	Species that regularly forage in the shrub or field layer
Ground foragers	Species that regularly forage on the ground
Wetland species	Species linked to wetland environments
Cavity nesters	Species that nest in cavities
Introduced species	Non-native species introduced by humans

6 · Boreal Forest Bird Assemblages and Their Conservation

JEAN-MICHEL ROBERGE, RAIMO
VIRKKALA AND MIKKO MÖNKKÖNEN

6.1 Introduction

The boreal biome encompasses 27% of the world's forests (Hansen *et al.* 2010). In Europe, boreal forests stretch in a west-east direction from Norway to the Ural Mountains in Russia, with a varying latitudinal extent within the range ~57°–69°N (Olson *et al.* 2001) (Fig. 5.1 in Chapter 5). The boreal region meets the temperate forest to the south (see Chapter 8 for an account of the temperate zone). The transition zone between the boreal and temperate regions, called the hemiboreal (or sometimes boreonemoral) zone, is characterised by a mixture of boreal and temperate elements (Nilsson 1997). In the present chapter, we focus mostly on the truly boreal forest located north of that transition zone, simply noting that many ecological patterns and conservation issues are shared with the hemiboreal zone. To the north and at high altitudes, the boreal forest meets the tundra. In this chapter, we will briefly cover some of the aspects of the northern European subalpine forests, which differ in many respects from subalpine ecosystems found at more southerly latitudes (e.g., in the Alps, Pyrenees and Carpathians; Chapter 7).

There is a relatively long history of avian ecological research in the boreal biome. Renowned ornithologists such as Sven Nilsson (1787–1883), Einari Merikallio (1888–1961), Boris Stegmann (1898–1975), Pontus Palmgren (1907–1993) and Svein Haftorn (1925–2003) all performed at least part of their classical works in the boreal region. There is also a long tradition of bird surveys in that biome, dating as far back as the 1930s in Finland (e.g., Palmgren 1930). Knowledge in boreal avian ecology developed gradually mostly during the 20th century and especially after World War II. Nearly three decades ago, Haila and Järvinen (1990) summarised much of that knowledge in their account of the composition and ecology of bird assemblages in northern coniferous forests. Conservation aspects became increasingly present in avian ecology research mostly from the 1980s–1990s, paralleling increasing concerns about the loss and fragmentation of old-growth forest due to industrial logging (Virkkala 1987a; Andrén 1994; Robinson *et al.* 1995). The research field continues to be very dynamic, spurred by recent advances in ecological theory and conservation biology as well as the recognition of threats arising from climate change and new forest management measures. In this chapter, we aim to synthesise accumulated knowledge about the ecology and conservation of boreal forest birds, with a special focus on Europe.

6.2 Boreal Forest Ecosystems

6.2.1 Natural Characteristics

The boreal biome is characterised by a relatively cold climate, large differences between summer and winter temperatures, and a persistent snow cover in winter. However, there are clear variations in climate at larger scales within the region. In boreal Europe, there is a gradient from a maritime climate in Norway to an increasingly continental climate eastwards into Russia (Tuhkanen 1980), as well as a latitudinal and altitudinal gradient from the south boreal zone to the north boreal zone (Moen 1999). Most of the area currently occupied by boreal forest in Europe was glaciated several times during the Pleistocene. The latest glacial period ended approximately 10,000 years ago, after which species gradually (re)colonised the region. As a consequence, boreal species assemblages can be considered relatively 'young' from a geological time perspective.

Depending on the location, boreal landscapes are naturally characterised by forest interspersed with various proportions of mires and other wetlands, water bodies and watercourses, as well as rocky outcrops. Naturally dynamic boreal forest ecosystems are shaped by a range of disturbances varying in size, severity and frequency, including fire, flooding, windthrow, snowbreak, avalanches, erosion, fungal diseases, outbreaks of defoliating and cambium-feeding insects, ungulate browsing and the actions of beaver (*Castor fiber* in Eurasia) (Esseen *et al.* 1997; Kuuluvainen 2002). Fire has historically been a major large-scale disturbance agent, especially on drier sites (Zackrisson 1977).

In terms of tree species composition, boreal forest landscapes are dominated by conifers with varying proportions of broadleaved deciduous trees, the latter (hereafter called deciduous trees) being most abundant in earlier stages of succession after disturbance. Compared to more southerly latitudes, forests in the boreal biome are home to relatively few tree species. In boreal Europe, the two main conifers are Scots pine *Pinus sylvestris* and Norway spruce *Picea abies*. The deciduous trees are silver birch *Betula pendula*, downy birch *Betula pubescens*, European aspen *Populus tremula*, rowan *Sorbus aucuparia*, grey alder *Alnus incana* and willows *Salix* spp. In high-altitude parts of Scandinavia, mountain birch *Betula pubescens* var. *czerepanovii* often dominates at the treeline, forming a subalpine belt of varying width separating the conifer-dominated boreal forest and the alpine tundra. In addition to the tree species above, some species with chiefly Siberian distributions appear in the eastern parts of European Russia close to the Ural Mountains (e.g., *Larix sibirica, Pinus sibirica, Abies sibirica*). Depending on site type and successional stage, understorey vegetation can be dominated by ericaceous shrubs and dwarf shrubs (e.g., *Vaccinium* spp., *Calluna vulgaris, Empetrum nigrum, Rhododendron tomentosum*), with varying cover of small trees and herbs. The forest floor is typically covered with mosses, lichens (mostly *Cladonia* spp.) or grasses.

The main factors influencing the local characteristics of natural boreal forests are (a) biogeographical patterns partly driven by climatic gradients, (b) the status of the soil's nutrient and moisture and their effects on tree growth and natural disturbances and (c) time since disturbance. According to Angelstam (1998), three main broad types of boreal forest can be defined based on natural disturbance regimes in northern Europe: (1) Norway spruce–dominated forest on wet and moist soils, characterised by internal gap dynamics and often forming more or less narrow elements in the landscape along depressions and water courses; (2) successional forest following stand-replacing disturbance (commonly on mesic soils), characterised by a gradual change from open conditions to closed forest and from more deciduous trees and pine shortly after disturbance to more Norway spruce after several decades; and (3) Scots pine–dominated forest on drier sites subjected to frequent low-intensity fires, with different cohorts of trees having survived past fire events (Fig. 6.1). Simulations suggest that old-growth forests dominated the natural landscapes of northern Europe under a wide range of fire frequencies (Pennanen 2002).

(a)

(b)

(c)

Figure 6.1 Three main types of naturally dynamic forests in boreal Europe.
(a) Norway spruce–dominated forest with internal gap dynamics (Kostomuksha
Nature Reserve, Russia); (b) birch-dominated successional forest following a stand-
replacing disturbance (Småland, Sweden); (c) Scots pine–dominated forest with
multiple tree cohorts and signs of past fire events (Kostomuksha Nature Reserve,
Russia). Photos: J.-M. Roberge.

6.2.2 Anthropogenic Impacts on the Forest

From a global perspective, the boreal biome is characterised by low human population density and a relatively low level of anthropogenic impact (Gauthier *et al.* 2015). Contrary to the temperate biome, only a minor proportion of the boreal forest has been converted to farmland. In boreal Europe, this has mostly occurred in the more fertile and accessible lowland areas along the seacoasts, near large lakes and in river valleys. Large parts of the European boreal forest have been influenced by a long history of shifting slash-and-burn agriculture (Myllyntaus *et al.* 2002) stretching into the early 20th century – with lasting local influences on the forest's structure and composition – as well as by reindeer husbandry. Most importantly, the largest part of the European boreal forest has been subjected to some form of logging or management for wood production (Bryant *et al.* 1997). In Fennoscandia, the history of logging is relatively long compared to other parts of the boreal biome. Already in the 17th to 19th centuries, forests were logged for charcoal production to supply the mining industry, and potash and tar production had large impacts on forests in some regions (Esseen *et al.* 1997; Östlund & Roturier 2011). Extensive logging for saw timber – typically diameter-limit cutting targeting the largest trees – increased mostly from the 19th century, spreading gradually from the south into the north and inland of Fennoscandia (Imbeau *et al.* 2001). Since the 1950s, even-aged forest management involving clearfelling and thinning has dominated. Forest management has aimed to control the forest for maximised economic output in terms of timber, wood fibre and biomass production. This has clearly affected the characteristics of the forest, and even resulted in the creation of some stand types not found in naturally dynamic forests. Young stands composed purely of Norway spruce and stands of the introduced lodgepole pine *Pinus contorta* constitute good examples of such artificial forest types in northern Europe. In Russia, the silvicultural management of forests has thus far been less intensive than in the Nordic countries (Elbakidze *et al.* 2013), although logging has affected most parts of the Russian boreal forest (Potapov *et al.* 2008; Gauthier *et al.* 2015). Moreover, forest fires have been suppressed very successfully in the Nordic countries since the later 19th century (Zackrisson 1977), whereas they still are a relatively common disturbance agent in Russia.

In today's boreal Europe, most of the naturally productive forest area is under management for timber production, while areas of low productivity are typically less affected by forestry. In Sweden, for example, forest areas with an annual tree volume growth ≤ 1 m^3ha^{-1} (mostly situated in the mountain regions, but also in wet and rocky lowland areas) are exempt from industrial logging by law. At a larger scale, there are still some relatively intact forest landscapes in the boreal region, unlike the situation in most of temperate Europe. However, these landscapes are confined to the northern parts of European Russia (Potapov *et al.* 2008) as well as to areas along the Finnish-Russian border and the Fennoscandian and Ural mountain ranges. The subalpine mountain birch forest of Fennoscandia has been largely exempt from industrial logging, although it has been influenced by low-intensity cutting for fuelwood.

In addition to industrial forest management, today's boreal forest ecosystems are subjected to a range of other anthropogenic impacts, including climate change, infrastructure development (e.g., roads, power facilities, buildings, mines) and recreational use. Their effects on boreal bird assemblages are described in Section 6.4.

6.3 Boreal Forest Bird Assemblages

6.3.1 Taxonomic Composition

Birds are the richest vertebrate taxonomic group in boreal forests, comprising 75% of all terrestrial vertebrate species in that biome (Mönkkönen & Viro 1997). A total of 160 forest bird species have breeding distribution ranges at least partly overlapping the European boreal zone. Taxonomically and ecologically, current bird assemblages consist of different elements reflecting the deep evolutionary history. The most common species in European boreal forests are habitat generalists with large European or Palearctic distributions, such as the common chaffinch *Fringilla coelebs*, willow warbler *Phylloscopus trochilus*, European robin *Erithacus rubecula*, tree pipit *Anthus trivialis* and spotted flycatcher *Muscicapa striata*. Yet, some typical taiga or northerly distributed species, such as the redwing *Turdus iliacus* and brambling *Fringilla montifringilla*, may locally constitute a large component of the assemblages. Most of the common boreal forest species are facultative forest species (cf. Chapter 5 for definition) which can breed in many other types of habitats than proper forest, e.g., gardens, hedgerows and wetlands with dispersed trees. On the other hand, 36 of Europe's 160 boreal bird species are forest specialists (cf. Chapter 5). Examples of relatively common and widespread forest specialists include the Eurasian siskin *Carduelis spinus*, goldcrest *Regulus regulus* and willow tit *Poecile montanus*. The boreal zone is home to 20 bird species which do not regularly breed in other biomes in Europe (Table 6.1; Fig. 6.2).

Table 6.1 *Forest bird species whose breeding ranges are normally restricted to the boreal zone in Europe.*

Resident species
Northern hawk owl[a] (*Surnia ulula*)
Siberian jay (*Perisoreus infaustus*)
Siberian tit (*Poecile cinctus*)
Pine grosbeak[a] (*Pinicola enucleator*)
Two-barred crossbill[a] (*Loxia leucoptera*)

Migrants occurring outside the boreal zone in winter
Smew (*Mergellus albellus*)
Himalayan cuckoo[b] (*Cuculus saturatus*)
Olive-backed pipit[b] (*Anthus hodgsoni*)
Bohemian waxwing (*Bombycilla garrulus*)
Black-throated accentor[b] (*Prunella atrogularis*)

Red-flanked bluetail (*Tarsiger cyanurus*)
Eastern stonechat (*Saxicola maurus*)

Scaly thrush[b] (*Zoothera dauma*)
Black-throated thrush[b] (*Turdus atrogularis*)
Lanceolated warbler[b] (*Locustella lanceolata*)
Yellow-browed warbler[b] (*Phylloscopus inornatus*)
Arctic warbler (*Phylloscopus borealis*)
Brambling (*Fringilla montifringilla*)
Rustic bunting (*Emberiza rustica*)
Little bunting (*Emberiza pusilla*)

---

[a] Mostly resident, but sometimes irrupts out of its usual range, which may lead to occasional breeding south of the boreal zone.
[b] Species whose European range is restricted to the eastern parts of European Russia.

Mönkkönen and Viro (1997) provided an overview of the taxonomic richness and composition of the avifauna across the Northern Hemisphere. Here we provide a summary of those results specifically for the boreal zone. Overall taxonomic diversity of boreal birds is lowest in the Western Palearctic (i.e., Europe in the case of boreal birds) and highest in the Eastern Palearctic region, with the Nearctic lying in between. In terms of taxonomic composition, the most remarkable difference between the regions is the higher degree of family-level endemism in the Nearctic. Nearctic bird assemblages are characterised by families such as Parulids (new-world warblers), Icterids (blackbirds), Thraupids (tanagers) and Cardinalids (grosbeaks) that do not occur in the Palearctic region. By contrast, only Prunellids (accentors) can be

Figure 6.2 The northern hawk owl (*Surnia ulula*) is a typical boreal bird species, although it occasionally makes irruptions farther south into the hemiboreal zone. Photo: J.-M. Roberge.

considered endemic to the Palearctic. It is striking that the interchange of taxa between the Nearctic and Palearctic regions has been rather asymmetric, many more Palearctic taxa having colonised the Nearctic than vice versa (Mayr 1990).

In spite of those differences, there are pronounced taxonomic similarities between the Palearctic and Nearctic regions. Taxonomic similarity increases towards the north; the avifauna of the boreal biome is taxonomically more uniform than that of the southern temperate biome. When comparing the avifaunas of Europe, eastern Asia, western North America and eastern North America as a whole, Mönkkönen and Viro (1997) found that among all bird taxa, 70% of the species and half of the genera are endemic, i.e., confined to only one of these regions. By comparison, in the boreal zone, less than half of the species and about one-quarter of genera occur in one region only. In European boreal forests, the proportion of endemic species (species confined to Europe or the Western Palearctic) is 28%, while 51% are also found in the Eastern Palearctic but not the Nearctic and 21% have a Holarctic distribution. At the genus level, the respective proportions are 5%, 46% and 49%. European endemics include, for example, the European crested tit *Lophophanes cristatus*, Eurasian blue tit *Cyanistes caeruleus*, dunnock

Prunella modularis and parrot crossbill *Loxia pytyopsittacus*. Examples of Holarctic species occurring in both the Nearctic and Palearctic boreal regions are the pine grosbeak *Pinicola enucleator*, two-barred crossbill *Loxia leucoptera*, Bohemian waxwing *Bombycilla garrulus*, northern goshawk *Accipiter gentilis* and five owl species (northern hawk owl *Surnia ulula*, great grey owl *Strix nebulosa*, long-eared owl *Asio otus*, short-eared owl *Asio flammeus* and Tengmalm's owl *Aegolius funereus*). Moreover, some common genera are represented by species with very similar ecologies in the two regions (e.g., black woodpecker *Dryocopus martius* and pileated woodpecker *D. pileatus*, as well as Eurasian treecreeper *Certhia familiaris* and brown creeper *C. americana* in the Palearctic and the Nearctic, respectively).

6.3.2 Large-scale Diversity Patterns

There is ample evidence for a global trend of decreasing species diversity towards higher latitudes, but exceptions also exist. Mönkkönen (1994) compared species diversity patterns in bird assemblages at different spatial scales in Europe and North America. This study did not unequivocally support the general latitudinal pattern of decreased species richness towards the north. On both continents, the largest regional species pools coincide with the areas where coniferous (boreal) forests meet deciduous (southern temperate) forests, i.e., the hemiboreal zone and regions with high altitudinal variation. Hence, habitat diversity is most likely the main driver underlying these large-scale regional patterns in forest bird species richness.

Interestingly, in boreal Fennoscandia there is an increase in regional species richness towards the east (cf. Fig. 5.2 in Chapter 5). The eastern parts of Fennoscandia (eastern Finland, western Russia) foster 10–20% more species than regions at the same latitude farther west (Sweden, Norway) (Mönkkönen 1994). This pattern is partially a consequence of many easterly distributed migrant species having distribution ranges that do not normally reach western Fennoscandia (e.g., red-flanked bluetail *Tarsiger cyanurus*, booted warbler *Iduna caligata*, greenish warbler *Phylloscopus trochiloides*, Blyth's reed warbler *Acrocephalus dumetorum*) (cf. Fig. 5.8 in Chapter 5). No boreal forest bird species is restricted to the western parts of Fennoscandia. There is a continent-wide pattern of increased species richness of tropical migrants towards the east, their richness peaking in eastern Siberia (Greenberg *et al.* 2008).

6.3.3 Seasonal Dynamics

A key characteristic of boreal bird assemblages is strong seasonal fluctuations, as many bird species that breed in the north migrate to spend the winter at lower latitudes. Thus, boreal forest bird assemblages show drastic annual dynamics: there is a striking contrast between the deafening early summer songbird concert and the tranquillity of the long boreal winter.

A wide spectrum of migratory habits typifies the boreal avifauna, with striking differences between continents. In Nearctic boreal forests, long-distance migrants (species that winter in the tropics) comprise 50% of the breeding species, followed by short-distance migrants (species that winter in temperate areas) at 30% and permanent residents at 20%. Among birds of European boreal forests, long-distance migrants (34%), short-distance migrants (35%) and residents (31%) comprise almost an equal share of all forest bird species. This intercontinental difference in the composition of bird assemblages likely stems from the Pleistocene history of forests and current climate (Mönkkönen & Welsh 1994). See Chapter 2 for a detailed account of the evolutionary background to these patterns.

If one accounts for abundance patterns, the broad picture about migratory habits changes substantially. Indeed, in the boreal regions of both the Palearctic and Nearctic, permanently resident species are disproportionately rare and migrants comprise ~90% of all breeding individuals (Mönkkönen & Forsman 2005; Greenberg *et al.* 2008). Further, this overall avifaunal composition changes dramatically if one considers only forest specialists. Among forest specialists in boreal regions (cf. Chapter 5), a large majority of bird species (69% in Finland) and breeding pairs (60%) are residents, and relatively few are long-distance migrants (17% of species, 5% of breeding pairs). Thus, in boreal Europe, forest specialists tend to be residents, whereas forest generalists are predominantly migrants wintering outside boreal forests. From a conservation perspective, this means that conservation actions in European boreal forests should pay particular attention to resident birds for which these forests constitute their only habitat.

The distribution of migratory strategies also varies across habitats in boreal forests. Once again, intercontinental differences are evident (Mönkkönen & Helle 1989; Böhning-Gaese 2005). In Europe, long-distance migrants are disproportionately common in early successional habitats (open, semi-open and shrubby habitats), while residents and short-distance migrants are overrepresented in late successional, more conifer-dominated habitats, where together they comprise on average

75% of the breeding pairs. This is in contrast to the boreal parts of the Nearctic, where long-distance migrants typically comprise some 50% – and locally up to 90% – of breeding pairs in mature boreal forests (Mönkkönen & Forsman 2005). Nevertheless, Imbeau *et al.* (2001) showed that tropical migrants commonly found in eastern Canadian boreal forests are usually not categorised as mature forest-interior specialists, but rather contain many species that use forest edges and other shrubby habitats. Consequently, tropical migrants can be a dominating group also in early successional forests.

Böhning-Gaese (2005) argued that macroecological evidence strongly supports the tropical origin of long-distance migrants. The difference in long-distance migrants' habitat preferences across continents likely stems from niche conservatism (Losos 2008). The current habitat preferences of the species reflect their habitat associations in their evolutionary past and, hence, historical habitat availability in their ancestral biomes. Stretching back to the Pliocene (2–5 Mya), forest cover has been at least twice as large in the Neotropics as in the Afrotropics (Böhning-Gaese & Oberrath 2003). Thus, the strong association of many European tropical migrants with open and shrubby habitat likely originates from the long-term dominance of such habitats in the Afrotropics. It is intriguing to realise how deep history in the tropical regions has modified the avifaunal composition of present-day high-latitude forests. For further discussion of these concepts, see Chapter 2.

6.3.4 Long-term Variation, Range Shifts and Interannual Dynamics

From a historical perspective, boreal bird assemblages have not been static. Järvinen and Ulfstrand (1980) studied species turnover in the avifauna of northern Europe between 1850 and 1970. Using faunistic information, they showed that Denmark, Norway, Sweden and Finland experienced more colonisations than extinctions of species, resulting in a net increase in total species richness. Each of these countries gained on average 2.8 species and lost 0.6 species per decade from 1850–1970.

Among boreal forest birds, about 15 species colonised either Finland, Sweden or Norway during the late 19th and 20th centuries. Most colonisations involved easterly distributed species expanding their range westwards into Fennoscandia (probably recolonising the region after the latest glaciations). For example, the greenish warbler, red-breasted flycatcher *Ficedula parva* and little bunting *Emberiza pusilla* started breeding in Sweden during the 20th century a few decades after colonising

Finland. Likewise, many species that already bred in the eastern parts of Fennoscandia prior to 1850 expanded further west, such as the common rosefinch *Carpodacus erythrinus* and the rustic bunting *Emberiza rustica*, which colonised Norway during the second half of the 20th century. More recently, several species have exhibited northward range shifts, most probably as a response to climate warming (Brommer *et al.* 2012; see Section 6.4.2). Examples of forest birds displaying striking northward expansion in the boreal zone during recent decades are Eurasian blue tit, European greenfinch *Chloris chloris* and the *europaea* subspecies of the Eurasian nuthatch *Sitta europaea* in Sweden and Norway. In spite of a number of population declines and range changes, we are not aware of any national-scale extinction event among boreal forest birds during modern times in Norway, Sweden, Finland or Russia.

At the level of interannual dynamics, northern animal populations are considered less stable than southern ones. Mönkkönen and Aspi (1998) tested the hypothesis that year-to-year variation in local bird assemblages increases towards the north. They found a positive correlation between latitude and annual assemblage variability. However, this increase seemed not to be linear. Variability among years in total bird abundance was high in the very north of the boreal zone (from 64°N and upwards). In contrast, variability in southern boreal assemblages seemed to be relatively low and at a similar level as in assemblages south of the boreal zone. Järvinen (1979) suggested that the main cause underlying the latitudinal difference in interannual variability is increased climatic unpredictability at northern latitudes. Extreme weather during the breeding season may influence reproductive success, and harsh winter conditions can result in very high mortality in small-bodied species such as the goldcrest and the Eurasian treecreeper (Svensson *et al.* 1999).

Another factor of importance which may or may not be related to climatic variations is fluctuations in food availability. For example, small rodent populations exhibit wider interannual fluctuations in the northern parts of boreal zones than in more southern regions (Hansson & Henttonen 1988), with clear influence on year-to-year variation in breeding performance and density of vole-feeding birds (e.g., many owls, the rough-legged buzzard *Buteo lagopus* and the common kestrel *Falco tinnunculus*). Southerly irruptions of owls during winter have been linked to small rodent population cycles in both Europe and North America (Cheveau *et al.* 2004). Moreover, several northern boreal bird species that feed on seeds (e.g., crossbills *Loxia* spp., Eurasian siskin, common redpoll *Carduelis flammea*) display strong year-to-year fluctuations and irruptive behaviour as a response to variations in tree seed crops (Bock & Lepthien 1976; Virkkala 1991), as do some berry-eating species, such as waxwing and bullfinch *Pyrrhula pyrrhula* (e.g., Fox *et al.* 2009). In mountain birch forest, the density of the brambling has been shown to increase strongly during outbreaks of the geometrid moth *Epirrita autumnata*, which occur at intervals of approximately 10 years (Enemar *et al.* 2004; Hogstad 2005). However, in contrast to the clear effects of increased food abundance during the outbreaks, the mass death of the trees occurring within a few years after the outbreak seems to have rather limited effects on the bird assemblages of mountain birch forest (Vindstad *et al.* 2015).

6.3.5 Fine-scale Variation in Bird Assemblages in Relation to Forest Characteristics

For local bird assemblages in European boreal forests, a typical species-abundance distribution is one characterised by two to five dominant species comprising about half of the pairs and most other species represented by only few pairs (Haila & Järvinen 1990; Hogstad 2013). Although knowledge about the habitat requirements of boreal birds is relatively good, little published data are available about absolute breeding densities for whole avian assemblages in different boreal forest types. This is due to the paucity of boreal studies making use of territory mapping with multiple visits. These few studies suggest widely varying bird densities, depending on broad geographical location and local forest characteristics (Table 6.2). At the scale of individual forest stands or patches within landscapes, the structure of bird assemblages is affected by a range of local-scale environmental variables. Among these, two general characteristics of the tree-layer vegetation are particularly important: tree species composition and forest age.

Tree species composition is mainly influenced by site-specific abiotic conditions in terms of nutrients and water, as well as the disturbance regimes (cf. Section 6.2.1 and Angelstam *et al.* 2005). Although Scots pine and Norway spruce have rather wide ecological amplitudes, the former often dominates on dry sandy or wet organic soils, while the latter often prevails on mesic to moist soils (Esseen *et al.* 1997; Angelstam 1998). Moreover, due to greater shade tolerance, Norway spruce has a greater ability to establish and grow under the tree canopy in stands subjected to internal gap-phase dynamics, whereas most boreal deciduous trees are shade-intolerant pioneer species which regenerate abundantly only after stand-replacing disturbances.

Table 6.2 *Estimates of absolute breeding densities for boreal forest bird assemblages based on multiple-visit territory mapping.*

Study	Vegetation zone[a]	Forest type	Mean density (pairs 10 ha^{-1})
Solonen (1996)	Hemiboreal to southern boreal (southern Finland)	*Dominating tree species*	
		Scots pine (L,M)[b]	74
		Norway spruce (M,H)[b]	123
		Deciduous (H,M)[b]	158
		Successional stage	
		Brush (M,H)[b]	71
		Young to middle-aged (H,M)[b]	158
		Old (M,H,L)[b]	143
Forslund (2003)	Southern boreal to hemiboreal (south-central Sweden)	*Dominating tree species*	
		Coniferous (>75% conifers)	68
		Mixed coniferous-deciduous (25–75% conifers)	74
		Deciduous (<25% conifers)	126
		Successional stage	
		Clearcut	13
		Young	47
		Young to middle-aged	73
		Middle-aged to mature	62
		Mature	91
		Older mature	53
Nordström (1953)	Southern boreal (western Finland)	*Dominating tree species*	
		Deciduous	44
		Mixed Norway spruce–deciduous	48
		Norway spruce with some Scots pine	24
Hogstad (2013)	Southern boreal (central Norway)	Single area of 100 ha: Mostly older Norway spruce–dominated forest >70 years, with some regenerating forest and minor proportion of peatland	17 (14–20)[c,d]

Table 6.2 (*cont.*)

Study	Vegetation zone[a]	Forest type	Mean density (pairs 10 ha^{-1})
Haila *et al.* (1994)	Border between southern boreal and middle boreal (south-central Finland)	Single area of 36 ha: One-third old-growth Norway spruce–dominated forest, two-thirds younger forest and small peatlands	33 (28–38)[c]
Edenius and Sjöberg (1997)	Northern boreal (northern Sweden)	Old-growth forest patches (dominated by Norway spruce) surrounded by mires or forest	18

[a] Moen (1999).
[b] Productivity of the study sites: L = low, M = medium, H = high (simplified version of the original classification used by Solonen (1996).
[c] Yearly mean and range over 13 years (Hogstad 2013) and 6 years (Haila *et al.* 1994).
[d] Passerines only.

Although several boreal bird species display preferences for particular tree species, there are few true specialists in that respect. Moreover, there is some geographic variation in habitat preferences even within northern Europe (Haila & Järvinen 1990). Nonetheless, some species seem to prefer specific forest types across most of their range in boreal Europe. The reasons vary, but they are usually linked to the species' foraging ecologies and nest-site selection. Species often associated with Norway spruce in boreal Europe include, among others, the coal tit *Periparus ater*, goldcrest and European robin (Haapanen 1966; Morozov 1992; Svensson *et al.* 1999). Species often linked to Scots pine include the western capercaillie *Tetrao urogallus* (especially in the winter), mistle thrush *Turdus viscivorus*, parrot crossbill and common redstart *Phoenicurus phoenicurus* (Haapanen 1966; Virkkala 1987b). Two species that prefer an open-forest canopy structure, the spotted flycatcher and tree pipit, often tend to dominate the assemblages of dry Scots pine stands with sparse crown cover (Haapanen 1966; Svensson *et al.* 1999). Examples of species that generally require the presence of deciduous trees within stands are the lesser spotted woodpecker *Dryobates minor*, white-backed woodpecker *Dendrocopos leucotos*, Eurasian blue tit, long-tailed tit *Aegithalos caudatus*,

Eurasian nuthatch (ssp. *europaea*), garden warbler *Sylvia borin* and Eurasian blackcap *Sylvia atricapilla* (Morozov 1992; Enoksson *et al.* 1995; Svensson *et al.* 1999). In north-west Europe, some bird species associated with deciduous trees reach their highest densities in the mountain birch forest of the Fennoscandian range. These include red-throated bluethroat *Luscinia svecica* ssp. *svecica*, common redpoll and willow grouse *Lagopus lagopus* (Svensson *et al.* 1999). In fact, the altitudinal transition from the conifer-dominated boreal forest to the subalpine mountain birch zone results in a very strong spatial turnover in bird-species composition along the Fennoscandian mountain range (cf. Fig. 5.10 in Chapter 5).

Although all the different boreal deciduous tree species may contribute to habitat quality for birds, two tree species deserve special consideration due to their keystone roles: aspen and rowan. The former is strongly overrepresented as a nesting tree for cavity nesters due to the frequent occurrence of heartwood rot in living trees (Rolstad *et al.* 2000; Andersson *et al.* 2017; Chapter 4), while the latter is by far the most abundant berry-producing tree, used largely by foraging thrushes, waxwings, bullfinches and pine grosbeaks, among others, during the autumn and winter (e.g., Fox *et al.* 2009).

The presence of an admixture of deciduous trees in conifer-dominated forest generally allows higher bird diversity compared to pure conifer stands (Stokland 1997; Felton *et al.* 2011). Moreover, bird densities and species richness are often higher in Norway spruce–dominated or deciduous forest than in Scots pine forest (e.g., Helle 1985a; Virkkala 1987b; Morozov 1992; Solonen 1996; Table 6.2). However, this is probably not just a pure effect of tree species. Indeed, at low elevations, spruce and deciduous trees often tend to dominate on more productive sites, and it has been shown that a significant part of the variation in boreal bird density and species richness can be explained directly by the density of productive energy (Elo *et al.* 2012).

Interestingly, the magnitude of the differences in local bird assemblages as a function of the dominating tree species seems to vary across continents. Mönkkönen (1994) compared the beta diversity component, i.e., the amount of spatial variation in bird assemblage composition between habitat types within a region. For western Palearctic boreal forest, this was done by measuring the differentiation in bird assemblage structure between Scots pine– and Norway spruce–dominated sites, and for Nearctic boreal forest between pine *Pinus* spp. and spruce-fir *Picea* spp.–*Abies balsamea*–dominated sites. The differentiation was far larger in the Nearctic, where about 70% of individuals represented different species in the two habitats, than in Europe, with just 36% differentiation between pine and spruce forests. On the other hand, local diversity (measured as the expected number of species in samples of 80 pairs) did not differ between Nearctic and western Palearctic boreal assemblages. In other words, in spite of there being similar local bird diversity on the two continents, there is much less compositional variation among local assemblages as a function of the dominating tree species in European boreal forests compared to North American forests. This is probably due to a lower level of habitat specialisation among European than North American boreal birds (see Chapter 2).

The other key stand-scale factor influencing the structure of bird assemblages is forest age. This factor is especially relevant to naturally dynamic forests influenced by stand-replacing disturbances such as high-intensity fire, as well as forest subjected to even-aged forest management. Some tree species are more common in particular successional stages (e.g., deciduous trees in early stages and spruce in older stages), and hence forest succession and tree species composition are not independent of each other. Nevertheless, some general patterns in bird assemblages can be identified along the forest succession. Helle (1985a,b) studied bird assemblages along a successional gradient in north-east Finland, where the youngest stages originated from clearfelling and the older stands developed after fire. He found that both bird density and species richness generally increased along the forest succession. During the first years following a stand-replacing disturbance, the habitat is largely open. The bird assemblages of this successional stage are distinct and character-ised by the highest number of species nesting or feeding on or near the ground (Helle 1985a). Examples of such species are the white and yellow wagtails *Motacilla alba* and *M. flava*, northern wheatear *Oenanthe oenanthe*, whinchat *Saxicola rubetra*, meadow pipit *Anthus pratensis* and ortolan bunting *Emberiza hortulana* (Haapanen 1966; Helle 1985b). Many of these species also breed in non-forest habitats such as mires, farmland or lakeshores (Helle 1985b). The second stage of forest succession is a transitional phase with brush and young trees. Bird densities in such young forest are typically lower than in the subsequent successional stages (Helle 1985a; Solonen 1996; Forslund 2003; Table 6.2). The pole and tall forest stages come next (often referred to as middle-aged forest), and finally the mature and old (overmature) forest stages. In boreal Europe, the proportion of species foraging or nesting in trees increases during the course of succession (Helle 1985a; Helle & Mönkkönen 1990). Examples of species dominating the assemblages of successional stages with a well-developed tree layer include common chaffinch and brambling (the latter mostly in the northern part of the boreal zone) (Helle 1985b). Some species, such as Eurasian treecreeper (Suorsa *et al.* 2005), require forest with an abundance of larger trees. Moreover, some species are specialised on habitat features which are particularly abundant in old forest, such as large-diameter nesting trees (e.g., golden eagle *Aquila chrysaetos* and black woodpecker), dead and dying trees (e.g., three-toed woodpecker *Picoides tridactylus*) and cavity-bearing trees (e.g., flycatchers and tits). However, most of these species have been shown to also breed in younger stages, provided that their specific resource requirements are met. For example, the three-toed woodpecker can forage and breed on clearcuts with retained trees (Helle 1985b; pers. obs.) and is abundant in recently storm-felled and burnt areas containing large amounts of deadwood (Virkkala *et al.* 1991; Fayt 2003). Similarly, cavity-nesters can often breed in younger forest if there is a sufficient supply of cavity trees or nest boxes (Virkkala 1990). This suggests that the autecological features of the bird species in relation to forest characteristics may be more important than forest age per se in explaining bird assemblage structure and composition (Helle & Mönkkönen 1990), and that the impact of forest management on the supply of different forest structures is an important factor to consider when analysing the effects of forest age on bird assemblages.

In addition to tree species composition and forest age, several other factors influence boreal bird assemblages at the local scale. One such factor is the landscape context, i.e., the characteristics of the wider area surrounding the focal forest stand. For example, Mönkkönen *et al.* (2014a) and Huhta and Jokimäki (2015) showed that resource availability in the surrounding landscape influences bird-species richness and abundance in old-forest fragments. Access to water is crucial to many boreal birds that breed in forest (e.g., common goldeneye *Bucephala clangula*, smew *Mergellus albellus*, osprey *Pandion haliaetus*, common sandpiper *Actitis hypoleucos*), and some species that regularly breed in forest forage mostly on agricultural or urbanised land (e.g., common starling *Sturnus vulgaris*, stock dove *Columba oenas*, western jackdaw *Coloeus monedula*). Moreover, the size of the forest area (i.e., patch size) and the level of fragmentation of the forest may influence boreal birds (Edenius & Elmberg 1996; Niemi *et al.* 1998; Virkkala & Rajasärkkä 2006). Finally, it must be emphasised that there is considerable stochastic variation in the actual composition of local assemblages, especially regarding the less common species (Haila & Järvinen 1990; Haila *et al.* 1996; Virkkala & Rajasärkkä 2006).

6.4 Conservation Issues

Since the late 20th century, the boreal forests have constituted a vibrant research scene in avian conservation research. Yet, from a global perspective, the boreal forest is far from being a biodiversity hotspot. As of 2014, only three bird species occurring in European boreal forests figured on the International Union for Conservation of Nature's red list of globally threatened species: the yellow-breasted bunting *Emberiza aureola* (endangered), greater spotted eagle *Aquila clanga* (vulnerable) and red-footed falcon *Falco vespertinus* (near-threatened). Although all three species may breed or forage in forest environments and hence qualify as forest birds (cf. definition in Chapter 5), none of them is a forest specialist. However, the limited number of globally Red-Listed boreal forest birds does not mean that conservation issues are few in the European boreal forest. As shown in Chapter 11, many forest birds of the boreal forest exhibit declining trends. Moreover, large numbers of species are Red-Listed at the national level: as of 2014, 30 boreal forest bird species were Red-Listed in Norway (Kålås *et al.* 2010), 39 in Sweden (Gärdenfors 2010) and 41 in Finland (Rassi *et al.* 2010). Of the 150 boreal forest bird species that have breeding populations in Fennoscandia west of Russia, 45% were Red-Listed and 25% were considered threatened (i.e., vulnerable, endangered or critically endangered) in at least one of these three Nordic countries. Several boreal bird species are also listed at the multinational level within Europe. Two countries dominated by boreal forest are members of the European Union (EU): Sweden and Finland. At the EU level, the Birds Directive (EU 2010) is one of two directives directly addressing the conservation of wildlife. Annex I of the Directive lists bird species 'which shall be the subject of special conservation measures concerning their habitat in order to ensure their survival and reproduction in their area of distribution'. A total of 37 boreal forest bird species are found on that list and hence are of special conservation concern in the EU.

There are multiple causes of threats to boreal forest birds. To obtain a coarse overview of the nature of those threats, we analysed information provided with the Swedish red list (Gärdenfors 2010). For each nationally Red-Listed species, a fact sheet has been published by the Swedish Species Information Centre. These fact sheets summarise the scientific literature and expert knowledge about the biology and conservation status of the species. To help identify the most important threats for boreal forest birds, we tallied the different threats mentioned in the fact sheets for all Red-Listed birds breeding in boreal forest (as of September

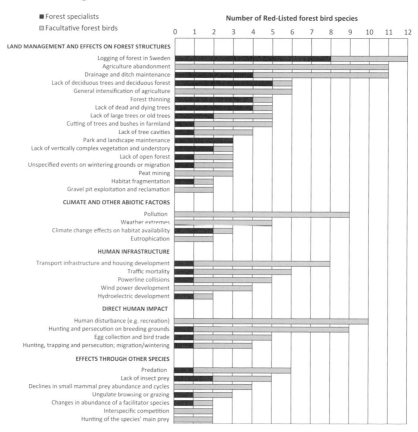

Figure 6.3 Main threats to Red-Listed boreal forest birds in Sweden according to the fact sheets published by the Swedish Species Information Centre. Only threats mentioned for more than one species are included. The number of forest specialists (out of 11 such species) affected by each threat is shown in black, and the number of facultative forest species (out of 28 such species) is depicted in grey.

2014) and summarised the data across species (Fig. 6.3). Evidently, the threats identified in Sweden may not directly apply to all parts of boreal Europe. Still, considering the similarities between Sweden and its neighbouring countries in terms of ecological settings and land-use patterns, we believe that this analysis provides a useful starting point to get an overview of the most important threats, at least for north-western Europe.

Different kinds of land management actions affecting forest and other land cover types were identified as important threats (Fig. 6.3). Among these, logging was the most commonly mentioned threat, both for forest birds in general and for forest specialists. Declines in the availability of key forest ecosystem structures (as a consequence of forest management) and forest drainage were recognised as important threats to many species. Another important driver threatening European boreal forest birds is climate change. Considering its more gradual impact, it is most often perceived as a long-term stress on boreal ecosystems rather than an immediate threat (e.g., Niemi et al. 1998). This is reflected by the fact that climatic factors are less commonly listed than land-management effects as threats to Swedish boreal birds (Fig. 6.3). Yet, wide-ranging impacts of climate change on boreal bird assemblages are already visible (Brommer et al. 2012; Lindström et al. 2013; Virkkala & Rajasärkkä 2011a; Virkkala & Lehikoinen 2014) and may represent a serious threat over a longer time perspective (Kujala et al. 2011; Virkkala et al. 2008, 2013). Additional threats to boreal forest birds include other kinds of changes in the abiotic environment (e.g., pollution), infrastructure development, direct impacts from humans (e.g., hunting or disturbance) and effects from other species. Acknowledging this variety of threats, forestry and climate change arguably represent the two most important drivers underlying the present or likely future endangerment of boreal birds.

6.4.1 Forestry

A key driver affecting boreal bird species is forestry, i.e., the management of forests for the extraction of wood-based products such as saw timber, pulpwood for papermaking and biomass for energy production. The effects of forestry differ considerably from those of natural disturbances to which boreal species are evolutionarily adapted, such as fire and flooding (Esseen et al. 1997; Niemi et al. 1998). Imbeau et al. (2001) assessed the sensitivity of boreal forest birds to forestry (based on habitat and nesting site) in relation to the types of changes that industrial forest management bring to the ecosystems. They found that the mean threat levels were higher for resident birds than short-distance or tropical migrants, in both Fennoscandia and eastern Canada. In Table 6.3, we summarise the range of management measures affecting compositional, structural and functional aspects of boreal forest ecosystems (*sensu* Noss 1990), with their potential effects on bird assemblages and possible mitigation actions.

In north-west Europe, boreal forest management is usually based on even-aged management systems involving a sequence of silvicultural

Table 6.3 *Effects of different boreal forest management measures on three forest biodiversity components (tree species composition, forest structure and natural processes; sensu Noss 1990[1]) and associated bird assemblages, and summary of the main actions that can be taken to mitigate negative effects on forest birds*

Forest management measures	Effects on the focal forest biodiversity component	Potential effects on bird assemblages	Mitigation measures for negative impacts
1. Measures influencing tree species composition			
Artificial regeneration through planting or sowing	Homogenisation of tree species composition within stands through planting or sowing of single species; introduction of non-native tree species or genotypes	Decreased habitat diversity; decreased habitat suitability for species disfavoured by non-native tree species	Promote natural regeneration; plant/sow material of local provenance
Thinning	Homogenisation of tree species composition within stands through removal of unwanted tree species (usually deciduous trees)	Decreased habitat diversity	Retain a variety of tree species at thinning, including deciduous trees
2. Measures influencing forest structure			
Clearfelling	Loss of forest cover; forest fragmentation at the landscape scale; simplification of within-stand age structure; disruption of temporal forest continuity at the local scale	Habitat loss for forest specialists; habitat fragmentation with effects on, e.g., movement behaviour; negative effects on species requiring vertically complex forest vegetation; increase in habitat area for open-habitat specialists (e.g., the declining ortolan bunting)	Retain trees at clearfelling (both as forest patches and solitary trees); retain or create snags and high stumps at clearfelling; plan spatially for ecological connectivity; use uneven-aged forest management methods such as single-tree selection cutting as alternatives to clearfelling

Harvesting at an age earlier than the old-growth stage	Paucity of old forest in the landscape, with associated impacts on the availability of old trees, large trees, cavity-bearing trees and dead/dying trees	Habitat loss for species requiring old, large, cavity-bearing or dying/dead trees, such as woodpeckers, secondary cavity nesters and large raptors	Prolong forestry rotations; retain trees at clearfelling; retain or create snags and high stumps at clearfelling; provide nest boxes and nest platforms
Thinning	Lowered stem density; simplification of within-stand structure through removal of smaller trees not belonging to the dominant layer	Decreased structural complexity of vegetation with effects on, e.g., predation risk; positive effects on species preferring more open stands (e.g., capercaillie, tree pipit)	Refrain from thinning; modify thinning methods to maintain structural complexity
Harvest of stumps, branches and tree tops after logging	Loss of deadwood substrates; homogenisation of habitat structure near ground	Decreased availability of stumps for foraging (e.g., black woodpecker) and nesting (e.g., robin); decreased cover near ground with potential negative impacts habitat suitability for, e.g., the wren *Troglodytes troglodytes*	Refrain from harvest of stumps, branches and tree tops after logging
Salvage logging after disturbance	Loss of deadwood substrates	Decreased abundance of feeding substrates (woodpeckers), perching posts and breeding substrates (woodpeckers, secondary cavity-nesters and the treecreeper)	Refrain from salvage logging; implement snag-retention measures during salvage logging
Soil scarification	Deadwood destruction	Decreased abundance of feeding substrates for woodpeckers	Refrain from scarification; modify scarification methods to minimise deadwood destruction

(cont.)

Table 6.3 (cont.)

Forest management measures	Effects on the focal forest biodiversity component	Potential effects on bird assemblages	Mitigation measures for negative impacts
Forest road construction	Forest fragmentation; changes to hydrology	Increased accessibility to humans, with potentially increased hunting pressure; increased habitat area for open-habitat specialists (e.g., white wagtail); access to grit for forest grouse and pigeons	Minimise road construction; implement road reclamation in some wilderness areas
3. Measures influencing natural processes			
Control of forest fires	Lesser frequency and extent of forest fires, causing decreased abundance of fire-injured and killed trees, burnt substrates and post-fire successional habitats rich in deciduous trees	Decreased abundance of feeding and nesting substrates for woodpeckers (and indirectly secondary cavity-nesters); decreased habitat area for deciduous forest specialists (e.g., white-backed woodpecker)	Implement prescribed forest burning; create sun-exposed deadwood; modify forest management methods to create deciduous-rich stands similar to post-fire succession
Clearfelling and salvage logging	Less frequent natural tree death and decay	Decreased abundance of feeding substrates for woodpeckers; decreased abundance of breeding substrates for woodpeckers, secondary cavity-nesters and the treecreeper	Refrain from clearfelling and salvage logging in some areas; retain living and dead trees at clearfelling; injure and kill trees mechanically at clearfelling
Thinning	Less frequent natural tree death and decay	Decreased abundance of feeding substrates for woodpeckers feeding on saproxylic insects; decreased abundance of	Refrain from thinning; retain dying and dead trees at thinning; injure and kill trees mechanically at thinning

Forest ditching and ditch maintenance	Reduced area of wet forest; decreased frequency of natural flooding events	breeding substrates for woodpeckers, secondary cavity-nesters and the treecreeper Reduced habitat area for wet forest specialists (e.g., little bunting, green sandpiper *Tringa ochropus* and the declining rustic bunting); decreased abundance of feeding and nesting substrates for woodpeckers (and, indirectly, secondary cavity-nesters) in the form of trees killed by flooding	Fill ditches or refrain from ditch maintenance
Forest fertilisation	Changes in site productivity, with effects on vegetation growth and composition	Increases in invertebrate prey for insectivorous birds; possible negative effects on species preferring open, low-productive forest	Refrain from fertilising dry, low-productive forest

[a] The same management measure may appear in two or all three categories if it is known to affect more than one type of biodiversity component.

measures applied in a cyclic pattern: clearfelling, soil scarification, regeneration through planting or sowing and thinning. Forest stands are typically clearfelled at an age of 60–120 years, depending on site type and location. Compared to naturally dynamic forest landscapes, this results in a truncated age-class distribution, with a reduced area of old-growth forest. In large parts of Finland and Sweden, for example, the mean forest age has decreased from the 1950s to the 2010s, with the share of young forests increasing and that of old forests decreasing (Vilén *et al.* 2012; Ecke *et al.* 2013). Due to a loss of old-growth forests, many boreal bird species associated with old-forest structures have declined (Helle & Järvinen 1986; Virkkala 1991; Väisänen *et al.* 1998; Imbeau *et al.* 2001; Laaksonen & Lehikoinen 2013).

To increase economic returns, stands are typically thinned two to three times during the rotation. As a result of thinning and clearfelling practices, the internal structure of the forest has been simplified towards a more or less even layer of similar-sized trees, with negative impacts on species requiring a vertically complex understorey (e.g., Eggers & Low 2014). Moreover, natural tree death and decay have been reduced, which affects birds that breed in tree cavities or feed on saproxylic insects in dying or dead trees (e.g., specialised woodpeckers; Roberge *et al.* 2008). In managed forest, tree-species composition is manipulated, both in the regeneration phase and when selecting trees to be retained during thinning. In particular, deciduous trees have been disadvantaged at the expense of conifers (Esseen *et al.* 1997). The associated decreases in tree-species diversity have affected many birds specialised on deciduous trees (Enoksson *et al.* 1995). Trees killed by disturbances (e.g., windthrow and fire) are often salvaged to avoid timber losses and to limit the risk of pest outbreaks. There is little knowledge about the effects of salvage logging on birds in boreal Europe, but North American studies show clear impacts of postfire salvage logging, especially on bark-foraging cavity-nesters (e.g., Hutto & Gallo 2006; Azeria *et al.* 2011).

An important factor influencing landscape patterns is habitat fragmentation, a process through which habitat patch size is reduced and patches are increasingly isolated from each other (Andrén 1994; Fahrig 1997). Habitat loss and fragmentation as a result of boreal forestry (e.g., Ecke *et al.* 2013) have had clear impacts on bird assemblages (Jokimäki & Huhta 1996; Kouki & Väänänen 2000; Schmiegelow & Mönkkönen 2002; Brotons *et al.* 2003). For example, forest fragmentation negatively affects the breeding success of forest grouse; it is believed that this is a major factor underlying the population declines of the western capercaillie and black grouse *Lyrurus tetrix* in Fennoscandia during the past decades (Kurki *et al.* 2000). Importantly, fragmentation may interact with climate change (cf. Section 6.4.2). Indeed, human-caused fragmentation of the boreal forest landscape may impede colonisation of new suitable habitat patches by bird species whose distribution ranges are shifting in response to a changing climate. In the Nordic countries, for example, old-growth boreal forest habitats are nowadays highly fragmented and found almost only in protected areas. Therefore, bird species with restricted dispersal ability (e.g., the Siberian jay *Perisoreus infaustus*; Griesser *et al.* 2014) or low population size may not be able to adapt their range to a northward shift of suitable climate.

Land-use change and climate effects can also act in parallel. Indeed, many northern boreal forest species suffer from both the loss of old-growth forests and a warming climate (e.g., Siberian jay; Edenius *et al.* 2004; Muukkonen *et al.* 2012). In a simulation study in western Canada, boreal bird species strongly associated with mature and old-forest habitats have been predicted to exhibit population declines over the coming 100 years (Mahon *et al.* 2014). However, some southern species that prefer old-growth or other natural boreal forests may also increase in numbers as the climate becomes more suitable for them, irrespective of effects on forest habitat structure per se. For example, mild winters may ameliorate the survival of individuals in resident species, thereby potentially mitigating some of the adverse effects of forestry practices on those species (Virkkala 2004).

In recent decades, there has been increasing concern for biodiversity in boreal forests, and far-reaching proposals have been made for ecologically sustainable management (Angelstam 1997, 1998; Angelstam & Pettersson 1997; Fries *et al.* 1997; Simberloff 1999, 2001; Larsson & Danell 2001; Niemelä *et al.* 2001; Angelstam *et al.* 2004a). To alleviate the negative effects of logging and forest management on ecosystems, new biodiversity conservation measures have been developed and implemented in practice. In the Nordic countries, for example, a range of conservation measures has been incorporated into forest legislation and certification standards since the early 1990s. These include maintaining key habitats of particular conservation value, implementing management that favours deciduous trees and retaining living and dead trees at clearfelling (e.g., Vanha-Majamaa & Jalonen 2001; Gustafsson *et al.* 2010; Timonen *et al.* 2010; Roberge *et al.* 2015; Bernes *et al.* 2015).

Although tree retention on clearcuts provides nest-cavities, these are generally not preferred by foliage-gleaning, cavity-nesting passerines (tit and flycatcher guilds; Carlson 1994). Most of these passerines appear to prefer closed forest and parts of the clearcut located within short distances (<25 m) from the forest edge for their breeding, probably due to enhanced foraging possibilities and predator avoidance, and it seems that only woodpeckers breed frequently in clearcuts with retention trees (Carlson 1994). However, Söderström (2009) found clear positive effects of tree retention on the abundance of late-successional forest bird species, as regards bird abundance both on the clearcuts with retained trees and in the directly adjacent forest.

One of the general aims of tree retention is to increase the volume of deadwood, which is currently very low in the managed forests of north-west Europe compared to the situation in unmanaged forests (Siitonen et al. 2000; Siitonen 2001). Retaining and creating deadwood at clearfelling is only one of several measures that can be used to increase deadwood availability. For example, Tikkanen et al. (2012) and Mönkkönen et al. (2014b) have shown that in managed forests, deadwood availability can efficiently be increased by refraining from silvicultural thinnings.

A study combining national forest inventory and bird survey data in Sweden has shown that recent increases in forest quality (as a result of the implementation of biodiversity conservation measures), forest quantity and temperature have coincided with population increases in forest birds (Ram et al. 2017). Although that study cannot demonstrate causality as such, the fact that forest birds had, on average, more positive trends than non-forest birds for a given climate sensitivity index suggests that structural improvements to the forest since the 1990s may have contributed to the observed population increases.

In contrast, in southern Finland, species with a preference for late successional habitats have shown negative population trends, on average, since the early 1990s (Fraixedas et al. 2015). In a study of 23 consecutive years (1993–2015) in a managed forest area in southern Finland, total bird density declined by almost 1% per year, with 7 of the 12 most abundant species declining and only one species increasing (Virkkala 2016). These changes in bird populations could be connected with both habitat alteration caused by forestry and climate change.

6.4.2 Climate Change

Climate change is the other key driver affecting bird assemblages in boreal forests (Jetz et al. 2007; Jiguet et al. 2010, 2013; Bellard et al. 2012).

According to the Intergovernmental Panel on Climate Change (IPCC), the projected annual warming estimated by the A1B ensemble mean scenario for the end of the 21st century is 5°C in the Arctic (including boreal areas), compared to 3.2–3.5°C in Europe in general (Christensen *et al.* 2007). From a global perspective, the boreal forest is the biome where climate is predicted to change most rapidly. In a comparison of the world's 14 main biomes and their respective protected areas, Loarie *et al.* (2009) showed that climate residence time (i.e., the expected time for current climate to cross a given area) was among the lowest in protected areas of the boreal biome.

At coarse scales, species distributions are largely restricted by climatic factors, each species being distributed according to its so-called bioclimatic envelope or niche (Heikkinen *et al.* 2006; Araújo & Peterson 2012), although other factors, such as habitat availability (Pearson *et al.* 2004), biotic interactions (Heikkinen *et al.* 2007; Wisz *et al.* 2013) and topography (Virkkala *et al.* 2010), are also highly important. Using bioclimatic envelope models, the relationships between present-day species distributions and current climate variables can be developed and then used to forecast future changes in suitable climate space for species under different climate scenarios. Based on such bioclimatic envelope models, bird species have been predicted to move their ranges in relation to expected climate change (Huntley *et al.* 2007, 2008; Virkkala *et al.* 2008, 2013; Barbet-Massin *et al.* 2012). In fact, species distributions have already been observed to shift polewards (latitudinally) and upwards (altitudinally) in several species groups (Hickling *et al.* 2006; Chen *et al.* 2011; Brommer *et al.* 2012).

Bird species distributions have been projected to change considerably over the 21st century throughout Europe as a consequence of climate change, with northern Europe gaining and southern Europe losing species, on average (Huntley *et al.* 2007, 2008; Barbet-Massin *et al.* 2012). In northern Europe, bird species that are particularly susceptible to the effects of climate warming are those with distributions concentrated in the northern boreal or Arctic zones, because the Arctic Ocean will effectively limit their range expansion northward (Virkkala *et al.* 2008, 2010). These prospects are also related to the severity of the climate change projections, in which the effect is predicted to be stronger for northern Europe than temperate and Mediterranean Europe (ACIA 2005; Christensen *et al.* 2007). Within the boreal zone, species ranges are predicted to shift during the 21st century, with ranges of forest species presently in the southern boreal zone moving towards middle and northern boreal zones (Virkkala *et al.* 2013). The composition of boreal bird assemblage composition has been shown to respond to temperature changes with a time lag of 1–3 years (Lindström *et al.* 2013).

Earlier studies based on bioclimatic envelope models and bird atlas data from 1974–1989 have suggested that northern-boreal bird species may face range contractions of 74%–82% by 2080, depending on the northern Europe climate scenario (Virkkala *et al.* 2008, 2010). Using new bird atlas data from Finland compiled in 2006–2010, Virkkala *et al.* (2014) showed that the ranges of these northern-boreal bird species (including forest species) have already contracted by 27% on average compared with 1974–1989. Thus the range changes of northern species are in the same direction as predicted by species-climate change models.

In addition to changes in species distribution ranges, densities of boreal bird species have also shifted northwards. In Finland, for example, the mean weighted latitude of density moved northwards by 1.3 km year^{-1} on average from the 1970s to the 2010s (45 km during the study period of 35 years) for the 94 most common landbird species (Virkkala & Lehikoinen 2014). This northward density shift was significantly stronger for northern species (ca. 70 km during the study period) than in southern species (ca. 30 km). Densities of the most abundant forest bird species distributed over the whole boreal region, such as the willow warbler, have also shifted northwards. Virkkala and Rajasärkkä (2011a) showed that populations of southern species (such as the chaffinch) had increased by 29% and northern species (such as the brambling) declined by 21% in a set of 96 Finnish protected areas between two time periods, 1981–1999 and 2000–2009. Temporal changes were most pronounced towards species range boundaries: southern birds increased most in northern protected areas, and northern species showed the greatest decrease in southern protected areas (Virkkala & Rajasärkkä 2011b).

In Finland, populations of northern bird species and of long-distance migrants declined during 1986–2012 (Laaksonen & Lehikoinen 2013), suggesting increased effects of climate change on birds that breed in boreal forests. This is supported by the fact that many northern bird species also declined in protected areas, where direct habitat use, such as logging or drainage of mires, does not take place (Virkkala & Rajasärkkä 2011a). Although logging in the managed forest matrix can also cause declines in forest birds inside the protected areas (e.g., Mönkkönen *et al.* 2014a; Huhta & Jokimäki 2015), the patterns for northern bird species of mires suggest that climate itself is an important driver: these species have also declined in protected areas in northernmost Finland, a region where direct habitat alteration through drainage of mires has not taken place at all, in contrast to more southerly regions (see Virkkala & Rajasärkkä 2012). Long-distance migrants have declined in large parts of Europe (e.g., Sanderson *et al.* 2006). Populations of species that winter in Africa and Asia are affected by climatic conditions not only in their breeding grounds, but also in their wintering grounds (Barbet-Massin *et al.* 2009) and along migration routes (Saino *et al.* 2011), as well as by direct habitat changes in non-breeding areas.

Population changes in forest birds have also been observed in the mountain birch zone, probably the most climatically extreme forest environment in Europe. Using data from systematic bird surveys stretching across the Fennoscandian mountain range, Lehikoinen *et al.* (2013) found that five of seven common bird species of mountain birch forest had suffered significant population declines (and none had increased significantly) during the period 2002–2012, which is in line with predictions based on climatic forecasting. Interestingly, these authors found that among alpine and subalpine birds, long-distance migrants declined less than short-distance migrants and residents, suggesting that for these species, the causes of decline may be found within Fennoscandia.

Climatic conditions may directly influence habitat suitability for birds. For example, snow depth probably restricts the northern range boundary of woodpeckers specialised on an ant (Hymenoptera: Formicidae) diet, such as the black woodpecker (Rolstad & Rolstad 2000) and grey-headed woodpecker *Picus canus* (Rolstad & Rolstad 1995). Both of these species – for which winter food availability probably is a critical factor – have expanded their ranges northwards during recent decades (e.g., Valkama *et al.* 2011). This is likely due to climate change resulting in milder winters with a thinner snow cover, which facilitates foraging on ants on the ground or in mounds, tree stumps or lying logs (Rolstad & Rolstad 1995, 2000; Mikusiński 1997).

More generally, climate change is expected to result in considerable changes in the characteristics of boreal forest vegetation, with probable implications for future habitat suitability for forest birds. Results of a dynamic vegetation model predict that forest vegetation zones will shift northwards, with the extent of boreal forests declining in Europe by 2085 due to climate change (Hickler *et al.* 2012). The hemiboreal zone is predicted to be a hotspot of change. In northern Europe, the proportion of Norway spruce is predicted to decline, particularly in the southern boreal zone, while the proportions of Scots pine and birch are forecast to increase (Kellomäki *et al.* 2008). Deadwood volume is predicted to increase by 2100, particularly for pine and birch (>60%) and less for spruce (26%), according to a simulation model (Mazziotta *et al.* 2014), although it should be kept in mind that in managed boreal forests, the volumes of deadwood are presently very low. These changes are likely to affect habitat suitability for bird species that depend on particular tree species and specific structures such as dead trees.

6.4.3 Pollution and Eutrophication

Populations of several boreal forest birds have been affected by environmental pollution. This is especially true for raptors such as eagles, harriers and falcons, for which contaminants such as dichlorodiphenyldichloroethene (DDE) and total polychlorinated biphenyl (PCB) have had strong negative impacts on breeding success in the past (e.g., Helander *et al.* 2008). Although the situation has improved dramatically following bans on the use of these chemicals, some other environmental contaminants, such as lead, are still problematic today.

Increasing eutrophication due to nitrogen deposition affects forests throughout Europe, including boreal areas (Dirnböck *et al.* 2014). Due to nitrogen deposition, oligotrophic plant species are replaced by eutrophic species. Hence, drier forest habitats become more mesic due to changes in forest floor vegetation, and particularly bird species that prefer dry pine-dominated habitats may suffer from this habitat change. Eutrophication is also connected with climate-induced vegetation dynamics in Europe (Hickler *et al.* 2012): eutrophication may exacerbate the northwards shift of more productive forest habitats. Another anthropogenic source of nitrogen in forest is silvicultural fertilisation, a tree-growth–enhancing measure which is common practice in many parts of north-west Europe. Fertilisation of young spruce forests may increase the abundance of arthropods in the branches and thus potentially increase the numbers of insectivorous birds in these forests (Edenius *et al.* 2011, 2012). Fertilisation reduces the concentration of phenolic compounds that trees use as a defence mechanism against herbivores, such as arthropods, which yields more prey for insectivores. On the other hand, fertilisation may be disadvantageous for species that prefer less productive forest habitats.

6.4.4 Human Infrastructure

The development of transport infrastructure and increasing urbanisation reduce the extent of boreal forest and may fragment boreal habitats.

Even though human population density is generally low in the boreal zone compared to the rest of Europe, infrastructure development may be important locally. This is especially true for the more ecologically productive parts of the boreal zone, which also tend to be most densely populated. However, some boreal forest species have adapted to urbanisation and successfully colonised urban areas (Jokimäki *et al.* 2011). These include common magpie *Pica pica* and, during more recent decades, common wood pigeon *Columba palumbus*, northern goshawk and Eurasian eagle owl *Bubo bubo*. Urban and built areas provide both food and suitable nesting sites for these species. For example, the goshawk has started to breed in mature woods in urban areas, probably benefiting from the fact that these woods are not managed for timber production and that the species is no longer persecuted by humans. It has even been found that goshawk brood size is larger in urban than in rural areas (Solonen 2008). In a northern boreal national park in Finland, human-favoured species (corvids, cavity-nesters and building-nesters) were in greater abundance in built areas than in the remainder of the park (Huhta & Sulkava 2014). However, densities of old-growth forest species did not differ between the disturbed and intact forest areas.

Infrastructure development for electricity production is a threat to some boreal forest birds. Wind power development in particular may affect populations of large raptors (e.g., Dahl *et al.* 2012). Considering the recent large-scale investments in wind power as a climate mitigation measure in northern Europe, this is likely to become an increasing concern in the coming decades. Other impacts of infrastructure on forest birds include collisions with power lines and traffic. The latter can be a significant cause of mortality in raptors that feed on animal carcasses by railways and roads (Tjernberg 2010).

6.4.5 Direct Human Impact

Direct human impact on boreal forest birds includes persecution, egg and bird collection, hunting and disturbance through, for example, recreational activities. The organised persecution of species, which used to be particularly common with birds of prey, has mostly ceased in Finland and other Nordic countries since the end of 1980s (Pohja-Mykrä *et al.* 2012). National legislation and the EU Birds Directive provide strong protection for birds in the Nordic countries, which limits persecution in north-west European boreal forests. In spite of that, some level of illegal persecution still occurs in these countries, as does the collection of eggs and birds for illegal trade.

Hunting can affect populations of game animals such as forest grouse (see also Chapter 12). A recent study based on 16 years of wildlife census data (1989 to 2004) in north-east Finland suggests that hunting influenced populations of four forest grouse (western capercaillie, black grouse, hazel grouse *Tetrastes bonasia*, willow grouse) in the short term, but did not result in a long-term declining trend in any of the grouse species (Lampila *et al.* 2011). A boreal forest species which may be threatened by hunting is the bean goose *Anser fabalis fabalis*, whose populations have declined during recent decades in northern Europe (BirdLife International 2014). In addition, some long-distance migrants are still subject to persecution and trapping at their stopover sites during migration and on their wintering grounds in Africa and Asia. For example, the globally endangered yellow-breasted bunting is trapped on a very large scale during fall migration in China (Kamp *et al.* 2015).

Boreal forest birds are also affected by disturbances due to recreational activities. According to a study in a northern boreal national park, recreation-induced disturbances affected the occurrence of certain species (open-cup–nesters breeding on the ground) and thus bird assemblage composition, but not bird species richness (Kangas *et al.* 2010). In northern Finland, territory occupancy rates of the golden eagle were lower around large tourist destinations, and disturbance levels at tourist destinations (measured as the length of skiing and snowmobile routes) negatively affected territory occupancy (Kaisanlahti-Jokimäki *et al.* 2008). These examples show that human recreation and nature tourism also affect boreal bird assemblages and species even within protected areas. Disturbances by birdwatchers at nesting sites can also be a conservation issue for species with very few breeding pairs, such as the white-backed woodpecker in Sweden (Mild & Stighäll 2005).

6.4.6 Effects through Other Species

Direct or indirect interspecific interactions can pose a threat to populations of some boreal forest bird species. These include predation, insufficient abundance of prey and habitat alterations due to the activities of other species. The introduction of invasive predator species such as the American mink *Mustela vison* can have a detrimental impact on the breeding success of some forest bird species, especially those that breed on the ground near water and wetlands (Nordström *et al.* 2003). The raccoon dog *Nyctereutes procyonoides*, a more recently invading species in the western parts of boreal Europe, is a potentially harmful predator, although the evidence is equivocal (Kauhala & Kowalczyk 2011). Predation by native predators can also be problematic for bird species with already small populations.

Several boreal forest birds are affected negatively by decreases in prey abundance. For example, the observed small-rodent density declines and disappearance of multiannual rodent population cycles in northern Fennoscandia may pose a threat to small-rodent specialists, including many owls (Hörnfeldt 2004). Moreover, changes in the characteristics of the forest can decrease the abundance of specific prey for insectivorous birds. For example, declines in the abundance of dead and dying trees decrease food abundance for the three-toed and white-backed woodpeckers, both of which are highly specialised on saproxylic insects (Aulén 1988; Fayt 2003; Roberge *et al.* 2008). Changes in the characteristics of the forest are usually a direct result of forest management, but they can also occur due to the actions of other vertebrate animals. For example, across much of boreal Sweden, very high densities of moose *Alces alces* led to excessive browsing pressure, impeding the recruitment of many deciduous tree species (Edenius *et al.* 2002), a key habitat component for several Red-Listed boreal birds.

6.4.7 The Role of Birds in Boreal Ecosystems

Most of the conservation discussion about forest birds has revolved around the value of birds in their own right. However, healthy bird assemblages are also important to the functioning of the broader boreal ecosystems (Niemi *et al.* 1998). Several studies have highlighted the fact that birds can reduce the densities of pest insects that damage boreal forest (e.g., Atlegrim 1989; Holmes 1990). Similarly, some predatory birds have the potential to exert a controlling influence on populations of small rodents at boreal latitudes (Korpimäki 1993), with follow-on effects on vegetation and tree regeneration. Another ecosystem service provided by boreal birds is seed dispersal, both on breeding grounds and during migration (e.g., fruit-eating thrushes and warblers). In boreal forests, woodpeckers play a key role as producers of cavities which are then used by a range of species from other taxonomic groups, including mammals (e.g., Siberian flying squirrel *Pteromys volans*) and insects. Birds are important also from a recreational perspective, and for human well-being for thousands of birdwatchers, naturalists and hunters. These multiple roles highlight the fact that the conservation of boreal avian assemblages stretches far beyond the birds themselves.

6.5 Conclusions

In spite of the large amount of knowledge about boreal forests and their avifauna, boreal bird assemblages face several major conservation challenges. Tackling these challenges will require novel approaches that are cost-effective enough to be implemented at large scales. In a comparison of different forest management scenarios, Mönkkönen *et al.* (2011) showed that conservation policies based on permanent protected areas are most cost-efficient when preserving species associated with deadwood in the long term. From a European perspective, the boreal biome presents the particularity of already hosting some of the largest and least fragmented forest areas under stronger forms of formal protection for biodiversity conservation, although there is currently a strong bias towards high altitudes and latitudes at the expense of more productive lowland forest (Virkkala & Rajasärkkä 2007; EEA 2012). To conserve boreal forest birds efficiently in the face of an intensification of forest management in the changing climate of the 21st century, there is a need to develop a spatially representative and well-connected protected area network (Angelstam *et al.* 2011; Kujala *et al.* 2011; Virkkala *et al.* 2013). Considering the ecological importance of the managed forest matrix outside of protected areas, we also call for the development and scientific validation of new conservation methods in managed forest (e.g., Mönkkönen *et al.* 2014b), including tools for the restoration of ecologically degraded boreal ecosystems.

Acknowledgements

This work was partly funded by grants from the Kempe Foundation (JMR) and the Academy of Finland (MM; project #275329). We thank Louis Imbeau, Esa Huhta, Grzegorz Mikusiński and Rob Fuller for constructive comments on the manuscript.

References

ACIA (2005) *Arctic Climate Impact Assessment*. Cambridge: Cambridge University Press.

Andersson, J., Domingo Gómez, E., Michon, S. & Roberge, J.-M. (2017) Tree cavity densities and characteristics in managed and unmanaged Swedish boreal forest. *Scandinavian Journal of Forest Research*. DOI: 10.1080/02827581.2017.1360389.

Andrén, H. (1994) Effects of habitat fragmentation on birds and mammals in landscapes with different proportions of suitable habitat: A review. *Oikos*, **71**, 355–366.

Angelstam, P. (1997) Landscape analysis as a tool for the scientific management of biodiversity. *Ecological Bulletins*, **46**, 140–170.

Angelstam, P.K. (1998) Maintaining and restoring biodiversity in European boreal forests by developing natural disturbance regimes. *Journal of Vegetation Science*, **9**, 593–602.

Angelstam, P., Andersson, K., Axelsson, R., Elbakidze, M., Jonsson, B.G. & Roberge, J.-M. (2011) Protecting forest areas for biodiversity in Sweden 1991–2010: The policy implementation process and outcomes on the ground. *Silva Fennica*, **45**, 1111–1133.

Angelstam, P., Persson, R. & Schlaepfer, R. (2004a) The sustainable forest management vision and biodiversity – barriers and bridges for implementation in actual landscapes. *Ecological Bulletins*, **51**, 29–49.

Angelstam, P. & Pettersson, B. (1997) Principles of present Swedish forest biodiversity management. *Ecological Bulletins*, **46**, 191–203.

Angelstam P., Roberge, J.-M., Ek, T. & Laestadius, L. (2005) Data and tools for conservation, management, and restoration of northern forest ecosystems at multiple scales. In *Restoration of Boreal and Temperate Forests*. Stanturf, J.A. & Madsen, P. (eds.). Boca Raton, FL: CRC Press/Lewis Publishers, pp. 269–283.

Araújo, M.B. & Peterson, A.T. (2012) Uses and misuses of bioclimatic envelope modeling. *Ecology*, **93**, 1527–1539.

Atlegrim, O. (1989) Exclusion of birds from bilberry stands: Impact on insect larval density and damage to the bilberry. *Oecologia*, **79**, 136–139.

Aulén, G. (1988) *Ecology and Distribution History of the White-Backed Woodpecker Dendrocopos leucotos in Sweden*. Report 14. Uppsala: Swedish University of Agricultural Sciences.

Azeria, E., Ibarzabal, J., Hébert, C., Boucher, J., Imbeau, L. & Savard, J.-P.L. (2011) Differential response of bird functional traits to post-fire salvage logging in a boreal forest ecosystem. *Acta Oecologica*, **37**, 220–229.

Barbet-Massin, M., Thuiller, W. & Jiguet, F. (2012) The fate of European breeding birds under climate, land-use and dispersal scenarios. *Global Change Biology*, **18**, 881–890.

Barbet-Massin, M., Walther, B.A., Thuiller, W., Rahbek, C. & Jiguet, F. (2009) Potential impacts of climate change on the winter distribution of Afro-Palaearctic migrant passerines. *Biology Letters*, **5**, 248–251.

Bellard, C., Bertelsmeier, C., Leadley, P., Thuiller, W. & Courchamp, F. (2012) Impacts of climate change on the future of biodiversity. *Ecology Letters*, **15**, 365–377.

Bernes, C., Jonsson, B., Junninen, K. *et al.* (2015) What is the impact of active management on biodiversity in boreal and temperate forests set aside for conservation or restoration? A systematic map. *Environmental Evidence*, **4**, 1.

BirdLife International (2014) *Species Factsheet: Anser fabalis*. Birdlife International.

Bock C.E. & Lepthien L.W. (1976) Synchronous eruptions of boreal seed-eating birds. *American Naturalist*, **110**, 559–571.

Böhning-Gaese, K. (2005) Influence of migrants on temperate bird communities. In *Birds of the Two Worlds*. Washington, DC: Johns Hopkins University Press, pp. 143–153.

Böhning-Gaese, K. & Oberrath, R. (2003) Macroecology of habitat choice in long-distance migratory birds. *Oecologia*, **137**, 296–303.

Brommer, J.E., Lehikoinen, A. & Valkama, J. (2012) The breeding ranges of Central European and Arctic bird species move poleward. *PLoS ONE*, **7(9)**, e43648.

Brotons, L., Mönkkönen, M., Huhta, E., Nikula, A. & Rajasärkkä, A. (2003) Effects of landscape structure and forest reserve location on old-growth forest bird species in Northern Finland. *Landscape Ecology*, **18**, 377–393.

Bryant, D., Nielsen, D. & Tangley, L. (1997) *The Last Frontier Forests: Ecosystems and Economies on the Edge*. Washington, DC: World Resource Institute.

Carlson, A. (1994) Cavity breeding birds and clearcuts. *Ornis Fennica*, **71**, 120–122.

Chen, I.-C., Hill, J.K., Ohlemüller, R., Roy, D.B. & Thomas, C.D. (2011) Rapid range shifts of species associated with high levels of climate warming. *Science*, **333**, 1024–1026.

Cheveau, M., Drapeau, P., Imbeau, L. & Bergeron, Y. (2004) Owl winter irruptions as an indicator of small mammal population cycles in the boreal forest of eastern North America. *Oikos*, **107**, 190–198.

Christensen, J.H., Hewitson, B., Busuioc, A. *et al.* (2007) Regional climate projections. In *Climate Change 2007: The Physical Science Basis. Contribution of Working Group I to the Fourth Assessment of the Intergovernmental Panel on Climate Change*. Cambridge: Cambridge University Press, pp. 847–940.

Dahl, E.L., Bevanger, K., Nygard, T., Roskaft, E. & Stokke, B.G. (2012) Reduced breeding success in white-tailed eagles at Smola windfarm, western Norway, is caused by mortality and displacement. *Biological Conservation*, **145**, 79–85.

Dirnböck, T., Grandin, U., Bernhardt-Römermann, M. *et al.* (2014) Forest floor vegetation response to nitrogen deposition in Europe. *Global Change Biology*, **20**, 429–440.

Ecke, F., Magnusson, M. & Hörnfeldt, B. (2013) Spatiotemporal changes in the landscape structure of forests in northern Sweden. *Scandinavian Journal of Forest Research*, **28**, 651–667.

Edenius, L., Bergman, M., Ericsson, G. & Danell, K. (2002) The role of moose as a disturbance factor in managed boreal forests. *Silva Fennica*, **36**, 57–67.

Edenius, L., Brodin, T. & White, N. (2004) Occurrence of Siberian jay *Perisoreus infaustus* in relation to amount of old forest at landscape and home range scales. *Ecological Bulletins*, **51**, 241–247.

Edenius, L. & Elmberg, J. (1996) Landscape level effects of modern forestry on bird communities in north Swedish boreal forests. *Landscape Ecology*, **11**, 325–338.

Edenius, L., Mikusiński, G. & Bergh, J. (2011) Can repeated fertilizer applications to young Norway spruce enhance avian diversity in intensively managed forests? *Ambio*, **40**, 521–527.

Edenius, L., Mikusiński, G., Witzell, J. & Bergh, J. (2012) Effects of repeated fertilization of young Norway spruce on foliar phenolics and arthropods: Implications for insectivorous birds' food resources. *Forest Ecology and Management*, **277**, 38–45.

Edenius, L. & Sjöberg, K. (1997) Distribution of birds in natural landscape mosaics of old-growth forests in northern Sweden: Relations to habitat area and landscape context. *Ecography*, **20**, 425–431.

EEA (European Environment Agency) (2012) *Protected Areas in Europe: An Overview*. Report No. 5/2012. Copenhagen: European Environmental Agency.

Eggers, S. & Low, M. (2014) Differential demographic responses of sympatric Parids to vegetation management in boreal forest. *Forest Ecology and Management*, **319**, 169–175.

Elbakidze, M., Andersson, K., Angelstam, P. *et al.* (2013) Sustained yield forestry in Sweden and Russia: How does it correspond to sustainable forest management policy? *Ambio*, **42**, 160–173.

Elo, M., Roberge, J.-M., Rajasärkkä, A. & Mönkkönen, M. (2012) Energy density and its variation in space limit species richness of boreal forest birds. *Journal of Biogeography*, **39**, 1462–1472.

Enemar, A., Sjöstrand, B., Andersson, G. & von Proschwitz, T. (2004) The 37-year dynamics of a subalpine passerine bird community, with special emphasis on the influence of environmental temperature and *Epirrita autumnata* cycles. *Ornis Svecica*, **14**, 63-106.

Enoksson, B., Angelstam, P. & Larsson, K. (1995) Deciduous forest and resident birds: The problem of fragmentation within a coniferous forest landscape. *Landscape Ecology*, **10**, 267–275.

Esseen, P.-A., Ehnström, B., Ericson, L. & Sjöberg, K. (1997) Boreal forests. *Ecological Bulletins*, **46**, 16–47.

EU (2010) *Directive 2009/147/EC of the European Parliament and of the Council of 30 November 2009 on the Conservation of Wild Birds*. Brussels: Official Journal of the European Union L20/7.

Fahrig, L. (1997) Relative effects of habitat loss and fragmentation on population extinction. *Journal of Wildlife Management*, **61**, 603–610.

Fayt, P. (2003) Insect prey population changes in habitats with declining vs. stable three-toed woodpecker *Picoides tridactylus* populations. *Ornis Fennica*, **80**,182–192.

Felton, A., Andersson, E., Ventorp, D. & Lindbladh, M. (2011) A comparison of avian diversity in spruce monocultures and spruce-birch polycultures in southern Sweden. *Silva Fennica*, **45**, 1143–1150.

Forslund, M. (2003) *Fågelfaunan i olika skogsmiljöer – en studie på beståndsnivå*. Report 2/2003. Jönköping: Swedish Forest Agency.

Fox, A.D., Kobro, S., Lehikoinen, A., Lyngs, P. & Väisänen, R.A. (2009) Northern bullfinch *Pyrrhula p. pyrrhula* irruptive behaviour linked to rowanberry *Sorbus aucuparia* abundance. *Ornis Fennica*, **86**, 51–60.

Fraixedas, S., Lindén, A. & Lehikoinen, A. (2015) Population trends of common breeding forest birds in southern Finland are consistent with trends in forest management and climate change. *Ornis Fennica*, **92**, 187–203.

Fries, C., Johansson, O., Pettersson, B. & Simonsson, P. (1997) Silvicultural models to maintain and restore natural stand structures in Swedish boreal forests. *Forest Ecology and Management*, **94**, 89–103.

Gärdenfors, U. (ed.) (2010) *The 2010 Red List of Swedish Species*. Uppsala: Swedish Species Information Centre, SLU.

Gauthier, S., Bernier, P., Kuuluvainen, T., Shvidenko, A.Z. & Schepaschenko, D.G. (2015) Boreal forest health and global change. *Science*, **349**, 819–822.

Greenberg, R., Kozlenko, A., Etterson, M. & Dietsch, T. (2008) Patterns of density, diversity, and the distribution of migratory strategies in the Russian boreal forest avifauna. *Journal of Biogeography*, **35**, 2049–2060.

Griesser, M., Halvarsson, P., Sahlman, T. & Ekman, J. (2014) What are the strengths and limitations of direct and indirect assessment of dispersal? Insights from a long-term field study in a group-living bird species. *Behavioral Ecology and Sociobiology*, **68**, 485–497.

Gustafsson, L., Kouki, J. & Sverdrup-Thygeson, A. (2010) Tree retention as a conservation measure in clear-cut forests of northern Europe: A review of ecological consequences. *Scandinavian Journal of Forest Research*, **25**, 295–308.

Haapanen, A. (1966) Bird fauna of the Finnish forests in relation to forest succession II. *Annales Zoologici Fennici*, **3**, 176–200.

Haila, Y., Hanski, I.K., Niemelä, J., Punttila, P., Raivio, S. & Tukia, H. (1994) Forestry and the boreal fauna: Matching management with natural forest dynamics. *Annales Zoologici Fennici*, **31**, 187–202.

Haila, Y. & Järvinen, O. (1990) Northern conifer forests and their bird species assemblages. In *Biogeography and Ecology of Forest Bird Communities*. Keast, A. (ed.). The Hague: SPB Academic Publishing, pp. 61–85.

Haila, Y., Nicholls, A.O., Hanski, I.K. & Raivio, S. (1996) Stochasticity in bird habitat selection: Year-to-year changes in territory locations in boreal forest bird assemblage. *Oikos*, **76**, 536–552.

Hansen, M.C., Stehman, S.V. & Potapov, P.V. (2010) Quantification of global gross forest cover loss. *Proceedings of the National Academy of Sciences*, **107**, 8650–8655.

Hansson, L. & Henttonen, H. (1988) Rodent dynamics as community processes. *Trends in Ecology and Evolution*, **3**, 195–200.

Heikkinen, R.K., Luoto, M., Araújo, M.B., Virkkala, R., Thuiller, W. & Sykes, M.T. (2006) Methods and uncertainties in bioclimatic envelope modelling under climate change. *Progress in Physical Geography*, **30**, 751–777.

Heikkinen, R.K., Luoto, M., Virkkala, R., Pearson, R.G. & Körber, J.H. (2007) Biotic interactions improve prediction of boreal bird distributions at macro-scales. *Global Ecology and Biogeography*, **16**, 754–763.

Helander, B., Bignert, A. & Asplund, L. (2008) Using raptors as environmental sentinels: Monitoring the white-tailed sea eagle *Haliaeetus albicilla* in Sweden. *Ambio*, **37**, 425–431.

Helle, P. (1985a) Effects of forest regeneration on the structure of bird communities in northern Finland. *Holarctic Ecology*, **8**, 120–132.

Helle, P. (1985b) Habitat selection of breeding birds in relation to forest succession in Northeastern Finland. *Ornis Fennica*, **62**, 113–123.

Helle, P. & Järvinen, O. (1986) Population trends of North Finnish land birds in relation to their habitat selection and changes in forest structure. *Oikos*, **46**, 107–115.

Helle, P. & Mönkkönen, M. (1990) Forest successions and bird communities: Theoretical aspects and practical implications. In *Biogeography and Ecology of Forest Bird Communities*. Keast, A. (ed.). The Hague: Academic Publishing, pp. 299–318.

Hickler, T., Vohland, K., Feehan, J. *et al.* (2012) Projecting the future distribution of European potential natural vegetation zones with a generalized, tree species–based dynamic vegetation model. *Global Ecology and Biogeography*, **21**, 50–63.

Hickling, R., Roy, D.B., Hill, J.K., Fox, R. & Thomas, C.D. (2006) The distributions of a wide range of taxonomic groups are expanding polewards. *Global Change Biology*, **12**, 450–455.

Hogstad, O. (2005) Numerical and functional responses of breeding passerine species to mass occurrence of geometrid caterpillars in a subalpine birch forest: A 30-year study. *Ibis*, **147**, 77–91.

Hogstad, O. (2013) Species richness and structure of a breeding passerine bird community in a spruce-dominated boreal forest in central Norway: Stability from 1960s to 2013. *Ornis Norvegica*, **36**, 52–60.

Holmes, R.T. (1990) Ecological and evolutionary impacts of bird predation on forest insects: An overview. *Studies in Avian Biology*, **13**, 6–13.

Hörnfeldt B. (2004) Long-term decline in numbers of cyclic voles in boreal Sweden: Analysis and presentation of hypotheses. *Oikos*, **107**, 376–392.

Huhta, E. & Jokimäki, J. (2015) Landscape matrix fragmentation effect on virgin forest and managed forest birds: A multiscale study. *Advances of Environmental Sciences*, **36**, 95–111.

Huhta, E. & Sulkava, P. (2014) The impact of nature-based tourism on bird communities: A case study in Pallas-Yllastunturi National Park. *Environmental Management*, **53**, 1005–1014.

Huntley, B., Collingham, Y.C., Willis, S.G. & Green, R.E. (2008) Potential impacts of climate change on European breeding birds. *PLoS ONE*, **3(1)**, e1439.

Huntley, B., Green, R.E., Collingham, Y.C. & Willis, S.G. (2007) *A Climatic Atlas of European Breeding Birds*. Barcelona: Lynx Edicions.

Hutto, R.L. & Gallo, S.M. (2006) The effects of postfire salvage logging on cavity-nesting birds. *Condor*, **108**, 817–831.

Imbeau, L., Mönkkönen, M. & Desrochers, A. (2001) Long-term effects of forestry on birds of the eastern Canadian boreal forests: A comparison with Fennoscandia. *Conservation Biology*, **15**, 1151–1162.

Järvinen O. (1979) Geographical gradients of stability in European land bird communities. *Oecologia*, **38**, 51–69.

Järvinen, O. & Ulfstrand, S. (1980) Species turnover of a continental bird fauna: Northern Europe, 1850–1970. *Oecologia*, **46**, 186–195.

Jetz, W., Wilcove, D.S. & Dobson, A.P. (2007) Projected impacts of climate and land-use change on the global diversity of birds. *PLoS Biology*, **5**, 1211–1219.

Jiguet, F., Barbet-Massin, M., Devictor, V., Jonzen, N. & Lindström, Å. (2013) Current population trends mirror forecasted changes in climatic suitability for Swedish breeding birds. *Bird Study*, **60**, 60–66.

Jiguet, F., Gregory, R.D., Devictor, V. *et al.* (2010) Population trends of European common birds are predicted by characteristics of their climatic niche. *Global Change Biology*, **16**, 497–505.

Jokimäki, J. & Huhta, E. (1996) Effects of landscape matrix and habitat structure on a bird community in northern Finland: A multi-scale approach. *Ornis Fennica*, **73**, 97–113.

Jokimäki, J., Kaisanlahti-Jokimäki, M.L., Suhonen, J., Clergeau, P., Pautasso, M. & Fernández-Juricic, E. (2011) Merging wildlife community ecology with animal behavioral ecology for a better urban landscape planning. *Landscape and Urban Planning*, **100**, 383–385.

Kaisanlahti-Jokimäki, M.L., Jokimäki, J., Huhta, E., Ukkola, M., Helle, P. & Ollila, T. (2008) Territory occupancy and breeding success of the golden Eagle (*Aquila chrysaetos*) around tourist destinations in northern Finland. *Ornis Fennica*, **85**, 2–12.

Kålås, J.A., Viken, Å., Henriksen, S. & Skjelseth, S. (eds.). (2010) *The 2010 Norwegian Red List for Species*. Trondheim: Norwegian Biodiversity Information Centre.

Kamp, J., Oppel, S., Ananin, A.A. *et al.* (2015) Global population collapse in a superabundant migratory bird and illegal trapping in China. *Conservation Biology*, **29**, 1684–1694.

Kangas, K., Luoto, M., Ihantola, A., Tomppo, E. & Siikamäki, P. (2010) Recreation-induced changes in boreal bird communities in protected areas. *Ecological Applications*, **20**, 1775–1786.

Kauhala, K. & Kowalczyk, R. (2011) Invasion of the raccoon dog *Nyctereutes procyonoides* in Europe: History of colonization, features behind its success, and threats to native fauna. *Current Zoology*, **5**, 584–598.

Kellomäki, S., Peltola, H., Nuutinen, T., Korhonen, K.T. & Strandman, H. (2008) Sensitivity of managed boreal forests in Finland to climate change, with implications for adaptive management. *Philosophical Transactions of the Royal Society B*, **363**, 2341–2351.

Korpimäki, E. (1993) Regulation of multiannual vole cycles by density-dependent avian and mammalian predation? *Oikos*, **66**, 359–363.

Kouki, J. & Väänänen, A. (2000) Impoverishment of resident old-growth forest bird assemblages along an isolation gradient of protected areas in eastern Finland. *Ornis Fennica*, **77**, 145–154.

Kujala, H., Araújo, M.B., Thuiller, W. & Cabeza, M. (2011) Misleading results from conventional gap analysis: Messages from the warming north. *Biological Conservation*, **144**, 2450–2458.

Kurki, S., Nikula, A., Helle, P. & Lindén, H. (2000) Landscape fragmentation and forest composition effects on grouse breeding success in boreal forests. *Ecology*, **81**, 1985–1997.

Kuuluvainen, T. (2002) Natural variability of forests as a reference for restoring and managing biological diversity in boreal Fennoscandia. *Silva Fennica*, **36**, 97–125.

Laaksonen, T. & Lehikoinen, A. (2013) Population trends in boreal birds: Continuing declines in agricultural, northern, and long-distance migrant species. *Biological Conservation*, **168**, 99–107.

Lampila, P., Ranta, E., Mönkkönen, M., Lindén, H. & Helle, P. (2011) Grouse dynamics and harvesting in Kainuu, northeastern Finland. *Oikos*, **120**, 1057–1064.

Larsson, S. & Danell, K. (2001) Science and the management of boreal forest biodiversity. *Scandinavian Journal of Forest Research, Suppl.* **3**, 5–9.

Lehikoinen, A., Green, M., Husby, M., Kålås, J.A. & Lindström, Å. (2013) Common montane birds are declining in northern Europe. *Journal of Avian Biology*, **45**, 3–14.

Lindström, Å., Green, M., Paulson, G., Smith, H.G. & Devictor, V. (2013) Rapid changes in bird community composition at multiple temporal and spatial scales in response to recent climate change. *Ecography*, **36**, 313–322.

Loarie, S.R., Duffy, P.B., Hamilton, H., Asner, G.P., Field, C.B. & Ackerly, D.D. (2009) The velocity of climate change. *Nature*, **462**, 1052–1055.

Losos, J.B. (2008) Phylogenetic niche conservatism, phylogenetic signal and the relationship between phylogenetic relatedness and ecological similarity among species. *Ecology Letters*, **11**, 995–1003.

Mahon, C.L., Bayne, E.M., Sólymos, P. *et al.* (2014) Does expected future landscape condition support proposed population objectives for boreal birds? *Forest Ecology and Management*, **312**, 28–39.

Mayr, E. (1990) Plattentektonik und die Geschichte der Vogel faunen. In *Proceedings of the International Centennial Meeting of the Deutsche Ornithologen-Gesellschaft, Current Topics in Avian Biology*. Stuttgart: Deutsche Ornithologen-Gesellshaft, pp. 1–17.

Mazziotta, A., Mönkkönen, M., Strandman, H., Routa, J., Tikkanen, O.-P. & Kellomäki, S. (2014) Modeling the effects of climate change and management on the dead wood dynamics in boreal forest plantations. *European Journal of Forest Research*, **133**, 405–421.

Mikusiński, G. (1997) Winter foraging of the black woodpecker *Dryocopus martius* in managed forest in south-central Sweden. *Ornis Fennica*, **74**, 161–166.

Mild, K. & Stighäll, K. (2005) *Action Plan for the Conservation of the Swedish Population of White-Backed Woodpecker (Dendrocopos leucotos)*. Stockholm: Swedish Environmental Protection Agency.

Moen, A. (1999) *National Atlas of Norway – Vegetation*. Hønefoss: Norwegian Mapping Authority.

Mönkkönen, M. (1994) Diversity patterns in Palaearctic and Nearctic forest bird assemblages. *Journal of Biogeography*, **21**, 183–195.

Mönkkönen, M. & Aspi, J. (1998) Sampling error in measuring temporal density variability in animal populations and communities. *Annales Zoologici Fennici*, **34**. 47–57.

Mönkkönen, M. & Forsman, J.T. (2005) Ecological and biogeographical aspects of the distribution of migrants vs. residents in European and North

American forest bird communities. In *Birds of the Two Worlds.* Greenberg, R. & Marra, P.P. (eds.). Washington, DC: Johns Hopkins University Press, pp. 131–142.

Mönkkönen, M. & Helle, P. (1989) Migratory habits of birds breeding in different stages of forest succession: A comparison between the Palaearctic and the Nearctic. *Annales Zoologici Fennici,* **26**, 323 330.

Mönkkönen, M., Juutinen, A., Mazziotta, A. *et al.* (2014b) Spatially dynamic forest management to sustain biodiversity and economic returns. *Journal of Environmental Management,* **134**, 80–89.

Mönkkönen, M., Rajasärkkä, A. & Lampila, P. (2014a) Isolation, patch size and matrix effects on bird assemblages in forest reserves. *Biodiversity and Conservation,* **23**, 3287–3300.

Mönkkönen, M., Reunanen, P., Kotiaho, J.S., Juutinen, A., Tikkanen, O.-P. & Kouki, J. (2011) Cost-effective strategies to conserve boreal forest biodiversity and long-term landscape-level maintenance of habitats. *European Journal of Forest Research,* **130**, 717–727.

Mönkkönen, M. & Viro, P. (1997) Taxonomic diversity in avian and mammalian faunas of the northern hemisphere. *Journal of Biogeography,* **24**, 603–612.

Mönkkönen, M. & Welsh, D. (1994) A biogeographical hypothesis on the effects of human caused habitat changes on the forest bird communities of Europe and North America. *Annales Zoologici Fennici,* **31**, 61–70.

Morozov, N.S. (1992) Breeding forest birds in the Valdai Uplands, north-west Russia: Assemblage composition, interspecific associations and habitat amplitudes. *Annales Zoologici Fennici,* **29**, 7–27.

Muukkonen, P., Angervuori, A., Virtanen, T., Kuparinen, A. & Merilä, J. (2012) Loss and fragmentation of Siberian jay (*Perisoreus infaustus*) habitats. *Boreal Environment Research,* **17**, 59–71.

Myllyntaus, T., Hares, M. & Kunnas, J. (2002) Sustainability in danger? Slash-and-burn cultivation in nineteenth-century Finland and twentieth-century Southeast Asia. *Environmental History,* **7**, 267–302.

Niemelä, J., Larsson, S. & Simberloff, D. (2001) Concluding remarks – finding ways to integrate timber production and biodiversity in Fennoscandian forestry. *Scandinavian Journal of Forest Research,* Suppl. **3**, 119–123.

Niemi, G., Hanowski, J., Helle, P. *et al.* (1998) Ecological sustainability of birds in boreal forests. *Conservation Ecology,* **2 (2)**, 17.

Nilsson, S.G. (1997) Forests in the temperate-boreal transition: Natural and man-made features. *Ecological Bulletins,* **46**, 61–71.

Nordström, G. (1953) Results of the census work on the birds breeding in three different forests during five years. *Ornis Fennica,* **30**, 56–67. [in Swedish, English summary]

Nordström, M., Högmander, J., Laine, J., Nummelin, J., Laanetu, N. & Korpimäki, E. (2003) Effects of feral mink removal on seabirds, waders and passerines on small islands in the Baltic Sea. *Biological Conservation,* **109**, 359–368.

Noss, R.F. (1990) Indicators for monitoring biodiversity: A hierarchical approach. *Conservation Biology,* **4**, 355–364.

Olson, D.M., Dinerstein, E., Wikramanayake, E.D. *et al.* (2001) Terrestrial ecoregions of the world: A new map of life on Earth. *Bioscience*, **51**, 933–938.

Östlund, L. & Roturier S. (2011) Forestry historical studies in the province of Västerbotten, Northern Sweden: A review of Lars Tirén (1937). *Scandinavian Journal of Forest Research*, **26** (Suppl. 10), 91–99.

Palmgren, P. (1930) Quantitative Untersuchungen über die Vogelfauna in den Wäldern Südfinnlands mit besonderer Berücksichtigung Ålands. *Acta Zoologica Fennica*, **7**, 1–218.

Pearson, R.G., Dawson, T.P. & Liu, C. (2004) Modelling species distributions in Britain: A hierarchical integration of climate and land-cover data. *Ecography*, **27**, 285–298.

Pennanen, J. (2002) Forest age distribution under mixed-severity fire regimes – a simulation-based analysis for middle boreal Fennoscandia. *Silva Fennica*, **36**, 213–231.

Pohja-Mykrä, M., Vuorisalo, T. & Mykrä, S. (2012) Organized persecution of birds of prey in Finland: Historical and population biological perspectives. *Ornis Fennica*, **89**, 1–19.

Potapov, P., Yaroshenko, A., Turubanova, S. *et al.* (2008) Mapping the world's intact forest landscapes by remote sensing. *Ecology and Society*, **13**, 51.

Ram, D., Axelsson, A.-L., Green, M., Smith, H.G. & Lindström, Å. (2017) What drives current population trends in forest birds – forest quantity, quality or climate? A large-scale analysis from northern Europe. *Forest Ecology and Management*, **385**, 177–188.

Rassi, P., Hyvärinen, E., Juslén, A. & Mannerkoski, I. (eds.). (2010) *The 2010 Red List of Finnish Species*. Helsinki: Ympäristöministeriö & Suomen ympäristökeskus.

Roberge, J.-M., Angelstam, P. & Villard, M.-A. (2008) Specialised woodpeckers and naturalness in hemiboreal forests – deriving quantitative targets for conservation planning. *Biological Conservation*, **141**, 997–1012.

Roberge, J.-M., Lämås, T., Lundmark, T., Ranius, T., Felton, A. & Nordin, A. (2015) Relative contributions of set-asides and tree retention to the long-term availability of key forest biodiversity structures at the landscape scale. *Journal of Environmental Management*, **154**, 284–292.

Robinson, S.K., Thompson, F.R.I., Donovan, T.M., Whitehead, D.R. & Faaborg, J. (1995) Regional forest fragmentation and the nesting success of migratory birds. *Science*, **267**, 1987–1990.

Rolstad, J. & Rolstad, E. (1995) Seasonal patterns in home range and habitat use of the grey-headed woodpecker *Picus canus* as influenced by the availability of food. *Ornis Fennica*, **72**, 1–13.

Rolstad, J. & Rolstad, E. (2000) Influence of large snow depths on black woodpecker *Dryocopus martius* foraging behavior. *Ornis Fennica*, **77**, 65–70.

Rolstad, J., Rolstad, E. & Saeteren, O. (2000) Black woodpecker nest sites: Characteristics, selection, and reproductive success. *Journal of Wildlife Management*, **64**, 1053–1066.

Saino, N., Ambrosini, R., Rubolini, D. *et al.* (2011) Climate warming, ecological mismatch at arrival and population decline in migratory birds. *Proceedings of the Royal Society B*, **278**, 835–842.

Sanderson, F.J., Donald, P.F., Pain, D.J., Burfield, I.J. & van Bommel, F.P.J. (2006) Long-term population declines in Afro-Palearctic migrant birds. *Biological Conservation*, **131**, 93–105.

Schmiegelow, F.K.A. & Mönkkönen, M. (2002) Habitat loss and fragmentation in dynamic landscapes: Avian perspectives from the boreal forest. *Ecological Applications*, **12**, 375–389.

Siitonen, J. (2001) Forest management, coarse woody debris, and saproxylic organisms: Fennoscandian boreal forests as an example. *Ecological Bulletins*, **49**, 11–41.

Siitonen, J., Martikainen, P., Punttila, P. & Rauh, J. (2000) Coarse woody debris and stand characteristics in mature managed and old-growth boreal mesic forests in southern Finland. *Forest Ecology and Management*, **128**, 211–225.

Simberloff, D. (1999) The role of science in the preservation of forest biodiversity. *Forest Ecology and Management*, **115**, 101–111.

Simberloff, D. (2001) Management of boreal forest biodiversity – a view from the outside. *Scandinavian Journal of Forest Research,* Suppl. **3**, 105–118.

Söderström, B. (2009) Effects of different levels of green- and dead-tree retention on hemi-boreal forest bird communities in Sweden. *Forest Ecology and Management*, **257**, 215–222.

Solonen, T. (1996) Patterns and variations in the structure of forest bird communities in southern Finland. *Ornis Fennica*, **73**, 12–26.

Solonen, T. (2008) Larger broods in the northern goshawk *Accipiter gentilis* near urban areas in southern Finland. *Ornis Fennica*, **85**, 118–125.

Stokland, J. (1997) Representativeness and efficiency of bird and insect conservation in Norwegian boreal forest reserves. *Conservation Biology*, **11**, 101–111.

Suorsa, P., Huhta, E., Jäntti, A. *et al.* (2005) Thresholds in selection of breeding habitat by the Eurasian treecreeper (*Certhia familiaris*). *Biological Conservation*, **121**, 443–452.

Svensson, S., Svensson, M. & Tjernberg, M. (1999) *Svensk fågelatlas*. Stockholm: Sveriges Ornitologiska Förening.

Tikkanen, O.-P., Matero, J., Mönkkönen, M., Juutinen, A. & Kouki, J. (2012) To thin or not to thin: Bio-economic analysis of two alternative practices to increase amount of coarse woody debris in managed forests. *European Journal of Forest Research*, **131**, 1411–1422.

Timonen, J., Siitonen, J., Gustafsson, L. *et al.* (2010) Woodland key habitats in northern Europe: Concepts, inventory and protection. *Scandinavian Journal of Forest Research*, **25**, 309–324.

Tjernberg, M. (2010) *Aquila chrysaetos* kungsörn – artfaktablad. Uppsala: Swedish Species Information Centre, SLU.

Tuhkanen, S. (1980) Climatic parameters and indices in plant geography. *Acta Phytogeographica Suecica*, **67**.

Väisänen, R.A., Lammi, E. & Koskimies, P. (1998) *Distribution, Numbers and Population Changes of Finnish Breeding Birds*. Helsinki: Otava. [in Finnish, English summary]

Valkama, J., Vepsäläinen, V. & Lehikoinen, A. (2011) *The Third Finnish Breeding Bird Atlas*. Helsinki: Finnish Museum of Natural History and Ministry of Environment.

Vanha-Majamaa, I. & Jalonen, J. (2001) Green tree retention in Fennoscandian forestry. *Scandinavian Journal of Forest Research*, **16** Suppl. **3**, 79–90.

Vilén, T., Gunia, K., Verkerk, P.J. *et al.* (2012) Reconstructed forest age structure in Europe 1950–2010. *Forest Ecology and Management*, **286**, 203–218.

Vindstad, O.P., Jepsen, J.U. & Ims, R.A. (2015) Resistance of a sub-arctic bird community to severe forest damage caused by geometrid moth outbreaks. *European Journal of Forest Research*, **134**, 725–736.

Virkkala, R. (1987a) Effects of forest management on birds breeding in northern Finland. *Annales Zoologici Fennici*, **24**, 281–294.

Virkkala, R. (1987b) Geographical variation in bird communities of old, intact forests in northern Finland. *Ornis Fennica*, **64**,107–118.

Virkkala, R. (1990) Ecology of the Siberian tit *Parus cinctus* in relation to habitat quality – effects of forest management. *Ornis Scandinavica*, **21**, 139–146.

Virkkala, R. (1991) Spatial and temporal variation in bird communities and populations in north-boreal coniferous forests: A multiscale approach. *Oikos*, **62**, 59–66.

Virkkala, R. (2004) Bird species dynamics in a managed southern boreal forest in Finland. *Forest Ecology and Management*, **195**, 151–163.

Virkkala, R. (2016) Long-term decline of southern boreal forest birds: Consequence of habitat alteration or climate change? *Biodiversity and Conservation*, **25**, 151–167.

Virkkala, R., Heikkinen, R.K., Fronzek, S., Kujala, H. & Leikola, N. (2013) Does the protected area network preserve bird species of conservation concern in a rapidly changing climate? *Biodiversity and Conservation*, **22**, 459–482.

Virkkala, R., Heikkinen, R.K., Lehikoinen, A. & Valkama, J. (2014) Matching trends between recent distributional changes of northern-boreal birds and species-climate model predictions. *Biological Conservation*, **172**, 124–127.

Virkkala, R., Heikkinen, R.K., Leikola, N. & Luoto, M. (2008) Projected large-scale range reductions of northern-boreal land bird species due to climate change. *Biological Conservation*, **141**, 1343–1353.

Virkkala, R., Heinonen, M. & Routasuo, P. (1991) The response of northern taiga birds to storm disturbance in the Koilliskaira National Park, Finnish Lapland. *Ornis Fennica*, **68**, 123–126.

Virkkala, R. & Lehikoinen, A. (2014) Patterns of climate-induced density shifts of species: Poleward shifts faster in northern boreal birds than in southern birds. *Global Change Biology*, **20**, 2995–3003.

Virkkala, R., Marmion, M., Heikkinen, R.K., Thuiller, W. & Luoto, M. (2010) Predicting range shifts of northern bird species: Influence of modelling technique and topography. *Acta Oecologica*, **36**, 269–281.

Virkkala, R. & Rajasärkkä, A. (2006) Spatial variation of bird species in landscapes dominated by old-growth forests in northern boreal Finland. *Biodiversity and Conservation*, **15**, 2143–2162.

Virkkala, R. & Rajasärkkä, A. (2007) Uneven distribution of protected areas in Finland: Consequences for boreal forest bird populations. *Biological Conservation*, **134**, 361–371.

Virkkala, R. & Rajasärkkä, A. (2011a) Climate change affects populations of northern birds in boreal protected areas. *Biology Letters*, **7**, 395–398.

Virkkala, R. & Rajasärkkä, A. (2011b) Northward density shift of bird species in boreal protected areas due to climate change. *Boreal Environment Research*, **16** (Suppl. B), 2–13.

Virkkala R. & Rajasärkkä, A. (2012) Preserving species populations in the boreal zone in a changing climate: Contrasting trends of bird species groups in a protected area network. *Nature Conservation*, **3**, 1–20.

Wisz, M.S., Pottier, J., Kissling, W.D. *et al.* (2013) The role of biotic interactions in shaping distributions and realised assemblages of species: Implications for species distribution modelling. *Biological Reviews*, **88**, 15–30.

Zackrisson, O. (1977) Influence of forest fires on the North Swedish boreal forest. *Oikos* **29**: 22–32.

7 · Subalpine Coniferous Forests of Europe

Avian Communities in European High-Altitude Woodlands

PIERRE MOLLET, KURT BOLLMANN, VERONIKA BRAUNISCH AND RAPHAËL ARLETTAZ

7.1 Forest Ecosystem

7.1.1 Introduction

Subalpine coniferous forests cover higher-altitudinal zones in various mountain ranges of Europe, notably in the Alps, Pyrenees and Carpathians, as well as some lower-elevation massifs in central and south-east Europe (defined as category 3 by the European map of natural vegetation; Bohn *et al.* 2000). These forests are characterised by a dominance of coniferous trees, compared to the lower-altitude montane forests, which are mainly composed of broadleaved trees (Ott *et al.* 1997; Landolt 2003). This distinction between montane and subalpine forests is important, because bird species assemblages generally differ quite markedly between conifer and broadleaved woodlands (Fuller *et al.* 2012; see also Chapters 6 and 8). Montane forests provide habitats supporting very rich bird assemblages linked to the presence of both coniferous and broadleaved forest features and thereby resemble forests of the hemiboreal (boreonemoral) zone (Nilsson 1997). Although a few studies have focused specifically on bird assemblages of montane forests in the Carpathians (e.g., Kropil 1996; Korňan & Adamík 2014) and the Alps (e.g., Archaux & Bakkaus 2007), montane forests are not treated separately in this book. The reader can refer to Chapter 8 (and to some extent Chapter 6) for content of relevance to the bird assemblages of these forests. Conifers tend to become dominant over broad-leaved trees under harsher environmental conditions (Ellenberg 2009). The principal environmental drivers of subalpine coniferous forest tree species composition are altitude, topography, soil conditions and natural history, particularly the history of recolonisation of mountain ranges by tree species after the Pleistocene ice ages. More specifically, climatic and weather conditions, ambient temperature, precipitation regime and type (snow *vs* rain), frost occurrence, air moisture and solar radiation all tightly correlate with altitude, topography and continentality, playing crucial roles in forest dynamics, notably in rejuvenation processes. This chapter considers the entire subalpine coniferous zone, including the ecologically distinctive ecotone along the upper treeline.

Subalpine coniferous forests occur within a given altitudinal belt, typically between the montane mixed forests and alpine grasslands. The absolute altitude and altitudinal range of this belt vary among the different mountain massifs considered. It tends to be situated higher and to extend across a broader altitudinal amplitude in areas where the climate is warmer or drier. This is the case, for instance, in the inner valleys of the Alps, due to the protective effect of high mountain ridges, which locally create a more continental climate. Thus, the limit between montane and subalpine forests almost never follows isotherms and shows great altitudinal variation. This is because of the manifold relationships between local climatic conditions, topographic circumstances, altitude and slope exposure typically encountered in mountain ranges with a complex topography (Körner 1998).

At first glance, the upper altitudinal limit of subalpine forest distribution seems evident. Worldwide, in all high massifs, there is a treeline somewhere above which tree growth is no longer possible (Fig. 7.1). However, this treeline is rarely a sharp line; it usually forms an ecotonal zone with gradual opening of the canopy and steadily wider spacing of individual trees as altitude increases (Körner 2012). The treeline belt can stretch across only a few metres under very steep conditions, whereas it can extend over several hundred metres in rather flat terrain. This natural zonal habitat heterogeneity is accentuated by uneven terrain and the resulting heterogeneous distribution of soil types. It is further modified by natural disturbances such as snow avalanches and landslides. Finally, it has been greatly influenced by human activity, since both timber production and grazing were important for the economy of Old World traditional mountain societies across centuries, if not millennia (Bugmann 2001; Bätzing 2005; Körner 2012). Given their pronounced habitat and structural heterogeneity, treeline ecosystems are inhabited by a rich species community in general, and a unique bird community in particular

(a)

(b)

Figure 7.1 (a) Looked at from far away, the upper altitudinal limit of a subalpine forest seems to be a more or less clearly defined line. (b) In reality, it's rather an ecotonal zone, with gradual opening of the canopy and steadily wider spacing of individual trees as altitude increases or productivity of the soil decreases, even in forests with no signs of past human intervention. (a) Val dal Spöl, Grisons, Switzerland and (b) pure larch forest on very rocky soil in the southern Alps, close to Alpe Magnello, Ticino, Switzerland. Photos: P. Mollet.

(Mattes *et al.* 2005). Here, birds with mainly Mediterranean distributions may live in sympatry with boreo-alpine species, and typical forest species meet species that are adapted to very open land with scattered single trees and grassy field layers.

7.1.2 Forest Cover

Traces of exploitation of subalpine forests by humans have been documented from the second millennium BC onwards, but large-scale landscape changes, resulting from burning and systematic tree felling, primarily to increase the area of grazed or mown grasslands, apparently accelerated in the 9th or 10th century AD; at least this has been documented for the Alps (Burga & Perret 1998). Forest conversion and exploitation continued unabated throughout the Middle Ages and the modern epoch until the late 19th and early 20th centuries (Parolini 2012). Later, during the 20th century, traditional silvi-agricultural land-use systems were progressively abandoned due to profound socioeconomic changes, but the magnitude of their effects depended on the geographic area or even the political system. Among other factors, the progressive reliance on petrol instead of wood fuel caused a dramatic release of the economic pressure formerly exerted upon subalpine forests. This development was paralleled by a progressive shift towards more sustainable forest management (see Johann 2006 for details), together resulting in an increase of forest extent and the stock of growing trees. Despite the abandonment of traditional agricultural and silvi-pastoral practices, the area covered by forest remains smaller today than what it would be naturally, i.e., without past human intervention. Some mountain areas, however, have recently undergone forestry intensification. In some regions of the Slovak and Romanian Carpathians, for instance, subalpine forests are being subjected to large-scale clearcutting by multinational companies, severely impacting the avifauna, as illustrated by the dramatic decline of local populations of capercaillie *Tetrao urogallus* (Mikoláš *et al.* 2015). A first crucial conservation issue is how a progressive reliance upon more renewable energy sources will affect subalpine forest management and its ecological community in the future. A second key issue is how land-use changes, notably the release of grazing pressure, will impact on species requiring semi-open and open grassy habitats (Chamberlain *et al.* 2013). These developments, and their consequences for subalpine birds, should be closely monitored.

7.1.3 Tree Species Composition

Tree species composition depends heavily on soil and local climate conditions. In general, European subalpine forests are dominated by four main tree species, while two additional species may be important locally. In the Alps and the Carpathians, Norway spruce *Picea abies* is the most widely distributed and most abundant tree. It is absent from the Pyrenees. After the last Pleistocene ice age, the Norway spruce recolonised the Alps and the Carpathians from the south-east (Burga & Perret 1998) and most likely never reached the Pyrenees. In many European subalpine forests, silver fir *Abies alba* is an important species, notably at lower altitudes and in rather humid and cool local climates. However, it rarely forms pure stands, being usually associated with other tree species, principally Norway spruce in subalpine conditions at higher altitudes. In inner alpine valleys, which are characterised by a pronounced continental climate (see above), the European larch *Larix decidua* may occupy vast areas. It requires very light conditions (i.e., it does not tolerate shade) and is usually associated with poor and shallow soils. Swiss stone pine *Pinus cembra* also covers wide areas at the treeline. This species is one of the most tolerant to cold temperatures and reaches the highest altitudes of any tree in the Alps, at slightly more than 2,500 m above sea level in

Valais, Switzerland. Stone pine can form pure, albeit mostly open or semi-open, stands, but is more often associated with larch. Neither the larch nor the stone pine occurs in the Pyrenees, but both have a fine-scale and spatially scattered distribution pattern in the Carpathians, including the High Tatra mountains.

Apart from these four dominant tree species, two other pines can be encountered in the subalpine zones of the Alps and on the southern slopes of the Pyrenees: Scots pine *Pinus sylvestris* and mountain pine *Pinus mugo* (var. *arborea, ssp. uncinata*, according to some sources), the latter in its upright growth form. In the Alps, however, they rarely cover large areas, occurring primarily on small patches of very poor soils, where they can break the dominance of the other four species. An exception is in the Swiss National Park, in south-east Switzerland next to the Italian border, where extensive pure stands of mountain pine dominate on a dolomitic substrate. On the southern slopes of the Pyrenees, where the climate is fairly dry (characterised by Mediterranean summers), the two species are widespread and predominant in subalpine woodlands. Mountain pine exists in another shrub-like form (*var. prostrata, ssp. mugo*, according to some sources), which covers large areas only in the eastern Alps and the Carpathians. Yet another potentially landscape-dominating element in the subalpine belt is the green alder *Alnus viridis*, a small bush-like tree that can form pure stands, particularly on cooler and steep slopes that are regularly exposed to snow avalanches.

At a local scale, tree-species composition depends not only on climatic and edaphic conditions, but also on historic and recent human activity. Silvi-agricultural land-use systems favour the larch over the Norway spruce (Mayer & Stöckli 2005), most probably due to both the enhanced light supply and the fact that many farmers spared the larches when cutting young trees (Janett 1943).

Finally, it is important to note that, in contrast to lower elevations, large-scale plantations of non-native tree species have never been important in subalpine forests, most likely as a consequence of the prevailing harsh climatic conditions.

7.1.4 Forest Structure

Structurally, subalpine forests can form two rather distinct types of stands. At lower elevations, close to the limits of montane woods, subalpine forests occasionally develop stands with a rather closed canopy, limited understorey and very scarce, if any, ground vegetation. At this elevation,

Figure 7.2 Typical subalpine forest stand with dominant conifers (*Picea abies*) in the tree layer at 1,200 m above sea level in Uaul Grond, Surselva, in Grisons, Switzerland. Microtopographic heterogeneity and disturbance agents support the development of semi-open stands with a well-developed ground layer and tree rejuvenation at microclimatic favoured sites. The avifaunistic diversity of such forests is high due to the availability of diverse ecological niches in the canopy, tree, shrub and ground layers. Photo: K. Bollmann.

more open stands only occur on poor soils or as a result of natural or anthropogenic disturbances such as avalanches, slope slides, fire, windthrow, bark beetle infestations or timber exploitation (Fig. 7.2).

In comparison, extensive closed stands are rare in the higher-altitude subalpine belt close to the treeline. Here, open stands predominate, typically accompanied by a rich understorey characteristic of early successional stages, consisting of small deciduous trees belonging to the genera *Betula*, *Sorbus*, *Salix* and *Alnus*, and dwarf shrubs such as *Vaccinium* ssp., *Rhododendron* ssp. and *Juniperus communis* (var. *saxatilis*). Many of these species provide important food resources for forest birds, notably various berries and buds (Turček 1961). Centuries-long grazing activity in those high-elevation forests, furthermore, has led to an even more open landscape, the woody vegetation being frequently intermixed with an extended grassy field layer (Fig. 7.3).

Human management of this zone has significantly lowered the treeline in many regions (Körner 2012). These profound structural differences between closed coniferous stands at lower elevations within the subalpine belt and very open vegetation in the treeline zone give rise to rather different bird assemblages, with typical forest guilds in the former and a dominance of ecotonal species in the latter habitat type.

Figure 7.3 Cattle grazing and browsing keep subalpine forests open through suppression of rejuvenation. Farmers sometimes also eliminate young trees actively. Forest with larch (*Larix decidua*), spruce (*Picea abies*) and some Scots pine (*Pinus sylvestris*) above Tschlin, Grisons, Switzerland. Photo: P. Mollet.

7.2 Bird Assemblages

7.2.1 Large-scale Variation in Species Richness and Abundance

Bird-species richness is lower in subalpine than in lowland and montane forests (Mosimann *et al*. 1987), which has been attributed to a decrease in net primary productivity – and therefore a decrease in the availability of ecological niches – with increasing altitude (Zbinden *et al*. 2010). According to presence–absence data from various breeding bird atlases (e.g., Dvorak *et al*. 1993; Niederfriniger *et al*. 1996; Schmid *et al*. 1998; Estrada *et al*. 2005), subalpine breeding bird assemblages are rather similar across European mountain ranges (Table 7.1), with a few noticeable exceptions:

a) Some species with a typical boreo-alpine distribution are absent from the Pyrenees: hazel grouse *Tetrastes bonasia*, black grouse *Lyrurus tetrix*, three-toed woodpecker *Picoides tridactylus* and pygmy owl *Glaucidium passerinum*.

b) Ural owl *Strix uralensis* is largely restricted to northern and eastern Europe, and in the Alps occurs only in Bavaria and in the far south-east of the massif.

c) Some species which are widespread throughout northern, central and eastern Europe have their western distribution limits in central France, thus not reaching the Pyrenean massif, e.g., willow tit *Poecile montanus* and lesser whitethroat *Sylvia curruca*.

d) Citril finch (*Serinus citrinella*) and western Bonelli's warbler *Phylloscopus bonelli* occur in south-western and southern Europe, respectively, but not in the Carpathians.

Table 7.1 Breeding bird species in European subalpine forests according to Catzeflis (1979), Estrada et al. (2005), Meier (1954), Mosimann et al. (1987), Müller-Buser (2002), Saniga (1995) and Schmid et al. (1998) and unpublished data by the authors. EU Bird Directive status according to Ddirective 2009/147/EC of the European Parliament and the Council of 30 November 2009 on the conservation of wild birds (http://ec.europa.eu/environment/nature/legislation/birdsdirective/index_en.htm, accessed 13 July 2015), SPEC categories according to Burfield and van Bommel (2004). All the species are classified as 'Least Concern' on the Red List (BirdLife International 2015).

	English	Scientific	Pyrenees	Jura & Alps	Carpathians	EU Bird Directive Annex I	SPEC
1	Northern goshawk	Acipiter gentilis	Yes	Yes	Yes	No	Non-SPEC
2	Eurasian sparrowhawk	Acipiter nisus	Yes	Yes	Yes	No	Non-SPEC
3	Hazel grouse	Tetrastes bonasia	No	Yes	Yes	Yes	Non-SPEC
4	Black grouse	Lyrurus tetrix	No	Yes	Yes	Yes	SPEC 3
5	Western capercaillie	Tetrao urogallus	Yes	Yes	Yes	Yes	Non-SPEC
6	Eurasian woodcock	Scolopax rusticola	Yes	Yes	Yes	No	SPEC 3
7	Common cuckoo	Cuculus canorus	Yes	Yes	Yes	No	Non-SPEC
8	Eurasian pygmy owl	Glaucidium passerinum	No	Yes	Yes	Yes	Non-SPEC
9	Tengmalm's owl	Aegolius funereus	Yes	Yes	Yes	Yes	Non-SPEC
10	Long-eared owl	Asio otus	Yes	Yes	Yes	No	Non-SPEC
11	Ural owl	Strix uralensis	No	Partly	Yes	Yes	Non-SPEC
12	European green woodpecker	Picus viridis	Yes	Yes	Yes	No	SPEC 2
13	Black woodpecker	Dryocopus martius	Yes	Yes	Yes	Yes	Non-SPEC
14	Great spotted woodpecker	Dendrocopos major	Yes	Yes	Yes	No	Non-SPEC
15	Three-toed woodpecker	Picoides tridactylus	No	Yes	Yes	Yes	SPEC 3
16	Tree pipit	Anthus trivialis	Yes	Yes	Yes	No	Non-SPEC
17	Eurasian wren	Troglodytes troglodytes	Yes	Yes	Yes	No	Non-SPEC
18	Dunnock	Prunella modularis	Yes	Yes	Yes	No	Non-SPEC

No.	Common name	Scientific name				Status
19	European robin	*Erithacus rubecula*	Yes	Yes	No	Non-SPEC
20	Ring ouzel	*Turdus torquatus*	Yes	Yes	No	Non-SPEC
21	Common blackbird	*Turdus merula*	Yes	Yes	No	Non-SPEC
22	Fieldfare	*Turdus pilaris*	No	Yes	No	Non-SPEC
23	Song thrush	*Turdus philomelos*	Yes	Yes	No	Non-SPEC
24	Mistle thrush	*Turdus viscivorus*	Yes	Yes	No	Non-SPEC
25	Lesser whitethroat	*Sylvia curruca*	No	Yes	No	Non-SPEC
26	Garden warbler	*Sylvia borin*	Yes	Yes	No	Non-SPEC
27	Blackcap	*Sylvia atricapilla*	Yes	Yes	No	Non-SPEC
28	Western Bonelli's warbler	*Phylloscopus bonelli*	Yes	No	No	SPEC 2
29	Chiffchaff	*Phylloscopus collybita*	Yes	Yes	No	Non-SPEC
30	Goldcrest	*Regulus regulus*	Yes	Yes	No	Non-SPEC
31	Firecrest	*Regulus ignicapilla*	Yes	Yes	No	Non-SPEC
32	Willow tit	*Poecile montanus*	No	Yes	No	Non-SPEC
33	Crested tit	*Lophophanes cristatus*	Yes	Yes	No	SPEC 2
34	Coal tit	*Periparus ater*	Yes	Yes	No	Non-SPEC
35	Eurasian nuthatch	*Sitta europaea*	Yes	Yes	No	Non-SPEC
36	Eurasian treecreeper	*Certhia familiaris*	Yes	Yes	No	Non-SPEC
37	Eurasian jay	*Garrulus glandarius*	Yes	Yes	No	Non-SPEC
38	Spotted nutcracker	*Nucifraga caryocatactes*	No	Yes	No	Non-SPEC
39	Common chaffinch	*Fringilla coelebs*	Yes	Yes	No	Non-SPEC
40	Citril finch	*Serinus citrinella*	Yes	No	No	Non-SPEC
41	Eurasian siskin	*Carduelis spinus*	Yes	Yes	No	Non-SPEC
42	Common linnet	*Carduelis cannabina*	Yes	Yes	No	Non-SPEC
43	Common redpoll	*Carduelis flammea*	No	Yes	No	Non-SPEC
44	Common crossbill	*Loxia curvirostra*	Yes	Yes	No	Non-SPEC
45	Eurasian bullfinch	*Pyrrhula pyrrhula*	Yes	Yes	No	Non-SPEC

In the lower subalpine forests (denser coniferous stands), most bird species are woodland generalists that occur in almost any type of forest, from the lowlands up to the treeline. Chaffinch *Fringilla coelebs* and coal tit *Periparus ater* are the two most widespread and abundant bird species of European subalpine forests, whether in the Jura (Catzeflis 1979), the Alps (Meier 1954; Mosimann *et al.* 1987; Schmid *et al.* 1998; Müller-Buser 2002), the Carpathians (Saniga 1995) or the Pyrenees (Estrada *et al.* 2005). Nevertheless, their populations can apparently undergo pronounced interannual demographic fluctuations (Müller-Buser 2002), most probably as a result of highly variable breeding success that might itself be dictated by variation in food supply. Another ubiquitous species, the blackbird *Turdus merula*, occurs at much lower abundance in subalpine than in montane and lowland forests. Although highly adaptable, since it occurs in private gardens and urban parks as well as in some treeline habitats, this species has its strongholds in deciduous forests.

Then there is a group of presumably more specialised species that are common in subalpine forests but absent or very rare in central European lowland and montane forests. Good examples are pygmy owl, three-toed woodpecker, citril finch and ring ouzel *Turdus torquatus*. As these species differ markedly in life history and foraging strategies (tree *vs* ground foraging), their preferences for coniferous forests probably have different ecological causes. Three-toed woodpecker and pygmy owl are emblematic inhabitants of conifer-dominated forests. They show a classical boreo-alpine distribution range in Europe, which is fairly congruent with the large-scale distribution of Norway spruce (Hess 1983). The three-toed woodpecker (Fig. 7.4) is a highly specialised forager that feeds on bark beetle larvae. It depends on high amounts of snags (Bütler *et al.* 2004) and often colonises forests after fires or heavy storms, which provide opportunities for massive bark beetle infestations. Its absence from most Norway spruce plantations at lower elevations in central Europe is therefore most likely due to an absence of sufficient natural forest disturbances and more intensive forest management (Glutz von Blotzheim & Bauer 1994). The pygmy owl prefers forest habitats with a pronounced vertical structure and high edge density (Braunisch *et al.* 2014), often occurring where coniferous stands are interspersed with clearings and grasslands (Brambilla *et al.* 2015). As a secondary cavity-nester, it also depends on the presence of rotting trees, snags and woodpecker cavities.

Subalpine and boreal ring ouzels belong to two phenotypically distinct subspecies: *T.t. alpestris* in central Europe and *T.t. torquatus* in Scandinavia

Figure 7.4 Three-toed woodpecker (*Picoides tridactylus*) is a common species in subalpine forests dominated by Norway spruce (*Picea abies*), as long as there is enough deadwood. As a highly specialised forager that feeds on bark beetle larvae, it usually does not occur in heavily managed Norway spruce stands in central European lowlands. Photo: M. Dorsch.

and the British Isles. The former is a typical inhabitant of semi-open subalpine conifer-dominated forests, while the latter prefers more open habitats such as heather-dominated moorland. The citril finch, endemic to Europe, is restricted to the Pyrenees, the Alps and some lower-elevation mountain ranges in Germany, France and Spain. Its typical habitat consists of open and semi-open coniferous stands and an extensive grassy field layer. Its large-scale distribution approximately coincides with that of the upright mountain pine, whose seeds indeed seem to be a crucial food source in winter (Borras *et al.* 2003), but its breeding range encompasses other woody formations, notably those dominated by larch and stone pine.

Treeline mosaics comprising very open coniferous stands and scattered trees within an extensive grass-shrub matrix represent other key habitats for bird species typical of semi-open habitats, such as black grouse (Signorell *et al.* 2010), fieldfare *Turdus pilaris*, lesser whitethroat and tree pipit *Anthus trivialis*. The latter was formerly widespread in lowland farmland (Schmid *et al.* 1998) but suffered large-scale decline due to agricultural intensification and now occurs mainly in semi-open sub-alpine areas. Some bird species that are not considered forest species can also be observed regularly in these semi-open habitats along the treeline. Black redstart *Phoenicurus ochruros*, for example, is quite widespread, at least in places where there are rocky outcrops between the trees. In rocky and very dry treeline habitats, rock bunting *Emberiza cia* is also not uncommon.

7.2.2 Fine-scale Variation and Seasonality in Species Richness and Abundance

Breeding bird species assemblages in subalpine forests seem to depend on forest structure and, to a lesser extent, edaphic conditions rather than on tree species composition (Mosimann *et al.* 1987; Müller-Buser 2002). However, as vegetation and soil structure are interlinked, it is difficult to disentangle the primary drivers of species' habitat selection. Important structural features in subalpine forests are similar to other forest types. Dense tree canopies provide abundant food supplies for needle-gleaners as well as varied nesting opportunities. Gaps in the canopy, in turn, allow ground vegetation to develop: pioneer trees, shrubs or grassy field layers represent crucial resources for foliage-gleaners, shrub-nesters and birds feeding on berries, and grass-dwelling arthropods, respectively (Signorell *et al.* 2010; Schäublin & Bollmann 2011; Patthey *et al.* 2012). Dense shrubs in clearings are inhabited by garden warbler *Sylvia borin*, blackcap *Sylvia atricapilla* and hazel grouse. Grassy field layers are important for ring ouzel, green woodpecker *Picus viridis*, tree pipit and citril finch. These ground foragers need free access to food resources, either invertebrates or seeds, and show a preference for patches with short grass or even bare soil, as do many insectivorous farmland birds (Schaub *et al.* 2010), although this preference still needs to be properly quantified for subalpine birds. Western Bonelli's warbler and, to a lesser extent, lesser whitethroat are principally found in relatively open and dry forests, with a predilection for sun-exposed areas. Among crucial forest structural features, old trees and snags are essential for woodpeckers and other cavity-breeders, either primary or secondary, such as pygmy owl, Tengmalm's owl *Aegolius funereus*, willow tit and crested tit *Lophophanes cristatus*.

Subalpine forests often offer very complex structured habitats, because they are regularly subjected to natural disturbances. Although fires remain rare in most subalpine coniferous forests, especially compared to Mediterranean pine woods, heavy winter snow cover and frequent storms cause branches, limbs and trunks to break. This offers fungi a portal to infect trees, weakening them and exposing them to bark beetle infestations, representing an accumulation of stress factors that can lead to a tree's death. This phenomenon increases the availability of snags, a key habitat feature for many bird species. In addition, the declining exploitation of timber in most European mountain ranges during the second half of the 20th century caused an accumulation of old, dead wood. As a result, these key structural habitat features important for birds occur nowadays almost everywhere in European subalpine forests. However, two grouse species that favour open stands seem to suffer a lot from a general increase in the standing stock following the progressive abandonment of timber exploitation. They have undergone a major range shrinkage in recent decades: both black grouse and capercaillie respond negatively to the closure of the forest canopy (Suchant & Braunisch 2004; Graf *et al.* 2007; Patthey *et al.* 2008).

There is no peer-reviewed literature about the seasonal variation of bird community composition in subalpine forests. Only qualitative information from citizen science platforms is available. The most widespread of these platforms in central and southern Europe is currently the 'www.ornitho.xx' family, where bird observation data, provided by the public, is validated by experts, and compilations of data are made publicly available. Generally, bird-species richness and abundance seem to be much lower there in winter than during the breeding season, probably due to a shortage of their principal food sources. Most insectivorous species, for instance from the genera *Anthus*, *Sylvia* and *Phylloscopus*, are migratory and thus absent from subalpine environments during the cold season. Even the majority of granivorous passerines, such as the siskin *Carduelis spinus*, citril finch or bullfinch *Pyrrhula pyrrhula*, leave subalpine forests in winter, moving to lower elevations or warmer latitudes. Those granivorous bird species that forage mostly on the ground can no longer access seeds when snow cover is both deep and persistent. Moreover, the amplitude of their winter dispersal and spatial movements varies from year to year due to fluctuating snow conditions. Thrushes adopt a similar seasonal spatial pattern, being short-distance migrants or simply altitudinal transhumants. Among seed-eaters, nutcrackers *Nucifraga caryocatactes* are a noticeable exception: they feed on tree seeds that are stored in ground caches at relatively high altitude, even if the food has been collected at lower elevation (e.g., hazel *Corylus avellana* nuts), which enables them to stay year-round in upper subalpine forests. The crossbill *Loxia curvirostra* is another year-round inhabitant of subalpine forests, due to its food specialisation on spruce, fir and larch seeds. Its local density varies a lot in response to the highly fluctuating yearly masting patterns of its favourite resource trees.

Only very few bird species of subalpine forests can be considered as sedentary. This concerns, for instance, the three-toed woodpecker, sightings of which are extremely rare in the lowlands of western and central Europe. Goldcrest *Regulus regulus*, treecreeper *Certhia familiaris*, nuthatch *Sitta europaea* and three species of tits (willow, crested and coal tit) do show some altitudinal movements, as they show up in the lowlands in winter. Still, regular observations show that quite a few individuals seem to stay in their high-altitude habitats in winter. These birds adopt specific behaviours that allow them to survive the low ambient temperatures and extreme food scarcity that characterise upland winters (Thaler-Kottek 1986). Among them are food hoarding, social aggregations at night roosts and a general reduction of activity, which all serve to save energy. Very little is known about seasonal movements of predatory birds such goshawk *Accipiter gentilis*, sparrowhawk *Accipiter nisus*, pygmy owl and Tengmalm's owl. Yet, observations suggest that they might also move to lower-elevation forests in winter. Finally, all central European grouse species except rock ptarmigan *Lagopus muta* are regularly observed in subalpine forests and treeline ecotonal woody formations all year round. They, too, have evolved specific physiological and behavioural adaptations to overcome the harsh winter conditions. For example, black grouse, hazel grouse and sometimes also capercaillie spend hours in self-burrowed 'igloos' in the snow, which is an efficient energy-saving strategy (Marti & Bossert 1985; Arlettaz *et al.* 2015).

Subalpine forests do not seem to play a major role as wintering grounds for northern migratory birds. Typical migrants from northern and north-east Europe that overwinter at lower latitudes in central Europe, such as waxwing *Bombycilla garrulus* and brambling *Fringilla montifringilla*, actually prefer to forage in deciduous and mixed forests at lower altitudes. During autumn and spring migrations, however, subalpine forests can provide good stopover sites for birds in transit.

7.2.3 Conservation Issues

In general, the current conservation status of birds in central European subalpine forests is favourable. According to BirdLife International (2015) and the IUCN Red List criteria, all species listed in Table 7.1 are considered 'least concern' at the pan-European scale. Some of them, however, have been classified as 'species of European conservation concern' (SPEC) by Burfield and van Bommel (2004), or they have been included in Annex I of the Birds Directive of the European Union (Directive 2009/147/EC of the European Parliament and the Council).

This reflects the fact that the current conservation status of a certain species can be much less favourable on a regional than the pan-European level. This is well illustrated by the capercaillie. It is classified as 'least concern' and 'non-SPEC' in the European Red List of birds, although it is included in Annex I of the EU Birds Directive. However, in the national Red Lists of Switzerland and France, for example, the capercaillie is classified as 'endangered' and 'vulnerable', respectively (Keller *et al.* 2010; UICN France *et al.* 2011), which has triggered intense conservation action in both countries (Mollet *et al.* 2008; Viry & Helderlé 2012).

Human land-use changes today represent the main threat for the avifauna of European subalpine forests, although climate change might represent an even greater challenge in the future (e.g., Braunisch *et al.* 2014). In contrast, there is currently no evidence that hunting, poaching, environmental pollution or diseases can represent any serious threat. The present situation differs greatly from historical times, when, for example, nutcrackers were persecuted as pests. Regional forest authorities, at least in Switzerland and Austria, used to pay a bounty for every killed nutcracker. Ironically, they recognised that this corvid massively exploits the cones of stone pines but misinterpreted the mechanism at play: actually, the winter caches of nutcrackers are often left behind unexploited, which represents the main mode of propagation of those rather heavy seeds (Mattes 1982; Tomback *et al.* 1993; Fig. 7.5). Today

Figure 7.5 Swiss stone pine (*Pinus cembra*) rejuvenation above the current timberline at 2,280 m above sea level in Val d'Anniviers, Valais, Switzerland. Birds, notably nutcrackers *Nucifraga caryocatactes*, collect the heavy seeds in the adult trees below and sometimes carry them to the upper slopes for hoarding. Non-harvested seeds germinate and grow. Photo: P. Mollet.

the species is protected in most areas and is thriving in subalpine forests in the Alps and Carpathians.

The two forms of land-use change which have most dramatically affected subalpine species in recent times are the abandonment of traditional silvi-agricultural practices and the sprawl of recreation activities, especially snow sports (Thiel *et al.* 2011; Arlettaz *et al.* 2013). Zbinden & Salvioni (2003), for instance, have documented the reduced reproductive success and long-term demographic decline of black grouse in the southernmost Swiss Alps (Ticino) after traditional grazing practices had ceased, which irremediably leads to the encroachment of semi-open treeline habitats by woody plants. Patthey *et al.* (2012) have shown that both vertical and horizontal structural heterogeneity in all vegetation layers within the treeline matrix (from grasslands through shrubs to trees) were the best predictors of the occurrence of both sexes in the black grouse. Chick-rearing black grouse hens, in particular, show a marked preference for the most heterogeneous habitat configuration. This habitat selection pattern is probably a result of a trade-off between food availability (invertebrates are crucial for chick growth, and these abound in grasslands) and shelter from predators, which is provided by shrubs and under low-branched trees (Signorell *et al.* 2010). Current action plans for restoring black grouse breeding habitat via management interventions, notably in the shrub layer and dense conifer stands, will probably benefit other bird species typical of very open forests, such as tree pipit and lesser whitethroat.

The sprawl of winter tourism, from the construction of ski infrastructure to the practice of snow sports (back-country skiing, snow-boarding and snow-shoeing) outside marked runs and trails, is considered to represent a new serious threat for subalpine wildlife (Arlettaz *et al.* 2007). Capercaillie and black grouse respond negatively to the regular presence of humans on their wintering grounds (Thiel *et al.* 2008; Braunisch *et al.* 2011). Due to their rather long flushing distances, they will eventually abandon otherwise suitable habitats if human pressure is too high (Thiel *et al.* 2007; Braunisch *et al.* 2011). Furthermore, disturbance by snow sport free-riders evokes endocrinological stress in capercaillie (Thiel *et al.* 2011) and black grouse (Arlettaz *et al.* 2007), which potentially affects population dynamics (Patthey *et al.* 2008). Specific wildlife winter refuges are currently deployed in the European Alps, with the objective of mitigating the impact of snow sports on alpine mammals and birds (Braunisch *et al.* 2011; Arlettaz *et al.* 2013).

Due to the rough terrain and limited accessibility of most subalpine woodland, forest exploitation is not economically viable in many areas. As a consequence, the pressure on subalpine forest ecosystems is much lower than on montane or lowland forests. Still, this may change with an increasing demand for timber, e.g., as a source of renewable energy. Recent evidence suggests that in the Carpathians, notably in Slovakia and Romania, forest loss, nowadays no longer occurring in other European subalpine forests, has become a serious threat for a majority of forest-dwelling wildlife (Mikoláš *et al.* 2015). Large areas of forest are being clearcut by companies that bought the rights to harvest timber. As a result, emblematic species such as capercaillie are becoming increasingly rare in these regions (Mikoláš *et al.* 2017).

Climate warming is much more pronounced in high mountainous environments than in lowland areas (Rebetez & Reinhard 2007). Faced with this, species have no other choice than to 'move, adapt or die'. Maggini *et al.* (2011) used data from the Swiss national common breeding bird survey to model elevational distributions of 95 bird species for two periods, 1999–2002 and 2004–2007. They found significant upward shifts for 33 out of the 95 species, among them bullfinch and ring ouzel, two typical species of subalpine forests and treeline ecosystems, respectively. These upward altitudinal shifts could eventually lead to a decrease in potential habitat and thus population size, simply because at higher altitudes the potential distribution area becomes smaller (habitat squeezing). These projections must be treated with caution, however. In effect, variable selection remains a great source of uncertainty for future range predictions in species distribution models (Braunisch *et al.* 2013), which even exceeds the variances introduced by different IPCC scenarios or circulation models (Thuiller 2004; Beaumont *et al.* 2007). In addition, most habitat suitability and distribution models are constructed from publicly available geodata that rarely include information about crucial species-specific ecological resources (e.g., the occurrence of an essential group of invertebrates for an insectivorous bird species). As a result, the variables used most of the time represent only rather crude proxies of actual species-specific ecological requirements. The good news is that predicted decreases in the habitat suitability and spatial range of emblematic, cold-adapted species such as pygmy owl, hazel grouse, capercaillie and three-toed woodpecker could, at least partially, be compensated by adaptive forest management enhancing the availability and quality of key species-specific structural elements (Braunisch *et al.* 2014). On the other hand, adaptive forestry practices implemented to cope with the economic risks of climate change, such as shortened harvesting periods or changes in the tree species portfolio, may represent an additional threat. The question of whether, and to what extent, climate warming will impact subalpine forest birds, and how this factor interacts with – or is even amplified by – other forms of global change (e.g., atmospheric nitrogen deposition, abandonment of pastoral systems, changes in forest exploitation) thus remain to be explored.

Acknowledgements

We are grateful to Aliki Buhayer for a thorough editing of the English and to Mattia Brambilla and Dan Chamberlain for helpful comments.

References

Archaux, F. & Bakkaus, N. (2007) Relative impact of stand structure, tree composition and climate on mountain bird communities. *Forest Ecology and Management*, **247**, 72–79.

Arlettaz, R., Nusslé, S., Baltic, M. *et al.* (2015) Disturbance of wildlife by outdoor winter recreation: Allostatic stress response and altered activity-energy budgets. *Ecological Applications*, **25**, 1197–1212.

Arlettaz,R., Patthey, P., Baltic, M. *et al.* (2007) Spreading free-riding snow sports represent a novel serious threat for wildlife. *Proceedings of the Royal Society*, **274**, 1219–1224.

Arlettaz, R., Patthey, P. & Braunisch, V. (2013) Impacts of outdoor winter recreation on alpine wildlife and mitigation approaches: A case study of the black grouse. In *The Impacts of Skiing and Related Winter Recreational Activities on Mountain Environments*. Rixen, C. & Rolando, A. (eds.) Bussum: Bentham eBooks, pp. 137–154.

Bätzing, W. (2005) *Die Alpen. Geschichte und Zukunft einer europäischen Kulturlandschaft*. 4th edition. Munich: C.H. Beck.

Beaumont, L.J., Pitman, A.J., Poulsen, M. & Hughes, L. (2007) Where will species go? Incorporating new advances in climate modelling into projections of species distributions. *Global Change Biology*, **13**, 1368–1385.

BirdLife International (2015) *European Red List of Birds*. Luxembourg: Office for Official Publications of the European Communities. http://bookshop.europa.eu.

Bohn, U., Gollub, G. & Hettwer, C. (2000) *Map of the Natural Vegetation of Europe.* Bonn: Federal Agency for Nature Conservation.

Borras, A., Cabrera, T., Cabrera, J. & Senar, J.C. (2003) The diet of the Citril Finch (*Serinus citrinella*) in the Pyrenees and the role of *Pinus* seeds as a key resource. *Journal of Ornithology,* **144**, 345–353.

Brambilla, M., Bergero, V., Bassi, E. & Falco, R. (2015) Current and future effectiveness of Natura 2000 network in the central Alps for the conservation of mountain forest owl species in a warming climate. *European Journal of Wildlife Research,* **61**, 35–44.

Braunisch, V., Coppes, J., Arlettaz, R., Suchant, R., Schmid, H. & Bollmann, K. (2013) Selecting from correlated climate variables: A major source of uncertainty for predicting species distributions under climate change. *Ecography,* **36**, 971–983.

Braunisch, V., Coppes, J., Arlettaz, R., Suchant, R., Zellweger, F. & Bollmann, K. (2014) Temperate mountain forest biodiversity under climate change: Compensating negative effects by increasing structural complexity. *PLoS ONE,* **9** (5), e97718.

Braunisch, V., Patthey, P. & Arlettaz, R. (2011) Spatially explicit modeling of conflict zones between wildlife and snow sports: Prioritizing areas for winter refuges. *Ecological Applications,* **21**, 955–967.

Bugmann, H. (2001) A comparative analysis of forest dynamics in the Swiss Alps and the Colorado Front Range. *Forest Ecology and Management,* **145**, 43–55.

Burfield, I. & van Bommel, F.P.J. (2004) *Birds in Europe: Population Estimates, Trends and Conservation Status.* BirdLife Conservation Series 12. Cambridge: BirdLife International.

Burga, C.A. & Perret, R. (1998) *Vegetation und Klima der Schweiz seit dem jüngeren Eiszeitalter (Vegetation and Climate History in Switzerland during the Later Pleistocene and Holocene).* Thun, Switzerland: Ott.

Bütler, R., Angelstam, P., Ekelund, P. & Schlaepfer, R. (2004) Dead wood threshold values for the three-toed woodpecker in boreal and sub-Alpine forest. *Biological Conservation,* **119**, 305–318.

Catzeflis, F. (1979) Etude qualitative et quantitative de l'avifaune de la pessière jurassienne du Chalet à Roch, Vaud. *Nos Oiseaux,* **35**, 75–84.

Chamberlain, D.E., Negro, M., Caprio, E. & Rolando, A. (2013) Assessing the sensitivity of alpine birds to potential future changes in habitat and climate to inform management strategies. *Biological Conservation,* **167**, 127–135.

Dvorak, M., Ranner, A. & Berg, H.-M. (1993) *Atlas der Brutvögel Österreichs.* Wien: Umweltbundesamt.

Ellenberg, H. (2009) *Vegetation Ecology of Central Europe.* Cambridge: Cambridge University Press.

Estrada, J., Guallar, S., Pedrocchi, V. & Brotons, L. (2005) *Atles dels Ocells Nidificants de Catalunya 1999–2002.* Barcelona: Lynx Edicions.

Fuller, R.J., Smith, K.W. & Hinsley, S.A. (2012) Temperate western European woodland as a dynamic habitat for birds: A resource-based view. In *Birds and Habitat: Relationships in Changing Landscapes.* Fuller, R.J. (ed.). Cambridge: Cambridge University Press, pp. 352–380

Glutz von Blotzheim, U.N. & Bauer, K.M. (1994) *Handbuch der Vögel Mitteleuropas. Vol. 9: Columbiformes – Piciformes.* 2nd ed. Wiesbaden: Aula.

Graf, R.F., Bollmann, K., Bugmann, H. & Suter, W. (2007) Forest and landscape structure as predictors of capercaillie occurrence. *Journal of Wildlife Management*, **71**, 356–365.

Hess, R. (1983) Verbreitung, Siedlungsdichte und Habitat des Dreizehenspechts *Picoides tridactylus alpinus* im Kanton Schwyz. *Der Ornithologische Beobachter*, **80**, 153–182.

Janett, A. (1943) Über die Regelungen von Wald und Weide. *Swiss Forestry Journal*, **94**, 105–117.

Johann, E. (2006) Historical development of nature-based forestry in Central Europe. In *Nature-based Forestry in Central Europe – Alternatives to Industrial Forestry and Strict Preservation*. Diaci, J. (ed.). Ljubljana: Studia Forestalia Slovenica, 126, pp. 1–17.

Keller, V., Gerber, A., Schmid, H., Volet, B. & Zbinden, N. (2010) *Rote Liste Brutvögel. Gefährdete Arten der Schweiz, Stand 2010*. Umwelt-Vollzug Nr. 1019. Bern & Sempach: Bundesamt für Umwelt und Schweizerische Vogelwarte.

Korňan, M. & Adamík, P. (2014) Structure of the breeding bird assemblage of a natural beech-spruce forest in the Šútovská dolina National Nature Reserve, the Malá Fatra Mts. *Ekológia, Bratislava*, **33**, 138–150.

Körner, C. (1998) A re-assessment of high-elevation treeline positions and their explanation. *Oecologia*, **115**, 445–459.

Körner, C. (2012) *Alpine Treelines: Functional Ecology of the Global High Elevation Tree Limits*. Basel: Springer.

Kropil, R. (1996) Structure of the breeding bird assemblage of the fir-beech primeval forest in the West Carpathians (Badin nature reserve). *Folia Zoologica*, **45**, 311–324.

Landolt, E. (2003) *Unsere Alpenflora*. Bern: SAC-Verlag.

Maggini, R., Lehmann, A., Kéry, M. *et al.* (2011) Are Swiss birds tracking climate change? Detecting elevational shifts using response curve shapes. *Ecological Modelling*, **222**, 21–32.

Marti, C. & Bossert, A. (1985) Beobachtungen zur Sommeraktivität und Brutbiologie des Alpenschneehuhns *Lagopus mutus* im Aletschgebiet (Wallis). *Der Ornithologische Beobachter*, **82**, 152–168.

Mattes, H. (1982) The coadaptive system of the nutcracker *Nucifraga caryocatactes* (L.) and the Swiss stone pine *Pinus cembra* (L.) and their importance to forestry in the upper mountain region. Report No. 241. Birmensdorf, Switzerland: Swiss Federal Institute of Forest, Snow and Landscape Research WSL. [in German, English summary]

Mattes, H., Maurizio, R. & Bürkli, W. (2005) *Die Vogelwelt im Oberengadin, Bergell und Puschlav*. Sempach: Schweizerische Vogelwarte.

Mayer, A.C. & Stöckli, V. (2005) Long-term impact of cattle grazing on subalpine forest development and efficiency of snow avalanche protection. *Arctic, Antarctic, and Alpine Research*, **37**, 521–526.

Meier, H. (1954) Über den Vogelbestand eines subalpinen Fichtenwaldes. *Der Ornithologische Beobachter*, **51**, 133–134.

Mikoláš, M., Svitok, M., Tejkal, M. *et al.* (2015) Evaluating forest management intensity on a umbrella species: Capercaillie persistence in central Europe. *Forest Ecology and Management*, **354**, 26–34.

Mikoláš, M., Tejkal, M., Kuemmerle, T. *et al.* (2017) Forest management impacts on capercaillie (*Tetrao urogallus*) habitat distribution and connectivity in the Carpathians. *Landscape Ecology*, **32**, 163–179.

Mollet, P., Stadler, B. & Bollmann, K. (2008) *Aktionsplan Auerhuhn Schweiz.* Umwelt-Vollzug Nr. 0804. Bern, Sempach & Zürich: Bundesamt für Umwelt, Schweizerische Vogelwarte, Schweizer Vogelschutz SVS/BirdLife Schweiz.

Mosimann, P., Naef-Daenzer, B. & Blattner, M. (1987) Die Zusammensetzung der Avifauna in typischen Waldgesellschaften der Schweiz. *Der Ornithologische Beobachter*, **84**, 275–299.

Müller-Buser, M. (2002) Die Avifauna der Bergföhrenwälder des Schweizer-ischen Nationalparks im Ofenpassgebiet. *Der Ornithologische Beobachter*, **99**, 1–18.

Niederfriniger, O., Schreiner, P. & Unterholzner, L. (1996) *Aus der Luft gegriffen. Atlas der Vogelwelt Südtirols.* Tappeiner, Lana d'Adige (Bolzano, Italy): Arbeits-gemeinschaft für Vogelkunde und Vogelschutz Südtirol.

Nilsson, S.G. (1997) Forests in the temperate-boreal transition: Natural and man-made features. *Ecological Bulletins*, **46**, 61–71.

Ott, E., Frehner, M., Frey, H.U. & Lüscher, P. (1997) *Gebirgsnadelwälder: praxisor-ientierter Leitfaden für eine standortgerechte Waldbehandlung.* Bern: Haupt.

Parolini, J.D. (2012) *Vom Kahlschlag zum Naturwaldreservat: Geschichte der Waldnut-zung im Gebiet des Schweizerischen Nationalparks.* Bern: Haupt.

Patthey, P., Signorell, N., Rotelli, L. & Arlettaz, R. (2012) Vegetation structural and compositional heterogeneity as a key feature in Alpine black grouse micro-habitat selection: Conservation management implications. *European Journal of Wildlife Research*, **58**, 59–70.

Patthey, P., Wirthner, S., Signorell, N. & Arlettaz, R. (2008) Impact of outdoor winter sports on the abundance of a key indicator species of alpine ecosystems. *Journal of Applied Ecology*, **45**, 1704–1711.

Rebetez, M. & Reinhard, M. (2007) Monthly air temperature trends in Switzerland 1901–2000 and 1975–2004. *Theoretical and Applied Climatology*, **91** (1–4), 27–34.

Saniga, M. (1995) Seasonal dynamics of the bird assemblages in the natural forests of the spruce vegetation tier. *Folia Zoologica*, **44**, 103–110.

Schaub, M., Martinez, N., Tagmann-Ioset, A. *et al.* (2010) Patches of bare ground as a staple commodity for declining ground-foraging insectivorous farmland birds. *PLoS ONE*, **5**, e13115.

Schäublin, S. & Bollmann, K. (2011) Winter habitat selection and conservation of Hazel Grouse (*Bonasa bonasia*) in mountain forests. *Journal of Ornithology*, **152**, 179–192.

Schmid, H., Luder, R., Naef-Daenzer, B, Graf, R. & Zbinden, N. (1998) *Schweizer Brutvogelatlas: Verbreitung der Brutvögel in der Schweiz und im Fürstentum Liechten-stein 1993–1996.* Sempach: Schweizerische Vogelwarte.

Signorell, N., Wirthner, S., Patthey, P., Schranz, R., Rotelli, L. & Arlettaz, R. (2010) Concealment from predators drives foraging habitat selection in brood-rearing Alpine black grouse *Tetrao tetrix* hens: Habitat management implica-tions. *Wildlife Biology*, **16**, 249–257.

Suchant, R. & Braunisch, V. (2004) Multidimensional habitat modelling in practical management: A case study on capercaillie in the Black Forest, Germany. *Ecological Bulletins*, **51**, 455–469.

Thaler-Kottek, E. (1986) Zum Verhalten von Winter- und Sommergoldhähnchen (*Regulus regulus, Regulus ignicapillus*) – etho-ökologische Differenzierung und Anpassung an den Lebensraum. *Der Ornithologische Beobachter*, **83**, 281–289.

Thiel, D., Jenni-Eiermann, S., Braunisch, V., Palme, R. & Jenni, L. (2008) Ski tourism affects habitat use and evokes a physiological stress response in capercaillie *Tetrao urogallus*: A new methodological approach. *Journal of Applied Ecology*, **45**, 845–853.

Thiel, D., Jenni-Eiermann, S., Palme, R. & Jenni, L. (2011) Winter tourism increases stress hormone levels in the Capercaillie *Tetrao urogallus*. *Ibis*, **153**, 122–133.

Thiel, D., Ménoni, E., Brenot, J.F. & Jenni, L. (2007) Effects of recreation and hunting on flushing distance of capercaillie. *Journal of Wildlife Management*, **71**, 1784–1792.

Thuiller, W. (2004) Patterns and uncertainties of species' range shifts under climate change. *Global Change Biology*, **10**, 2020–2027.

Tomback, D.F., Holtmeier, F.-K., Mattes, H., Carsey, K.S. & Powell, M.L. (1993) Tree clusters and growth form distribution in *Pinus cembra*, a bird-dispersed pine. *Arctic and Alpine Research*, **25**, 374–381.

Turček, F.J. (1961) Ökologische Beziehungen der Vögel und Gehölze. Bratislava, Verlag der slowakischen Akademie der Wissenschaften. 285 S.

UICN France, MNHN, LPO, SEOF, ONCFS (2011) *La liste rouge des espèces menacées en France – chapitre oiseaux de France métropolitaine*. Paris.

Viry, B. & Helderlé, C.L. (eds.) (2012) *Des forêts pour le Grand Tétras: Guide de sylviculture*. Metz: Edition La Région Lorraine.

Zbinden, N., Kéry, M., Keller, V., Brotons, L., Herrando, S. & Schmid, H. (2010) Species richness of breeding birds along the altitudinal gradient: An analysis of atlas databases from Switzerland and Catalonia (NE Spain). In *Data Mining for Global Trends in Mountain Biodiversity*. Spehn, E.M. & Körner, C. (eds.). Boca Raton, FL: Taylor & Francis, pp. 65–73.

Zbinden, N. & Salvioni, M. (2003) Verbreitung, Siedlungsdichte und Fortpflanzungserfolg des Birkhuhns *Tetrao tetrix* im Tessin 1981–2002. *Der Ornithologische Beobachter*, **100**, 211–226.

8 · *Temperate Forests*

A European Perspective on Variation and Dynamics in Bird Assemblages

TOMASZ WESOŁOWSKI, ROBERT J. FULLER
AND MARTIN FLADE

8.1 Natural Forest Cover

In the post-glacial period, ca. 7,000 years ago, before humans substantially transformed landscapes, predominantly broadleaved forests occupied most of Europe's temperate zone, the middle latitude belt situated roughly between 55–60°N and 45°N. This forest formation covered the vast European lowland plains and the lower mountain slopes, stretching from the Pyrenees in the west to the Ural Mountains in the east (Chapter 5; Podbielkowski 1987). To the north, the temperate forest bordered the boreal coniferous (taiga) forests. The transition between these two zones was formed by an extensive belt of mixed deciduous-coniferous forests (the hemiboreal, boreonemoral zone). To the south, the lowland temperate forests bordered either montane forests (reaching the height of 500–1,200 m above sea level) or the eastern European forest-steppe zone.

The temperate forests developed across a huge range of climatic conditions, from mild oceanic climates along the Atlantic coasts, with relatively little winter snow, to strongly continental climates in the east of their range, where sub-zero temperatures and snow cover could last three to five months. However, conditions in the growing period were relatively similar in all these areas, permitting broadleaved trees to spread. The forests managed to develop in almost all types of soil and hydrological conditions, from regularly flooded riverine forests on nutrient-rich alluvial soils to infertile sand dunes. On the more productive soils, these were presumably tall, predominantly closed-canopy forests, mostly of deciduous trees (Iversen 1973; Bobiec 2002a; Svenning 2002; Smirnova 2004; Hodder *et al.* 2005; Mitchell 2005). Permanently or temporarily open non-wooded areas (saltmarshes, lakes, big rivers, mires, extremely infertile grounds and herbivore-made glades) punctuated extensive forest cover. Along the south-eastern edge of the temperate forest distribution – in the forest-steppe zone – the forests were naturally fragmented. Here they formed tree-covered islands within the treeless matrix (e.g., Novikov 1959; Smirnova & Turubanova 2004).

Controversy surrounds the status of open treeless areas within the forests at this time. Vera (2000) proposed that large herbivores maintained dynamic patchworks of open parkland and wooded groves, and that continuous forest was not typical of the ancient post-glacial landscapes before the advent of Neolithic farming. This concept, at least as a general view of post-glacial landscapes, has been hotly contested. The arguments are summarised by Kirby and Watkins (2015), who conclude that current evidence points to early Neolithic landscapes being predominantly wooded, but with a higher degree of openness than has often been recognised. Large herbivores may have driven forest dynamics at particular places at particular times, but there is no reason to assume that this was the primary mechanism determining the pattern and structure of forests across Europe. Disease, storms, drought and fire are just as likely to have been major agents of disturbance. In this chapter, we focus on the contemporary condition, i.e., forest and woodland where regeneration is driven mainly by natural gap dynamics or by forest management actions. For a discussion of the implications of different models of historic landscape structures for the European temperate avifauna, see Hinsley *et al.* (2015).

Well-drained mineral soils, the most widespread soil type, were occupied by broadleaved deciduous trees of several species, usually forming multispecies stands. Oaks *Quercus* spp. and small-leaved lime *Tilia cordata* were important tree species throughout the whole temperate range. Other dominating species were more geographically restricted, notably beech *Fagus sylvatica* in western Europe and hornbeam *Carpinus betulus* in central Europe. The dominants were frequently accompanied by maples *Acer* spp., elms *Ulmus* spp., ash *Fraxinus excelsior*, birches *Betula* spp. and aspen *Populus tremula* (Podbielkowski 1987; Jahn 1991; Kirby & Watkins 2015).

Poorly drained places were covered by riverine or swampy forests. They developed in regularly flooded or waterlogged areas, such as floodplains and lake shores, as well as in depressions with a permanently high water table. Poplar *Populus alba* and *P. nigra* and willow *Salix alba* and *S. fragilis* forests developed in frequently inundated places in large river valleys. Less frequently flooded locations were covered with ash-elm *Fraxinus excelsior-Ulmus* spp. forest, whereas ash-alder *F. excelsior-Alnus glutinosa* forest developed in slow-running/stagnating water (Ellenberg 1986; Podbielkowski 1987).

Coniferous forests were confined to unproductive places, especially on sandy soils, where nutrient levels were generally too poor for broad-leaved forest to develop. They were composed almost exclusively of Scots pine *Pinus sylvestris*. Conifers otherwise occurred only in the transitional hemiboreal zone (Norway spruce *Picea abies*), in the transition to the montane forests (Norway spruce and silver fir *Abies alba*), at the margins of mires (spruce, pine) and on subcontinental and continental forest bogs (pine) (Ellenberg 1986; Podbielkowski 1987). Due to extensive planting, coniferous forests are now widespread, replacing deciduous trees over a wide range of habitats (see Chapter 10).

8.2 Historical Changes and Current Forest Cover

The temperate zone supports the largest areas of rich soils in Europe and has attracted the densest settlement of humans, with consequent massive reduction and exploitation of forest. By 4,000 years ago, farming societies existed in all parts of the temperate forest zone (Smirnova &Turubanova 2004). Deforestation rates were higher in north-west Europe than in eastern Europe. By ca. 1100 AD, forest cover in England was only 15% (Rackham 2003), whereas the eastern part of the continent was still extensively forested (Gatter 2000; Smirnova & Turubanova 2004). Eastern Europe lost more than half of its temperate forests during the 18th and 19th centuries (Smirnova *et al.* 2004). By this time, most remaining forests were heavily modified by humans. Livestock grazing had created open woodland pastures, coppicing kept large areas at early stages of growth and drainage works had destroyed much riverine forest. The area of temperate forest reached its historical minimum at the end of the nineteenth century, by which time some countries (e.g., Ireland, the Netherlands) were virtually deforested. Patches of primeval forests (i.e., forests that have been allowed to develop largely through a long history of natural processes in the absence of substantial human intervention) survived on higher land in parts of central and south-east Europe, especially in the Czech Republic and Slovakia, as well as Romania and Bulgaria (Veen *et al.* 2010), but primeval forests were virtually eliminated throughout the temperate lowlands (Peterken 1996). The striking exception is Białowieża Forest, where some fragments of primeval character survive (Box 8.1).

Box 8.1 *Białowieża National Park (BNP), a benchmark primeval (wildwood) forest.*

Our knowledge of the ecology and behaviour of birds in pristine European temperate forests is very limited, for the simple reason that most such forest had been transformed extensively by humans before modern research started. However, without gaining data on the functioning and natural dynamics of forest ecosystems free of direct human impact and without studying ecological and behavioural adaptations of birds in their evolutionary settings, our comprehension of patterns and processes in contemporary European forests would be highly limited, or sometimes even wrong (e.g., Baker 1938; Lack 1965; Wesołowski 1983, 2007a; Stutchbury & Morton 2001). The research conducted in remnants of the ancient lowland temperate forests is of both fundamental and applied importance, providing crucial baseline data against which to measure results from secondary or 'man-modified' woodlands (Tomiałojć *et al.* 1984; Blondel 1995; Angelstam *et al.* 1997). Data from such reference areas are necessary if we wish to direct management of secondary woods so as to 'imitate the natural spatial and temporal patterns of forest regeneration and development' (e.g., Hunter 1990; Angelstam 1996; Rebane *et al.* 1997; Winter *et al.* 2015).

Fortunately, there is one extensive area in Europe where the forests have retained their primeval features: the Białowieża Forest, situated on the Polish-Belarussian border. The forest owes its survival to around 500 years of consistent protection, initially as a prestigious hunting ground for Lithuanian grand dukes, Polish kings and, later, Russian tsars. In the twentieth century, the care by rulers was replaced by formal nature protection. After World War II, the forest was divided between Poland (613 of 1,500 km^2) and Belarus (ca. 60%). Commercial timber exploitation started during World War I, and most of the forest in the Polish part has since been managed for timber (Wesołowski 2005; Latałowa *et al.* 2015). The Belarussian part used to be a hunting reserve, affected by extensive drainage works in Soviet times. Later on, its timber was heavily exploited but, since 2014, 38% of the area has been designated as a strictly protected zone.

A small part of the forest in the Polish fragment, some 47.5 km^2, has been strictly protected since 1921 as Białowieża National Park (BNP). Apart from some limited intrusion by humans (a few small clearcut or

Box 8.1 (cont.)

burnt patches), this area has remained continuously under forest cover for approximately seven millennia (Tomiałojć & Wesołowski 2004). The conditions existing within BNP are indicative of those that are likely to have existed in many areas of primeval forest before widespread clearance and modification, though it is increasingly accepted that open areas were more frequent than is currently evident (Kirby & Watkins 2015) and that the vegetation structure of other naturally occurring forests could differ to some extent (e.g., beech forests; M. Flade pers. obs.).

Białowieża Forest is located in the middle of the vast European lowlands, approximately at the same latitude as Amsterdam and a few hundred kilometres south of Moscow (the Białowieża village coordinates are 52°41′ N and 23°52′ E). Biogeographically, the area is situated at the southern border of the mixed (nemoral-boreal) forest zone containing some native Norway spruce *Picea abies* in almost all types of tree stands (Faliński 1986). For more details and photographs, see Tomiałojć *et al.* (1984), Faliński (1986) and Tomiałojć and Wesołowski (1990, 2004, 2005). The relief of this forest is flat, mostly between 165 and 170 m above sea level. The climate is subcontinental, with a mean annual precipitation of 624 (425–940) mm, long-term average annual temperature of +6.6°C and average January temperature of −4.8 (−16.8 to 1.8) °C. Snow cover (up to 95 cm deep) lasts up to 92 days; morning ground frost occurs as late as mid-May, even to mid-June (during the 1970s). Snow melt occurs between around 10 March (early) and 20 April (exceptionally late), based on a 49-year time series (see Faliński 1986 and Jędrzejewska *et al.* 1997 for more information). Some warming was observed over the last 20 to 30 years (Wesołowski & Cholewa 2009), but temperatures have remained within the historic range already recorded during the previous warm period (1820–1870; Jędrzejewska *et al.* 1997).

The forest contains the last surviving extensive fragments of primeval forest in the temperate zone. It is a relic of the vast forests which once extended across the European lowlands and is home to many species that are rare or extinct elsewhere, including the largest terrestrial European animal, the bison *Bison bonasus*, and large predators (wolf *Canis lupus* and lynx *Lynx lynx*; Jędrzejewska & Jędrzejewski 1998). It contains a very diverse breeding avifauna (ca. 111 forest species; Tomiałojć & Wesołowski 2004) and a large

Box 8.1 (cont.)

assemblage of predators, more than 30 species, using a diverse range of detection and attack techniques (Tomiałojć et al. 1984; Tomiałojć & Wesołowski 1990; Wesołowski 2002). All other agents and processes (except forest fires) known to influence the dynamics and structure of forests and the living conditions of birds still operate there (Wesołowski 2007a).

The tree stands of primeval character are an unparalleled living museum and research laboratory, offering a valuable 'window into the past' through which we can gain insights into the ecology and adaptations of temperate forest birds living in as near to pristine circumstances as can still be found in Europe (Tomiałojć et al. 1984; Tomiałojć & Wesołowski 1990; Wesołowski 1983, 2002, 2003, 2005, 2007a, 2007b; Stutchbury & Morton 2001). The BNP stands are distinguished among European temperate forests by features which seem typical of most rich primeval forests. These are:

Large size of trees: The maximum height for Białowieża Norway spruce is 52 m, and 40–45 m for some other tree species; the largest trunk circumference at breast height can be 741 cm in pedunculate oak *Quercus robur* and 585 cm in small-leaved lime *Tilia cordata* (Niechoda & Korbel 2011).

Multistorey profile of stands: In particular, stands of the lime-hornbeam *Tilio-Carpinetum* forest can be subdivided into five or six layers. The huge Norway spruce which rise 10–15 m above the main canopy are the temperate forest equivalents of the emergent trees of tropical forests.

Diverse tree community: Białowieża stands harbour 26 species of trees and 55 of shrubs (Faliński 1991). The *Tilio-Carpinetum* stands alone may be composed of a dozen or so tree species, including small-leaved lime, pedunculate oak, hornbeam *Carpinus betulus*, Norway maple *Acer platanoides*, elms *Ulmus* spp., birches *Betula* spp., aspen *Populus tremula* and ash *Fraxinus excelsior*. They are also strongly diversified as regards the age and size of trees. Several individuals are up to 500 years old. Since the early 1990s, a widespread dieback of ash trees, especially severe in the riverine stands, has been observed (T. Wesołowski, unpubl.)

Large amount of deadwood and uprooted trees: There are many dead standing stems, stumps, freshly uprooted trees and fallen logs

Box 8.1 (cont.)

(on average $130\,\mathrm{m}^3$/ha in lime-hornbeam stands; Bobiec 2002b). There are many root pads, discs of flat root systems that belong to fallen trees, chiefly Norway spruce (see Photo D). These rise vertically up to 7.5 m, forming walls up to 10–20 m long and constitute a special stratum intermediate between the ground and tree layers.

High abundance of tree holes: Many and diverse excavated and non-excavated tree holes are found throughout most of the stands (Walankiewicz *et al.* 2007; Wesołowski 2007b, 2011a, 2012; Chapter 4).

Most of the BNP area is covered by three types of old-growth stands, illustrated in photographs A to C: (1) lime-hornbeam *Tilio-Carpinetum* forest (Photo A), the richest in tree species and structurally the most diverse and extensive forest type, which covers 44% of the total area; (2) swampy deciduous forests, *Circaeo-Alnetum* riverine stands and alder *Alnus glutinosa* carrs (Photo B), with the highest amount of dead wood, covering 22% of the area; and (3) mixed coniferous forests, dominated by Norway spruce and Scots pine *Pinus sylvestris* (Photo C), covering 28%. The remaining areas are covered by old meadows partially overgrown by secondary woods.

Intensive studies of birds in the primeval fragments of Białowieża Forest were commenced in 1975 (Tomiałojć *et al.* 1977, 1984) and continue to the present day. Most of the observations were carried out within several large (33–54 ha) permanent plots in the strictly preserved part of the Białowieża National Park. These studies aimed to describe patterns and processes found in breeding bird assemblages in the primeval forest and understand population ecology and the behaviour of birds living under such conditions. They combine long-term (40-year) studies of the structure and dynamics of the whole breeding bird assemblage (see Wesołowski *et al.* 2002, 2010, 2015a) with long-term studies of the population dynamics of individual species. In addition to bird data, information on potentially relevant resources such as tree holes (Wesołowski 1989; Walankiewicz 1991; Maziarz *et al.* 2016), tree masting (Wesołowski 1994; Wesołowski *et al.* 2015b), folivorous caterpillars (Rowiński & Wesołowski 1999; Wesołowski *et al.* 2009) and small rodents (Walankiewicz 2002; Wesołowski *et al.* 2009) has also been gathered. Shorter intensive population studies on the breeding ecology and behaviour of a

Box 8.1 (cont.)

dozen or so species, mostly passerines, have also been conducted (Wesołowski & Tomiałojć 1995, 2005), and some other aspects of the Białowieża work have been reviewed (Tomiałojć & Wesołowski 1990; Tomiałojć 1995; Wesołowski & Tomiałojć 1995, 1997; Wesołowski 2003, 2007a, 2007b; Czeszczewik & Walankiewicz 2003; Mitrus & Soćko 2008).

The future of this forest is, unfortunately, still far from secure. The majority of the Białowieża Forest is, as previously mentioned, managed by forestry authorities as a commercial timber-producing forest, involving logging in the surviving patches of old growth. These activities are strongly opposed by biologists and public opinion (Wesołowski *et al.* 2016).

Major habitat types of the BNP. (A) Lime-hornbeam *Tilio-Carpinetum* forest, an early May aspect. Numerous dead trees, which tend to be removed from managed woods, are important as foraging and nesting places for many species (Photo: J. Walencik /www.zubrowa10.pl). (B) Riverine habitat alongside a small stream, supporting the most luxuriant vegetation (Photo: T. Gmerek). (C) Coniferous habitat (Photo: T. Gmerek). (D) Uprooted tree. Soil-covered root pads are a common and preferred nesting place for several bird species (Photo: T. Gmerek). After Tomiałojć and Wesołowski (2004).

These massive changes in habitat extent and character, coupled with exploitation of birds and mammals (for meat, fur, eggs, etc.) and persecution of predatory birds and mammals, hugely impacted on forest biodiversity (Tomiałojć 1980; Gatter 2000; Rutz *et al.* 2006; Hinsley *et al.* 2015). By the onset of the twentieth century, the situation was changing in several respects. Extensive afforestation resulted in expansion of tree-covered land in most European countries. As the century progressed, the total area of forest was further supplemented by natural succession in areas where traditional farming and livestock grazing had ceased. In both newly established and existing forests, intensive forestry methods were being widely adopted, creating strikingly different structures to those that existed under primeval or even medieval conditions, and often involving plantations of non-native conifers (see Chapters 10 and 13).

Currently, about 26% of the European temperate zone is forested, and much of the forest exists as patches embedded in anthropogenic landscapes (Spiecker 2003). Forest cover tends to increase from west to east, from ca. 10% in Ireland, the United Kingdom and the Netherlands to more than 40% in Belarus (Spiecker 2003). The current tree species composition is mainly determined by human management (Ellenberg 1986; Jahn 1991; Gatter 2000). The area covered by old-growth forests in western Europe is only 1.9% of the total extent of forests (Ibero 1994). The loss of old-growth lowland forest has been almost as great in eastern Europe, though data are elusive (Rebane *et al.* 1997). Riverine forests have been especially severely affected; most of the original alluvial forests have been destroyed. In Europe (outside Russia), their remnants now barely cover 20,000 km^2 (Iremonger *et al.* 1996). Former broadleaved forests have frequently been replanted with relatively fast-growing conifers. Today, the area covered by coniferous species expands far beyond the limits of their natural range. In consequence, the tree species composition of temperate forests can resemble more that of the boreal forests than of the temperate zone 'wildwood'. In summary, the forests existing in the temperate zone nowadays constitute an impoverished, highly simplified version of forests which once covered the European lowlands.

8.3 Breeding Birds of Different Temperate Forest Types

How do breeding bird assemblages (defined in terms of species richness, densities, ecological guilds) vary with the forest type? To remove confounding effects of varying tree age (discussed separately below), we compare here, as far as possible, data from mature and old-growth stands, i.e., forest fragments that contain at least some very old trees that have grown beyond commercial harvesting age. An enormous diversity of forest plant associations has been distinguished (Ellenberg 1986; Podbielkowski 1987; Jahn 1991), but to provide a tractable overview of the general characteristics of the temperate forest avifauna, we group them into fewer broad categories. Inevitably this is a simplification, because current European forests represent a kaleidoscope of vegetation structures and tree species mixtures.

Some caveats are required when it comes to comparing bird densities derived from different studies. Even after controlling for stand age, within each of the forest types considered below, there will be variation in bird assemblages caused by many factors, including tree species composition, stand and foliage structure, soil type, forest patch size, landscape context and management system (Fuller 1995; Fuller *et al.* 2012). Note that variants of forest type and structure created through forest management are beyond the scope of this chapter, but information is provided in Chapter 13. Whilst there have been many assessments of numbers of breeding birds in various European temperate forests, these have used diverse methods (mainly variants of territory mapping, point counts and transects). When coupled with the above factors that cause variation in bird assemblages, these methodological differences make comparisons of estimated bird densities fraught with difficulty. Furthermore, there have been large temporal changes in bird assemblages in some regions in recent decades (e.g., Britain: Fuller *et al.* 2005; Hewson & Noble 2009; Balmer *et al.* 2013), which adds to the difficulty of making valid comparisons of densities and assemblage structures from studies conducted at different times. For these reasons, we have confined our attention to a relatively small number of studies, mainly based on multiple-visit territory mapping, where the habitat type and context are well documented and we consider are likely to be representative of different forest types.

8.3.1 Riverine and Swampy Forests

Riverine and swampy forests (also known as alluvial, gallery or riparian forests) develop in areas regularly flooded or waterlogged, such as floodplains, lake shores and depressions with a permanently high water table. Several broad types of such 'wet forests' can be distinguished based on landscape context and tree species composition.

Willow and poplar forests grow in regularly inundated fragments in large river valleys. This is probably the most dynamic of all forest types in temperate Europe. The damage done by floods and ice floes creates a complex mosaic of habitat conditions; plant composition and forest stature can change rapidly over space and time. Such forests always border open flowing waters and often contain water bodies (old river beds, side channels, flooded depressions). They are very fertile, with a rich, lush field layer. In large areas of central and eastern Europe, it is the only forest type that contains vines (mostly *Humulus lupulus*). The willow-poplar forests have largely been destroyed, and knowledge of their avifauna is scanty. Wösendorfer (1985) and Randik (1985) provide semi-quantitative lists of breeding birds in the Danube valley (Austria, Slovakia), and Hudek (1985) in the Morava/Dyje valley (former Czechoslovakia). Bohuš *et al.* (1999) present results of mapping censuses in the young floodplain forests in the Danube valley. The results of censuses in Germany are summarised by Flade (1994a), and in the former Czechoslovakia by Korňan (2011). However, some of these lists do not differentiate between birds that breed in the willow-poplar forests and in other habitat types on the floodplains. Similarly, the census plots were often very small (<10 ha), and some were situated in rather young tree stands or consisted of a mosaic of different habitats. Therefore, these results have to be interpreted with caution.

The breeding avifauna is very species-rich, the richest of all local forest types: for example, approximately 80 breeding species in the Inn valley (lower Bavaria) compared with 55 in mixed woodland nearby (Reich-holf 1985) and up to 89 in the former Czechoslovakia (review in Hudek 1985). Also, breeding densities are very high, reaching 150–180 territories/10 ha in plots of ca. 10 ha in size (and 200–320 territories/10 ha in plots of 4–6 ha). Almost no species is confined to this forest type. River warbler *Locustella fluviatilis*, penduline tit *Remiz pendulinus* and azure tit *Cyanistes cyanus* (Nikiforov *et al.* 1989) are the best candidates to be regarded as riverine forest specialists, though azure tit only reaches the extreme east of the European temperate zone. However, the breeding bird assemblage differs from that in other forest types in several important respects, the most striking being a high proportion of non-passerines. Such forests are used for breeding by cormorant *Phalacrocorax carbo*, white stork *Ciconia ciconia,* black stork *C. nigra*, grey heron *Ardea cinerea*, other species of herons and several Anseriformes, including goosander *Mergus merganser* and goldeneye *Bucephala clangula*. It is also used by a diverse array of birds of prey, including white-tailed eagle *Haliaeetus albicilla*, osprey *Pandion haliaetus*, lesser spotted eagle *Aquila pomarina*, black kite *Milvus migrans*, red kite *M. milvus* and several *Falco* spp. Some rallids and waders besides woodcock *Scolopax rusticola* are also reported, but it is unclear if they actually breed in the tree-covered parts or in the adjoining open wetlands. A high diversity of hole-nesting birds is another feature of the willow-poplar forests. In Austria (Wösendorfer 1985), all locally occurring excavating species (six woodpeckers and willow tit *Poecile montanus*, plus an additional 16 non-excavator species, including starling *Sturnus vulgaris* and tree sparrow *Passer montanus*) use this habitat type.

This high species richness is due to a combination of factors. This forest type is always close to open water, and sometimes marshes, so species which require open wetlands (for foraging) and trees (for breeding) can breed in close proximity. Moreover, a high microhabitat variation within the forest enables birds with very different requirements (e.g., kingfisher *Alcedo atthis*, penduline tit, willow tit) to share the same forest patches. Many of these forests show the rare combination of large trees towering above complex understorey structures that develop on the fertile soils beneath trees that tend not to cast dense shade. Hence, the requirements of many bird species can be met within relatively small areas of forest. Furthermore, the major tree species have soft wood that decays easily, creating diverse deadwood microhabitats and facilitating hole excavation. Quantities of dead and decaying wood tend to be high due to unstable soils and the presence of relatively short-lived trees. Last but not least, due to its inaccessibility to humans, this forest type provides a secure breeding refuge for large and shy birds.

Ash-elm forests develop on the upper, infrequently flooded alluvial soils. In major river valleys, they are usually situated between willow-poplar forests close to the river and deciduous forests on 'upland' mineral soils. These forests can also develop in valleys of smaller rivers, as well as in depressions or on slopes where rainwater accumulates. The dominant tree species are elms, ash and pedunculate oak *Quercus robur*. The shrub layer is typically well developed and the field layer is luxuriant, but less so than in willow-poplar forest. Of all riverine forests, this is most similar to the oak-hornbeam (*Quercus-Carpinus betulus*) type (see below). Bird assemblages of this forest type have been extensively studied in Germany (reviews in Wesołowski 1985; Flade 1994a). They are species-rich; in the study by Flade (1994a), 78 species were found breeding in all 19 study areas (jointly about 500 ha), and the expected number of breeding species in a 20 ha patch amounted to 38. Starling and chaffinch *Fringilla coelebs* were most numerous, with 14 other species reaching high densities (>3 territories/10 ha) (Table 8.1). In consequence, the overall density (mean 140, maximum 314 territories/10 ha on plots ≥10 ha) was amongst the highest recorded for any European forest type. Data from a single French study (Dronneau 2007) are broadly consistent with these patterns, though starling was relatively scarce (Table 8.1). For many of the most numerous species, the ash–elm forest is the habitat in which they reach the highest density of all forest types (Flade 1994a, though figures from old willow–poplar forests are unavailable). As with willow-poplar forest, ash–elm forest is used by a diverse set of hole-nesters (including seven woodpecker species) and birds of prey. Species dependent on heterogeneous shrub and field layer vegetation also reach high densities; such species include blackbird *Turdus merula*, blackcap *Sylvia atricapilla*, wren *Troglodytes troglodytes*, chiffchaff *Phylloscopus collybita*, dunnock *Prunella modularis* and nightingale *Luscinia megarhynchos*. These species are also likely to be abundant in willow-poplar forest, though less data are available.

Tree diseases have led to striking ecological impacts in the ash–elm forests. Effects of Dutch elm disease were studied by Gnielka (1965, 1978) in eastern Germany. The resulting thinning of tree stands and formation of canopy gaps resulted in increases of great spotted woodpecker *Dendrocopos major,* garden warbler *Sylvia borin,* blackcap, icterine warbler *Hippolais icterina,* dunnock, serin *Serinus serinus,* goldfinch *Carduelis carduelis* and tree sparrow, but declines of chaffinch, great tit *Parus major,* azure tit and pied flycatcher *Ficedula hypoleuca.* The effects on birds of the recent widespread dieback of ash remain to be studied in any forest types. This disease, which first appeared in Poland in 1992 and rapidly spread west across Europe, is caused by an introduced fungal pathogen (Pautasso *et al.* 2013; Gross *et al.* 2014).

Ash-alder forests develop in flat, swampy valleys of slow-flowing streams, in places with moving ground water. They contain one or two layers of trees composed almost exclusively of alder, ash and, in the northern transitional zone, Norway spruce. The shrub layer is well developed and the herb layer is composed of tall perennials. Ash-alder forests, of all wet forests, are most similar to alder carrs or alder swamps. Alder carrs are more strongly dominated by alder and develop in depressions filled (almost permanently) with stagnating water. In some alder carrs, the ground consists of a patchwork of relatively dry, tree-covered islets and (almost permanently) water-filled pools; in other cases, it can exist more as a tree-covered swamp.

Table 8.1 *Breeding bird assemblages in old-growth riverine and swampy forests. Densities of the most numerous species (≥3.0 territories/10 ha) are arranged in descending order of abundance, followed by the combined density of all species.*

France[1] Ash-elm forest		Germany[2] Ash-elm forest		Slovakia[3] Alder swamp[a]		Białowieża Nat. Park (Poland)[4] Ash-alder (edge)		Alder swamp (interior)	
Species	t/10 ha	Species	t/10 ha	Species	t/10 ha	Species	t/10 ha	Species	t/10 ha
F. coelebs	18.2	S. vulgaris	27.0	S. vulgaris	22.5	F. coelebs	18.2	F. coelebs	15.1
S. atricapilla	16.9	F. coelebs	11.7	A. platyrhynch.	15.8	S. vulgaris	9.6	E. rubecula	6.9
T. philomelos	13.8	P. major	9.7	F. albicollis	10.6	E. rubecula	8.3	F. albicollis	5.0
E. rubecula	11.1	T. merula	7.2	F. coelebs	10.5	S. atricapilla	6.5	Ph. collybita	4.9
P. major	10.7	S. atricapilla	7.1	Ph. collybita	10.3	F. albicollis	6.2	S. atricapilla	4.1
C. caeruleus	6.7	C. caeruleus	7.0	P. major	7.4	Ph. collybita	4.7	T. philomelos	3.5
T. merula	5.6	T. troglodytes	6.2	S. atricapilla	7.2	T. philomelos	4.7	T. merula	3.3
S. europaea	5.3	Pas. montanus	5.8	E. rubecula	6.4	Ph. sibilatrix	3.8	P. major	3.1
C. coccothr.	5.3	Ph. collybita	5.6	C. caeruleus	4.6	P. major	3.8	P. modularis	3.0
P. palustris	4.4	P. modularis	5.0	C. familaris	4.0	P. modularis	3.7	C. caeruleus	3.0
D. major	4.2	S. europaea	4.8			C. coccothraust.	3.6		
T. troglodytes	3.5	E. rubecula	4.5			T. troglodytes	3.5		
S. vulgaris	3.5	T. philomelos	4.5			C. caeruleus	3.5		
Ph. collybita	3.1	C. palumbus	4.3			T. merula	3.1		
		M. striata	3.4						
		C. brachydact.	3.3						
All species	129.3	All species	145.4	All species	125.1	All species	112.2	All species	79.5

[1] France, Rhine valley, Alsace, mean transect density in two years (Dronneau 2007).

[2] Germany, ash-elm forests, mean values from 17 plots in north and central Germany (recalculated from Flade 1994a).

[3] Slovakia, mean values for 1992–1995, 16 ha plot (Korňan 2009a).

[4] Białowieża National Park (Poland), mean values for 1975–2009; forest edge, plot K (33 ha), forest interior, plot L (25 ha). Recalculated from Tomiałojć et al. (1984); Tomiałojć & Wesołowski (1994, 1996); Wesołowski et al. (2002, 2006, 2010).

[a] Plot situated 250–300 m from the forest edge (Korňan 2009a).

In the Białowieża National Park, the ash-alder forest abutting the forest edge supports the largest number of species (Fig. 8.1), with almost 50 species breeding there in a single year and a total of 78 species recorded breeding there during 40 years (Wesołowski et al. 2015). Chaffinch and starling are the two most numerous species, but 12 additional species reach densities of >3 territories/10 ha. These are birds that use different forest strata, species that breed close to the ground, in tree crowns and in tree holes. Hole-nesters, including nine woodpecker species, contribute almost 40% of the breeding pairs in the whole assemblage. Overall bird density, 112 territories/10 ha (maximum 144/10 ha), is also highest there (Fig. 8.1). In the alder swamp forest, situated in the forest interior, the forest edge species (e.g., starling; Table 8.1) do not occur, so it is relatively species-poor, and overall bird density (<100 territories/10 ha) is lower (Fig. 8.1).

In a Slovakian alder forest more than 100 years old, both overall density (125 territories/10 ha) and species richness (33 species/year) were high (Korňan 2009b). This was partially due to its position within a few hundred metres of the forest edge – starling and mallard *Anas platyrhynchos* were the two most numerous species there (Table 8.1). Data from alder carrs in Germany (summarised in Oelke 1987 and Flade 1994a) are hardly comparable, as they probably come mostly from rather young, disturbed and highly fragmented woodlots. This is suggested by their species composition, willow warbler *Phylloscopus trochilus* being the most numerous species, with tree pipit *Anthus trivialis* a regular breeder. Therefore, the low overall densities in the alder woods in Germany (mean 67 territories/10 ha, maximum 117.5 territories/10 ha; Flade 1994a) could result more from their stage of development than from any geographical differences.

Green sandpiper *Tringa ochropus* and forest-breeding crane *Grus grus* seem to be restricted to alder woods in both the BNP and Germany. Otherwise, the same species of birds breed in both of these wet forest types (Table 8.1). A comparison of breeding bird assemblages in the ash-elm forests in Germany with those in Białowieża riverine forests shows that, despite being >1,000 km apart and containing some differences in tree composition, they are similar in their most abundant species (Table 8.1). There are a few differences, though: willow tit and short-toed treecreeper *Certhia brachydactyla* do not breed in the wet forests of Białowieża, while collared flycatcher *Ficedula albicollis* is not found in central/ northern Germany.

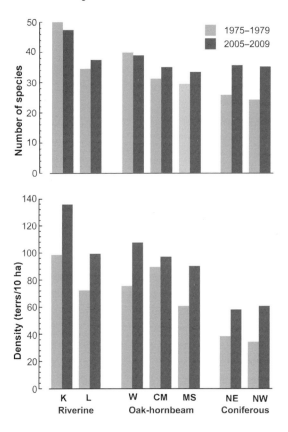

Figure 8.1 Species richness of breeding bird assemblage (upper) and total density of breeding birds (lower) and their long-term change in different forest types in Białowieża National Park. Mean 5-year values for individual plots (24–33 ha) sampled 30 years apart. Plot K and plot W are situated at the forest edge, the remaining ones in the forest interior. After Tomiałojć *et al.* (1984) and Wesołowski *et al.* (2010).

Beavers *Castor fiber* were once distributed throughout the whole temperate forest zone (Halley & Rosell 2012), damming streams and small rivers and creating numerous ponds. These permanent small bodies of standing water formed a unique riverine 'forest' habitat. Unfortunately, the beavers were extirpated long before the start of quantitative ornithology, therefore no data on the effects of beaver-induced habitat changes on forest birds seem to be available. The current recolonisation of Europe by beavers (Halley & Rosell 2012) offers a chance to fill this gap in knowledge. Recent observations from north-east Germany (M. Flade unpubl.) show that forests flooded by beaver dams are regularly used by goldeneye, little grebe *Tachybaptus ruficollis,* kingfisher, grey wagtail *Motacilla cinerea* and white wagtail *M. alba.* A typical feature is the high density of pied flycatchers in these stands, which consist almost completely of standing deadwood over water. Such stands are also intensively used by foraging woodpeckers, especially black *Dryocopus martius,* middle spotted *Leiopicus medius,* lesser spotted *Dryobates minor* and great spotted woodpeckers.

8.3.2 Broadleaved Forests on Well-drained Mineral Soils

Forests of this type once covered the largest areas of the temperate zone. They are usually formed by several tree species. Oaks (mostly pedunculate and sessile *Quercus petraea*) and small-leaved lime are important tree species in the whole range of temperate forests. However, stands consisting purely of oak are likely to be a consequence of selective forest management (Jahn 1991). Other species usually grow in an admixture: maples, elms, ash, birches and aspen. Overall, this mixed deciduous forest type harbours the most species-rich tree assemblages of the European temperate zone; 12 or so different species can co-occur in the same forest patch (Faliński 1986), although tree diversity is considerably lower than in the North American temperate zone (Askins 2014). Other dominant species are more restricted. Beech occurs in western and western-central European forests and hornbeam mainly in central Europe. In this account, we make a broad distinction between beech forests and mixed deciduous forests, the latter embracing both oak- and hornbeam-dominated stands.

Contemporary beech forests are often almost monodominant stands forming a single closed-canopy tree layer largely devoid of undergrowth (reviewed in Flade 1994a). However, these hall-like, rather uniformly structured stands are merely a result of forest management by clearcuts or shelterwood cuttings. By comparison, natural beech forests show a much more fine-grained pattern of forest development phases (Figs. 8.2, 8.3). In long-term unmanaged beech forests, the complete set of forest development phases occurs on each 100×100 m^2 (Begehold *et al.* 2016, submitted). Probably due to the structural simplicity of conventionally managed mature beech forests, the number of species that breed (ca. 26 in a 20 ha plot; Flade 1994a) and the average density of breeding birds of 55 territories/10 ha (Table 8.2) within them are rather low, comparable

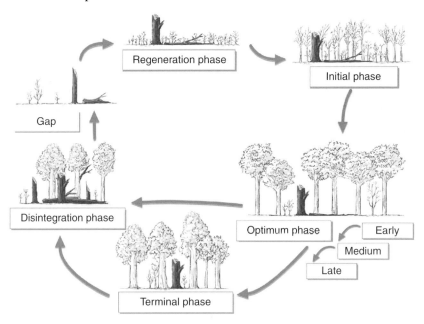

Figure 8.2 Forest life cycle in unmanaged beech forests in north-east Germany (from Begehold *et al.* 2015). Developmental phases differed in canopy cover, tree size, quantity of deadwood and understorey regeneration. In this study, most of the 37 bird species examined showed a preference for the terminal or disintegration phase, though some preferred younger growth, such as gaps and regeneration phases. Each bird species showed an individual profile with respect to its distribution across phases. See also Fig. 8.3.

to those in some coniferous forests (see below). Species numbers and abundances in German montane beech forests are even lower, on average 20 species on a 20 ha plot, 34 territories/10 ha (Flade 1994a). Crown-nesting chaffinches and ground-nesting wood warblers *Phylloscopus sibilatrix* and robins *Erithacus rubecula* are amongst the most numerous species in central European beech forests, but hole-nesting birds are prominent (Table 8.2).

In contrast, near-natural beech forests found, for example, in old strict forest reserves have higher species numbers and a higher total abundance of breeding birds. The strict forest reserves of Heilige Hallen and Fauler Ort in north-east Germany contain beeches up to 350 years old, as well as numerous snags and root pads of fallen trees and a deadwood volume of 220–255 m³/ha, and have been the subject of several studies (Schumacher 2001; Begehold *et al.* 2015; Begehold & Schumacher 2017).

Figure 8.3 Typical pictures of different forest development phases in lowland beech forests of the Schorfheide-Chorin Biosphere Reserve, north-east Germany (see also Fig. 8.2). Top left: Regeneration phase (Photo: J. Donath). Top right: Late optimum phase (Photo: M. Paulat). Bottom left: Terminal phase with gap, >100 years without exploitation (Photo: R. Kant). Bottom right: Disintegration (decay) phase, >100 years without exploitation (Photo: S. Winter).

A total of 32 breeding species have been recorded in both sites (maximum 30 in a single year), reaching a joint density of 67–98 territories/10 ha in Heilige Hallen and 76–153 territories/10 ha in the Fauler Ort (ranges describe annual variation in 5 study years). Among them were 19 species of hole-nesters (59% of the assemblage). Regular breeding species included ones that require rough bark (middle spotted woodpecker, nuthatch *Sitta europaea*, treecreepers *Certhia* spp.) as well as ones that depend on well-structured low vegetation (e.g., wren, blackcap); the latter are usually missing or less abundant in structurally more uniform beech woods.

In managed beech forests of the same region, in which a proportion of 'late' (terminal and disintegration; Fig. 8.2) forest development phases was retained for conservation reasons, 27–34 species were breeding, on

Table 8.2 *Breeding bird assemblages in mature deciduous forests on mineral soils. Densities of the most numerous species (≥ 3 territories/10 ha) are arranged in descending order of abundance, followed by the combined density of all species.*

Beech[1]				Oak & Oak–Hornbeam[2]							
Germany (N and Central)		Germany (NE)		France		Germany		Białowieża Nat. Park (Poland)			
Species	t/10 ha	Species	t/10 ha	Species	t/10 ha	Species	t/10 ha	Species (edge)	t/10 ha	Species (interior)	t/10 ha
F. coelebs	6.7	*F. coelebs*	8.9	*C. caeruleus*	12.6	*S. vulgaris*	6.7	*F. coelebs*	18.3	*F. coelebs*	17.4
P. major	5.5	*S. vulgaris*	6.1	*F. coelebs*	5.6	*F. coelebs*	6.4	*P. sibilatrix*	9.6	*F. albicollis*	8.4
S. vulgaris	5.4	*P. major*	5.9	*P. major*	4.7	*P. major*	5.5	*F. albicollis*	7.3	*E. rubecula*	6.8
P. sibilatrix	3.8	*E. rubecula*	5.0	*S. vulgaris*	3.9	*E. rubecula*	4.2	*E. rubecula*	6.2	*P. sibilatrix*	5.1
E. rubecula	3.7	*S. atricapilla*	4.2	*S. europaea*	3.8	*C. caeruleus*	4.0	*C. coccothraustes*	5.9	*C. coccothraustes*	4.9
C. caeruleus	3.4	*C. caeruleus*	4.1			*T. merula*	3.7	*T. philomelos*	5.4	*P. major*	3.7
T. merula	3.4	*T. troglodytes*	3.6			*P. sibilatrix*	3.2	*P. major*	3.6	*C. caeruleus*	3.7
F. hypoleuca	3.1	*S. europaea*	3.2			*C. brachydactyla*	3.2	*S. vulgaris*	3.3	*T. philomelos*	3.2
						F. hypoleuca	3.0	*C. caeruleus*	3.3		
						S. europaea	3.0	*S. atricapilla*	3.2		
All species	55.0	All species	60.3	All species	58.9	All species	74.0	All species	92.1	All species	77.3

[1] Beech forests: mean values from 34 plots in north and central Germany (1955–1985, recalculated from Flade 1994a), and mean values of 18 plots in north-east Germany 1999–2013 (Schumacher 2006; Begehold pers. comm.).

[2] Oak and oak-hornbeam forests: France (Burgundy), 150–200 years old, *Quercus robur* stands, densities derived from point counts (Futaie VII, Ferry & Frochot 1970); Germany, mean values from 70 plots in north and central Germany (recalculated from Flade 1994a); Białowieża National Park (Poland), mean values for 1975–2009; forest edge, plot W (25.5 ha), forest interior, plot MS (30 ha). Recalculated from Tomiałojć *et al.* (1984); Tomiałojć & Wesołowski (1994, 1996); Wesołowski *et al.* (2002, 2006, 2010).

average, at a total density of 60–97 territories/10 ha (means from nine 40 ha plots; Schumacher 2001; Begehold *et al.* 2015, and unpublished data). These values were intermediate between those found in purely conventionally managed forests and in strictly protected reserves (see above).

The middle spotted woodpecker turned out to be the best indicator species for naturalness, deadwood volume and age of trees in lowland beech forests. In conventionally managed forests, the species was almost absent, and whilst it was present at low densities (<1 ter/10 ha) in the forests managed for conservation, it reached the highest densities, up to 1.6 and 2.9 territories/10 ha, in the strictly protected old-growth areas (Schumacher 2001; Hertel 2003; Flade *et al.* 2004).

Begehold *et al.* (2015) showed that all breeding-bird species of beech forests select or avoid particular forest development phases within a natural forest cycle that includes gaps and various intermediate phases, concluding with terminal and decay (disintegration) phases (Fig. 8.2). Whereas the wren, for instance, prefers gaps, swamps and the decay phase and avoids the middle and late optimum phase, the wood warbler selects the initial and early optimum phases and avoids the middle and late optimum and terminal phases. The hawfinch *Coccothraustes coccothraustes*, in contrast, prefers the late optimum phase.

Among the 24 most abundant beech forest bird species, a majority prefer the terminal and decay phases, which are characterised by old massive trees and high amounts of deadwood, whereas a considerable number of species avoid the earlier younger phases (Begehold *et al.* 2015; Fig. 8.2). The entire species set of beech forest birds can only exist in stands that consist of a mosaic of all forest development phases. Since the terminal and decay phases are almost missing in conventionally managed forests, these preferences explain the differences between managed and strictly protected forests in species number and abundance.

Old deciduous forest stands consist of patches at different stages of growth following natural disturbances (tree diseases and windblow) and contain large quantities of standing and grounded deadwood. These form a fine-grained mosaic of structurally diverse patches which can still be seen in the BNP (Bobiec *et al.* 2000). Such diversity of structural features provides breeding opportunities for numerous birds with different requirements, as described above for beech forests. Forest stands of this type in the BNP harbour 33–36 species in the forest interior and ca. 39 species/year at the forest edge (Wesołowski *et al.* 2010), at mean densities of 77 and 92 territories/10 ha, respectively (Table 8.2). Crown nesters, including chaffinch (the most numerous species, densities of which regularly exceed 10 territories/10 ha, Table 8.2), hawfinch and song thrush *Turdus philomelos* form about 40% of the whole assemblage. Hole-nesters, dominated by very numerous collared flycatchers, are equally abundant, and ground-nesting birds (wood warbler, robin) form the remaining 20%. A few species, including starling, are restricted to the forest edges. Thus, the common occurrence of the latter species, which feeds mainly on open ground outside the forest, in all other beech and oak-hornbeam forests (Table 8.2) suggests that these study areas were situated in patchy landscapes with open areas nearby.

Breeding densities (74 territories/10 ha) and number of species (30 species) recorded in broadleaved forests on mineral soils in central and north Germany (Table 8.2) were similar to those found in the BNP. Also, the species most numerous in Germany occurred regularly (though not always in similar densities) in BNP, and vice versa. There were however two differences: short-toed treecreeper was found breeding only in Germany, whereas collared flycatcher occurred only in BNP. Results from French oak forest suggest much lower densities (59 territories/10 ha, Table 8.2), though it should be noted that this density value was derived from point counts, whereas territory mapping was the method used in the other studies. However, the most numerous bird species breeding in France were abundant in all the other areas. Hole-nesting birds, forming 58% of pairs in the assemblage (Ferry & Frochot 1970), were relatively more numerous than elsewhere.

British mature deciduous woodlands are dominated by the same group of species (Table 8.3; Fuller 1982); chaffinch, robin, great tit and blue tit are usually most abundant. Species living close to the forest floor (e.g., wren, blackbird, dunnock) are frequently more numerous there than in other areas. However, wood warbler and pied flycatcher are largely confined to oak-dominated stands in the western and northern upland regions of Britain (Balmer et al. 2013), and starling has become a scarce breeder in many British woods in recent decades (RJF pers. obs.). Some 2,500 km to the east, in forest parks of Moscow, a similar set of commonest species is found (Morozov 2009): chaffinch, great tit and blue tit are most numerous, followed by robin, song thrush, pied flycatcher and wood warbler. Additionally, starling and tree sparrow reach high numbers along forest edges.

In summary, across the whole lowland temperate zone, the bulk of the breeding avifauna in broadleaved forests on well-drained mineral soils consists of a very similar set of species. The breeding bird assemblages

Table 8.3 *Densities of dominant breeding species (≥3 territories/10 ha) in two contrasting woods in southern England. Both woods are fragments surrounded by farmland. The mature oak wood has been largely unmanaged for several decades and is predominantly closed-canopy pedunculate oak* Quercus robur *with some areas dominated by ash* Fraxinus excelsior *and field maple* Acer campestre; *the study plot includes a network of tracks and several open canopy patches with young trees. The coppiced wood is a mixture of ash, birch* Betula spp., *hazel* Corylus avellana *and alder* Alnus glutinosa *cut on a 25-year rotation. For details of study areas, see Hinsley* et al. *(2009). The densities are means for three widely spaced years: 1987, 2003 and 2013 (R.J. Fuller, unpubl. data). Asterisks indicate species mainly associated with shrubby vegetation, e.g., in patches of young growth and the edges of glades and tracks.*

Mature oak (49.5 ha)		Coppiced mixed broadleaves (63.5 ha)	
Species	t/10 ha	Species	t/10 ha
Cyanistes caeruleus	9.5	*Erithacus rubecula*	8.1
Erithacus rubecula	6.9	*Cyanistes caeruleus*	6.7
Parus major	6.1	*Troglodytes troglodytes*	4.7
Troglodytes troglodytes	5.4	*Phylloscopus trochilus*★	4.5
Fringilla coelebs	5.0	*Sylvia atricapilla*★	4.4
Turdus merula	3.2	*Parus major*	4.3
Sylvia atricapilla★	3.1	*Turdus merula*	3.8
		Sylvia borin★	3.4
		Phylloscopus collybita★	3.1
All species[a]	61.8	All species[a]	65.8

[a] The total densities are minimum estimates, because there was no census of pheasant *Phasianus colchicus* and woodpigeon *Columba palumbus*; the latter has a longer breeding season and later peak breeding activity than other species, making it difficult to estimate realistic numbers of different individuals. Densities of blue tit *Cyanistes caeruleus* may be underestimated, because conventional territory mapping, without nest location, does not work well for this species. Densities of blue tit and great tit *Parus major* in the coppiced broadleaved plot may have been influenced in some years by the presence of nest boxes.

of such forests are intermediate between the species-rich, very dense assemblages of riverine forests (see above) and low-density ones found in the coniferous forests (see below). Although the dominant bird species are similar throughout temperate forests, there is a striking east–west gradient in the diversity of bird species within European temperate forests, as described below (see also Chapter 5).

8.3.3 Broadleaved Forests in the Forest-steppe Zone

Over most areas of the temperate zone, fragmentation of broadleaved forests is a relatively recent human-induced phenomenon. However, along the south-east edge of the temperate forest distribution, due to climatic conditions, the forests were naturally fragmented in post-glacial times. Here they are thought to have existed as tree-covered 'islands' embedded within the treeless matrix (e.g., Novikov 1959; Smirnova & Turubanova 2004). This landscape presumably provided ideal conditions for 'edge' species that require forests (for breeding) and open areas (for feeding) in close proximity. No intact forest-steppe forest landscapes survive, but data collected in old-growth fragments of the Les na Vorskle reserve (Russia, 51°N, 36°E) give clues to the character of their avifauna (Novikov 1959). These old-growth patches were dominated by pedunculate oak and small-leaved lime. Unusually high overall densities of 200–400 territories/10 ha were reported from two one-hectare plots. These figures are derived from very small census plots and may not be comparable with data from larger and more typical census plots. Nevertheless, they indicate the existence of very high bird densities. These could be largely a result of the presence of several semi-colonial (jackdaw *Coloeus monedula,* tree sparrow, starling) or colonial (rook *Corvus frugilegus,* kestrel *Falco tinnunculus,* red-footed falcon *F. vespertinus*) breeding species. On the other hand, the large number of species, more than 70, breeding in the Les na Vorskle reserve may also contribute to the exceptional density. All the commonly breeding species of oak-hornbeam forests (cf. Table 8.2) bred there, but were accompanied by additional species, such as black kite, roller *Coracias garrulus,* hooded crow *Corvus cornix* and turtle dove *Streptopelia turtur.*

In terms of high species richness and high bird density, the forest islands in the forest-steppe zone match those found in the riverine and swampy forests (see above). As deforestation and agriculture expanded, numerous species originally inhabiting the forest-steppe zone were able to spread into their current large ranges (Vladiševskij 1975; reviewed in Gatter 2000).

8.3.4 Coniferous Forests

Remnants of natural pine-dominated stands are extremely rare in the temperate zone of Europe. As such forests were limited to the poorest soils, it seems reasonable to assume that these were monodominant pine forests with very little or no broadleaved undergrowth. In north Germany (summarised by Flade 1994a), these forests harbour species-poor (ca. 20 species/20 ha) and low-density (ca. 30–35 territories/10 ha) breeding assemblages, with only chaffinch exceeding 3 territories/10 ha. These densities are similar to those observed in European boreal coniferous forests (see Chapter 6). Hole-nesters, mostly excavators, form a smaller part of the breeding assemblages than in the deciduous forests. Characteristic species for this forest type are crested tit *Lophophanes cristatus*, coal tit *Periparus ater*, capercaillie *Tetrao urogallus* and Tengmalm's owl *Aegolius funereus*. Addition of Norway spruce increases both bird-species richness and overall bird density. Mixed pine-spruce forests with an admixture of deciduous trees tend to be richer in species and hold denser populations (ca. 35 species, up to 55–60 territories/10 ha) in a natural situation (Fig 8.1) and when man-modified (north Germany; Flade 1994a). In such mixed-conifer forests, additional species breed that are more dependent on the presence of Norway spruce; these include goldcrest, siskin *Carduelis spinus*, pygmy owl *Glaucidium passerinum*, nutcracker *Nucifraga caryocatactes* and crossbill *Loxia curvirostra*. However, such habitat associations can vary regionally. Some species that are most typical of coniferous forest in central and eastern parts of the temperate zone can use purely deciduous forests and other habitats in England (Table 8.4).

8.3.5 Mixed Deciduous-coniferous Forests

Forests composed of a mixture of deciduous and coniferous trees occurred naturally only locally, at transitions between pine and deciduous forests. Norway spruce also co-occurred with deciduous trees in the hemiboreal zone and in the transition to montane forests (Norway spruce and silver fir). However, mixed forests are now widespread in the European lowlands as a result of planting (see Chapter 10); consequently, they represent an important ingredient of contemporary forest landscapes.

Mature mixed forests allow species that are mainly associated with broadleaved trees and ones more dependent on conifers to breed side-by-side in the same patch. Additionally, some species benefit from the juxtaposition of broadleaved and coniferous trees. Willow tits may forage in conifers but excavate nests in broadleaves. Hazel grouse *Tetrastes bonasia* forage in deciduous trees but obtain cover from spruce. Firecrests *Regulus ignicapilla* reach highest densities in some regions in

Table 8.4 *Contrasts in breeding habitat associations and nest sites used by birds in a primeval forest, Białowieża National Park (Poland), and in England. If not shown otherwise, data from Białowieża are extracted from Tomiałojć et al. (1984), Tomiałojć and Wesołowski (1990) and Wesołowski et al. (2003, 2010), and data for England extracted from Fuller (1995) and Robinson (2005). Modified after Wesołowski and Fuller (2012).*

Species	Białowieża Forest	England
Buteo buteo	Inside extensive old-growth stands, forages under tree canopy, nests high in trees (Jędrzejewski *et al.* 1994b)	Nests in mature woodlands, mainly forages outside woodland; in open country also nests on cliffs, in isolated trees and bushes, or on the ground where fox *Vulpes vulpes* absent
Columba palumbus	As above, nests in trees above 10 m, forages in and under canopy, rarely in fields (Tomiałojć 1980)	Wide range of woodland and scrub, also in hedgerows and parkland; forages mostly outside woods, nests in bushes and trees, usually up to 10 m
Columba oenas	Mostly in coniferous forest; forages under tree canopy, nests in tree holes (mainly excavated by *Dryocopus martius*)	Woodland and farmland with some trees, nests in tree holes, also farm buildings, cliffs or rabbit holes; forages mainly outside woodland
Apus apus	Nests in holes in emergent trees inside extensive old-growth stands	Nests entirely in buildings in towns and villages, absent from woods (although tree-nesting occurs in northern Scotland)
Troglodytes troglodytes	Mostly in riverine or other broadleaved forests; nests in root pads of fallen trees, fallen logs, etc. (Wesołowski 1983)	Woodland, scrub, gardens, hedgerows; uses wide range of nest sites in dense vegetation and artefacts
Prunella modularis	Mostly riverine forests; sites with lush ground vegetation	Scrub, young woodland, gardens, hedges; in mature woodland often confined to the edge; now most abundant in non-woodland situations, especially urban and suburban

Table 8.4 (*cont.*)

Species	Białowieża Forest	England
Erithacus rubecula	All old-growth forest types; nests on the ground, in root pads of uprooted trees, commonly in tree holes	All types of woodland, scrub, gardens, hedgerows, other places with bushes and trees; typically nests on or close to the ground, also open cavities (natural and man-made)
Phoenicurus phoenicurus	Mature coniferous and some deciduous (with sparse understorey) stands	Mature open woodland, upland *Betula* and *Quercus petraea*, wood-pasture and northern *Pinus sylvestris* woods, also southern heaths with mature *Pinus* and (formerly) in hedgerows with pollarded trees
Turdus merula	Mostly deciduous (riverine and oak-hornbeam) old-growth forests; often in tree holes and root pads of uprooted trees (Tomiałojć 1993)	In all rural and urban habitats with trees or bushes; in many woods highest densities at the edge, nests usually in shrubs, below 4 m
Turdus philomelos	All types of old-growth forest, nests in tree crowns, half of them in spruces (Tomiałojć 1992)	Similar to *Turdus merula*
Turdus viscivorus	Mature coniferous woods	Wide range of woodland and lightly wooded country, feeding also on open land, avoids extensive forest
Regulus regulus	Mature coniferous and broadleaved with admixture of *Picea abies*	Highest densities in mature coniferous forest, but breeds also in pure broadleaved woods at low density
Regulus ignicapilla	Mostly mature riverine deciduous-coniferous woods	Mature coniferous or mixed woods (especially *Picea abies* and *Pseudotsuga menziesii*), rarely in broadleaved woods with *Ilex aquifolium*

Table 8.4 (*cont.*)

Species	Białowieża Forest	England
Periparus ater	Old-growth coniferous forest, temporary colonisation of *Quercus–Carpinus* habitats with admixture of *Picea*	Coniferous woodland, common also in a wide range of pure broadleaved and mixed woods
Poecile palustris	Broadleaved old-growth forest with sparse understorey	Broadleaved woodland, avoids sites with very little understorey (Broughton & Hinsley 2015)
Poecile montanus	Mainly coniferous stands with admixture of *Betula*	Mostly broadleaved scrub and woodland, though local populations occur in some coniferous stands with broadleaved stumps and snags
Pyrrhula pyrrhula	Mature coniferous and broadleaved with admixture of spruce *Picea abies*	Scrub, hedgerows and woodland; mainly in broadleaved woods, but also in thicket-stage conifers
Sturnus vulgaris	Mature broadleaved stands along forest edge; nests in tree holes, forages in forest glades or tree crowns	Mostly human settlements; feeds mainly on farmland; now a scarce nester in much woodland, where it usually nests at edges
Corvus corax	Inside extensive old-growth stands; nests high in trees, forages mostly in forest (Rösner *et al.* 2005)	Moorland, bogs, coast, increasingly in wooded landscapes: nests either on tall trees, cliffs or buildings

mixed stands, possibly because they forage in the broadleaved trees but nest in the conifers (M. Flade pers. obs.). Consequently, one might expect to find more breeding species (higher species richness) and higher overall densities of breeding birds in the mixed forests. This has been observed in mixed pine-oak forests in Germany (review in Flade 1994a), which are inhabited both by conifer-dependent crested tits and coal tits, as well as by wood warbler and several other species that generally require deciduous foliage, for example some other warblers. In Germany, a 10–33 ha patch of such habitat can be used by 30–35 species, at a mean assemblage density of 60 territories/10 ha. These values exceed those in the coniferous forests in the region and approach those found in rich deciduous forests on the mineral soils there (see above). The same pattern was revealed in former coniferous old-growth patches in BNP that changed into mixed deciduous-coniferous forests following extensive windfalls. The formerly present 'coniferous' species continued to breed, but the areas were colonised by additional 'deciduous forest' species. In consequence, the species richness substantially increased, from a mean of 26 species/plot in 1975–1979 to 37 species in 2010–2014, and the overall density rose from 36 to 55 territories/10 ha on average (cf. Tomiałojć *et al.* 1984; Wesołowski *et al.* 2015a).

Birds of the mixed forests in the montane zones show a similar pattern of high species richness, due to cohabitation by birds with different habitat affinities (e.g., beech-spruce-fir forests in the western Carpathians; Korňan & Adamík 2007, 2014; Chapter 7).

There are, however, some exceptions to the above pattern. In managed forest in western Britain, Donald *et al.* (1998) could find little difference between broadleaved, coniferous and mixed stands in species number and overall abundance of breeding birds. Similarly, Archaux & Bakkaus (2007) found that mixed stands in mountains of southern France did not have higher avian species richness than pure stands.

8.4 Breeding Birds of Mature and Old-growth Forests – Overview

With the exception of the geographically restricted beech forests and forest-steppe broadleaved forests, the above forest types can co-occur anywhere in the temperate zone. Their spatial distribution follows moisture/fertility gradients, from floodplain forests in valley bottoms to conifers on sandy plateaus. Within the space of a few kilometres, one can observe how the composition of the breeding bird assemblages changes in relation to habitat variation, but the BNP data show that these changes are generally small (Tomiałojć & Wesołowski 2004). When moving from one forest type to another, only a few species are replaced. Some specialists are found only in a single habitat type, such as green sandpiper (alder swamp forests) or pygmy owl (conifers). However, most of the other species breed in the majority of primeval forest habitats (Wesołowski *et al.* 2003; Tomiałojć & Wesołowski 2004). In the BNP, even dramatic changes in forest structure induced by the appearance of large treefall gaps (up to several hectares in area) after storms result in colonisation by just a handful of new species (Fuller 2000; see below). The gaps are still inhabited by a subset of species typical of the mature forest. As a result of this high plasticity of individual species, the combined number of species breeding in all woodland habitats is only a third higher than their number in the single richest plot (cf. Fig. 8.1). Due to this high similarity of species composition across forest types, it could be argued that a single bird assemblage inhabits all the forest types within this large primeval forest (Tomiałojć *et al.* 1984; Wesołowski *et al.* 2002, 2006).

This relative uniformity of composition of the breeding avifauna of mature European temperate forests is also visible at much broader geographical scales, as evidenced by the similarity of the commonest species in the breeding assemblages in Britain, northern Germany, eastern Poland and western Russia. There is also a high level of constancy in the types of species – in terms of taxonomic, ecological and life-history groups – that occur in forest bird assemblages across the European temperate zone (Fuller *et al.* 2007). The occurrence of less numerous species shows much more variation, as there are large geographic differences in the pool of available species (see 'West-east trends' below).

No species seems to be restricted to the lowland temperate forests of Europe, but there is a group of species whose distribution is concentrated in the deciduous forests of this zone, with the majority of their European populations occurring there. Tucker and Evans (1997) count the following species as concentrated in 'lowland temperate forest' (all types and age classes lumped): red kite, lesser spotted eagle, tawny owl *Strix aluco*, green woodpecker *Picus viridis*, grey-headed woodpecker *P. canus*, middle spotted woodpecker, lesser spotted woodpecker, common nightingale, thrush nightingale *Luscinia luscinia*, river warbler, icterine warbler, garden warbler, red-breasted flycatcher *Ficedula parva*, collared flycatcher, blue tit, azure tit, nuthatch, both European treecreeper species, golden oriole *Oriolus oriolus* and hawfinch. Of these species, the two nightingales, river warbler and garden warbler are largely associated with young growth stages.

It is difficult to propose a consistent list of 'indicator species' (i.e., species that strongly prefer certain habitat types over most others) for individual temperate forest types which would be valid across the continent. Due to large interregional contrasts in habitat use by many species (see below), this is more readily achievable at a regional scale. For example, Flade (1994a, b) has proposed such a list for central and north Germany. In that region, there is a core group of species that prefer ash-elm alluvial forests, oak-hornbeam and beech forests, consisting of middle spotted and green woodpeckers, nuthatch, short-toed treecreeper, pied flycatcher and wood warbler. Red-breasted flycatcher, stock dove *Columba oenas* and Tengmalm's owl are indicator species of pure beech forests; lesser spotted woodpecker, golden oriole, river warbler, thrush nightingale, icterine warbler and penduline tit are indicators of alluvial forests, while crane is an exclusive indicator species of alder carrs.

8.5 Ecological Guild Structure of Temperate Forest Bird Assemblages

Groups of species with similar ecological requirements or niches represent the basic functional units of forest bird assemblages. In the case of nest sites, three main groups can be identified in European mature forests: (i) ground-nesters, birds that use open or domed nests on the ground or in low vegetation up to 1.5 m above the ground which are accessible to all classes of predators; (ii) crown-nesters, birds that construct open or domed nests in high bushes or in trees, accessible to climbing or flying predators; and (iii) hole-nesters.

Species that nest on the ground (e.g., grouse species, woodcock, chiffchaff and wood warbler) and hole-nesters seldom use other nest sites, while some canopy-nesters show great variability and will nest from near ground level to more than 20 m above it (e.g., chaffinch, song thrush and blackbird). Some species nevertheless breed mostly in the upper tree canopy (e.g., hawfinch, mistle thrush *Turdus viscivorus*, swift *Apus apus*, corvids, large birds of prey).

Hole-nesters are most dependent upon availability of specific nest sites. They constitute an important component of the breeding bird assemblages in all mature temperate forest types. In BNP, ca. 36% of breeding species use holes to some extent, and up to 45% of all pairs breed in holes (Chapter 4). The situation looks similar in other old-growth deciduous and mixed forests in Europe (see above). In some places, up to 60% of pairs can use tree holes. Only a minority of hole-nesters are excavators. Their distribution and numbers may be constrained by the availability of suitable substrates for excavation. The majority of hole-nesting species are non-excavators and have to rely on existing holes. Thus the availability and diversity of holes could be critical in shaping the composition and numbers of the latter group of species. However, observations in old-growth deciduous forests show that holes are generally superabundant there and that non-excavators are not limited by a shortage of nest sites (Chapter 4). The excavators tend to be critical ('keystone') hole providers only in conifer-dominated forests, or in young forest patches. By contrast, non-excavators in old-growth deciduous forests mostly use 'decay' holes. These holes take a long time to form, but are rather persistent. These differences in hole-use patterns have profound conservation implications (see Chapter 4).

The foraging guild structure of bird assemblages has been worked out objectively in just a handful of European temperate forests. In a Hungarian oak forest, Székely and Moskát (1991) proposed that resident species fell into two general guilds: bark-foraging (nuthatch, treecreeper, woodpeckers) and foliage-gleaning (tits and goldcrest). Summer visitors (warblers and flycatchers) were included in the foliage-gleaning guild rather than as an aerial feeding group. More detailed analyses of guild structure are available for a plot of primeval beech-fir forest in the Carpathian mountains (Korňan & Adamík 2007; Korňan et al. 2013).

The exact guild structure of forest birds, with respect to both nest sites and foraging sites, will depend on the impacts of forest management on the vegetation structure and resources available (Chapter 13). The maturity of forests will have an obvious strong influence on the availability of nesting and foraging substrates (see below). Furthermore, as discussed later, there may be geographical variation in the niches occupied by individual species.

8.6 Temporal Variation of Bird Assemblages

We have so far examined spatial variation in the breeding bird assemblages of mature forest stands across geographical regions and major habitats. However, there is another important dimension of variation, namely temporal changes in bird assemblages. The changes can occur at different time scales, ranging from geological to seasonal. Here we concentrate on three levels, long-term (decadal) variation in mature forests, long-term successional changes or ones associated with tree growth, and seasonal variation in bird assemblages, concentrating on the winter season.

8.6.1 Long-term Variation in Mature Forests

Even with no major changes in the forest structure and no direct human intervention, the composition of bird assemblages would vary over time.

What is the magnitude of this variation? Are changes in composition directional? How fast does the composition of bird assemblages change over time?

Several decades-long series of observations collected in various temperate forests allow these questions to be addressed. The longest-running census, in a 13 ha mixed-deciduous forest island in south Sweden, started in 1953 and still continues (Enemar *et al.* 1994; Svensson *et al.* 2010). The ongoing studies in BNP (Box 8.1) encompass 40 years (Wesołowski *et al.* 2015a). Birds in a secondary isolated oak wood in England were studied for 30 years (Beven 1976; Gaston & Blackburn 2000), and in a small lime-oak wood on an Estonian island for 27 years (Leito *et al.* 2006). See also the review of long-term studies by Kampichler *et al.* (2014). The forest structure in these areas was changing slowly through the ageing and dying of trees.

In the Swedish study, over 57 years the overall density or number of species of small passerines remained constant over the first 40 years. However, in the last 17 years there was an increase in both density and species number; in each case the annual means in the second time period were approximately 20% higher. The eight most numerous species bred there in all years and an additional seven in more than 80% of the years. Numerically, these 'core' species formed ca. 74% of the assemblage (Svensson *et al.* 2010). Gaston and Blackburn (2000) found in England that a third of 45 species bred there every year and ca. 46% used the wood in more than 27 of 30 study years. Leito *et al.* (2006) observed in Estonia that over 27 years, variation in the number of species/year (CV = 11%) as well as in the total density (CV = 15%) was rather small.

Overall composition of the breeding avifauna in BNP did not change substantially during 40 years (Wesołowski *et al.* 2015a), and no colonisation of forest areas by a new species or extinction of a formerly widespread species, except tree pipit, was observed. The core assemblage of breeding birds in BNP was very stable, with almost 40% of species found breeding somewhere in the study plots during the 40 years of study and 57% of the species breeding in at least 35 years. These 'constant species' formed ca. 97% of the pairs in the breeding assemblage and included all of the most numerous species, but also some that bred in low numbers, such as three-toed woodpecker *Picoides tridactylus* (only two pairs per season, on average). Crown insectivores, crown-nesters and short-distance migrants remained the most numerous foraging, nesting and migratory groups during the whole period. The density gradient across habitats – highest in the riverine, lowest in the coniferous stands – was retained (Wesołowski *et al.* 2015a). The compositional change over time was very small, though fastest in the coniferous habitat, which had experienced relatively large natural disturbances from a European spruce bark beetle *Ips typographus* outbreak and windfalls in recent decades (Kampichler *et al.* 2014; Wesołowski *et al.* 2015a).

In summary, the composition of the breeding bird assemblages in mature temperate forests, even in small areas, appears to remain remarkably stable over a timescale of several decades. In the absence of major disturbances (see below), their composition changes only gradually, at slow rates (Kampichler *et al.* 2014).

8.6.2 Tree Growth Stages and Forest Succession

Local exchange of tree generations and replacement of dying mature (senile) trees by juvenile individuals adds another axis of temporal variation. As structure (forest architecture) changes substantially with the stage of tree growth, within the same forest, neighbouring patches containing trees of different ages can have contrastingly different three-dimensional structure. Developmental phases differ in canopy cover, tree size, quantity of deadwood and understorey regeneration (Fig. 8.2). Individual species of birds use only parts of this gradient, as illustrated by unmanaged beech forests in north-east Germany (Begehold *et al.* 2015, see above).

Patches of young trees develop mainly in canopy gaps formed by the death or removal of mature trees. In natural conditions, several mortality (disturbance) factors could be involved. Disease and parasites, as well as strong winds uprooting/breaking trees, are apparently important in all types of temperate forests. Additionally, floodwaters and ice floes are mortality agents in floodplain riverine forests, whereas fires were relevant only in Scots pine–dominated forests (Niklasson *et al.* 2010). Depending on the number of trees involved, the size of gaps can vary from tens of square meters (replacement of single trees) to thousands of hectares (large fires, tornadoes).

There seem to be no studies of birds in canopy gaps created by floods or fires in temperate forests (but see Chapter 9 for a discussion of fire in Mediterranean forests), but we have some glimpses of what happens in windfall gaps. Fuller (2000) compared birds that breed in windfall gaps (up to ca. 15 hectares in size) with surrounding closed-canopy, old-growth lime-hornbeam stands in BNP. Canopy cover in the old growth (ca. 90%) was far higher than in gaps (ca. 15%), whereas understorey density and the number of fallen trees was three times higher in the gaps. Despite these profound changes of habitat structure and the large size of some gaps, broadly the same set of woodland species utilised gaps and non-gaps, though the relative abundance of some species differed: dunnock, blackcap and chiffchaff were more abundant in gaps, whereas wood warbler and red-breasted flycatcher were more abundant in closed-canopy forest. Strikingly, several species that commonly breed in forest edges and young tree plantations in the managed parts of the Białowieża Forest, such as whitethroat *Sylvia communis*, red-backed shrike *Lanius collurio*, linnet *Carduelis cannabina* and yellowhammer *Emberiza citrinella*, were not recorded in these treefall gaps.

Similar robustness of the breeding avifauna to large-scale canopy destruction was observed in other windfall areas. Żmihorski (2008) found that five years after a storm which affected ca. 30,000 ha of managed Scots pine forest in Puszcza Piska (north Poland) and damaged ca. 70% of trees, woodland species, such as chaffinch, robin, great tit and song thrush, still formed ca. 70% of the breeding assemblage. The area was partially cleared by sanitary fellings, yet birds that use mostly open ground or bushy areas (willow warbler, tree pipit, woodlark *Lullula arborea,* wheatear *Oenanthe oenanthe,* white wagtail, red-backed shrike) contributed only ca. 30% of territories in the assemblage. Muller (2002) studied 140-year-old beech forest and 50-to-80-year-old Scots pine plantation in the northern Vosges Mountains of France (ca. 400 m above sea level) in the spring following a storm, which downed ca. 80% of trees. The broken trees had been already partially removed in sanitary fellings. Though some woodland species disappeared from the area (firecrest, wood warbler, pied flycatcher, marsh tit *Poecile palustris*), the most numerous remaining species were forest birds (great tit, chaffinch, robin). However, species of more open areas (white wagtail, tree pipit) or of dense undergrowth (garden warbler, chiffchaff) colonised the area. In Germany, similar observations have been made in storm-affected forests. Despite the downing of 80–90% of trees in oak-hornbeam forests of the upper Rhine valley (Hohlfeld 2006) and in beech forests in north-east Germany (Lutz 2014; M. Flade pers. obs.), the composition and total abundance of the breeding avifauna on the study plots did not differ substantially before and after windfall. In the upper Rhine valley, the abundance of some tree-inhabiting and hole-nesting species declined (e.g., nuthatch, woodpeckers) and some species of early successional stages and clearings, such as turtle dove, green woodpecker, white wagtail, garden warbler, red-backed shrike, yellowhammer, serin and greenfinch *Chloris chloris*, colonised the plots. In the German beech forests, typical species of forest gaps and clearings, such as red-backed shrike, woodlark, yellowhammer and grasshopper warbler *Locustella nae-via*, were absent in the first two years after windfall (Lutz 2014). All these studies indicate that wind-created gaps, even when 80% of the canopy is lost, continue to be suitable habitat for the majority of woodland birds and, without human intervention (see below), are largely unsuitable for the birds of open land. Patches of bare land, totally devoid of vegetation (sandbars), appeared regularly only in floodplain forests. Very intensive canopy fires could possibly have similar effects. Therefore, in pre-human times, species such as woodlark, wheatear and red-backed shrike presumably found rather few opportunities to breed within continuous tracts of forest; they were probably mainly limited to permanently, or semi-permanently, open areas.

The main disturbance factor creating canopy gaps in temperate forests nowadays is forestry operations. Gaps created by clearcutting have been frequently replanted with a single tree species, producing even-aged monocultures (note that diversification of tree species is becoming recognised as a means of adapting forestry to climate change and 'continuous cover systems', as an alternative to clearcutting, are now widespread; see Chapter 13). Clearcuts, however, differ massively from natural gaps. The latter usually retain most elements of the pre-disturbance forest, but with a reduced three-dimensional structure. Treefall gaps usually contain a substantial number of snags and living standing trees, many of which have damaged limbs. There is a low tangle of downed tree stems mixed with the original shrub layer and regenerating tree saplings. The presence of such complex structures in the natural gaps allows woodland birds to persist, and some may use treefall gaps as concentrations of resources associated with deadwood and dense understorey vegetation (Fuller 2000). This is not the case in clearcuts. Unless there is a policy of leaving snags and retentions (see Chapter 13), nothing of the former forest cover is left, all woody material is removed and, in the process of soil preparation for replanting, the ground vegetation is often largely destroyed. This is a completely recent type of habitat that offers no opportunity for true woodland birds, but opens an avenue for colonisation of the area by birds of open habitats, such as woodlark, wheatear, even skylark *Alauda arvensis* (e.g., Flade 1994a; Fuller 1995; Żmihorski 2010; Fig. 8.4). Comparing a windfall area left for natural recovery with a windfall subjected to salvage logging (clearcutting) and replanting, the breeding bird assemblage in intact managed Scots pine forest was shown to be more similar to that in windfall left for natural regeneration than to that in salvage-logged windfall; the bird assemblages 'were affected more profoundly by

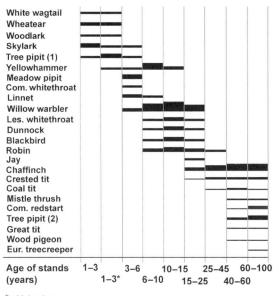

Figure 8.4 Distribution of breeding birds in relation to age (stage of growth) of tree stands in managed Scots pine forests in north Germany. For each age class, only dominant species (>5% numerical share in the assemblage) and subdominant species (2–5% share) occurring with a frequency of ≥50% are shown. Height of bars is proportional to breeding density of species, with a range of 0.5–12 territories/10 ha. Modified after Dierschke (1973).

the salvage logging and replanting following a windstorm than by the natural windstorm itself' (Żmihorski 2010).

This difference between human- and wind-created gaps has to be kept in mind in the following discussion about 'successional' changes in bird assemblages. Most studies of 'forest succession' deal not with the temporal progression of organisms in response to natural forest dynamics, but with responses to age-related changes in physiognomy (architecture) of the same tree species in managed forests. These studies mostly take a replanted clearcut as an initial stage of 'succession' (e.g., lime-hornbeam, Poland, Głowaciński 1975; oak forest, France, Ferry & Frochot 1970, 1990; Scots pine forests, north Germany, Dierschke 1973; south-west Poland, Borowiec & Grabiński 1982). A review by Helle and Mönkkönnen (1990) of such studies found that despite differences in tree species and geographical position, the progression of changes was very repeatable, related to progressive development of foliage stratification (an example is presented in Fig. 8.4). Similar, but faster, turnover in bird assemblages as a result of changing vegetation architecture occurs in coppiced woodland (Fuller 1995; Fuller & Rothery 2013). However, as many coppiced woods tend to retain mature trees (standard trees) throughout the rotation, they remain useable by a majority of mature forest bird species even after harvesting (cf. Table 8.3), so the structural change in habitat is not as profound as in the case of complete tree removal.

The turnover of bird assemblages in forests managed by clearcutting follows a broadly predictable path. Initially, if just a single layer of low vegetation is available, only ground-nesting and ground-foraging birds occur (e.g., woodlark) and both diversity and density of nesting birds are at their lowest. If scattered snags, seed trees or standard trees are left, these can provide some limited resources for hole-nesters and other tree-dependent species. When growing trees reach the stature of bushes, areas are colonised by 'scrub or shrubland' birds, which replace the former ground dwellers. Several species of mostly long-distance migrant warblers typify this stage (Helle & Fuller 1988), the most ubiquitous being willow warbler, though this species is now strongly decreasing in some southern parts of its range (Balmer *et al.* 2013). The next major transition occurs when trees change their stature from bush to tree form (a closed canopy with crowns raised above the ground on trunks). Dense low vegetation becomes sparser due to shading, and 'scrub' species are replaced by typical woodland ones. The onset of this stage is marked by the appearance of chaffinch (Fig. 8.4), probably the most ubiquitous woodland species in temperate forests. Hole-nesters, which have to wait for holes in trees to form, and specialised seed-eaters are the last groups to appear. Their arrival, though, does not coincide with the disappearance of the woodland species that colonised earlier, so the numbers of breeding species increases. As shown by Begehold *et al.* (2015), the majority of forest-inhabiting species actually prefer to breed in forest fragments containing the oldest (large and senile) trees, both alive and dead (Figs. 8.2, 8.3). Hence, over several decades, a complete turnover of species takes place. No single species utilises all growth stages for nesting, unless measures such as snag or green tree retention are adopted (see Chapter 13).

The number of years that it takes for trees to reach consecutive developmental stages is variable across tree species, soil nutrient status and climate. However, structural changes in the early stages are faster than in the later ones. Changes in bird assemblages follow this pattern, with species turnover rates declining with increasing tree age (Helle & Mönkkönen 1990). Overall, there is a tendency for species richness and assemblage density to increase with tree age (Helle & Mönkkönnen 1990). In reality, for commercial reasons, many forests are managed on rather short rotations, and over-mature stands are frequently absent. This results in a predominance of younger stages of tree growth, with large implications for the overall bird assemblage composition. This is well illustrated in coppiced broadleaved woodland, which is managed on extremely short rotations, resulting in bird assemblages being relatively biased towards the 'scrub' phase compared with mature mixed broad-leaved forest (Table 8.3).

There has been relatively little attention paid to the factors that influence variation in bird assemblages within 'young-growth' habitats compared to mature forests. The resource and structure requirements of early successional species can be just as precise as those of mature forests; indeed, in a successional gradient study, Reif et al. (2013) found that early successional bird species had higher levels of habitat specialisation than species associated with later stages. In many landscapes, early successional species find suitable habitat only at the edges of forest or in non-forest vegetation such as hedgerows. This can result in such species being referred to as 'edge' species, when in fact they are young-growth specialists; true edge species are those that benefit from the close proximity of fundamentally different resources or habitat types found at many edges (Imbeau et al. 2003; Fuller 2012).

8.6.3 Seasonal Changes: Winter Bird Assemblages in Temperate Forests

Deciduous forests are probably the most seasonally variable of all forest types. Periodic appearance and disappearance of leaves causes dramatic changes in the habitat architecture, affecting the lives of birds in many ways. To survive year-round in such forests, birds have to be able to adapt to extremely different conditions. In spring and summer, lush foliage provides birds with food, hiding places and a benign microclimate. With the disappearance of leaves, tree crowns become very transparent, exposed places, with invertebrate food available exclusively on or inside twigs and buds, though tree seeds and fruits become accessible in some seasons (e.g., Wesołowski et al. 2015b). The only remaining green patches are bunches of mistletoe Viscum spp. and, in the western part of the zone, offshoots of ivy Hedera helix, leaves of

Figure 8.5 Lime-hornbeam *Tilio-Carpinetum* forest in BNP in winter (left photo). The ground can be covered by a thick layer of snow for up to three months, and temperatures can fall below −20°C (Tomiałojć *et al.*, 1984; Wesołowski *et al.*, 2006). Photo: B. Hyży-Czołpińska. The photograph on the right shows a woodland in southern England in midwinter, typically with no snow and dense ground cover of *Rubus fruticosus* with leaves; winter daytime temperatures here rarely remain below 0°C for more than a few days. Photo: R.J. Fuller. These situations provide extremely contrasting environments for forest birds in winter.

bramble *Rubus fruticosus*, holly *Ilex aquifolium* and yew *Taxus baccata*. Snow cuts off access to resources on the ground for the majority of birds. The importance of snow varies geographically, from almost no snow in winter along Atlantic coasts to snow cover lasting 3–5 months in the continental eastern parts of the temperate forest zone (Fig. 8.5).

Wintering in deciduous forests in the continental part of their range is consequently only possible for a score of species. The few year-round residents in the deciduous forests in BNP illustrate these constraints well (Wesołowski *et al.* 2010). The wintering avifauna there is mostly composed of bark-/twig-foraging birds (nuthatch, treecreeper, marsh tit, several woodpeckers), rodent-eating owls and, due to the presence of Norway spruce, species that depend on conifers: goldcrest, crested tit, coal tit, hazel grouse, pygmy owl. Hawfinch overwinters mostly in hornbeam masting years (Tomiałojć 2012). Some other species, like blue and great tit, do not spend winter in the forest, even though they overwinter in anthropogenic landscapes in the vicinity. Overall, the year-round residents constitute less than a quarter of species (<10% of pairs) breeding there in the spring (recalculated from Wesołowski *et al.* 2010). The winter avifauna is supplemented by immigrants from boreal forests: mistle thrushes and waxwings *Bombycilla garrulus* eating mistletoe fruits, and flocks of siskins and redpolls *Carduelis flammea* foraging on alder and birch seeds in mast years.

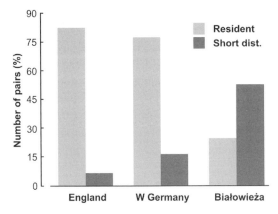

Figure 8.6 Proportion of residents and short-distance migrants in old-growth or mature forest breeding bird assemblages situated at approximately the same latitude but different longitudes (after Tomiałojć & Wesołowski 2004). Due to displacement of a large fraction of the 'resident' birds to other habitats (see the text for details), the actual proportion of birds staying year-round in the woods is much less than the figure suggests.

In the western part of the temperate forest range, where the forest floor remains mostly snow-free and ground resources are available for the birds, the situation looks different. In German forests, the number of wintering bird species is distinctly higher than in eastern Poland. In addition to the species wintering farther east, several ground-foraging, mostly seed-eating birds occur, such as woodpigeon *Columba palumbus,* stock doves, great tits and several finches. Some individuals of the partially migratory blackbirds, wrens and robins also overwinter within the forest. Temperate western Europe constitutes the major wintering area for large numbers of birds that breed in boreal forests, and it is likely that many of these birds make use of forests for roosting or feeding for at least part of the winter.

Numerous species of birds that are short-distance migrants in the east remain sedentary in the west (Fig. 8.6). However, even in these areas, the diversity and density of birds within the forests appear to be at their lowest in winter (e.g., France, Frochot 1971; north Germany, Oelke 1987; England, Fuller 1995). Whilst many 'resident' birds in England appear to remain in winter in the general vicinity of their woodland breeding areas, they may use a wider range of habitats, and some, such as chaffinch, typically leave the woods altogether (Fuller 1995). Frochot (1971) found a similar pattern in an old oak forest in Burgundy (France).

There, the majority of individuals of 15 'sedentary' species left the forest and wintered in other habitats. Woodpeckers, bark-gleaning species and tits tend to be amongst the most characteristic bird species in western European winter forests. The winter woodland bird assemblage can be dominated more by ground-, and near-ground-feeding and canopy-feeding species (including bark- and deadwood-dependent species) than is the case in the breeding season, when more shrub-dependent and insectivorous species are present (Holt *et al.* 2014). Winter territoriality is confined to a handful of species, and many join nomadic multi-species feeding flocks. Large numbers of woodpigeons, chaffinches, bramblings *Fringilla montifringilla* and jays *Garrulus glandarius* can be drawn into beech woods in mast years (e.g., Nilsson 1985; Jenni 1986; Fuller 1995), while alder and birch seeds can attract siskins and redpolls.

Such patterns of distribution indicate that the temperate deciduous forests, at least in low mast years (see below), are rather unfavourable wintering habitats for many species, and that the birds can profit by emigrating to man-made habitats, some containing copious food provided by humans for birds. This, however, is the current situation, and it raises the question of where these birds wintered before anthropogenic habitats appeared. Did they stay year-round in forests or migrate to some other areas? Were their breeding numbers lower, controlled by winter mortality?

Even nowadays, the breeding numbers of resident forest birds in Britain are strongly dependent on the severity of the previous winter (Lack 1966; Greenwood & Baillie 1991; Newton 1998). Similarly, in Germany, harsh and long winters, especially those with long periods of snow cover and/or late onset of spring, negatively affect numbers of insectivorous and frugivorous birds, such as wren, chiffchaff, blackcap, robin, blackbird, mistle thrush and song thrush (Bauer & Berthold 1996; Flade & Schwarz 2004). However, variation in numbers of the seed-eaters in the German forests is mainly driven by fluctuations in the availability of tree seeds (Flade & Schwarz 2004; see below).

These findings from Germany are partially confirmed by studies from eastern Poland and western Europe. The yearly mortality of nuthatch, a year-round resident in BNP (Wesołowski & Stawarczyk 1991), is no higher than that of the majority of British sedentary birds (Dobson 1990) or in the Belgian population (Matthysen 1998). Moreover, the mortality of this species in BNP is not concentrated in winter, thus failing to support the idea that heavy winter mortality is controlling numbers (Wesołowski & Stawarczyk 1991). Indirect observations also indicate that harsh local winters are not as detrimental as one might think. Changes in overall numbers of local residents in BNP are positively correlated with the temperature of the preceding winter for only two residents, goldcrest and middle spotted woodpecker (Wesołowski 1994; Wesołowski & Tomiałojć 1997). Others either do not show any correlation (e.g., great spotted woodpecker, nuthatch, treecreeper), or their numbers are only moderately correlated with winter temperatures (great tit, blue tit, marsh tit). Deep, long-lasting snow cover can, however, lead to food shortages for rodent-eating tawny owls, as suggested by the strong decline in numbers of this species after the unusually snowy winter of 1995–1996 (Jędrzejewska & Jędrzejewski 1998).

The above discussion suggests that many birds can adapt to harsh conditions that are a regular winter occurrence, but are less able to cope with more sporadic effects. After a run of mild winters, a severe one, especially with snow cover and ice glazing on vegetation, could be particularly destructive for birds that are, in effect, naive with respect to such conditions. This may be the case in Britain, where mild winters are the norm but occasional harsh winters result in very high mortality of resident species, such as wren, goldcrest and long-tailed tit *Aegithalos caudatus*. Exactly how winter climate will change across Europe in the coming decades and what the implications for distribution and population dynamics of birds might be are still very uncertain.

8.6.4 Multi-year Variation in Tree Seed Production and Birds

Seeds of trees constitute an important food source for numerous birds in the non-breeding season. Trees in the temperate forests tend to produce abundant seed crops only in some (mast) years, separated by several years without almost any fructification (e.g., Gatter 2000; Flade & Schwarz 2004). In mixed forests, individual tree species may fructify out of synchrony (Wesołowski et al. 2015b), which to some extent smooths out interannual variation in seed production and its impact on birds (Wesołowski 1994). However, where a single species predominates, such as in a majority of beech forests, the mast years (in Germany, once in three to seven years, Flade & Schwarz 2004; Grendelmeier et al. submitted) are separated by 'trough' years, when few or almost no tree seeds are available. This variation has a profound effect on the birds. In Germany, short-term fluctuations in the breeding numbers of woodpigeon, stock dove, great spotted woodpecker, great tit, blue tit, nuthatch, jay, chaffinch and probably other species of finches are apparently driven by variations in the fructification of beech and, to a lesser extent, oak (Flade & Schwarz 2004; Grendelmeier *et al.* submitted). The effects of variation in seed availability on the birds' numbers are much stronger than the effects of winter weather. In the period 1990–2003, there was even a positive correlation between harsh winters and population peaks of these seed-eating bird species in the following springs, because most harsh winters (characterised by a high number of ice days and days with snow cover) coincided with bumper crops of beech and oak (Flade & Schwarz 2004). Similarly, the numbers of breeding nuthatches in Sweden (Nilsson 1985) and great tits in England (Perrins 1979) were higher in springs that followed good beech mast. However, as their numbers fluctuated in parallel with the beech mast even in areas outside the range of beeches (Perrins 1979; Enoksson 1990), the birds could actually have been responding to other food resources that fluctuated in parallel with the beech seed crop.

Mast years can also have cascading indirect effects on birds via the food chain. As the number of seed-eating rodents tends to increase after autumns with abundant seed supplies, the reproductive output of rodent-eating birds of prey and owls tends to fluctuate with the variation in tree seed supply (Gatter 2000; Wesołowski 2007a). The increased rodent numbers also affect the numbers of wood warblers. Ground-nesting wood warblers assess the numbers of rodents within the area and avoid settling in areas with high rodent density (Wesołowski *et al.* 2009; Pasinelli *et al.* 2016), which they apparently perceive as places where the predation risk is too high (Grendelmeier *et al.* 2015, submitted). Thus, abundant tree fructification in the autumn would indirectly worsen conditions for breeding wood warblers in the following spring. Other indirect effects could exist, but little is known about them. Studies aimed at disentangling the multisided effects of tree masting on birds in temperate forests could be rewarding.

8.7 Geographical Trends in the Temperate Forest Avifauna

Despite considerable consistency in the dominant breeding species within the various types of temperate forests, there is large-scale longitudinal variation in species richness, habitat associations and population densities. We conclude this chapter with an exploration of these patterns.

8.7.1 West-east Trends in Breeding Species Richness

The number of breeding species is a third lower in western than in equivalent eastern European forests (120–127 species; Tomiałojć 2000a; Chapter 5). The contrast between England and Białowieża Forest is very instructive. During the twentieth century, 111 forest/forest-edge species were recorded breeding in that forest (Tomiałojć & Wesołowski 2004); almost all of them still breed there (Tomiałojć 1995; Wesołowski *et al.* 2003, 2006). A 33 ha old-growth patch of the forest-edge riverine forest can harbour 52 species in a single year, and a total of 78 species was found to breed there at least once during 40 years (Wesołowski *et al.* 2015a). The latter figure can be compared with ca. 81 forest, shrubland and forest-edge species breeding in the *whole* of Britain (Fuller 1995). Moreover, the contemporary British avifauna constitutes an impoverished version of that in the Białowieża Forest – as all but a few British breeding species (e.g., Scottish crossbill *Loxia scotica*) also nest there, whereas numerous species that breed in Białowieża Forest do not nest in Britain (cf. Fuller 1995; Tomiałojć 1995; Tomiałojć & Wesołowski 2005). The same longitudinal trend is visible in woodpeckers (Mikusiński & Angelstam 1997, 1998). Only three species breed regularly in Britain (Balmer *et al.* 2013), five in the Netherlands (Bijlsma *et al.* 2001) and seven in central and north Germany (Gedeon *et al.* 2014), while up to nine or ten breed in eastern Europe.

The contrast between Britain and eastern Poland is part of a continuum of increasing diversity that stretches from Ireland through Britain and across western Europe (Fuller *et al.* 2007). Insularity is therefore unlikely to be the sole explanation for the low richness of forest birds in Britain and Ireland, though it undoubtedly does contribute. Some species, such as three-toed woodpecker and red-breasted flycatcher, may never have colonised the Atlantic islands. Furthermore, stochastic extinctions of scarce species may have been more likely on islands with no nearby source populations. However, some 'sedentary' species can successfully cross sea barriers, as shown by woodpeckers: white-backed woodpecker *Dendrocopos leucotos* breeding on Corsica (Tomiałojć 2000b), black woodpecker colonising Bornholm in the Baltic (Hansen 1984) and great spotted woodpecker recently colonising Ireland (Mcdevitt *et al.* 2011).

As far as we are aware, all structures and processes that shape forests and birds' breeding conditions were similar in England and BNP in the past (Table 8.5), except that the climate changes from oceanic in England to continental in the BNP. Usually, species richness is inversely related to

Table 8.5 *A comparison of patterns and processes known to influence forest structure and the living conditions of birds in primeval forest (Białowieża National Park) with those found (paleobiological data) or presumed to occur (judging by their presence in current English woods) in the pristine English forests (ca. 6,000 yr BP). Modified after Wesołowski (2007a).*

Feature	Białowieża NP	England
Major tree species	See Box 8.1	Same species, but *Picea abies* absent and *Fagus sylvatica* present (Peterken 1996)
Ungulate diversity	Five species: *Bison bonasus, Alces alces, Cervus elaphus, Capreolus capreolus, Sus scrofa* (Jędrzejewska & Jędrzejewski 1998)	Same species, but *B. bonasus* absent (Yalden 1999)
Predator diversity	>30 species of birds and mammals important as bird and/or nest predators, from *Lynx lynx* and *Canis lupus* to rodents (Tomiałojć *et al.* 1984)	Similar set of carnivores and rodents (Yalden 1999), and of raptors and owls (judging from their current presence in parts of Britain (Balmer *et al.* 2013)
Leaf-eating caterpillars	Important as nestling food, cyclic defoliation (Rowiński & Wesołowski 1999; Rowiński 2001; Wesołowski & Rowiński 2006)	The same (Perrins 1991; Peterken 1996)
Tree masting	Cyclic: *P. abies, Q. robur, C. betulus* (Pucek *et al.* 1993: Wesołowski *et al.* 2015b)	Especially of *F. sylvatica* (Perrins 1966)
Wood-decomposing fungi	High diversity (Faliński 1994), main hole-producing agents (Wesołowski 1989, 2002; Walankiewicz 2002)	Possibly equally important, but data scarce (Peterken 1996)
Windfalls/tree uprootings	Major gap-forming factors in all forest types (Fuller 2000; Bobiec 2002b)	The same (Peterken 1996)
Cyclical rodent dynamics	Every few years outbreaks following tree masting (Pucek *et al.* 1993; Wesołowski *et al.* 2009)	Recorded in mature woodlands (Southern 1959 in Lack 1966)

climatic severity (e.g., at high altitudes or latitudes). However, in the temperate forests, we observe the opposite pattern (Mikusiński & Angelstam 1998; Tomiałojć 2000b). Insularity and historical variations in human land use may contribute to this pattern, as discussed further below.

There is evidence indicating that the current avifauna of western European forests constitutes a depauperate version of originally much richer assemblages. Some of the 'missing species' may have become extinct due to the negative impact of deforestation, intensification of forest management and/or persecution. Mikusiński and Angelstam (1998) found that the woodpecker richness in continental Europe was strongly negatively affected by intensity of land use (higher human population density, more urbanisation, less remaining forest cover, stronger forest fragmentation). All these factors changed directionally, between the most transformed western European landscapes to the least altered areas in eastern Europe. The difference in woodpecker richness was mostly due to species extinctions, which were concentrated in the more intensively transformed regions (Mikusiński & Angelstam 1998; Tomiałojć 2000b). Apart from woodpeckers, extinctions in parts of western Europe have been documented for several, mostly large, species: black stork, crane, black grouse *Lyrurus tetrix*, capercaillie, hazel grouse, white-tailed eagle, golden eagle *Aquila chrysaetos*, lesser spotted eagle, short-toed eagle *Circaetus gallicus*, red kite, osprey, peregrine falcon *Falco peregrinus*, goshawk *Accipiter gentilis*, eagle owl *Bubo bubo*, raven *Corvus corax* (Tomiałojć 2000a). Additional missing species could have disappeared before ornithological records began; possible candidates are green sandpiper, forest breeding swifts and collared flycatcher. Some recent colonisations of parts of western Europe (honey buzzard *Pernis apivorus*, eagle owl, pied flycatcher, firecrest; Hagemeijer & Blair 1997) may actually be re-colonisations (Tomiałojć 2000b).

8.7.2 Geographically Variable Habitat Associations of Forest Birds

If the prehistoric western European lowland forests and their avifauna were similar to those persisting in the near-primeval condition of Białowieża Forest (see above), then bird–habitat relationships found there may be regarded as broadly ancestral. If this view is correct, the habitat associations of birds found nowadays in anthropogenic lowland landscapes are at least partly a consequence of adaptation to a long period of landscape modification. A comparison of birds' habitat associations in

BNP and England (Table 8.4) demonstrates an array of differences. These are close to the extremes of what is probably an east-west gradient in patterns of habitat association in European forest birds (Fuller *et al.* 2007). Numerous species which in eastern and central Europe are confined to large forest tracts (e.g., woodpigeon, dunnock, song thrush, mistle thrush) are widespread in anthropogenic habitats and landscapes of western Europe including small woods, gardens and parks (England, Table 8.4; the Netherlands, Bijlsma *et al.* 2001; Germany, Flade 1994a). Some of these species – wren, blackbird, robin – are actually regarded in Britain as the most widespread habitat generalists (Fuller 1995).

Striking contrasts are evident in the use of broadleaved and coniferous forest between lowland Britain and BNP (Table 8.4). Several species that are strongly dependent on conifers in the latter area (e.g., goldcrest, coal tit, bullfinch *Pyrrhula pyrrhula*, redstart *Phoenicurus phoenicurus*) use a wider range of forest types in Britain, including purely deciduous forests (Fuller 1995). Some other species (e.g., wood warbler, willow tit, pied flycatcher) in the east or north of Europe use both broadleaves and conifers, but are more strongly, though not exclusively, dependent on broadleaves in the extreme west of their range (Fuller 2002). Furthermore, several species that are typically confined to forest in some parts of their ranges also breed in treeless or almost treeless areas in other parts of their ranges (see Wesołowski & Fuller 2012 for details and references). These include some island populations of wrens, urban breeding swifts and stock doves nesting among dunes in rabbit holes.

There is a common thread to these patterns: in almost every case, species which had been initially (forest) habitat specialists have substantially broadened their range of utilised habitats. In some cases, this was probably necessary for survival in largely deforested landscapes. For other species, new landscapes created opportunities to colonise new habitats. The plasticity of species varied, and, as discussed above, some will have become extinct while others prospered through behavioural adaptation. Expansion into new habitats could be facilitated by reduction in predation pressure and increased productivity of broods (see below) in remnants of traditional habitats.

8.7.3 Regional Variation in Bird Densities

Apart from being poorer in species, forests in western Europe tend to contain a higher proportion of species which can develop dense populations where habitat is suitable, compared with BNP, where the majority of birds breed at very low densities. Only a few numerically dominant species breed regularly in BNP in densities exceeding 5 territories/10 ha (Table 8.1 and Table 8.2). Species that breed at densities less than 3 territories/10 ha contribute on average 58% of the species list in the riverine and up to 71% in the coniferous forest (Tomiałojć & Wesołowski 2004).

There are indications that several of the species which occur at low density in BNP can reach much higher densities in some lowland English woods. Caution is required in generalising about breeding bird densities, because, as mentioned above, there is huge variation resulting from many different factors. Particularly relevant here is the fact that few English woods have vegetation structures comparable with the old-growth stands of Białowieża, and most are set in an entirely different landscape context, typically small fragments surrounded by agricultural land. Nonetheless, some comparative examples of densities are given as follows, where densities for BNP have been extracted from Wesołowski and Tomiałojć (1997) and Wesołowski et al. (2003, 2006). Nest densities of woodpigeons currently frequently exceed 10 nests/10 ha in lowland English woods (RJF pers. obs.), and Murton (1965) gave a mean density of 79 nests/10 ha for deciduous woodland in eastern England. This compares with a mean of 1 and a maximum of 3.4 territories/10 ha in BNP. Wrens can exceed 15 territories/10 ha in Britain (Armstrong 1955; Garson 1978), compared with a mean of 3.2 and a maximum of 5.5 in BNP. Respective mean densities of great tits and blue tits in an English wood were 13.7 and 32.9 territories/10 ha (birds using natural nest sites in 1982–1984 in a 9 ha area; East & Perrins 1988). Densities of blue tits in mature oak woodland in Britain probably widely exceed 10 territories/10 ha, though the behaviour of this species makes an accurate census hard to achieve. These compare with means of 3.4 and 3.2 territories/10 ha of great and blue tits, respectively, in BNP. Whilst exceptionally high densities of these and other species, such as robin and blackbird, can occur in British woods, especially in small woods with complex foliage structures, it is suggested that the densities documented in Table 8.3 are now more typical of woods of moderate and large size in lowland England.

What could cause these differences? Longitudinally, the harshness of winter and the proportion of migrants in local assemblages could have some effect (see above), but another important gradient is detectable.

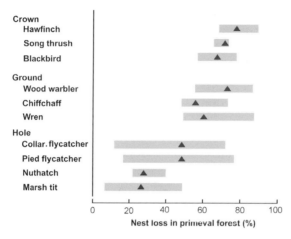

Figure 8.7 Nesting losses of passerines in BNP in relation to nest type and localisation. From top to bottom: three crown–nesters with open nests, three near-ground-nesters with domed nests and four hole-nesters. Medians (triangles) and ranges of values (bars) observed in individual seasons are shown. Original sources, sample sizes and methods of loss calculation are given in Wesołowski and Tomiałojć (2005).

Persecution of predatory birds and mammals took place all over Europe, but it was most efficient in densely populated regions such as Britain (Lovegrove 2007). Numerous species of predators have been exterminated across large stretches of western Europe, but they have managed to survive in at least some parts of eastern Europe (reviews in Tomiałojć 1980; Gatter 2000; Rutz *et al.* 2006). Predator diversity in BNP is two to three times higher than in most western European forests (Tomiałojć *et al.* 1984), and breeding birds have to cope with this diverse assemblage of predators (>30 species; see Wesołowski & Tomiałojć 2005). Nest mortality rates in BNP (Fig. 8.7) are high and exceed, or are equal to, the highest loss rates recorded for the same species in man-transformed areas (Wesołowski & Tomiałojć 1995). Predation is the most important factor limiting avian productivity in BNP, responsible for 65–95% of nest loss in different species (Wesołowski & Tomiałojć 2005; Wesołowski 2011b; Wesołowski & Rowiński 2012; Maziarz *et al.* 2016). Nests are mostly robbed during the nestling stage, making the losses especially costly, because it limits further nesting attempts. Heavy predation continues during the post-fledgling period, when several birds of prey, owls and pine martens

Martes martes hunt juvenile birds (Jędrzejewski *et al.* 1994a, b; Zalewski *et al.* 1995; van Manen 2003).

Relatively low productivity, a consequence of heavy predation, combined with low breeding densities results in low production of young per unit area, sometimes by an order of magnitude lower than that recorded in other areas (Wesołowski 1983; Wesołowski *et al.* 1987; Tomiałojć 1994). This low productivity, even without heavy mortality in the non-breeding season, leads to few potential recruits in the following spring and, in turn, could result in permanent under-saturation and low breeding numbers. In the case of wrens, British birds can produce 10–20 times more fledglings than their counterparts from the primeval forest. Because they have reasonably high survival, this high productivity translates into many birds establishing territories in the following spring and high breeding densities relative to BNP (Wesołowski 1983). A similar sequence of events (man-induced weakening of predator pressure, increase in productivity, more potential recruits, increased densities) may have contributed to relatively high numbers of woodpigeon (Tomiałojć 1976, 1980) and blackbird (Tomiałojć 1993, 1994) in small British woods, though the former species has increased since oilseed rape, introduced in the 1970s, created an important new winter food source (Inglis *et al.* 1997).

A causal link between inflated production of young and relatively high population density seems to be well established. It is observed not only in the temperate forests, but in situations where some birds switch to breed in places devoid of, or inaccessible to, predators, such as islands and urban areas (Tomiałojć & Wesołowski 1990). The numbers of birds in such highly productive populations can increase up to some new limit set by other factors, such as food resources, nest sites and/or interspecific competition for resources (Newton 1998).

In the case of temperate forests, additional mechanisms may serve to enhance forest bird densities in landscapes that have been modified by man for long periods of time. First, small woodland patches often have very complex vegetation structures at their edges, providing the preferred microhabitats of several understorey-dependent and early successional species, which can reach high densities in such situations (Fuller 2012). Because edge-affected vegetation contributes a relatively high proportion of the total area of many small woods, this mechanism can result in relatively high overall bird densities where the forest cover is highly fragmented. Second, especially in Britain and parts of western France, agricultural landscapes are characterised by dense networks of hedges that can provide additional resources for woodland birds and cover for dispersal movements (Hinsley & Bellamy 2000). Third, birds in ancient cultural landscapes that are not heavily persecuted or exploited may have evolved a relatively high tolerance for the close proximity of humans.

8.7.4 West-east Gradients in the Bird Assemblages – Conclusions

It seems likely that the longitudinal gradients in breeding bird assemblages in temperate forests have been generated mostly by spatial variations in the intensity of human impact. The influence of anthropogenic factors has been so strong that it may even have overshadowed biogeographic processes and climatic variation, though these factors will also have played a part.

The pattern observed in temperate Europe, that bird assemblages in highly man-transformed (fragmented, simplified, predator-poor) forests differ from those in the more pristine (primeval) ones in a predictable fashion (fewer species, higher densities), probably constitutes the specific case of a more general phenomenon. Primeval forests, irrespective of their geographical location, seem to share the same suite of characters that strongly contrast with those found in the secondary or cultural ones (Table 8.6). Wesołowski (2007a) terms this 'primeval forest syndrome'. It is also the case that in tropical forests, bird assemblages dominated by large numbers of species occurring at low density are most typical of pristine situations (Thiollay 1992).

Table 8.6 *Major differences between primeval and secondary states in temperate forests (modified after Tomiałojć et al. 1984, Tomiałojć & Wesołowski 1990; Wesołowski 2003).*

Variable	Primeval	Secondary
Forest size	Large, continuous	Fragmented, isolated
Predator diversity	High	Low
Availability of holes	Excess	Shortage
Avian species richness	High	Low
Bird density	Low	high
Production of young birds	Low	high
Interspecific competition	Seldom, insignificant	Frequent, eminent

Acknowledgements

We are grateful to Shelley Hinsley and Martin Korňan for many helpful comments and suggestions which have greatly improved the chapter.

References

Angelstam, P. (1996) Ghost of forest past – natural disturbance regimes as a basis for reconstruction of biologically diverse forests in Europe. In *Conservation of Faunal Diversity in Forested Landscapes*. DeGraaf, R.M. & Miller, R.I. (eds.). London: Chapman and Hall, pp. 287–336.

Angelstam, P., Anufriev, V., Balciauskas, L. *et al.* (1997) Biodiversity and sustainable forestry in European forests – how West and East can learn from each other. *Wildlife Society Bulletin*, **25**, 38–48.

Archaux, F. & Bakkaus, N. (2007) Relative impact of stand structure, tree composition and climate on mountain bird communities. *Forest Ecology and Management*, **247**, 72–79.

Armstrong, E.A. (1955) *The Wren*. London: Collins.

Askins, R.A. (2014) *Saving the World's Deciduous Forests: Perspectives from East Asia, North America, and Europe*. London: Yale University Press.

Baker, J.R. (1938) The evolution of breeding seasons. In *Evolution. Essays on Aspects of Evolutionary Biology*. de Beer, G.R. (ed.). Oxford: Clarendon Press, pp. 161–177.

Balmer, D.E., Gillings, S., Caffrey, B.J., Swann, R.L., Downie, I.S. & Fuller, R.J. (2013) *Bird Atlas 2007-11: The Breeding and Wintering Birds of Britain and Ireland*. Thetford: BTO Books.

Bauer, H.-G. & Berthold, P. (1996) *Die Brutvögel Mitteleuropas: Bestand und Gefährdung*. 2nd ed. Wiesbaden: Aula-Verlag.

Begehold, H., Rzanny, M. & Flade, M. (2015) Forest development phases as an integrating tool to describe habitat preferences of breeding birds in lowland beech forests. *Journal of Ornithology*, **156**, 19–29.

Begehold, H., Rzanny, M. & Winter, S. (2016) Patch patterns of lowland beech forests in a gradient of management intensity. *Forest Ecology and Management*, **360**, 69–79.

Begehold, H., Rzanny, M. & Winter, S. (submitted) Impact of naturalness-promoting forest management on forest structure.

Begehold, H. & Schumacher, H. (2017) Impact of different management as well as management abandonment on breeding birds in lowland beech forests of north-eastern Germany. *Vogelwelt*, **137**, 227–235.

Beven, G. (1976) Changes in breeding bird populations of an oak-wood on Bookham Common, Surrey, over twenty-seven years. *London Naturalist*, **55**, 23–42.

Bijlsma, R.G., Hustings, F. & Camphuysen, C.J. (2001) *Algemene en schaarse vogels van Nederland*. Haarlem/Utrecht: GMB Uitgeverij/KNNV Uitgeverij.

Blondel, J. (1995) *Biogéographie: Approche écologique et évolutive*. Paris: Masson.

Bobiec, A. (2002a) 'Grazing ecology' from the Białowieża Primeval Forest perspective. *Acta Theriologica*, **47**, 509–511.

Bobiec, A. (2002b) Living stands and dead wood in the Białowieża Forest: Suggestions for restoration management. *Forest Ecology and Management*, **165**, 121–136.

Bobiec, A., van der Burgt, H., Meijer, K. & Zuyderduyn, C. (2000) Rich deciduous forests in Białowieża as a dynamic mosaic of developmental phases: Premises for nature conservation and restoration management. *Forest Ecology and Management*, **130**, 159–175.

Bohuš, M., Baloghová, A., Illavský, J. & Kalúsová, E. (1999) Contribution to knowledge of breeding bird communities of selected Danubian flood plain forests. *Tichodroma*, **12**, 61–91. [in Slovak]

Borowiec, M. & Grabiński, W. (1982) Avifauna of ponds and forests of the Ziemia Niemodlińska including a quantitative study in mixed forests. *Acta Universitatis Wratislaviensis*, **12**, 3–54. [in Polish]

Broughton, R.K. & Hinsley, S.A. (2015) The ecology and conservation of the Marsh Tit in Britain. *British Birds*, **108**, 12–29.

Czeszczewik, D. & Walankiewicz, W. (2003) Natural nest sites of the Pied Flycatcher *Ficedula hypoleuca* in a primeval forest. *Ardea*, **91**, 221–230.

Dierschke, F. (1973) Die Sommervogelbestände nordwestdeutscher Kieferforsten. *Vogelwelt*, **94**, 201–225.

Dobson, A. (1990) Survival rates and their relationship to life-history traits in some common British birds. *Current Ornithology*, **7**, 115–146.

Donald, P.F., Fuller, R.J., Evans, A.D. & Gough, S.J. (1998) Effects of forest management and grazing on breeding bird communities in plantations of broadleaved and coniferous trees in western England. *Biological Conservation*, **85**, 183–197.

Dronneau, C. (2007) Peuplement d'oiseaux nicheurs d'une forêt alluviale du Rhin (première partie). *Alauda*, **75**, 215–226.

East, M.L. & Perrins, C.M. (1988) The effect of nestboxes on breeding populations of birds in broadleaved temperate woodlands. *Ibis*, **130**, 393–401.

Ellenberg, H. (1986) *Vegetation Mitteleuropas mit den Alpen*. 4th ed. Stuttgart: Ulmer.

Enemar, A., Cavallin, B., Nyholm, E., Rudebeck, I. & Thorner, A.M. (1994) Dynamics of a passerine bird community in a small deciduous wood, S. Sweden, during 40 years. *Ornis Svecica*, **4**, 65–104.

Enoksson, B. (1990) Autumn territories and population regulation in the Nuthatch *Sitta europaea*: An experimental study. *Journal of Animal Ecology*, **59**, 1047–1062.

Faliński, J.B. (1986) *Vegetation Dynamics in Temperate Forests (Ecological Studies in Białowieża Forest)*. Dordrecht: Dr W Junk Publishers.

Faliński, J.B. (1991) Le Parc National de Białowieża et le systeme intégral des espaces protégés en Pologne. *Revue Forestiére Française*, **43**, 190–206.

Faliński, J.B. (1994) Concise geobotanical atlas of Białowieża Forest. *Phytocenosis*, **6** (Suppl.), 3–34.

Ferry, C. & Frochot, B. (1970) L'avifaune nidificatrice d'une foret de chenes pedoncules en Bourgogne: etude de deux successions ecologiques. *La Terre et la Vie*, **2**, 153–250.

Ferry, C. & Frochot, B. (1990) Bird communities of the forests of Burgundy and the Jura (Eastern France). In *Biogeography and Ecology of Forest Bird Communities*. Keast, A. (ed.). The Hague: SPB Academic Publishers, pp. 183–194.

Flade, M. (1994a) *Die Brutvogelgemeinschaften Mittel- und Norddeutschlands*. Eching: IHW – Verlag.

Flade, M. (1994b) The identification of indicator species for landscape planning in Germany. In *Bird Numbers 1992, Proceedings of the 12th Conference of IBCC and EOAC*. Hagemeijer, E.J.M. & Verstrael, T.J. (eds.). Voorburg/Heerlen: Statistics Netherlands, pp. 371–381.

Flade, M., Hertel, F., Schumacher, H. & Weiß, S. (2004) Einer, der auch anders kann: Der Mittelspecht und seine bisher unbeachteten Lebensräume. *Der Falke*, **51**, 82–86.

Flade, M. & Schwarz, J. (2004) Results of the German Common Birds Census, part II: Population changes in German forest birds 1989–2003. *Vogelwelt*, **125**, 177–213. [In German]

Frochot, B. (1971) L'evolution saisonniere de l'avifaune dans une futaie de chenes en Bourgogne. *La Terre et la Vie*, **2**, 145–182.

Fuller, R.J. (1982) *Bird Habitats in Britain*. Calton, UK: Poyser.

Fuller, R.J. (1995) *Bird Life of Woodland and Forest*. Cambridge: Cambridge University Press.

Fuller, R.J. (2000) Influence of treefall gaps on distributions of breeding birds within interior old-growth stands in Białowieża forest, Poland. *Condor*, **102**, 267–274.

Fuller, R.J. (2002) Spatial differences in habitat selection and occupancy by woodland bird species in Europe: A neglected aspect of bird-habitat relationships. In *Avian Landscape Ecology – Pure and Applied Issues in the Large-scale Ecology of Birds*. Chamberlain, D. & Wilson, A. (eds.). Thetford: International Association for Landscape Ecology (UK), pp. 101–111.

Fuller, R.J. (2012) Avian responses to transitional habitats in temperate cultural landscapes: woodland edges and young-growth. In *Birds and Habitat: Relationships in Changing Landscapes*. Fuller, R.J. (ed.). Cambridge: Cambridge University Press, pp. 125–149.

Fuller, R.J., Gaston, K.J. & Quine, C.P. (2007) Living on the edge: British and Irish woodland birds in a European context. *Ibis*, **149** (Suppl. 2), 53–63.

Fuller, R.J., Noble, D.G., Smith, K.W. & Vanhinsbergh, D. (2005) Recent declines in populations of woodland birds in Britain: A review of possible causes. *British Birds*, **98**, 116–143.

Fuller, R.J. & Rothery, P. (2013) Temporal consistency in fine-scale habitat relationships of woodland birds during a period of habitat deterioration. *Forest Ecology and Management*, **289**, 164–174.

Fuller, R.J., Smith, K.W. & Hinsley, S.A. (2012) Temperate western European woodland as a dynamic environment for birds: A resource-based view. In *Birds and Habitat: Relationships in Changing Landscapes*. Fuller, R.J. (ed.). Cambridge: Cambridge University Press, pp. 352–380.

Garson, P.J. (1978) *A Study of Territorial and Breeding Behaviour in the Wren*, Troglodytes troglodytes (L.). University of Oxford: Unpublished DPhil thesis.

Gaston, K.J. & Blackburn, T.M. (2000) *Pattern and Process in Macroecology*. Oxford: Blackwell Science.

Gatter, W. (2000) *Vogelzug und Vogelbestände in Mitteleuropa*. Wiebelsheim: Aula-Verlag.

Gedeon, K., Grüneberg, C., Mitschke, A. *et al.* (2014). *Atlas Deutscher Brutvogelarten*. Münster: Stiftung Vogelmonitoring Deutschland & Dachverband Deutscher Avifaunisten.

Głowaciński, Z. (1975) Succession of bird communities in the Niepołomice Forest (southern Poland). *Ekologia Polska*, **23**, 231–263.

Gnielka, R. (1965) Die Vögel der Rabeninsel bei Halle (Saale). Ergebnisse ganzjähriger quanitativer Bestandsaufnahmen in einem Stieleichen-Eschen-Ulmen-Auwald. *Hercynia NF*, **2**, 221–254.

Gnielka, R. (1978) Der Einfluß des Ulmensterbens auf den Brutvogelbestand eines Auwaldes. *Apus*, **4**, 49–66.

Greenwood, J.J.D. & Baillie, S.R. (1991) Effects of density-dependence and weather on population changes of English passerines using a non-experimental paradigm. *Ibis*, **133** (Suppl. 1), 121–133.

Grendelmeier A., Arlettaz, R., Gerber, M. & Pasinelli, G. (2015) Reproductive performance of a declining forest passerine in relation to environmental and social factors: Implications for species conservation. *PLoS ONE*, **10**, e0130954.

Grendelmeier, A., Flade, M. & Pasinelli, G. (submitted) Of seed mast, rodents and songbirds: How populations relate to resource pulses.

Gross, A., Holdenrieder, O., Pautasso, M., Queloz, V. & Sieber, T.N. (2014) *Hymenoscyphus pseudoalbidus*, the causal agent of European ash dieback. *Molecular Plant Pathology*, **15**, 5–21.

Hagemeijer, W.J.M. & Blair M.J. (eds.) (1997) *The EBCC Atlas of European Breeding Birds: Their Distribution and Abundance*. London: Poyser.

Halley, D. & Rosell, D. (2012) The beaver's reconquest of Eurasia: Status, population development and management of a conservation success. *Mammal Review*, **32**,153–178.

Hansen, F. (1984) Der Schwarzspecht *Dryocopus martius* als Brutvogel auf der Dänischen Insel Bornholm. *Annales Zoologici Fennici*, **21**, 431–433.

Helle, P. & Fuller, R.J. (1988) Migrant passerine birds in European forest successions in relation to vegetation height and geographical position. *Journal of Animal Ecology*, **57**, 565–579.

Helle, P. & Mönkkönen, M. (1990) Forest successions and bird communities: Theoretical aspects and practical implications. In *Biogeography and Ecology of Forest Bird Communities*. Keast, A. (ed.). The Hague: SPB Academic Publishers, pp. 299–318.

Hertel, F. (2003) Habitatnutzung und Nahrungserwerb von Buntspecht *Picoides major*, Mittelspecht *Picoides medius* und Kleiber *Sitta europaea* in bewirtschafteten und unbewirtschafteten Buchenwäldern des nordostdeutschen Tieflandes. *Vogelwelt*, **124**, 111–132.

Hewson, C.M. & Noble, D.G. (2009) Population trends of breeding birds in British woodlands over a 32-year period: Relationships with food, habitat use and migratory behaviour. *Ibis*, **151**, 464–486.

Hinsley, S.A. & Bellamy, P.E. (2000) The influence of hedge structure, management and landscape context on the value of hedges to birds: A review. *Journal of Environmental Management*, **60**, 33–49.

Hinsley, S.A., Fuller, R.J. & Ferns, P.N. (2015) The changing fortunes of woodland birds in temperate Europe. In *Europe's Changing Woods and Forests: From Wildwood to Managed Landscapes*. Kirby, K.J. & Watkins, C. (eds.). Wallingford, UK: CABI, pp. 154–173.

Hinsley, S.A., Hill, R.A., Fuller, R.J., Bellamy, P.E. & Rothery, P. (2009) Bird species distributions across woodland canopy structure gradients. *Community Ecology*, **10**, 99–110.

Hodder, K.H., Bullock, J.M., Buckland, P.C. & Kirby, K.J. (2005) *Large Herbivores in the Wildwood and Modern Naturalistic Grazing Systems*. English Nature Research Reports, No. 648. Peterborough: English Nature.

Hohlfeld, F. (2006) Ornithological studies in a strict forest reserve and a managed forest before and after a storm. *Vogelwelt*, **127**, 51–64.

Holt, C.A., Fuller, R.J. & Dolman, P.M. (2014) Exclusion of deer affects responses of birds to woodland regeneration in winter and summer. *Ibis*, **147**, 116–131.

Hudek, K. (1985) The Morava-Dyie riverine forest system, Czechoslovakia. In *Riverine Forests in Europe: Status and Conservation*. Imboden, E. (ed.). Cambridge: ICBP, pp. 38–42.

Hunter, M.L. (1990) *Wildlife, Forests and Forestry: Principles of Managing Forests for Biological Diversity*. Englewood Cliffs, NJ: Prentice-Hall.

Ibero, C. (1994) *The Status of Old-Growth and Semi-Natural Forests in Western Europe*. Gland, Switzerland: World Wide Fund for Nature.

Inglis, I.R., Isaacson, A.J., Smith, G.C., Haynes, P.J. & Thearle, R.J.P. (1997) The effect on the woodpigeon *(Columba palumbus)* of the introduction of oilseed rape into Britain. *Agriculture, Ecosystems and Environment*, **61**, 113–121.

Imbeau, L., Drapeau, P. & Mönkkönen, M. (2003) Are forest birds categorised as 'edge species' strictly associated with edges? *Ecography*, **26**, 514–520.

Iremonger, S., Kapos, V., Rhind, J. & Luxmoore, R. (1996) A global overview of forest conservation. *Proceedings of the XI World Forestry Congress, Antalya, Turkey*. Vol. 2, 103–145.

Iversen, J. (1973) The development of Denmark's nature since the last glacial. *Danmarks Geoolgiske Undersøgelse Series V*, **7**, 1–126.

Jahn, G. (1991) Temperate deciduous forests of Europe. In *Temperate Deciduous Forests*. Röhrig, E.S. & Ulrich, B. (eds.). Amsterdam: Elsevier, pp. 377–502.

Jędrzejewska, B. & Jędrzejewski, W. (1998) *Predation in Vertebrate Communities. The Białowieża Primeval Forest as a Case Study*. Berlin: Springer Verlag.

Jędrzejewska, B., Jędrzejewski, W., Bunevich, A.N., Miłkowski, L. & Krasiński, Z.A. (1997) Factors shaping population densities and increase rates of ungulates in Białowieża Primeval Forest (Poland and Belarus) in the 19th and 20th centuries. *Acta Theriologica*, **42**, 399–451.

Jędrzejewski, W., Jędrzejewska, B., Zub, K., Ruprecht, A.L. & Bystrowski, C. (1994a) Resource use by Tawny Owls *Strix aluco* in relation to rodent fluctuations in Białowieża National Park, Poland. *Journal of Avian Biology*, **25**, 308–318.

Jędrzejewski, W., Szymura, A. & Jędrzejewska, B. (1994b) Reproduction and food of the Buzzard *Buteo buteo* in relation to the abundance of rodents and birds in Białowieża Nat. Park, Poland. *Ethology, Ecology and Evolution*, **6**, 179–190.

Jenni, L. (1986) The importance of large roosts of bramblings (*Fringilla montifringilla*) in beech-mast areas. *Ornithologische Beobachter*, **83**, 267–286. [in German, English summary]

Kampichler, C., Angeler, D.G., Holmes, R.T. *et al.* (2014) Temporal dynamics of bird community composition: An analysis of baseline conditions from long-term data. *Oecologia*, **175**, 1301–1313.

Kirby, K.J. & Watkins, C. (2015) The forest landscape before farming. In *Europe's Changing Woods and Forests: From Wildwood to Managed Landscapes*. Kirby, K.J. & Watkins, C. (eds.). Wallingford, UK: CABI, pp. 33–45.

Korňan, M. (2009a) Structure of the breeding bird assemblage of a primeval alder swamp in the Šúr National Nature Reserve. *Biologia Bratislava*, **64**, 165–179.

Korňan, M. (2009b) Comparison of bird assemblage structure between forest eco-tone and interior of an alder swamp. *Sylvia*, **45**, 151–176. [in Slovak]

Korňan, M. (2011) Breeding bird assemblage of a secondary ash-willow floodplain forest along the Morava River, Slovakia. *Sylvia*, **47**, 103–122. [in Slovak]

Korňan, M. & Adamík, P. (2007) Foraging guild structure within a primaeval mixed forest bird assemblage: A comparison of two concepts. *Community Ecology*, **8**, 133–249.

Korňan, M. & Adamík, P. (2014) Structure of the breeding bird assemblage of a natural beech-spruce forest in the Šútovská dolina National Nature Reserve, the Malá Fatra Mts. *Ekológia Bratislava*, **33**, 138–150.

Korňan, M., Holmes, R., Recher, H., Adamík, P. & Kropil, R. (2013) Convergence in foraging guild structure of forest breeding bird assemblages across three continents is related to habitat structure and foraging opportunities. *Community Ecology*, **14**, 89–100.

Lack, D. (1965) Evolutionary ecology. *Journal of Applied Ecology*, **2**, 247–255.

Lack, D. (1966) *Population Studies of Birds*. Oxford: Clarendon Press.

Latałowa, M., Zimny, M., Jędrzejewska, B. & Samojlik, T. (2015) Białowieża Primeval Forest: A 2000-year interplay of environmental and cultural forces in Europe's best preserved temperate woodland. In *Europe's Changing Woods and Forests: From Wildwood to Managed Landscapes*. Kirby, K.J. & Watkins, C. (eds.). Wallingford: CAB International, pp. 243–264.

Leito, A., Truu, J., Roosaluste, E., Sepp, K. & Poder, I. (2006) Long-term dynamics of breeding birds in broad-leaved deciduous forest on Hanikatsi Island in the West-Estonian archipelago. *Ornis Fennica*, **83**, 124–130.

Lovegrove, R. (2007) *Silent Fields: The Long Decline of a Nation's Wildlife*. Oxford: Oxford University Press.

Lutz, E. (2014) *Vergleichende avifaunistische Untersuchungen von naturbelassenen und stammholzberäumten Windwurfflächen in Tieflandbuchenwäldern*. University of Applied Science Eberswalde: Bachelor thesis.

Matthysen, E. (1998) *The Nuthatches*. London: Poyser.

Maziarz, M., Wesołowski, T., Hebda, G., Cholewa, M. & Broughton, R.K. (2016) Breeding success of the Great Tit *Parus major* in relation to attributes of natural nest cavities in a primeval forest. *Journal of Ornithology*, **157**, 343–354.

Mcdevitt, A.D., Kajtoch, L., Mazgajski, T.D. *et al.* (2011) The origins of great spotted woodpeckers *Dendrocopos major* colonizing Ireland revealed by mitochondrial DNA. *Bird Study*, **58**, 361–364.

Mikusiński, G. & Angelstam, P. (1997) European woodpeckers and anthropogenic habitat change: A review. *Vogelwelt*, **118**, 277–283.

Mikusiński, G. & Angelstam, P. (1998) Economic geography, forest distribution, and woodpecker diversity in Central Europe. *Conservation Biology*, **12**, 200–208.

Mitchell, F.J.G. (2005) How open were European primeval forests? Hypothesis testing using palaeoecological data. *Journal of Ecology*, **93**, 168–177.

Mitrus, C. & Soćko, B. (2008) Breeding success and nest-site characteristics of Red-breasted Flycatchers *Ficedula parva* in a primeval forest. *Bird Study*, **55**, 203–208.

Morozov, N.S. (2009) A city as an object for synecological studies: A search for density compensation among birds breeding in urban woodlands. In *Species and Communities in Extreme Environments*. Golovatch, S.I., Makarova, O.L., Babenko, A.B. & Penev, L.D. (eds.). Sofia: Pensoft Publishers & KMK Scientific Press, pp. 459–520.

Muller, Y. (2002) L'ouragan Lothar et l'avifaune forestiere nicheuse. I. Effets immédiates dans deux zones fortement perturbées. *Ciconia*, **26**, 73–84.

Murton, R.K. (1965) *The Woodpigeon*. London: Collins.

Newton, I. (1998) *Population Limitation in Birds*. London: Academic Press.

Niechoda, T. & Korbel, J. (2011) *Puszczańskie olbrzymy*. Białowieża: Towarzystwo Ochrony Krajobrazu.

Nikiforov, M.E., Yaminski, B.V. & Sklyarow, L.P. (1989) [*Birds of Byelorusia*]. Minsk: Visheishaya Shkola. [in Russian]

Niklasson, M., Zin, E., Zielonka, T. *et al.* (2010) A 350-year tree-ring fire record from Białowieża Primeval Forest, Poland: Implications for Central European lowland fire history. *Journal of Ecology*, **98**, 1319–1329.

Nilsson, S.G. (1985) Ecological and evolutionary interactions between reproduction of beech *Fagus sylvatica* and seed eating animals. *Oikos*, **44**, 157–164.

Novikov, G.A. (1959) *Ekologiâ zverej i ptic lesostepnyh dubrav.* Leningrad: Izd. Leningradskogo Universiteta.

Oelke, H. (1987) Bird structures of wet woodland stands (*Alnion glutinosae*) in Europe. *Acta Oecologica*, **8**, 191–199.

Pasinelli, G., Grendelmeier, A., Gerber, M. & Arlettaz, R. (2016) Rodent-avoidance, topography and forest structure shape territory selection of a forest bird. *BioMed Central Ecology*, **16**, 24.

Pautasso, M., Aas, G., Queloz, V. & Holdenrieder, O. (2013) European ash (*Fraxinus excelsior*) dieback – a conservation biology challenge. *Biological Conservation*, **158**, 37–49.

Perrins, C.M. (1966) The effect of beech crops on Great Tit populations and movements. *British Birds*, **59**, 419–432.

Perrins, C.M. (1979) *British Tits.* London: Collins.

Perrins, C.M. (1991) Tits and their caterpillar food supply. *Ibis*, **133** (Suppl.), 49–54.

Peterken, G.F. (1996) *Natural Woodland: Ecology and Conservation in Northern Temperate Regions.* Cambridge: Cambridge University Press.

Podbielkowski, Z. (1987) *Fitogeografia części świata.* Vol. 1. Warszawa: Państwowe Wydawnictwo Naukowe.

Pucek, Z., Jędrzejewski, W., Jędrzejewska, B. & Pucek, M. (1993) Rodent population dynamics in a primeval deciduous forest (Białowieża National Park) in relation to weather, seed crop, and predation. *Acta Theriologica*, **38**, 199–232.

Rackham, O. (2003) *Ancient Woodland.* 2nd ed. Dalbeattie: Castlepoint Press.

Randik, A. (1985) The bird fauna of the riverine forests along the Danube in Czechoslovakia. In *Riverine Forests in Europe: Status and Conservation.* Imboden, E. (ed.). Cambridge: ICBP, pp. 43–45.

Rebane, M., Waliczky, Z. & Turner, R. (1997) Boreal and temperate forests. In *Habitats for Birds in Europe: A Conservation Strategy for the Wider Environment.* Tucker, G.M. & Evans, M.I. (eds.). Cambridge: BirdLife International, pp. 203–238.

Reichholf, J.H. (1985) Composition of bird fauna in riverine forests. In: *Riverine Forests in Europe: Status and Conservation.* Imboden, E. (ed.). Cambridge: ICBP, pp. 16–21.

Reif, J., Marhoul, P. & Koptík, J. (2013) Bird communities in habitats along a successional gradient: Divergent patterns of species richness, specialization and threat. *Basic and Applied Ecology*, **14**, 423–431.

Robinson, R.A. (2005) *BirdFacts: Species Profiles of Birds Occurring in Britain and Ireland.* BTO Research Report 407. Thetford: BTO. (www.bto.org/birdfacts).

Rösner, S., Selva, N., Müller, T., Pugacewicz, E. & Laudet, F. (2005) Raven *Corvus corax* ecology in a primeval temperate forest. In *Corvids of Poland*. Jerzak, L., Kavanagh, B.P. & Tryjanowski, P. (eds.). Poznań: Bogucki Wydawnictwo Naukowe, pp. 385–405.

Rowiński, P. (2001) [*Timing of Breeding of Nuthatch* Sitta europaea *in Relation to Food Resources in a Natural Forest.*] Warsaw: Unpubl. doctoral thesis, SGGW. [in Polish]

Rowiński, P. & Wesołowski, T. (1999) Timing of Marsh Tit (*Parus palustris*) and Nuthatch (*Sitta eruropaea*) breeding in relation to their caterpillar food in primaeval conditions – preliminary data. *The Ring*, **21**, 126.

Rutz, C., Bijlsma, R.G., Marquiss, M. & Kenward, R.E. (2006) Population limitation in the Northern Goshawk in Europe: A review with case studies. *Studies in Avian Biology*, **31**, 158–197.

Schumacher, H. (2001) Zur avifaunistischen Bedeutung des alten Naturschutzgebietes 'Heilige Hallen'. *Labus*, **13**, 32–41.

Schumacher, H. (2006) *Zum Einfluss forstlicher Bewirtschaftung auf die Avifauna von Rotbuchenwäldern im nordostdeutschen Tiefland*. PhD thesis. University of Göttingen: Cuvillier Verlag.

Smirnova, O.V. (2004) Prirodnaâ organizaciâ biogeocenotičeskogo pokrova lesnogo poâsa Vostočnoj Evropy. In *Vostočnoevropejskie Lesa: Istoriâ v Golocene i Sovremennost*. Vol. 1. Smirnova, O.V. (ed.). Moskva: Nauka, pp. 16–58.

Smirnova, O.V., Bobrovskij, V.M., Turubanova, S.A. & Kalâkin V.N. (2004) Sovremennaâ zonalnost' Vostočnoj Evropy kak rezul'tat prirodnogo i antropogennogo preobarzovaniâ pozdneplejstocenvogo kompleksa klûčevyh vidov. In *Vostočnoevropejskie Lesa: Istoriâ v Golocene i Sovremennost*. Vol. 1. Smirnova, OV. (ed.). Moskva: Nauka, pp. 134–144.

Smirnova, O.V. & Turubanova, S.A. (2004) Izmenenie vidovogo sostava i raspostraneniâ klûčevyh vidov derev'ev (èdifikatorov) lesnogo poâsa s konca plejstocena do pozdnego golocena. In *Vostočnoevropejskie Lesa: Istoriâ v Golocene i Sovremennost*. Vol. 1. Smirnova, O.V. (ed.). Moskva: Nauka, pp. 118–133.

Spiecker, H. (2003) Silvicultural management in maintaining biodiversity and resistance of forest in Europe – temperate zone. *Journal of Environmental Management*, **67**, 55–65.

Stutchbury, B.J.M. & Morton, E.S. (2001) *Behavioral Ecology of Tropical Birds*. San Diego: Academic Press.

Svenning, J.-C. (2002) A review of natural vegetation openness in north-western Europe. *Biological Conservation*, **104**, 133–148.

Svensson, S., Thorner, A.M. & Nyholm, N.E.I. (2010) Species trends, turnover and composition of a woodland bird community in southern Sweden during a period of fifty-seven years. *Ornis Svecica*, **20**, 31–44.

Székely, T. & Moskát, C. (1991) Guild structure and seasonal changes in foraging behaviour of birds in a central-European oak forest. *Ornis Hungarica*, **1**, 10–28.

Thiollay, J.M. (1992) Influence of selective logging on bird species diversity in a Guianan rainforest. *Conservation Biology*, **6**, 47–63.

Tomiałojć, L. (1976) The urban population of the Woodpigeon *Columba palumbus* Linnaeus, 1758, in Europe – its origin, increase and distribution. *Acta Zoologica Cracoviensia*, **21**, 585–632.

Tomiałojć, L. (1980) The impact of predation on urban and rural woodpigeon (*Columba palumbus* (L.)) populations. *Polish Ecological Studies*, **5**, 141–220.

Tomiałojć, L. (1992) Colonization of dry habitats by the Song Thrush *Turdus philomelos*: Is the type of nest material an important constraint? *Bulletin of the British Ornithologists' Club*, **112**, 27–34.

Tomiałojć, L. (1993) Breeding ecology of the Blackbird *Turdus merula* studied in the primaeval forest of Białowieża (Poland). Part I. Breeding numbers, distribution and nest sites. *Acta Ornithologica*, **27**, 131–157.

Tomiałojć, L. (1994) Breeding ecology of the Blackbird *Turdus merula* studied in the primaeval forest of Białowieża (Poland). Part 2. Reproduction and mortality. *Acta Ornithologica*, **29**, 101–121.

Tomiałojć, L. (1995) The birds of the Białowieża Forest – additional data and summary. *Acta Zoologica Cracoviensia*, **38**, 363–397.

Tomiałojć, L. (2000a) An east-west gradient in the breeding distribution and species richness of the European woodland avifauna. *Acta Ornithologica*, **35**, 3–17.

Tomiałojć, L. (2000b) Did White-backed Woodpeckers ever breed in Britain? *British Birds*, **93**, 452–456.

Tomiałojć, L. (2012) Reproduction and population dynamics of Hawfinches *Coccothraustes coccothraustes* in the primeval forest of Białowieża National Park (NE Poland). *Acta Ornithologica*, **47**, 63–78.

Tomiałojć, L., Walankiewicz., W. & Wesołowski, T. (1977) Methods and preliminary results of the bird census work in primeval forest of Białowieża National Park. *Polish Ecological Studies*, **3**, 215–223.

Tomiałojć, L. & Wesołowski, T. (1990) Bird communities of the primaeval temperate forest of Białowieża, Poland. In *Biogeography and Ecology of Forest Bird Communities*. Keast, A. (ed.). The Hague: SPB Academic Publishers, pp. 141–165.

Tomiałojć, L. & Wesołowski, T. (1994) Die Stabilität der Vogelgemeinschaft in einem Urwald der gemässigten Zone: Ergebnisse einer 15 jährigen Studie aus dem Nationalpark von Białowieża (Polen). *Ornithologische Beobachter*, **91**, 73–110.

Tomiałojć, L. & Wesołowski, T. (1996) Structure of a primaeval forest bird community during 1970s and 1990s (Białowieża National Park, Poland). *Acta Ornithologica*, **31**, 133–154.

Tomiałojć, L. & Wesołowski, T. (2004) Diversity of the Białowieża Forest avifauna in space and time. *Journal of Ornithology*, **145**, 81–92.

Tomiałojć, L. & Wesołowski, T. (2005) The avifauna of the Białowieża Forest: A window into the past. *British Birds*, **98**, 174–193.

Tomiałojć, L., Wesołowski, T. & Walankiewicz, W. (1984) Breeding bird community of a primaeval temperate forest (Białowieża National Park, Poland). *Acta Ornithologica*, **20**, 41–310.

Tucker, G.M. & Evans, M.I. (eds.) (1997) *Habitats for Birds in Europe: A Conservation Strategy for the Wider Environment*. Cambridge: BirdLife International.

van Manen, W. (2003) *Notes on Raptorial Birds in Białowieża Forest (NE Poland) in 2003*. Assen: Privately published.

Veen, P., Fanta, J., Raev, I., Biris, I.-A., de Smidt, J. & Maes, B. (2010) Virgin forests in Romania and Bulgaria: Results of two national inventory projects and their implications for protection. *Biodiversity and Conservation*, **19**, 1805–1819.

Vera, F.W.M. (2000) *Grazing Ecology and Forest History*. Wallingford: CABI.

Vladiševskij, D.V. (1975) *Pticy v antropogennom Landšafte*. Novosibirsk: Nauka.

Walankiewicz, W. (1991) Do secondary-cavity nesting birds suffer more from competition for cavities or from predation in primaeval deciduous forest? *Natural Areas Journal*, **11**, 203–212.

Walankiewicz, W. (2002) Nest predation as a limiting factor to the breeding population size of the Collared Flycatcher *Ficedula albicollis* in the Białowieża National Park (NE Poland). *Acta Ornithologica*, **37**, 91–106.

Walankiewicz, W., Czeszczewik, D. & Mitrus, C. (2007) Natural nest sites of the Collared Flycatcher *Ficedula albicollis* in lime-hornbeam-oak stands of a primeval forest. *Ornis Fennica*, **84**, 155–162.

Wesołowski, T. (1983) The breeding ecology and behaviour of Wrens *Troglodytes troglodytes* under primaeval and secondary conditions. *Ibis*, **125**, 499–515.

Wesołowski, T. (1985) Riverine forests in Poland and the German Democratic Republic – their status and avifauna In *Riverine Forests in Europe: Status and Conservation*. Imboden, E. (ed.). Cambridge: ICBP, pp. 48–54.

Wesołowski, T. (1989) Nest-sites of hole-nesters in a primaeval temperate forest (Białowieża National Park, Poland). *Acta Ornithologica*, **25**, 321–351.

Wesołowski, T. (1994) Variation in the numbers of resident birds in a primaeval temperate forest: Are winter weather, seed crop, caterpillars and interspecific competition involved? In *Bird Numbers 1992, Proceedings of the 12th Conference of IBCC and EOAC*. Hagemeijer, E.J.M. & Verstrael, T.J. (eds.). Voorburg/Heerlen: Statistics Netherlands, pp. 203–211.

Wesołowski, T. (2002) Antipredator adaptations in nesting marsh tits *Parus palustris* – the role of nest site security. *Ibis*, **144**, 593–601.

Wesołowski, T. (2003) Bird community dynamics in a primaeval forest – is interspecific competition important? *Ornis Hungarica*, **12–13**, 51–62.

Wesołowski, T. (2005) Virtual conservation: How the European Union is turning a blind eye on its vanishing primeval forests. *Conservation Biology*, **19**, 1349–1358.

Wesołowski, T. (2007a) Primeval conditions – what can we learn from them? *Ibis*, **149** (Suppl. 2), 64–77.

Wesołowski, T. (2007b) Lessons from long-term hole-nester studies in a primeval temperate forest. *Journal of Ornithology*, **148** (Suppl. 2), 395–405.

Wesołowski, T. (2011a) 'Lifespan' of woodpecker-made holes in a primeval temperate forest: A thirty year study. *Forest Ecology and Management*, **262**, 1846–1852.

Wesołowski, T. (2011b) Blackcap *Sylvia atricapilla* numbers, phenology and reproduction in a primeval forest – a 33-year study. *Journal of Ornithology*, **152**, 319–329.

Wesołowski, T. (2012) 'Lifespan' of non-excavated holes in a primeval temperate forest: A 30 year study. *Biological Conservation*, **153**, 118–126.

Wesołowski, T. & Cholewa, M. (2009) Climate variation and birds' breeding seasons in a primeval temperate forest. *Climate Research*, **38**, 199–208.

Wesołowski, T., Czeszczewik, D., Hebda, G., Maziarz, M., Mitrus, C. & Rowiński, P. (2015a) 40 years of breeding bird community dynamics in a primeval temperate forest (Białowieża National Park, Poland). *Acta Ornithogica*, **50**, 95–120.

Wesołowski, T., Czeszczewik, D., Mitrus, C. & Rowiński, P. (2003) Birds of the Białowieża National Park. *Notatki Ornitologiczne*, **44**, 1–31. [in Polish, English summary]

Wesołowski, T. & Fuller, R.J. (2012) Spatial variation and temporal shifts in habitat use by birds at the European scale. In *Birds and Habitat: Relationships in Changing Landscapes*. Fuller, R.J. (ed.). Cambridge: Cambridge University Press, pp. 63–92.

Wesołowski, T., Kujawa, A., Bobiec, A. *et al.* (2016) Dispute over the future of the Białowieża Forest: Myths and facts. A voice in the debate. www.forestbiology.org, **Article 2**, 1–19.

Wesołowski, T., Mitrus, C., Czeszczewik, D. & Rowiński, P. (2010) Breeding bird dynamics in a primeval temperate forest over 35 years: Variation and stability in a changing world. *Acta Ornithologica*, **45**, 209–232.

Wesołowski, T. & Rowiński, P. (2006) Tree defoliation by winter moth *Operophtera brumata* L. during an outbreak affected by structure of forest landscape. *Forest Ecology and Management*, **221**, 299–305.

Wesołowski, T. & Rowiński, P. (2012) The breeding performance of Blue Tits *Cyanistes caeruleus* in relation to the attributes of natural holes in a primeval forest. *Bird Study*, **59**, 437–448.

Wesołowski, T., Rowiński, P. & Maziarz, M. (2009) Wood warbler *Phylloscopus sibilatrix* – a nomadic insectivore in search of safe breeding grounds? *Bird Study*, **56**, 26–33.

Wesołowski, T., Rowiński, P. & Maziarz, M. (2015b) Interannual variation in tree seed production in a primeval temperate forest: Does masting prevail? *European Journal of Forest Research*, **134**, 99–112.

Wesołowski, T., Rowiński, P., Mitrus, C. & Czeszczewik, D. (2006) Breeding bird community of a primeval temperate forest (Białowieża National Park, Poland) at the beginning of the 21st century. *Acta Ornithologica*, **41**, 55–70.

Wesołowski, T. & Stawarczyk, T. (1991) Survival and population dynamics of Nuthatches *Sitta europaea* breeding in natural cavities in a primeval temperate forest. *Ornis Scandinavica*, **22**, 143–154.

Wesołowski, T. & Tomiałojć, L. (1995) Ornitologische Untersuchungen im Urwald von Białowieża – eine Übersicht. *Ornithologische Beobachter*, **92**, 111–146.

Wesołowski, T. & Tomiałojć, L. (1997) Breeding bird dynamics in a primaeval temperate forest: Long-term trends in Białowieża National Park (Poland). *Ecography*, **20**, 432–453.

Wesołowski, T. & Tomiałojć, L. (2005) Nest sites, nest predation, and productivity of avian broods in a primeval temperate forest: Do the generalisations hold? *Journal of Avian Biology*, **36**, 361–367.

Wesołowski, T., Tomiałojć, L., Mitrus, C., Rowiński, P. & Czeszczewik, D. (2002) Breeding bird community of a primeval temperate forest (Białowieża National Park, Poland) at the end of XXth century. *Acta Ornithogica*, **37**, 27–45.

Wesołowski, T., Tomiałojć, L. & Stawarczyk, T. (1987) Why low numbers of *Parus major* in Białowieża Forest – removal experiments. *Acta Ornithogica*, **23**, 303–316.

Winter, S., Begehold, H., Herrmann, M. *et al.* (2015) *Praxishandbuch – Naturschutz im Buchenwald. Naturschutzziele und Bewirtschaftungsempfehlungen für reife Buchenwälder Nordostdeutschlands*. Potsdam: Ministerium für Ländliche Entwicklung, Umwelt und Landwirtschaft Brandenburg.

Wösendorfer, J. (1985) Austria with reference to Hainburg and Marchegg. In: *Riverine Forests in Europe: Status and Conservation*. Imboden, E. (ed.). Cambridge: ICBP, pp. 22–28.

Yalden, D. (1999) *The History of British Mammals*. London: Poyser.

Zalewski, A., Jędrzejewski, W. & Jędrzejewska, B. (1995) Pine marten home ranges, numbers and predation on vertebrates in a deciduous forest (Białowieża National Park, Poland). *Annales Zoologici Fennici*, **32**, 131–144.

Żmihorski, M. (2008) Breeding bird community of the windthrow in the Piska Forest (NE Poland). *Notatki Ornitologiczne*, **49**, 39–56. [in Polish, English summary]

Żmihorski, M. (2010) The effect of windthrow and its management on breeding bird communities in a managed forest. *Biodiversity and Conservation*, **19**, 1871–1882.

9 · *Mediterranean Forest Bird Communities and the Role of Landscape Heterogeneity in Space and Time*

LLUÍS BROTONS, SERGI HERRANDO,
CLÉLIA SIRAMI, VASSILIKI KATI
AND MARIO DÍAZ

9.1 Introduction

Bird communities need to be interpreted in the context and characteristics of the ecosystems in which they occur. In the case of bird communities of Mediterranean forests, this is especially relevant given the particular nature of these ecosystems in terms of both a marked spatial heterogeneity and a particularly variable temporal dynamics related to a long and intense history of human influence. The Mediterranean region is located at the intersection of three major landmasses: Europe, Africa and Asia. It includes areas associated with a Mediterranean climate as well as nearby areas in transition to other climates (e.g., the extreme eastern Pyrenees; Blondel *et al.* 2010). The region is topographically very diverse; the many mountain chains and plateaux and the different sizes and shapes of its peninsulas and islands produce environmental heterogeneity levels higher than anywhere else in Europe (Metzger *et al.* 2005). This, together with its long history of climatic variations and human activities, has resulted in high levels of endemism in many groups of terrestrial plants and animals. As a result, the Mediterranean Basin is considered to be one of the biodiversity hotspots of the world, and is the only one in Europe apart from the Caucasus region (Myers *et al.* 2000). Whereas the level of endemism is very high for plants, amphibians and reptiles, it is much lower for mammals and birds, suggesting that evolutionary processes in relation to dispersal and geographical aspects of the Basin have been key factors behind diversity patterns in the region (Blondel *et al.* 2010; Chapter 2).

Defining forests in this complex ecoregion requires some degree of flexibility to take into account its high levels of tree species diversity, spatial heterogeneity and temporal dynamics. Indeed, the Mediterranean region includes up to 130 tree species, against only 30 in temperate forests. Most Mediterranean tree species are evergreen, 'semi-deciduous' or conifers. The majority of Mediterranean forests are usually lower in canopy height, and more open and structurally and floristically heterogeneous than other European forests. Moreover, fine-grained mosaics and high disturbance levels traditionally characterise Mediterranean landscapes. Therefore, we consider that Mediterranean forests also include shrublands and open, even savanna-like, woodlands. Nowadays, forests and shrublands cover 32–55% of the total area in Mediterranean European countries. Primary Mediterranean forests are virtually non-existent, however, and most of the forested area corresponds to naturally regenerated forest. Dense forests occur in areas where rainfall is sufficient and human activities have ceased, as well as along rivers. Shrublands replace arboreal formations in the driest and warmest areas, but also widely occur as post-disturbance transitional phases resulting from the actions of natural or anthropogenic processes. Shrublands are more diverse and widespread in the Mediterranean than anywhere else in Europe, including endemic types such as garrigue, matorral and maquis, and play a crucial role for birds in both evolutionary and ecological terms (Blondel *et al.* 2010). Planted forests (usually consisting of non-native pine plantations; Chapter 10) form less than 20% of the total forest area, and are mostly concentrated in parts of the Iberian Peninsula (FAO 2013). Several tree crops widespread in the Mediterranean, such as olive groves, are not included in our definition of Mediterranean forests because of the strong level of human intervention on their functional processes. However, these non-forest habitats and their avian inhabitants are occasionally mentioned in this chapter, due to their spatial extent and their ecological importance for some species of forest birds.

9.2 Factors Driving the Dynamics of Mediterranean Forests

The extent and characteristics of current forests in the Mediterranean can only be understood in the context of the historical development of Mediterranean socio-ecosystems. Self-sustainability at both the family and village level has been traditionally achieved through three main traditional activities: cultivating, grazing and harvesting of forest products (Blondel *et al.* 2010). These three activities and associated management practices have noticeable implications in terms of the overall ecosystem functioning, and specifically on the ecology of forest bird species. The first type of agro-silvo-pastoral system corresponds to the triad forest-pasture-field, which was traditionally implemented at the scale of the village and its surrounding land. Exploitation of forest, livestock husbandry and production of arable crops were undertaken at distinct sites according to the spatial distribution of the best microclimatic and edaphic conditions for each activity. Nowadays, many of the pastures have been abandoned and the above triad is increasingly becoming a forest-field duet. At the level of the forest patches, humans have altered the tree species composition according to various forestry aims. Often, pines have been selected for the production of timber for building, while oaks have been favoured for uses such as the production of charcoal, cork or acorns. Traditionally, forest management has also involved removal of the forest understorey, which represented either a source of firewood, a grazing resource for livestock or simply an inconvenience for forestry practices. This practice has usually been associated with negative impacts on forest bird communities (Camprodon & Brotons 2006).

In some parts of the Basin, particularly in south-west Iberia, another type of agro-silvo-pastoral system, called *dehesa* (Spain) or *montado* (Portugal), has been developed. Here, the three main rural activities of generating forest product, livestock husbandry and agriculture have not been segregated in space but coexist at small spatial scales. The resulting landscape is an oak woodland with a savanna-like structure, created and maintained over time by low-intensity management practices such as livestock grazing, tree pruning and thinning, and shrub removal. Dehesas and montados maintain more diverse bird communities than those harboured by the closed-canopy and shrubby Mediterranean forests, to the point that they are one of the few man-made habitats that qualify for protection under the European Habitats Directive (Díaz & Pulido 2009). High levels of biological diversity observed in dehesas and montados can be explained by the coexistence of species that depend on forests and grasslands at scales ranging from fields and stands to whole landscapes (review in Díaz *et al.* 2013; Moreno *et al.* 2016). Insufficient tree recruitment and the corresponding slow decrease of tree cover, conversion to other land-uses and shrub encroachment after the abandonment of livestock rearing are the main threats to this land-use system (Campos *et al.* 2013). Similar trends occur in other small-scale management systems equivalent to dehesas and montados (the so-called pastoral woodlands) found outside the Iberian peninsula (Eichhorn *et al.* 2006; Rossetti & Bagella 2014).

These two broad types of agro-silvo-pastoral systems (triads and pastoral woodlands) explain the occurrence of the two main types of forest in the Mediterranean human-shaped landscapes, as well as its spatial patterning and admixture with other land uses. It should be recognised that tree-based perennial crops, although not treated in detail in this chapter, form a widespread landscape component that can provide suitable habitat for many forest species. The best example is olive groves, but many others should be considered too, including carob, almond and fig trees. Here, the degree of management of trees is higher than in the dehesa and montado woodlands, but often moderate enough to provide important resources for forest species, particularly during the fruiting season. For instance, winter densities of many forest birds are much higher in olive groves than in any other forest type (e.g., Herrando *et al.* 2011).

The spatial distribution of Mediterranean socio-related forest ecosystems is strongly associated with the physical heterogeneity of the region. Indeed, the locations of forests, pastures and crops, or mosaics of these ecosystems, are strongly influenced by the locations of plains, mountains and valleys, with their different soils and climates. Due to the strong orographic heterogeneity of the Mediterranean region, Mediterranean forests have been fragmented for millennia. As a result, their biotas have evolved in a far more complex physical context than their northern European counterparts. In fact, most Mediterranean forest species, including birds, tend to be habitat generalists, exploiting not only forests, but also shrublands and even open habitats (e.g., Díaz *et al.* 1998; Santos *et al.* 2006). This has major consequences for the current sensitivity of bird communities to landscape or land-cover modifications (Fraser *et al.* 2015); the effects of habitat fragmentation are much less severe in Mediterranean than in temperate or boreal forests (Blondel *et al.* 2010).

9.3 Historical Dynamics of Mediterranean Forests

The impact of human activities on forests has been both deep and fluctuating since the Neolithic, leading Corvol (1987) to write, 'forests are mirrors of societies'. It can be argued that this statement applies more strongly to the forests of the Mediterranean than anywhere else in Europe. Mediterranean forests have undergone several 'ups and downs' since the Neolithic, associated not only with climatic fluctuations but also with the flourishing and decline of human societies (Thirgood 1981; Mercuri & Sadori 2014). The times of the Roman Empire were characterised by intensive agricultural development and forest destruction across the Basin, and its decline in the western Mediterranean coincided with a spontaneous recovery of forest that lasted until a resurgence of human activities at the end of the Middle Ages. With the development of powerful naval empires during the Age of Discoveries, all easily accessible timber was employed for ship-building initiatives. The Industrial Revolution needed enormous quantities of wood for manufacturing, and also triggered a substantial increase in human population. These factors brought severe destruction of forests in the western part of the Basin during the nineteenth century and the first half of the twentieth century.

By contrast, as industrial development was never pronounced in the eastern Mediterranean, the agricultural income crisis in the less productive mountainous areas led to massive rural depopulation over the same period, as well as after the Second World War, resulting in substantial forest expansion on formerly grazed and cultivated land (Tzanopoulos *et al.* 2011; Zakkak *et al.* 2014). In most Euro-Mediterranean countries, the massive substitution of wood and charcoal by fossil fuels after the Second World War further encouraged the recovery of forests across the region (Blondel *et al.* 2010), as well as strong changes in the traditional uses of extensive silvo-pastoral systems such as dehesas and montados (Grove & Rackham 2003; Campos *et al.* 2013). Trends in cover of Mediterranean forests differ to the north and south and east of the Mediterranean Sea shores: northern forest cover is currently increasing by an average rate of 0.33% per year, which contrasts with a much lower 0.07% increase in southern and eastern forest cover (Mazzoleni *et al.* 2004). Large-scale increases in forest cover have also led to recent increases in fire impact over large regions of the northern Mediterranean, with wildfires becoming one of the most significant factors determining forest dynamics in the region (Mouillot *et al.* 2005). The proportions of the various forest types – conifers, broadleaved deciduous and broadleaved sclerophyllous – have also changed dramatically over the last decades with complex spatial patterns derived from the impacts of land-use changes and disturbances such as fire (Colombaroli & Tinner 2013). At the same time that abandonment has occurred in many marginal areas, land-use intensification (including agriculture intensification and urbanisation) has occurred in the most productive areas, especially along coastlines (Blondel *et al.* 2010).

Human-related driving forces have been so strong across recent millennia that forests can be regarded as part of the cultural heritage of

Mediterranean landscapes. This is highly relevant when it comes to implementing conservation strategies. Baseline references in the form of ancient wilderness areas are generally lacking. The amount, type and landscape structure of forests have been so closely linked to spatial and temporal variation in human activities in the Mediterranean region since the last glaciation that finding suitable reference points from the past would depend on our (inevitably subjective) time-window selection. The historical rise and decline of civilisations and their consumption of forest resources have greatly affected the extent and nature of Mediterranean forests (Thirgood 1981; Grove & Rackham 2003). Forests are not isolated elements of landscapes, and the way human societies have used and lived with forests represents a good example of socio-ecological systems in which the dynamics of ecological components cannot be understood without keeping their social context in mind (e.g., Campos et al. 2013).

9.4 Future Scenarios for Mediterranean Forests

9.4.1 Land Use

Although land abandonment started more than 50 years ago in some areas, its effects on ecosystems are associated with important time lags. Consequently, afforestation resulting from the widespread collapse of farming in many areas currently represents the main land-cover transition in European Mediterranean countries (Feranec et al. 2010). Land abandonment is still ongoing in many areas, especially where topography is complex and farming less profitable. Future models predict that farming activities will keep decreasing in many areas and further increases in forest cover should be expected. At the same time, urbanisation is also predicted to increase considerably in Mediterranean regions, possibly triggering local decreases in forest cover (Catalán et al. 2008). Finally, agricultural intensification could locally influence the extent of tree-based perennial crops. For example, large irrigation plans are expected to trigger an expansion of such crops that are currently suffering large-scale decreases across the region (e.g., olive and almond tree plantations in the western Mediterranean). Of particular interest in the context of a weak forestry sector is the potential impact of forest biomass for energy uses on the future dynamics of Mediterranean forests. In recent years, regional and national authorities have promoted the use of firewood and wood pellets as a source of renewable energy. In a context of expensive fossil fuels, forest exploitation for energy production could strongly alter the structure and, via interaction with other disturbances, the composition of forests over large areas of the Mediterranean.

9.4.2 Climate and Fire Regime

Climate projections consistently predict significant increases in temperature and decreases in precipitation in the Mediterranean Basin (Gibelin & Deque 2003; IPCC 2014). Such potential changes could have a profound effect on Mediterranean forests. Projections concerning trees seem to differ considerably, depending on the ecology of the species. Mediterranean mountain species, such as the black pine *Pinus nigra* and the Pyrenean oak *Quercus pyrenaica*, could show the largest reduction of their distribution ranges (Benito-Garzón *et al.* 2008). Recent models suggest a general increase of unsuitable areas, even for the most widespread tree species, such as holm oak *Q. ilex* and Aleppo pine *P. halepensis*, although there is still a high degree of uncertainty about these range constraints (Keenan *et al.* 2011).

The Mediterranean is a fire-prone region as a result of its particular climate, which makes vegetation highly flammable during the summer drought. Decadal-scale droughts, sometimes associated with global-scale climatic oscillations, create high fire hazard years, leading to approximately half a million hectares of land being burned by wildfires in southern Europe yearly (Moreira *et al.* 2011; Xystrakis *et al.* 2014). Land abandonment is triggering an increase in the amount of fuel (vegetation), which, combined with the inclination of the terrain, can increase both fire speed and severity. Generally, surface fires are smaller and patchier than crown fires, which are often more associated with large fires impelled by strong winds overcoming potential barriers to fire passage (Keeley *et al.* 2012). Fires can shape forested landscapes in very different ways and, depending on the characteristics of both the landscape and the fire itself, can homogenise the mosaic of habitats or act in exactly the opposite direction. There is evidence that humans have altered natural fire regimes since the Neolithic, and this interaction has been maintained until the present day (Vannière *et al.* 2008). Mediterranean societies have often increased fire frequency but have also served as effective fire extinguishers, particularly of small-intensity fires. As a result, the mosaic of recently burnt areas, shrublands and forests is strongly influenced by human activity (Keeley *et al.* 2012).

The number of fires in southern Europe has substantially increased since 1980 (Venäläinen *et al.* 2014). One of the main causes affecting this recent trend is fuel accumulation caused by vegetation encroachment in the context of land abandonment (Pausas & Vallejo 1999). Large wild-fires have homogenised landscapes over large areas in recent decades, with a general negative impact on biodiversity, which contrasts with the positive effects reported for the heterogeneity created by traditional carefully controlled burns on small areas (Moreno & Oechel 1994). Finally, the fire regime depends on a number of interactions among key factors such as climate, land use, vegetation type, and ignition and extinction patterns (Minnich 1983). While accurate forecasts are difficult to make, the predicted climatic scenarios in the Mediterranean point to an increased duration of dry spells (IPCC 2014), suggesting an increasing frequency of large wildfires in the coming decades (Doblas-Miranda *et al.* 2015). Increases in storm incidence and insect outbreaks have been reported elsewhere in Europe and could also impact Mediterranean forests, but increasing fire risk is the main consequence of warming climate conditions likely to impact Mediterranean forests (Seidl *et al.* 2014). Future changes in fire regimes associated with climate changes and extreme climate events, combined with land-use changes leading to more extensive forest, are likely to lead to a more dramatic impact of large fires on Mediterranean forests (Doblas-Miranda *et al.* 2015).

9.4.3 Invasive Species

Mediterranean forests are considered to be resistant to biological invasions as a result of a long-lasting history of intermediate levels of disturbance and constant immigration rates of taxa that originated within the region and nearby areas (di Castri *et al.* 1990). Plant communities show this high resistance particularly well, since apart from some exotics in riparian forests (e.g., locust tree *Robinia pseudoacacia*) or warm maquis (*Opuntia* spp. or *Agave* spp.), the occurrence of invaders within native ecosystems is relatively low (di Castri *et al.* 1990). Although invasive species do not currently seem to pose serious problems in Mediterranean forests, large-scale plantations of exotic trees (e.g., eucalypts in the western Iberian peninsula) have negative effects on forest bird communities (Chapter 10).

Many of the bird species recently introduced into the Mediterranean Basin have a high potential to establish self-sustaining populations and could eventually have a detrimental impact on native species (Kark & Sol 2005). Compared with other habitats, forest ecosystems do not seem particularly prone to the invasion of exotic bird species, at least compared with urban or agricultural habitats (Case 1996). Nevertheless, some invasive species can already be found in forest edges, and the red-billed leiothrix *Leiotrix lutea* represents a very successful case of invasion of holm-oak forests in the north-west of the Basin (Herrando *et al.* 2010).

9.5 Biogeography of Mediterranean Forest Birds

At large scales, bird species diversity and composition vary in both space and time due to the geographic location of the Mediterranean region, its spatial heterogeneity and its history. At the scale of the entire Mediterranean biome, the species richness of breeding birds shows a general decreasing trend from central and eastern Europe towards the south and west (Araújo *et al.* 2005), a pattern that also holds true when considering forest bird communities (Covas & Blondel 1998; Tellería 2001; Box 9.1). This pattern of richness is related to a decreasing trend in the abundance of most European forest birds in the same direction (Covas & Blondel 1998; Chapter 5), from maximum values in central Europe to minimum values in southern Europe and northern Africa. Some common European breeding forest birds reach their southern range limit in the northern Mediterranean (e.g., three out of the seven woodpeckers that occupy the Iberian Peninsula) or in humid locations further south, such as mountain, coastal or riverine forests (e.g., Díaz *et al.* 1996; Tellería *et al.* 1999 for the Iberian Peninsula). Fewer species show the opposite pattern, with maximum abundances in the south decreasing northwards, but examples include several *Sylvia* warblers (*S. sarda, S. balearica, S. undata, S. conspicillata, S. melanothorax, S. cantillans, S. subalpina, S. hortensis, S. crassirostris, S. rueppelli, S. melanocephala;* Fig. 9.1); several buntings, finches, starlings and shrikes; and some large forest raptors (imperial eagles *Aquila heliaca* and

---

Box 9.1 *Geographical patterns in Mediterranean forest bird assemblages.*

Data from the European Breeding Bird Atlas (Hagemeijer & Blair 1997) represent a useful dataset to depict patterns of richness for Mediterranean forest species, both in general and for those whose distribution in Europe is mainly concentrated in the Mediterranean Basin (listed in Box 9.2). Although the completeness of coverage in this

Box 9.1 (cont.)

atlas differs greatly among squares and robust comparisons are difficult to assess, these data suggest that the observed number of Mediterranean forest species is higher in Iberia and Greece than in the central part of the northern Mediterranean Basin (see maps below). This geographical pattern could be related to both environmental patterns and its close relationship with biogeographical processes. Large tracts of Italy and the western Balkans have a more humid character than the other two peninsulas and thus, in general, have fewer Mediterranean forest species. Despite speciation processes allowing the evolution of a few endemics (see Box 9.2), islands are associated with a lower richness of Mediterranean forest species than the mainland.

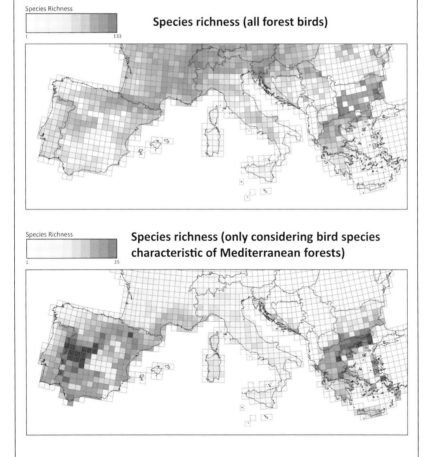

Species Richness

1   133

Species richness (all forest birds)

Species Richness

1   25

Species richness (only considering bird species characteristic of Mediterranean forests)

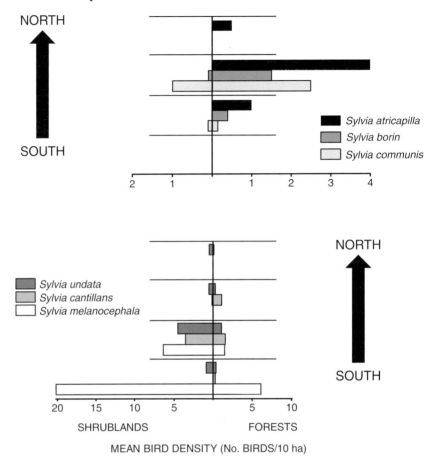

Figure 9.1 Mean bird densities (bars) for the six most common *Sylvia* warblers in forests and shrublands of the Iberian Peninsula. Densities of each species are ordered along the vertical axis according to four biogeographic regions within the Iberian peninsula; note that in some regions densities are zero for some species. (From north to south: Eurosiberian, Supra-, Meso- and Thermomediterranean regions. Eurosiberian sites have no summer drought, the extent and severity of which increase from Supra- to Thermomediterranean). Bars on the right side of the vertical axis represent densities in forest; bars on the left represent densities in shrubland. The top figure corresponds to the three species of temperate origin and the bottom figure to the three species of Mediterranean origin. Unexpected low mean abundance of warblers of temperate origin in the Iberian Eurosiberian region may be related to a local scarcity of well-developed temperate broadleaved forests because of its usual substitution by pine and eucalypt plantations (see Chapter 10). Note differences in density scales between the bottom and top figures (horizontal axis scales). After Tellería *et al.* (1999) and Díaz (2004).

A. adalberti, short-toed eagle *Circaetus gallicus* and black vulture *Aegypius monachus*). All these 'southern' species characteristically occupy shrublands and other open habitats, either as alternative or complementary habitats to forests, whereas 'northern' bird species are typically forest specialists (Fig. 9.1; Box 9.2; Covas & Blondel 1998; Díaz 2004).

Patterns of decreasing abundance towards the borders of distributional ranges may be explained by different hypotheses, such as the productivity hypothesis and the niche hypothesis (Brown 1984). At the community level, the productivity hypothesis states that large population sizes related to ecosystem productivity lead to a higher probability of different species coexisting at a site and a lower extinction rate per species. These two mechanisms drive forest-species richness in the Iberian Peninsula, with lower species richness in less productive, more marginal forests (Carnicer *et al.* 2008). At the species level, the niche hypothesis states that the optimal environmental conditions for each species – the fundamental niche in which the species evolved – occur at the centre of its range, with conditions deteriorating towards the margins. Abundance patterns match these geographical patterns due to the effect of environmental conditions on reproductive output and survival. According to this hypothesis, the specialist bird species currently found in Mediterranean forest bird communities should have evolved in the cold-humid forests that are currently found in central Europe. Increased temperatures and decreased rainfall southwards produce changes in forest composition and structure that decrease its suitability for these 'northern' forest birds (e.g., Carbonell & Tellería 1998). 'Southern' species should have evolved in drier and more open vegetation types, thus showing an opposite response to geographical change in temperature and rainfall (and also to ongoing and expected climate change; Huntley *et al.* 2007; Devictor *et al.* 2012). This hypothesis would also explain local exceptions to the latitudinal gradient in abundance or species richness, i.e., local peaks of abundance, species richness and even changes in morphology and migratory behaviour of 'northern' species, associated with cold-humid mountain, riverine and coastal forests located even at the southernmost border of the Mediterranean region (Díaz 2004; Pérez-Tris *et al.* 2004).

The current dominance of 'northern' over 'southern' specialist breeding bird species in Mediterranean forests seems to be due to the fact that these 'northern' species moved south during, and north after, Pleistocene glaciations (Covas & Blondel 1998; Blondel *et al.* 2010). Forest birds of northern origin survived in humid forest relicts around the Mediterranean during the glacial maxima, later recolonising southern, central and even northern Europe following the northward expansion of these forests. East-west barriers, such as most European mountain ranges, the Mediterranean Sea and the Sahara Desert, precluded the north-south movement of species of tropical origin, thus increasing the extinction rates of these species (Mönkkönen 1994). Maintenance of forest birds of southern origin and vicariant evolution in the south seem to have been reduced to a handful of groups: small *Sylvia* warblers, imperial eagles, the Iberian azure-winged magpie *Cyanopica cooki*, forest passerines such as the Corsican nuthatch *Sitta whiteheadi* and Corsican finch *Serinus corsicana* in Mediterranean peninsulas and large islands, laurel-forest pigeons (*Columba junionae, C. bollii* and *C. trocaz*) and some small passerines (*Cyanistes teneriffae, Phylloscopus canariensis, Regulus madeirensis, Pyrrhula murina*) in Macaronesia (e.g., Martín *et al.* 2000; Päckert *et al.* 2006; Hansson *et al.* 2014; Box 9.2). Contrarily, Mediterranean bird endemisms evolved in open habitats such as grassland and steppe (Box 9.2), a fact that explains the contrasting homogeneity of forest bird communities and the uniqueness of open-land bird communities around the Mediterranean Basin (Blondel & Farré 1988). Thus, the general patterns of decreasing species richness south- and westwards in Mediterranean forest can disappear, or

---

Box 9.2 *Bird species characteristic of main Mediterranean forest types.*

As a result of complex evolutionary processes, many of the bird species located in Mediterranean forests and shrublands are a subset of European forest bird species. However, a number of forest species have a major part of their distribution range within the Mediterranean zone or are entirely confined to it. Although classifications are difficult to make and could change with accumulated knowledge or future changes in species distribution, it is important to build a potential list of species for which the Mediterranean region has a considerable responsibility for their conservation and associated habitat. These species concentrate their distribution in the Mediterranean either all year round or only during the breeding or the winter season. The number of island endemics is relatively low and concentrated in Macaronesia.

Forest bird species characteristic of the Mediterranean zone (i.e., whose distribution in Europe is concentrated in the Mediterranean region, during either the breeding or winter season or both) are listed below. Each species is associated with its main habitat based on its highest abundance. Species marked with ★ are species for which this

Box 9.2 (cont.)

pattern exclusively occurs during the winter season, whereas species marked with **!** are only present during the breeding season. The symbol **+** indicates island endemics.

Shrublands (various levels of development)	Open woodland ("dehesa")	Forests (canopy closed)

Shrublands	Open woodland	Forests
Alectoris chukar	*Aegypius monachus*	*Scolopax rusticola* *
Alectoris graeca	*Elanus caeruleus*	*Columba trocaz* +
Alectoris barbara	*Milvus milvus* *	*Columba bollii* +
Alectoris rufa	*Circaetus gallicus* !	*Columba junoniae* +
Aquila fasciata	*Buteo rufinus* !	*Picus sharpei*
Caprimulgus ruficollis !	*Accipiter brevipes* !	*Turdus iliacus* *
Galerida theklae	*Aquila pennata* !	*Phylloscopus bonelli* !
Prunella modularis *	*Aquila chrysaetos*	*Phylloscopus orientalis* !
Erithacus rubecula *	*Aquila adalberti*	*Phylloscopus ibericus* !
Turdus torquatus *	*Falco biarmicus*	*Phylloscopus canariensis* +
Iduna opaca !	*Grus grus* *	*Regulus madeirensis* +
Iduna pallida !	*Clamator glandarius* !	*Cyanistes teneriffae* +
Sylvia sarda +	*Otus scops* !	*Sitta krueperi*
Sylvia balearica +	*Columba oenas* *	*Sitta whiteheadi* +
Sylvia undata	*Apus caffer* !	*Fringilla teydea* +
Sylvia cantillans !	*Dendrocopos syriacus*	*Serinus citrinella* *
Sylvia melanocephala	*Lullula arborea* *	*Serinus corsicana* +
Lanius meridionalis	*Luscinia megarhynchos*!	*Pyrrhula murina* +
Emberiza hortulana !	*Cettia cetti*	
	Turdus philomelos *	
	Turdus viscivorus *	
	Hippolais olivetorum !	
	Hippolais polyglotta !	
	Sylvia rueppelli !	
	Sylvia hortensis !	
	Sylvia crassirostris !	
	Sylvia atricapilla *	
	Phylloscopus collybita *	
	Poecile lugubris	
	Lanius senator !	
	Lanius nubicus !	
	Cyanopica cooki	
	Sturnus vulgaris *	
	Sturnus unicolor	
	Serinus serinus *	
	Serinus canaria +	
	Emberiza cirlus	
	Emberiza melanocephala !	

DRAWINGS: Toni Llobet.

even change, when considering generalist and shrubland birds of southern origin, and when the analyses are restricted to rare birds (Chapter 2). This changing pattern is due to the varying geographical effects in recent history on birds of different origins and habitat affinities which currently coexist in Mediterranean forests (Covas & Blondel 1998; Blondel *et al.* 2010).

Future climatic scenarios for forest bird species distributions suggest that range expansions at the European level will be particularly large for Mediterranean species (Huntley *et al.* 2007), but accurate predictions are impossible to make, partly because of the difficulty of incorporating current distribution and environmental data from northern Africa in these models (Barbet-Massin *et al.* 2012). Behavioural and ecological flexibility of plants and animals along food chains (e.g., phenological adjustments to increasing temperature and time lags) make it even harder to predict how the abundance, distribution and community structure of Mediterranean forest birds will respond to climate change (Sanz 2002; Devictor *et al.* 2012).

The niche hypothesis may also explain the strong seasonal changes experienced by Mediterranean forest bird communities. In fact, the pattern of southerly decline in abundance and species richness of breeding communities vanishes with the end of the Mediterranean summer drought (Tellería 1988, 2001). After the first autumn rains, large numbers of birds that bred in temperate and boreal forests arrive in the lowlands and on the coasts of the Mediterranean peninsulas and islands, as well as in northern Africa. In parallel, resident Mediterranean forest species tend to abandon forests to occupy more open habitats, such as grassland, crops (both annual and perennial), scrub and open woodland (Herrando *et al.* 2011). Both large- and local-scale movements blur the southward pattern of decreasing abundance and richness during the winter period. Clear examples of these changes are common starlings *Sturnus vulgaris* and red kites *Milvus milvus* wintering in open grassland or fallow, thrushes in olive groves, warblers in fruit-rich scrub, and woodpigeons *Columba palumbus* and chiffchaffs *Phylloscopus collybita* wintering in dehesas. The ultimate cause of these medium-distance migratory movements is the seasonal complementarity in primary production between the temperate forests, limited by low winter temperatures (see also Chapter 8), and the Mediterranean forest systems, limited by summer drought. Many plants in the Mediterranean lowlands produce large autumn crops of fruits that depend on migratory birds for seed dispersal (Jordano 2013). Fruit and seed crops are usually larger in open woodland and shrubland than in forests due to relaxed plant-plant competition (Jordano 2013; Koenig *et al.* 2013), a fact that helps to explain habitat shifts of birds from forest to more open habitats, as well as dietary shifts from insects to seeds and fruits between the breeding and wintering periods (Díaz 1996; Jordano 2013). Starlings, warblers, thrushes and robins *Erithacus rubecula* shift from insect-gleaning in forests to a fruit diet in shrubland and open woodland. Many finches, pigeons, cranes *Grus grus* and even tits shift to a diet based on seeds, produced either by herbs and forbs in grassland or by oaks and some pines in dehesas and open woodlands. The ability of forest birds to track changes in primary productivity, together with their plastic diet, produces changes in distribution and abundance patterns consistent with tracking a seasonally 'moving niche' (Rey 1995).

9.6 The Role of Birds in the Maintenance of Mediterranean Forests

Birds are not only strongly influenced by vegetation patterns, they also, in turn, play an important role in key forest processes. Due to their high mobility, birds provide key ecosystem services, such as nutrient transport by scavengers and marine birds, ecosystem engineering by nest excavation (see Chapter 4) and propagule dispersal (Sekercioglu 2006). One of the most remarkable functions birds play in Mediterranean forests is seed dispersal: many Mediterranean plants depend on keystone bird and mammal dispersers for their long-term maintenance (Herrera 1995; Purves *et al.* 2007; Jordano 2013). While some flesh-fruiting plants are efficiently dispersed by generalist carnivores such as foxes *Vulpes vulpes* (e.g., Jordano *et al.* 2007; Fedriani & Wiegand 2014), they are often mainly dispersed by bird species such as thrushes *Turdus* spp. or warblers *Sylvia* spp. (García *et al.* 2014; Pías *et al.* 2014). Frugivorous birds and flesh-fruiting plants often form mutualistic associations, making the conservation of frugivore bird communities necessary for the conservation of Mediterranean forests (Telleria *et al.* 2005). Dry-fruiting dominant trees such as oaks are preferentially dispersed by jays *Garrulus glandarius*, which tend to scatter acorns at sites usually favourable to oak regeneration (Gómez 2003; Purves *et al.* 2007; Puerta-Piñero *et al.* 2012b). In turn, the presence of large patches of continuous tall forest within open woodland or shrubland matrices influences the abundance and foraging behaviour of jays (review in Morán-López *et al.* 2015). The potential role of the jay as a keystone species in Mediterranean forests needs to be further investigated, as it is likely to be critical in our understanding of the responses of Mediterranean forests to global change (Valladares *et al.* 2014).

Insectivorous birds have long been regarded as efficient control agents against forest insect pests (Atlegrim 1992). In fact, there have been multiple incentives to install nest boxes to favour them despite the lack of evidence that nest boxes will necessarily increase bird densities or that bird densities influence insect abundance or damage. Some studies suggested that birds play a significant but rather modest role in pest control in Mediterranean forests (Sanz 2001). This result could be explained by the generally low levels of insect herbivory on Mediterranean trees, likely due to compensation mechanisms associated with important stored resources (Díaz *et al.* 2004). Alternatively, this result could be explained by generalised mismatches between tree, insect and bird phenologies, such that birds tend to prey on low-damage stages of insect life cycles (e.g., adult moths instead of caterpillars; García-Navas & Sanz 2011).

9.7 Major Drivers of Finer-scale Variation in Mediterranean Forest Bird Communities

At local scales, bird species diversity and composition vary in space as a result of the fine-scale heterogeneity of Mediterranean landscapes and, in time, as a result of strong landscape dynamics mainly resulting from human activities. We now describe the main drivers of these variations.

9.7.1 Forest Management: The Role of Forest Patch Characteristics

Forest management practices strongly influence critical components of forest bird habitat, such as the vertical structure of the vegetation, the tree species composition and the availability of old trees and snags.

Complex forest vertical structure positively influences Mediterranean forest bird communities (López & Moro 1997; Camprodon & Brotons 2006; Kati *et al.* 2009). In many Mediterranean regions where dense oak forests prevail, understorey clearing is a widespread technique to reduce vegetation, and hence reduce fuel availability to prevent fires (Moreira *et al.* 2011). This practice results in a significant simplification of the vertical structure of the forest, which is even more pronounced when tree thinning is applied. This simplification leads to reduced foraging opportunities and breeding resources for bird species that depend on the understorey (e.g., wren *Troglodytes troglodytes*, robin, blackbird *Turdus merula*) or species that favour bushes (e.g., subalpine warbler *Sylvia cantillans* and Sardinian warbler *S. melanocephala*). However, both understorey clearing and tree thinning tend to temporarily favour open-habitat and mosaic species such as turtle dove *Streptopelia turtur*, mistle thrush *Turdus viscivorus* and cirl bunting *Emberiza cirlus* (Camprodon & Brotons 2006). As a result, tree thinning in pine forests tends to temporarily increase rather than decrease bird species richness at the stand level (Díaz 2006).

Forest tree composition also affects Mediterranean forest bird communities through its influence on forest vegetation structure (Brotons &

Herrando 2001). For example, the vertical structure of pine plantations is simpler than that of natural mixed pine-broadleaved woods or oak-woods, leading to lower forest bird species richness (Díaz 2006; Kati et al. 2006, 2009; Bergner et al. 2015). In the western Mediterranean, pine plantations on formerly arable land are also generally less suitable for Mediterranean shrubland birds, unless pine trees are small or young, but can benefit some specialist forest species of northern origin, like short-toed treecreeper *Certhia brachydactyla* and coal tit *Periparus ater* (Santos et al. 2006; Chapter 10).

Finally, forest age and the diversity of tree microhabitats (deadwood, cavities, mature trees with loose bark) are of particular importance, since old-growth stands provide feeding and nesting places for a number of cavity-dwelling bird species (Regnery et al. 2013; Touihri et al. 2014). In Greece, several old-growth stands have been preserved by local societies, either because they represent sacred groves around churches and chapels, which were preserved by orthodox religious rules since the 15th century, or because these woodlands prevented landslides, erosion and floods (Stara et al. 2012). These locally managed ancient woods can function as 'habitat islands', providing shelter for species that favour old trees, such as cavity-dwelling passerines and woodpeckers (Gil-Tena et al. 2009).

9.7.2 Human Activities and the Role of Landscape Heterogeneity

Human activities including forestry and agro-silvo-pastoral practices, create landscape heterogeneity at different spatial scales. Creating land-scape heterogeneity implies some degree of habitat fragmentation, which can have either negative or positive effects on Mediterranean forest birds, depending on the species considered.

At the patch scale, bird species richness decreases with forest patch size following a nested pattern, so that the bird communities that occupy small patches are nested subsets of the communities that occupy the largest local forest patch. The minimum size of fragments occupied by each species is inversely related to their regional abundance in large forest tracts. As a result, the smallest fragments are occupied by a handful of generalist abundant species of tits and finches, whereas large forest fragments (more than 100 ha) are needed to maintain most forest bird species (Díaz et al. 1998; Santos et al. 2006). Fragmentation effects are strongest towards the south (i.e., species-area relationships are steeper), due to the north-south species richness gradient explained above, and stronger in forest-cropland than in forest-shrubland mosaics (Herrando & Brotons 2002; Santos *et al.* 2006). Habitat fragmentation has been largely exacerbated by road development to facilitate timber extraction. In fact, road development, foreseen to increase by 60% until 2050, has a suite of negative impacts on biodiversity and ecosystem functionality, whilst the biome of Mediterranean forests, woodlands and scrub is among the most fragmented in the world (Ibisch *et al.* 2016).

At the landscape scale, mosaics of forest, shrubland and open land allow for the coexistence of larger numbers of species than the sum of species observed in either forest, shrubland or grassland patches. This phenomenon can be explained by the fact that some species require resources found in distinct land covers, a process known as landscape complementation. At the smallest scale (0.5 ha plots), trees scattered in grassland typical of dehesa and montado systems allow for the coexistence of generalist forest species, such as tits, pigeons or finches, with open-ground birds such as Thekla larks *Galerida theklae* or partridges. At this scale, species richness increases with tree density following a nested pattern (Díaz *et al.* 2013). At larger scales (hundreds of hectares), shrubby or cultivated plots within dehesas, as well as farmhouses, ponds or stone walls, maintain forest or open habitat specialists such as *Sylvia* warblers or corn buntings *Emberiza calandra*, as well as house sparrows *Passer domesticus*, herons or even cormorants. Finally, large-sized endangered species such as Spanish imperial eagles, black vultures, cranes and white-rumped swifts *Apus caffer* depend on land-cover mixes at landscape scales of thousands of hectares, since they are using open woodlands for foraging and surrounding undisturbed forests or reservoirs for nesting and resting (Díaz *et al.* 2013).

9.7.3 Fire Regimes: The Joint Role of Habitat Changes in Time and Space

Fires trigger secondary succession processes for both plant and animal communities, including birds (Prodon & Lebreton 1981; Prodon *et al.* 1984; 1987). Mediterranean forests are generally perceived as highly resilient to fires, thanks to resprouting and seedling mechanisms (Puerta-Piñero *et al.* 2012a). Jacquet and Prodon (2009) assessed the recovery times of both vegetation and bird communities after fire in holm oak forests and found that while vegetation took ca. 50 years to reach pre-fire stages, the bird community took ca. 35 years. The return of many forest bird species is effective as soon as the vegetation profile becomes 'forest-like' (i.e., presents a closed canopy and a clear undergrowth) irrespective of whether the trees have reached their full size. The relatively strong resilience of bird communities can be explained by the strong regeneration capacity of Mediterranean vegetation, but is also due to bird site fidelity (Prodon *et al.* 1987; Pons & Prodon 1996) and the strong ability of birds to recolonise a burnt patch from nearby population sources (Brotons *et al.* 2005). Although Mediterranean forests are generally resilient, regeneration of pre-fire vegetation is not universal and can lead to alternative successional trajectories for bird communities. For instance, relatively young pine forests (especially black pine forests) do not always regenerate well after a crown fire and then get replaced by oak forests, which results in a dramatic change in bird species composition (Zozaya *et al.* 2011). Fire should therefore not unequivocally be seen as a driver of general loss or increase in bird diversity. Moreover, fires also increase the spatial and seasonal heterogeneity of bird communities, which was shown to be higher in burnt than in unburnt patches (Herrando *et al.* 2002, 2003; Sitters *et al.* 2015). Finally, spatial variations in fire extent and intensity greatly contribute to Mediterranean landscape heterogeneity, creating landscape mosaics necessary to maintain bird diversity (Herrando & Brotons 2002; Tews *et al.* 2004; Kati *et al.* 2010; Zozaya *et al.* 2012). Climate changes are therefore likely to induce large-scale indirect effects on birds via large-scale changes in perturbation regimes linked to extreme climate events (Brotons *et al.* 2012).

9.7.4 Land Abandonment

Like fire, land abandonment triggers a secondary succession, ultimately resulting in forest regeneration. Land abandonment has been a key driver of forest and forest bird dynamics in the Mediterranean over the last decennia. The overall effects of land abandonment on bird communities at the north-west rim of the Mediterranean were examined by Sirami *et al.* (2008). They found that woodland and shrubland species showed the strongest increases in occurrence, in contrast to farmland species, for which no change in overall occurrence was detected. Changes in species occurrence were also related to initial landscape composition, with larger increases for species that occur in landscapes initially dominated by woodland or mixed landscapes. Woodland species increased in all landscape types, whereas shrubland species increased only in mixed landscapes. In the eastern Mediterranean, forest encroachment following land abandonment at local scales did not strongly influence bird community structure (Mikulić *et al.* 2014; Dulgerova *et al.* 2015), although increases in diversity and abundance of forest-dwelling species have been reported (Zakkak *et al.* 2014). When examined at a regional cross-national scale, such as in the Balkan Peninsula, agricultural land abandonment has a negative effect on overall bird diversity, but it significantly increases forest bird abundance (Zakkak *et al.* 2015).

Recent results show that forest maturation and forest expansion, mostly linked to land abandonment, have played a critical role in shaping changes in forest bird communities in the Mediterranean region (Gil-Tena *et al.* 2009; Zakkak *et al.* 2015). Forest maturation was a major driver of these dynamics, which is consistent with the fact that most forest bird species in the Mediterranean, as elsewhere in Europe, are strongly associated with advanced forest development stages rather than with initial successional stages typical of young (recently colonised) forests (Blondel & Farré 1988; Suárez-Seoane *et al.* 2002). Mature forest stands are characterised by a more complex forest structure and therefore provide a diversity of microhabitats for species with very different resource needs (Herrando & Brotons 2002; Kati *et al.* 2009). Forest maturation is important in the Mediterranean, because old-growth forests are scarce due to long-lasting human interference.

9.8 Bird Conservation Issues in Mediterranean Forests

As stressed throughout this chapter, the dynamics of most Mediterranean forests are strongly determined by human activities. Biogeography and recent land-use history explain why, in many areas of the Mediterranean region, currently existing forest bird communities are not especially interesting from a conservation viewpoint, because they tend to be dominated by widespread European forest species. Changes from forest to more open habitats, such as mixed arable-grassland or post-fire recovering forests, tend to be associated with a marked increase in the overall conservation value of the bird community (Clavero *et al.* 2011). This is easily explained, because in Europe, early successional bird species are generally more narrowly confined to particular habitat structures or stages of vegetation development than other species are (Blondel & Farré 1988). Important land-cover types for these species are shrublands and agricultural land; intensification of the latter has been the main threat to European birds in recent decades (Donald *et al.* 2001). Disturbed forests, in many instances, tend to be colonised by these early successional species

(Brotons *et al.* 2005), thus inducing an increase in the overall conservation value of the system after fire (Clavero *et al.* 2011) or under moderate disturbance linked to extensive agricultural and livestock uses in agro–silvo-pastoral systems (Díaz *et al.* 2013).

This apparent contradiction between 'naturalness' and conservation value in Mediterranean ecosystems offers a caution against uncritical generalised application of IUCN-type species conservation status based on population trends. Thus, nationally or regionally based categorisations of open habitat species as 'threatened' and of forest species as 'least concern' reflect a necessarily narrow temporal perspective. In these ecosystems, forest bird species have probably experienced large historical reductions in population size but have started to recover in recent decades (Gil-Tena *et al.* 2009). In contrast, historical increases in the populations of open habitat and early successional bird species have recently shifted to population declines due to land-use abandonment. The questions of which time reference we should choose and how we should interpret and respond to recent changes in bird communities associated with increases in fire, land abandonment and changes in agriculture remain open (Díaz & Concepción 2016).

In our opinion, making judgements based only on traditional conservation criteria could lead to misleading decision-making. We need to change our perspective and aim at integrating socio–economic changes for more effective conservation action (see also Chapter 13). Forest systems that need to be maintained through sustained conservation action will likely fail to deliver conservation value in the long term. Therefore, we need to promote transitions to new equilibriums between ecological processes and the new set of socio-economic factors shaping Mediterranean landscapes (Campos *et al.* 2013). A good example of this is the interaction between land abandonment and fire. Wildfire is starting to be used as a management action in protected areas to compensate for vegetation encroachment and favour early successional species, when elsewhere in the Mediterranean region, the current fire regime is creating open habitat in large quantities (Brotons *et al.* 2005). In the same context, subsidies may target specific forestry practices, especially within protected areas or for highly threatened species, but these practices may be difficult to maintain and are likely to fail in periods of economic crisis. Our view is that integrated forestry practices aimed at sustaining socio-economic systems should be developed and assessed for their biodiversity value (Fischer *et al.* 2012; Campos *et al.* 2013, 2014; Díaz *et al.* 2015). Targeting protected areas for management actions that aim at counteracting large-scale socio-economic changes might overlook the fact that these same socio-economic changes could be creating opportunities for conservation elsewhere (i.e., a conservation trap; *sensu* Cardador *et al.* 2015). These reactive strategies aim at ensuring short-term benefits to the threatened species, but it is highly uncertain whether those species would benefit in the long term, especially if financial resources run out.

In 'traditional' anthropogenic landscapes undergoing rapid change, such as Mediterranean landscapes, knowledge of ecosystem states from the recent past can offer a biased, incomplete framework to guide current management of forest systems. The lack of a clear reference state and the high uncertainty of future environmental threats and ecosystem responses make it difficult to determine conservation policy. Mediterranean forests have been strongly modified for centuries, in terms of both distribution and stand structure. Moving towards a better understanding of possible future landscape states, searching for sustainable solutions to maintain landscape heterogeneity and evaluating their long-term implications could help reduce the risk of conservation traps, in which expensive conservation actions target threats derived from socio-economic drivers that are hard to modify (Cardador *et al.* 2015). This approach would help identify opportunities to create transitions from present situations threatening species to new, less-threatening states. A key challenge of such an approach would be to develop interdisciplinary knowledge, so that assumptions of different stakeholders can be discussed and potential consequences of various management plans evaluated. Indeed, is it of paramount importance that new conservation approaches take full account of the socio-economic context of forests both now and in the long term (Fischer *et al.* 2012; Campos *et al.* 2014).

Acknowledgements

This work is a contribution to the projects VULGLO (CGL2010-22180-C03-03), RISKDISP (CGL2009-08430), VEABA (ECO2013-42110-P), FORESTERRA-ERANET project INFORMED and FORESTCAST (CGL2014-59742), funded by the Spanish Ministry of Science and Innovation; REMEDINAL 3 (S2013/MAE-2719), funded by the Comunidad de Madrid; and RECAMAN (NET165602) funded by the Junta de Andalucía. We also thank Jacques Blondel and Luis Maria Carrascal for constructive comments on earlier versions of the chapter.

References

Araújo, M.B., Thuiller, W., Williams, P.H. & Reginster, I. (2005) Downscaling European species atlas distributions to a finer resolution: Implications for conservation planning. *Global Ecology and Biogeography*, **14**, 17–30.

Atlegrim, O. (1992) Mechanisms regulating bird predation on a herbivorous larva guild in boreal coniferous forests. *Ecography*, **15**, 19–24.

Barbet-Massin, M., Thuiller, W. & Jiguet, F. (2012) The fate of European breeding birds under climate, land-use and dispersal scenarios. *Global Change Biology*, **18**, 881–890.

Benito-Garzón, M., Sánchez-de Dios, R. & Sáinz-Ollero, H. (2008) Effects of climate change on the distribution of Iberian tree species. *Applied Vegetation Science*, **11**, 169–178.

Bergner, A., Avcı, M., Eryiğit, H. *et al.* (2015) Influences of forest type and habitat structure on bird assemblages of oak (*Quercus* spp.) and pine (*Pinus* spp.) stands in southwestern Turkey. *Forest Ecology and Management*, **336**, 137–147.

Blondel, J., Aronson, J., Boudiou, J.Y. & Boeuf, G. (2010) *The Mediterranean Basin: Biological Diversity in Space and Time.* Oxford: Oxford University Press.

Blondel, J. & Farré, H. (1988) The convergent trajectories of bird communities along ecological successions in European forests. *Oecologia*, **75**, 83–93.

Brotons, L., de Cáceres, M., Fall, A. & Fortin, M.J. (2012) Modeling bird species distribution change in fire prone Mediterranean landscapes: Incorporating species dispersal and landscape dynamics. *Ecography*, **35**, 458–467.

Brotons, L. & Herrando, S. (2001) Factors affecting bird communities in fragments of secondary pine forests in the north-western Mediterranean basin. *Acta Oecologica*, **22**, 21–31.

Brotons, L., Pons, P. & Herrando, S. (2005) Colonization of dynamic Mediterranean landscapes: Where do birds come from after fire? *Journal of Biogeography*, **32**, 789–798.

Brown, J.H. (1984) On the relationship between abundance and distribution of species. *American Naturalist*, **124**, 255–279.

Campos, P., Caparrós, A., Beguería, S. *et al.* (2014) *RECAMAN: Manufactured and Environmental Total Incomes of Andalusian Forest.* Madrid: CSIC. www.recaman.es/sites/default/files/RECAMAN_SUMMARY_02_04_14.pdf.

Campos, P., Huntsinger, L., Oviedo, J.L. *et al.* (eds.) (2013) *Mediterranean Oak Woodland Working Landscapes: Dehesas of Spain and Ranchlands of California.* New York: Springer.

Camprodon, J. & Brotons, L. (2006) Effects of undergrowth clearing on the bird communities of the Northwestern Mediterranean Coppice Holm oak forests. *Forest Ecology and Management*, **221**, 72–82.

Carbonell, R. & Tellería, J.L. (1998) Increased asymmetry of tarsus-length in three populations of Blackcaps *Sylvia atricapilla* as related to proximity to range boundary. *Ibis*, **140**, 331–333.

Cardador, L., Brotons, L., Mougeot, F. *et al.* (2015) Conservation traps and long-term species persistence in human-dominated systems. *Conservation Letters*, **8**, 456–462.

Carnicer, J., Brotons, L., Sol, D. & De Cáceras, M. (2008) Random sampling, abundance-extinction dynamics and niche-filtering immigration constraints explain the generation of species richness gradients. *Global Ecology and Biogeography*, **17**, 352–362.

Case, T.J. (1996) Global patterns in the establishment and distribution of exotic birds. *Biological Conservation*, **78**, 69–96.

Catalán, B., Saurí, D. & Serra P. (2008) Urban sprawl in the Mediterranean? Patterns of growth and change in the Barcelona Metropolitan Region 1993–2000. *Landscape and Urban Planning*, **85**, 174–184.

Clavero, M., Brotons, L. & Herrando, S. (2011) Bird community specialization, bird conservation and disturbance: The role of wildfires. *Journal of Animal Ecology*, **80**, 128–136.

Colombaroli, D. & Tinner, W. (2013) Determining the long-term changes in biodiversity and provisioning services along a transect from Central Europe to the Mediterranean. *Holocene*, **23**, 1625–1633.

Corvol, A. (1987) *L'Homme aux bois. Histoire des relations de l'homme et de la forêt XVII-XXème siècle.* Paris: Fayard.

Covas, R. & Blondel, J. (1998) Biogeography and history of the Mediterranean bird fauna. *Ibis*, **140**, 395–407.

Devictor, V., van Swaay, C., Brereton, T. *et al.* (2012) Differences in the climatic debts of birds and butterflies at a continental scale. *Nature Climate Change*, **2**, 121–124.

di Castri, R., Hansen, A.J. & Debussche, M. (eds.) (1990) *Biological Invasions in Europe and the Mediterranean Basin.* Dordrecht: Kluwer Academic Publishers.

Díaz, L. (2006) Influences of forest type and forest structure on bird communities in oak and pine woodlands in Spain. *Forest Ecology and Management*, **223**, 54–65.

Díaz, M. (1996) Food choices by seed-eating birds in relation to seed chemistry. *Comparative Biochemistry and Physiology*, **113A**, 239–246.

Díaz, M. (2004) Comunidad de aves de las formaciones arbóreas. In *El Bosque Mediterráneo Andaluz.* Herrera, C.M. (ed.). Sevilla: Estación Biológica de Doñana-Junta de Andalucía, pp. 89–101.

Díaz, M., Asensio, B. & Tellería, J.L. (1996) *Aves Ibéricas. I. No paseriformes.* Madrid: J.M. Reyero Editoral.

Díaz, M., Carbonell, R., Santos, T. & Tellería. (1998) Breeding bird communities in pine plantations of the Spanish plateaux: Biogeography, landscape and vegetation effects. *Journal of Applied Ecology*, **35**, 562–574.

Díaz, M. & Concepción, E.D. (2016) Enhancing the effectiveness of CAP greening as a conservation tool: A plea for regional targeting considering landscape constraints. *Current Landscape Ecology Reports*, **1**, 168–177.

Díaz, M., Concepción, E.D. & Alonso, C.L. (2015) Conservación de la biodiversidad en los sistemas forestales de Andalucía. In *Biodiversidad, Usos del Agua Forestal y Recolección de Setas Silvestres en los Sistemas Forestales de Andalucía.* Campos P. & Díaz, M. (eds.). Memorias científicas de RECAMAN. Vol. 2. Memoria 2.1. Madrid: Editorial CSIC, pp. 7–101.

Díaz, M. & Pulido, F.J. (2009) Dehesas perennifolias de *Quercus* spp. En *Bases Ecológicas Preliminares para la Conservación de los Tipos de Hábitat de Interés Comunitario en España.* Madrid: Dirección General de Medio Natural y Política Forestal, Ministerio de Medio Ambiente, y Medio Rural y Marino.

Díaz, M., Pulido, F.J. & Møller, A.P (2004) Herbivore effects on developmental stability and fecundity of *Quercus ilex*. *Oecologia*, **139**, 224–234.

Díaz, M., Tietje, W.D. & Barrett, R.H. (2013) Effects of management on biological diversity and endangered species. In *Mediterranean Oak Woodland Working Landscapes: Dehesas of Spain and Ranchlands of California*. Campos, P., Huntsinger, L., Oviedo, J.L. *et al.* (eds.). Dordrecht: Springer, pp. 213–243.

Doblas-Miranda, E., Martínez-Vilalta, J., Álvarez, A. *et al.* (2015) Reassessing global change research priorities in the Mediterranean Basin: How far have we come and where do we go from here? *Global Ecology and Biogeography*, **24**, 25–43.

Donald, P.F., Green, R.E. & Heath, M.F. (2001) Agricultural intensification and the collapse of Europe's farmland bird populations. *Proceedings of the Royal Society of London B*, **268**, 25–29.

Dulgerova, S., Gramatikov, M. Pedashenko, H. Vassilev, K. Kati, V. & Nikolov, S.C. (2015) Farmland birds and agricultural land abandonment: Evidences from Bulgaria. *Acta Zoologica Bulgarica*, **67**, 223–234.

Eichhorn, M.P., Paris, P., Herzog, F. *et al.* (2006) Silvoarable systems in Europe – past, present and future prospects. *Agroforestry Systems*, **67**, 29–50.

FAO (2013) The State of Mediterranean Forests. www.fao.org/docrep/017/i3226e/i3226e.pdf.

Fedriani, J. M. & Wiegand, T. (2014) Hierarchical mechanisms of spatially contagious seed dispersal in complex seed-disperser networks. *Ecology*, **95**, 514–526.

Feranec, J., Jaffrain, G., Soukup, T. & Hazeu, G. (2010) Determining changes and flows in European landscapes 1990–2000 using CORINE land cover data. *Applied Geography*, **30**, 19–35.

Fischer, J., Hartel, T. & Kuemmerle, T. (2012) Conservation policy in traditional farming landscapes. *Conservation Letters*, **5**, 167–175.

Fraser, H., Garrard, G.E., Rumpff, L., Hauser, C.E. & McCarthy, M.A. (2015) Consequences of inconsistently classifying woodland birds. *Frontiers in Ecology and Evolution*, **3**, 1–8.

García, C., Moracho, E., Díaz-Delgado, R. & Jordano, P. (2014) Long-term expansion of juniper populations in managed landscapes: Patterns in space and time. *Journal of Ecology*, **102**, 1562–1571.

García-Navas, V. & Sanz, J.J. (2011) The importance of a main dish: Nestling diet and foraging behaviour in Mediterranean blue tits in relation to prey phenology. *Oecologia*, **165**, 639–649.

Gibelin, A.L. & Deque, M. (2003) Anthropogenic climate change over the Mediterranean region simulated by a global variable resolution model. *Climate Dynamics*, **20**, 327–339.

Gil-Tena, A., Brotons, L. & Saura, S. (2009) Mediterranean forest dynamics and forest bird distribution changes in the late 20th century. *Global Change Biology*, **15**, 474–485.

Gómez, J.M. (2003) Spatial patterns in long-distance dispersal of *Quercus ilex* acorns by jays in a heterogeneous landscape. *Ecography*, **26**, 573–584.

Grove, T. & Rackham, O. (2003) *The Nature of Mediterranean Europe: An Ecological History*. New Haven: Yale University Press.

Hagemeijer, E.J.M. & Blair, M.J. (eds.) (1997) *The EBCC Atlas of European Breeding Birds: Their Distribution and Abundance*. London: T. & A.D. Poyser.

Hansson, B., Ljungqvist, M., Illera, J.C. & Kvist, L. (2014) Pronounced fixation, strong population differentiation and complex population history in the Canary Islands blue tit subspecies complex. *PLoS One* 9:e90186.

Herrando, S. & Brotons, L. (2002) Forest bird diversity in Mediterranean areas affected by wildfires: A multi-scale approach. *Ecography*, **25**, 161–172.

Herrando, S., Brotons, L., Estrada, J., Guallar, S. & Anton, M. (eds.) (2011) *Atles dels ocells de Catalunya a l'hivern 2006–2009*. Barcelona: Institut Català d'Ornitologia/Lynx Edicions.

Herrando, S., Brotons, L. & Llacuna, S. (2002) Does fire increase the seasonal variability of bird communities? A case in Mediterranean shrublands. *Revue d'Écologie*, **57**, 151–163.

Herrando, S., Brotons, L. & Llacuna, S. (2003) Does fire increase the spatial heterogeneity of bird communities in Mediterranean landscapes? *Ibis*, **145**, 307–317.

Herrando, S., Llimona, F., Brotons, L. & Quesada, J. (2010) A new exotic bird in Europe: Recent spread and potential range of Red-billed Leiothrix *Leiothrix lutea* in Catalonia (northeast Iberian Peninsula). *Bird Study*, **57**, 226–235.

Herrera, C.M. (1995) Plant-vertebrate seed dispersal systems in the Mediterranean: Ecological, evolutionary, and historical determinants. *Annual Review of Ecology and Systematics*, **26**, 705–727.

Huntley, B., Green, R.E., Collingham, Y.C. & Willis, S.G. (2007) *A Climatic Atlas of European Breeding Birds*. Barcelona: Lynx Edicions.

Ibisch, P.L., Hoffmann, M., Kreft, S. *et al.* (2016). A global map of roadless areas and their conservation status. *Science*, **354**, 1423–1427.

IPCC (2014) *Climate Change 2014: Impacts, Adaptation, and Vulnerability*. Cambridge: Cambridge University Press.

Jacquet, K. & Prodon, R. (2009) Measuring the postfire resilience of a bird-vegetation system: A 28-year study in a Mediterranean oak woodland. *Oecologia*, **161**, 801–811.

Jordano, P. (2013) Fruits and frugivory. In *Seeds: The Ecology of Regeneration in Plant Communities*, 3rd ed. Gallagher, R.S. (ed.). Wallingford, UK: CAB International, pp. 18–91.

Jordano, P., García, C., Godoy, J.A. & García-Castaño, J.L. (2007) Differential contribution of frugivores to complex seed dispersal patterns. *Proceedings of the National Academy of Sciences*, **104**, 3278–3282.

Kark, S. & Sol, D. (2005) Establishment success across convergent Mediterranean ecosystems: An analysis of bird introductions. *Conservation Biology*, **19**, 1341–1678.

Kati, V., Dimopoulos, P., Papaioannou, H. & Poirazidis, K. (2009) Ecological management of a Mediterranean mountainous reserve (Pindos National Park, Greece) using the bird community as an indicator. *Journal for Nature Conservation*, **17**, 47–59.

Kati, V. Poirazidis, K., Dufrêne, M. *et al.* (2010) Towards the use of ecological heterogeneity to design reserve networks: A case study from Dadia National Park, Greece. *Biodiversity and Conservation*, **19**, 1585–1597.

Kati, V. & Sekercioglu, C.H. (2006) Diversity, ecological structure, and conservation of the landbird community of Dadia reserve, Greece. *Diversity and Distributions*, **12**, 620–629.

Keeley, J.E., Bond, W.J., Bradstock, R.A., Pausas, J.G. & Rundel, P.W. (2012) *Fire in Mediterranean Ecosystems: Ecology, Evolution and Management*. Cambridge: Cambridge University Press.

Keenan, T., Serra, J.M., Lloret, F., Ninyerola, M. & Sabaté, S. (2011) Predicting the future of forests in the Mediterranean under climate change, with niche- and process-based models: CO_2 matters! *Global Change Biology*, **17**, 565–579.

Koenig, W.D., Díaz, M., Pulido, F., Alejano, R., Beamonte, E. & Knops, J.M.H. (2013) Acorn production patterns. In *Mediterranean Oak Woodland Working Landscapes: Dehesas of Spain and Ranchlands of California*. Campos, P., Huntsinger, L., Oviedo, J.L. *et al.* (eds.). New York: Springer, pp. 181–209.

López, G. & Moro, M.J. (1997) Birds of Aleppo pine plantations in south-east Spain in relation to vegetation composition and structure. *Journal of Applied Ecology*, **34**, 1257–1272.

Martín, A., Hernández, M.A., Lorenzo, J.A., Nogales, M. & González, C. (2000) *Las palomas endémicas de Canarias*. Santa Cruz de Tenerife: Consejería de Política Territorial y Medio Ambiente del Gobierno de Canarias/SEO-Birdlife.

Mazzoleni, S., di Pasquale, G., Mulligan, M., di Martino, P. & Rego, F. (2004) *Recent Dynamics of Mediterranean Vegetation and Landscape*. Chichester, UK: John Wiley & Sons.

Mercuri, A.M. & Sadori, L. (2014) Mediterranean culture and climatic change: Past patterns and future trends. In *The Mediterranean Sea: Its History and Present Challenges*. Goffredo, S. & Dubinsky, Z. (eds.). Dordrecht: Springer, pp. 507–527.

Metzger, M.J., Bunce, R.G.H., Jongman, R.H.G., Mucher, C.A. & Watkins, J.W. (2005) A climatic stratification of the environment of Europe. *Global Ecology and Biogeography*, **14**, 549–563.

Mikulić, K., Radović, A., Kati, V., Jelaska, S.D. & Tepić, N. (2014) Effects of land abandonment on bird communities of smallholder farming landscapes in postwar Croatia: Implications for conservation policies. *Community Ecology*, **15**, 169–179.

Minnich, R.A. (1983) Fire mosaics in southern California and northern Baja California. *Science*, **219**, 1287–1294.

Mönkkönen, M. (1994) Diversity patterns in Palaearctic and Nearctic forest bird assemblages. *Journal of Biogeography*, **21**, 183–195.

Morán-López, T., Alonso, C.L. & Díaz, M. (2015) Landscape effects on jay foraging behavior decrease acorn dispersal services in dehesas. *Acta Oecologica*, **69**, 52–64.

Moreira, F., Viedma, O., Arianoutsou, M. *et al.* (2011) Landscape-wildfire interactions in southern Europe: Implications for landscape management. *Journal of Environmental Management*, **92**, 2389–2402.

Moreno, G., González-Bornay, G., Pulido, F. *et al.* (2016) Exploring the causes of high biodiversity of Iberian dehesas: The importance of wood pastures and marginal habitats. *Agroforestry Systems*, **90**, 87–105.

Moreno, J.M. & Oechel, W.C. (eds.) (1994) *The Role of Fire in Mediterranean-Type Ecosystems*. New York: Springer-Verlag, Ecological Studies 107.

Mouillot, F., Ratte, J.P., Joffre, R., Mouillot, D., Rambal, S. (2005) Longterm forest dynamic after land abandonment in a fire prone Mediterranean landscape (central Corsica, France). *Landscape Ecology*, **20**, 101–112.

Myers, N., Mittermeier, R.A., Mittermeier, C.G., da Fonseca, G.A.B. & Kent, J. (2000) Biodiversity hotspots for conservation priorities. *Nature*, **403**, 853–858.

Päckert, M., Dietzen, C., Martens, J., Wink, M. & Kvist, L. (2006) Radiation of Atlantic goldcrests *Regulus regulus* spp.: Evidence of a new taxon from the Canary Islands. *Journal of Avian Biology*, **37**, 364–380.

Pausas, J.G. & Vallejo, V.R. (1999) Remote sensing of large wildfires in the European Mediterranean basin. In *The Role of Fire in European Mediterranean Ecosystems*. Chuvieco E. (ed.), New York: Springer-Verlag, pp. 3–16.

Pérez-Tris, J., Bensch, S., Carbonell, R., Helbig, A.J. & Tellería, J.L. (2004) Historical diversification of migration patterns in a passerine bird. *Evolution*, **58**, 1819–1832.

Pías, B., Escribano-Avila, G., Virgós, E., Sanz-Pérez, V., Escudero, A. & Valladares, F. (2014) The colonization of abandoned land by Spanish juniper: Linking biotic and abiotic factors at different spatial scales. *Forest Ecology and Management*, **329**, 186–194.

Pons, P. & Prodon, R. (1996) Short-term temporal patterns in a Mediterranean shrubland bird community after wildfire. *Acta Oecologica*, **17**, 29–41.

Prodon, R., Fons, R. & Athias-Binche, F. (1987) The impact of fire on animal communities in Mediterranean area. In *The Role of Fire on Ecological Systems*. Trabaud, L. (ed.). The Hague: SPB Academic Publishing, pp. 121–157.

Prodon, R., Fons, R. & Peter, A.M. (1984) L'impact du feu sur la vegetation, les oiseaux et les micromamifères dans diverses formations des Pyrénées-Orientales: Premiers résultats. *Revue d'Écologie*, **39**, 129–158.

Prodon, R. & Lebreton, J.D. (1981) Breeding avifauna of a Mediterranean succession: the holm oak and the cork oak series in eastern Pyrenees. Analysis and modelling structure gradient. *Oikos*, **37**, 21–38.

Puerta-Piñero, C., Espelta, J.M., Sánchez-Humanes, B., Rodrigo, A., Coll, L. & Brotons, L. (2012a) History matters: Previous land use changes determine post-fire vegetation recovery in forested Mediterranean landscapes. *Forest Ecology and Management*, **279**, 121–127.

Puerta-Piñero, C., Pino, J. & Gómez, J.M. (2012b) Direct and indirect landscape effects on *Quercus ilex* regeneration in heterogeneous environments. *Oecologia*, **170**, 1009–1020.

Purves, D.W., Zavala, M.A., Ogle, K., Prieto, F. & Rey, J.M. (2007) Environmental heterogeneity, bird-mediated directed dispersal, and oak woodland dynamics in Mediterranean Spain. *Ecological Monographs*, **77**, 77–97.

Regnery, B., Couvet, D., Kubarek, L., Julien, J.F. & Kerbiriou, C. (2013) Tree microhabitats as indicators of bird and bat communities in Mediterranean forests. *Ecological Indicators*, **34**, 221–230.

Rey, P.J. (1995) Spatio-temporal variation in fruit and frugivorous bird abundance in olive orchards. *Ecology*, **76**, 1625–1635.

Rossetti, I. & Bagella, S. (2014) Mediterranean *Quercus suber* wooded grasslands risk disappearance: New evidences from Sardinia (Italy). *Forest Ecology and Management*, **329**, 148–157.

Santos, T., Tellería, J.L., Díaz, M. & Carbonell, R. (2006) Evaluating the environmental benefits of CAP reforms: Can afforestations restore forest bird communities in Mediterranean Spain? *Basic and Applied Ecology*, **7**, 483–495.

Sanz, J.J. (2001) Experimentally increased insectivorous bird density results in a reduction of caterpillar density and leaf damage to Pyrenean oak. *Ecological Research*, **16**, 387–394.

Sanz, J.J. (2002) Climate change and birds: have their ecological consequences already been detected in the Mediterranean region? *Ardeola*, **49**, 109–120.

Seidl, R., Schelhaas, M.-J., Rammer, W. & Verkerek, P.J. (2014) Increasing forest disturbances in Europe and their impact on carbon storage. *Nature Climate Change*, **4**, 806–810.

Sekercioglu, C.H. (2006) Increasing awareness of avian ecological function. *Trends in Ecology & Evolution*, **21**, 464–471.

Sirami, C., Brotons, L., Burfield, I., Fonderflick, J. & Martin, J.-L. (2008) Is land abandonment having an impact on biodiversity? A meta-analytical approach to bird distribution changes in the north-western Mediterranean. *Biological Conservation*, **141**, 450–459.

Sitters, H., Di Stefano, J., Christie, F.J., Sunnucks, P. & York, A. (2015) Bird diversity increases after patchy prescribed fire: Implications from a before-after control-impact study. *International Journal of Wildland Fire*, **24**, 690–701.

Stara, K., Tsiakiris, R. & Wong, J. (2012) Sacred trees and groves in Zagori, Northern Pindos National Park, Greece. In *Sacred Species and Sites*. Pungetti, G.l., Oviedo, G. & Hooke, D. (eds.). Cambridge: Cambridge University Press, pp. 392–396.

Suárez-Seoane, S., Osborne, P.E. & Baudry, J. (2002) Responses of birds of different biogeographic origins and habitat requirements to agricultural land abandonment in northern Spain. *Biological Conservation*, **105**, 333–344.

Tellería, J.L. (1988) Caracteres generales de la invernada de las aves en la península Ibérica. In *Invernada de Aves en la Península Ibérica*. Tellería, J.L. (ed.), Madrid: Sociedad Española de Ornitología, pp. 13–22.

Tellería, J.L. (2001) Passerine birds communities of Iberian dehesas: A review. *Animal Biodiversity and Conservation*, **24**, 67–78.

Tellería, J.L., Asensio, B. & Díaz, M. (1999) *Aves Ibéricas. II. Passeriformes*. Madrid: J.M. Reyero Editoral.

Tellería, J.L., Ramirez, A. & Perez-Tris, J. (2005) Conservation of seed-dispersing migrant birds in Mediterranean habitats: Shedding light on patterns to preserve processes. *Biological Conservation*, **124**, 493–502.

Tews, J., Brose, U., Grimm, V. *et al.* (2004) Animal species diversity driven by habitat heterogeneity/diversity: The importance of keystone structures. *Journal of Biogeography*, **31**, 79–92.

Thirgood, J.V. (1981) *Man and the Mediterranean Forest*. New York: Academic Press.

Touihri, M., Villard, M.A. & Charfi, F. (2014) Cavity-nesting birds show threshold responses to stand structure in native oak forests of northwestern Tunisia. *Forest Ecology and Management*, **325**, 1–7.

Tzanopoulos, J., Kallimanis, A.S., Bella, I., Labrianidis, L., Sgardelis, S. & Pantis, J.D. (2011) Agricultural decline and sustainable development on mountain areas in Greece: Sustainability assessment of future scenarios. *Land Use Policy*, **28**, 585–593.

Valladares, F., Benavides, R., Rabasa, S. *et al.* (2014) Global change and Mediterranean forests: current impacts and potential responses. In: *Forests and Global Change*. Coomes, D.A., Burslem, D.F.R.P. & Simonson, W.D. (eds.), Cambridge: Cambridge University Press, pp. 47–75.

Vannière, B., Colombaroli, D., Chapron, E., Leroux, A., Tinner, W. & Magny, M. (2008) Climate versus human-driven fire regimes in Mediterranean landscapes: The Holocene record of Lago dell'Accesa (Tuscany, Italy). *Quaternary Science Reviews*, **27**, 1181–1196.

Venäläinen, A., Korhonen, N., Hyvärinen, O. *et al.* (2014) Temporal variations and change in forest fire danger in Europe for 1960–2012. *Natural Hazards and Earth System Sciences*, **14**, 1477–1490.

Xystrakis, F., Kallimanis, A.S., Dimopoulos, P., Halley, J.M. & Koutsias, N. (2014) Precipitation dominates fire occurrence in Greece (1900–2010): Its dual role in fuel build-up and dryness. *Natural Hazards and Earth System Sciences*, **14**, 21–32.

Zakkak, S., Kakalis, E., Radović, A., Halley, J.M. & Kati, V. (2014) The impact of forest encroachment after agricultural land abandonment on passerine bird communities: The case of Greece. *Journal for Nature Conservation*, **22**, 157–165.

Zakkak, S., Radovic, A., Nikolov, S.C., Shumka, S., Kakalis, L. & Kati, V. (2015) Assessing the effect of agricultural land abandonment on bird communities in southern–eastern Europe. *Journal of Environmental Management*, **164**, 171–179.

Zozaya, E.L., Brotons, L & Saura, S. (2012) Recent fire history and connectivity patterns determine bird species distribution dynamics in landscapes dominated by land abandonment. *Landscape Ecology*, **27**, 171–184.

Zozaya, E.L., Brotons, L. & Vallecillo, S. (2011) Bird community responses to vegetation heterogeneity following non-direct regeneration of Mediterranean forests after fire. *Ardea*, **99**, 73–84.

10 · *Plantations of Non-native Tree Species*

Opportunities and Limitations for Birds in Intensively Managed Forests

JOHN CALLADINE, MARIO DÍAZ,
LUÍS REINO, DAVID JARDINE
AND MARK WILSON

10.1 Plantation Forest Ecosystems

Plantations of exotic tree species are arguably the most 'unnatural' forest habitats. Not only do tree species originate from areas different to where they are planted, often from different continents and with different supporting and supported biota, but typically such plantations are intensively managed and include rather different structures and levels of structural heterogeneity than are found in more natural forests. These plantations are likely to present different food sources, risks and niches to occupy, and different combinations of these, than are found in other forest types. It might be expected that non-native plantations would be more challenging habitats than natural forests for some forest birds, and also that they would provide opportunities for others, including some facultative forest species. Exotic plantations often include areas that are homogeneous in either tree species composition or age (or both) and can, depending on cropping regime, be subject to intensive management. As a result, some of the opportunities (and limitations) for birds have more in common with agricultural systems than with more natural forests. In this chapter, we describe some forms of management carried out in plantation forests, the resulting structures and the bird assemblages that can be supported by them at different stages of their management, and the issues and opportunities that exotic plantations present for the distribution and conservation of birds in Europe.

The term 'plantation' is typically applied to forests where trees have been established directly by man. There is, however, a continuum, from forests that have resulted from natural processes, to those that include some selective felling, supplementary planting and nurturing of saplings, to those that have been exclusively planted and managed by man. Also, it is often difficult to be definitive about whether (and to what extent) a tree species is non-native in a particular area. Most forests in Europe are modified by humans to some extent, and their current conditions are dependent on past and proposed future management (Kirby & Watkins 2015). This can lead to the introduction or removal of certain tree species and changes in the relative dominance of naturally occurring species. These changes result directly from selective planting, nurturing and harvesting, but can also arise gradually due to differences between tree species in their responses to the ecological effects of forest management (e.g., Urbieta *et al.* 2008). As a result of such management, many semi-natural forests include tree species growing at different locations and altitudes from those at which they would occur under entirely natural circumstances. Plantations can include native species (sometimes creating extensive pure stands that generally do not occur naturally, and often comprising non-local genetic stock); non-locally native species (for example, conifers outside of their naturally occurring altitudinal range); or exotic tree species that are not native to the region, country or even continent where they are planted (Hartley 2002). The selection of tree species for planting, and of cultivars of those species, is driven by eco-nomic and environmental considerations. Where non-native species pro-vide greater or more rapid economic returns or some other strategic resource, or are better suited to the sites available for afforestation, they may be selected in preference to native trees. To increase the likelihood that they will thrive in the environment where they are planted, such species are typically selected from similar bioclimatic zones. Selection often involves trials of different species, provenances and sometimes hybrids, in order to determine productivity as well as resistance and resilience to pests and diseases. Preferred species that are planted also can change over time, depending on the relative demand for different forest products (or other ecosystem services), the economic returns of these products and the prevailing environmental conditions (including climate, pests and diseases). In modern times, most plantations are designed and managed for fast growth and relatively rapid economic returns.

This chapter focuses on 'extreme' plantations, in terms of both the non-native provenance of their tree species and the management regimes applied to them. In some parts of Europe, plantations of non-native species comprise the majority of forest cover. For example, plantations of various kinds account for about 90% of Britain's forest cover (Donald *et al.* 1997; Hartley 2002), and 43% of all woodland cover in Britain in 2010 was coniferous or mostly coniferous (Forestry Commission 2013). Most of these conifer forests were dominated by non-native species originating from western North America (e.g., Sitka spruce *Picea sitchensis*, lodgepole pine *Pinus contorta*, Douglas fir *Pseudotsuga menziesii*) or Eurasia (e.g., Corsican pine *Pinus nigra*, Norway spruce *Picea abies*, larch *Larix* species and cultivars) (Petty & Avery 1990). Elsewhere in Europe, other examples are plantations of black locust *Robinia pseudoacacia* (an American species), which make up 20% of Hungarian forests; plantations of Australasian *Eucalyptus* species, which make up about 10% of Iberian forests; and approximately 600,000 ha of *Pinus contorta* in Sweden.

Many plantations differ from more natural forests in the denser spacing of trees and the comparatively simple structure of forest stands, deriving from uniformity of tree species and/or age. However, some native woodlands can be similarly even-aged at certain stages of their development, particularly in areas where disturbance events such as fires or high winds result in re-establishment of forest over a large area. Previous land-use history can be an important influence on plantation ecosystems. For example, a plantation that replaces established forest (often converting broadleaved forests to conifers) could inherit some of the original forest's biota, though many plantations are established on sites with no recent history of forest (Figure 10.1). In Europe, typical planting habitats include blanket mires, moorland, heath and various types of grassland (Petty & Avery 1990; Stroud *et al.* 1990; Diaz *et al.* 1998; Shochat *et al.* 2001).

The structure of most plantations (in terms of spatial layout, tree density, tree size and foliage characteristics) is predominantly determined by commercial management rather than by natural forest processes. Drivers and constraints of management include markets for timber, pulp and fibre (determining the target stem size of trees to be achieved before harvesting and the frequency of management interventions); the location of processing facilities to deal with extracted timber; risks of windblow (determining where trees are planted and their silviculture) and disease (influencing species, phenotypes and cultivars that are planted); watershed management; rural employment; sport (hunting); and other recreation, such as walking and mountain biking. Some plantation management has taken on board aims and incentives to deliver biodiversity (now an explicit deliverable of the forest industry in many EU countries) as well as tax and carbon-capture benefits. Although many of these economic and social pressures limit the extent to which natural forest

(a)

(b)

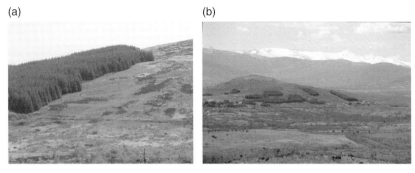

Figure 10.1 Plantations of exotic tree species are often planted on semi-natural open habitats, creating fragmented landscapes. (a) A Sitka spruce plantation replaces moorland in Scotland (Photo: J. Calladine), and (b) pine plantations have been created on grasslands in central Spain (Photo: M. Díaz). The influence on birds of neighbouring habitats can extend beyond the immediate footprint of the plantations.

processes are allowed to operate in most plantations, there is a range of silvicultural systems which can introduce or simulate some natural processes (O'Hara 2001). We describe the contrasting influences on forest structure of three systems for cultivating timber crops, which are not necessarily mutually exclusive (clearcutting and replanting rotations, continuous cover forestry and coppicing), and two further techniques that are applied within a range of silviculture currently used in European plantations (thinning and coppicing). Each has a marked influence on forest age structure, the lower layers of vegetation, soil properties and processes and their patterns of occurrence in forests over space and time. For further discussion of these and other aspects of forest management, see Chapter 13.

10.1.1 Clearcutting and Replanting Rotations

Intensive management based on clearcutting and replanting is typical for plantations dedicated to the production of fibre or pulp, as is the case, for example, for eucalypts and pines in sub-humid Mediterranean regions, and for many conifer plantations in Britain and Ireland. Management of these forests is characterised by high-density planting and fairly short rotations. In most British and Irish conifer plantations, for instance, trees are planted at around 2,500 stems per hectare (Brazier & Mobbs 1993)

(a)   (b)

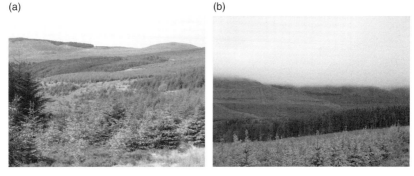

Figure 10.2 Plantations managed by rotations of clearcutting and replanting can create discrete stands, each of which differs from its neighbours in structure and supports a different assemblage of birds. (a) Areas of young growth can support shrubland and other open habitat species, while (b) older stands can progressively support an assemblage of more typically forest birds. Photos: J. Calladine.

and clearfelled on 35- to 60-year rotations. After felling, the remaining brash is either cleared or stacked, and the area is replanted with second or subsequent rotations. Larger plantations can comprise multiple management blocks or coupes. This results in plantations that consist of adjacent but discrete blocks or stands, each of which differs from its neighbours in tree age and forest structure but is internally homogeneous (Figure 10.2). This is an important silvicultural consideration, in order to ensure that stands yield a uniform quality of wood, avoiding or minimising costs imposed by the need for sorting and selecting timber during or after harvesting. Stand sizes vary from less than one hectare to several hundred hectares. Young stands of saplings (in pre-thicket growth stages) are ecologically similar to open habitats, with increasing shrubland characteristics as the saplings grow. At about 12–15 years (for conifers in northwest Europe, but earlier for eucalypt plantations), a thicket stage is formed which can resemble dense shrubland. This develops into pole-stage forest, in which ground vegetation can be severely suppressed and even excluded through a combination of lack of light and smothering with leaf litter (and bark, in the case of eucalypts). Trees in such clearcut rotation systems do not achieve ecological maturity; the size at which they are felled (typically 35–50 cm diameter at breast height) is determined primarily by economic and logistic considerations (e.g., MacDonald *et al.* 2009).

Clearcut forests on even shorter rotations, which are managed to produce biomass energy crops, are currently less widespread. Planting densities in these biomass crops can be even higher than in 'standard' clearcut systems, at up to 5,000 stems per hectare. Clearcutting occurs at 8–20 years, when the stem size is in the order of 10–20 cm diameter at breast height. Faster growing trees are best suited to short-rotation forestry, with ongoing trials in Britain including a number of non-native broadleaved species such as the southern beech *Nothofagus procera* and several *Eucalyptus* species (Harrison 2008). Short rotations of 10–12 years are more widely established in Iberia, where eucalypts (originally introduced to the Iberian Peninsula as ornamental trees in the mid-19th century; Radich 2007) are exploited as raw material for the pulp industry due to fast growing rates under the dominant climate in the west and north-west of the peninsula (Pina 1989). The main *Eucalyptus* species planted in Iberia is *Eucalyptus globulus*, which is by far the most commonly grown eucalypt outside Australia and achieves a mean height of about 20 m during a typical short rotation.

10.1.2 Continuous-Cover Forestry

The term 'continuous-cover forestry' comprises several different silvicultural systems and traditions, including 'low-intensity silvicultural systems', 'uneven-aged silviculture', 'jardinage' and 'plenterwald' (O'Hara 2001; Pommerening & Murphy 2004; Pukkala 2006). Most of these are broadly distinguished from large-scale clearfelling by much greater selectivity at harvesting, ranging from removal of single trees to small felling coupes up to about 0.25 hectares. However, some strip systems of selective harvesting can create larger, though still narrow, coupes, and some shelterwood systems can be extensive (Klopcic & Boncina 2012). Continuous cover forestry is widely established in mainland Europe, and its use is increasingly advocated in Britain. However, its suitability in many parts of north-west Europe may be limited by factors such as risk of windthrow or the feasibility of the required timber extraction operations. Where browsing pressure and seed sources permit, trees can self-seed and naturally regenerate in harvested areas, but in other situations they can be established on site by planting. During closed-canopy management, the principal aims are to maintain close to continuous forest canopy cover across the plantation and, if tree establishment is by natural regeneration, to maintain a crown structure that encourages fruit production. Forest structural diversity is more finely grained than within large-scale clearcut systems, such that relatively small areas within a forest, typical of the size of many passerine territories, can

(a)   (b)

Figure 10.3 Plantations approaching 'commercial maturity'. (a) A continuous-cover system, on the left, with selective felling and a regenerating understorey of young trees can support a relatively diverse assemblage of shrub and forest dependent species. (b) A stand of a similar age, on the right, but managed to be clearcut, can support some forest birds but has a simple single-level canopy, other than where light can penetrate through rides, and support few species typical of lower-level shrubland. Photos: J. Calladine.

encompass a range of structural features, such as multilayered canopies, woody understories, and fallen and standing deadwood. Some trees may be allowed to grow older than they would within a large-scale clearcutting system, with maximum harvestable size being effectively limited by the ease with which they can be felled and extracted with available machinery. Continuous-cover forestry can promote tree species diversity (Pommerening & Murphy 2004), in particular by increasing the establishment of broadleaved trees within conifer plantations (Calladine *et al.* 2015). In general, continuous-cover management is more labour-intensive than clearcutting systems (except during tree establishment) but provides greater opportunities for the growth of large-diameter trees. Continuous-cover forestry will therefore tend to be favoured when and where there is a market for high-quality timber, but it can also be favoured by biodiversity and landscape aesthetic considerations (Figure 10.3). However, the feasibility of this forestry system may be dependent on site condition factors such as wind risk, soil type and regeneration potential.

10.1.3 Thinning

Commercially managed plantations are often managed to achieve high densities of sapling trees, in order to minimise the time taken to canopy closure and to optimise wood quality important for timber and fibre production. High tree-stocking densities suppress competitive ground vegetation that could otherwise compete with growing crop trees for light and nutrients, as well as reduce the proportion of 'juvenile' wood within the final crop (Hamilton 1974). Thinning is the process of removing a portion of the trees from late thicket and older stands, primarily to optimise the quality and marketability of the final crop. Although markets (such as fibre or biomass for fuel) are often found for the products of thinning, the process is primarily aimed at promoting the quality of the remaining trees by increasing girth and improving growth form (e.g., Fuller 2013). Thinning can achieve this, in all harvesting systems, by reducing competition between trees and removing undesirable tree species or individuals with poor growth form (Hamilton 1974). Other reasons for thinning are to reduce risks to tree crops from fire and disease, to carry out targeted management for nature conservation (Macmillan & Marshall 2004; Garcia del Rey et al. 2010) or to improve access for recreation. Removal of canopy cover through thinning can, depending on tree species and thinning regime, increase the light reaching lower vegetation layers for a time, until the canopies of the remaining trees grow into the gaps created by the thinning. This, in turn, can promote or permit the development of ground vegetation and shrub layers (Sakura et al. 1985). However, the extent of early thinning in commercially managed plantations can sometimes be insufficient to have much effect on lower layers of vegetation, especially where the interventions are limited to relatively young crops (Calladine et al. 2009).

10.1.4 Coppicing

Coppicing, as opposed to felling, retains live stumps following harvesting and uses the regeneration of roots and stumps for the successor crops rather than using replacement successor plants. Typically carried out in broadleaf crops, harvesting (of regrown stems) can be done on a much more frequent basis than in alternative forest management regimes, with rotations as short as three years in forests coppiced for biofuel (McKay et al. 2003; Suttie et al. 2009). Traditional coppice rotations can be much longer, but are typically less than 30 years (Rackham 2006). Coppicing can lead to contrasting mosaics of different foliage profiles within a forest, but is probably more widely practiced in semi-natural woodlands

(Fuller & Green 1998), except where short rotations are practised (Dhondt et al. 2004; Sage & Robertson 2006).

10.2 Bird Assemblages

As in all forests, the avifauna supported by a plantation is locally determined by species–specific responses to its structure and floristic composition (Hewson et al. 2011). There can be individual associations between bird species and the size of the forest (Díaz et al. 1998; Magura et al. 2008), management practices, habitats and features in the landscape surrounding the plantation (Gjerde & Sætersdal 1997) and the presence of non-plantation habitats within it (Wilson et al. 2010). Many other, wider-scale factors, including climate, socioeconomics and the regional population sizes of relevant bird species, all potentially influence bird assemblages occupying plantations (Petty & Avery 1990; Patterson et al. 1995; Díaz et al. 1998; Donald et al. 1998; Summers et al. 1999; Poulsen 2002; Fuller & Browne 2003; Santos et al. 2006; Wilson et al. 2006). However, compared to more natural forests, managed plantations often support a relatively impoverished avifauna. The difference in bird species richness between planted and natural pine forests in Spain tends to be greatest in those plantations that are managed more intensively for commercial purposes (Martínez-Jauregui 2016a). A meta-analysis of 76 published studies of birds in commercial plantations found that species richness tended to be greater in natural forests than in plantations, but overall bird abundance did not differ significantly (Nájera & Simonetti 2009). However, both bird species richness and abundance tended to be greater in those plantations with greater structural complexity. An important aspect of structural complexity is the vertical foliage profile; forests of high complexity tend to have multiple vertical layers of vegetation, which may include field layer vegetation, understorey shrubs and different canopy strata.

Despite a reduced avifauna compared to natural forests, commercially managed plantations of exotic conifer species can support a reasonably high diversity of birds in some situations. The communities of birds that can be found within plantations differ markedly between different growth stages (or seres), and although they are generally dominated by common and/or widespread species, they can include nationally important populations of scarce or declining species (e.g., Fuller & Browne 2003 for Britain). Commercially mature conifer plantations in Britain can be important for goshawk *Accipiter gentilis*, capercaillie *Tetrao urogallus*, long-eared owl *Asio otus*, firecrest *Regulus ignicapilla*, crested tit *Lophophanes cristatus* and crossbills *Loxia* spp., though most of these species remain localised in distribution. In areas where plantations form the majority of forest cover (as in many upland parts of Britain and Ireland), plantations of exotic conifers support a considerable proportion of the populations of many common woodland birds, such as song thrush *Turdus philomelos*, goldcrest *Regulus regulus*, siskin *Carduelis spinus* and chaffinch *Fringilla coelebs*. Young growth stages can be important for scarce or declining species, such as hen harrier *Circus cyaneus*, black grouse *Lyrurus tetrix*, short-eared owl *Asio flammeus*, nightjar *Caprimulgus europaeus*, woodlark *Lullula arborea*, tree pipit *Anthus trivialis*, whinchat *Saxicola rubetra*, grasshopper warbler *Locustella naevia* and lesser redpoll *Carduelis cabaret* (Fuller & Browne 2003), though some of these species also remain quite localised. Although forests managed by clearfelling are often regarded as having low conservation value (Brockerhoff *et al.* 2008), some conifer plantations have received statutory nature conservation designation in recognition of their value for protected bird species either at commercial maturity (e.g., for capercaillie; Broome *et al.* 2014) or at younger growth stages (e.g., for hen harrier, nightjar and woodlark; Conway *et al.* 2007; Wilson *et al.* 2009). Some other species of conservation concern (e.g., lesser grey shrike *Lanius minor* and red-footed falcon *Falco vespertinus*) are able to breed in *Robinia* plantations (József 1992), but the relative importance of those plantations in maintaining populations of facultative forest birds such as these remains unclear. In some situations where plantations are used by birds that are typically associated with non-forest habitats, they may even act as ecological traps, providing secure areas for nesting but seemingly poor-quality feeding opportunities (Bártol & Lovászi 2000; Wilson *et al.* 2012a).

Within northern and central Europe, plantations have predominantly been of tree species from northern Eurasia or North America (Holarctic) or of cultivars derived from them. In parts of southern Europe, there are extensive plantations of *Eucalyptus* species of Australasian origin (Radich 2007), which are now also being planted in north-west Europe, especially where biomass energy crops are the intended output (Harrison 2008). While some conifer and *Robinia* plantations can support representative species of regional forest avifaunas, plantations of eucalypts appear to be especially poor habitats for birds. Studies in Portugal, Spain, Brazil and Tanzania suggest that *Eucalyptus* plantations support particularly impoverished bird populations even when compared to plantations of some other locally non-native trees (Barlow *et al.* 2007; John & Kabigumila 2007;

Proença *et al.* 2010; Calvino-Cancela 2013). Comparisons of Iberian eucalypt plantations with nearby native forests (either pine or oak woods), agro-forest systems (Portuguese *montados* or Spanish *dehesas*) and plantations of other tree species found them to support a very restricted avifauna, in terms of both species richness and abundance (Pina 1982; Santos & Álvarez 1990; Tellería & Galarza 1990; Araújo 1995). In contrast to conifer and *Robinia* plantations, very few breeding species were detected in eucalypt plantations that were older than about 12 years. The degree of exoticness of tree species in a forest stand probably affects the bird assemblages it supports. In the Czech Republic, the differences in bird species between stands of *Robinia* and native oak were greater than those between Corsican pine and native Scots pine (Hanzelka & Reif 2016). *Robinia* is native to North America, while the native distribution of Corsican pine is reasonably close to the Czech Republic. Some initial assessments of birds using small *Eucalyptus* plantations in England similarly found that their avifauna was impoverished compared to some nearby plantations of non-native pine. Although they still included a few species of conservation importance, these were invariably present at lower densities than in plantations of other species, and the extent to which the birds in and around the eucalypts were making active use of resources in these forests is unclear (Calladine & Bray 2011). As well as having low structural diversity (in common with most intensively managed plantations), eucalypts are likely to support relatively few invertebrates (reducing food availability for insectivorous birds) due to effective physical and chemical defences. They also have a particularly sparse ground flora and soil fauna due to suppression of plant growth by the bark and leaves shed by eucalypt trees (El-Darier 2002; Fikreyesus *et al.* 2011; de la Hera *et al.* 2013; Aslam *et al.* 2015).

10.2.1 Young Growth Stages

All forests are dynamic habitats, with birds shifting their local distributions and abundances as conditions become less or more suitable for them. In managed plantations, the effects of management for timber production on bird populations can greatly outweigh the effects of natural processes. Most plantations lack ecologically mature forest stands, as opposed to commercially mature stands, in which the trees are of sufficient size to be harvested. They can, however, include extensive areas of young trees (pre-thicket and thicket growth stages) that, in terms of habitats for birds, are essentially shrublands. Extensive blocks of young growth stage forest occur when large plantations are first established and, in plantations managed by clearcutting and restocking, at the start of each rotation. These support a distinct assemblage of birds, including species of conservation interest (Paquet *et al.* 2006).

The breeding bird communities of young plantations, up to the thicket stage, are often comparable with those of scrub and more open habitats. Areas of low shrubs or young trees are important habitats, notably (but not exclusively) for long-distance migrant passerines (Helle & Fuller 1988; Fuller 2012). The typical breeding birds of open ground and/or shrubland have been recorded during studies of pre-thicket conifer plantations in Scotland (Moss *et al.* 1979), Wales (Bibby *et al.* 1985), Ireland (Wilson *et al.* 2006), France (Marion & Frochot 2001), Portugal (Reino *et al.* 2009) and Spain (Rey Benayas *et al.* 2010). Frequently recorded species in north-west Europe included willow warbler *Phylloscopus trochilus*, wren *Troglodytes troglodytes*, tree pipit, meadow pipit *Anthus pratensis*, whitethroat *Sylvia communis*, grasshopper warbler, bullfinch *Pyrrhula pyrrhula*, whinchat, lesser redpoll, linnet *Carduelis cannabina*, reed bunting *Emberiza schoeniclus* and stonechat *Saxicola torquatus*. The use of young conifer plantations by birds in winter has been less studied than during the breeding season. However, reed bunting and bullfinch were more abundant in winter than they were in the breeding season in pre-thicket conifer plantations in south-west Scotland, an area where both species are present throughout the year (Calladine *et al.* 2013). This suggests local dispersal by some species into shrub-dominated habitats at that time of year.

Other species that can thrive in young pre-thicket plantations include black grouse, hen harrier and short-eared owl. The extent and distribution of pre-thicket plantations influence the suitability of this habitat for some species. For example, the smallest individual patch of young forest occupied by breeding short-eared owls in south-west Scotland was 62 ha (Shaw 1995) and by black grouse in Scotland and northern England about 200 ha (except where a similar total area of suitable habitat was available in combination with adjacent open habitats) (Garson & Starling 1990; Haysom 2002). Tree pipits breeding within young restocked plantations in the south-east of England occurred at highest densities when suitable coupes were located within the largest plantation forest blocks, indicating that the total extent of suitable habitat available at a local or regional scale influenced the use of that resource by a species at the site level (Burton 2007). However, as well as nesting in larger stands, hen harriers in Ireland and western Scotland frequently nest in small pre-thicket stands of just a few hectares (Haworth & Fielding 2009; Wilson *et al.* 2009).

The distribution of young growth stage trees within plantations changes as crops grow, are harvested and are restocked. 'Shrubland' birds become displaced as trees grow and canopies close, with birds adapted to more open, scrub-dominated habitats peaking and declining earlier than those suited to denser scrub-woodland. For black grouse in northern Britain, displacement occurs at 12–20 years of age (Pearce-Higgins *et al.* 2007; White *et al.* 2013), while at lower altitudes in southern Britain, tree pipit densities start to decline in plantations older than six years (Burton 2007). Short-eared owls do not use plantations after canopy closure (Shaw 1995), and although hen harriers have been known to nest in the canopies of post-thicket stands (Scott *et al.* 1993; Sim *et al.* 2007), such stands are less useful for both nesting and foraging than areas of clearcut and pre-thicket growth stages (Madders 2000; Redpath *et al.* 2002; Wilson *et al.* 2009). Several species occur in both pre-thicket and post-thicket plantations. Some of these can be more abundant in young growth stages, while others are more numerous in older plantations. For example, Calladine *et al.* (2013) found that wren, willow warbler and lesser redpoll were 18%–66% more abundant in young than relatively old plantations, whereas robin *Erithacus rubecula*, blackbird *Turdus merula* and chaffinch were 76%–96% more abundant in older plantations.

At least in some situations, the number of shrubland birds and species occurring in young second-rotation plantations may be greater than in newly afforested sites (Bibby *et al.* 1985; Sweeney *et al.* 2010). This could be due to a relative lack of woodland and shrubland habitats in the vicinity of many newly afforested sites, and therefore a lack of birds that are associated with those habitats within a distance from which they are readily capable of dispersing. Second and subsequent rotation plantings usually form part of a mosaic of differently aged management coupes. This is because, in all but the smallest plantations, harvesting and replanting take place over years or decades and are often a more or less continuous process. Furthermore, changes in soil conditions and associated ground vegetation of afforested sites after three or more decades under the first rotation of crop trees may create more suitable conditions for shrubland species (Sweeney *et al.* 2010). Some birds of more open habitats, such as black grouse, short-eared owl, meadow pipit and skylark *Alauda arvensis*, are likely either to re-colonise second-rotation plantings at lower densities or to abandon forests after the first rotation. Possible reasons for this include the displacement of these birds by commercially mature forest plantations (leading to a reduced source population from which to colonise newly created open habitats), increased risk (actual or perceived) of predation (predator density and activity can be higher in and around plantations than in open habitats; Hancock & Avery 1998; Smedhaug *et al.* 2002) and, particularly for predators, intra-guild competition from species that have colonised the new forests, for example goshawks (Petty *et al.* 2003; Sergio & Hiraldo 2007). Plantations can also host higher densities of ticks than are found in some open habitats, such as peatlands (Gilbert 2013). Tick infestation, especially on chicks of ground-nesting birds (Newborn *et al.* 2009), may act as a further deterrent to recolonisation of second and subsequent rotation plantations. Second and subsequent rotation plantings can provide habitat suitable for birds of open and shrubland habitats, but the surrounding landscape and its fauna will often have undergone extensive changes since a site was originally planted. Nevertheless, some species which are typical of more open habitats readily re-colonize clearfelled plantations. Such habitats can support important populations of species of conservation concern, such as nightjar (Langston *et al.* 2007), woodlark (Bowden 1990) and hen harrier (Wilson *et al.* 2009). The dispersal capability of an individual species is an important factor in determining its likelihood of colonising temporarily available habitats created by clearcutting and restocking (Baillie *et al.* 2000; Bailey 2007).

10.2.2 Age and Structural Heterogeneity in Plantations

The development of native trees and shrubs within or adjacent to a plantation can enhance its bird diversity and be an effective mechanism for increasing the value of otherwise commercially managed plantations for nature conservation (Bibby *et al.* 1989; Barrientos 2010; Wilson *et al.* 2010; Calladine *et al.* 2013). The responses of birds to the development of shrubs within or by plantations can vary according to the habitat preferences of individual species. Species that have a high affinity for shrubland habitats may gravitate towards shrub-dominated areas. Other species that are more associated with woodland or woodland edge habitats may respond by exploiting additional nearby shrub habitats and associated resources, allowing them to increase in number along the edges of plantations (Imbeau *et al.* 2003; Calladine *et al.* 2013). The size and shape of plantations, and the distribution of non-crop features within them, will have both positive and negative effects, depending on how individual species exploit those features.

Where plantation management aims for more uneven-aged and complex-structured stands (such as through continuous-cover forestry), young trees tend to be distributed at a finer patch scale through the forest. They occur as an understorey beneath older trees and in relatively small felled areas where trees have seeded and regenerated or else been planted. This can result in greater stand-level structural diversity than in plantations managed by clearcutting, but without the extensive 'shrublands' of the thicket and pre-thicket growth stages. Studies of birds in semi-natural forests that are either managed by clearcutting or selectively felled to maintain uneven-aged stands with near continuous cover have identified potential conflicts of interest between management for mature forest birds and maintenance of habitats for birds of woody, early successional communities (Costello *et al.* 2000; Thompson & DeGraaf 2001; Gram *et al.* 2003).

A study in Britain compared breeding bird abundances in plantations dominated by non-native Sitka spruce that were managed either as continuous-cover forestry or through clearcutting rotations and identified some differences between them (Calladine *et al.* 2015). Although the shrub understorey of continuous-cover plantations supported densities of some 'shrubland' species comparable to those found in the young growth stages of plantations managed by clearcutting, other species reached higher levels of abundance in the young growth stages of more extensive even-aged plantations. For example, willow warbler and lesser redpoll were, respectively, 49% and 60% less abundant in understorey shrub than in thicket and younger growth stage plantation rotations. Overall, however, species richness was greatest in continuous-cover plantations with shrub understorey (followed by continuous-cover forests without shrubs, then young growth stage clearfell plantations and, finally, older clear-felled plantations approaching commercial maturity). Conversely, species richness throughout the whole harvest cycle of non-native Norway spruce stands in the Belgian Ardennes was found to be greater in forests managed on clearcut rotations than in stands managed as continuous-cover forests. There was little difference in bird communities between management treatments in older growth stages, but several open habitat and shrubland species present in young restocked areas after clearfelling were absent from the continuous cover forests (du Bus de Warnaffe & Deconchat 2008).

The atmospheric nitrogen-fixing ability of *Robinia* can lead to an enhanced shrubby understorey within plantations that can in turn support an enhanced assemblage of shrub-foraging birds, where this was studied in the Czech Republic. Comparisons were made with particularly homogeneously structured forests of native species, however, and despite a greater structural diversity of the non-native plantations, that did not necessarily translate into differences in birds species richness and community assemblages, other than the occurrence of some shrub foragers such as blackcap and chiffchaff (Hanzelka & Reif 2016).

10.2.3 Post-thicket or Mature Plantations

As plantations mature, species more typical of forests become predominant. Older plantations can support a number of 'mature forest' birds (Petty & Avery 1990; Marion & Frochot 2001). However, the potential of most plantations harvested by clearcutting to provide habitat similar to more natural forests for these species is limited by the fact that forests are typically felled before understorey vegetation has had much chance to develop. Approaches such as continuous-cover forestry, which promote structural diversity in plantations, can increase their capacity to support mature forest birds. As noted above, continuous cover can also support relatively high levels of broadleaved trees, which can increase the diversity and abundance of some bird species. A diverse mix of tree species can increase bird diversity through increased availability of food (e.g., seeds and invertebrates) in forest canopies with a more complex structure (Donald et al. 1998; Brotons & Herrando 2003).

Tree and forest structure, which in plantations is heavily influenced by silvicultural management, can also affect the suitability of a forest for different bird species. In Scotland, plantations of native Scots pine (and also those dominated by exotic conifer species) differ from nearby ancient native pine woods in having higher and less variable tree densities, less developed and less rounded canopy crowns, more homogeneous structure and a field layer dominated by needle litter and/or bryophytes rather than ericaceous dwarf shrubs (Summers et al. 1999b). The average density of crested tits in these plantations was about 10 times lower than in native woodlands. Availability of ground vegetation and standing deadwood were the main factors limiting crested tit numbers in plantations (Summers et al. 1999a; Summers 2000). Although some plantations include relatively high volumes of deadwood, especially where they have not been thinned or affected by windthrow, snags of suitable size and locations for use as nest sites by crested tits are normally absent. Forest structure can also play a role in determining whether plantations are suitable for breeding by large tree-nesting birds. For example, goshawks in Britain mostly breed in conifer plantations (Balmer et al. 2013), where they generally require good aerial access and space around the nest where young birds can practice flying (Petty 1989; Hardey et al. 2006).

Other large raptors are likely to have similar requirements. Tall and fast-growing stands of eucalypts (which are otherwise rather poor for birds) can provide large trees suitable for species such as Bonelli's eagle *Aquila fasciata*, Iberian imperial eagle *Aquila adalberti* and goshawk, especially where there are no other large trees available nearby (Onofre 1990; Luís Palma and Juan Carlos Epifanio, pers. comm.). However, the usefulness of these plantations to large raptors is probably restricted to nest site provision, as hunting potential is very limited (as noted above, they can support very limited numbers of birds in Europe).

Thinning of closed-canopy plantations managed by clearcutting can increase light penetration and shrub-layer development (Summers *et al.* 1999b; Broome *et al.* 2014). This, in turn, can potentially increase their value for forest birds (Fuller 2013), as described above in relation to plantations managed for continuous cover. Some studies have found that thinning has a positive influence on birds (for example, an increase in the abundance of blue chaffinch *Fringilla teydea* on Gran Canaria; Garcia-Del-Rey *et al.* 2010). However, no such effect was found in commercially managed plantations in Scotland, where thinning tends to be aimed at maximising crop output while maintaining suppression of potentially competitive ground vegetation (Calladine *et al.* 2009). Thinning for conservation purposes does have the potential to improve the shrub layer of closed-canopy forests, but evidence for its effectiveness in European forests is, as yet, rather limited (Fuller 2013).

Tree species composition is an important factor in determining the suitability of forests for different bird species (e.g., Hewson *et al.* 2011). It might be assumed that plantations of native tree species would tend to support higher abundance and diversity of birds than those of exotic trees. However, a comparison of plantations of exotic Sitka spruce and native ash *Fraxinus excelsior* in Ireland (a country with a restricted and generalist forest avifauna) found no differences in the species assemblages supported by either forest type across a wide range of taxa, including birds (Wilson *et al.* 2006). In Britain (also with a relatively restricted forest avifauna), there were no overriding differences in bird species richness between stands of Sitka spruce and native trees (Quine & Humphrey 2010). An assessment of bird-foraging preferences in a mixed plantation in northern England (Peck 1989) found that European larch *Larix decidua*, sycamore *Acer pseudoplatanus* and Scots pine (all not native to England) tended to be selected in preference to native trees (e.g., oak *Quercus* spp., rowan *Sorbus aucuparia*, ash) and other non-native trees (e.g., western hemlock *Tsuga heterophylla*, Norway spruce). The inclusion of non-native tree species within a plantation need not prevent it from being a valuable habitat for birds (Baguette *et al.* 1994). Even within an already forested landscape, the introduction of non-native species can influence the diversity of birds present. The introduction of spruce plantations within native Scots pine forests in western Norway reduced local bird diversity (the number of species found within the spruce plantations was less than that within the native pine stands), but at a landscape scale species richness actually increased (Gjerde & Sætersdal 1997). The spruce plantations were dominated by generalist bird species (e.g., woodpigeon *Columba palumbus*, sparrowhawk *Accipiter nisus*, magpie *Pica pica*, coal tit *Periparus ater*, but also nutcracker *Nucifraga caryocatactes* and lesser whitethroat *Sylvia curruca*), while some species were found mostly in the native pine forests (e.g., capercaillie, redstart *Phoenicurus phoenicurus*, pied flycatcher *Ficedula hypoleuca*, tree pipit and wryneck *Jynx torquilla*). Interestingly, however, mosaic areas (of both native pine and spruce plantation) supported a range of species not found in pure blocks of either native or non-native trees alone (e.g., chiffchaff *Phylloscopus collybita*, icterine warbler *Hippolais icterina*, grey-headed woodpecker *Picus canus* and tawny owl *Strix aluco*). The introduction of blue spruce *Picea pungens* stands, a tree native to North America, to expand remaining native forest patches of Norway spruce in the Czech Republic influenced the behaviour of Tengmalm's owl *Aegolius funereus*, apparently in response to contrasting predation risks within the different stands (Zárybnická *et al.* 2015). Nest-predation risk (predominantly by pine marten *Martes martes*) was lower within stands of blue spruce, while the predation risk of roosting adults (by avian predators) was lower in old Norway spruce stands. The introduction of forest stands with contrasting structures into otherwise naturally forested areas appears to offer opportunities for some species to exploit niches resulting from the juxtaposition of different forest types, though this is likely to be as much a result of different forest ages and management as of the introduction of non-native tree species *per se*.

There is also an interesting example of a bird species favoured by non-native trees having a positive effect on nearby native forest habitats. The Eurasian jay *Garrulus glandarius* is a keystone species for oak dispersal and regeneration due to its scatter-hoarding of acorns (Bossema 1979; Gómez 2003; Purves *et al.* 2007). The abundance and foraging behaviour of this species is positively affected by the presence of large patches of tall forest within habitat matrices (e.g., forest-shrub-pasture mosaics) (Andrén 1992; Pons & Pausas 2008; Puerta-Piñero *et al.* 2012; Morán-López *et al.* 2015), especially at the fringes of its geographical range (Santos *et al.* 2002; Lundberg *et al.* 2008). Further, oak seedlings recruit in greater numbers under pine than under oak canopies or in open sites due to lower post-dispersal seed predation by mice and boar *Sus scrofa* and reduced susceptibility to summer drought (Puerta-Piñero *et al.* 2007). Long-term management or recovery of oak forests, at least in dry Mediterranean open areas, may benefit from a transitional stage of pine growth (including non-natives), after which pines can be cleared to allow the development of oak-dominated forests from the high densities of oak seedlings established under the pine canopy (Ruiz-Benito *et al.* 2012). Managing for keystone bird dispersers in forests could prove important in making some forests resilient in Mediterranean habitats in the face of ongoing global change (Valladares *et al.* 2014).

10.3 Influences on Bird Distribution and Conservation Issues

Plantations, including those of non-native tree species, can contribute to bird conservation by providing habitat required by some forest specialists, facilitating connectivity between existing patches of other forest types and, at least on a temporary or intermittent basis, creating areas of shrublands. On the other hand, they can also reduce and fragment valuable non-forest habitats and native forests, in situations where these are replaced with exotic tree species. Moreover, positive and negative influences of a plantation can extend beyond that of its immediate footprint.

10.3.1 Forest Expansion

Most of the bird species found in plantations tend to be species that would normally be found in woodlands and other habitats in the surrounding landscape (Diaz *et al.* 1998). In Britain, for example, turtle dove *Streptopelia turtur*, firecrest, marsh tit *Poecile palustris*, willow tit *Poecile montanus* and lesser whitethroat occur locally in some exotic plantations in the south and east (where their distribution is concentrated), but are typically absent from plantations in other regions. Similarly, some species that are restricted to northern Britain (e.g., capercaillie and crested tit) occur in plantations only in areas where they occur in native woodlands, with the result that plantations do not effectively increase the geographical range of these birds (Balmer *et al.*

2013). The bird communities of plantations tend to follow the same general patterns of occurrence as are apparent for the wider forest avifauna across Europe (Fuller & Browne 2003). In general, bird species richness declines from east to west (Mönkkönen 1994), and is especially poor in Britain and Ireland due to the additional influence of insularity (Fuller et al. 2007). Within Iberia, as another example, plantation avifauna reflects the more general distributions of birds as they are influenced by the Atlantic and Mediterranean climates (Díaz et al. 1998; Martínez-Jauregui et al. 2016b).

Although many aspects of the bird communities that are supported by exotic plantations reflect their geographic locations, a few species have expanded their range because of the particular environments created by non-native tree species. In Belgium, the introduction of stands of non-native spruce added new species to an otherwise native broadleaved forest landscape, including nutcracker *Nucifraga caryocatactes*, goldcrest, common crossbill *Loxia curvirostra* and crested tit (Baguette et al. 1994; du Bus de Warnaffe & Deconchat 2008). In modern-day Britain and Ireland, indigenous coniferous forests are restricted to fragments in the Highlands of Scotland. However, plantations of non-native conifers have become extensive over the past century and continue to expand in total area and range. Common crossbills, arboreal granivores that are specialised to forage on seeds from the cones of coniferous trees, were formerly scarce over much of Britain and Ireland. A recent atlas survey found them in 35% of the 10 km squares covering Britain and Ireland, with their distribution broadly reflecting the distribution of coniferous plantations and representing an increase in range of 331% from 1970 to 2010 (Figure 10.4) (Balmer et al. 2013). Siskin, another specialist of coniferous forests, though not as exclusively restricted to this habitat as crossbills, had similarly expanded its range (measured by occupancy of 10 km squares) by 166% across Britain and Ireland over the same 40-year period (Balmer et al. 2013). Both species now occupy plantations in extensive tracts of land where conifers were absent in historical times, and also show marked regional population fluctuations in response to inter-annual variation in the cone crop of these plantations. The establishment of conifer plantations is likely to have allowed some other species, such as goldcrest and coal tit, which can be especially abundant in this habitat, to increase their British and Irish populations. However, absolute range expansions in response to the establishment of plantations are less obvious for these species (Balmer et al. 2013) due to their frequent occurrence in other woodland types.

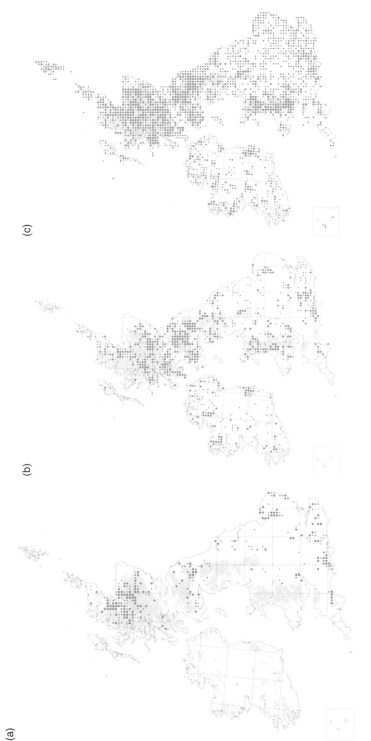

Figure 10.4 Common crossbill *Loxia curvirostra* breeding range has expanded in Britain and Ireland in response to the expansion and maturation of exotic conifer plantations. (a) Dots show occupied 10 km squares in 1968–1972; (b) 1988–1991; and (c) 2008–2011. Shading indicates 'uplands' with altitude at least 200 m. Increased dot size represents increasing evidence for breeding, the largest being confirmed. Note that in the 2008–2011 map, the smallest dots show non-breeding presence only, a category not included in the other maps (after Sharrock 1976, Gibbons *et al.* 1993, Balmer *et al.* 2013; maps reproduced with permission of the British Trust for Ornithology).

(a)　(b)　(c)

An interesting example of how crossbills exploit exotic coniferous crop species is the way two closely related types in Scotland, common crossbill and Scottish crossbill *Loxia scotica*, use them. The endemic Scottish crossbill evolved in relative isolation in the remnant Scots pine forests of the Scottish Highlands with larger bills that are better able to exploit those trees' cones (Nethersole-Thompson 1975). The more widespread common crossbill, with its finer bill, is better adapted to exploit the cones of spruce trees (in Europe, Norway spruce). Where both forms occur in Scotland, Scottish crossbills tended to be found more frequently in plantations of lodgepole pine, while common crossbills tended to occur more frequently in Sitka spruce, even though both Scots pine (native stands and plantations) and Norway spruce (plantations only) were available and producing cones. Although the variation in preference for cone structure between these forms appears to be related to bill size, both forms favoured cones with finer scales than those of their native forage species (Summers & Broome 2012).

For the majority of forest birds, the main positive influence of plantations is through the expansion and re-establishment of forest habitats in areas where they would previously have been present, although the avifaunas of these plantations may be somewhat impoverished and different compared to those of native forests. In Britain and Ireland regionally, and even nationally, important populations of some species are associated with plantations of non-native conifers, including those of breeding goshawk and honey buzzard *Pernis apivorus*, and wintering woodcock *Scolopax rusticola* (Balmer *et al.* 2013). It is unlikely, however, that these species genuinely favour plantations of non-native species over natural forests. Rather, plantations probably provide these species with extensive tracts of habitat in areas where they have few alternatives. The role of plantations in re-establishing forest cover, and associated forest avifaunas, is most clear in areas that have been severely denuded of natural forest cover, such as Britain and, even more markedly, Ireland (Wilson *et al.* 2006). A still more extreme example of such an area is Iceland, where the establishment of forest plantations since the 1950s, often with non-native species, has resulted in the colonisation of birds that were previously absent from the island, including blackbird, siskin and goldcrest, as well as an increase in redwings *Turdus iliacus* (Stefansson & Bjarnadottir 2005; Jonsson *et al.* 2006; Prainsson *et al.* 2013).

10.3.2 Impacts of Plantations on Other Habitats

Although plantations can create habitats for some forest and shrubland birds, they can replace and impact upon other habitats of conservation importance for birds and other taxa. This can include the replacement of natural or semi-natural forests, resulting in multi-scale changes in the forest avifauna (e.g., Gjerde & Sætersdal 1997). Also, plantations have frequently been established in open and semi-natural habitats (typically moorland, heathland, grassland and shrubland), typically reducing or eliminating the original nature conservation value of those habitats (Petty & Avery 1990; Stroud et al. 1990; Díaz et al. 1998; Shochat et al. 2001; Hancock et al. 2009; Wilson et al. 2012b).

The relative abundance of tall forest specialist, shrubland specialist and forest generalist species varies latitudinally in Europe (see Chapter 5). In southern Europe, species linked to shrubby and open patches are usually of a Mediterranean origin, whereas species depending on full-grown mature forests generally derive from the temperate communities that remained in the Pleistocene forest refuges of central and southern Europe (see Chapters 2 and 9). Consequently, the birds available to colonise plantations in some Mediterranean areas are likely to be drawn from relatively impoverished communities of forest birds. At the same time, these plantations could be replacing relatively rich bird communities of high conservation value for shrubland and steppe bird species (Díaz et al. 1998; Reino et al. 2009; Rey Benayas et al. 2010). The establishment of plantations on natural and semi-natural open and shrubland habitats is therefore likely to have more negative consequences in southern Europe than in the north (Santos et al. 2006; Reino et al. 2009).

In addition to the direct replacement of habitats, the influence of plantations on birds can extend beyond the footprint of the plantation itself, particularly in adjacent non-forest habitats. Fragmentation of open habitats due to afforestation can be associated with increased real and perceived risks of predation (Stroud et al. 1990; Hancock et al. 2009; Reino et al. 2009, 2010; Wilson et al. 2012a). Planting can cause changes in populations of birds and other taxa supported by the remaining adjacent open habitats, through shading and changes in use of that land (Newton et al. 1982; Marquiss et al. 1978, 1985; Smith & Charman 1988; Madders & Walker 2002; Bieringer & Zulka 2004). Changes in water quality may also be associated with expansion of forestry in terms of sediment load, acidification and physical alteration of water courses that can lead to changes in hydrology, and in the birds and other taxa supported by mires, rivers and other wetland habitats (Ormerod & Tyler 1989; Fox & Bell 1994; Giller & O'Halloran 2004).

In Britain, the most extensive semi-natural habitat to have been replaced by plantations of non-native conifers has been moorland, a cultural plagioclimax vegetation that occurs on peat-based and other acidic soils in areas of high precipitation. Nearly all British moorland lies below the natural tree line, but a long history of anthropogenic deforestation, grazing and burning has created extensive open habitats dominated by graminoid and ericaceous vegetation (Smout 2005; Brooker 2011) that supports a unique community of breeding birds characterised by relatively high densities of breeding waders, gamebirds, raptors and some passerines (Thompson *et al.* 1995). In Galloway (south-west Scotland) it was estimated that about 5,000 pairs of breeding curlews *Numenius arquata* were directly displaced by afforestation of moorland with conifer plantations during the second half of the 20th century (Ratcliffe 2010). In addition to direct habitat loss, proximity to plantations has also been associated with declining populations, lower densities and reduced breeding success of curlews, with predation by predators harboured in small plantations considered a plausible causal mechanism (Douglas *et al.* 2013). Population densities and breeding success of ground-nesting moorland waders, gamebirds and passerines can be limited by predators (Thirgood *et al.* 2000; Amar *et al.* 2008; Baines *et al.* 2008; Park *et al.* 2008; Fletcher *et al.* 2010), which, in turn, can be harboured in even small plantations. Consequently, the surrounding land may be avoided by birds that perceive them as likely sources of predators. Reduced breeding density and the success of some moorland breeding waders have been associated with proximity to forest edges (Avery 1989; Stroud *et al.* 1990; Parr 1992; Finney *et al.* 2005), and similar patterns have been found for other bird species of open habitats (Shochat *et al.* 2001; Buchanan *et al.* 2003; Reino *et al.* 2009). In addition to increased levels of predation (or perceived risk of predation), suggested mechanisms for this relationship include the drying of mires and other vegetation modifications (Lavers & Haines-Young 1996), and potentially enhanced tick infestation (Wilson *et al.* 2013). Greenshank *Tringa nebularia*, however, is thought to be a species that is more effective at driving off predators than some other wader species that breed on moorland, and typically breeds within forests across much of its range (Nethersole-Thompson & Nethersole-Thompson 1979), even in open areas within a few conifer plantations in Scotland. This probably explains a lack of apparent effects of proximity to plantation edges for greenshanks breeding on moorland (Hancock *et al.* 2009; Wilson *et al.* 2013).

Proximity to plantations (non-native eucalypts and native oak) was demonstrated to have a negative influence on some steppe birds in open agricultural landscapes in Portugal (calandra lark *Melanocorypha calandra* and short-toed lark *Calandrella brachydactyla*). Densities of these birds increase with distance from plantations, though other species (little bustard *Tetrax tetrax* and tawny pipit *Anthus campestris*) were not so affected (Reino *et al.* 2009). Such edge effects also appear to interact with both the structure of the plantation edge and the wider landscape. 'Soft-edged' oak plantations appeared to exert a less pronounced negative influence on steppe birds than 'hard-edged' eucalyptus plantations (Reino *et al.* 2009). The potential for benefitting birds that inhabit both plantations and open habitats through management and restructuring of the interface between them deserves further study (Calladine *et al.* 2013).

10.3.3 Exotic Plantations and Future Bird Conservation

Future preferred tree species and their management in plantation forests are likely to depend on changes in climate, tree diseases, demands for forest products, and economic and social pressures and incentives. These will, in turn, influence the supported bird populations of plantation forests and consequently the value of these forests for bird conservation. The majority of studies of birds in European plantations have been in the British Isles or the Iberian Peninsula, but even within these regions, knowledge is lacking in some key areas. To increase the opportunities for plantations to contribute to bird conservation (and to minimise their negative impact on other habitats), some areas that deserve attention include:

- Landscape scale analyses to assess the potential biodiversity gains and losses that would result from further afforestation, including the interactions between new plantations, natural forests and non-forested environments.
- More extensive studies on the occurrence and densities of bird species supported by different crop tree species (including novel crop species being promoted in response to changing climatic scenarios and plant health threats), and how these are influenced by different combinations of crop trees and their management.

- Further investigation of how changes in management, especially in the spatial and temporal frequency of harvesting, can influence birds. The retention of trees beyond their commercially optimal age for harvesting can increase forest bird species diversity (Currie & Bamford 1982), but the contribution of young growth stages (by benefitting birds of shrubland and open habitats) should also be considered. Within continuous cover systems, there is a need to assess the responses of birds to the scale on which trees are harvested, i.e., single tree harvesting or patch felling (see also Chapter 13).

- Management of plantations lends itself to creating many and extensive edges. These can be at coupe interfaces, rides that facilitate forest management and external edges. Edge effects can be important for birds (Fuller & Whittington 1987; Patterson et al. 1995; Hawrot & Niemi 1996; McCollin 1998; Reino et al. 2009; Calladine et al. 2013), and more information on how birds respond to them and different treatments applied to them would inform the design and management of forest plantations at multiple scales.

- Empirical evidence for positive contributions of thinning operations to the delivery of conservation objectives in plantation management, including the interaction between canopy openness and deer browsing and its effect on understorey structures (Fuller 2013).

- The nature, distribution and ecological role of deadwood within managed plantations, particularly in relation to its use by birds.

- Dynamic modelling of coupled bird-tree interactions, particularly in the case of seed dispersers, to assess their role in mitigation strategies to conserve forests in response to changing climates (Valladares et al. 2014).

- The role, influence and effectiveness of policy and incentive instruments such as forest certification schemes (Ozinga 2001; Rametsteiner & Simula 2003; Auld et al. 2008) in delivering enhanced biodiversity within plantation forests.

Studies of the above topics should not be restricted to studying assemblages of breeding birds, but should include their use of plantations year round. Additionally, the information to inform these studies should be collected from across Europe, with comparisons of plantations from two or more biogeographical zones being particularly valuable.

Acknowledgements

Paul Bellamy and Tom Gittings provided valuable comments on an earlier draft of this chapter. Luís Reino was supported by the post-doc fellowship (SFRH/BPD/62865/2 SFRH/BPD/62865/2009009) and the project PTDC/BIA-BIC/2203/2012, both funded by the Portuguese Science and Technology Foundation (FCT). Mario Díaz was supported by projects Consolider Montes (CSD2008-00040), VULGO (CGL2010-C03-03), REMEDINAL3-CM (S2013/MAE-2719) and BACCARA (CE: FP7-226299,7FP). John Calladine received support from the J. & J.R. Wilson Trust.

References

Amar, A., Thirgood, S., Pearce-Higgins, J.W. & Redpath, S. (2008) The impact of raptors on the abundance of upland passerines and waders. *Oikos*, **117**, 1143–1152.

Andrén, H. (1992) Corvid density and nest predation in relation to forest fragmentation; a landscape perspective. *Ecology*, **73**, 794–804.

Araújo, M.B. (1995) *The effect of* Eucalyptus globulus *Labill. plantations on biodiversity: A case study in Serra de Portel (South Portugal).* Master thesis, University College London.

Aslam, T.J., Benton, T.G., Nielsen, U.N. & Johnson, S.N. (2015) Impacts of eucalypt plantation management on soil faunal communities and nutrient availability: Trading function for dependence? *Biology and Fertility of Soils*, **51**, 637–644.

Auld, G., Gulbrandsen, L.H. & McDermott, C.L. (2008) Certification schemes and the impacts on forests and forestry. *Annual Review of Environment and Resources*, **33**, 187–211.

Avery, M.I. (1989) Effects of upland afforestation on some birds of adjacent moorland. *Journal of Applied Ecology*, **26**, 957–996.

Baguette, M., Deceuninck, B. & Muller, Y. (1994) Effect of spruce afforestation on bird community dynamics in a native broad-leaved forest area. *Acta Oecologica*, **15**, 275–288.

Bailey, S. (2007) Increasing connectivity in fragmented landscapes: An investigation of evidence for biodiversity gain in woodlands. *Forest Ecology and Management*, **238**, 7–23.

Baillie, S.R., Sutherland, W.J., Freeman, S.N., Gregory, R.D. & Paradis, E. (2000) Consequences of large-scale processes for the conservation of bird populations. *Journal of Applied Ecology*, **37**, 88–102.

Baines, D., Redpath, S., Richardson, M. & Thirgood, S. (2008) The direct and indirect effects of predation by Hen Harriers *Circus cyaneus* on trends in breeding birds on a Scottish grouse moor. *Ibis*, **150** (Suppl. 1), 27–36.

Balmer, D., Gillings, S., Caffrey, B., Swann, B., Downie, I. & Fuller, R.J. (2013) *Bird Atlas 2007–11: The Breeding and Wintering Birds of Britain and Ireland.* Thetford: BTO Books.

Barlow, J., Mestre, L.A.M., Gardner, T.A. & Peres, C.A. (2007) The value of primary, secondary and plantation forests for Amazonian birds. *Biological Conservation*, **136**, 212–231.

Barrientos, R. (2010) Retention of native vegetation within the plantation matrix improves its conservation value for a generalist woodpecker. *Forest Ecology and Management*, **260**, 595–602.

Bártol, I. & Lovászi, P. (2000) Habitat selection and reproductive success of the Lesser Grey Shrike (*Lanius minor*) in the Kiskunság area. *Ornis Hungarica*, **10**, 87–91. [in Hungarian, English summary]

Bibby, C.J., Aston, N. & Bellamy, P.E. (1989) Effects of broadleaved trees on birds of upland conifer plantations in North Wales. *Biological Conservation*, **49**, 17–29.

Bibby, C.J., Philips, B.N. & Seddon, A.J.E. (1985) Birds of restocked conifer plantations in Wales. *Bird Study*, **22**, 619–633.

Bieringer, G. & Zulka, K.P. (2004) Shading out species richness: Edge effect of a pine plantation on the Orthoptera (*Tettigoniidae* and *Acrididae*) assemblage of an adjacent dry grassland. *Biodiversity and Conservation*, **12**, 1481–1495.

Bossema, I. (1979) Jays and oaks. Eco-ethological study of a symbiosis. *Behaviour*, **70**, 1–117.

Bowden, C.G.R. (1990) Selection of foraging habitats by woodlarks (*Lullula arborea*) nesting in pine plantations. *Journal of Applied Ecology*, **27**, 410–419.

Brazier, J.D. & Mobbs, I.D. (1993) The influence of planting distance on structural yields of unthinned Sitka spruce. *Forestry*, **66**, 333–352.

Brockerhoff, E.G., Jactel, H., Parrotta, J.A., Quine, C.P., Sayer, J. & Hawkesworth, D. (2008) Plantation forests and biodiversity: Oxymoron or opportunity? *Biodiversity and Conservation*, **17**, 925–951.

Brooker, R. (2011) The changing nature of Scotland's uplands – an interplay of processes and timescales. In *The Changing Nature of Scotland*. Marrs, S.J., Foster, S., Hendrie, C., Mackey, E.C. & Thompson, D.B.A. (eds.). Edinburgh: The Stationary Office, pp. 381–396.

Broome, A., Connolly, T. & Quine, C.P. (2014) An evaluation of thinning to improve habitat for capercaillie (*Tetrao urogallus*). *Forest Ecology and Management*, **314**, 94–103.

Brotons, L. & Herrando, S. (2003) Effect of increased food abundance near forest edges on flocking patterns of Coal Tit *Parus ater* winter groups in mountain coniferous forests. *Bird Study*, **50**, 106–111.

Buchanan, G.M., Pearce-Higgins, J.W., Wotton, S.R., Grant, M.C. & Whitfield, D.P. (2003) Correlates of change in Ring Ouzel *Turdus torquatus* abundance in Scotland from 1988–1991 to 1999. *Bird Study*, **50**, 97–105.

Burton, N.H.K. (2007) Influences of restock age and habitat patchiness on Tree Pipits *Anthus trivialis* breeding in Breckland pine plantations. *Ibis*, **149** (Suppl. 2), 193–204.

Calladine, J., Bielinski, A. & Shaw, G. (2013) Effect on bird abundance and species richness of edge restructuring to include shrubs at the interface between conifer plantations and open moorland. *Bird Study*, **60**, 345–356.

Calladine, J. & Bray, J. (2011) *Bird communities in and around short-rotation forestry energy crops in Britain: Baseline surveys in 2009–11 and an initial assessment of Eucalyptus plantations.* BTO Research Report No. 596, Stirling: BTO.

Calladine, J., Bray, J., Broome, A. & Fuller, R.J. (2015) Implications for breeding birds of continuous cover forestry compared with clear-felling in upland conifer plantations. *Forest Ecology and Management*, **344**, 20–29.

Calladine, J., Humphreys, E.M, Jardine, D. & Strachan, F. (2009) Forestry thinning in commercial conifer plantations has little effect on breeding bird abundance and species richness in northern Scotland. *Bird Study*, **56**, 137–141.

Calvino-Cancela, M. (2013) Effectiveness of eucalypt plantations as a surrogate habitat for birds. *Forest Ecology and Management*, **310**, 692–699.

Conway, G., Wotton, S., Henderson, I., Langston, R., Drewitt, A. & Currie, F. (2007) Status and distribution of European Nightjars *Caprimulgus europaeus* in the UK in 2004. *Bird Study*, **54**, 98–111.

Costello, C.A., Yamasaki, M., Pekins, P.J., Leak, W.B. & Neefus, C.D. (2000) Songbird response to group selection harvests and clearcuts in a New Hampshire northern hardwood forest. *Forest Ecology and Management*, **127**, 41–54.

Currie, F.A. & Bamford, R. (1982) The value to birdlife of retaining small conifer stands beyond normal felling age within forests. *Quarterly Journal of Forestry*, **6**, 153–160.

de la Hera, Arizag, J & Galarze, A. (2013) Exotic tree plantations and avian conservation in northern Iberia: A view from a nest box study. *Animal Biodiversity and Conservation*, **36**, 153–163.

Dhondt, A.A., Wrege, P.H., Sydenstricker K.V. & Cerretani, J. (2004) Clone preference by nesting birds in short-rotation coppice plantations in central and western New York. *Biomass and Bioenergy*, **27**, 429–435.

Díaz, M., Carbonell, R., Santos, T. & Tellería. (1998) Breeding bird communities in pine plantations of the Spanish plateaux: Biogeography, landscape and vegetation effects. *Journal of Applied Ecology*, **35**, 562–574.

Donald, P.F., Fuller, R.J., Evans, A.D. & Gough, S.J. (1998) Effects of forest management and grazing in plantations of broadleaved and coniferous trees in western England. *Biological Conservation*, **85**, 183–197.

Donald, P.F., Haycock, D. & Fuller, R.J. (1997) Winter bird communities in forest plantations in western England and their response to vegetation, growth stage and grazing. *Bird Study*, **44**, 206–219.

Douglas, D.J.T., Bellamy, P.E., Stephen, L.S., Pearce-Higgins, J.W., Wilson, J.D. & Grant, M.C. (2013). Upland land use predicts population decline in a globally near-threatened wader. *Journal of Applied Ecology*, **51**, 194–203.

du Bus de Warnaffe, G.D. & Deconchat, M. (2008) Impact of four silvicultural systems on birds in the Belgian Ardenne: Implications for biodiversity in plantation forests. *Biodiversity and Conservation*, **17**, 1041–1055.

El-Darier, S.M. (2002) Allelopathic effects of *Eucalyptus rostrata* on growth, nutrient uptake and metabolite accumulation of *Vicia faba* L. and *Zea mays* L. *Pakistan Journal of Biological Sciences*, **5**, 6–11.

Fikreyesus, S., Kebebew, Z., Nebiyu, A., Zeleke, N. & Bogale, S. (2011) Allelopathic effects of *Eucalyptus camaldulensis* Dehnh. on germination and growth of tomato. *American-Eurasian Journal of Agricultural and Environmental Sciences*, **11**, 600–608.

Finney, S.K., Pearce-Higgins, J.W. & Yalden, D.W. (2005) The effect of recreational disturbance on an upland breeding bird, the golden plover *Pluvialis apricaria*. *Biological Conservation*, **121**, 53–63.

Fletcher, K., Aebischer, N.J., Baines, D., Foster, R. & Hoodless, A.N. (2010) Changes in breeding success and abundance of ground-nesting moorland birds in relation to the experimental deployment of legal predator control. *Journal of Applied Ecology*, **47**, 263–272.

Forestry Commission (2013) *National Forest Inventory*. Edinburgh: Forestry Commission.

Fox, A.D. & Bell, M.C. (1994) Breeding bird communities and environmental variable correlates of Scottish peatland wetlands. *Hydrobiologia*, **279–280**, 297–307.

Fuller, R.J. (2012) Avian responses to transitional habitats in temperate cultural landscapes: Woodland edges and young growth. In *Birds and Habitat: Relationships in Changing Landscapes*. Fuller, R.J. (ed.). Cambridge: Cambridge University Press, pp. 125–149.

Fuller, R.J. (2013) Searching for biodiversity gains through woodfuel and forest management. *Journal of Applied Ecology*, **50**, 1295–1300.

Fuller, R.J. & Browne, S. (2003) Effects of plantation structure and management on birds. In *Biodiversity in Britain's Planted Forests*. Humphrey, J., Ferris, R. & Quine, C.P. (eds.). Edinburgh: Forestry Commission, pp. 93–99.

Fuller, R.J., Gaston, K.J. & Quine, C.P. (2007) Living on the edge: British and Irish woodland birds in a European context. *Ibis*, **149** (Suppl. 2), 53–63.

Fuller, R.J. & Green, G.H. (1998) Effects of woodland structure on breeding bird populations in stands of coppiced lime (*Tilia cordata*) in western England over a 10-year period. *Forestry*, **71**, 199–218.

Fuller, R.J. & Whittington, P.A. (1987) Breeding bird distribution within Lincolnshire ash-lime woodlands: The influence of rides and the woodland edge. *Acta Oecologica*, **8**, 259–268.

Garcia-Del-Rey, E., Otto, R. & Fernández-Palacios, J.M. (2010) Medium-term response of breeding Blue Chaffinch *Fringilla teydea teydea* to experimental thinning in a *Pinus canariensis* plantation (Tenerife, Canary Islands). *Ornis Fennica*, **87**, 180–188.

Garson, P.J. & Starling, A.E. (1990) Explaining the present distribution black grouse in northeast England. In *De toekomst van de wilde hoenerachtigen in Nederland*. Lumeij, J.T. & Hoogeveen, Y.R. (eds.). Amersfoort: Organisatieconnissie Nedrlandse Wilde Hoenders pp. 97–105.

Gibbons, D.W., Reid, J.B. & Chapman, R.A. (1993) *The New Atlas of Breeding Birds in Britain and Ireland: 1988–91*. London: T. & A. D. Poyser.

Gilbert, L. (2013) Can restoration of afforested peatland regulate pests and disease? *Journal of Applied Ecology*, **50**, 1226–1233.

Giller, P.S. & O'Halloran, J. (2004) Forestry and the aquatic environment: Studies in an Irish context. *Hydrology and Earth System Sciences*, **8**, 314–326.

Gjerde, I. & Sætersdal, M. (1997) Effects on avian diversity of introducing spruce *Picea* spp. plantations in the native Pine *Pinus sylvestris* forests of western Norway. *Biological Conservation*, **79**, 241–250.

Gómez, J.M. (2003) Spatial patterns in long-distance dispersal of *Quercus ilex* acorns by jays in a heterogeneous landscape. *Ecography*, **26**, 573–584.

Gram, W.K., Porneluzi, P.A., Clawson, R.L., Faaborg, J. & Richter, S.C. (2003) Effects of experimental forest management on density and nesting success of bird species in Missouri Ozark forests. *Conservation Biology*, **17**, 1324–1337.

Hamilton, G.J. (1974) Aspects of thinning. *Forestry Commission Bulletin No. 55* London: HMSO.

Hancock, M.H. & Avery, M. (1998) Changes in breeding bird populations in peatland and young forestry in north east Sutherland and Caithness between 1988 and 1995. *Scottish Birds*, **19**, 195–205.

Hancock, M.H., Grant, M.C. & Wilson, J.D. (2009) Associations between distance to forest and spatial and temporal variation in abundance of key peatland breeding bird species. *Bird Study*, **56**, 53–64.

Hanzelka, J. & Reif, J. (2016) Effects of vegetation structure on the diversity of breeding bird communities in forest stands of non-native black pine (*Pinus nigra* A.) and black locust (*Robinia pseudoacacia* L.) in the Czech Republic. *Forest Ecology and Management*, **379**, 102–113.

Hardey, J., Crick, H., Wernham, C., Riley, H. & Thompson, D. (2006) *Raptors: A Field Guide to Survey and Monitoring*. Edinburgh: The Stationary Office.

Harrison, A. (2008) *Operational Guidance for Establishing Energy Forestry Trial*. Edinburgh: Forestry Commission Scotland.

Hartley, M.J. (2002) Rationale and methods for conserving biodiversity in plantation forests. *Forest Ecology and Management*, **155**, 81–95.

Haworth, P.F. & Fielding, A.H. (2009) *An assessment of woodland habitat utilisation by breeding Hen Harriers*. Report to SNH Project no. 24069. Edinburgh: Scottish Natural Heritage.

Hawrot, R.Y. & Niemi, G.J. (1996) Effects of edge type and patch shape on avian communities in a mixed conifer-hardwood forest. *The Auk*, **113**, 586–598.

Haysom, S.L. (2002) *Aspects of the ecology of black grouse* Tetrao tetrix *in plantation forests in Scotland*. PhD thesis, University of Stirling.

Helle, P. & Fuller, R.J. (1988) Migrant passerine birds in European forest successions in relation to vegetation height and geographic position. *Journal of Animal Ecology*, **57**, 565–579.

Hewson, C.M., Austin, G.E., Gough, S.J. & Fuller, R.J. (2011) Species-specific responses of woodland birds to stand-level habitat characteristics: The dual importance of forest structure and floristics. *Forest Ecology and Management*, **261**, 1224–1240.

Imbeau, L., Drapeau, P. & Mönkkönen, M. (2003) Are forest birds categorised as 'edge species' strictly associated with edges? *Ecography*, **21**, 514–552.

John, J.R.M. & Kabigumila, J.D.L. (2007) The impact of Eucalyptus plantations on the avian breeding community in the East Usambaras, Tanzania. *Ostrich*, **78**, 265–269.

Jonsson, J.A., Sigurdsson, B.D. & Hallorsson, G. (2006) Changes in bird life, surface fauna and ground vegetation following afforestation by black cottonwood (*Populus trichocarpa* Torr. & Gray) *Icelandic Agricultural Sciences*, **19**, 33–41.

József, R. (1992) Data on the bird-life of the locust-tree forests of the Southern Alföld (Great Hungárián Plain). *Aquila*, **99**, 137–148. [in Hungarian, English summary]

Kirby, K.J. & Watkins, C. (eds.) (2015) *Europe's Woods and Forests: From Wildwood to Cultural Landscapes*. Wallingford: CABI.

Klopcic, M. & Boncina, A. (2012) Recruitment of tree species in mixed selection and irregular shelterwood forest stands. *Annals of Forest Science*, **69**, 915–925.

Langston, R.H.W., Wotton, S.R., Conway, G.J. et al. (2007) Nightjar *Caprimulgus europaeus* and Woodlark *Lullula arborea* – recovering species in Britain? *Ibis*, **149**, 250–260.

Lavers, C.P. & Haines-Young, R.H. (1997) Displacement of dunlin *Calidris alpina schinzii* by forestry in the flow country and an estimate of the value of moorland adjacent to plantations. *Biological Conservation*, **79**, 87–90.

Lundberg, J., Andersson, E., Cleary, G. & Elmqvist, T. (2008) Linkages beyond borders: Targeting spatial processes in fragmented urban landscapes. *Landscape Ecology*, **23**, 717–726.

Macdonald, E., Gardiner, B. & Mason, W. (2009) The effects of transformation of even-aged stands to continuous cover forestry on conifer log quality and properties in the UK. *Forestry*, **83**, 1–16.

Macmillan, D.C. & Marshall, K. (2004) Optimising capercaillie habitat in commercial forestry plantations. *Forest Ecology and Management*, **198**, 351–365.

Madders, M. (2000) Habitat selection and foraging success of Hen Harriers *Circus cyaneus* in west Scotland. *Bird Study*, **47**, 32–40.

Madders, M. & Walker, D. (2002) Golden Eagles in a multiple land-use environment: A case study in conflict management. *Journal of Raptor Research*, **36**, 55–61.

Magura, T., Báldi, A. & Horváth, R. (2008) Breakdown of the species-area relationship in exotic but not in native forest patches. *Acta Oecologica*, **33**, 272–279.

Marion, P. & Frochot, B. (2001) L'avifaune nicheuse de la succession écologique du sapin de Douglas en Morvan (France). *Revue d'ecologie – La Terre et la Vie*, **56**, 53–79.

Marquiss, M., Newton, I. & Ratcliffe, D.A. (1978) The decline of the raven, *Corvus corax*, in relation to Afforestation in southern Scotland and northern England. *Journal of Applied Ecology*, **15**, 129–144.

Marquiss, M., Ratcliffe, D.A. & Roxburgh, R. (1985) The numbers, breeding success and diet of Golden Eagles in southern Scotland in relation to changes in land use. *Biological Conservation*, **33**, 1–17.

Martínez-Jauregui, M., Díaz, M., Sánchez de Ron, D. & Soliño, M. (2016b) Plantations or natural recovery? Relative contribution of planted and natural pine forest to the maintenance of regional bird diversity along ecological gradients in Southern Europe. *Forest Ecology and Management*, **376**, 183–192.

Martínez-Jauregui, M., Soliño, M. & Díaz, M. (2016a) Geographical variation in the contribution of planted and natural pine forests to the conservation of bird diversity. *Diversity and Distributions*, **22**, 1255–1265.

McCollin, D. (1998) Forest edges and habitat selection in birds: A functional approach. *Ecography*, **21**, 247–260.

McKay, H., Bijlsma, A., Bull, G. *et al.* (2003) *Woodfuel Resources in Britain*. Edinburgh: Forestry Commission.

Mönkkönen, M. (1994) Diversity patterns in Palearctic and Nearctic forest bird assemblages. *Journal of Biogeography*, **21**, 193–195.

Moran-Lopez, T., Alonso, C.L. & Diaz M. (2015) Landscape effects on jay foraging behavior decrease acorn dispersal services in dehesas. *Acta Oecologica*, **69**, 52–64.

Moss, D., Taylor, P.N. & Easterbee, N. (1979) Effects on song-bird populations of upland afforestation with spruce. *Forestry*, **52**, 129–150.

Nájera, A & Simonetti, J.A. (2009) Enhancing avifauna in commercial plantations. *Conservation Biology*, **24**, 319–324.

Nethersole-Thompson, D. (1975) *Pine Crossbills*. Berkhamsted: T. & A. D. Poyser.

Nethersole-Thompson, D. & Nethersole-Thompson, M. (1979) *Greenshanks*. Berkhamsted: T. & A.D. Poyser.

Newborn, D., Fletcher, K.L., Beeston, R. & Baines, D. (2009) Occurrence of sheep ticks on moorland wader chicks. *Bird Study*, **56**, 401–404.

Newton, I., Davis, P.E. & Davis, J.E. (1982) Ravens and Buzzards in relation to sheep farms and forestry in Wales. *Journal of Applied Ecology*, **19**, 681–706.

O'Hara, K.L. (2001) The silviculture of transformation – a commentary. *Forest Ecology and Management*, **151**, 81–86.

Onofre, N. (1990) *Sobre o valor relativo de algumas áreas florestais para as comunidades de falconiformes: Breve caracterização das exigências de habitat de algumas rapinas dependentes de biótopos florestais*. Porto: II Congresso Florestal.

Ormerod, S.J. & Tyler, S.J. (1989) Long-term change in the suitability of Welsh streams for Dippers *Cinclus cinclus* as a result of acidification and recovery – a modelling study. *Environmental Pollution*, **62**, 171–182.

Ozinga, S. (2001) *Behind the Logo: An Environmental and Social Assessment of Forest Certification Schemes*. Moreton-in-Marsh: FERN.

Paquet, J.Y., Vandevyvre, X., Delahaye, L. & Rondeux, J. (2006) Bird assemblages in a mixed woodland-farmland landscape: The conservation value of silviculture-dependant open areas in plantation forest. *Forest Ecology and Management*, **227**, 59–70.

Park, K.J., Graham, K.E., Calladine, J. & Wernham, C.V. (2008) Impacts of birds of prey on gamebirds in the UK: A review. *Ibis*, **150** (Suppl. 1), 9–26.

Parr, R. (1992) The decline to extinction of a population of golden plover in north-east Scotland. *Ornis Scandinavica*, **23**, 152–158.

Patterson, I.J., Ollason, J.G. & Doyle, P. (1995) Bird populations in upland spruce plantations in northern Britain. *Forest Ecology and Management*, **79**, 107–131.

Pearce-Higgins, J.W., Grant, M.C., Robinson, M.C. & Haysom, S.L. (2007) The role of forest maturation causing the decline of Black Grouse *Tetrao tetrix*. *Ibis*, **149**, 143–155.

Peck, K.M. (1989) Tree species preferences shown by foraging birds in forest plantations in northern England. *Biological Conservation*, **48**, 41–57.

Petty, S.J. (1989) *Goshawks: Their Status, Requirements and Management*. Forestry Commission Bulletin 81. London: HMSO.

Petty, S.J., Anderson, D.I.K., Davison, M. *et al.* (2003) The decline of Common Kestrels *Falco tinnunculus* in a forested area of northern England: The role of predation by Northern Goshawks *Accipiter gentilis*. *Ibis*, **145**, 472–483.

Petty, S.J. & Avery, M.I. (1990) *Forest Bird Communities:A Review of the Ecology and Management of Forest Bird Communities in Relation to Sylvicultural Practices in the British Uplands*. Forestry Commission Occasional Paper 26. Edinburgh: Forestry Commission.

Pina, J.P. (1982) *Avifauna nidificante de povoamentos artificiais de* Pinus pinaster *Aiton e* Eucalyptus globulus *Labill*. Lisboa: Rel. Activ. do Curso de Eng. Silvicultor.

Pina, J.P. (1989) Breeding bird assemblages in eucalyptus plantations in Portugal. *Annales Zoologici Fennici*, **26**, 287–290.

Pommerening, A. & Murphy, S.T. (2004) A review of the history, definitions and methods of continuous cover forestry with special attention to afforestation and restocking. *Forestry*, **77**, 27–44.

Pons, J. & Pausas, J.G. (2008) Modelling jay (*Garrulus glandarius*) abundance and distribution for oak regeneration assessment in Mediterranean landscapes. *Forest Ecology and Management*, **256**, 578–584.

Poulsen, B.O. (2002) Avian richness and abundance in temperate Danish forests: Tree variables important to birds and their conservation. *Biodiversity and Conservation*, **11**, 1551–1566.

Prainsson, G., Kolbeinsson, Y. & Petursson, G. (2013) Rare birds in Iceland in 2008. *Bliki*, **32**, 11–30.

Proença, V.M., Pereira, H.M., Guilherme, J. & Vicente, L. (2010) Plant and bird diversity in natural forests and in native and exotic plantations in NW Portugal. *Acta Oecologica*, **36**, 219–226.

Puerta-Piñero, C., Gómez, J. M. & Valladares, F. (2007). Irradiance and oak seedling survival and growth in a heterogeneous environment. *Forest Ecology and Management*, **242**, 462–469.

Puerta-Piñero, C., Pino, J. & Gómez, J.M. (2012) Direct and indirect landscape effects on *Quercus ilex* regeneration in heterogeneous environments. *Oecologia*, **170**, 1009–1020.

Pukkala, T. (2006) Optimising semi-continuous cover forestry of Finland. *Allgemeine Forest und Jagdzeitung*, **177**, 141–149.

Purves, D.W., Zavala, M.A., Ogle, K., Prieto, F. & Rey, J.M. (2007) Environmental heterogeneity, bird-mediated directed dispersal, and oak woodland dynamics in Mediterranean Spain. *Ecological Monographs*, **77**, 77–97.

Quine, C.P. & Humphrey, J.W. (2010) Plantations of exotic tree species in Britain: Irrelevant for biodiversity or novel habitat for native species. *Biodiversity and Conservation*, **19**, 1503–1512.

Rackham, O. (2006). *Woodlands*. London: Collins.

Radich, M.C. (2007) Introdução e expansão do eucalipto em Portugal. In *Árvores e Florestas de Portugal, Pinhais e Eucaliptais – A floresta cultivada*. Silva, J.S. (Coord.). Lisboa: Edição Público, Comunicação Social, SA & Fundação Luso-Americana para o Desenvolvimento, pp. 151–165.

Rametsteiner, E. & Simula, M. (2003) Forest certification – an instrument to promote sustainable forest management? *Journal of Environmental Management*, **67**, 87–98.

Ratcliffe, D. 2010. *Galloway and the Borders*. London: Harper Collins.

Redpath, S., Amar, A., Madders, M., Leckie, F. & Thirgood, S. (2002). Hen harrier foraging success in relation to land use in Scotland. *Animal Conservation*, **5**, 113–118.

Reino, L., Beja, P., Osborne, P.E., Morgado, R., Fabião, A. & Rotenberry, J.T. (2009) Distance to edges, edge contrast and landscape fragmentation: Interactions affecting farmland birds around forest plantations. *Biological Conservation*, **142**, 824–838.

Reino, L., Porto, M., Morgado, R., Carvalho, F., Mira, A. & Beja, P. (2010) Does afforestation increase nest predation risk in surrounding farmland? *Forest Ecology and Management*, **160**, 1359–1386.

Rey Benayas, J.M., Galván, I. & Carrascal, L.M. (2010) Differential effects of vegetation restoration in Mediterranean abandoned cropland by secondary succession and pine plantations on bird assemblages. *Forest Ecology and Management*, **260**, 87–95.

Ruiz-Benito, P., Gómez-Aparicio, L. & Zavala, M.A. (2012) Large-scale assessment of regeneration and diversity in Mediterranean planted pine forests along ecological gradients. *Diversity and Distributions*, **18**, 1092–1106.

Sage, R. & Robertson, P.A. (1996) Factors affecting songbird communities using new short rotation coppice habitats in spring. *Bird Study*, **43**, 201–213.

Sakura, T., Gimingham, C.H. & Millar, C.S. (1985) Effects of tree density on ground vegetation in a Japanese larch population. *Scottish Forestry*, **39**, 191–198.

Santos, T. & Alvarez, G. (1990) Efectos de las repoblaciones con eucaliptos sobre las comunidades de aves forestales en un maquis mediterráneo (Montes de Toledo). *Ardeola*, **37**, 319–324.

Santos, T., Tellería, J.L. & Carbonell, R. (2002) Bird conservation in fragmented Mediterranean forests of Spain: Effects of geographical location, habitat and landscape degradation. *Biological Conservation*, **105**, 113–125.

Santos, T., Tellería, J.L., Díaz, M. & Carbonell, R. (2006) Evaluating the environmental benefits of CAP reforms: Can afforestations restore forest bird communities in Mediterranean Spain? *Basic and Applied Ecology*, **7**, 483–495.

Scott, D., Clark, R. & Shawyer, C. (1993) Tree-nesting Hen Harriers – evolution in the making? *Raptor*, **21**, 53–56.

Sergio, F. & Hiraldo, F. (2007) Intraguild predation in raptor assemblages: A review. *Ibis*, **150**, 132–145.

Sharrock, J.T.R. (1976) *The Atlas of Breeding Birds in Britain and Ireland.* Berkhamsted: T. & A. D. Poyser.

Shaw, G. (1995) Habitat selection by Short-eared Owls *Asio flammeus* in young coniferous forests. *Bird Study*, **42**, 158–164.

Shochat, E., Abramsky, Z. & Pinshow, B. (2001) Breeding bird species diversity in the Negev: Effects of scrub fragmentation by planted forests. *Journal of Applied Ecology*, **38**, 1135–1147.

Sim, I.M.W., Dillon, I.A., Eaton, M.A. *et al.* (2007) Status of the Hen Harrier *Circus cyaneus* in the UK and Isle of Man in 2004, and a comparison with the 1988/99 and 1998 surveys. *Bird Study*, **54**, 256–267.

Smedhaug, C.A., Lund, S.E., Brekke, A., Sonerud, G. & Rafoss, T. (2002) The importance of farmland-forest edge for area use of breeding hooded crows as revealed by radio telemetry. *Ornis Fennica*, **79**, 1–13.

Smith, R.S. & Charman, D.J. (1988) The vegetation of upland mires within conifer plantations in Northumberland, Northern England. *Journal of Applied Ecology*, **25**, 579–594.

Smout, T.C. (2005) *Nature Contested. Environmental History in Scotland and Northern England since 1600.* Edinburgh: Edinburgh University Press.

Stefansson, R.A. & Bjarnadottir, S. (2005) The distribution of Goldcrest in W-Iceland. *Bliki*, **26**, 5–10.

Stroud, D.A., Reed, T.M. & Harding, N.J. (1990) Do moorland breeding waders avoid plantation edges? *Bird Study*, **37**, 177–186.

Summers, R.W. (2000) The habitat requirements of the crested tit *Parus cristatus* in Scotland. *Scottish Forestry*, **54**, 197–201.

Summers, R.W. & Broome, A. (2012) Associations between crossbills and North American conifers in Scotland. *Forest Ecology and Management*, **271**, 37–45.

Summers, R.W., Mavor, R.A., Buckland, S.T. & MacLennan, A.M. (1999a) Winter population size and habitat selection of Crested Tits *Parus cristatus* in Scotland. *Bird Study*, **46**, 230–242.

Summers, R.W., Mavor, R.A., MacLennan, A.M. & Rebecca, G.W. (1999b) The structure of ancient native pinewoods and other woodlands in the Highlands of Scotland. *Forest Ecology and Management*, **119**, 231–245.

Suttie, E., Taylor, G., Livesey, K. & Tickell, F. (2009) Potential of forest products and substitution for fossil fuels to contribute to mitigation. In *Combating Climate Change − A Role for UK Forests. An Assessment of the Potential of the UK's Trees and Woodlands to Mitigate and Adapt to Climate Change.* Read, D.J., Freer-Smith, P.H., Morison, J.I.L., Hanley, N., West, C.C. & Snowdon, P. (eds.). Edinburgh: The Stationary Office.

Sweeney, O.F.McD., Wilson, M.W., Irwin, S., Kelly, T.C. & O'Halloran, J. (2010) Breeding bird communities of second-rotation plantations at different stages of the forest cycle. *Bird Study*, **57**, 301–314.

Tellería, J.L. & Galarza, A. (1990) Avifauna y paisaje en el norte de España: Efecto de las repoblaciones con árboles exóticos. *Ardeola*, **37**, 229–245.

Thirgood, S.J., Redpath, S.M., Rothery, P. & Aebischer, N.J. (2000) Raptor predation and population limitation in red grouse. *Journal of Animal Ecology*, **69**, 504–516.

Thompson, D.B.A., MacDonald, A.J., Marsden, J.H. & Galbraith, C.A. (1995) Upland heather moorland in Great Britain: A review of international importance, vegetation change and some objectives for nature conservation. *Biological Conservation*, **71**, 163–178.

Thompson, F.R. & DeGraaf, R.M. (2001) Conservation approaches for woody, early successional communities in the eastern United States. *Wildlife Society Bulletin*, **29**, 483–494.

Urbieta, I.R., Zavala, M.A. & Marañón, T. (2008) Human and non-human determinants of forest composition in southern Spain: Evidence of shifts towards cork oak dominance as a result of management over the past century. *Journal of Biogeography*, **35**, 1688–1700.

Valladares, F., Benavides, R., Rabasa, S. *et al.* (2014) Global change and Mediterranean forests: Current impacts and potential responses. In: *Forests and Global Change*. Coomes, D.A., Burslem, D.F.R.P. & Simonson, W.D. (eds.). Cambridge: Cambridge University Press, pp. 47–75.

White, P.J.C., Warren, P. & Baines, D. (2013) Forest expansion in Scotland and its potential effects on black grouse *Tetrao tetrix* conservation. *Forest Ecology and Management*, **308**, 145–152.

Wilson, J.D., Anderson, R., Bailey, S. *et al.* (2013) Modelling edge effects of mature forest plantations on peatland waders informs landscape-scale conservation. *Journal of Applied Ecology*, **51**, 204–213.

Wilson, M.W., Gittings T, Kelly T.C. & O'Halloran J. (2010) The importance of non-crop vegetation for bird diversity in Sitka spruce plantations in Ireland. *Bird Study*, **57**, 116–120.

Wilson, M.W., Gittings, T., Pithon, J., Kelly, T.C., Irwin, S. & O'Halloran, J. (2012b) Bird diversity of afforestation habitats in Ireland: Current trends and likely impacts. *Biology and Environment: Proceedings of the Royal Irish Academy*, **112**, 1–14.

Wilson, M.W., Irwin, S., Norriss, D.W. *et al.* (2009) The importance of pre-thicket conifer plantations for nesting Hen Harriers *Circus cyaneus* in Ireland. *Ibis*, **151**, 332–343.

Wilson, M.W., O'Donoghue, B., O'Mahony, B. *et al.* (2012a) Mismatches between breeding success and habitat preferences in Hen Harrier *Circus cyaneus* breeding in forested landscapes. *Ibis*, **154**, 578–589.

Wilson, M.W., Pithon, J., Gittings, T., Kelly, T.C., Giller, P.S. & O'Halloran, J. (2006) Effects of growth stage and tree species composition on breeding bird assemblages of plantation forests. *Bird Study*, **53**, 225–236.

Zárybnická, M, Riegert, J. & Šťastný, K. (2015) Non-native spruce plantations represent a suitable habitat for Tengmalm's Owl (*Aegolius funereus*) in the Czech Republic, central Europe. *Journal of Ornithology*, **156**, 457–468.

Part III

Conservation and Management

11 · *Population Trends and Conservation Status of Forest Birds*

ALEKSI LEHIKOINEN AND
RAIMO VIRKKALA

11.1 Introduction

Bird populations can have large temporal variations both in the short term, from year to year, and in the long term, producing trends. The exact reason behind these temporal variations often remains unclear, although there are several suggestions as to the cause of the temporal patterns (Wiens 1989; Newton 1998; Eglington & Pearce-Higgins 2012; Ram *et al.* 2017).

Environmental variation, such as differences in weather conditions and food availability, has a profound effect on birds (Newton 1998; Møller *et al.* 2010). A high proportion of the bird species in Europe are migratory, particularly in temperate and boreal areas, so many birds are affected by environmental variation over extremely large areas of the planet (Newton 2008). Long-distance migrants that breed in the Northern Hemisphere meet environmental variation in three areas: the breeding areas, migratory areas and wintering areas in the tropics. As a classic example, the numbers of the common whitethroat *Sylvia communis* collapsed in Britain in the late 1960s and early 1970s as a consequence of extreme drought in the Sahel region of Africa, the main wintering area of the species (Winstanley *et al.* 1974; Batten & Marchant 1977). Similarly, in North America, survival and breeding success of American redstarts *Setophaga ruticilla* are influenced by climatic conditions in the wintering grounds (Norris *et al.* 2004; Marra *et al.* 2015).

Many of the recent population changes of forest birds are connected with large-scale habitat alteration caused by human activities (Butchart *et al.* 2010; Hoffman *et al.* 2010) and the effects of climate change (Crick 2004; Gregory *et al.* 2009; Jiguet *et al.* 2010). Although climate change has been observed to affect both population trends (Gregory *et al.* 2009; Devictor *et al.* 2012; Pearce-Higgins & Green 2014) and range shifts of bird species (Chen *et al.* 2011; Brommer *et al.* 2012), protected areas seem to alleviate the negative effects of climate change on the occurrence of boreal bird species (Virkkala *et al.* 2014). The main purpose of this chapter is to summarise recent population trends of forest birds in the different parts of Europe and draw attention to species that are in need of particular conservation actions. We also draw comparisons with the situation in other continents in the Northern Hemisphere.

11.2 Monitoring Bird Populations

Although human activities have affected forest birds for thousands of years, bird populations have only been monitored accurately during recent decades. On a national level, most of the longest continuous monitoring schemes have existed since the 1960s, but in many countries monitoring activity started much later.

In Europe, the national breeding bird count data of common birds is collated by the European Bird Census Council (EBCC). Based on census data from different countries, EBCC calculates combined population trends, so-called status indicators, of common forest and farmland species (hereafter 'bird indicators') at both the European and regional level (methodology in Gregory *et al.* 2005, 2007). These international multi-species bird indicators, as well as pan-European species-specific trends, are regularly updated and published on the EBCC website (www.ebcc.info). The website also shows which species, countries and time spans are included in the analyses to build the bird indicators. Although these indicators do not cover all European countries, they generally provide good information about the status of common forest birds in different parts of the continent. Here we refer to the EBCC bird indicators for forest birds; the species included in these indicators have been classified by EBCC as forest species throughout their European ranges. In North America, birds are monitored by the North American Breeding Bird Survey (BBS), which is a roadside survey primarily covering the continental United States and southern Canada. The BBS was started in 1966 and now contains more than 5,000 survey routes which are surveyed in June by experienced birders (Link & Sauer 1998). This survey regularly delivers estimates of population trends and annual indices of abundance and population change (also in the form of maps) for a variety of regions for more than 400 bird species (www.mbr-pwrc.usgs .gov/bbs/). In both Europe and North America, census data are collected mainly by volunteers, making bird monitoring a long-standing example of successful citizen science.

In this chapter, we summarise the recent population changes in forest birds in Europe based on EBCC data, but have also added information derived from more specific forest bird studies published during recent decades. To do this, we did a literature search (on 10 February 2015) from Web of Knowledge using the keywords 'forest + bird + population + trend'. We review this knowledge on both whole European and regional scales, but also provide an overview of population trends of forest birds in North America and boreal and temperate Asia.

Furthermore, we have investigated the conservation status of forest birds using information about globally Red-Listed species provided by the International Union for Conservation of Nature (IUCN). This information can be obtained from the websites of IUCN and BirdLife International (http://discover.iucnredlist.org/ BirdLife International 2013). In the latter part of this chapter, we summarise the geographic location and key threats of the globally Red-Listed forest species in the Northern Hemisphere and compare Red-Listed species of different continents (Europe including North Africa, Asia and North America).

To describe a change in population size with any level of certainty requires quantitative data from a series of years. Since it is often impossible to estimate the size of the total population, trend estimates are usually based on a sampling of a subset of the population. Typically, this sampling unit is some form of a census, which has been repeated in the same area during different years using the same methods (for reviews of census methods, see Verner 1985 and Bibby *et al.* 2000). In Europe, censuses of forest birds are conducted mainly during the breeding season, but census methods differ between countries. The most commonly used census types are line transects and point counts, but territory mapping is used in some countries (Voříšek *et al.* 2008).

Although the counts are generally undertaken by volunteers, the sampling design of the monitoring schemes is developed by professional researchers. In recent decades, there has been a general tendency to improve the schemes using systematic sampling to produce a spatially and temporally unbiased sampling procedure. The number of sampling sites per country varies from tens to hundreds or even thousands (e.g., United States), covering all kinds of habitats including forests.

In addition, in certain countries wintering populations of forest birds are also monitored (e.g., Fraixedas *et al.* 2015a). In Canada, monitoring of migratory songbirds is also based on trapping and banding of birds during spring along the migration bottlenecks, since the boreal forest zone is way too large and inaccessible to be covered solely by counts from the breeding grounds (Dunn *et al.* 2006). Also, in Europe, standardised migration counts and mist-netting provide information on long-term changes of forest bird species (e.g., Kjellén & Roos 2000; Eglington *et al.* 2015).

11.3 Population Trends in Different Regions

11.3.1 Europe in General

Europe is very diverse in terms of vegetation, forest cover, human population densities, sizes of countries and conservation policies. The literature search revealed that, in general, articles that dealt with population trends of multiple forest bird species within large areas, such as an entire country, were rare. Multinational studies were even more uncommon, but several single-species case studies have been published. At the European scale, common forest birds, defined as ones that use trees in various kinds of woodlands for at least part of the year for feeding and/or nesting, declined by 13% from 1980 to 2003 (Gregory *et al.* 2007). Furthermore, forest specialists, defined as ones with a dependence on, or specialisation to, various kinds of forests, declined by 18%. However, the decline of forest birds was much lower than that of farmland species (Gregory *et al.* 2007). Since 2003, monitoring data from 27 countries and 33 species indicates that populations of common forest birds have been relatively stable at the pan-European level (www.ebcc.info). Among common European forest birds, long-distance migrants and residents show, on average, the strongest declines, whereas populations of short-distance migrants have been relatively stable or have increased. There is also evidence that, on average, ground- or low-nesting species and insectivorous forest birds have declined relatively strongly (Gregory *et al.* 2007; Vickery *et al.* 2014).

The most recent account from the EBCC, covering the period 1980–2012, clearly shows that trends vary considerably among forest species, also between different periods (Appendix 11.1). Of the species that are considered as forest birds for the purpose of this book (see Chapters 1 and 5) and that are surveyed by EBCC (114 species), there is roughly an even split between ones that have experienced long-term population declines and ones undergoing population increases. The most distinct population declines among species classified as forest specialists were reported for rustic bunting *Emberiza rustica*, lesser spotted woodpecker *Dryobates minor*, willow tit *Poecile montanus*, European crested tit *Lophophanes cristatus* and goldcrest *Regulus regulus*. On the other hand, grey-headed woodpecker *Picus canus*, collared flycatcher *Ficedula albicollis*, black woodpecker *Dryocopus martius* and long-tailed tit *Aegithalos caudatus* are examples of forest specialists that have undergone long-term population increases in Europe as a whole. Notwithstanding these Europe-wide patterns, there is considerable regional variation in the trends for particular species and ecological groups, as discussed below.

11.3.2 Northern Europe

The northern European forest bird indicator of the EBCC is based on census data from Norway, Sweden and Finland, covering mainly boreal taiga. The combined abundance index of 26 species from these three countries shows a decline of ca. 25% during 1980–2012 (Fig. 11.1a). However, much larger forest bird datasets are also available, especially from Finland.

In south-west Finland, populations of breeding forest birds were studied in nine forest habitats in 1926–1927 and 1975. Over this period,

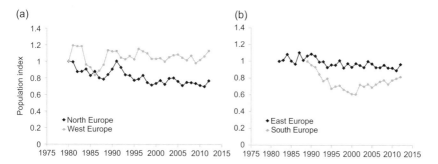

Figure 11.1 Combined population dynamics of common forest birds in (a) northern and western Europe, and (b) southern and eastern Europe. The lines are geometric means of annual population indices of forest species. Redrawn from European common forest bird status indicators of the European Bird Census Council (region and species definitions are more thoroughly explained in the text; see also www.ebcc.info and Gregory *et al.* 2007). Index starts from 1.0, and a value of 0.5 means that population sizes have, on average, declined by half.

non-passerines decreased, but passerines greatly increased their populations. The decreasing non-passerines included forest grouse, birds of prey and woodpeckers. These changes of passerines were thought to be linked with abandonment of forest grazing as well as an increase of Norway spruce *Picea abies* within forests (Haila *et al.* 1980).

Furthermore, both the breeding and wintering counts suggest long-term declines among residents or partially migratory species. Wintering forest bird species in Finland have been counted since the late 1950s (see Fig. 11.2). Combined populations of 17 wintering bird species, which prefer forest habitats during wintertime, declined by half from the 1950s and 1960s to the 2010s, with no clear break-point in the trend (continuous decline). A reduction in the area of closed-canopy forest (see Chapter 6) was likely the main reason, as the relative winter bird densities of these 17 forest species were eight times higher in forest areas (trees >5 m) than relative densities in clearcuts and stands of saplings (Fraixedas *et al.* 2015a). Correspondingly, based on breeding counts, many boreal bird species associated with old-forest structures have declined in Finland due to fragmentation and loss of old-growth forests (see Chapter 6). Furthermore, the Finnish breeding population trends of 32 forest bird species were negatively linked with their preference for older forests in 1984–2013 (Fraixedas *et al.* 2015b).

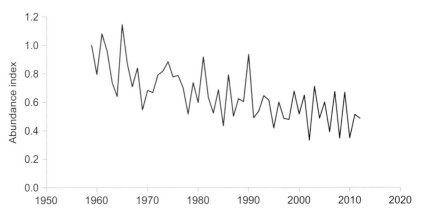

Figure 11.2 Combined population dynamics of 17 forest bird species in Finland during 1959–2012 based on national winter bird counts. The large annual variation in the index is driven by changes in numbers of crossbills and pine grosbeak *Pinicola enucleator*, which are affected by fluctuating seed crops of trees and berry yields (e.g., Newton 2008). Index starts from 1.0, and a value of 0.5 means that population sizes have, on average, declined by half. Redrawn from Fraixedas *et al.* (2015a).

In Sweden, Ottvall *et al.* (2009) found that during the period 1977–2006, 42% of all forest species showed a declining trend, 27% were stable and 26% increased. However, populations of both forest generalists and specialists have increased in Sweden since the mid-1990s, when systematic monitoring started, but these increases levelled off during the mid-2000s. These changes are likely linked with increased forest quantity and quality, and temperature in the area (Ram *et al.* 2017).

Changes in forested landscapes are thought to be a key driver of declines in forest grouse (see Chapter 6), but relationships are not necessarily related simply to changes in age structure of forests or the loss of old semi-natural forest (Sirkiä *et al.* 2010; Wegge & Rolstad 2011). Other factors, such as amount of forest cover, are likely to be involved (Sirkiä *et al.* 2010). The Swedish capercaillie *Tetrao urogallus* population has even increased since the late 1990s (Ottosson *et al.* 2012).

Based on breeding counts, populations of common forest generalists remained stable during 1986–2012 in Finland, but species that prefer coniferous forests declined during 2001–2012 (Laaksonen & Lehikoinen 2013). Importantly, populations of many migratory raptors increased from the 1960s and 1970s due to reductions in pesticide levels, but for some forest birds of prey, such as European honey buzzard *Pernis apivorus* and common buzzard *Buteo buteo*, continuous declines have occurred potentially due to the declining proportion of old forests in Fennoscandia (Kjellén & Roos 2000; Hakkarainen *et al.* 2004). In addition, Tengmalm's owl *Aegolius funereus* has declined since the 1980s in Finland, at least partly due to the loss of old forest (Saurola 2009; Korpimäki & Hakkarainen 2013).

In central Sweden, forest thinning, the removal of small-diameter trees, caused lower reproduction output and survival of adult willow tits, but not European crested tits, which suggests that forest management practices could be a major driver of population decline in willow tits (Eggers & Low 2014; see also Box 11.1). In the closely related northern species, Siberian tit *Poecile cinctus*, heavy thinning can also reduce breeding success and could be one cause of the long-term decline of the species (Virkkala 1990). Studies in Sweden have also demonstrated the preference of Siberian jays *Perisoreus infaustus* for feeding in multi-storey forests and that their breeding success was better there than in forests that had been thinned (Edenius & Meyer 2002; Griesser *et al.* 2007).

The birds of mountain forest habitats have been poorly monitored. However, common species in the subalpine birch forest of the Fennoscandian mountain range, such as willow grouse *Lagopus lagopus*,

Box 11.1 *Case study of the declining willow tit*

Willow tit *Poecile montanus* is a species that inhabits coniferous, broadleaved and mixed forests in Europe. The species has a large range, with southern limits in Greece and southern France (Hagemeijer & Blair 1997). The largest populations are found in northern and eastern Europe: between 0.5 and 1.0 million pairs are present in Finland and Sweden, but the Russian population in Europe exceeds 25 million pairs (BirdLife International 2015; European Union 2015).

European willow tit populations have been declining over the long term (1980–2013) and the short term (2004–2013) by 69% and 33%, respectively (European Bird Census Council 2015). As a consequence, willow tit is listed as vulnerable in the EU (27 countries; BirdLife International 2015). Of the 17 countries with long-term data, willow tits declined in nine countries, remained stable in seven and increased in only one. Numbers declined in all the countries with large populations (>0.2 million pairs in Finland, Sweden and Poland; European Union 2015). In Finland, willow tits had declined already by half between 1945 and 1975 (Järvinen & Väisänen 1977).

In many regions, the decline of willow tits is most probably largely connected with forestry practices causing forest habitat degradation, but in Britain the causes are unclear (Balmer *et al.* 2013). Nest and adult survival of willow tits are both reduced in coniferous forest when the understorey density of spruce is reduced as a consequence of thinning (Eggers & Low 2014). Thus, the long-term decline of willow tits in boreal forest is linked to large-scale harvesting of small-diameter spruce trees that provide important understorey vegetation. Furthermore, willow tits usually excavate their nesting cavities in decaying birch stumps, which are often destroyed during modern mechanical logging procedures (Hautala *et al.* 2004; see also Virkkala 2004). Forestry practices have also reduced suitable wintering habitat and carrying capacity in the forest area (Siffczyk *et al.* 2003).

In Europe, willow tit is a mostly northerly species which is probably also affected negatively by climate warming. If climate warming was an important factor, the species would have been expected to decline also in protected areas, where logging is not allowed and forest habitat thus not degraded. Virkkala (2016) studied population changes of boreal forest birds in southern Finland and observed that willow tit declined both in a managed study area and in protected areas.

Box 11.1 (cont.)

Moreover, the mean weighted density of the willow tit shifted northwards over 150 km in Finland between 1970–1989 and 2000–2012, suggesting that climate change affects population dynamics of the species (Lehikoinen & Virkkala 2016).

Photo: Lars Edenius.

brambling *Fringilla montifringilla* and common redpoll *Carduelis flammea*, have declined in Finland, Sweden and Norway (Lehikoinen *et al.* 2014).

In general, these findings suggest that common forest bird species in northern Europe have been declining for decades, at least partly due to changes in forest structure and management, though there have been some recent positive developments in Sweden (Ram *et al.* 2017). Warming climate has also affected population trends of boreal birds, and will probably do so increasingly in the future (see Chapter 6).

Other positive examples from northern Europe exist too. For instance, osprey *Pandion haliaetus* numbers have been increasing since the 1970s, at least partly due to conservation actions, such as the building of artificial nests and new guidelines for foresters to avoid clearcuttings close to nest trees (Saurola 1997). In addition, the population size of the endangered white-backed woodpecker *Dendrocopos leucotos*, which prefers mature deciduous forest, tripled in Finland from 1991 to 2010 after a long-term decline from the 1950s. The increase was driven partly by large-scale conservation measures and partly by increased immigration from Russia (Virkkala *et al.* 1993; Lehikoinen *et al.* 2011).

11.3.3 Eastern Europe

The EBCC forest bird indicator for eastern Europe includes census contributions from the Czech Republic, Estonia, the former East Germany, Hungary, Latvia, Lithuania, Poland and Slovakia. The combined forest bird abundance of 27 species from these countries shows a stable or a slightly declining trend during 1982–2012 (Fig. 11.1b). Gregory *et al.* (2007) found that population trends of forest bird species in eastern Europe tend to have greater stability compared with other European regions, but the set of species varies between regions. Angelstam *et al.* (2004) showed that population trends of 18 forest birds in Estonia, Latvia, Lithuania and Poland were significantly more positive than in Denmark, Finland and Sweden, likely due to stronger forest management activity in the latter north-western areas.

National data showed that some common forest bird species were stable or even increasing. For instance, national atlas work in the former Czechoslovakia in the late 1980s and early 2000s revealed increasing occupancy of grid squares by forest birds (Koleček *et al.* 2010). These general increases amongst forest birds were probably due to the increase in forest cover (Reif *et al.* 2007; Koleček & Reif 2011). However, this has not necessarily benefited forest specialists (Reif *et al.* 2013). In addition, in the Czech Republic, species that prefer broadleaved forest showed more positive trends than species that prefer conifers or mountain forests, which is likely caused by the gradual replacement of coniferous by deciduous forests (Reif *et al.* 2008). The common forest birds increased also in Estonia during 1983–2000, but showed sharp declines between 2009 and 2010, possibly due to one severe winter (Kuresoo *et al.* 2011).

Forest bird species also seem to do well in one of the largest protected areas of temperate forest in Europe, Białowieża National Park (BNP), Poland. The numbers of 18 out of 26 common breeding forest bird species inside BNP showed increasing trends, and only three species declined during the period 1975–2009. All three declining species were long-distance migrants (Wesołowski *et al.* 2010; see also Wesołowski & Tomiałojć 1997). Nevertheless, BNP does not seem to represent the general pattern of forest birds in Poland. The slopes of population trends of 22 forest bird species in BNP and the rest of Poland were not significantly correlated during 2000–2009 ($F_{1,20}$ = 0.57, b = 0.21, P = 0.46), but the population trends in general were neither more positive nor more negative in BNP compared to the rest of Poland (data from Wesołowski *et al.* 2010). These differences could be driven by many types of landscape change, including an increasing area of plantations outside BNP (Wesołowski *et al.* 2010).

As with northern Europe, some species in eastern European countries appear to be negatively affected by forestry. As an example, the black stork *Ciconia nigra* population in Lithuania decreased by at least 20% between the periods 1978–1996 and 2005–2006. Shifts in forest structure due to timber harvest are likely to be implicated. The nest sites of black storks were situated significantly more often in younger forest and closer to the forest edge during the latter period than the first study period (Treinys *et al.* 2008).

11.3.4 Western Europe

For the purposes of EBCC monitoring, western Europe includes Austria, Belgium, Denmark, former West Germany, Luxembourg, the Netherlands, Republic of Ireland, Switzerland and United Kingdom. The combined common forest bird indicator of 27 species showed rather strong fluctuations but no clear trends during 1980–2012 Fig. 11.1a).

In Ireland, a programme of afforestation has increased the proportion of forest cover from 1% to more than 10% within a century. Not surprisingly, this has led to increasing population densities of several bird species (Wilson *et al.* 2012). Moreover, great spotted woodpecker *Dendrocopos major* recently colonised Ireland, probably due to afforestation there and increased production of dispersing individuals in Great Britain (Mcdevitt *et al.* 2011). In contrast, common bird monitoring in Denmark has shown a declining trend of species living in coniferous forests during 1986–2009 (Larsen *et al.* 2011). Also, in Britain there have been marked declines and range contractions over the last 30 years in populations of several woodland species, including residents such as willow tit, lesser spotted woodpecker and hawfinch *Coccothraustes coccothraustes* and most long-distance migrants (Hewson *et al.* 2007; Hewson & Noble 2009; Balmer *et al.* 2013).

Several studies have shown habitat-specific population trends of forest species. In the Netherlands over the period 1984–2004, forest populations of 10 long-distance migratory species had a more negative trend than populations of the same species that breed in marshlands (Both *et al.* 2010). This has been interpreted in terms of changes in the timing of food availability driven by climate change. In highly seasonal forest landscapes, a mismatch has developed between a relatively narrow peak in food availability and the timing of breeding in migrants, whereas in marshland, food is more evenly distributed through the spring and summer (Both *et al.* 2010). Population trends of migratory species can also be linked with their habitat selection during the non-breeding season. British studies show that more species that overwinter in west Africa in humid forests and humid savannah, as well as scarce and specialist (e.g., scrub and understorey) woodland species, have declined compared to species that overwinter in arid savannah habitat and ones that are relatively common or generalist (Hewson *et al.* 2007; Hewson & Noble 2009; Thaxter *et al.* 2010). Most western European areas lack large areas of unbroken forest, which may explain why the status of forest grouse species is critical in many countries. For instance, capercaillie was reintroduced in Scotland in the 1830s after becoming extinct in the late 18th century. The re-established population has been declining since the 1970s due to poor breeding success, climate change and the high mortality of full-grown birds colliding with forest fences (Moss 2001). The UK black grouse *Lyrurus tetrix* population has also been in long-term decline (Sim *et al.* 2008; Balmer *et al.* 2013).

11.3.5 Southern Europe

The forest bird indicator for southern Europe shows contrasting trends in recent decades. The combined population trends of 24 species from Portugal, Spain, France and Italy showed a clear increase in the 2000s (Fig. 11.1b). However, there was a decline throughout the 1990s, partly driven by the situation in France, where forest specialists in particular showed declining trends (Julliard *et al.* 2003).

The positive signs in the populations of forest birds are likely linked with changes in agricultural practices, which have caused forest expansion, at least in France and in Catalonia, north-east Spain (see Chapter 9). Large-scale forest maturation mainly due to land abandonment has caused distributions of many forest species to expand despite the negative effects of forest fires (Gil-Tena *et al.* 2009; Herrando *et al.* 2015). In France, these changes have caused declines of open-habitat species, such as tawny pipit *Anthus campestris* and common linnet *Carduelis cannabina*, but, on the other hand, increases of common forest species such as common chiffchaff *Phylloscopus collybita* and Eurasian wren *Troglodytes troglodytes* from the mid-1980s to the early 2000s. However, several species associated mainly with mountains in this region have declined, including capercaillie, Eurasian bullfinch *Pyrrhula pyrrhula* and citril finch *Serinus citrinella* (Fonderflick *et al.* 2010; Fernández-Olalla *et al.* 2012).

There are also some positive signs from the Atlantic islands. The population of the endemic Azores bullfinch *Pyrrhula murina,* although threatened by habitat destruction due to land-use changes and invasion of the native laurel forest by exotic plants (Bastos *et al.* 2012), has increased about six-fold since the early 1990s, probably due to improved survival.

11.3.6 Summary of Regional Variation in Population Changes

In Europe, the strongest declines in recent decades have been found in northern Europe, especially in Finland, at least partly due to changes in forest structure (see Box 11.1). In contrast, the general status of common forest birds has improved in southern Europe due to abandonment of cultivated areas, although long-term changes in south-eastern Europe (Greece and the Balkans) are not known. Population trends of common forests birds are most stable on a regional scale in eastern Europe, but even there trends of forest birds differ locally, which could be due to the fact that timber harvesting has increased in certain areas and the amount of forest cover has increased in others. Common forest birds seem to succeed moderately well also in western Europe, and at least in some countries the amount of deadwood has increased (Hess 2009, cited in Spühler *et al.* 2015; Amar *et al.* 2010), producing positive population trends, such as an increase of middle spotted woodpecker *Leiopicus medius* in most parts of central and southern Europe (Box 11.2). Nevertheless, due to historical heavy fragmentation of forests, especially in western and southern Europe, specialists of larger uniform forest areas, such as capercaillie and black grouse, are in danger and retreated into isolated forests, often in the mountain areas, such as the Alps and the Pyrenees. In general, over recent decades European forest birds have fared better than farmland species (Gregory *et al.* 2007).

In some species, there are also variations in population trends between countries. For instance, European green woodpecker *Picus viridis* has considerably decreased in Estonia, Denmark and Sweden, whereas it has increased in Germany and the UK (Hewson *et al.* 2007; European Union 2015). Where declines of the green woodpecker have occurred, these are probably associated with the loss of semi-natural wooded grasslands (Lõhmus *et al.* 2016). On the other hand, hawfinch has decreased in Germany and the UK, but increased in France, Belgium, Latvia and Finland (European Union 2015). In Britain, hawfinches preferred areas where woodland cover was higher (Kirby *et al.* 2015). Originally, hawfinch may have been a species that preferred old, tall

Box 11.2 *Population recovery and range expansion of middle spotted woodpecker*

Middle spotted woodpecker *Leiopicus medius* is a Eurasian forest species whose distribution covers large parts of Europe from northern Spain and France to western Russia and the Middle East. The species has been classified as an excellent avian indicator of forest bird diversity and abundance (Roberge & Angelstam 2006), because it requires mature broadleaved forests (Pasinelli 2000; Robles & Ciudad 2012). Due to large-scale loss and fragmentation of mature forests, especially oak forests, the species was in decline during the 20th century in many European countries (39% of the 23 countries showed a negative trend during the period 1970–1990; Mikusiński & Angelstam 1997). During this period, the species became extinct in Sweden in 1983 (last individual observed in 1982) as a consequence of a combination of isolation and sporadic cold winters (Pettersson 1985). Due to its unfavourable population status, the species has been listed in Annex 1 of the European Union Birds Directive, which requires conservation actions in the member countries (2009/147/EC).

The latest EU Birds Directive report, which gathered information from the member states, showed that the population status of the species had clearly improved in recent decades. The species was increasing in nine countries out of 16 with available population trend data and declining only in two during the 21st century (European Union 2015). Furthermore, the information from outside the EU also appears positive, such as range expansion in western Russia (Zav'yalov *et al.* 2010), and the species' conservation status was classified in the latest European and EU Red Listing as 'least concern' (BirdLife International 2015).

Population increases and range expansion (such as colonisation of Estonia; European Union 2015) in the northern and eastern edge of the range could be partly linked with warming climate, since both winter survival and breeding success are positively correlated with temperature (Pettersson 1985; Pasinelli 2001). However, the population has been increasing also in western and south-western areas, as well as in some core breeding countries, which suggests that the population recovery is not driven solely by climate. Importantly, several studies suggest that habitat quality has improved in some areas. For instance, population increase in the Spanish Pyrenees between

Box 11.2 (cont.)

1990 and 2010 was likely due to an increasing presence of mature oak forests (Romero *et al.* 2013). Correspondingly, an increase in the amount of deadwood in Switzerland is at least partly responsible for the positive trend in a local middle spotted woodpecker population (Spühler *et al.* 2015). Robles and Ciudad (2012) showed that habitat patch quality is more important than patch size or connectivity of patches in explaining the patch occupancy of the species. We can only hope that this positive tendency will continue and will be reflected in the population trends of common forest species and other specialists that depend on mature forests.

Photo: Z. Hanč

forest, because the densities of hawfinch in the old-growth forest of Białowieża National Park are very high (Tomiałojć 2005). Thus, European green woodpecker and hawfinch are examples of species that appear to be affected by forest management and land use practices which may differ between countries.

11.4 A Wider Geographical Perspective

Several regional-scale studies dealing with forest bird population trends have been published in North America (e.g., Holmes & Sherry 2001; King et al. 2008; McNulty et al. 2008; Blodget et al. 2009; Brooks et al. 2010). However, we concentrate here on the continent-scale analyses. In North America, the BBS has provided important information on population trends, although coverage for the very northern species is limited (Machtans et al. 2014). In continent-wide analyses for the period 1968–2008, Sauer & Link (2011) showed that eastern forest-obligate species (n = 25) had declined on average about 26%, but western forest-obligate species (n = 37) showed a stable trend. Trends of boreal-forest-obligate species (n = 24) showed a negative tendency (–18%), but due to large species-specific variation, this was not significant.

Environmental changes in the wintering areas and along the migration routes can likely explain part of the declines (Norris et al. 2004; Kirby et al. 2008; Marra et al. 2015). Combined data of 26 studied wood warbler species from central and eastern North American breeding grounds that migrate to the Neotropics showed declining trends in the 1970s in the Appalachian Mountains and Eastern Foothills (James et al. 1996). On a continental scale, the general trend of Neotropical migrants was also negative from the late 1960s until the late 1980s, but has been stable since then, whereas populations of temperate migrants and residents were stable or showed increasing trends (Robbins et al. 1989; Askins et al. 1990; Sauer & Link 2011; however, see Valiela & Martinetto 2007).

Population trends of forest birds can also be affected by environmental changes in the breeding grounds. For instance, Robbins et al. (1989) and Askins et al. (1990) suggested that habitat loss and fragmentation in both breeding and wintering grounds had caused declines of forest species between the 1940s and the 1980s. Using BBS data, Pidgeon et al. (2014) showed that species richness of forest birds depends on housing density. In the early stages of human settlement, housing density is low and can be positively linked with species richness, but in later stages, increased density of settlements is usually detrimental to forest-species richness. Declines of North American forest species could also be linked with increased deer populations. A continent-wide relationship has been established between deer abundance and the status of understorey-dependent bird species (i.e., species that are potentially most sensitive to vegetation removal by deer); the proportion of understorey-dependent species that has declined over the period 1966–2009 is higher in areas with the greatest biomass of deer (Chollet & Martin 2013).

We are not aware of any paper that has investigated long-term abundance trends of breeding Asian forest birds at a large spatial scale in the boreal or temperate zone. Nevertheless, investigation of the changes in range size among Japanese forest birds showed that species that prefer early successional habitats have decreased, whereas short-distance migrants and residents that prefer mature forest habitats have increased. This is due to the cessation of most forestry actions since the 1970s as most of the wood has been imported from southern latitudes (Yamaura et al. 2009). However, long-distance migratory species in Japan showed declining trends, probably as a consequence of drastic loss of tropical forests in south and south-east Asia (Yamaura et al. 2009). It seems inevitable that logging of tropical forest has reduced many other populations of tropical migrants in Asia (Kirby et al. 2008; Li Yong et al. 2015). In general, east Asian migratory songbirds are more dependent on mature forests than are European songbirds that migrate to the Afrotropics (Li Yong et al. 2015). Some forest birds that winter in Asia but breed in Europe, such as rustic bunting *Emberiza rustica* and scarlet rosefinch *Carpodacus erythrinus* (forest species in the wintering grounds), have decreased in the European breeding areas in recent decades (Laaksonen & Lehikoinen 2013).

In general, these findings suggest that many common forest bird species have declined in the long term in Europe, North America and Asia. Outside Europe, population trends of boreal and temperate forest birds in North America are much better known than in Asia. Furthermore, the North American surveys show small long-term decline with regional differences. In Asia, the limited information suggests population decline, much of which is caused by drastic habitat loss in the wintering grounds of tropical migrants.

11.5 Conservation Status of Forest Bird Species

BirdLife International (2015) has recently published a European Red List of birds. Among the 232 native forest bird species, 15 (6%) were Red-Listed. Inside the EU, the list was even longer, 26 species, despite the lower number of considered species, 217 (12%; Appendix 11.2). This is mainly because several non-EU eastern European countries, such as Russia, have important and relatively secure forest bird populations.

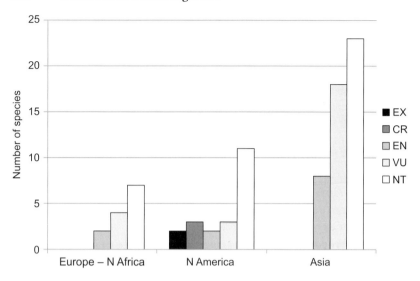

Figure 11.3 Number of globally Red-Listed forest bird species in the Northern Hemisphere. EX, extinct; CR, critically endangered; EN, endangered; VU, vulnerable; NT, near-threatened. Please note that some Red-Listed species occur on two continents and are counted twice.

Altogether, 76 globally Red-Listed forest bird species occur in the Northern Hemisphere outside the tropical and subtropical forests (Fig. 11.3, Appendix 11.3). Forest landscapes are or have been important habitat for these species for at least part of their annual life cycle. Two forest species, Carolina parakeet *Conuropsis carolinensis* and passenger pigeon *Ectopistes migratorius*, both from North America, became extinct about a century ago (in 1910 and 1900, respectively), mainly because of large-scale reduction of their forest habitats and hunting (Saikku 1990; Bucher 1992). Interestingly, all three critically endangered (CR) species are from North America, too. However, possibly two of them, Bachman's warbler *Vermivora bachmanii* and ivory-billed woodpecker *Campephilus principalis*, have also become extinct, since the last confirmed records of these species are from the 1980s. Habitat loss due to logging and clearance for agriculture is thought to be the main reason for their demise. Altogether, 12 species are listed as endangered (EN), 8 of which occur in Asia; 23 species are listed as vulnerable (VU); and 36 are classified as near threatened (NT).

IUCN has classified threats of Red-Listed species according to 12 factors, 9 of which relate to the forest species considered here. The five most common threats were biological resource use (mainly loss of forests due to logging, etc.; 73 species out of 76), agriculture and aquaculture (mainly conversion of forests into agricultural land, 54 species) and natural system modifications (including degradation of forest habitats, 29 species). Biological resource use and agriculture–aquaculture were the most important threats on all four continents.

The largest number of Red-Listed forest species in temperate and boreal zone is found in Asia: 49 species altogether, compared to North America (21), Europe (12) and Africa (3). However, the number of forest bird species is also higher in Asia; central and south-central Asia in particular have several diversity hotspots, including the Himalayas in Tibet, Shaanxi, Sichuan and northern Yunnan (17 species altogether). In addition, forests of the Arabian Peninsula (3 threatened species) and Japanese islands (9 species) hold important concentrations of Red-Listed species.

No Red-Listed grouse, partridge or pheasant species occur in North America, whereas nine are listed in Asia, one of which occurs in Europe too, in the Caucasus mountains (Caucasian black grouse *Lyrurus mlokosiewiczi*). In contrast, in Europe, half of the Red-Listed species are raptors, which is partly because of the long history of persecution of raptor species (e.g., Newton 1998), but also because these species have large territory sizes and habitat loss has caused fragmentation of natural environments. Furthermore, in Asia, seven forest species that spend part of their life cycle in water ecosystems but are threatened by deforestation in the breeding grounds are Red-Listed. However, only one species connected with water ecosystems occurs in other continents.

11.6 Conclusions

Great progress has been made in monitoring and evaluating Red-Listed forest species in recent decades. The citizen science monitoring network has widely improved and is still expanding. The monitoring data have revealed several large-scale issues. First, decline of common long-distance migratory forest birds seems to be a general problem in Europe, Asia and North America (Gregory *et al.* 2007; Sauer & Link 2011; Li Yong *et al.* 2015). Loss of tropical forests is a considerable threat for several endangered species, especially in Asia (Kirby *et al.* 2008; Li Yong *et al.* 2015). This underlines the need to target conservation actions not only on breeding areas, but also on the protection of wintering and migration staging areas (Sanderson *et al.* 2006; Gregory *et al.* 2007; Kirby *et al.* 2008; Laaksonen & Lehikoinen 2013). In general, bird-monitoring schemes are poorest in Asia, where there is the highest number of endangered species.

Monitoring schemes and conservation actions of both endangered and common species should be urgently improved in this region.

Second, on the European scale, the monitoring data reveal that the poorest situation among forest birds in terms of declining trends is in the northern part of the continent. At least in Finland, the declines of forest bird species have gradually continued since the 1950s (Fraixedas *et al.* 2015a); also, the combined population trends from Norway, Sweden and Finland show decreasing trends for the last three decades (Fig. 11.1a). In contrast, the most pronounced recent improvements in the state of common forest birds are evident in some central and southern European countries, such as Ireland, the Czech Republic, north-east Spain and France (Gil-Tena *et al.* 2009; Fonderflick *et al.* 2010; Koleček & Reif 2011). Fortunately, the coverage of monitoring schemes across many European countries has greatly improved in recent years and several of these schemes are still growing, which will further improve our knowledge of the status of European common forest birds in the future.

Third, population trends of species can vary spatially, as shown by the population dynamics of European green woodpecker and hawfinch across their European ranges. Land use and forestry can differ between countries, causing different population trends. In addition, due to climate change, a species could increase at the leading edge and decrease at the trailing edge of its range (Jiguet *et al.* 2010).

Monitoring work will be increasingly vital because of ongoing habitat change and loss, but also to assess responses to climate change. Forest bird populations are being affected by climate change now, and its impacts are expected to intensify in the future. For instance, based on both climate and habitat variables, Barbet-Massin *et al.* (2012) predicted that by 2050, the ranges of 71% of bird species in Europe (409 species in various habitat types) would be reduced by an average of 14%. Climate-change effects can be even more pronounced and more clearly observed in population densities and trends than in species range shifts (see Gregory *et al.* 2009; Virkkala & Lehikoinen 2014).

Although huge progress has been made in monitoring the status of forest birds, there is still much to be done to improve the quality of monitoring schemes. A high priority is to adopt systematic sampling instead of free choice of locations. New schemes are needed in areas which currently have no structured monitoring, though this can be challenging due to a lack of observers or political instability. Future issues that require research are discussed in Chapter 14, and it is clear that data derived from monitoring have an important role to play in much of this research. Monitoring will give insights into the large-scale joint effects of climate change and shifts in forest management, including potential negative effects of introducing non-native stands and positive effects of continuous cover forestry. Monitoring can also help to evaluate the risks and impacts from forest diseases, as well as potential non-native predators, such as the spread of grey squirrel *Sciurus carolinensis* in Europe.

Acknowledgements

Comments by Jiří Reif and an anonymous referee improved the clarity of the paper. Jana Skorpilova kindly provided the EBCC indices for Fig. 11.1. We are very grateful to Grzegorz Mikusiński for preparing Appendix 1. Alexi Lehikoinen has received economical support from the Academy of Finland (grant 275606). Our knowledge of forest bird populations would be minimal without the efforts of huge numbers of skilled volunteers - we warmly thank them all.

References

Amar, A., Smith, K.W., Butler, S. *et al.* (2010) Recent patterns of change in vegetation structure and tree composition of British broadleaved woodland: Evidence from large-scale surveys. *Forestry*, **83**, 345–356.

Angelstam, P., Roberge, J.-M., Lõhmus, A. *et al.* (2004) Habitat modelling as a tool for landscape-scale conservation – a review of parameters for focal forest birds. *Ecological Bulletins*, **51**, 427–453.

Askins, R.A., Lynch, J.F. & Greenberg, R. (1990) Population declines in migratory birds in eastern North America. *Current Ornithology*, **7**, 1–57.

Balmer, D.E., Gillings, S., Caffrey, B.J., Swann, R. L., Downie, I.S. & Fuller, R.J. (2013) *Bird Atlas 2007–2011: The Breeding and Wintering Birds of Britain and Ireland*. Thetford: BTO Books.

Barbet-Massin, M., Thuiller, W. & Jiguet, F. (2012) The fate of European breeding birds under climate, land-use and dispersal scenarios. *Global Change Biology*, **18**, 881–890.

Bastos, R., Santos, M., Ramos, J.A. *et al.* (2012) Testing a novel spatially-explicit dynamic modelling approach in the scope of the laurel forest management for the endangered Azores bullfinch (*Pyrrhula murina*) conservation. *Biological Conservation*, **147**, 243–254.

Batten, L.A. & Marchant, J.H. (1977) Bird population changes for the years 1965–75. *Bird Study*, **24**, 55–61.

Bibby, C.J., Burgess, N.D., Hill, D.A. & Mustoe, S.H. (2000) *Bird Census Techniques* (2nd ed.). London: Academic Press.

BirdLife International (2013) The IUCN Red List of Threatened Species. Version 2014.3. www.iucnredlist.org. Accessed 21 January 2015.

BirdLife International (2015) *European Red List of Birds*. Luxembourg: Office for Official Publications of the European Communities.

Blodget, B.G., Dettmetrs, R. & Scanlon, J. (2009) Status and trends of birds in an extensive Western Massachusetts Forest. *Northeastern Naturalist*, **16**, 423–422.

Both, C., van Turnhout, C.A.M., Bijlsma, R.G., Siepel, H., Van Strien, A.J. & Foppen, R.P.B. (2010) Avian population consequences of climate change are most severe for long-distance migrants in seasonal habitats. *Proceedings of the Royal Society London B*, **277**, 1259–1266.

Brommer, J.E., Lehikoinen, A. & Valkama, J. (2012) The breeding ranges of Central European and Arctic bird species move poleward. *PLoS ONE* **7**(9), e43648.

Brooks, E.W. & Bonter, D.N. (2010) Long-term changes in avian community structure in a successional, forested, and managed plot in a reforesting landscape. *Wilson Journal of Ornithology*, **122**, 288–295.

Bucher, E.H. (1992) The causes of extinction of the passenger pigeon. *Current Ornithology*, **9**, 1–36.

Butchart, S.H.M., Walpole, M., Collen, B. *et al.* (2010) Global biodiversity: Indicators of recent declines. *Science*, **328**, 1164–1168.

Chen, I.-C., Hill, J.K., Ohlemüller, R., Roy, D.B. & Thomas, C. D. (2011) Rapid range shifts of species associated with high levels of climate warming. *Science*, **333**, 1024–1026.

Chollet, S. & Martin, J.-L. (2013) Declining woodland birds in North America: Should we blame Bambi? *Diversity and Distribution*, **19**, 481–483.

Crick, H.Q.P. (2004) The impact of climate change on birds. *Ibis*, **146** (Suppl. 1), 48–56.

Devictor, V., Swaay, C., Brereton, T. *et al.* (2012) Differences in the climatic debts of birds and butterflies at a continental scale. *Nature Climate Change*, **2**, 121–124.

Dunn, E.H., Hobson, K.A., Wassanaar, L., Hussell, D.J.T. & Allan, M.L. (2006) Identification of summer origins of songbirds migrating through southern Canada in autumn. *Avian Conservation and Ecology*, **1**(2), 4.

Edenius, L. & Meyer, C. (2002) Activity budgets and microhabitat use in the Siberian Jay *Perisoreus infaustus* in managed and unmanaged forest. *Ornis Fennica*, **79**, 26–33.

Eggers, S. & Low, M. (2014) Differential demographic responses of sympatric Parids to vegetation management in boreal forest. *Forest Ecology and Management*, **319**, 169–175.

Eglington, S.M., Julliard, R., Gargallo, G. *et al.* (2015) Latitudinal gradients in the productivity of European migrant warblers have not shifted northwards during a period of climate change. *Global Ecology and Biogeography* **24**, 427–436.

Eglington, S.M. & Pearce-Higgins, J.W. (2012) Disentangling the relative importance of changes in climate and land-use intensity in driving recent bird population trends. *PLoS ONE*, **7**, e30407.

European Bird Census Council (2015) Trends of common birds in Europe, 2015 update. www.ebcc.info/index.php?ID=587. Accessed 26 September 2015.

European Union (2015) Bird Directive article 12 reporting. http://bd.eionet .europa.eu/article12/summary?period=1&subject=A238. Accessed 25 September 2015.

Fernández-Olalla, M., Martínez-Abraín, A., Canut, J., García-Ferré, D., Afonso, I. & González, L. M. (2012) Assessing different management scenarios to reverse the declining trend of a relict capercaillie population: A modelling approach within an adaptive management framework. *Biological Conservation*, **148**, 79–87.

Fonderflick, J., Caplat, P., Lovaty, F., Thévenot, M. & Prodon, R. (2010) Avifauna trends follow changes in a Mediterranean upland pastoral system. *Agriculture, Ecosystems and Environment*, **137**, 337–347.

Fraixedas, S., Lehikoinen, A., Lindén, A. (2015a) Impact of climate and land use change on wintering bird populations in Finland. *Journal of Avian Biology*, **46**, 63–72.

Fraixedas, S., Lindén, A. & Lehikoinen, A. (2015b) Recent population trends of common breeding birds in southern Finland correspond with trends in forest management and climate change. *Ornis Fennica*, **92**, 187–203

Gil-Tena, A., Brotons, L. & Saura, S. (2009) Mediterranean forest dynamics and forest bird distribution changes in the late 20th century. *Global Change Biology*, **15**, 474–485.

Gregory R.D., van Strien A. J., Voříšek P. *et al.* (2005) Developing indicators for European birds. *Philosophical Transactions of the Royal Society Series B*, **360**, 269–288.

Gregory, R.D., Voříšek, P., Van Strien, A. *et al.* (2007) Population trends of widespread woodland birds in Europe. *Ibis*, **149** (Suppl. 2), 78–97.

Gregory, R.D., Willis, S.G., Jiguet, F. *et al.* (2009) An indicator of the impact of climatic change on European bird populations. *PLoS ONE* **4 (3)**, e4678.

Griesser, M., Nystrand, M., Eggers, S. & Ekman, J. (2007) Impact of forestry on fitness correlates and population productivity in an open-nesting bird species. *Conservation Biology*, **21**, 767–774.

Hagemeijer, W.J.M. & Blair, M.J. (eds.) (1997) *The EBCC Atlas of European Breeding Birds: Their Distribution and Abundance*. London: Poyser.

Haila, Y., Järvinen, O. & Väisänen, R.A. (1980) Effects of changing forest structure on long-term trends in bird populations in SW Finland. *Ornis Scandinavica*, **11**, 12–22.

Hakkarainen, H., Mykrä, S., Kurki, S., Tornberg, R. & Jungell, S. (2004) Competitive interactions among raptors in boreal forests. *Oecologia*, **141**, 420–424.

Hautala H., Jalonen, J., Laaka-Lindberg, S. & Vanha-Majamaa, I. (2004) Impacts of retention felling on coarse woody debris (CWD) in mature boreal spruce forests in Finland. *Biodiversity and Conservation*, **13**, 1541–1554.

Herrando, S., Brotons, L., Anton, M. *et al.* (2015) Assessing impact of land abandonment on Mediterranean biodiversity using indicators based on bird and butterfly monitoring data. *Environmental Conservation*, DOI: 10.1017/S0376892915000260.

Hewson, C.M., Amar, A., Lindsell, J.A. *et al.* (2007) Recent changes in bird populations in British broadleaved woodland. *Ibis*, **149** (Suppl. 2), 14–28.

Hewson, C.M. & Noble, D.G. (2009) Population trends of breeding birds British woodlands over a 32-year period: Relationships with food, habitat use and migratory behaviour. *Ibis*, **151**, 464–486.

Hoffmann, M., Hilton-Taylor, C., Angulo, A. *et al.* (2010) The impact of conservation on the status of the world's vertebrates. *Science*, **330**, 1503–1509.

Holmes, R.T. & Sherry, T.W. (2001) Thirty-year bird population trends in a unfragmented temperate deciduous forest: Importance of habitat change. *Auk*, **118**, 589–609.

James, F.C., McCulloch, C. & Widenfeld, D.A. (1996) New approaches to the analysis of population trends in land birds. *Ecology*, **77**, 13–27.

Järvinen, O. & Väisänen, R.A. (1977) Recent quantitative changes in the populations of Finnish land birds. *Polish Ecological Studies*, **3**, 177–188.

Jiguet F., Gregory R.D., Devictor V. *et al.* (2010) Population trends of European common birds are predicted by characteristics of their climatic niche. *Global Change Biology*, **16**, 497–505.

Julliard, R., Jiguet, F. & Couvet, D. (2003) Common birds facing global changes: What makes a species at risk. *Global Change Biology*, **10**, 148–154.

King, D.I., Lambert, J.D., Buonaccorsi, J.P. & Prout, L.S. (2008) Avian population trends in the vulnerable montane forests of the Northern Appalachians, USA. *Biodiversity and Conservation*, **17**, 2691–2700.

Kirby, J.S., Stattersfield, A.J., Butchart, S.H.M. *et al.* (2008) Key conservation issues for migratory land- and waterbird species on the world's major flyways. *Bird Conservation International*, **18**, S49–S73

Kirby, W.B., Bellamy, P.E., Stanbury, A.J., Bladon, A.J., Grice, P.V. & Gillings, S. (2015) Breeding season habitat associations and population declines of British Hawfinches *Coccothraustes coccothraustes*. *Bird Study*, **62**, 348–357.

Kjellén, N. & Roos, G. (2000) Population trends in Swedish raptors demonstrated by migration counts at Falsterbo, Sweden 1942–1997. *Bird Study*, **47**, 195–211.

Koleček, J. & Reif, J. (2011) Differences between the predictors of abundance, trend and distribution as three measures of avian population change. *Acta Ornithologica*, **46**, 143-153.

Koleček, J., Reif, J., Šťastný, K. & Bejček, V. (2010) Changes in bird distribution in Central European country between 1985–1989 and 2001–2003. *Journal of Ornithology*, **151**, 923–932.

Korpimäki, E. & Hakkarainen, H. (2013) *The Boreal Owl: Ecology, Behaviour, and Conservation of a Forest-Dwelling Predator*. New York: Cambridge University Press.

Kuresoo, A., Pehlak, H. & Nellis, R. (2011) Population trends of common birds in Estonia in 1983–2010. *Estonian Journal of Ecology*, **60**, 88–110.

Laaksonen, T.K. & Lehikoinen, A. (2013) Population trends in boreal birds: Continuing declines in long-distance migrants, agricultural and northern species. *Biological Conservation*, **168**, 99–107.

Larsen, J.L., Heldbjerg, H. & Eskildsen, A. (2011) Improving national habitat specific biodiversity indicators using relative habitat use for common birds. *Ecological Indicators*, **11**, 1459–1466.

Lehikoinen, A., Green, M., Husby, M., Kålås, J.A. & Lindström, Å. (2014) Common montane birds are declining in North Europe. *Journal of Avian Biology*, **45**, 3-14.

Lehikoinen, A., Lehikoinen, P., Lindén, A. & Laine, T. (2011) Population trend and status of the endangered White-backed Woodpecker *Dendrocopos leucotos* in Finland. *Ornis Fennica*, **88**, 195–207.

Lehikoinen, A. & Virkkala, R. (2016) North by northwest: Climate change and directions of density shifts in birds. *Global Change Biology*, **22**, 1121–1129.

Li Yong, D., Liu, Y., Wen Low, B., Española, C.P., Choi, C.-Y. & Kawakami, K. (2015) Migratory songbirds in the East Asian-Australasian Flyway: A review from a conservation perspective. *Bird Conservation International*, **25**, 1–37.

Link, W.A. & Sauer, J.R. (1998) Estimating population change from count data: Application to the North American Breeding Bird Survey. *Ecological Applications*, **8**, 258–268.

Lõhmus, A., Nellis, R., Pullerits, M. & Leivits, M. (2016) The potential for long-term sustainability in seminatural forestry: A broad perspective based on woodpecker populations. *Environmental Management*, **57**, 558–571.

Machtans, C.S., Kardynal, K.J. & Smith, P.A. (2014) How well do regional or national Breeding Bird Survey data predict songbird population trends at an intact boreal site? *Avian Conservation and Ecology*, **9** (1), Article 5.

Marra, P.P., Studds, C., Wilson, S., Sillett, T.S., Sherry, T.W. & Holmes, R.T. (2015) Non-breeding season habitat quality mediates the strength of density-dependence for a migratory bird. *Proceedings of the Royal Society London B*, **282**, 20150624.

Mcdevitt, A.D., Kajtoch, Ł., Mazgajski, T.D. *et al.* (2011) The origins of Great Spotted Woodpeckers *Dendrocopos major* colonizing Ireland revealed by mitochondrial DNA. *Bird Study*, **58**, 361–364.

McNulty, S.A., Droege, S. & Masters, R.D. (2008) Long-term trends in breeding birds in an old-growth Adirondack forest and the surrounding regions. *Wilson Journal of Ornithology*, **120**, 153–158.

Mikusiński, G. & Angelstam, P. (1997) European woodpeckers and anthropogenic habitat change: A review. *Vogelwelt*, **118**, 277–283.

Møller, A.P., Fiedler, W. & Berthold, P. (2010) *Effects of Climate Change on Birds*. Oxford: Oxford University Press.

Moss, R. (2001) Second extinction of capercaillie (*Tetrao urogallus*) in Scotland? *Biological Conservation*, **101**, 255–257.

Newton, I. (1998) *Population Limitation in Birds*. London: Academic Press.

Newton, I. (2008) *The Migration Ecology of Birds*. London: Academic Press.

Norris, D.R., Marra, P.P., Kyser, T.K. *et al.* (2004) Tropical winter habitat limits reproductive success on the temperate breeding grounds in migratory bird. *Proceedings of the Royal Society B*, **271**, 59–64.

Ottosson, U., Ottvall, R., Elmberg, J. *et al.* (2012) *The Birds in Sweden – Numbers and Occurrence*. Halmstad: SOF. [in Swedish]

Ottvall R., Edenius L., Elmberg J. *et al.* (2009) Population trends for Swedish breeding birds. *Ornis Svecica*, **19**, 117–192.

Pasinelli, G. (2000) Oaks (*Quercus* sp.) and only oaks? Relations between habitat structure and home range of the middle spotted woodpecker (*Dendrocopos medius*). *Biological Conservation*, **93**, 227–235.

Pasinelli, G. (2001) Breeding performance of the Middle Spotted Woodpecker *Dendrocopos medius* in relation to weather and territory quality. *Ardea*, **89**, 353–361.

Pearce-Higgins, J.W. & Green, R.E. (2014) *Birds and Climate Change: Impacts and Conservation Responses*. Cambridge: Cambridge University Press.

Pettersson, B. (1985) Extinction of an isolated population of the Middle Spotted Woodpecker *Dendrocopos medius* (L.) in Sweden and its relation to general theories on extinction. *Biological Conservation*, **32**, 335–353.

Pidgeon, A.M., Flather, C.H., Radeloff, V.C. *et al.* (2014) Systematic temporal patterns in the relationship between housing development and forest bird biodiversity. *Conservation Biology*, **28**, 1291–1301.

Ram, D., Axelsson, A.-L., Green, M., Smith, H.G. & Lindström, Å. (2017) What drives current population trends in forest birds – forest quantity, quality or climate? A large-scale analyses from northern Europe. *Forest Ecology and Management*, **385**, 177–188.

Reif, J., Prylová, K., Šizling, A. L., Vermouzek, Z., Šťastný, K. & Bejček, V. (2013) Changes in bird community composition in the Czech Republic from 1982 to 200: Increasing biotic homogenization, impacts of warming climate, but no trend in species richness. *Journal of Ornithology*, **154**, 359–370.

Reif, J., Storch, D., Voříšek, P., Šťastný, K. & Bejček (2008) Bird-habitat associations predict population trends in central European forest and farmland birds. *Biodiversity and Conservation*, **17**, 3307–3319.

Reif, J., Voříšek, P., Šťastný, K., Bejček V. & Petr, J. (2007) Population increase of forest birds in the Czech Republic between 1982–2003. *Bird Study*, **54**, 248–255.

Robbins, C.S., Sauer, J.R., Greenberg, R.S. & Droege, S. (1989) Population declines in North American birds that migrate to the Neotropics. *Proceedings of the National Academy of Sciences*, **86**, 7658–7662.

Roberge, J.M. & Angelstam, P. (2006) Indicator species among resident forest birds – A cross-regional evaluation in northern Europe. *Biological Conservation*, **130**, 134–147.

Robles, H. & Ciudad, C. (2012) Influence of habitat quality, population size, patch size, and connectivity on patch-occupancy dynamics of the Middle Spotted Woodpecker. *Conservation Biology*, **26**, 284–293.

Romero, J.L., Lammertink, M. & Cañestro, J.P. (2013) Population increase and habitat use of the Middle Spotted Woodpecker *Dendrocopos medius* in the Aran Valley, Spanish Pyrenees. *Ardeola*, **60**, 345–355.

Saikku, M. (1990) The Extinction of the Carolina Parakeet. *Environmental History Review*, **14** (3), 1–18.

Sanderson, F.J., Donald, P.F., Pain, D.J., Burfield, I.J. & van Bommel, F.P.J. (2006) Long-term population declines in Afro-Palaearctic migrant birds. *Biological Conservation*, **131**, 93–105.

Sauer, J.R. & Link, W.A. (2011) Analysis of the North American Breeding Bird Survey using hierarchical models. *Auk*, **128**, 87–98.

Saurola, P. (1997) The osprey (*Pandion haliaetus*) and modern forestry: A review of population trends and their causes in Europe. *Journal of Raptor Research*, **31**, 129–137.

Saurola, P. (2009) Bad news and good news: Population changes of Finnish owls during 1982–2007. *Ardea*, **97**, 469–482.

Siffczyk, C., Brotons, L., Kangas, K. & Orell, M. (2003) Home range size of willow tits: A response to winter habitat loss. *Oecologia*, **136**, 635–642.

Sim, I.M.W., Eaton, M.A., Setchfield R.P., Warren, P.K. & Lindley, P. (2008) Abundance of male Black Grouse *Tetrao tetrix* in Britain in 2005, and change since 1995–1996. *Bird Study*, **55**, 304–313.

Sirkiä, S., Lindén, A., Helle, P., Nikula, A., Knape, J. & Lindén, H. (2010) Are the declining trends in forest grouse populations due to changes in the forest age structure? A case study of Capercaillie in Finland. *Biological Conservation*, **143**, 1540–1548.

Spühler, L., Krüsi, B.O. & Pasinelli, G. (2015) Do Oaks *Quercus* spp., dead wood and fruiting Common Ivy *Hedera helix* affect habitat selection of the Middle Spotted Woodpecker *Dendrocopos medius*. *Bird Study*, **62**, 115–119.

Thaxter, C.B., Joys, A.C., Gregory, R.D., Baillie, S.R. & Noble, D. (2010) Hypotheses to explain patterns of population changes among breeding bird species in England. *Biological Conservation*, **143**, 2006–2019.

Tomiałojć, L. (2005) Distribution, breeding density and nest sites of Hawfinches *Coccothraustes coccothraustes* in the primeval forest of Białowieża National Park. *Acta Ornithologica*, **40**, 127–138.

Treinys, R., Lõhmus, A., Stoncius, D. *et al.* (2008) At the border of ecological change: Status and nest sites of Lithuanian Black Stork *Ciconia nigra* population 2000–2006 versus 1976–1992. *Journal of Ornithology*, **149**, 75–81.

Valiela, I. & Martinetto, P. (2007) Changes in bird abundance in Eastern North America: Urban sprawl and global footprint. *Bioscience*, **57**, 360–370.

Verner, J. (1985) Assessment of counting techniques. In *Current Ornithology*. Johnston, R.F. (ed.). New York: Plenum Press, pp. 247–302.

Vickery, J.A., Ewing, S.R., Smith, K.W. *et al.* (2014) The decline of Afro-Palaearctic migrants and an assessment of potential causes. *Ibis*, **156**, 1–22.

Virkkala, R. (1990) Ecology of the Siberian Tit *Parus cinctus* in relation to habitat quality: Effects of forest management. *Ornis Scandinavica*, **21**, 139–146.

Virkkala, R. (2004) Bird species dynamics in a managed southern boreal forest in Finland. *Forest Ecology and Management*, **195**, 151–163.

Virkkala, R. (2016) Long-term decline of southern boreal forest birds: Consequence of habitat alteration or climate change? *Biodiversity and Conservation*, **25**, 151–167.

Virkkala, R., Alanko, T., Laine, T. & Tiainen, J. (1993) Population contraction of the white-backed woodpecker *Dendrocopos leucotos* in Finland as a consequence of habitat alteration. *Biological Conservation*, **66**, 47–53.

Virkkala, R. & Lehikoinen, A. (2014) Patterns of climate-induced density shifts of species: Poleward shifts faster in northern boreal birds than in southern birds. *Global Change Biology*, **20**, 2995–3003.

Virkkala, R., Pöyry, J., Heikkinen, R.K., Lehikoinen, A. & Valkama, J. (2014) Protected areas alleviate climate change effects on northern bird species of conservation concern. *Ecology and Evolution*, **4**, 2991–3003.

Voříšek, P., Klvanová, A., Wotton, S. & Gregory, R.D. (eds.) (2008) *A Best Practice Guide for Wild Bird Monitoring Schemes*. Třeboň, Czech Republic: CSO/RSPB.

Wegge, P. & Rolstad, J. (2011) Clearcutting forestry and Eurasian boreal forest grouse: Long-term monitoring of sympatric capercaillie *Tetrao urogallus* and black grouse *T. tetrix* reveals unexpected effects on their population performance. *Forest Ecology and Management*, **261**, 1520–1529.

Wesołowski, T., Mitrus, C., Czeszczewik, D. & Rowiński, P. (2010) Breeding bird dynamics in a primeval temperate forest over thirty-five years: Variation and stability in the changing world. *Acta Ornithologica*, **45**, 209–232.

Wesołowski, T. & Tomiałojć, L. (1997) Breeding bird dynamics in a primaeval temperate forest: Long-term trends in Białowieża National Park (Poland). *Ecography*, **20**, 432–453.

Wiens, J.A. (1989). *The Ecology of Bird Communities. Vol. 2. Processes and Variations*. Cambridge: Cambridge University Press.

Wilson, M.W., Gittings, T., Pithon, J., Kelly, T.C., Irwin, S. & O'Halloran, J. (2012) Bird diversity of afforestation habitats in Ireland: Current trends and likely impacts. *Biology and Environment – Proceedings of the Royal Irish Academy*, **112B**, 55–68.

Winstanley, D., Spencer, R. & Williamson, K. (1974) Where have all the Whitethroats gone? *Bird Study*, **21**, 1–14.

Yamaura, Y., Amano, T., Koizumi, T., Mitsuda, Y., Taki, H. & Okabe, K. (2009) Does land-use change affect biodiversity dynamics at a macroecological scale? A case study of birds over the past 20 years in Japan. *Animal Conservation* **12**, 110–119.

Zav'yalov, E.V., Shlyakhtin, G.V., Tabachishin, V.G., Yakushev, N.N. & Mosolova, E.Y. (2010) Ecological aspects of the dynamics of Middle Spotted Woodpecker (*Dendrocopos medius*) expansion in the lower Volga region. *Russian Journal of Ecology*, **41**, 71–74.

Appendix 11.1

Population trends of common forest birds in Europe according to EBCC (www.ebcc.info/index.php?ID=557) and their conservation status and presence in Annex 1 of the Birds Directive (BirdLife International 2015). VU, vulnerable; NT, near threatened; LC, least concern.

English name	Scientific name	Forest specialist	Long-term trend (%)	10-year trend (%)	Threat level Europe	Threat level EU	Annex I
Azure-winged magpie	Cyanopica cyanus		61	21	LC	LC	
Barn swallow	Hirundo rustica		−25	4	LC	LC	
Barred warbler	Sylvia nisoria		−63	16	LC	LC	x
Black grouse	Lyrurus tetrix		20	54	LC	LC	x
Black woodpecker	Dryocopus martius	x	110	11	LC	LC	x
Black-eared wheatear	Oenanthe hispanica		−25	−18	LC	LC	
Black-headed bunting	Emberiza melanocephala			−4	LC	LC	
Bluethroat	Luscinia svecica		−22	−7	LC	LC	x
Bohemian waxwing	Bombycilla garrulus	x	199	−39	LC	LC	
Brambling	Fringilla montifringilla		−44	−22	LC	VU	
Carrion crow	Corvus corone		21	4	LC	LC	
Cattle egret	Bubulcus ibis		14	28	LC	LC	
Cirl bunting	Emberiza cirlus		49	5	LC	LC	
Coal tit	Periparus ater		−2	2	LC	LC	
Collared flycatcher	Ficedula albicollis	x	171	46	LC	LC	x
Common blackbird	Turdus merula		17	5	LC	LC	
Common buzzard	Buteo buteo		119	5	LC	LC	
Common chaffinch	Fringilla coelebs		13	5	LC	LC	
Common chiffchaff	Phylloscopus collybita	x	87	−8	LC	LC	
Common crane	Grus grus		386	52	LC	LC	x

Common name	Scientific name						
Common cuckoo	*Cuculus canorus*		-26	LC	-6	LC	
Common firecrest	*Regulus ignicapilla*	x	-20	LC	16	LC	
Common grasshopper warbler	*Locustella naevia*		-53	LC	15	LC	
Common greenshank	*Tringa nebularia*		-12	LC	-7	LC	
Common house martin	*Delichon urbicum*		-18	LC	11	LC	
Common kestrel	*Falco tinnunculus*		-31	LC	6	LC	
Common linnet	*Carduelis cannabina*		-56	LC	7	LC	
Common magpie	*Pica pica*		4	LC	5	LC	
Common nightingale	*Luscinia megarhynchos*		-63	LC	12	LC	
Common raven	*Corvus corax*		108	LC	17	LC	
Common redpoll	*Carduelis flammea*		-71	LC	-51	LC	
Common redstart	*Phoenicurus phoenicurus*		26	LC	66	LC	
Common reed bunting	*Emberiza schoeniclus*		-35	LC	-18	LC	
Common rosefinch	*Carpodacus erythrinus*		-27	LC	-24	VU	
Common sandpiper	*Actitis hypoleucos*		-38	LC	-33	NT	
Common snipe	*Gallinago gallinago*		-54	LC	-33	LC	
Common starling	*Sturnus vulgaris*		-58	LC	-5	LC	
Common swift	*Apus apus*		1	LC	2	LC	
Common whitethroat	*Sylvia communis*		25	LC	3	LC	
Common wood pigeon	*Columba palumbus*		103	LC	32	LC	
Dartford warbler	*Sylvia undata*		-32	NT	-24	NT	
Dunnock	*Prunella modularis*		-38	LC	-7	LC	x

(cont.)

(cont.)

English name	Scientific name	Forest specialist	Long-term trend (%)	10-year trend (%)	Threat level Europe	Threat level EU	Annex I
Eurasian blackcap	Sylvia atricapilla		144	36	LC	LC	
Eurasian blue tit	Cyanistes caeruleus		44	12	LC	LC	
Eurasian bullfinch	Pyrrhula pyrrhula		−45	−13	LC	LC	
Eurasian collared dove	Streptopelia decaocto		102	39	LC	LC	
Eurasian golden oriole	Oriolus oriolus		19	21	LC	LC	
Eurasian jay	Garrulus glandarius		28	16	LC	LC	
Eurasian nuthatch	Sitta europaea		115	39	LC	LC	
Eurasian siskin	Carduelis spinus	x	32	32	LC	LC	
Eurasian sparrowhawk	Accipiter nisus	x	22	5	LC	LC	
Eurasian tree sparrow	Passer montanus		−52	17	LC	LC	
Eurasian treecreeper	Certhia familiaris		3	17	LC	LC	
Eurasian wren	Troglodytes troglodytes		31	−13	LC	LC	
Eurasian wryneck	Jynx torquilla		−54	24	LC	LC	
European crested tit	Lophophanes cristatus	x	−37	−2	LC	LC	
European goldfinch	Carduelis carduelis		18	1	LC	LC	
European green woodpecker	Picus viridis		48	0	LC	LC	
European greenfinch	Chloris chloris		22	−5	LC	LC	
European pied flycatcher	Ficedula hypoleuca		−23	0	LC	LC	

Common name	Scientific name		Change 1	Change 2	Status 1	Status 2	
European robin	*Erithacus rubecula*		14	−3	LC	LC	
European serin	*Serinus serinus*		−42	−17	LC	LC	
European turtle dove	*Streptopelia turtur*		−77	−21	VU	NT	
Fieldfare	*Turdus pilaris*		0	−29	LC	VU	
Garden warbler	*Sylvia borin*		−21	−9	LC	LC	
Goldcrest	*Regulus regulus*	x	−33	−25	LC	NT	
Great spotted woodpecker	*Dendrocopos major*		80	29	LC	LC	
Great tit	*Parus major*		22	13	LC	LC	
Green sandpiper	*Tringa ochropus*	x	−2	−8	LC	LC	
Grey heron	*Ardea cinerea*		127	−12	LC	LC	
Grey-headed woodpecker	*Picus canus*	x	349	−2	LC	LC	x
Hawfinch	*Coccothraustes coccothraustes*		343	18	LC	LC	
Hazel grouse	*Tetrastes bonasia*	x	−10	−13	LC	LC	x
Hoopoe	*Upupa epops*		148	4	LC	LC	
Icterine warbler	*Hippolais icterina*		−36	5	LC	LC	
Lesser spotted woodpecker	*Dryobates minor*	x	−77	−4	LC	LC	
Lesser whitethroat	*Sylvia curruca*		−21	−4	LC	LC	
Little egret	*Egretta garzetta*			−30	LC	LC	x
Long-tailed tit	*Aegithalos caudatus*		92	7	LC	LC	
Marsh tit	*Poecile palustris*	x	−20	25	LC	LC	
Marsh warbler	*Acrocephalus palustris*		5	−1	LC	LC	
Meadow pipit	*Anthus pratensis*		−70	−32	NT	VU	
Middle spotted woodpecker	*Leiopicus medius*	x	11	48	LC	LC	x

(cont.)

(cont.)

English name	Scientific name	Forest specialist	Long-term trend (%)	10-year trend (%)	Threat level Europe	Threat level EU	Annex I
Mistle thrush	Turdus viscivorus		−24	4	LC	LC	
Northern nutcracker	Nucifraga caryocatactes	x	68	8	LC	LC	
Northern wheatear	Oenanthe oenanthe		−59	−2	LC	LC	
Ortolan bunting	Emberiza hortulana		−88	−14	LC	LC	x
Red-backed shrike	Lanius collurio		−35	10	LC	LC	x
Redwing	Turdus iliacus		−17	−25	NT	VU	
Ring ouzel	Turdus torquatus		6	10	LC	LC	
River warbler	Locustella fluviatilis		−64	−29	LC	VU	
Rook	Corvus frugilegus		170	−11	LC	LC	
Rustic bunting	Emberiza rustica		−84	−48	VU	VU	
Sardinian warbler	Sylvia melanocephala	x	98	−1	LC	LC	
Short-toed treecreeper	Certhia brachydactyla		4	20	LC	LC	
Song thrush	Turdus philomelos		10	17	LC	LC	
Spotless starling	Sturnus unicolor		27	26	LC	LC	
Spotted flycatcher	Muscicapa striata		−42	0	LC	LC	
Stock dove	Columba oenas		28	14	LC	LC	
Subalpine warbler	Sylvia cantillans		68	25	LC	LC	
Syrian woodpecker	Dendrocopos syriacus			−73	LC	LC	x
Thrush nightingale	Luscinia luscinia		−16	−7	LC	LC	

Common name	Scientific name						
Tree pipit	*Anthus trivialis*		−55	−8	LC	LC	
Western Bonelli's warbler	*Phylloscopus bonelli*	x	−19	59	LC	LC	
Western jackdaw	*Coloeus monedula*		22	4	LC	LC	
Western orphean warbler	*Sylvia hortensis*		106	62	LC	LC	
Western yellow wagtail	*Motacilla flava*		−52	12	LC	LC	
Whimbrel	*Numenius phaeopus*		19	17	LC	LC	
Whinchat	*Saxicola rubetra*		−76	−27	LC	LC	
White wagtail	*Motacilla alba*		−11	−7	LC	LC	
Willow tit	*Poecile montanus*	x	−63	−20	LC	VU	
Willow warbler	*Phylloscopus trochilus*		−38	−7	LC	LC	
Woodlark	*Lullula arborea*		50	16	LC	LC	x
Wood sandpiper	*Tringa glareola*		−13	14	LC	LC	x
Wood warbler	*Phylloscopus sibilatrix*	x	−35	16	LC	LC	
Woodchat shrike	*Lanius senator*		−13	−13	LC	LC	
Yellowhammer	*Emberiza citrinella*		−44	−12	LC	LC	

Appendix 11.2

Red-Listed species in Europe and the EU area that use forest during part of their life cycle, based on BirdLife International (2015). Note that in some cases (e.g., gyr falcon), forests are a very minor constituent of the habitats used by a species. CR, critically endangered; EN, endangered; VU, vulnerable; NT, near threatened.

English name	Scientific name	Europe	EU
Willow grouse	*Lagopus lagopus*	VU	VU
Rock partridge	*Alectoris graeca*	NT	VU
Red kite	*Milvus milvus*	NT	NT
Rough-legged buzzard	*Buteo lagopus*	–	EN
Greater spotted eagle	*Aquila clanga*	EN	CR
Bonelli's eagle	*Aquila fasciata*	NT	NT
Eastern imperial eagle	*Aquila heliaca*		NT
Spanish imperial eagle	*Aquila adalberti*	VU	VU
Red-footed falcon	*Falco vespertinus*	NT	VU
Gyr falcon	*Falco rusticolus*	–	VU
Iberian green woodpecker	*Picus sharpei*	NT	NT
Siberian accentor	*Prunella montanella*	NT	–
Fieldfare	*Turdus pilaris*	–	VU
Redwing	*Turdus iliacus*	NT	VU
Arctic warbler	*Phylloscopus borealis*	–	VU
Goldcrest	*Regulus regulus*	–	NT
Willow tit	*Poecile montanus*	–	VU
Siberian tit	*Poecile cinctus*	–	VU
Krüper's nuthatch	*Sitta krueperi*	–	NT
Corsican nuthatch	*Sitta whiteheadi*	VU	VU
Great grey shrike	*Lanius excubitor*	VU	VU
Brambling	*Fringilla montifringilla*	–	VU
Common rosefinch	*Carpodacus erythrinus*	–	VU
Azores bullfinch	*Pyrrhula murina*	EN	EN
Pine bunting	*Emberiza leucocephalos*	VU	–
Rustic bunting	*Emberiza rustica*	VU	VU

Appendix 11.3

Breeding regions of global Red-Listed forest birds species based on the IUCN database (31 March 2015). As, Asia; Eur, Europe; N Afr, North Africa; N Am, North America; EX, extinct; CR, critically endangered; EN, endangered; VU, vulnerable; NT, near threatened.

Common name	Scientific name	Region	Status
Ala Shan redstart	*Phoenicurus alaschanicus*	As	NT
Arabian tit-warbler	*Sylvia buryi*	As	VU
Arabian woodpecker	*Dendropicos dorae*	As	VU
Asian crested ibis	*Nipponia nippon*	As	EN
Black-throated blue robin	*Luscinia obscura*	As	VU
Blakiston's eagle-owl	*Bubo blakistoni*	As	EN
Brown-eared pheasant	*Crossoptilon mantchuricum*	As	VU
Chinese grouse	*Tetrastes sewerzowi*	As	NT
Copper pheasant	*Syrmaticus soemmerringii*	As	NT
Firethroat	*Luscinia pectardens*	As	NT
Giant babax	*Babax waddelli*	As	NT
Gray-tailed tattler	*Heteroscelus brevipes*	As	NT
Grey-sided thrush	*Turdus feae*	As	VU
Izu leaf warbler	*Phylloscopus ijimae*	As	VU
Izu thrush	*Turdus celaenops*	As	VU
Japanese night heron	*Gorsachius goisagi*	As	EN
Japanese paradise flycatcher	*Terpsiphone atrocaudata*	As	NT
Japanese waxwing	*Bombycilla japonica*	As	NT
Japanese wood pigeon	*Columba janthina*	As	NT
Japanese yellow bunting	*Emberiza sulphurata*	As	VU
Long-billed murrelet	*Brachyramphus perdix*	As	NT
Nordmann's greenshank	*Tringa guttifer*	As	EN
Emei Shan liocichla	*Liocichla omeiensis*	As	VU
Oriental white stork	*Ciconia boyciana*	As	EN
Reeve's pheasant	*Syrmaticus reevesii*	As	VU
Rufous-headed robin	*Luscinia ruficeps*	As	EN
Rusty-throated parrotbill	*Paradoxornis przewalskii*	As	VU
Scaly-sided merganser	*Mergus squamatus*	As	EN
Siberian grouse	*Falcipennis falcipennis*	As	NT
Sichuan partridge	*Arborophila rufipectus*	As	EN
Sinchuan grey jay	*Perisoreus internigrans*	As	VU
Sinhuan treecreeper	*Certhia tianquanensis*	As	NT
Snowy-cheeked laughingthrush	*Garrulax sukatschewi*	As	VU
Syrian serin	*Serinus syriacus*	As	VU

(*cont.*)

Common name	Scientific name	Region	Status
Tibetan eared pheasant	*Crossoptilon harmani*	As	NT
Tytler's leaf warbler	*Phylloscopus tytleri*	As	NT
White-eared pheasant	*Crossoptilon crossoptilon*	As	NT
White-speckled laughingthrush	*Garrulax bieti*	As	VU
Yemen thrush	*Turdus menachensis*	As	VU
Yunnan nuthatch	*Sitta yunnanensis*	As	NT
Caucasian black grouse	*Tetrao mlokosiewiczi*	As, Eur	NT
Cinereous vulture	*Aegypius monachus*	As, Eur	NT
Eastern imperial eagle	*Aquila heliaca*	As, Eur	VU
European roller	*Coragias garrulus*	As, Eur	NT
Greater spotted eagle	*Aquila clanga*	As, Eur	VU
Krueper's nuthatch	*Sitta krueperi*	As, Eur	NT
Red kite	*Milvus milvus*	As, Eur	NT
Red-footed falcon	*Falco vespertinus*	As, Eur	NT
Semi-collared flycatcher	*Ficedula semitorquata*	As, Eur	NT
Azores bullfinch	*Pyrrhula murina*	Eur	EN
Corsican nuthatch	*Sitta whiteheadi*	Eur	VU
Spanish imperial eagle	*Aquila adalberti*	Eur	VU
Algerian nuthatch	*Sitta ledanti*	N Afr	EN
Blue chaffinch	*Fringilla teydea*	N Afr	NT
Laurel pigeon	*Columba junoniae*	N Afr	NT
Bachman's sparrow	*Peucaea aestivalis*	N Am	NT
Bachman's warbler	*Vermivora bachmanii*	N Am	CR
Bicknell's thrush	*Catharus bicknelli*	N Am	VU
California condor	*Gymnogyps californianus*	N Am	CR
Carolina parakeet	*Conuropsis carolinensis*	N Am	EX
Cassin's finch	*Haemorhous cassinii*	N Am	NT
Cerulean warbler	*Dendroica cerulea*	N Am	VU
Chimney swift	*Chaetura pelagica*	N Am	NT
Golden-cheeked warbler	*Setophaga chrysoparia*	N Am	EN
Golden-winged warbler	*Vermivora chrysoptera*	N Am	NT
Ivory-billed woodpecker	*Campephilus principalis*	N Am	CR
Kirtland's warbler	*Setophaga kirtlandii*	N Am	NT
Marblet murrelet	*Brachyramphus marmoratus*	N Am	EN
Olive-sided flycatcher	*Contopus cooperi*	N Am	NT
Passenger pigeon	*Ectopistes migratorius*	N Am	EX
Pinyon jay	*Gymnorhinus cyanocephalus*	N Am	VU
Red-cockaded woodpecker	*Leuconotopicus borealis*	N Am	NT
Red-headed woodpecker	*Melanerpes erythrocephalus*	N Am	NT
Spotted owl	*Strix occidentalis*	N Am	NT
Wood thrush	*Hylocichla mustelina*	N Am	NT
Yellow-billed magpie	*Pica nuttalli*	N Am	NT

12 · *Hunting and Other Forms of Exploitation and Persecution of Forest Birds*

ILSE STORCH

12.1 Introduction

Humans most likely have exploited and persecuted birds throughout their existence. People killed birds to eat them, or to eliminate them as vermin or predators. People live-trapped birds to keep them in cages and to train them as hunting and fishing partners. Historic bird-hunting techniques ranged from simple snares and deadfall traps to elaborate devices such as telescopic sticks with birdlime, and sophisticated trapping groves for songbirds and duck decoys for catching wildfowl (Lindner 1940, 1973; Shrubb 2013). Some of these types of hunting became local traditions and are maintained in parts of Europe to the present day (Hirschfeld & Heyd 2005). Other types of bird exploitation found in Europe include the collection of eggs for food; the removal of eggs, nestlings and adults for the pet bird trade and for falconry; the capture of specimens for aviaries and museums; and the collection of feathers for decoration, fishing flies and clothing. Finally, birdwatching is a type of exploitation, however non-consumptive, that has developed into a major recreational activity and a growing international business (Roth & Merz 1996; BirdLife International 2004).

In most European countries, many historic types of consumptive exploitation and persecution of wild birds are now prohibited by law. Yet the pursuit, capture and killing of birds is still commonly practised, both legally and illegally, in all parts of Europe. Grouse shooting is a popular sport in the boreal forest and the arctic tundra, and shooting of waterfowl is valued along the seacoasts and lakeshores. In parts of western Europe, hunting of woodcocks *Scolopax rusticola* is a major sport, and in the Mediterranean, millions of passerines are killed each year for food consumption. Also, the persecution of raptors and corvids as predators of valued small game or domestic poultry continues to be practised.

Historically, food consumption has been the major motivation for all these types of bird exploitation and persecution. In the rich European societies of today, however, the subsistence hunting of the past has turned into a leisure activity of major social and cultural, and hence also economic, importance (Roth & Merz 1996). This transformation of hunting into a sport was first carried out by noblemen, later by the urban bourgeoisie who adopted upper-class habits, and more recently by farmers and the working class (Hudson *et al.* 1989).

The long established cultural importance of many types of bird exploitation may explain why legal hunting is often maintained even where harvested populations become threatened. Although there are millions of bird shooters in Europe (Hirschfeld & Heyd 2005), the proportion of hunters in European societies is less than 2%; only in a few countries, including Ireland (8.3%), Finland (5.9%), Norway (4.8%) and Sweden (3.2%), are hunters still more numerous (FACE 2017). In many European countries, the numbers of bird watchers and preservationists probably far exceed the numbers of bird hunters, although these two groups are not mutually exclusive. For example, in the UK, there are 800,000 members of hunting associations (FACE 2017), whereas the membership of BirdLife partner the Royal Society for the Protection of Birds (RSPB) exceeds 1 million (RSPB 2017); in Germany, there are 380,000 hunters (DJV 2017) and 620,000 members of BirdLife partner Naturschutzbund Deutschland (NABU 2017). Consequently, conflicts over whether hunting of birds is right or wrong are inevitable (Verissimo & Campbell 2015). Many bird species in Europe are declining and their ranges contracting. At the same time, wider public attitudes in Europe towards hunting and fishing in general are gradually changing, in particular against sport hunting of Red-Listed species (Manfredo *et al.* 2003; Hirschfeld & Heydt 2005; Knezevic 2009; Riepe & Arlinghaus 2014; Gamborg & Jensen 2016).

Hunting remains a strong tradition in many rural parts of Europe, and thus may contribute to local economies. Income generated from hunting may create an incentive for habitat preservation among land-owners. In Great Britain, for example, red grouse *Lagopus lagopus scoticus* moors on private lands are intensively managed for shooting (Tharme *et al.* 2001). In Austria, landowners can make several thousand Euros from the shooting of a single capercaillie *Tetrao urogallus* or black grouse

Lyrurus tetrix cock. Advocates of hunting interests argue that hunting will secure time and money invested in maintaining bird populations, whereas hunting bans would cause hunters and landowners to lose interest. This argument is also advanced in current policies such as the Sustainable Hunting Initiative of the European Union, which acknowledges that in some situations, moderate levels of hunting can have an overall favourable effect on conservation, even of threatened bird populations (EU Commission 2014). Nevertheless, hunting as a means of conservation continues to be fiercely debated (Knezevic 2009). The debate often focuses on the question of the morality of sport hunting. Scientific studies can inform this debate by providing insights into questions about the effects of exploitation and persecution on individuals, populations and communities of birds. This chapter summarises some of this knowledge in relation to forest birds. Ecological research, however, cannot provide normative guidance. Whether and under which circumstances exploitation and persecution of wild birds can be considered to be justified is a matter of human values, beliefs and attitudes, which change over time and vary among societies and cultures (Decker *et al.* 2012).

This chapter cannot provide a full account of all the forest bird species that are presently hunted, or otherwise exploited or persecuted. Readers who are interested in details on human utilisation and management of particular species are referred to the Internet. My aspiration here is rather to draw attention to the wide range of effects that exploitation and persecution can have on wildlife. Using some of the most heavily hunted forest bird taxa as examples, I will synthesise published knowledge on how human exploitation and persecution can affect individuals and populations of European forest birds and their communities and ecosystems. The largest available evidence comes from studies of the effects of hunting on game species. However, I also attempt to cover other forms of exploitation and persecution. Regardless of the motivation of the people concerned, hunting can be described as a sport or a form of land use 'that involves the seeking, pursuing, and killing of wild animals' (Encyclopædia Britannica 2017). I adopt this broad and descriptive definition for the purpose of this chapter. Fig. 12.1 summarises the conceptual understanding of hunting and its effects on forest birds.

This chapter is based on journal articles retrieved from the Web of Knowledge (https://apps.webofknowledge.com; last updated March 2017) and cited references in those papers. For publications on the effects

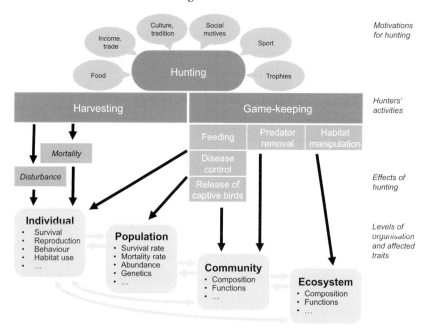

Figure 12.1 Conceptual model of hunting and its effects on wildlife, such as forest birds. Harvesting and the mortality and disturbance it causes affect individuals of the target species, whereas game-keeping activities affect organisational levels from individual to ecosystem (dark arrows). Changes caused by hunting at one organisational level will indirectly extend through all others (light arrows).

of hunting and other forms of exploitation and persecution on the various forest bird species, I used the Web of Knowledge title search function, combining species vernacular name with (hunt★ OR harvest★ OR shoot★ OR exploit★ OR persecut★), and excluded papers reporting on regions other than Europe. In addition, I used a few books and various Internet sources that provided relevant information on the topic.

12.2 Effects of Human Persecution on Bird Populations

From an ecological perspective, hunters are predators. Hunting, just as other kinds of predation (Cresswell 2008), can influence wildlife in many ways. Hunting mortality and its consequences for the structure and dynamics of populations is just the most obvious effect. Hunting can change the behaviour and habitat use of individuals (Stankowich & Blum-stein 2005) and the distribution, activity pattern and social organisation of populations (Byers 1998; Brown *et al.* 1999), and can present a strong selection pressure that changes the evolutionary pathway of populations (Allendorf *et al.* 2008). Hunted populations may differ from non-hunted ones in many ways. This also holds where hunting of a particular species or population is considered sustainable. According to current understanding, hunting is considered sustainable as long as it does not lead to a long-term decline of biodiversity (Council of Europe 2007), which, in practice, will largely be assessed based on conservation status and population numbers of hunted species.

12.2.1 Behavioural Effects

Imagine you come across a grouse before the bird notices you. What response would you expect once it does? Flushing is likely, but indifference too, and even approach cannot be excluded. Responses to humans vary greatly even within the same species, not only in grouse. Rock ptarmigan *Lagopus muta* in the European Alps are likely to hide or flush from a hiker, whereas the same species in the Japanese Alps may tolerate humans at arm's length (Storch 2013). Such differences in behaviour towards humans have much to do with whether or not wildlife perceive humans as predators (Frid & Dill 2002). Inevitably, the perceived predation risk, and thus an animal's response in a human–wildlife encounter, will be influenced by hunting.

Most bird species are potential prey to a wide range of predators, including humans. Prey species have evolved numerous ways to avoid and escape their predators. Examples of predator-avoiding traits range from morphological adaptations, such as camouflage plumage, to behaviours such as long flight-initiation distances and the selection of low-risk habitat. Prey can distinguish dangerous predators and situations from less dangerous ones, and adjust their predation-avoidance investment accordingly (Stankowich & Blumstein 2005).

Researchers have long focused on hunting mortality. More recently, ecologists have intensified efforts to assess the non-lethal effects of human predators on wildlife. According to predation risk theory (Brown *et al.* 1999), anti-predator behaviours are based on genetic predisposition and learning. Prey can evolve predator-specific responses which may persist long after isolation from the predator (Byers 1998; Blumstein 2006). The learning part of anti-predator behaviour is highly flexible (Frid & Dill 2002; Blumstein *et al.* 2004), but can also be lost quickly. It is important to note, however, that learned anti-predator responses can be maintained by tradition across generations after isolation from the predator (Maloney & McLean 1995). This is particularly likely in birds; social learning is common, and there is evidence for both inter-generation and intra-population transmission of anti-predator behaviours (Griffin 2004; Slagsvold & Wiebe 2011).

For some populations of birds, hunting presents a major cause of mortality, and hunting can be hypothesised as a key to understanding variation in their responses towards humans. In ungulates, hunted populations adjust their behaviour to the hunting method humans apply (Sand *et al.* 2006; Thurfjell *et al.* 2013) and show greater 'flight responses' towards humans than do populations in protected areas, but responses may relax in areas with frequent contact with non-hunting humans (Stankowich 2008; Ciuti *et al.* 2012). Studies on the behaviour of hunted bird populations report similar findings (Madsen & Fox 1995; Magige *et al.* 2009; Brøseth & Pedersen 2010). In waterbirds, disturbance by hunters has been shown to affect habitat use (Madsen 1998a, b; Bregnballe *et al.* 2004), time and energy budgets (Guillemain *et al.* 2007; Madsen 1998a) and migration dates (Gunnarsson *et al.* 2006). So far, only a few studies have looked into the effects of hunting on the behaviour of European forest birds. There is evidence that hunted populations of grouse adjust their escape behaviour (Thiel *et al.* 2007; Moss *et al.* 2014) and make greater use of dense cover (Olsson *et al.* 1996; Brøseth & Pedersen 2010). A study on the effects of hunting on the behaviour of woodcocks concluded that habitat quality may reduce negative effects of hunting disturbance in this species (Ferrand *et al.* 2013).

Disturbance caused by human leisure activities is increasingly viewed as a threat to wildlife in many parts of Europe (Ingold 2005). Recreationists may be the proximate cause of disturbances, but ultimately, hunting and persecution have caused wildlife to perceive humans as predators. For conservation managers, it is important to note that the behavioural consequences of hunting may prevent forest birds and other wildlife from habituating to outdoor recreation and tourism activities (Storch 2013). This certainly holds for continued hunting of the population of concern; however, as mentioned above, anti-predator behaviours can persist long after a predator disappears or hunting is banned. Genetic predispositions evolved during a long history of hunting, coupled with predator-avoidance behaviours developed by inter-generational social learning, may prevent quick habituation to humans (Maloney & McLean 1995; Blumstein *et al.* 2004; Griffin 2004).

12.2.2 Effects on Population Abundance and Dynamics

Hunting mortality can be high in hunted populations, and there are numerous cases of wildlife populations extirpated by hunters. Hunting may be particularly harmful for populations already at risk from threats such as habitat fragmentation (Sreekar *et al.* 2015). A challenge for managers, therefore, is to regulate hunting in a way that allows for sustainable yields without compromising a population's viability. To base hunting planning on realistic assumptions, a central question is whether or not hunting mortality is additive or compensatory to natural mortality. The concept suggests that the hunting mortality a population is exposed to may be at least partly compensated by density-dependent changes in reproduction, survival or dispersal (Burnham & Anderson 1984; Aebischer 1997). Numerous studies on a large range of taxa, including forest birds, have addressed this issue. Their results indicate that hunting mortality can vary greatly, from fully additive to fully compensatory (Ellison 1991; Sandercock *et al.* 2011).

In grouse, at least the ptarmigan *Lagopus* spp., species are thought to be capable of compensating for hunting mortality where there is a surplus of birds that are prevented from breeding by territory holders (Pedersen *et al.* 2014). However, in Scandinavia, telemetry studies on the effects of hunting on ptarmigan populations reported evidence of additive hunting mortality, whereas data from larger-scale annual counts suggested almost complete compensation. This seeming contradiction may result from seasonal movements, which re-distribute birds across the landscape (Hörnell-Willebrand *et al.* 2014). Local declines in abundance caused by intensive hunting may be balanced by dispersing birds within a relatively short time (Pedersen *et al.* 2004). Still, without hunting, overall abundance would likely be higher, as experimental studies suggested that hunting of ptarmigan is only partially compensatory (Pedersen *et al.* 2004; Sandercock *et al.* 2011).

Studies on American species of grouse report mixed results regarding the question of compensatory hunting mortality: whereas Small *et al.* (1991) suggested additive hunting mortality in ruffed grouse *Bonasia umbellus*, Sedinger *et al.* (2010) found no such evidence in greater sage-grouse *Centrocercus urophasianus*. For woodcocks, hunting appears to be at least partly additive to natural mortality (Duriez *et al.* 2005; Peron *et al.* 2011; Bruggink *et al.* 2013). For doves and pigeons, data are lacking on the effects of shooting on population dynamics. However, at least in Britain, woodpigeons *Columba palumbus* have increased in abundance despite heavy shooting mortality (Aebischer 1995).

Population-level effects of hunting can be strongly linked to variation in social behaviour and population composition. For example, large black grouse leks attract disproportionally many females during their autumn dispersal (Alatalo *et al.* 1992), and therefore are of major importance for local-scale population growth. Hunting on large leks in autumn is likely to kill those dominant older males, which are the ones that would attract the most females (Kervinen 2013). Thus, the effects of hunting can be significant at the local scale (H. Siitari, pers. comm. 2014), although landscape-scale abundance might seem unchanged, at least in the short to medium term.

The diverse outcomes of all these studies indicate that compensation effects may depend on the spatial and temporal scales of analysis, and also vary among sites and possibly species. Studies in Finland and the UK suggest that the dynamics of hunted populations of grouse may be significantly affected by hunting, even if their abundance appears to be stable. Hunting effects can show up in modified population fluctuation patterns and increased risk of extinction (Bunnefeld *et al.* 2011; Lampila *et al.* 2011). In conclusion, it is safe to assume that a hunted population is more likely than not to differ from a non-hunted population in its spatial and/or temporal demographic patterns.

12.2.3 Genetic Effects of Hunting

Because hunting can be expected to be at least unintentionally selective, it is likely to cause genetic change in wildlife (Milner *et al.* 2007; Allendorf *et al.* 2008). Just as prey species evolve predispositions for responses to specific predators, hunting will present a selection pressure favouring traits which are related to lower mortality risk. This is most obvious in highly selective hunting regimes such as trophy hunting, which can result in rapid evolutionary change in morphological traits, such as body mass and antler size, of the hunted populations (Coltman *et al.* 2003; Darimont *et al.* 2009; Mysterud & Bischof 2010; Monteith *et al.* 2013). Hunting is likely to have evolutionary consequences for behavioural traits as well. Existing evidence for evolutionary change caused by hunting comes from a wide range of taxa (Allendorf *et al.* 2008), but until now, there have been few examples of studies that assessed genetic effects of hunting in birds (Little *et al.* 1993). Elsewhere, I have speculated that the longer history and greater intensity of human hunting in Europe compared with North America may have selected European grouse species for a disposition of stronger escape behaviours towards humans (Storch 2013).

12.2.4 Community- and Ecosystem-level Effects of Hunting

The effects of hunting can reach far beyond the hunted populations. Predation risk can cause trophic cascades and alter the structure of ecosystems (Brown *et al.* 1999; Ripple & Beschta 2004, 2012; Laundré *et al.* 2014). Hunting can therefore be assumed to show effects at the community and ecosystem levels. Predators create 'landscapes of fear', and prey adjust their whereabouts accordingly (Brown *et al.* 1999; Beschta & Ripple 2009). Likewise, a hunted population will change its habitat in favour of lower-risk habitat types, and thereby redirect its effects on the ecosystem caused by feeding, trampling, scratching and depositing faeces and parasites. Trophic cascades caused by hunting have been discussed for various ecosystem types and taxa (Proffitt *et al.* 2009; Effiom *et al.* 2014), but forest bird examples are lacking. However, since hunting can change the habitat use of birds, trophic cascades caused by forest bird hunting are likely. Likewise, shifts in ecosystem functions of hunted forest bird species, such as seed dispersal, can be assumed. Further, hunting can confound the relationships between forest birds and their predators. Strong hunting pressure can prevent prey from developing effective anti-predator behaviours against their natural predators (Sand *et al.* 2006; Lone *et al.* 2014). Likewise, hunting of predators can confound the habitat use of their prey; where predators avoid humans, areas with human presence can become attractive habitats for prey (Berger 2007) such as grouse (Storch 2013). It should also be recognised that hunting of game mammals can have indirect effects on forest birds. High deer populations can reduce habitat quality for bird species that depend on understorey vegetation (Fuller 2001; Côté *et al.* 2004). Hunting pressure on deer can therefore potentially influence ecosystem structure, with cascading ecological effects.

The community- and ecosystem-level effects of hunting described above are unintended. However, hunters commonly also manipulate their hunting grounds intentionally in order to boost the abundance of game species. In favour of small game, including forest birds such as grouse, hunters remove predators (Fletcher *et al.* 2013), and provide food (Marjakangas & Aspegren 1991) and medication against parasites (Newborn & Foster 2002). Habitat management in favour of game species (Baines 1996) can dominate the characteristics of entire landscapes. An extreme example is heather *Calluna vulgaris* moorland in the north of Britain, which is intensively managed on a large scale for red grouse hunting (Tharme *et al.* 2001). Hunters also directly manipulate the availability of game birds for shooting. In parts of Europe, the release of large numbers of captive-bred Galliformes is common practice (Sokos *et al.* 2008) and a dividing issue among hunters and the general public (Gamborg *et al.* 2016). Competition and breeding between released and wild birds can affect the native population in many ways (Ford 2002; Barilani *et al.* 2007; Puigcerver *et al.* 2007), but indirect community-level effects are also likely. Predators (and scavengers) can increase in numbers, predator communities can change in composition and, finally, predator-prey relationships may change fundamentally (Kenward *et al.* 2001; Sokos *et al.* 2008). Hunting-motivated mass release of pheasants *Phasianus colchicus* into woodland habitats has also been shown to at least locally affect the vegetation (Sage *et al.* 2005; Draycott *et al.* 2008).

This section sketched out some of the effects hunting can have at the community and ecosystem levels. Although studies on forest birds are lacking, there is little doubt that hunting has the potential to affect not only hunted populations, but many other species and their interactions and functions as well.

12.3 Hunted Species and Their Management

Throughout European history, numerous species of birds, ranging from large raptors to small songbirds, have been hunted (Lindner 1940, 1973; Shrubb 2013). There is probably not a single bird species that has never been utilised or persecuted by humans. Among forest birds, however, a few taxa have been especially valued as game birds for centuries and are still hunted today. These are primarily the grouse species and the woodcock. Particular hunting cultures have developed around these species, including specialised techniques, tools and dog breeds. In the following sections, I give short accounts on the hunting and hunting management of grouse and woodcock in Europe, the persecution of raptors and corvids as a means of predator control, and the practice of trapping and hunting migratory birds in the Mediterranean. Further, I briefly refer to other forest-inhabiting species of birds that are regularly hunted in Europe.

12.3.1 Hunting of Grouse

There are five species of grouse in Europe. The capercaillie, the black grouse and the hazel grouse *Tetrastes bonasia* are forest birds, associated with various successional stages of coniferous and mixed forests. The rock ptarmigan is confined to Arctic and alpine tundra, whereas the willow grouse *Lagopus l. lagopus* inhabits northern and alpine treeline and forest-edge habitats rich in willows *Salix* spp. and birches *Betula* spp (with its subspecies, red grouse, mentioned earlier which is associated with British moorland). All five species of European grouse have large distribution ranges from westernmost Europe through eastern Asia (Storch 2007a). In Europe, they have their strongholds in the boreal forests of Fennoscandia, but also occur in some mountain ranges of the temperate zone, such as the Alps and the Carpathians. Only a few lowland populations, largely in secondary habitats, remain in central Europe (Storch 2007a). Except for seasonal migrations that rarely exceed 20 km, grouse are non-migratory in Europe (Storch & Segelbacher 2000; Storch 2007a). They are well adapted to harsh winter conditions and survive on diets of seeds, conifer needles and buds of shrubs or deciduous trees.

Globally, due to their large distribution ranges, capercaillie, black grouse and hazel grouse are species classified as Least Concern (IUCN, 2017). At the European level, however, all grouse species, except for the willow grouse, are listed in the European Union's Birds Directive Annex I (special habitat conservation measures required). Further, grouse are listed as threatened species in the Red Data books of numerous European countries. Major declines in grouse numbers occurred from about 1950 in temperate Europe, presumably caused by major and large-scale changes in human land-use practices. As a response to declining population numbers, hunting has been banned in a number of European countries since the 1970s. In some countries, however, grouse species are still legally hunted, although they are listed as threatened in the national Red Data books (Storch 2007a).

Grouse are traditional game species over most of their distribution ranges, and, particularly in the boreal forest, grouse hunting is culturally important (Fig. 12.2). All grouse species of Europe have long been valued by hunters for their meat, and grouse and grouse hunting still play a role in local folklore in parts of Europe. This is particularly true for capercaillie and black grouse; their display behaviour and traditional communal mating grounds, or leks, have long fascinated people and attracted hunters. Today, sport is the major motivation for grouse hunting in Europe. In Fennoscandia, hunting of grouse is commonplace and popular, and the willow grouse is the principal quarry of many hunters (Pedersen 2007; Wam et al. 2013). Unrivalled is the enormous cultural and economic significance of red grouse shoots in northern Britain; yet to many hunters, particularly in central Europe, stuffed black grouse and capercaillie males, mounted in display posture, are prestigious trophies for which they are willing to pay high prices (Storch 2007a). Historically, the hunt for capercaillie was reserved for noblemen, and still today the species is counted as 'high game' by central European hunters.

Figure 12.2 Grouse hunting has a long tradition and, particularly in the boreal forest, still is culturally important. Here, father and son carry their bag after an autumn hunt of black grouse and capercaillie in Norway. Photo: T. Storaas.

Traditional grouse hunting practices vary considerably across Europe. In northern Europe, but also in southern Europe, grouse have always been hunted in autumn and winter, often with the help of special breeds of hunting dogs. In central Europe, capercaillie and black grouse hunters traditionally focused on displaying males in spring, which were shot during morning display on the leks. The non-lekking hazel grouse was also shot in spring, and hunters used special whistles to imitate the territorial song of male hazel grouse (Storch 2007a).

The European Union recognises hunting as legitimate as long as hunting practices are sustainable. All species of grouse are listed in Annex II of the EU Birds Directive, according to which hunting is not permitted during the reproduction period, which, by definition, begins with courtship display (*Tetrao, Lyrurus, Bonasa*) and continuous occupation of the breeding territory (*Lagopus*), and ends with independence of the young (European Commission 2009). Thus, spring hunting of grouse is no longer permitted under European law. Nevertheless, some countries, such as Austria, where lek hunting of displaying male capercaillie and black grouse is considered a valued tradition, have requested a spring hunting derogation based on the argument that the hunters' motivation for grouse-friendly land management would depend on continued permission of spring hunting (Storch 2007a).

Estimated annual hunting bags of forest grouse add up to about 1.5 million individuals shot in the European Union, Switzerland and Norway (Hirschfeld & Heydt 2005). Excluding >400,000 red grouse shot annually in the UK, the largest numbers of grouse are killed in Fennoscandia, where grouse are most common and grouse hunting is most popular. There are many differences in the ways that grouse hunting is managed in Europe. In most countries, government authorities are in charge of setting hunting seasons and bag limits (Baines & Lindén 1991; Andersen *et al.* 2014). Despite the importance of grouse as game birds in Europe, only a few countries have established science-based monitoring systems which are used as a basis to plan hunting. With its wildlife-triangle scheme, Finland maintains the most extensive country-wide monitoring system for grouse and other wildlife (Lindén *et al.* 1996), which allows for analysis of population abundance, composition and trends at regional and country-wide levels.

In large parts of central Europe, however, the hunting of grouse has been banned in response to their unfavourable conservation status (Storch 2007a). The major causes of decline and local extinctions are seen in the deterioration and fragmentation of habitats as a consequence of altered and intensified forestry and agricultural practices. Although hunting in most countries is not considered a major cause of decline, it will cause additional mortality and disturbance. Grouse management in most of central Europe is oriented towards halting declines and re-establishing viable, self-sustaining populations. Because some argue that hunted species could profit from interest in conservation among hunters (Watson & Moss 2008; Knezevic 2009), hunting of Red-Listed grouse species continues in a few countries. In the Pyrenees, France, for example, a low level of capercaillie hunting is maintained despite a questionable conservation status. Lek counts in spring and population surveys in autumn are used as a basis for capercaillie hunting plans, and modelling studies have suggested that currently low levels of capercaillie hunting in the Pyrenees may be compensatory (Ménoni & Defos Du Rau 2003). Similarly, in Austria, shooting of displaying male capercaillie and black grouse is maintained, and hunting regulation is based on numbers of displaying males counted by the hunters (Storch 2007a). In both France and Austria, legal shooting of threatened capercaillie persists for cultural reasons. Although some grouse hunting continues also in central Europe (Storch 2007a), maintaining and improving suitable habitat structures is the major conservation approach for grouse in Europe. Additional measures include reducing human disturbance from tourism and recreational activities and controlling predators (Storch 2007b). None of the many recent attempts to re-establish grouse populations in various parts of Europe by release of captive-bred or translocated birds has so far been successful (Ludwig & Storch 2011; Siano & Klaus 2013).

Numerous case studies have been conducted on the effects of hunting on grouse. Most research, however, has been published on the ptarmigan species, particularly the willow grouse, which is the grouse species with by far the largest hunting bags in Europe. Based on figures published for the early 2000s (Hirschfeld & Heyd 2005), one can assume hunting bags of more than 1 million willow grouse shot in Europe annually, including the British subspecies red grouse. Major research questions have been in regard to the effects of grouse hunting on survival rates and population dynamics in order to derive sustainable hunting strategies (Baines & Lindén 1991; Aanes *et al.* 2002; Lampila *et al.* 2011; Sandercock *et al.* 2011). More recently, behavioural effects of hunting (Storch 2013) and the effects of unintentional selectivity of hunting (Bunnefeld *et al.* 2011; Asmyhr *et al.* 2012) have also received attention.

12.3.2 Hunting of Eurasian Woodcock

Woodcocks are solitary, migratory waders. Because hunters consider them 'good sport' and because they are good to eat, woodcocks are among the major game birds of Europe. Woodcocks inhabit extensive forests with dense undergrowth, good ground cover and soil rich in earthworms, their staple food throughout the year (Johnsgard 1981; Hoodless & Hirons 2007). In the non-breeding season, woodcocks also use smaller woods, plantations and hedges as daytime resting habitat, and at night they feed in grassland and cultivated fields (Duriez *et al.* 2005).

The breeding range of the Eurasian woodcock spans all of temperate and boreal Eurasia, from the coasts of the North Sea in the west to the coasts of the Okhotsk Sea in the east. In Europe, the largest breeding densities occur in the north-east, including the Baltic states, Fennoscandia and Russia (BirdLife International 2017). European woodcocks migrate across the continent between summer ranges in the north-east to winter ranges in the south and west. During winter, woodcocks are particularly numerous along the coasts of the North Sea, the Mediterranean Sea and the Black Sea.

Due to its huge distribution range and its large and presumably generally stable population, the Eurasian woodcock is globally listed as a species of Least Concern by the IUCN (BirdLife International 2017). The European population, however, has repeatedly been assessed as threatened. The latest status assessment for birds in the European Union determined an unfavourable conservation status for the woodcock based on a large decline of wintering numbers between 1970 and 1990. Major threats are seen in the fragmentation, loss and deterioration of habitats (BirdLife International 2017). In the European Union, the woodcock is listed in Annex II/1 of the EU Birds Directive as a species of which hunting is permitted. However, member states have to ensure that hunting is conducted sustainably, and it is not permitted 'during the periods of their greatest vulnerability, such as the return migration to the nesting areas, reproduction and the raising of chicks' (European Commission 2014, http://ec.europa.eu/environment/nature/legislation/birdsdirective/index_en.htm; accessed 8 October 2014).

For the woodcock, the reproduction period, during which hunting is banned, is defined as beginning with roding behaviour and the occupation of breeding sites in late February (European Commission 2009). In some European countries, however, including Hungary and Austria, where spring shooting of woodcocks is considered a tradition, spring hunting of woodcocks is continued under national law (FACE 2014).

European hunters shoot an estimated 3–4 million woodcocks annually, and woodcock hunting is particularly valued in the species' wintering range, i.e., the Mediterranean region and westernmost Europe (Ferrand & Gossmann 2001; Hirschfeld & Heyd 2005). In Ireland, Britain, Denmark, Greece, Italy, France and Spain, woodcocks are a preferred quarry, and annual hunting bags in each of these countries comprise tens of thousands to more than a million birds. Only in small areas within Europe, such as Slovenia, the Netherlands and parts of Belgium and Switzerland, is woodcock hunting banned. In the woodcock's Russian breeding range, shooting of males in spring, during their crepuscular display flights, is popular. Elsewhere, woodcocks are shot primarily during migration. In the wintering areas, e.g., in France, woodcocks are primarily hunted by solitary hunters with pointing dogs (Duriez *et al.* 2005). In high-density areas in autumn and winter, driven hunts with dogs are common. Hunters consider the shooting of woodcocks excellent sport because of the birds' elusive behaviour, unpredictable occurrence and fast and erratic flight movements.

In general, hunting mortality of woodcocks is regulated by season length and bag limits, i.e., the maximum number of birds permitted to shoot per day or season. However, population surveys and monitoring are difficult for both breeding populations and migrants because of the species' behaviour, polygamous mating system and unspecific and variable flyways. In most European countries, there is no systematic monitoring of woodcock populations that would allow an annual adjustment of hunting regulations. Some countries, such as Germany, do not restrict woodcock hunting except through the setting of a hunting season (www.jagdverband.de/content/waldschnepfe-scolopax-rusticola). Others, such as France, also limit the number of woodcocks permitted to be shot per hunter or hunting party, and per day or season (www.oncfs.gouv.fr/Connaitre-les-especes-ru73/La-Becasse-des-bois-ar113#mesure_regle). In France, the country where the largest numbers of woodcocks are shot inwoodcocks in France Europe (Hirschfeld & Heyd 2005), a systematic monitoring and hunting planning system is in place, combining surveys of roding males, woodcocks flushed and/or shot during hunting and ringing data. Results suggest stable wintering and breeding populations in France (Ferrand et al. 2008). Systematic surveys and population estimates have also been conducted in a few other European countries (Heward et al. 2015). In the US, American woodcocks are monitored based on surveys of singing males in spring and of wing collections from hunters in autumn (McAuley et al. 2005). These data allow annual population estimates, hunting bag estimates and information on recruitment and distribution, and provide the basis for harvest planning (Cooper & Rau 2014). In a study that assessed current hunting regulations, McAuley et al. (2005) reported similar survival of American woodcocks in hunted versus non-hunted populations.

Only a few studies have assessed the effects of hunting on woodcocks in Europe. A study from Greece listed the woodcock among the migratory birds most likely to be negatively impacted by hunting (Sokos et al. 2013). Based on radio-tagged birds in hunting areas and protected reserves in France, Duriez et al. (2005) suggested there were additive effects of hunting on overall mortality in winter and called for caution in hunting planning. Based on a study of radio-tagged woodcocks in France, Ferrand et al. (2013) pointed to non-lethal, yet potentially significant, behavioural effects of hunting on woodcocks and concluded that good feeding conditions might help woodcocks to better withstand disturbances from hunting.

12.3.3 Persecution of Raptors and Corvids

The killing of raptors and corvids has long been common practice. In past farming-dominated societies of Europe, people had the desire not only to control, but to extirpate all predators. Particularly those species that were known, or believed, to kill livestock, poultry and game were heavily persecuted as vermin, and many became locally extinct. Until the 1960s and 1970s, state agencies of many European countries paid hunters to kill predators, including raptors and corvids (Kenward 2006; Pohja-Mykrä et al. 2012). In Britain, the killing of predators became especially severe in the 19th century, in parallel with the fashion of organised hunting of gamebirds (Lovegrove 2007). While today most raptor species are legally protected in Europe and have recovered from former population lows, attitudes have not changed completely. Most corvid species are still legally hunted at least in parts of Europe, and illegal killing of raptors has remained common (Marquiss et al. 2003; Kenward 2006; Pohja-Mykrä et al. 2012; Holá et al. 2015). Effects may be significant. Marquiss et al. (2003), for example, analysed contrasting trends in two re-colonising goshawk *Accipiter gentilis* populations in northern Britain. Despite similar breeding success and fledgling rates, one of the populations remained at low numbers, while the other increased steadily. The authors concluded that these differences resulted from different levels of illegal persecution: the first area was dominated by privately owned land used for shooting game, whereas in the latter area, goshawks were more secure in state-owned forests.

In parts of Europe where game bird hunting is a major part of the local economy, such as Britain and Ireland, professional gamekeepers may still spend much of their time reducing predator numbers. However, predator control is not only implemented as a measure of small game management, but today is also commonly advocated for conservation purposes. For example, many threatened populations of ground-nesting birds appear to be limited by high rates of predation on nests and chicks (Fletcher et al. 2010; Madden et al. 2014).

Whether attempts to enforce predator control are likely to show the desired effects on threatened bird populations is unclear and remains heavily debated. Several reviews have addressed the effectiveness of predator removal as a conservation measure for threatened species. All concluded that predator removal could significantly enhance productivity in prey bird species, whereas effects on population abundance are less clear (Côté & Sutherland 1997; Smith et al. 2010). In a recent review of the effects of corvid predation, Madden *et al.* (2014) found that only about one-fifth of all studies reported evidence of negative impacts of corvids on prey bird populations; however, effects were more common on productivity than on abundance. It is important to note, however, that most studies addressed single predator taxa. Existing evidence suggests that removing multiple predator species will generate significantly stronger effects on prey populations than removing a single species (Newton 1998; Fletcher *et al.* 2010; Madden *et al.* 2014).

The magnitude of the numbers of corvids and raptors killed in Europe remains obscure. With regard to forest-living species, annual bag records for the jay *Garrulus glandarius* have been estimated to exceed 1 million individuals (www.komitee.de/en/projects/hunting-bags/passerines).

12.3.4 Trapping and Shooting of Migratory Birds

Hunting of migratory birds is a powerful element of human culture in southern Europe and the entire Mediterranean region (Falzon 2008; Verissimo & Campbell 2015; Brochet *et al.* 2016). Among the numerous passerines targeted, there are also many forest-bird species, such as thrushes (Turdidae) and buntings (Emberizidae). Among the European countries, Italy, Malta and Cyprus, but also France and Spain, have strong traditions of netting, trapping and shooting of birds. Passerines are considered delicacies, and numerous species are also captured or killed in large numbers for sport, or for use as cage birds or decoys (Hirschfeld & Heyd 2005; Brochet *et al.* 2016).

Based on EU legislation, the hunting of most passerine species has become illegal; however, strong traditions are hard to eliminate and illegal hunting continues to be an issue (http://ec.europa.eu/environment/nature/conservation/wildbirds/illegal_killing.htm). Also, in some Mediterranean EU member states, derogations from EU legislation, justified by 'traditional practices', allow for continued legal killing of passerines (Brochet *et al.* 2016). Bird hunting is a significant issue not only in the European, but also the Middle Eastern and North African countries of the Mediterranean region.

The first comprehensive assessment of the extent of illegal killing and trapping of birds across the Mediterranean, which includes estimates of numbers of birds killed by country and species, has been provided by Brochet *et al.* (2016). The authors estimated that annually, 11–36 million individual birds are taken illegally in the region.

Trapping and shooting of migrants focuses on not only passerines. Along the coast of the Black Sea, for example, large numbers of sparrowhawks *Accipiter nisus* are trapped for traditional falconry, whereas other migratory raptors are indiscriminately shot or trapped and killed (Van Maanen *et al.* 2001). Similar cases of illegal trapping and killing of birds, including forest species, likely occur in other parts of Europe, and the extent can vary, depending on culture, tradition, economic situation and law enforcement (Hirschfeld & Heyd 2005; Brochet *et al.* 2016).

The effects of trapping and shooting may especially impact migratory bird species in the Mediterranean (Brochet *et al.* 2016). Many of the most heavily exploited species are not globally threatened. However, because hunting mortality is rarely fully compensatory (see above), population-level effects are likely to exist, and the abundance of a hunted population will be reduced below the level of a non-hunted population (Aebischer 1997). Furthermore, trapping and shooting during migration will also affect non-target species, some of which will be rare and threatened (Van Maanen *et al.* 2001). Some authors assume that hunting will accelerate population declines in species with unfavourable conservation status (Hirschfeld & Heyd 2005; Brochet *et al.* 2016). Rigorously measuring the effects of hunting on survival rates and population abundance is diffi-cult, and ideally hunted and non-hunted populations should be compared (Aebischer *et al.* 1999). A few studies on migrants have used this approach. For example, in the 1960s and 1970s, first-year survival rates of hunted migratory song thrushes *Turdus philomelos* in the Baltic region were signifi-cantly lower than those of a non-hunted, largely resident population in the UK (annual survival rates 0.411 vs. 0.529); adult survival was similar, however. Whether poor survival in Baltic region first-year thrushes was related to hunting pressure remains unclear (Payevsky & Vysotsky 2003).

12.3.5 Exploitation and Persecution of Other Forest Bird Species

Numerous other species of birds which use forests as well as other habitat types are hunted or persecuted in Europe. Two such species which are commonly hunted are woodpigeon and turtle dove *Streptopelia turtur*. Both are hunted for sport and for their meat, but also as agricultural pests, and several million individuals of each species are shot annually (Hirsch-feld & Heyd 2005). Among the few studies that assessed the effects of hunting on pigeons and doves in Europe, Aebischer *et al.* (1995) came to the conclusion that hunting had no measurable effect on the population size of woodpigeon in the UK, which increased in abundance despite heavy shooting. For the turtle dove, which is Red-Listed as Vulnerable (IUCN 2017), hunting during migration and in its wintering ranges is believed to contribute significantly to recent population declines (Bird-Life International 2017).

12.4 Conclusions

This review indicates that a hunted population will inevitably be different from a non-hunted one (Fig. 12.1). Hunting can also change the functions of hunted species in their communities and ecosystems. Further, hunting impairs how wild animals interact with humans. Outdoor recreationists and tourists are commonly blamed for disturbing wildlife, while ultimately hunting is the reason why wildlife is susceptible to disturbance by humans. Wildlife ecologists have only started to explore and understand the full effects of hunting. Until recently, researchers have focused on hunting mortality and its consequences for the abundance and composition of populations. Hunting management generally aims at providing hunters with maximum yields without compromising the viability of hunted populations, and hunting is considered sustainable as long as the hunted populations do not decline (Milner-Gulland & Akcakaya 2001). In the light of recent evidence of the large non-lethal effects that hunting can have on hunted populations and their interactions with other species, including humans, this exclusively demographic rationale for sustainability appears to be outdated.

Critics of hunting are commonly motivated by moral concerns (Knezevic 2009). However, it should be recognised that hunting has significant and complex effects on wildlife and ecosystems. Thus, it may be time to debate, develop and implement broader concepts of sustainability in the context of wildlife management.

Acknowledgements

I thank the editors for inviting me to contribute this chapter, and to Hans-Christian Pedersen and Andrew Hoodless for reviewing a draft of the manuscript.

References

Aanes, S., Engen, S., Saether, B.E., Willebrand, T. & Marcstrom, V. (2002) Sustainable harvesting strategies of willow ptarmigan in a fluctuating environment. *Ecological Applications*, **12**, 281–290.

Aebischer, N.J. (1995) Investigating the effects of hunting on the survival of British pigeons and doves by analysis of ringing recoveries. *Journal of Applied Statistics*, **22**, 923–934.

Aebischer, N.J. (1997) Impact of hunting on the population dynamics of wild birds. *Gibier Faune Sauvage*, **14**, 183–200.

Aebischer, N.J., Potts, G.R. & Rehfisch, M. (1999) Using ringing data to study the effect of hunting on bird populations. *Ringing and Migration*, **19** (Suppl.), S67–S81.

Alatalo R.V., Höglund J., Lundberg A. & Sutherland W.J. (1992) Evolution of black grouse leks – female preferences benefit males in larger leks. *Behavioural Ecology*, **3**, 53–59.

Allendorf, F.W., England, P.R., Luikart, G., Ritchie, P.A. & Ryman, N. (2008) Genetic effects of harvest on wild animal populations. *Trends in Ecology and Evolution*, **23**, 327–337.

Andersen, O., Kaltenborn, B.P., Vittersø, J. & Willebrand, T. (2014) Preferred harvest principles and regulations amongst willow ptarmigan hunters in Norway. *Wildlife Biology*, **20**, 285–290.

Asmyhr, L., Willebrand, T. & Hörnell-Willebrand, M. (2012) Successful willow grouse are exposed to increased harvest risk. *Journal of Wildlife Management*, **76**, 940–943.

Baines, D. (1996) The implications of grazing and predator management on the habitats and breeding success of black grouse *Tetrao tetrix*. *Journal of Applied Ecology*, **33**, 54–62.

Baines, D. & Lindén, H. (1991) The impact of hunting on grouse population dynamics. *Ornis Scandinavica*, **22**, 245–246.

Barilani, M., Bernard-Laurent, A., Mucci, N. *et al.* (2007) Hybridisation with introduced chukars (*Alectoris chukar*) threatens the gene pool integrity of native rock (*A. graeca*) and redlegged rufa partridge populations. *Biological Conservation*, **137**, 57–69.

Berger, J. (2007) Fear, human shields and the redistribution of prey and predators in protected areas. *Biology Letters*, **3**, 620–623.

Beschta, R.L. & Ripple, W.J. (2009) Large predators and trophic cascades in terrestrial ecosystems of the western United States. *Biological Conservation*, **142**, 2401–2414.

BirdLife International (2004) *Birds in the European Union: A Status Assessment*. Wageningen: BirdLife International. http://birdsineurope.birdlife.org.

BirdLife International (2017) *IUCN Red List for Birds*. www.birdlife.org. Accessed 9 March 2017.

Blumstein, D.T. (2006) The multipredator hypothesis and the evolutionary persistence of antipredator behavior. *Ethology*, **112**, 209–217.

Blumstein, D.T., Daniel, J.C. & Springett, B.P. (2004) A test of the multi-predator hypothesis: Rapid loss of antipredator behavior after 130 years of isolation. *Ethology*, **110**, 919–934.

Bregnballe, T., Madsen, J. & Rasmussen, P.A.F. (2004) Effects of temporal and spatial hunting control in waterbird reserves. *Biological Conservation*, **119**, 93–104.

Brochet, A.-L. van Den Bossche, W., Jbour, S. *et al.* (2016) Preliminary assessment of the scope and scale of illegal killing and taking of birds in the Mediterranean. *Bird Conservation International*, **26**, 1–28.

Brøseth, H. & Pedersen, H.C. (2010) Disturbance effects of hunting activity in a willow ptarmigan *Lagopus lagopus* population. *Wildlife Biology*, **16**, 241–248.

Brown, J.S., Laundré, J.W. & Gurung, M. (1999) The ecology of fear: Optimal foraging, game theory, and trophic interactions. *Journal of Mammalogy*, **80**, 385–399.

Bruggink, J.G., Oppelt, E.J., Doherty, K.E., Andersen, D.E., Meunier, J. & Lutz, R.S. (2013) Fall survival of American woodcock in the western Great Lakes region. *Journal of Wildlife Management*, **77**, 1021–1030.

Bunnefeld, N., Reuman, D.C., Baines, D. & Milner-Gulland, E.J. (2011) Impact of unintentional selective harvesting on the population dynamics of red grouse. *Journal of Animal Ecology*, **80**, 1258–1268.

Burnham, K.P. & Anderson, D.R. (1984) Tests of compensatory vs. additive hypotheses of mortality in mallards. *Ecology*, **63**, 105–112.

Byers, J.A. (1998) *American Pronghorn: Social Adaptations and the Ghosts of Predators Past*. Chicago: University of Chicago Press.

Ciuti, S., Northrup, J.M., Muhly, T.B. *et al.* (2012) Effects of humans on behaviour of wildlife exceed those of natural predators in a landscape of fear. *PLoS ONE* **7** (11), e50611.

Coltman, D.W., O'Donoghue, P., Jorgenson, J.T., Hogg, J.T., Strobeck, C. & Festa-Bianchet, M. (2003) Undesirable evolutionary consequences of trophy harvesting. *Nature*, **426**, 655–658.

Cooper, T.R. & Rau, R.D. (2014) *American Woodcock Population Status, 2014.* Laurel, MD: US Fish and Wildlife Service.

Côté, I.M. & Sutherland, W.J. (1997) The effectiveness of removing predators to protect bird populations. *Conservation Biology*, **11**, 395–405.

Côté, S.D., Rooney, T.P., Tremblay, J.-P., Dussault, C. & Waller, D.M. (2004) Ecological impacts of deer overabundance. *Annual Review of Ecology, Evolution and Systematics*, **35**, 113–147.

Council of Europe (2007) European Charter on Hunting and Biodiversity. www .face.eu/sites/default/files/attachments/charter.en-fr.fin_.pdf.

Cresswell, W. (2008) Non-lethal effects of predation in birds. *Ibis*, **150**, 3–17.

Darimont, Ch.T., Carlson, S.M., Kinnison, M.T., Paquet P.C., Reimchen Th.E. & Wilmers, Ch.C. (2009) Human predators outpace other agents of trait change in the wild. *Proceedings of the National Academy of Sciences*, **106(3)**, 952–954.

Decker, D.J., Riley, S.J. & Siemer, W.F. (2012) *Human Dimensions of Wildlife Management,* 2nd ed. Baltimore: John Hopkins University Press.

DJV (2017) www.jagdverband.de/content/jagdscheininhaber-deutschland. Accessed 9 March 2017.

Draycott, R.A., Hoodless, A.N. & Sage, R.B. (2008) Effects of pheasant management on vegetation and birds in lowland woodlands. *Journal of Applied Ecology*, **45**, 334–341.

Duriez, O., Eraud, C., Barbraud, C. & Ferrand, Y. (2005) Factors affecting population dynamics of Eurasian woodcocks wintering in France: Assessing the efficiency of a hunting-free reserve. *Biological Conservation*, **122**, 89–97.

Effiom, E.O., Birkhofer, K., Smith, H.G. & Olsson, O. (2014) Changes of community composition at multiple trophic levels due to hunting in Nigerian tropical forests. *Ecography*, **37**, 367–377.

Ellison, L.N. (1991) Shooting and compensatory mortality in tetraonids. *Ornis Scandinavica*, **22**, 229–240.

Encyclopædia Britannica (2017) www.britannica.com/EBchecked/topic/277043/hunting. Accessed 9 March 2017.

European Commission (2009) Key concepts of article 7(4) of directive 79/409/EEC. Period of reproduction and prenuptial migration of Annex II bird species in the 27 EU member states. http://ec.europa.eu/environment/nature/conservation/wildbirds/hunting/docs/reprod_intro.pdf.

European Commission (2014) http://ec.europa.eu/environment/nature/conservation/wildbirds/hunting/index_en.htm. Accessed 3 September 2014.

FACE (2014) www.face.eu/sites/default/files/hungary_en.pdf. Accessed 9 October 2014.

FACE (2017) www.face.eu/about-us/members/across-europe/census-of-the-number-of-hunters-in-europe-september-2010. Accessed 9 March 2017.

Falzon, M.-A. (2008) Flights of passion. Hunting, ecology and politics in Malta and the Mediterranean. *Anthropology Today*, **24**, 15–20.

Ferrand, Y., Aubry, P., Landry, P. & Priol, P. (2013) Responses of Eurasian woodcock *Scolopax rusticola* to simulated hunting disturbance. *Wildlife Biology*, **19**, 19–29.

Ferrand, Y. & Gossmann, F. (2001) Elements for a woodcock (*Scolopax rusticola*) management plan. *Game and Wildlife Science*, **18**, 115–139.

Ferrand, Y., Gossmann, F., Bastat, C. & Guénézan, M. (2008) Monitoring of the wintering and breeding woodcock populations in France. *Revista Catalana d'Ornitologia*, **24**, 44–52.

Fletcher, K.L., Aebischer, N.J., Baines, D., Foster, R. & Hoodless, A.N. (2010) Changes in breeding success and abundance of ground-nesting moorland birds in relation to the experimental deployment of legal predator control. *Journal of Applied Ecology*, **47**, 263–272.

Fletcher, K., Hoodless, A.N. & Baines, D. (2013) Impacts of predator abundance on red grouse *Lagopus lagopus scotica* during a period of experimental predator control. *Wildlife Biology*, **19**, 248–256.

Ford, M.J. (2002) Selection in captivity during supportive breeding may reduce fitness in the wild. *Conservation Biology*, **16**, 815–825.

Frid, A. & Dill, L.M. (2002) Human-caused disturbance stimuli as a form of predation risk. *Conservation Ecology*, **6**, 11.

Fuller, R.J. (2001) Responses of woodland birds to increasing numbers of deer: A review of evidence and mechanisms. *Forestry*, **74**, 289–298.

Gamborg, C. & Jensen, F.S. (2016) Wildlife value orientations among hunters, landowners, and the general public: A Danish comparative quantitative study. *Human Dimensions of Wildlife*, **21**, 328–344.

Gamborg, C., Jensen, F.S. & Sandøe, P. (2016) A dividing issue: Attitudes to the shooting of rear and release birds among landowners, hunters and the general public in Denmark. *Land Use Policy, 57,* 296–304.

Griffin, A.S. (2004) Social learning about predators: A review and prospectus. *Learning and Behaviour, 32,* 131–140.

Guillemain, M., Blanc, R., Lucas, C. & Lepley, M. (2007) Ecotourism disturbance to wildfowl in protected areas: Historical, empirical and experimental approaches in the Camargue, Southern France. *Biodiversity Conservation, 16,* 3633–3651.

Gunnarsson, T.G., Gill, J.A., Atkinson, P.W. *et al.* (2006) Population-scale drivers of individual arrival times in migratory birds. *Journal of Animal Ecology, 75,* 1119–1127.

Heward, C.J., Hoodless, A.N., Conway, G.J., Aebischer, N.J., Gillings, S. & Fuller, R.J. (2015) Current status and recent trend of the Eurasian woodcock *Scolopax rusticola* as a breeding bird in Britain. *Bird Study, 62,* 535–551.

Hirschfeld, A. & Heyd, A. (2005) Mortality of migratory birds caused by hunting in Europe: Bag statistics and proposals for the conservation of birds and animal welfare. *Berichte zum Vogelschutz, 42,* 47–74.

Hoodless, A.N. & Hirons, G.J.M. (2007) Habitat selection and foraging behaviour of breeding Eurasian Woodcock *Scolopax rusticola*: A comparison between contrasting landscapes. *Ibis,* **149** (Suppl. 2), 234–249.

Holá, M., Zíka, T., Šálek, M. *et al.* (2015) Effect of habitat and game management practices on ring-necked pheasant harvest in the Czech Republic. *European Journal of Wildlife Research, 61,* 73–80.

Hörnell-Willebrand, M., Willebrand, T. & Smith, A.A. (2014) Seasonal movements and dispersal patterns: Implications for recruitment and management of willow ptarmigan (*Lagopus lagopus*). *Journal of Wildlife Management, 78,* 194–201.

Hudson, R.J., Drew, K.R. & Baskin, L.M. (1989) *Wildlife Production Systems: Economic Utilisation of Wild Ungulates.* Cambridge: Cambridge University Press.

Ingold, P. (2005) *Freizeitaktivitäten im Lebensraum der Alpentiere.* Bern: Haupt.

IUCN (2017) Red List of Threatened Species. www.iucnredlist.org. Accessed 9 March 2017.

Johnsgard, P.A. (1981) *The Plovers, Sandpipers and Snipes of the World.* Lincoln and London: University of Nebraska Press.

Kenward, R.E. (2006) *The Northern Goshawk.* London: Poyser.

Kenward, R.E., Hall, D.G., Walls, S.S. & Hodder, K.H. (2001) Factors affecting predation by buzzards *Buteo buteo* on released pheasants *Phasianus colchicus. Journal of Applied Ecology, 38,* 813–822.

Kervinen, M. (2013) Fitness in Male Black Grouse (*Tetrao tetrix*): Effects of life histories and sexual selection on male lifetime mating success. *Jyväskylä Studies in Biological and Environmental Science,* **271**.

Knezevic, I. (2009) Hunting and environmentalism: Conflict or misperceptions. *Human Dimensions of Wildlife, 14,* 12–20.

Lampila, P., Ranta, E., Mönkkönen, M., Lindén, H. & Helle, P. (2011) Grouse dynamics and harvesting in Kainuu, northeastern Finland. *Oikos,* **120,** 1057–1064.

Laundré, J.W., Hernandez, L., Lopez Medina, P. *et al.* (2014) The landscape of fear: The missing link to understand top-down and bottom-up controls of prey abundance? *Ecology*, **95**, 1141–1152.

Lindén, H., Helle, E., Helle, P. & Wikman, M. (1996) Wildlife triangle scheme in Finland: Methods and aims for monitoring wildlife populations. *Finnish Game Research*, **49**, 4–11.

Lindner, K. (1940) *Die Jagd im frühen Mittelalter*. Berlin: Walter de Gruyter.

Lindner, K. (1973) *Beiträge zu Vogelfang und Falknerei in Altertum*. Berlin and New York: Walter de Gruyter.

Little, R.M., Crowe, T.M. & Grant, W.S. (1993) Does hunting affect the demography and genetic-structure of the greywing francolin *Francolinus africanus*? *Biodiversity and Conservation*, **2**, 567–585.

Lone, K., Loe, L.E., Gobakken, T. *et al.* (2014) Living and dying in a multi-predator landscape of fear, roe deer are squeezed by contrasting pattern of predation risk imposed by lynx and humans. *Oikos*, **123**, 641–651.

Lovegrove, R. (2007) *Silent Fields: The Long Decline of a Nation's Wildlife*. Oxford: Oxford University Press.

Ludwig, T. & Storch, I. (2011) Re-introduction and re-enforcement as a conservation measure for grouse? *G@llinformed*, **4**, 18–20.

Madden, C.F., Arroyo, B. & Amar, A. (2014) A review of the impacts of corvids on bird productivity and abundance. *Ibis*, **157**, 1–16.

Madsen, J. (1998a) Experimental refuges for migratory waterfowl in Danish wetlands. I. Baseline assessment of the disturbance effects of recreational activities. *Journal of Applied Ecology*, **35**, 386–397.

Madsen, J. (1998b) Experimental refuges for migratory waterfowl in Danish wetlands. II. Tests of hunting disturbance effects. *Journal of Applied Ecology*, **35**, 398–417.

Madsen, J. & Fox, A.D. (1995) Impacts of hunting disturbance on waterbirds – a review. *Wildlife Biology*, **1**, 193–207.

Magige, F.J., Holmern, T., Stokke, S., Mlingwa, C. & Røskaft, E. (2009) Does illegal hunting affect density and behaviour of African grassland birds? A case study on ostrich (*Struthio camelus*). *Biodiversity Conservation*, **18**, 1361–1373.

Maloney, R.F. & McNeal, I.G. (1995) Historical and experimental learned predator recognition in free-living New Zealand robins. *Animal Behaviour*, **50**, 1193–1201.

Manfredo M., Teela, T. & Bright, A. (2003) Why are public values toward wildlife changing? *Human Dimensions of Wildlife*, **8**, 287–306.

Marjakangas, A. & Aspegren, H. (1991) Responses of black grouse *Tetrao tetrix* hens to supplemental winter food. *Ornis Scandinavica*, **22**, 282–283.

Marquiss, M., Petty, S.J., Anderson, D.I.K. & Legge, G. (2003) Contrasting population trends of the northern goshawk (*Accipiter gentilis*) in the Scottish/English borders and north-east Scotland. In *Birds of Prey in a Changing Environment*. Thompson, D.B.A., Redpath, S.M., Fielding, A.H., Marquiss, M. & Galbraith, C.A. (eds.). Edinburgh: The Stationery Office, pp. 143–148.

McAuley, D.G., Longcore, J.R., Clugston, D.A. *et al.* (2005) Effects of hunting on survival of American woodcock in the Northeast. *Journal of Wildlife Management*, **69**, 1565–1577.

Ménoni, E. & Defos Du Rau, P. (2003) Démographie pyrénéenne du Grand Tétras Tetrao urogallus, quel impact de la chasse et des infrastructures. In *Proceedings of Premières rencontres Naturalistes de Midi-Pyrénées*. Cahors: Naturalistes de Midi-Pyrénées, pp. 113–119.

Milner, J.M., Nilsen, E.B. & Andreassen, H.P. (2007) Demographic side effects of selective hunting in ungulates and carnivores. *Conservation Biology*, **21**, 36–47.

Milner-Gulland, E.J. & Akcakaya, H.R. (2001) Sustainability indices for exploited populations. *Trends in Ecology and Evolution*, **16**, 686–692.

Monteith, K.L., Long, R.A., Bleich, V.C., Heffelfinger, J.R., Krausman, P.R. & Bowyer, R.T. (2013) Effects of harvest, culture, and climate on trends in size of horn-like structures in trophy ungulates. *Wildlife Monographs*, **183**, 1–28.

Moss, R., Leckie, F., Biggins, A., Poole, T., Baines, D. & Kortland, K. (2014) Impacts of human disturbance on capercaillie *Tetrao urogallus* distribution and demography in Scottish woodland. *Wildlife Biology*, **20**, 1–18.

Mysterud, A. & Bischof, R. (2010) Can compensatory culling offset undesirable evolutionary consequences of trophy hunting? *Journal of Animal Ecology*, **79**, 148–160.

NABU (2017) www.nabu.de/wir-ueber-uns/was-wir-tun/00357.html. Accessed 9 March 2017.

Newborn, D. & Foster, R. (2002) Control of parasite burdens in wild red grouse *Lagopus lagopus scoticus* through the indirect application of anthelmintics. *Journal of Applied Ecology*, **39**, 909–914.

Newton, I. (1998) *Population Limitation in Birds*. London: Academic Press.

Olsson, G.E., Willebrand, T. & Smith, A.A. (1996) The effects of hunting on willow grouse movements. *Wildlife Biology*, **2**, 11–15.

Payevsky, V.A. & Vysotsky, V.G. (2003) Migratory song thrushes *Turdus philomelos* hunted in Europe: Survival rates and other demographic parameters. *Avian Science*, **3**, 13–20.

Pedersen, A.O., Soininen, E.M., Unander, S., Hörnell-Willebrand, M. & Fuglei, E. (2014) Experimental harvest reveals the importance of territoriality in limiting the breeding population of Svalbard rock ptarmigan. *European Journal of Wildlife Research*, **60**, 201–212.

Pedersen, H.C. (2007) *Alt om rypa – biologi, jakt, forvaltning*. Oslo: Tun forlag.

Pedersen, H.C., Steen, H., Kastdalen, L. *et al.* (2004) Weak compensation of harvest despite strong density-dependent growth in willow ptarmigan. *Proceedings of the Royal Society B*, **271**, 381–385.

Peron, G., Ferrand, Y., Gossmann, F., Bastat, C., Guenezan, M. & Gimenez, O. (2011) Nonparametric spatial regression of survival probability: Visualization of population sinks in Eurasian woodcock. *Ecology*, **92**, 1672–1679.

Pohja-Mykrä, M., Vuorisalo, T. & Mykrä, S. (2012) Organized persecution of birds of prey in Finland: Historical and population biological perspectives. *Ornis Fennica*, **89**, 1–19.

Proffitt, K.M., Grigg, J.L., Hamlin, K.L. & Garrott, R.A. (2009) Contrasting effects of wolves and human hunters on elk behavioral responses to predation risk. *Journal of Wildlife Management*, **73**, 345–356.

Puigcerver, M., Vinyoles, D. & Rodríguez-Teijeiro, J.D. (2007) Does restocking with Japanese quail or hybrids affect native populations of common quail *Coturnix coturnix*? *Biological Conservation*, **136**, 628–635.

Riepe, C. & Arlinghaus, R. (2014) Explaining anti-angling sentiments in the general population of Germany: An application of the cognitive hierarchy model. *Human Dimensions of Wildlife*, **19**, 371–390.

Ripple, W.J. & Beschta, R.L. (2004) Wolves and the ecology of fear: Can predation risk structure ecosystems? *Bioscience*, **54**, 755–766.

Ripple, W.J. & Beschta, R.L. (2012) Trophic cascades in Yellowstone: The first 15 years after wolf reintroduction. *Biological Conservation*, **145**, 205–213.

Roth, H.H. & Merz, G. (1996) *Wildlife Resources: A Global Account of Economic Use.* Berlin: Springer.

RSPB (2017) www.rspb.org.uk/. Accessed 9 March 2017.

Sage, R.B., Ludolf, C. & Robertson, P.A. (2005) The ground flora of ancient semi-natural woodlands in pheasant release pens in England. *Biological Conservation*, **122**, 243–252.

Sand, H., Wikenros, C., Wabakken, P. & Liberg, O. (2006) Cross-continental differences in patterns of predation: Will naive moose in Scandinavia ever learn? *Proceedings of the Royal Society B*, **273**, 1421–1427.

Sandercock, B.K., Nilsen, E.B., Brøseth, H. & Pedersen, H.C. (2011) Is hunting mortality additive or compensatory to natural mortality? Effects of experimental harvest on the survival and cause-specific mortality of willow ptarmigan. *Journal of Animal Ecology*, **80**, 244–258.

Sedinger, J.S., White, G.C., Espinosa, S., Partee, E.T. & Braun, C.E. (2010) An approach to assessing compensatory versus additive harvest mortality: An example using greater sage-grouse *Centrocercus urophasianus. Journal of Wildlife Management*, **74**, 326–332.

Shrubb, M. (2013) *Feasting, Fowling and Feathers: A History of the Exploitation of Wild Birds*. London: Poyser.

Siano, R. & Klaus, S. (2013) Auerhuhn Wiederansiedlungs- und Bestandesstützungs-projekte in Deutschland nach 1950 – eine Übersicht. *Vogelwelt*, **134**, 3–18.

Slagsvold, T. & Wiebe, K.L. (2011) Social learning in birds and its role in shaping a foraging niche. *Philosophical Transactions of the Royal Society B*, **366**, 969–977.

Small, R.J., Holzwart, J.C. & Rusch, D.H. (1991) Predation and hunting mortality of ruffed grouse in central Wisconsin. *Journal of Wildlife Management*, **55**, 512–520.

Smith, R.K., Pullin, A.S., Stewart, G.B. & Sutherland, W.J. (2010) Effectiveness of predator removal for enhancing bird populations. *Conservation Biology*, **24**, 820–829.

Sokos, C.K., Birtsas, P.K., Connelly, J.W. & Papaspyropoulos, K.G. (2013) Hunting of migratory birds: disturbance intolerant or harvest tolerant? *Wildlife Biology*, **19**, 113–125.

Sokos, C.K., Birtsas, P.K. & Tsachalidis, E.P. (2008) The aims of galliforms release and choice of techniques. *Wildlife Biology*, **14**, 412–422.

Sreekar, R., Huang, G., Zhao, J.-B. *et al.* (2015) The use of species-area relationships to partition the effects of hunting and deforestation on bird extirpations in a fragmented landscape. *Diversity and Distributions*, **21**, 441–450.

Stankowich, T. (2008) Ungulate flight responses to human disturbance: A review and meta-analysis. *Biological Conservation*, **141**, 2159–2173.

Stankowich, T. & Blumstein, D.T. (2005) Fear in animals: A metaanalysis and review of risk assessment. *Proceedings of the Royal Society B*, **272**, 2627–2634.

Storch, I. (2007a) *Grouse Status Survey and Conservation Action Plan 2006–2010.* Switzerland and Cambridge: IUCN; Reading: World Pheasant Association.

Storch, I. (2007b) Conservation status of grouse worldwide: An update. *Wildlife Biology*, **13**, 9–17.

Storch, I. (2013) Human disturbance of grouse – why and when? *Wildlife Biology*, **19**, 390–403.

Storch, I. & Segelbacher, G. (2000) Genetic correlates of spatial population structure in central European capercaillie *Tetrao urogallus* and black grouse *T. tetrix*: A project in progress. *Wildlife Biology*, **6**, 305–310.

Tharme, A.P., Green, R.E., Baines, D., Bainbridge, I.P. & O'Brien, M. (2001) The effect of management for red grouse shooting on the population density of breeding birds on heather-dominated moorland. *Journal of Applied Ecology*, **38**, 439–457.

Thiel, D., Menoni, E., Brenot, J.F. & Jenni, L. (2007) Effects of recreation and hunting on flushing distance of capercaillie. *Journal of Wildlife Management*, **71**, 1784–1792.

Thurfjell, H., Spong, G. & Ericsson, G. (2013) Effects of hunting on wild boar *Sus scrofa* behaviour. *Wildlife Biology*, **19**, 87–93.

Van Maanen, E., Goradze, I., Gavashelishvili, A. & Goradze, R. (2001) Trapping and hunting of migratory raptors in western Georgia. *Bird Conservation International*, **11**, 77–92.

Verissimo, D. & Campbell, B. (2015) Understanding stakeholder conflict between conservation and hunting in Malta. *Biological Conservation*, **191**, 812–818.

Wam, H.K., Andersen, O. & Pedersen, H.C. (2013) Grouse hunting regulations and hunter typologies in Norway. *Human Dimensions of Wildlife*, **18**, 45–57.

Watson, A. & Moss, R. (2008) *Grouse*. London: Harper Collins.

13 · Conservation Strategies and Habitat Management for European Forest Birds

ROBERT J. FULLER AND HUGO ROBLES

13.1 Introduction

Human activities over many centuries have modified forests throughout Europe. Spreading exploitation grossly altered the extent, age structures, tree species and physical structures of the primeval forest, with massive consequences for bird assemblages (Hinsley *et al.* 2015). Only about 0.4% of the remaining European temperate forests can be regarded as 'virgin' (Parviainen 2005). Forest cover in Europe is now extremely uneven and is heavily concentrated in Fennoscandia and European Russia. Recent decades have seen continuing impacts of human activity on forest birds as demands for timber and wood-based products have intensified. These historical and recent impacts have operated at different scales, ranging from alteration of specific niches or microhabitats through to macro-scale alteration of landscapes.

Most countries have designated areas of 'protected' forest, but the function and status of these areas vary greatly and present a rather complex picture. At the end of the 20th century, less than 2% of Europe's present forest area, excluding Russia, was strictly protected in 'areas in which neither silvicultural measures nor any other avoidable human impacts are allowed' (Parviainen *et al.* 2000). The forests and their dynamics within most of these strict reserves have not escaped past modification by humans. Protected forest areas are strongly biased towards mountains, areas with poor soils and inaccessible places; relatively few are on rich soils or in the lowlands (Halkka & Lappalainen 2001). By 2010, about 10% of Europe's forest area, excluding Russia, received some level of formal protection for biodiversity and landscape (Parviainen & Schuck 2011). Protection in a high proportion of these forests is achieved by 'conservation through active management', where their dynamics are regulated through human activities in ways that are considered ecologically sympathetic.

It is clear that strictly protected areas can only support extremely small proportions of the European populations of forest birds. Moreover, their typical function is to conserve rare ecosystems rather than to protect specific taxa. Wider and complementary measures for conserving forest biodiversity that are integrated into multipurpose forestry and wider land management across a range of strategies and scales are needed (Lindenmayer *et al.* 2006; Bollmann & Braunisch 2013). Policies aiming to minimise negative impacts of forestry through adoption of best management practices now exist in many countries, though these do not necessarily address the specific needs of birds or any other wildlife group.

Birds are the subject of a major research and conservation effort, but the reality is that they will rarely be the exclusive focus of conservation policy in forests. Nonetheless, knowledge of how birds respond to forest environments will continue to be valuable in developing principles for maintaining and restoring forest biodiversity. Many studies have examined how forest management affects avian species richness and diversity, but maximising species numbers is not necessarily a sound basis for nature conservation in forests. A general principle that applies to all taxa, not just birds, is that strategies should avoid increasing species diversity by creating conditions that favour common species if this is to the detriment of endangered or threatened populations of old-forest specialists.

Forest bird conservation across Europe has broadly developed in two directions which are loosely associated with the degree of human impact on the landscape. In regions that still support populations of specialist forest birds of high conservation concern (see Chapter 5), research and management actions tend to focus on maintaining habitat quality for those birds (e.g., white-backed woodpecker *Dendrocopos leucotos* or three-toed woodpecker *Picoides tridactylus* in Scandinavia, Eastern Europe and the Alps). Conversely, in regions where large, mature forests are relatively scarce or absent (e.g., Ireland, Britain and parts of mainland western Europe), conservation and research actions in forests are frequently aimed at (i) enhancing bird diversity and (ii) improving habitat suitability for birds of conservation concern that are associated with the early successional stages of the forests (e.g., nightingale *Luscinia megarhynchos*).

These two strategies are complementary and are not exclusively adopted within particular regions. The protection of extensive old forests and the specialist species that depend on them often is the highest priority for forest conservation (Wesołowski 2005). Nonetheless, sensitive forest management has a role in maintaining habitat suitability for some old-forest specialists, perhaps especially through forms of so-called close-to-nature silviculture, ecological forestry or retention forestry (Schütz 1999; Seymour & Hunter 1999; Lindenmayer *et al.* 2012), which may also have wider benefits for bird diversity. In both Europe and North America, there is concern that many young-growth species have recently declined and that conservation should be taking more account of their needs (Askins 2001; Thompson & DeGraaf 2001; Fuller 2012a). In this chapter, therefore, we emphasise the resource needs and conservation actions for species associated with both the earliest and latest stages of succession.

Integrating patch-level and landscape-level conservation approaches is essential. The former is concerned mainly with local habitat suitability (quality), the latter with ensuring that sufficient habitat exists, in appropriate configurations, to sustain viable populations. Hence, in this chapter, 'habitat suitability' or 'habitat quality' refers mainly to the patch level rather than the landscape level. For our purposes, we regard habitat 'patches' as areas of vegetation/land use that are distinct from their surroundings in their general spatial pattern, vegetation structure or plant composition. Because habitat is a species-specific attribute, individual habitat patches will obviously be suitable for some bird species but not for others. Furthermore, a given species may require complementary resources from different kinds of patches, or it may have large area requirements that cannot be met by small patches.

The structure of the chapter reflects these two levels at which conservation science must operate and conservation solutions be sought. In the first part, we explore the relationships between forest management and the critical resources required by birds which influence the quality of individual forest patches. Ways that management can improve habitat quality through resource enhancement are outlined. We then explore broader-scale issues connected with how the carrying capacity of landscapes for forest birds has been reduced through land-use change in many regions of Europe. Approaches to mitigating negative land-use effects and specific conservation actions that are possible at the landscape level are discussed, and knowledge gaps that currently hinder effective conservation are identified. We conclude with comments about the development of habitat-based strategies for conserving forest birds that reflect different but complementary paradigms.

13.2 Resources and Habitat Suitability for Forest Birds

A resource-based approach to conservation of bird habitats within forests has the advantage that it directly links with habitat quality and individual fitness (Fuller 2012b). However, the provision of resources consistent with high habitat quality does not guarantee that target species will colonise or thrive. If a declining population is primarily limited by factors not related to resource availability at the patch level, such as pressures in winter, or on migration in the case of migrant birds, then delivery of high quality breeding habitat will do little to improve population status. Similarly, populations in high-quality habitat could be constrained or suppressed by a range of other factors, some of which interact in various ways with resource use, including competition, predation, parasites or disturbance by people (Fuller 2012b). Nonetheless, we believe that enhancing local habitat quality by increasing the availability of resources that are needed at different times of the year is essential for bird conservation, because this is a prerequisite for maintaining sustainable populations at the landscape scale. Forest management has especially profound effects on resource availability, which are summarised below.

13.2.1 Forest Management Systems and Resources

Forestry takes many forms, depending on local environment, intended products and markets, tree species, human history and culture. The various approaches to growing and harvesting trees can create strikingly different forest structures (Fig. 13.1). Where conservation is the main objective and forest production a relatively minor consideration, the range of potential structures is broadened further, and we return to this possibility later. Despite this variation, it is useful to identify the broad types of systems used in commercial forestry or woodland management. The resulting structures probably account for most forest cover, with the exception of regions where historical management has been abandoned, as is the case in many former coppiced woods in western Europe and the extensive forest regeneration on former grazing land in parts of southern and eastern Europe.

We consider four basic management systems, which are characterised below in terms of their resources and their conservation value for birds.

Figure 13.1 Different woodland structures created under different management systems: (a) hazel *Corylus avellana* coppice with scattered oak trees in southern England; (b) oak managed by clearfelling and replanting in eastern England; (c) continuous cover management involving patch felling of mature conifers and natural regeneration in gaps, southern England; (d) irregular forest management in central Sweden with small retentions, unevenly sized coupes and many retained stumps and snags; (e) wood-pasture forested landscape in Romania, with areas of clearfelling visible at the top left; (f) traditional Pyrenean oak dehesa wood-pasture system, northern Spain, with a relatively low density of trees. Photos: (a–e) R.J. Fuller, (f) H. Robles.

For more information on these systems, see, for example, Peterken (1993) and Harmer *et al.* (2010). *Rotational clearfelling systems* involve harvesting relatively large patches of trees (typically >1 ha in size) on a cycle that can be as long as 150 years (oak *Quercus* spp.) or as short as 40 years (some conifers). In some regions, conifers tend to be managed in larger patch sizes than broadleaves. Regeneration is usually done by planting one or a few species of trees. 'Shelterwood' systems are a variant of rotational clearfelling in which some trees are left unharvested to provide seeds for regeneration. *Coppice* is a short-rotation felling system in broadleaved woodland designed to produce crops of poles or firewood. The felling cycle is usually less than 30 years. Patch size is typically smaller than clearfelling, and regrowth is from cut stumps rather than planting. Coppice is frequently grown amongst scattered large trees termed 'standards'. *Continuous cover systems* do not involve rotational felling; they utilise small patch felling (group felling or group selection) or selective single-tree harvesting, which maintains relatively high canopy cover, resulting in no dramatic change to the overall appearance of the forested landscape. *Wood-pasture systems* combine the growth of trees with livestock grazing. The trees are typically scattered at low density and are often old. These systems are now rare in Europe, though examples survive especially in eastern Europe and Iberia (see below).

Large differences exist between these production systems in their gross structures. Canopy opening sizes (associated with regeneration) and tree sizes (associated with growth stage and forest maturity) are especially variable (Fig. 13.2). Growth stage is a basic attribute of woodland that affects the bird assemblage composition, because the types of available resources, especially nesting and feeding sites, change strikingly as the forest matures (Fuller *et al.* 2012). There have been rather few direct comparisons of bird assemblages, either breeding or wintering, associated with fundamentally different management systems. However, based on gross structures and their consequences for resource availability, simple predictions can be made. In the case of rotational systems, bird assemblages must be assessed at the scale of the full management cycle in order to account for all the habitat types that may be provided by the system. Within each system, there is much variation in implementation, for example in tree species composition, regeneration gap size, timing and intensity of thinning, treatment of deadwood and timing of harvesting. These factors all affect resources and birds in ways outlined below. Additionally, bird species composition varies regionally and bird–habitat associations are not geographically constant (Wesołowski & Fuller 2012).

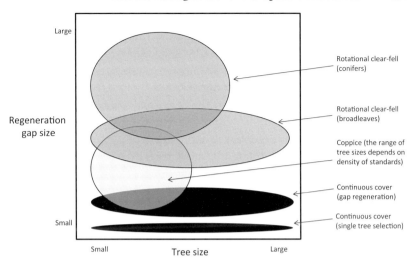

Figure 13.2 Schematic representation of different broad management systems in terms of the range of regeneration gap sizes and stature of trees. Regeneration gaps are open-canopy patches of young planted or regenerating trees. Ellipses indicate relative characteristics of each system and do not indicate frequency or density of gaps or trees of different size. For the sake of clarity, wood-pastures are not shown; these can be highly variable in both gap size and tree size distributions. However, large veteran trees typify long-established wood-pastures. Wood-pastures grazed at low intensity may contain many patches of small regenerating trees, whereas more intensively grazed systems frequently lack regeneration.

Consequently, only general assessments are possible about how management systems influence the characteristics of assemblages; these are summarised below for the breeding season.

Rotational clearfelling provides a diversity of growth stages, from open low shrubby stands to mature closed-canopy stands. Potentially, therefore, the diversity of bird assemblages is relatively high in these systems; this is especially the case in broad-leaved systems where trees are grown on long rotations and achieve considerable stature. Shelterwood systems are similar to plantation clearfelling, except that the early regeneration stages can support a higher diversity of birds due to the presence of seed trees (Ferry & Frochot 1990). By contrast, coppice systems are managed on much shorter rotations, and where mature trees (standards) are present, they are grown at low densities so as not to shade the regenerating coppiced trees. At the whole-system level, young-growth species are potentially more strongly represented in terms of their overall contribution of birds than in rotational clearfell. Even where standard trees are present, the representation of hole-nesting species is expected to be lower in coppice than in the later stages of rotational clearfell and in continuous cover. This is likely to be especially true of hole-nesters that generally require large trees or mature stands (e.g., nuthatch *Sitta europaea*, flycatchers and some woodpeckers).

Continuous cover is different to the rotational systems in that it does not exhibit spatial separation of growth stages. However, the physical complexity of foliage is potentially high, with multilayered strata created by the juxtaposition of differently aged trees. If the MacArthur and MacArthur (1961) model of vertical foliage complexity as a main predictor of bird species diversity is valid when applied to European forests, then continuous cover systems could maximise alpha species diversity. However, it is unclear whether this model does have universal application when applied to forest vegetation (e.g., Erdelen 1984; Verner & Larson 1989; Mills *et al.* 1991). A study in the Belgian Ardennes found that continuous cover did not result in more diverse bird assemblages in conifer plantations relative to clearfelling, and that clear differences in bird assemblages were not evident between these systems when applied to beech *Fagus sylvatica* forest (du Bus de Warnaffe & Deconchat 2008). Furthermore, there is a question as to whether continuous cover can provide suitable habitats for early successional species that avoid small gaps or that need dense thickets of shrubs. Calladine *et al.* (2015) reported that whilst bird assemblages in continuous cover conifer forests in Britain were richer in bird species and held a higher abundance of 'mature forest birds', rotational clearfells were preferred by a small number of young-growth species. Evidence from US forests indicates that clearfelling rotational systems offer more opportunities for early successional species than continuous cover managed by group-felling or tree selection (Costello *et al.* 2000; Thompson & DeGraaf 2001; Gram *et al.* 2003). Other studies in the United States have examined responses of birds to management *within* continuous cover systems and shown that early successional species can respond favourably to selection harvesting (e.g., Holmes & Pitt 2007).

Finally, wood-pasture systems offer structures ranging from parkland (scattered trees and grass) to far more complex mosaics with patches of scrub and tree regeneration. Examples include traditional agroforestry systems and wood-pastures such as *dehesas* and *montados* in Iberia (Camprodón *et al.* 2007; Robles *et al.* 2007a, 2011), and wood-pastures and traditional village systems in central and eastern Europe (Palang *et al.* 2006; Fischer *et al.* 2012; Hartel *et al.* 2013). The bird assemblages of parkland are low in species and density and are dominated by small numbers of hole-nesting species. Mosaic structures, however, can support a much wider range of species, including both shrub-dependent birds and hole-nesters (Hartel *et al.* 2014; Robles *et al.* 2007a, 2011). In Transylvania, wood-pastures were found to have higher absolute species richness and showed higher spatial turnover in species than nearby closed forests (Hartel *et al.* 2014).

The very early and late stages of succession, referred to here as young-growth and mature-growth[1], are particularly important in a conservation context, because these stages support sets of resources that are typically otherwise scarce in timber production forests (Fuller *et al.* 2007, 2012). Young-growth occurs mainly in man-made gaps and at woodland edges; it usually contains the greatest concentrations of dense shrubby vegetation, fruits and bare ground, but many factors affect the availability of these resources (Fuller 2012a). Natural tree-fall gaps can also contain vigorous regeneration, but these generally occur in late successional stages so are best regarded as a mature-growth feature. Mature-growth potentially offers dead and decaying wood, with major concentrations in tree-fall gaps, plus a range of microhabitats associated with large trees. Whilst many species are strongly associated with either the early or the late successional stage, relatively few species are specialists of the intermediate stages (Fuller *et al.* 2007; Begehold *et al.* 2015). Intermediate stages typically form the greatest proportion of forests managed as rotational clearfell. They are characterised by a relatively uniform closed canopy, heavy shading and minimal understorey structures (Quine *et al.* 2007).

The longevity of individual trees varies depending on factors such as soils, climate and competition, but in commercially managed forests, trees are harvested long before their natural age span. For example, oak *Quercus robur* and Scots pine *Pinus sylvestris* can live to at least 300 years, and beech and Norway spruce *Picea abies* to more than 200 years. Typical felling ages can be as short as 40–60 years for the conifers and 100–150 years for the broadleaves. The harvesting of trees well before biological maturity reduces the availability of cavities and deadwood that might otherwise be provided by old trees.

---

[1] We prefer the term 'mature-growth' to 'old-growth', because the latter tends to be applied to structures that appear to have been little modified by humans and are characterised by natural dynamics with stand-scale patchiness, massive trees, and large quantities of decaying wood in various states. Mature-growth encompasses such forests but also can be applied to pre-harvesting stages of productive forests managed on long rotations.

This sketch of bird assemblages indicates that different management systems are somewhat complementary in their bird assemblages, despite overlap in the structures and potential resources they offer (Fig. 13.2). Where a range of different management systems is adopted within a region, or even within a single forest area, one might therefore expect the diversity of bird species to be relatively high at that scale. However, the frequent reality is that in any particular region, one or two systems predominate for economic reasons. For example, to maximise the diversity of structures and avian resources in the lowlands of western Europe, a mixture of clearfelling, continuous cover, coppice and wood-pasture could create highly complementary habitats for birds. Unfortunately, the latter two systems are scarce, whereas clearfelling or forms of continuous cover are typically dominant. More importantly, within each of these systems there is variation in implementation and context. For instance, within coppice, differences in density of standards, patch size, tree density, tree species, rotation length and grazing pressure have large influences on habitat suitability for bird species (Fuller 1992; Holt *et al.* 2013a, b). Whilst broad management systems provide an initial framework for thinking about the potential quality of forest habitats for birds, it is essential to understand how management actions affect the resources available to birds within these systems. The following section considers various approaches to optimising the resources for forest birds and the limits to achieving this within economically productive forestry.

13.2.2 Management Interventions to Improve Habitat Suitability for Birds

Conservation interventions are most likely to focus on (i) increasing the *quantity* of young- and mature-growth vegetation, (ii) improving the *quality of resources* in young-growth and mature-growth and (iii) enhancing the range of resources in intermediate growth stages. Decisions and actions undertaken regarding how to manage any area of forest have complex implications for the characteristics of the forest environment and the functional resources available for biodiversity. Some likely pathways between management and resource quantity and quality are summarised in Fig. 13.3. Specific management interventions that can potentially increase habitat availability and quality for particular groups of forest birds are summarised below. This text is not intended to provide practical management guidance, but rather to indicate the diversity of potential interventions and identify information needs.

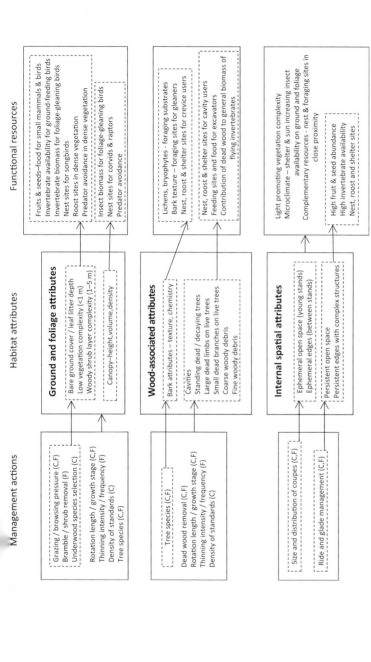

Management actions   Habitat attributes   Functional resources

Figure 13.3 Likely relationships between forest management actions, habitat features and functional resources relevant to birds. The diagram is structured around three broad types of habitat features affected by forest management: ground/foliage attributes, wood-associated attributes and spatial attributes. Relevance of management actions to active coppice (C) and high forest (F) is indicated. Adapted from Fuller (2013).

Experimental tests of how birds respond to these management interventions are rare and can take an exceedingly long time to deliver results, so evidence rests mainly on observation/comparative studies or expert judgement concerning resource development. Much conservation management in forests involves some form of manipulating rotation length; for a review of the ecological implications from a Fennoscandian perspective, see Roberge *et al.* (2016).

Young-growth resources

Manipulating rotation length: Much of the available young-growth in landscapes will be determined by silvicultural practices. The age at which trees are harvested is usually determined by products and markets, so the scope for altering rotation length is limited. However, where conservation is an objective, it may be possible to manage a part of the forest on a shorter rotation in order to increase the absolute area of young-growth. Sometimes it may be possible to achieve this and sell the resulting harvested material (e.g., for firewood), but in most cases it is likely to require a commercial sacrifice.

Edge management: Resources delivered at habitat edges are frequently similar to those in shrubland and early-regeneration patches (Fuller 2012a). Actions aimed at increasing vegetation complexity at edges (Fig. 13.4) can occur in three situations: (i) at the interface of tree-covered land and open land, (ii) between forest patches of different ages and (iii) along the edges of forest tracks and roads. In each case, some sacrifice of productive forest is required. Shrubs and trees are cut at frequent intervals to create strips or bays of regenerating vegetation. Persistence of shrubland structures can be encouraged by selective removal of trees. Elaborate designs can be employed involving differential cutting of various vegetation bands (Warren & Fuller 1993), but these are expensive to maintain. An example of successful edge management is given by Calladine *et al.* (2013), who found that creating shrubby edges at the interface of Scottish Sitka spruce *Picea sitchensis* plantations and moorland considerably diversified the bird assemblages. However, many edge treatments create rather narrow bands of young-growth and may not provide sufficient habitat extent for many specialist birds. Fuller (2012a) argues that in European forests, the majority of bird species associated with edges are essentially young-growth specialists. There is a need to quantify the relative benefits of providing young-growth vegetation at edges (e.g., Pietzarka & Roloff 1993) compared with more extensive habitat patches created by manipulating rotation length.

Figure 13.4 Some interventions that can enhance habitat quality for bird species at the margins and inside forest stands. 'Hard' forest edges, such as example (a) from north-west Spain, offer little suitable habitat for shrub-dependent species and fruit-eating birds. They can be improved by managing woody regeneration at the edge to create more complex 'soft' margins, as shown in (b), which is a woodland glade in Norfolk, England. Where conservation is a primary objective, there may be scope for using heavy thinning to create innovative structures within stands. Compare the broadleaved stands (c) and (d), which are in southern England. The former stand was planted more than 120 years ago and has not been managed for many decades; it is heavily shaded with little undergrowth. Stand (d) has been transformed into a far more complex structure that offers resources for both species that depend on large trees and ones that require dense undergrowth. An alternative treatment for stand (c) would be to leave it indefinitely to acquire old-growth characteristics through the senescence of trees and the natural formation of gaps. Photos: (a) C. Ciudad, (b–d) R.J. Fuller.

Maximise regeneration gap size: In continuous cover systems, young-growth is limited to small patches in regeneration gaps (typically < 0.2 ha). These are unlikely to offer high-quality resources for species that need substantial areas of dense shrubby vegetation or bare ground. However, studies are needed that compare the diversity of bird assemblages across a range of structures within European continuous cover systems; the expectation would be that group-felling would support higher diversity than individual tree selection. In North America, DeGraaf and Yamasaki (2003) recommended that gap sizes should be at least 0.8 ha for early successional specialists. In South Carolina, Moorman and Guynn (2001) examined birds using gap sizes from 0.06 to 0.5 ha and concluded that scattered gaps of at least 0.5 ha would result in satisfactory tree regeneration and increase bird diversity by providing habitat for both edge and interior species.

Provision of bare ground: Several species require bare ground or very short vegetation for feeding (e.g., green and grey-headed woodpeckers *Picus viridis* and *P. canus*, woodlark *Lullula arborea*, tree pipit *Anthus trivialis*). High patch quality could potentially be maintained by grazing, inter-row ploughing or herbicide use (Langston *et al.* 2007). Moderate grazing pressure in wood-pasture systems can create areas of bare ground surrounded by trees and shrubs (Robles *et al.* 2007a, 2011), a structure that can provide habitat for an array of species (Hartel *et al.* 2014).

Reduction of grazing pressure: High grazing pressure by wild ungulates can profoundly affect low vegetation structures by reducing tree and shrub growth and encouraging the growth of unpalatable vegetation (Gill & Fuller 2007). This can reduce the density of shrub-dependent bird species (McShea & Rappole 2000; Holt *et al.* 2013a, b). Where deer pressure severely impacts on habitat structures, reducing the numbers of deer or excluding them with fencing can potentially increase resources for birds in young-growth. Both approaches have limitations. Relationships between deer abundance and biodiversity can be non-linear (Foster *et al.* 2014), and ideally the form of this relationship needs to be understood in order to deliver the most effective management. Total exclusion by fencing is expensive and does not allow development of complex habitat mosaics that can occur under light browsing. Fences can cause additional mortality to birds, notably forest grouse, as a result of collisions (Baines & Summers 1997). A third approach is to introduce predators such as wolves *Canis lupus* or lynx *Lynx lynx*, but this is controversial and we are unaware of situations where this has been implemented specifically to reduce the impact of deer.

Mature-growth resources
Green-tree retentions: Allowing groups of trees to persist beyond commercial harvesting age has long been advocated as a positive intervention for birds in clearfelling systems as a means of retaining canopy volume and the resources linked with large trees (Currie & Bamford 1982). More recently, many variants have been proposed for retaining live tree cover

in clearfelling (see Rosenvald & Lõhmus 2008; Lindenmayer *et al.* 2012). A meta-analysis of 944 studies conducted across a wide range of taxa indicated that retention forestry can potentially reduce some undesirable effects of clearcutting on biodiversity, though it tends not to provide suitable habitats for specialised young-growth or forest-interior species (Fedrowitz *et al.* 2014). The taxa-specific results were complex, but overall species richness and abundance of birds were higher in retention cuts than in clearcuts. Whilst mature forest birds were found to be more abundant in retentions than in clearcuts, they were less abundant than in unharvested forest. An earlier meta-analysis suggested that the overall species richness of birds can be enhanced relative to clearfelling as a result of greater structural complexity, and that mature trees within clearfells may benefit some raptors and woodpeckers (Rosenvald & Lõhmus 2008). In Estonia, raptors generally only nest in stands less than 80 years old if large trees, typically spruces, are present, so green-tree retention can improve forest conditions for these species (Lõhmus 2006). In slow-growing forests, retentions may be valuable in creating high quality habitat for species such as Siberian jay *Perisoreus infaustus* (Griesser & Lagerberg 2012).

Green-tree retention can potentially benefit birds in the post-breeding period as well as the breeding season (McDermott & Wood 2011). Whilst retentions frequently improve habitat for mature forest birds, some studies have failed to record positive responses (e.g., Otto & Roloff 2012). As with most forestry-wildlife interactions, the fine details are important, in particular the numbers of retained trees or the proportion of the original tree density retained; as one might expect, larger-scale retentions appear to provide greater benefits (Linden *et al.* 2012; Söderström 2009).

Maintaining individual trees: Certain trees may be of particular biodiversity and cultural value because of their exceptional size or age (Blicharska & Mikusiński 2014; Lindenmayer *et al.* 2014). This is especially true with regard to some scarce invertebrates, and maintaining the quality of such trees is important for saproxylic species (Alexander *et al.* 2010; Koch Widerberg *et al.* 2012). Although it is sometimes assumed that 'ancient' or 'legacy' trees are important for woodpeckers and other hole-nesting birds, we are unaware that this has been demonstrated in Europe. We suspect that any benefits they do provide will be context-specific. For example, scattered ancient trees may provide the main sources of food and nest sites for hole-nesters in parkland, some wood-pastures and some stands of young or middle-aged uniform trees. Trees with decaying heartwood form a key resource for woodpeckers (Zahner *et al.* 2012), but such trees are not necessarily 'ancient', and secondary hole-nesters appear to prefer living medium-sized trees for nesting (Remm *et al.* 2006; Robles *et al.* 2011). It is clear, however, that the canopies of exceptionally large trees provide important nest sites for diurnal open-nesting raptors (Lõhmus 2006), while large hollow trees give nest sites for some owl species.

Provision of snags and decaying wood: It is widely assumed that maximising the volume of decaying wood, and providing it in diverse contexts (snags, limbs, fallen) and at different stages of decay, must enhance invertebrate food supplies for many birds and assist cavity-nesting species, as well as provide habitats for saproxylic invertebrates. However, rather few studies have demonstrated a general link between overall bird assemblages and deadwood. Nilsson (1979) found that across eight Swedish forest plots, the richness and density of birds were more strongly correlated with the quantity of standing deadwood than with other vegetation variables. The cause of these relationships is unclear, and it is uncertain how general they might be. A large, predominantly North American, body of literature exists on the use of decaying wood by birds and on relationships between snags and bird assemblages. The retention of snags within clearfells, the provision of artificial snags and the creation of dead trees by girdling are long-standing management practices in North American and, less frequently, European forests, with the aim of enhancing habitats for woodpeckers and other hole-nesting and bark-gleaning species (e.g., Dickson *et al.* 1983; Petit *et al.* 1985). There appear to be fewer snag-dependent woodpeckers in forests in Europe than in North America; furthermore, many European secondary cavity nesters prefer living trees to snags (Remm *et al.* 2006; Robles *et al.* 2011). However, at least in Britain, dead trees are commonly, but not exclusively, used for nesting by great spotted woodpecker *Dendrocopos major* and especially by lesser spotted woodpecker *Dryobates minor* (Smith 2007). The availability of deadwood in various forms also provides especially important food resources for feeding woodpeckers outside the breeding season (Smith 2007). Deadwood on live trees is an important feeding substrate; for example, lesser spotted woodpeckers can feed heavily on beetle larvae within small dead branches on live trees (Olsson *et al.* 2001).

The effects on biodiversity of salvage logging following insect outbreaks, fires or storms have received increasing attention, leading to insights into the relationships between birds and deadwood resources (Fig. 13.5). Snag-dependent species in North America appear to show

Figure 13.5 Forest fires can create new opportunities for birds, as shown in these photographs of a large burn in a central Swedish conifer forest taken in September 2015, approximately one year after the fire occurred. (a) and (b) are salvage logged areas with much temporary bare ground that provides habitat for ground-feeders such as pipits. Within a few years, habitat quality is likely to be high for many shrub-nesters. Unharvested burnt forest can be seen in the background of (b). (c) The interiors of such stands quickly develop many foraging opportunities for species dependent on deadwood invertebrates; black woodpecker *Dryocopus martius* and three-toed woodpecker *Picoides tridactylus* were using the standing dead trees at this site. Two of the editors are examining black woodpecker excavations in (d). Photos: R.J. Fuller.

general negative responses to salvage logging (Rost *et al.* 2013). However, avian responses can be complex. For example, in Oregon conifer forests, Cahall and Hayes (2009) found that some species were apparently unaffected, others decreased and still others increased. Interestingly, species that responded negatively to salvage logging did not benefit from leaving a higher density of snags (30 ha^{-1} compared to 5–6 ha^{-1}).

Prescribed burning: Controlled fires are widely used in North American pine and oak forests to improve regeneration and forest structure and reduce the risk of wildfire. By removing much of the litter layer and low vegetation, burning could potentially reduce densities of ground- and shrub-nesting birds (Artman *et al.* 2001). However, some studies have explored whether prescribed burning could be used to enhance habitat quality for birds. Jentsch *et al.* (2008) considered that canopy gaps maintained by prescribed fires could promote the growth of large oaks considered important to several bird species. James *et al.* (2001) proposed that a combination of burning and thinning could create high-quality habitat for red-cockaded woodpeckers *Picoides borealis* in longleaf pine forest. Prescribed burning is now adopted in Fennoscandian conifer forests for both silvicultural and conservation purposes; for example, it is one of the recovery plan measures for the white-backed woodpecker in Sweden (Blicharska *et al.* 2014). Potential benefits to birds include an increased broadleaved component and bare ground which can enhance food availability for ground foragers, while burnt trees can provide foraging habitat for bark and canopy foragers. We are unaware of any European studies of prescribed burning, but wildfires in Sweden provide insights into changes in resources following fire (Fig. 13.5). Edenius (2011) found striking short-term differences in bird assemblages in burned areas and nearby unburned conifer forest in northern Sweden.

Thinning as a conservation tool

Commercial forestry uses thinning in a variety of contexts and management systems, usually to promote the growth of selected trees. At one level, this is detrimental for biodiversity, in that it removes future dead-tree biomass. Nevertheless, in the context of managed forests, it potentially increases shade-sensitive vegetation and associated animals. Many studies, mainly in North America, have examined biodiversity responses to thinning, and a review by Verschuyl *et al.* (2011) considered that thinning treatments tend to have 'positive or neutral effects on diversity and abundance across all taxa'. However, the literature indicates that bird species differ considerably in their response to thinning, and several studies have found no measurable effects (Fuller 2013). Much silvicultural thinning does not create sufficiently large canopy openings to stimulate sufficient understorey development to benefit early successional species or ones that require complex field- or shrub-layer vegetation (Fuller 2013). One exception is the use of thinning and small-patch clearfelling to enhance field-layer food supplies for capercaillie *Tetrao urogallus*, which can be compatible with productive forestry (Broome *et al.* 2014).

Where conservation is a primary objective and maximising economic returns is less important, thinning has considerable potential to create novel habitat structures of high biodiversity value. Variable density thinning can be used to create mosaics of closed- and open-canopy patches, with gap sizes larger than those typically adopted in continuous cover systems. Innovative thinning could create stand structures in broadleaved woodland that are valuable for both young-growth and mature-growth species (Fig. 13.4).

Tree species diversification
Despite the undeniable importance of vegetation structure at both the macro and micro scale, there are additional effects of tree species composition on habitat quality for many bird species. It is well recognised that deciduous and coniferous stands frequently differ in their bird assemblages, but more subtle effects of tree species are undoubtedly widespread. Links between tree species and birds operate through variations in type and quantity of food resources, provision of shelter and availability of nest sites. The process of disentangling these relationships has barely started, which is unfortunate, because enhancing the tree diversity of managed forests is already being adopted as one of the main routes to achieving higher resilience in the face of changing climate and escalating tree diseases.

Some studies have reported that the addition of broadleaved trees to conifer forests can do much to increase avian diversity in conifer forests (Bibby *et al.* 1989; Wilson *et al.* 2010), but others have not found such clear support (Archaux & Bakkaus 2007). There is a logical preference for using native species and provenances wherever possible, on the assumption that these will favour local invertebrates, lichens, fungi, etc. Irrespective of whether the species are native, some mixtures of tree species could provide economic resilience as well as constitute diverse environments for birds. Tree-species mixtures could help to increase the seasonal availability of insects, enhance the provision of seeds, diversify microstructures through variation in canopy and bark texture and contribute different kinds of decaying wood. However, the exact benefits, if any, will depend on the details of tree composition and the scale and pattern of implementation. It has been suggested that the provision of mixtures as blocks of different tree species rather than intimate mixtures may be preferable (Archaux & Bakkaus 2007). It remains an open question as to whether this is generally true in European forests.

13.3 The Landscape Level: Habitat Loss, Habitat Fragmentation and the Matrix

13.3.1 Habitat Loss and Fragmentation

Human-induced landscape changes have driven large loss and fragmentation of habitat, which is a major driver of biodiversity decline (Groom *et al.* 2006). Habitat loss is associated with a reduction in the amount of habitat at the landscape level. Habitat fragmentation is typically defined as the subdivision of continuous habitat into a number of separate smaller habitat patches or fragments, which results in increased edge-interior habitat ratios and inter-patch distances. All these spatial processes can impose new selection pressures on birds that can lead to the decline, and eventual extinction, of local populations, with a consequent reduction in species richness of local communities. The main mechanisms and selection pressures involved are summarised below and in Fig. 13.6.

Allee effect and increased impacts of stochasticity
Habitat loss and fragmentation inevitably reduces the size of populations. Because population growth is often positively related to population size (i.e., the Allee effect), small populations are more likely to become extinct due to a reduction in bird reproduction and/or survival. Different mechanisms can explain the Allee effect in small breeding populations (Swift & Hannon 2010). The most common mechanism is the disappearance or high mortality of individuals of one sex associated with high demographic stochasticity, leading to biased sex ratios and, ultimately, reduced fecundity in small populations. Small populations can also be exposed to high inbreeding depression and disruption of social information (see below). Most studies have focused on variation in fecundity and mortality of the breeders (Penteriani *et al.* 2011). However, simulation studies suggest that the Allee effect in breeding populations can be explained by a high mortality of floaters, i.e., nonbreeding but sexually mature individuals able to enter the breeding population when a vacancy becomes available (Penteriani *et al.* 2008, 2011). Indeed, a surplus of floaters can buffer small breeding populations from extinction by replacing the lost breeders in populations subjected to the individual and synergic impacts of the Allee effect and demographic/environmental stochasticity (Robles & Ciudad 2017); thus, a high mortality of floaters could reduce the resilience and stability of small populations.

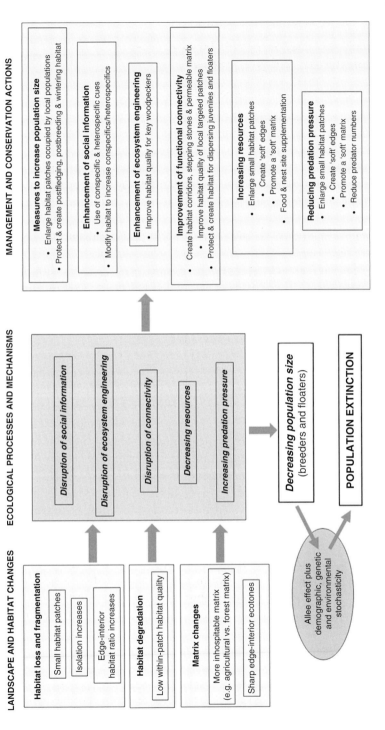

Figure 13.6 Ecological mechanisms underlying population extinction and management actions aimed at palliating adverse effects of landscape and habitat changes on birds. Rather than an accurate description of the ecological mechanisms and management actions involved, this figure is just an example of the complexity inherent in the persistence of avian populations in heterogeneous landscapes and habitats. See the text for more explanations of the linkages.

Reduction in food supply

According to the resource concentration hypothesis (Root 1973; Lampila *et al.* 2005), small habitat patches are less likely to hold sufficient essential resources than large habitat patches. The availability of some resources in small habitat patches could be further reduced due to the increase of edge habitat in fragmented landscapes. For example, ground invertebrates may not survive well under warmer and drier conditions along the edges compared to interior habitat, causing a reduction in food biomass for some insectivorous birds (Burke & Nol 1998), with possible negative effects on reproductive parameters associated with food supply, such as nestling size (Zanette *et al.* 2000). However, a meta-analysis suggests that habitat fragmentation effects on forest birds are not generally driven by reduced food resources in small patches, as several demographic parameters associated with food supply do not show strong responses to fragmentation (Lampila *et al.* 2005). While this may be true for many birds, a reduction in food supply near edges and in small habitat patches may well explain negative fragmentation effects in some species.

Increase of predation pressure

To date, the best-documented negative effect of habitat fragmentation on forest birds is increased nest predation pressure (Lampila *et al.* 2005). This can be associated with an increase in either the number of predators or their efficiency as the amount of edge habitat increases (Chalfoun *et al.* 2002). The effects of habitat loss and fragmentation on nest predation depend on specific traits of birds. Open-nesting birds are more likely to be affected by an increase in predation pressure than cavity-nesters (Lampila *et al.* 2005), as cavities provide birds with relatively safe nesting opportunities (Mitrus 2003). This may explain why nesting success is not strongly affected by fragmentation in European cavity-nesting birds (Matthysen & Adriaensen 1998; Lampila *et al.* 2005; Robles *et al.* 2008). Moreover, most studies reporting a negative effect of fragmentation on nesting success come from North America, and the results cannot necessarily be extrapolated to Europe, given the intercontinental differences in fragmentation histories and avian life-history traits.

Juvenile birds undergo high mortality associated with predation during the first weeks after fledging, which matches the dependence period before dispersal (Götmark 2002; Sunde 2005; Robles *et al.*

2007b). Could this mortality be enhanced by habitat loss and frag-mentation? The few Palaearctic studies that have assessed the influence of fragmentation on juvenile survival failed to find a negative response to fragmentation-related variables (Currie & Matthysen 1998; Mat-thysen 1999; Robles *et al.* 2007b). Compared to juveniles, adult survival is relatively high in forest birds (e.g., Robles *et al.* 2007b). There is no evidence of negative fragmentation effects on adult survival in the middle spotted woodpecker *Leiopicus medius* (Robles *et al.* 2007b) or the nuthatch (Matthysen 1999), but more studies are needed to understand the global effect of fragmentation on avian survival.

Disruption of connectivity and dispersal

Dispersal is a crucial process influencing gene flow, population dynamics and species distributions (Hanski & Gilpin 1997; Bowler & Benton 2005; Clobert *et al.* 2009). At the population level, immigration may rescue declining or sink populations from extinction (the 'rescue effect'; *sensu* Brown & Kodric-Brown 1977) or favour the (re)colonisation of empty patches, balancing extinctions in other patches in meta-populations (Hanski & Gilpin 1997; Robles & Ciudad 2012). Thus, enhancing functional connectivity could have positive consequences for the persist-ence of populations.

A major fragmentation–related hypothesis, often taken as dogma by wildlife managers, is that increasing the isolation of habitat patches (the inverse of connectivity) disrupts functional connectivity among local populations. However, empirical tests of the hypothesis provide contrast-ing results. Cooper and Walters (2002) showed experimentally that disruption in the connectivity of fragmented habitats led to short natal dispersal distances and low recruitment of females in the cooperatively breeding brown treecreeper *Climacteris picumnus*. Likewise, disperser suc-cess in juvenile nuthatches was lower in a highly fragmented landscape compared to a large forest, through reductions in the number of settlers and mating opportunities (Matthysen & Currie 1996). Conversely, Robles and Ciudad (2012) did not find a strong effect of connectivity on the probability of patch colonisation by middle spotted woodpeckers in a highly fragmented landscape where only 4% of the area provided habitat. Instead, high-quality patches (those with a higher density of large oaks) were more likely to be colonised by woodpeckers. This suggests that habitat quality may be more relevant than connectivity in colonisation of local patches by habitat specialists with relatively high dispersal ability (Robles & Ciudad 2012).

Disruption of social information

The disruption of social information is a largely neglected subject in fragmentation studies. Because habitat loss and fragmentation typically reduce the size of local populations, and several ecological processes require social information associated with large population sizes, one can expect disruption of social interactions that contribute to population cohesion. Fletcher (2009) showed experimentally that a reduced attraction of conspecifics during habitat selection in small habitat patches with small populations explained the sensitivity of some forest birds to habitat fragmentation. Conspecific attraction can be an efficient habitat selection mechanism, because juvenile birds (the majority of dispersers) may not be proficient in identifying suitable habitat (Ahlering & Faaborg 2006). In addition, conspecific attraction could be a potential explanation for the reduction in pairing success of male birds in more fragmented habitats, as females may use the proximity and abundance of neighbouring territorial males as an index of habitat quality (Villard *et al.* 1993; Robles *et al.* 2008). Consequently, females may judge small patches with few neighbours to be of low quality.

Forest birds may use heterospecific cues during settlement (i.e., heterospecific attraction; Mönkkönen *et al.* 1990; Fletcher 2007). Moreover, the use of heterospecific information may shape community structure through the formation and organisation of mixed-species groups. Species with a poor ability to detect information such as predation risk may benefit from using information provided by other species (Goodale *et al.* 2010). If fragmentation diminishes heterospecific populations or communities, species that rely on heterospecific information for habitat selection may lack cues for settling.

Disruption of ecosystem engineering

An important fraction of avian diversity is structured within 'cavity-nest web communities', where avian excavators, mostly woodpeckers, and other agents (e.g., rot-fungi/insects, wind, snow) act as cavity producers (i.e., ecosystem engineers) that facilitate nest sites for secondary cavity-nesting birds in forests (Robles & Martin 2013; Chapter 4). The associations between particular species of ecosystem engineers and cavity users will depend on the quantity and quality of cavities that each ecosystem engineer provides to each cavity user in each habitat type (Robles &

Martin 2013, 2014). By changing the abundance and composition of ecosystem engineers, habitat loss and fragmentation are expected to shape the cavity-nest web community structure.

13.3.2 The Matrix

Traditionally, habitat fragmentation studies have been carried out within the context of metapopulation (Hanski & Gilpin 1997) and island bio-geography (MacArthur & Wilson 1967) theories. Both theories assume that species survive in habitat fragments or 'islands' surrounded by an inhospitable matrix (i.e., non-habitat). This dichotomous perspective (habitat vs. non-habitat) is challenged and complemented by landscape ecology, which recognises the heterogeneity inherent in most real-world landscapes. Thus, fragmented landscapes are composed of habitat patches surrounded by a heterogeneous matrix that can influence the survival of local bird populations (Åberg et al. 1995). This can operate through at least three major mechanisms (Fig. 13.6).

First, differences in the matrix can affect nest predation pressures to which birds are subjected in the habitat patches. Nest predation for ground-nesting forest birds is expected to be greater in small habitat fragments surrounded by an open agricultural matrix than in habitat patches embedded within forest (Chalfoun et al. 2002). This effect arises from the abundance or the efficiency of predators being relatively high along edges where forest meets open country. Second, the matrix can influence the amount of resources available for birds by altering the abiotic and biotic components in the habitat patches. In particular, 'hard', abrupt boundaries (Fig. 13.4) can generate severe changes in soil and vegetation structure, which in turn can reduce the availability of food and nest sites for birds (Burke & Nol 1998). The third mechanism concerns the influence of the matrix on the ability of organisms to move through it. Large errors in estimations of inter-patch connectivity can occur if it is assumed that the matrix is homogeneous (Revilla et al. 2004). Indeed, some empirical studies have found that bird movements are strongly affected by the composition of the matrix (Richard & Armstrong 2010; Aben et al. 2012).

13.3.3 Management Actions for Bird Conservation at the Landscape Level

General principles for improving the biodiversity and ecological function of landscapes are widely accepted (Fischer et al. 2006; Lindenmayer et al.

2008). These are not elaborated here but should be recognised as a starting point in landscape restoration and improvement. Instead, we identify several actions that have value for birds in particular contexts (summarised below and in Fig. 13.6).

Increasing resource availability in small habitat patches
Because small habitat patches may hold insufficient critical resources, such as food and nest-sites (Lampila *et al.* 2005), increasing the size of individual patches may be beneficial. In particular, small patches (ca. <10 ha) do not allow some birds with relatively large home ranges, such as woodpeckers, to establish, probably due to a scarcity of resources (Robles & Ciudad 2012). Likewise, a reduction in the amount of habitat at the landscape level under a certain threshold may exclude some forest birds (Jansson & Angelstam 1999). Habitat patches can be enlarged by planting trees or encouraging regeneration around the patches. The latter is cheaper than planting but depends on high natural regeneration. For example, in north-west Spain the middle spotted woodpecker occupies patches with large (≥37 cm diameter at breast height) Pyrenean oaks *Quercus pyrenaica*, which are often surrounded by dense forests composed of small-diameter oaks that originate from vegetative regeneration (Robles *et al.* 2007a). Tree competition in these dense forests suppresses tree growth, but low-intensity thinning and selective cutting stimulate faster growth of the remaining trees, eventually enlarging the patches of large-diameter oaks suitable for the woodpecker and secondary cavity-nesters (Robles *et al.* 2011; Robles & Ciudad 2012).

The negative effects of 'hard' edges described above can be reduced by several interventions. The availability of resources (nest sites, insect food, berries) for some forest specialists can be enhanced by creating 'soft' edges (Fig. 13.4, Section 13.2.2). Complex edge structures can also create a more favourable internal microclimate through reduction of exposure to wind and rain. Converting the agricultural matrix itself to a 'softer' matrix, for example one that contains increased quantities of forest or shrubland, may yield even more positive results than just managing 'hard' boundaries, as a 'soft' matrix can provide continuous habitats for arthropods and, in some contexts, reduce the abundance or activity of some predators (Chalfoun *et al.* 2002).

Other options include the artificial supplementation of food or nest sites in small habitat patches. Nest-box provisioning has been shown to increase the occupancy and density of breeding great tits in small patches (Loman 2006). Supplementary feeding has rescued the small population of the Spanish imperial eagle *Aquila adalberti* from short-term extinction (Ferrer *et al.* 2013) and can increase breeding success in the great spotted woodpecker (Smith & Smith 2013). Nevertheless, the use of these techniques has been questioned, because a substantial 'artificial' increase of the population could occur (e.g., Robles *et al.* 2012), which could, in turn, disrupt critical density-dependent processes, such as dispersal (Matthysen 2005) and reproduction (Pöysä & Pöysä 2002), with potential negative consequences for the long-term viability of populations.

Reducing predation pressure
Controlling predators can be an option where an increase in the number or efficiency of predators is causing severe declines of avian populations or communities in fragmented habitats. However, the long-term effectiveness of directly controlling predators is questionable, partly because of the high cost and the fact that some predators are themselves endangered. Any programme of predator control should take into account that predators can provide complex ecosystem functions, for example through trophic interactions involving top predators, mesopredators and their prey (Elmhagen *et al.* 2010).

Predation pressure can be controlled indirectly by modifying habitat attributes to reduce the efficiency of predators in fragmented habitats. Such indirect control of predation may be more effective in the long term and is expected to have less impact on predator populations than direct control. Converting 'hard' edges to 'softer' boundaries and planting more woodland and shrubs in the matrix (see above) may help to reduce nest predation pressure for ground-nesting birds. In addition, management actions aimed at enlarging small patches will reduce the edge-interior habitat ratio, which in turn may reduce the efficiency of predators in fragmented habitats.

Identifying and protecting non-breeding areas critical for dispersing juveniles and floaters
Bird conservation requires the protection of critical resources through all life stages (Anders *et al.* 1998; Vega Rivera *et al.* 1998; Ciudad *et al.* 2009). Non-breeding floaters and post-fledging juveniles are often transient birds that disperse through habitats or areas not used by the breeding adults (Anders *et al.* 1998; Robles & Olea 2003; Penteriani *et al.* 2011). Because juveniles and floaters largely influence population growth and turnover (Porneluzi & Faaborg 1999; Robles & Ciudad 2017), identifying and protecting areas and habitats where these birds can meet

their requirements, either in spring or in the critical post-fledging and winter periods, are important for population persistence (Robles *et al.* 2007b; Ciudad *et al.* 2009; Penteriani *et al.* 2011; Porneluzi *et al.* 2014). Indeed, conservation strategies based exclusively on the protection of breeding habitats can be unsuccessful in maintaining bird populations (Penteriani *et al.* 2011). This is particularly relevant in fragmented landscapes, where juveniles and floaters are more likely to use different habitats and areas than those adults use for breeding (e.g., Robles & Olea 2003).

Improving functional connectivity

Improving functional connectivity in fragmented and heterogeneous landscapes is a major challenge, partly because of the practical difficulties of implementing conservation actions in real landscapes and partly because knowledge of dispersal processes and behaviours is limited. Connectivity enhancement will have the most positive effects for dispersing juveniles and floaters that move among habitat patches in search of a vacant territory or a mate. Approaches proposed so far to enhance functional connectivity are of three broad kinds, each intended to facilitate movements of individuals through landscapes: (i) 'habitat corridors', (ii) 'stepping stones' and (iii) enhanced permeability of the matrix.

Corridors, typically defined as linear structures of native vegetation connecting habitat patches, appear to have relatively low efficiency in facilitating movements of birds compared to other vertebrates, invertebrates and plants (Gilbert-Norton *et al.* 2010). This is partly due to the fact that birds are relatively mobile organisms. Furthermore, individuals that use narrow corridors may experience high predation risk. Nonetheless, corridors could be useful in promoting inter-patch movements that connect local populations of habitat specialists that experience reduced survival when travelling through the matrix (Haddad & Tewksbury 2006). Stepping stones are discrete habitat patches embedded within the matrix that promote individual movements between local populations (Bennett 1999; Noss & Daly 2006). The effectiveness of stepping stones depends on birds' willingness to cross the matrix and efficiency at detecting them (Noss & Daly 2006). The third approach, establishing a 'soft' matrix composed of a mosaic of structures offering low resistance to bird movements, may provide the greatest benefits for birds that are able to use a wide variety of environments in the matrix.

Enhancing social information

Conspecific cues can be enhanced by broadcasting vocalisations of conspecifics to attract juveniles to high-quality empty areas (Ward & Schlossberg 2004) or to increase the pairing success of solitary males in small patches with few or no neighbours (Robles *et al.* 2008). This approach requires caution because ecological traps can potentially be created by attracting birds to areas where their survival or reproduction can be seriously compromised (Ahlering & Faaborg 2006). In the case of species that use heterospecific cues for habitat selection, broadcasting vocalisations of heterospecifics can be effective, but again, there is a risk of creating ecological traps. An alternative way to use vocalisations, or other surrogates of social information, is to enlarge local patches already occupied by focal species. Although this can take a long time, it is expected to enhance the carrying capacity of populations or communities, and therefore the quantity and strength of conspecific/heterospecific cues available for the settlement of dispersers during habitat selection.

Enhancing ecosystem engineering

As primary cavity excavators, woodpeckers act as keystone ecosystem engineers, providing cavities for the community of secondary cavity-nesting birds (see above and chapter 4). Accordingly, simplifying and reducing woodpecker assemblages under habitat loss and fragmentation could have negative consequences for secondary cavity-nesting birds. However, while most cavities are provided by avian excavators in North America (Cockle *et al.* 2011), the role of woodpeckers as key ecosystem engineers for cavity-nesting bird communities in Europe is restricted to forests where other types of cavities are very scarce. For example, in Estonian riverine forests, woodpeckers provided 88% of cavities suitable for passerines (Remm *et al.* 2006). In this instance, other agents of cavity formation (e.g., rot-fungi/insect decay, windstorms, snow) created only a few cavities. The quality of woodpecker cavities for secondary cavity-nesting passerines in temperate Europe seems to be low or not particularly high, as passerines either prefer cavities not excavated by woodpeckers (Wesołowski 2002; Remm *et al.* 2006) or have no particular preference for cavities according to their origin (Robles *et al.* 2011). Thus, enhancing woodpecker habitat quality with the aim of benefitting the assemblage of secondary cavity-nesters is only appropriate for those European forests with low availability of other natural cavities; for example, managed forests composed of relatively small-diameter trees where rot-fungi/insects or windstorms have a limited influence to create cavities (e.g. Andersson *et al.* 2017). Having said that, some large wood-peckers probably do produce important cavities used by other species. For example, the black woodpecker *Dryocopus martius* provides key nesting cavities for jackdaws *Coloeus monedula*, stock doves *Columba oenas* and Tengmalm's owls *Aegolius funereus* in many European forests (Korpimäki 1987; Johnsson *et al.* 1993; Mikusiński 1995; Kosiński *et al.* 2010). Overall, management actions should consider the specific links between particular species of woodpeckers and the target species of secondary cavity users (Robles & Martin 2013).

13.4 Knowledge Gaps, Misconceptions and Methodological Problems Limiting Conservation Delivery

The emphasis, scale and conclusions of conservation research in boreal forests have been similar in North America and Europe (Martin *et al.* 2012). However, in temperate conifer and broadleaved forests, Europe lags behind North America in terms of knowledge (Fuller 2013). There have been systematic attempts in North America to understand the consequences for birds and other wildlife of using different forest-management treatments. These have involved experimental and com-parative studies of species abundance, assemblage composition, breeding performance and home-range movements.

In Europe, there is a need to improve the understanding of effects on birds of factors such as thinning intensity, green-tree retention and regeneration gap sizes in continuous cover management, all of which have been the subject of detailed attention in North America. At present, ecologists are especially poorly equipped to predict the impacts on forest-bird populations of two of the main trends in temperate forest manage-ment: the expansion of continuous cover management systems and the use of new mixtures of tree species in forestry. A more specific know-ledge gap concerns the implications of disturbance created by forestry activities (e.g., Lõhmus 2005) or increased human recreation in forests as they become increasingly multifunctional. Furthermore, the effects of some original disturbance agents such as forest fire, potentially useful as a management tool in some contexts, are largely unknown (but see Chap-ter 9 for the case of Mediterranean forests and a discussion of prescriptive burning in this chapter).

The extent to which the findings of work conducted in North America and other continents can be readily applied to European contexts is unclear. The historical pattern of habitat change as a result of human activity and the intensity of land use is frequently very different to that in much of Europe. Species have had much longer periods to adapt to man-made environments in some regions and consequently may have evolved behaviours such as predator avoidance and dispersal that make them more successful in the modified landscapes. Equally, forest species on different continents have evolved in historically different assemblages of tree species, competitors, predators and pathogens. Basic habitat relationships could therefore be fundamentally different in many contexts. Further transcontinental comparisons of habitat management, habitat loss and habitat fragmentation are highly desirable in order to assess the extent to which general patterns exist (Martin *et al.* 2012).

Despite a plethora of studies, the underlying mechanisms of bird population declines operating at the landscape level through habitat loss and fragmentation remain poorly understood. A major issue of many fragmentation studies is the use of 'forest loss and fragmentation' (or loss and fragmentation of 'native vegetation') as a proxy for 'habitat loss and fragmentation' (Lindenmayer & Fischer 2006, 2007). While 'forest' refers to a vegetation type, 'habitat' is a species-specific feature that does not necessarily match a particular forest type. For example, the middle spotted woodpecker is a specialist of deciduous forests, mainly oak forests. In north-west Spain, oak forest covers 34% of the area, but only 4% is covered by old oak forest with large trees that provide breeding habitat for this woodpecker (Robles *et al.* 2007b). Thus, in this case, the extent of oak forest loss and fragmentation is not a good proxy for habitat loss and fragmentation, which can lead to incorrect or confusing conclusions when the effects of patch size are assessed.

Several theoretical models and simulation studies point to the importance of floaters in population dynamics (e.g., Kokko & Sutherland 1998; Penteriani *et al.* 2008), but to our knowledge there is only one empirical study that strongly supports the hypothesis that floaters effectively buffer the extinction risk of small populations in fragmented habitats (Robles & Ciudad 2017). Unravelling the general buffer effect of floaters will require studies on a wide array of species in different landscape contexts. Likewise, how habitat loss and fragmentation influence floater distribution and mortality remains poorly studied. Robles and Ciudad (2017) found a strong positive effect of patch size, population size and intrinsic patch quality (density of oaks ≥ 37 cm diameter at breast height) on floater occurrence in the middle spotted woodpecker, whereas connectivity of populations did not have a strong influence. Thus, habitat loss, subdivision and degradation, but not increased isolation, are behind the distribution pattern of woodpecker floaters. In line with these results, removal experiments in the ovenbird *Seiurus aurocapillus* demonstrated that floaters were more likely to occur in contiguous forests than in fragments (Bayne & Hobson 2001). But do these findings apply to other birds?

More research is needed to fully understand how habitat loss and fragmentation influence the dispersal and survival of juvenile birds in their early stages of life. More generally, knowledge of habitat use by forest birds in the critical post-fledging period is extremely weak. While numerous studies in North American forests have assessed habitat use, movements and survival of post-fledging juvenile birds, just a few studies have addressed these issues in Europe (e.g., Robles *et al.* 2007b; Ciudad *et al.* 2009). Similarly, changes in habitat quality between winter and breeding seasons have been scarcely studied, despite the importance of winter habitat quality in limiting populations of some resident birds in northern Europe (e.g., nuthatch in Sweden; Nilsson 1987).

The use of conspecific and heterospecific information for habitat selection deserves more attention, especially whether, and to what extent, it is disrupted by habitat loss and fragmentation. Moreover, we need data that clarify the consequences of artificially attracting birds to particular areas or habitats by using social cues.

The role of woodpeckers as key ecosystem engineers in different types of forests is uncertain (Robles & Pasinelli 2014). Experiments that manipulate access to cavities provided by woodpeckers would be informative in evaluating the influence of habitat fragmentation and forest management practices on assemblages of cavity-nesting birds.

Several methodological issues have hampered our understanding of how habitat and landscape changes affect forest birds. The first concerns the calculation of connectivity indexes on the basis of habitat selection of non-dispersing individuals. A proper assessment of functional connectivity requires an understanding of how real dispersers, which exhibit different physiological characteristics and motivations to non-dispersers, move among patches in heterogeneous landscapes (Richard & Armstrong 2010). Translocation and playback experiments that force territorial birds to move through the matrix can provide misleading results that do not reflect dispersal decisions and movements conducted by real dispersers in heterogeneous landscapes.

Second, the use of artificial nest experiments can lead to large errors in our understanding of the mechanisms underlying population declines, because conditions in artificial nests do not always reflect those in real nests. For example, different types of predators may be attracted to artificial nests and real nests of ground-nesting songbirds (Thompson & Burhans 2004). Fortunately, this problem is now widely recognised. However, the use of nest boxes is still relatively frequent in European fragmentation studies. Predation in artificial nest boxes, where nests are well protected from predators, may not reflect real conditions in natural breeding cavities (Møller 1989; Mitrus 2003). Moreover, nest-box size and material influence the clutch size of some forest birds (Møller *et al.* 2014). Further, as mentioned above, the addition of nest boxes can markedly increase the breeding densities of cavity-nesting birds (Robles *et al.* 2012), with potential implications for population dynamics. The artificial increase of population densities is unlikely to reflect real conditions in habitat fragmentation scenarios.

Finally, avian survival and dispersal in fragmentation studies are frequently estimated by recovering or re-sighting individually marked birds in small study plots. Such plots often cover the whole area of habitat in more fragmented landscapes, which makes it possible to cover more extensive study areas in fragmented landscapes, compared with landscapes containing tracts of continuous habitat. Consequently, marked birds can be searched for in a smaller fraction of the habitat available in continuously forested landscapes. This can lead to a greater underestimation of survival rates, dispersal distances and home ranges in continuous landscapes, because long dispersal events are more likely to be missed (Koenig *et al.* 1996).

13.5 Conservation Action for Declining Species

This chapter emphasises the importance of habitat-based interventions, but recovery plans may include other actions of which we have not attempted a comprehensive review. As discussed elsewhere in the chapter, these actions can include predator control and the provision of supplementary food and artificial nest sites (typically nest boxes; see also Chapter 4). These actions can be adopted alongside habitat-based approaches and have the greatest value where they address a critical limiting factor (e.g., the absence of nest sites for large cavity-nesting birds in forest lacking large trees).

Plans for effective conservation actions for declining or vulnerable birds should ideally be based on a proper identification of the negative effects of land uses to be mitigated at whatever spatial level these operate.

Because the necessary knowledge will never be comprehensive, an element of pragmatism in finding solutions will often be needed. Nonetheless, it is useful to recognise that three interrelated approaches can form a framework for determining the most appropriate course of action, taking account of local or regional priorities for conservation.

13.5.1 The Species–centred Approach

Quantifying landscapes by human-defined land-cover types may not reflect how organisms perceive the distribution of their habitats (Betts *et al.* 2014). Likewise, habitat degradation within the local patches is not always associated with the human perception of forest degradation. Treating 'habitat' and 'forest/vegetation' as synonymous has often led to confusing conclusions about the effects of habitat changes on biodiversity (Lindenmayer & Fischer 2007; Betts *et al.* 2014). When delineating habitat distribution and landscape composition, a species-centred approach that recognises habitat as species-specific will considerably improve our understanding of species responses to landscape structure (Betts *et al.* 2014). This in turn will have substantial benefits for understanding the mechanisms that underlie population declines, which is crucial for establishing adequate management plans for conservation. However, in the real world, human-defined cover types are often easier to integrate into conservation policies. Betts *et al.* (2014) therefore proposed combining species-centred approaches with ones based on landscape changes as perceived by humans.

13.5.2 The Mechanism–oriented Approach

Conservation management plans not based on knowledge of the underlying mechanisms of population declines can lead to misguided actions that waste limited resources. Let´s illustrate this issue as follows. We aim to establish a management plan for a forest bird species that avoids habitat patches that have been degraded by human activity. Typically, there are multiple plausible explanations for the observed spatial distribution pattern of any bird species (see Fig. 13.6). Habitat degradation can diminish resources in the local patches (food, nest sites, shelter from predators), which in turn can have an impact on various demographic parameters, such as clutch size, nestling conditions, the ratio of breeders to non-breeders, nest losses due to predation, fledgling survival and adult survival. Habitat degradation can also promote dispersal (emigration) from local patches as a behavioural mechanism to avoid adverse conditions (Dickinson & McGowan 2005; Baglione *et al.* 2006). Likewise, habitat degradation can reduce immigration into low-quality patches, which in turn can reduce the (re)colonisation of empty patches, and ultimately the persistence of populations (Robles & Ciudad 2012). However, from a conservation perspective, mitigating these negative outcomes caused by different mechanisms can require substantially different management actions. Food supplementation during the pre-breeding season can increase clutch sizes by improving the body condition of female breeders, but would not have the desired effect when low food availability during the breeding season prevents parents from providing enough food for nestlings. Controlling nest predators can improve nesting success under particular conditions, but may not reduce fledgling or adult survival if the types of predators or their predation pressure differs from that acting on the nests and so on.

13.5.3 The Multilevel Approach

Further complexity arises from the infinitely variable spatial patterning of habitats in real landscapes. Local habitat quality, patch size and isolation are often highly interrelated, making it difficult to disentangle which variables and mechanisms are responsible for the decline of bird populations in habitat loss, fragmentation and degradation scenarios (Fahrig 2003; Lindenmayer & Fischer 2006). A reduction in patch sizes associated with habitat loss and subdivision could lead to similar demographic responses to those associated with habitat degradation, as both low quality and small patch size can reduce the quantity of resources in the local patches, especially for forest specialists. In addition, both increasing isolation and a reduction in the size and quality of habitat patches could prevent occupation and/or (re)colonisation by birds. However, tackling the effects of a reduction in habitat quality generally requires very different actions to those needed to address the consequences of habitat loss, subdivision and isolation (Lens *et al.* 2002; Lindenmayer & Fischer 2006). Awareness that birds may respond at multiple levels of the spatial arrangement of habitats (within-patch habitat structure, patch size and connectivity, amount of habitat at the landscape level) will help in making appropriate decisions for conservation.

13.6 Concluding Comments about Conservation Strategies

Once the focus of conservation moves away from a target species, the objectives become less clear and even more challenging to deliver: how can suitable conditions be established simultaneously for large numbers of species with contrasting requirements? In practice, much conservation effort in forests is directed not at single species, but rather at maintaining conditions for particular suites of species that are especially sensitive to intensive forest management, or at providing conditions that benefit even wider assemblages of species. The latter is usually justified in terms of 'maximising diversity', though the scale on which diversity should be maximised is often not specified. In these final sections, we make some general observations, many of which relate to these 'higher-level' aspects of strategy, where conservation activities are not targeted at particular species of forest birds.

13.6.1 Protection, Preservation, Transformation or Integration?

In many areas across Europe, globalised markets have inexorably led to the demise of long-established relatively wildlife-friendly land uses. As an example, Cevasco and Moreno (2015) describe the historical complexity of agro-silvo-pastoral systems in what is now Italy. In response, much conservation policy has followed two approaches: (i) protecting relatively small areas covered by particular habitats (e.g., through Natura 2000 or strict forest reserves), and (ii) encouraging local people to continue with low-intensity wildlife-friendly production practices in wider areas (Fischer *et al.* 2012; Palomo *et al.* 2014). Both approaches, but especially the second, pursue biodiversity conservation through direct financial incentives, often for the preservation of ancient practices that would otherwise disappear. This 'preservation strategy' (*sensu* Fischer *et al.* 2012) does not recognise that across centuries, people have obtained goods and services from nature by managing the environment in a sustainable way that guarantees the long-term renovation of resources. Because direct financial incentives do not promote long-term links between nature and people, conservation strategies that only consider monetary incentives seem destined to fail (Fischer *et al.* 2012).

As an alternative, Fischer *et al.* (2012) propose a 'transformation' strategy that acknowledges unavoidable changes in the social structure of rural communities while recognising the benefits of extensive land uses for conservation. The idea is to facilitate new relationships between nature and society that not only promote wildlife-friendly land uses, but also provide people with goods and services. The transformation strategy aims to encourage local communities to seek strong links between nature and the new social environment (Fischer *et al.* 2012; Palomo *et al.* 2014).

Typical examples are policies that develop eco-tourism or niche markets for local, often organic, products.

In regions where population density is high and habitat loss and fragmentation are at an advanced stage, a preservation strategy may be the only realistic approach, whereas in regions with relatively high cover of non-intensively managed land, a transformation strategy may be feasible. Indeed, Fischer *et al.* (2012) proposed the transformation strategy as a means of tackling changes in social-ecological systems in traditional farming landscapes. However, transformation may also have relevance in some landscapes subjected to more intensive land uses. For example, forests managed intensively for timber could potentially become more wildlife-friendly by leaving deciduous trees along woodland margins, integrating other land uses compatible with conservation (e.g., honey production or extensive livestock grazing) and simultaneously promoting the self-organisation of local communities to exploit these forest resources in ways that favour the long-term sustainability of a social-ecological system. Education is essential to the development of attitudes that transcend the generation of money and reinforce sustainable relationships between people and nature.

In practice, a dichotomy of preservation and transformation greatly simplifies how conservation approaches have developed with respect to forests. First, a variant of the preservation strategy involves linking protected areas to form ecological habitat networks, within which forests and shrublands often play key roles (Bailey 2007; Dolman *et al.* 2007; Gimona *et al.* 2012). Habitat networks are intended simultaneously to increase the extent of wildlife habitat and facilitate the movement of individuals through impoverished landscapes. Improving functional connectivity through ecological networks could enhance the persistence of species that inhabit patchy and fragmented landscapes as well as accommodate species' responses to climate change (note, though, that Hodgson *et al.* [2009] place a stronger emphasis on the importance of habitat area and habitat quality).

Second, integrating conservation measures into productive forestry (Bollmann & Braunisch 2013) is also distinct from both the preservation and transformation strategies of Fischer *et al.* (2012); relevant interventions and actions are outlined above for young-growth and mature-growth resources. There has been a large research effort focused on this topic, yet it is unclear how extensively such measures are adopted across Europe and whether they are implemented on a sufficient scale to either increase populations of species of conservation interest or enhance

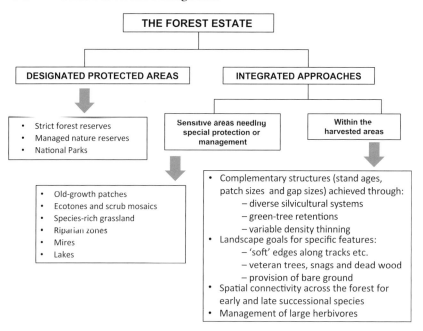

Figure 13.7 A framework that incorporates both protection and integration approaches for biodiversity conservation within extensively forested areas (based on Lindenmayer *et al.* 2006).

diversity. There is also a question as to whether such strategies are defined in terms that will be readily understood by foresters (Poulsen 2002). In practice, integration is best regarded as a complementary approach to protecting specific areas of forest (Bollmann & Braunisch 2013; Lindenmayer *et al.* 2006, 2012). A framework of protection and integration approaches is illustrated in Fig. 13.7.

Adopting integrated approaches requires modifying forestry practices and potentially sacrificing some production. Any attempt to assess the economic implications should take into account social and human well-being benefits that cannot be readily quantified in monetary terms (Nilsson *et al.* 2011; Blicharska & Mikusiński 2014). Persuasive arguments for integrating conservation measures into forestry may eventually come from demonstrating how, and under what circumstances, they can have major ecosystem service benefits or increase resilience to diseases and/or climate change. For example, the extent to which insectivorous birds could reduce commercial damage from insects in forests was a topic of considerable interest to foresters in the mid-20th century (Mackenzie

1951). It was only several decades later that evidence emerged that birds can, under some circumstances, have a positive influence on tree growth (Marquis & Whelan 1994; Bridgeland *et al.* 2010; Morrison & Lindell 2012). Further research in European forests on the links between trees, their herbivorous insects and the birds that feed on them is most desirable. Habitat management (rather than mere provision of nest boxes) that enhances breeding populations of insectivorous birds within commercially managed forests could potentially benefit forest production in some contexts.

13.6.2 Rewilding, Land Sparing and Land Sharing

With such a long and deep history of human interference in our landscapes, it is perhaps unsurprising that many see the rewilding movement as the 'big idea' for taking European conservation forward into the 21st century. The notion of allowing 'natural processes' to hold sway over large tracts of land is alluring, and has been given some theoretical underpinning by Vera's (2000) assertion that large herbivores were responsible for creating far greater vegetation diversity in primeval post-glacial landscapes than has been traditionally assumed. The nature of these past landscapes is a hot topic (Sandom *et al.* 2014; Kirby & Watkins 2015). Semi-open landscapes probably held bird assemblages that were considerably more diverse than those occurring in closed-canopy forest (Hinsley *et al.* 2015). It is difficult to predict how future landscapes and their birds might appear under rewilding – much depends on factors such as grazing intensity, soil type and altitude. Nonetheless, the potential exists for the development of structurally heterogeneous landscapes benefitting both early and late successional species.

At first sight, rewilding seems to fit with a land sparing, rather than land sharing, approach to conserving nature (Green *et al.* 2005). Rewilding is likely to find space in the less productive regions of Europe. These include regions that are already substantially forested, as well as ones largely denuded of any natural forest cover, such as the British mountains. However, the relationship of rewilding with sparing or sharing of land is not clear-cut. Rewilding does not have to mean pure non-intervention; it could involve various shades of extensive production compatible with the transformation strategy of Fischer *et al.* (2012). In essence, this is a form of extensive land sharing.

Conversely, land sparing strategies do not necessarily apply exclusively to situations where areas of high production and rich biodiversity are spatially separated and each large in scale. Klein *et al.* (2014) pointed out that land sparing involving forests could potentially operate at relatively small scales, with patches of forest interspersed with agricultural land. This could simultaneously enhance biodiversity and production, the former through providing habitat, the latter through increasing populations of desirable insects (pollinators, beneficial predators, etc.) that spill over from forest to adjacent farmland.

13.6.3 Management for Habitat Heterogeneity and Habitat Quality

No single forest structure or management system can deliver suitable habitat for all species. Additionally, there is much uncertainty about how climate change will alter the future quality of different vegetation types for birds. It seems very unlikely that current patterns of microclimate, insect abundance, predation risk and parasite burden will remain the same in the forests of the future. Maintaining the diversity of resources and vegetation structures within different regions should therefore be an important component of conservation thinking; this will enable species to shift niches if they have the behavioural and morphological flexibility to do so. Habitat heterogeneity may be one of the best ways at our disposal to buffer biodiversity against climate change (Hodgson *et al.* 2009). The types of interactions between forest management and functional resources summarised in Fig.13.3 can form a useful starting point for developing approaches that provide habitat heterogeneity within forests.

Habitat heterogeneity is a multilevel concept that is difficult to define and delimit. It ranges across microstructures (e.g., decaying wood), macrostructures (e.g., regeneration gap sizes, tree-size diversity, understorey complexity) and tree-species composition (many mixtures are possible). Hence, heterogeneity can be viewed as continua of variation along multiple axes of vegetation structure and composition. In any conservation project, it will be necessary to ask: what is the best range and balance of habitat diversity? Also, on what spatial scale and pattern should the different habitat types be maintained? What are the relative benefits of extensive ecotones, rather than discrete blocks of different habitat structures?

The practical design and implementation of habitat heterogeneity is a subject that requires more attention from ecologists, with the aim of developing guidance that will help conservation planners to develop appropriate forms of habitat heterogeneity. Different types of heterogeneity will be needed in different regions and landscapes. A policy of maximising heterogeneity on all areas of land could be harmful, because this could benefit generalists at the expense of specialists (Batáry *et al.* 2011). Rather than maximising heterogeneity in small blocks of woodland, a better strategy for forest birds is more likely to involve creating complementary structures across a range of locations, or in different parts of extensive forested tracts. Working towards high beta and gamma diversity would seem especially valuable.

Improving habitat quality as a management strategy for avian conservation deserves special attention. Even in highly fragmented landscapes, local habitat quality may be a primary driver of patch–occupancy dynamics (Robles & Ciudad 2012), yet most fragmentation studies have assumed that habitat quality in local patches is uniform. Future research and conservation plans for bird populations in fragmented landscapes should consider not only patch geometry (patch size and connectivity), but also the effects of habitat quality in local patches. Where information is lacking on the factors underlying the decline of avian populations in fragmented habitats, we suggest that improving habitat quality for target species in local patches may be more successful than enhancing connectivity. Nonetheless, every case requires careful evaluation of the potential factors involved in population declines.

13.6.4 The Strategy Should Fit the Context

An array of human activities determines landscape composition, which in turn influences avian population and community dynamics within forests. Examples are the widespread substitution of native forests by exotic plantations, the expansion of agriculture in previously forested landscapes and the exponential rise of urbanisation and 'hard infrastructure' (Groom *et al.* 2006). The strength of these drivers varies across Europe, depending on human population density, the occurrence of natural and human-induced disturbances, the types of natural resources available and cultural variation in the use of these resources. Recognition of this regional variation, which is well illustrated by the chapters in Part 2 of this book, is essential for establishing conservation priorities and appropriate actions for birds and other wildlife. As mentioned in the introduction of this chapter, a diversity-led approach is mainly appropriate in regions where large tracts of forest are scarce and populations of mature forest specialists are absent. Where regionally threatened species or habitat types are present, these clearly should be the priority for conservation efforts. This applies in terms of both habitat protection and continuing to search for ways of making forestry more compatible with the needs of specialist forest species.

Acknowledgements

We thank Tibor Hartel and Sven G. Nilsson for helpful comments on a draft of the chapter.

References

Aben, J., Adriaensen, F., Thijs, K.W. *et al.* (2012) Effects of matrix composition and configuration on forest bird movements in a fragmented Afromontane biodiversity hotspot. *Animal Conservation*, **15**, 658–668.

Åberg, J., Jansson, G., Swenson, J.E. & Angelstam, P. (1995) The effect of matrix on the occurrence of hazel grouse (*Bonasa bonasia*) in isolated habitat fragments. *Oecologia*, **103**, 265–269.

Ahlering, M.A. & Faaborg, J. (2006) Avian habitat management meets conspecific attraction: If you build it, will they come? *Auk*, **123**, 301–312.

Alexander, K., Stickler, D. & Green, T. (2010) Is the practice of haloing successful in promoting extended life? A preliminary investigation of the response of veteran oak and beech trees to increased light levels in Windsor Forest. *Quarterly Journal of Forestry*, **104**, 257–266.

Anders, A.D., Faaborg, J. & Thompson, F.R. III (1998) Postfledging dispersal, habitat use, and home-range size of juvenile wood thrushes. *Auk*, **115**, 349–358.

Andersson, J., Domingo Gómez, E., Michon, S. & Roberge, J.-M. (2017) Tree cavity densities and characteristics in managed and unmanaged Swedish boreal forest. *Scandinavian Journal of Forest Research*. DOI: 10.1080/02827581.2017.1360389.

Archaux, F. & Bakkaus, N. (2007) Relative impact of stand structure, tree composition and climate on mountain bird communities. *Forest Ecology and Management*, **247**, 72–79.

Artman, V.L., Sutherland, E.K. & Downhower, J.F. (2001) Prescribed burning to restore mixed-oak communities in Southern Ohio: Effects on breeding-bird populations. *Conservation Biology*, **15**, 1423–1434.

Askins, R.A. (2001) Sustaining biological diversity in early successional communities: The challenge of managing unpopular habitats. *Wildlife Society Bulletin*, **29**, 407–412.

Baglione, V., Canestrari, D., Marcos J.M. & Ekman J. (2006) Experimentally increased food resources in the natal territory promotes offspring philopatry and helping in cooperatively breeding carrion crows. *Proceedings of the Royal Society London B*, **273**, 1529–1535.

Bailey, S. (2007) Increased connectivity in fragmented landscapes: An investigation of evidence for biodiversity gain in woodlands. *Forest Ecology and Management*, **238**, 7–23.

Baines, D. & Summers, R.W. (1997) Assessment of bird collisions with deer fences in Scottish forests. *Journal of Applied Ecology*, **34**, 941–948.

Batáry, P., Fischer, J., Báldi, A., Crist, T.O. & Tscharntke, T. (2011) Does habitat heterogeneity increase farmland biodiversity? *Frontiers in Ecology and the Environment*, **9**, 152–153.

Bayne, E.M. & Hobson, K.A. (2001) Effects of habitat fragmentation on pairing success of Ovenbirds: The importance of male age and floater behavior. *Auk*, **118**, 380–388.

Begehold, H., Rzanny, M. & Flade, M. (2015) Forest development phases as an integrating tool to describe habitat preferences of breeding birds in lowland beech forests. *Journal of Ornithology*, **156**, 19–29.

Bennett, A.F. (1999) *Linkages in the Landscape: The Role of Corridors and Connectivity in Wildlife Conservation*. Gland, Switzerland: IUCN.

Betts, M.G., Fahrig, L., Hadley, A.S. *et al.* (2014) A species–centered approach for uncovering generalities in organism responses to habitat loss and fragmentation. *Ecography*, **37**, 517–527.

Bibby, C.J., Aston, N. & Bellamy, P.E. (1989) Effects of broadleaved trees on birds of upland conifer plantations in North Wales. *Biological Conservation*, **49**, 17–29.

Blicharska, M., Baxter, P.W.J. & Mikusiński, G. (2014) Practical implementation of species' recovery plans: Lessons from the White-backed Woodpecker action plan in Sweden. *Ornis Fennica*, **91**, 108–128.

Blicharska, M. & Mikusiński, G. (2014) Incorporating social and cultural significance of large old trees in conservation policy. *Conservation Biology*, **28**, 1558–1567.

Bollmann, K. & Braunisch, V. (2013) To integrate or to segregate: Balancing commodity production and biodiversity conservation in European forests. In *Integrative Approaches as an Opportunity for the Conservation of Forest Biodiversity*. Kraus, D. & Krumm, F. (eds.). Barcelona: European Forest Institute, pp. 18–31.

Bowler, D.E. & Benton, T.G. (2005) Causes and consequences of animal dispersal strategies: Relating individual behaviour to spatial dynamics. *Biological Reviews*, **80**, 205–225.

Bridgeland, W.T., Beier, P., Kolb, T. & Whitham, T.G. (2010) A conditional trophic cascade: Birds benefit faster growing trees with strong links between predators and plants. *Ecology*, **91**, 73–84.

Broome, A., Connolly, T. & Quine, C.P. (2014) An evaluation of thinning to improve habitat for capercaillie (*Tetrao urogallus*). *Forest Ecology and Management*, **314**, 94–103.

Brown, J.H. & Kodric-Brown, A. (1977) Turnover rates in insular biogeography: Effect of immigration on extinction. *Ecology*, **58**, 445–449.

Burke, D.M. & Nol, E. (1998) Influence of food abundance, nest-site habitat, and forest fragmentation on breeding Ovenbirds. *Auk*, **115**, 96–104.

Cahall, R.E. & Hayes, J.P. (2009) Influences of postfire salvage logging on forest birds in the Eastern Cascades, Oregon, USA. *Forest Ecology and Management*, **257**, 1119–1128.

Calladine, J., Bielinski, A. & Shaw, G. (2013) Effects on bird abundance and species richness of edge restructuring to include shrubs at the interface between conifer plantations and moorland. *Bird Study*, **60**, 345–356.

Calladine, J., Bray, J., Broome, A. & Fuller, R.J. (2015) Comparison of breeding bird assemblages in conifer plantations managed by continuous cover forestry and clearfelling. *Forest Ecology and Management*, **344**, 20–29.

Camprodón, J., Campión, D., Martínez-Vidal, R. *et al.* (2007) Habitat selection and conservation of the Iberian woodpeckers. In *Conservación de la Biodiversidad, Fauna Vertebrada y Gestión Forestal*. Camprodón, J. & Plana, E. (eds.). Barcelona: Centro Tecnológico Forestal de Cataluña–University of Barcelona, pp. 391–434. [in Spanish]

Cevasco, R. & Moreno, D. (2015) Historical ecology in modern conservation in Italy. In *Europe's Changing Woods and Forests: From Wildwood to Managed Landscapes*. Kirby, K.J. & Watkins, C. (eds.). Wallingford, UK: CABI, pp. 227–242.

Chalfoun, A.D., Thompson, F.R. & Ratnaswamy, M.J. (2002) Nest predators and fragmentation: A review and meta-analysis. *Conservation Biology*, **16**, 306–318.

Ciudad, C., Robles, H. & Matthysen, E. (2009) Postfledging habitat selection of juvenile middle spotted woodpeckers: A multi-scale approach. *Ecography*, **32**, 676–682.

Clobert, J., Le Galliard, J.-F., Cote, J., Meylan S. & Massot, M. (2009) Informed dispersal, heterogeneity in animal dispersal syndromes and the dynamics of spatially structured populations. *Ecology Letters*, **12**, 197–209.

Cockle, K.L., Martin, K. & Wesołowski, T. (2011) Woodpeckers, decay, and the future of cavity-nesting vertebrate communities worldwide. *Frontiers in Ecology and the Environment*, **9**, 377–382.

Cooper, C.B. & Walters, J.R. (2002) Experimental evidence of disrupted dispersal causing decline of an Australian passerine in fragmented habitat. *Conservation Biology*, **16**, 471–478.

Costello, C.A., Yamasaki, M., Pekins, P.J., Leak, W.B. & Neefus, C.D. (2000) Songbird response to group selection harvests and clearcuts in a New Hampshire northern hardwood forest. *Forest Ecology and Management*, **127**, 41–54.

Currie, D. & Matthysen, E. (1998) Nuthatches do not delay postfledging dispersal in isolated forest fragments. *Belgian Journal of Zoology*, **128**, 49–54.

Currie, F.A. & Bamford, R. (1982) The value to bird life of retaining small conifer stands beyond normal felling age within forests. *Quarterly Journal of Forestry*, **76**, 153–160.

DeGraaf, R.M. & Yamasaki, M. (2003) Options for managing early-successional forest and shrubland bird habitats in the northeastern United States. *Forest Ecology and Management*, **185**, 179–191.

Dickinson, J.L. & McGowan, A. (2005) Winter resource wealth drives delayed dispersal and family-group living in western bluebirds. *Proceedings of the Royal Society London B*, **272**, 2423–2428.

Dickson, J.G., Conner, R.N. & Williamson, J.H. (1983) Snag retention increases bird use of a clear-cut. *Journal of Wildlife Management*, **47**, 799–804.

Dolman, P.M., Hinsley, S.A., Bellamy, P.E. & Watts, K. (2007) Woodland birds in patchy landscapes: The evidence base for strategic networks. *Ibis*, **149** (Suppl. 2), 146–160.

du Bus de Warnaffe, G. & Deconchat, M. (2008) Impact of four silvicultural systems on birds in the Belgian Ardenne: Implications for biodiversity in plantation forests. *Biodiversity and Conservation*, **17**, 1041–1055.

Edenius, L. (2011) Short-term effects of wildfire on bird assemblages in old pine- and spruce-dominated forests in northern Sweden. *Ornis Fennica*, **88**, 71–79.

Elmhagen, B., Ludwig, G., Rushton, S.P., Helle, P. & Lindén, H. (2010) Top predators, mesopredators and their prey: Interference ecosystems along bioclimatic productivity gradients. *Journal of Animal Ecology*, **79**, 785–794.

Erdelen, M. (1984) Bird communities and vegetation structure: I. Correlations and comparisons of simple and diversity indices. *Oecologia*, **61**, 277–284.

Fahrig, L. (2003) Effects of habitat fragmentation on biodiversity. *Annual Review of Ecology, Evolution, and Systematics*, **34**, 487–515.

Fedrowitz, K., Koricheva, J., Baker, S.C. *et al.* (2014) Can retention forestry help conserve biodiversity? A meta-analysis. *Journal of Applied Ecology*, **51**, 1669–1679.

Ferrer, M., Newton, I. & Muriel, R. (2013) Rescue of a small declining population of Spanish imperial eagles. *Biological Conservation*, **159**, 32–36.

Ferry, C. & Frochot, B. (1990) Bird communities of the forests of Burgundy and the Jura (Eastern France). In *Biogeography and Ecology of Forest Bird Communities*. Keast, A. (ed.). The Hague: SPB Academic Publishing, pp. 183–195.

Fischer, J., Hartel, T. & Kuemmerle, T. (2012) Conservation policy in traditional farming landscapes. *Conservation Letters*, **5**, 167–175.

Fischer, J., Lindenmayer, D.B. & Manning, A.D. (2006) Biodiversity, ecosystem function, and resilience: Ten guiding principles for commodity production landscapes. *Frontiers in Ecology and the Environment*, **4**, 80–86.

Fletcher, R.J. (2007) Species interactions and population density mediate the use of social cues for habitat selection. *Journal of Animal Ecology*, **76**, 598–606.

Fletcher, R.J. (2009) Does conspecific attraction explain the patch-size effect? An experimental test. *Oikos*, **118**, 1139–1147.

Foster, C.N., Barton, P.S. & Lindenmayer, D.B. (2014) Effects of large native herbivores on other animals. *Journal of Applied Ecology*, **51**, 929–938.

Fuller, R.J. (1992) Effects of coppice management on woodland breeding birds. In *The Ecology and Management of Coppice Woodlands*. Buckley, G.P. (ed.). London: Chapman & Hall, pp. 169–192.

Fuller, R.J. (2012a) Avian responses to transitional habitats in temperate cultural landscapes: Woodland edges and young-growth. In *Birds and Habitat: Relationships in Changing Landscapes*. Fuller, R.J. (ed.). Cambridge: Cambridge University Press, pp. 125–149.

Fuller, R.J. (2012b) Habitat quality and habitat occupancy by birds in variable environments. In *Birds and Habitat: Relationships in Changing Landscapes*. Fuller, R.J. (ed.). Cambridge: Cambridge University Press, pp. 37–62.

Fuller, R.J. (2013) Searching for biodiversity gains through woodfuel and forest management. *Journal of Applied Ecology*, **50**, 1295–1300.

Fuller, R.J., Smith, K.W. & Hinsley, S.A. (2012) Temperate western European woodland as a dynamic environment for birds: A resource-based view. In *Birds and Habitat: Relationships in Changing Landscapes*. Fuller, R.J. (ed.). Cambridge: Cambridge University Press, pp. 352–380.

Fuller, R.J., Smith, K.W., Grice, P.V., Currie, F.A. & Quine, C.P. (2007) Habitat change and woodland birds in Britain: Implications for management and future research. *Ibis*, **149** (Suppl. 2), 261–268.

Gilbert-Norton, L., Wilson, R., Stevens, J.R. & Beard, K.H. (2010) A meta-analytic review of corridor effectiveness. *Conservation Biology*, **25**, 660–668.

Gill, R.M.A. & Fuller, R.J. (2007) The effects of deer browsing on woodland structure and songbirds in lowland Britain. *Ibis*, **149** (Suppl. 2), 119–127.

Gimona, A., Poggio, L., Brown, I. & Castellazzi, M. (2012) Woodland networks in a changing climate: Threats from land use change. *Biological Conservation*, **149**, 93–102.

Goodale, E., Beauchamp, G., Magrath, R.D., Nieh, J.C. & Ruxton, G.D. (2010) Interspecific information transfer influences animal community structure. *Trends in Ecology and Evolution*, **25**, 354–361.

Götmark, F. (2002) Predation by sparrowhaws favours early breeding and small broods in great tits. *Oecologia*, **130**, 25–32.

Gram, W.K., Porneluzi, P.A., Clawson, R.L., Faaborg, J. & Richter, S.C. (2003) Effects of experimental forest management on density and nesting success of bird species in Missouri Ozark forests. *Conservation Biology*, **17**, 1324–1337.

Green, R.E., Cornell, S.J., Scharlemann, J.P.W. & Balmford, A. (2005) Farming and the fate of wild nature. *Science*, **307**, 550–555.

Griesser, M. & Lagerberg, S. (2012) Long-term effects of forest management on territory occupancy and breeding success of an open-nesting boreal bird species, the Siberian jay. *Forest Ecology and Management*, **271**, 58–64.

Groom, M.J., Meffe, G.K. & Carroll, C.R. (2006) *Principles of Conservation Biology*. Sunderland, MA: Sinauer Associates.

Haddad, N.M. & Tewksbury, J.J. (2006) Impacts of corridors on populations and communities. In *Connectivity Conservation*. Crooks, K.R. & Sanjayan, M. (eds.). Cambridge: Cambridge University Press, pp. 390–415.

Halkka, A. & Lappalainen, I. (2001) *Insight into Europe's Forest Protection*. Gland, Switzerland: WWF.

Hanski, I. & Gilpin, M.E. (1997) *Metapopulation Biology: Ecology, Genetics and Evolution*. San Diego: Academic Press.

Harmer, R., Kerr, G. & Thompson, R. (2010) *Managing Native Broadleaved Woodland*. Edinburgh: The Stationery Office.

Hartel, T., Dorresteijn, I., Klein, C. *et al.* (2013) Wood-pastures in a traditional rural region of Eastern Europe: Characteristics, management and status. *Biological Conservation*, **166**, 267–275.

Hartel, T., Hanspach, J., Abson, D.J., Máthé, O., Moga, C.I. & Fischer, J. (2014) Bird communities in traditional wood-pastures with changing management in eastern Europe. *Basic and Applied Ecology*, **15**, 385–395.

Hinsley, S.A., Fuller, R.J. & Ferns, P.N. (2015) The changing fortunes of woodland birds in temperate Europe. In *Europe's Changing Woods and Forests: From Wildwood to Managed Landscapes*. Kirby, K.J. & Watkins, C. (eds.). Wallingford, UK: CABI, pp. 154–173.

Hodgson, J.A., Thomas, C.D., Wintle, B.A. & Moilanen, A. (2009) Climate change, connectivity and conservation decision making: Back to basics. *Journal of Applied Ecology*, **46**, 964–969.

Holmes, S.B. & Pitt, D.G. (2007) Response of bird communities to selection harvesting in a northern tolerant hardwood forest. *Forest Ecology and Management*, **238**, 280–292.

Holt, C.A., Fuller, R.J. & Dolman, P.M. (2013a) Exclusion of deer affects responses of birds to woodland regeneration in winter and summer. *Ibis*, **156**, 116–131.

Holt, C.A., Fuller, R.J. & Dolman, P.M. (2013b) Deer reduce habitat quality for a woodland songbird: Evidence from settlement patterns, demographic parameters, and body condition. *Auk*, **130**, 13–20.

James, F.C., Hess, C.A., Klicklighter B.C. & Thum, R.A. (2001) Ecosystem management and the niche gestalt of the Red-cockaded woodpecker in longleaf pine forests. *Ecological Applications*, **11**, 854–870.

Jansson, G. & Angelstam, P. (1999) Threshold levels of habitat composition for the presence of the long-tailed tit (*Aegitalus caudatus*) in a boreal landscape. *Landscape Ecology*, **14**, 283–290.

Jentsch, S., Mannan, R.W., Dickson, B.G. & Block, W.M. (2008) Associations among breeding birds and gambel oak in southwestern ponderosa pine forests. *Journal of Wildlife Management*, **72**, 994–1000.

Johnsson, K., Nilsson, S.G. & Tjernberg, M. (1993) Characteristics and utilization of old Black Woodpecker *Dryocopus martius* holes by hole-nesting species. *Ibis*, **135**, 410–416.

Kirby, K.J. & Watkins, C. (2015) The forest landscape before farming. In *Europe's Changing Woods and Forests: From Wildwood to Managed Landscapes*. Kirby, K.J. & Watkins, C. (eds.). Wallingford, UK: CABI, pp. 33–45.

Klein, A.M., Boreux, V., Bauhus, J., Jahi-Chappell, M., Fisher, J. & Philpott, S.M. (2014) Forest islands in an agricultural sea. In *Global Forest Fragmentation*. Kettle, C.J. & Koh, L.P. (eds.). Wallingford, UK: CABI, pp. 79–95.

Koch Widerberg, M., Ranius, T., Drobyshev, I., Nilsson, U. & Lindbladh, M. (2012) Increased openness around retained oaks increases species richness of saproxylic beetles. *Biodiversity and Conservation*, **21**, 3035–3059.

Koenig, W., Van Vuren, D. & Hooge, P.N. (1996) Detectability, philopatry, and the distribution of dispersal distances in vertebrates. *Trends in Ecology and Evolution*, **11**, 514–517.

Kokko, H. & Sutherland, W.J. (1998) Optimal floating and queuing strategies: Consequences for density dependence and habitat loss. *American Naturalist*, **152**, 354–366.

Korpimäki, E. (1987) Clutch size, breeding success and brood size experiments in the Tengmalm´s owl *Aeolius funereus*: A test of hypotheses. *Ornis Scandinavica*, **18**, 277–284.

Kosiński, Z., Bilińska, E., Dereziński, J., Jeleń, J. & Kempa, M. (2010) The Black Woodpecker *Dryocopus martius* and the European Beech *Fagus sylvatica* as keystone species for the Stock Dove *Columba oenas* in western Poland. *Ornis Polonica*, **51**, 1–13.

Lampila, P., Mönkkönen, M. & Desrochers, A. (2005) Demographic responses by birds to forest fragmentation. *Conservation Biology*, **19**, 1537–1546.

Langston, R.H.W., Wotton, S.R., Conway, G.J. *et al.* (2007) Nightjar *Caprimulgus europaeus* and Woodlark *Lullula arborea* – recovering species in Britain? *Ibis*, **149**, 250–260.

Lens, L., Van Dongen, S., Norris, K., Githiru, M. & Matthysen, E. (2002) Avian persistence in fragmented rainforest. *Science*, **298**, 1236–1238.

Linden, D.W., Roloff, G.J. & Kroll, A.J. (2012) Conserving avian richness through structure retention in managed forests of the Pacific Northwest, USA. *Forest Ecology and Management*, **284**, 174–184.

Lindenmayer, D.B. & Fischer, J. (2006) *Habitat Fragmentation and Landscape Change: An Ecological and Conservation Synthesis*. Washington, DC: Island Press.

Lindenmayer, D.B. & Fischer, J. (2007) Tackling the habitat fragmentation panchreston. *Trends in Ecology and Evolution*, **22**, 127–132.

Lindenmayer, D.B., Franklin, J.F. & Fischer, J. (2006) General management principles and a checklist of strategies to guide forest biodiversity conservation. *Biological Conservation*, **131**, 433–445.

Lindenmayer, D.B., Franklin, J.F., Lõhmus, A. *et al.* (2012) A major shift to the retention approach in forestry can help resolve global forest sustainability issues. *Conservation Letters*, **5**, 421–431.

Lindenmayer, D., Hobbs, R.J., Montague-Drake, R. *et al.* (2008) A checklist for ecological management of landscapes for conservation. *Ecology Letters*, **11**, 78–91.

Lindenmayer, D.B., Laurance, W.F., Franklin, J.F. *et al.* (2014) New policies for old trees: averting a global crisis in a keystone ecological structure. *Conservation Letters*, **7**, 61–69.

Lõhmus, A. (2005) Are timber harvesting and conservation of nest sites of forest-dwelling raptors always mutually exclusive? *Animal Conservation*, **8**, 443–450.

Lõhmus, A. (2006) Nest-tree and nest-stand characteristics of forest dwelling raptors in east-central Estonia: Implications for forest management and conservation. *Proceedings of the Estonian Academy of Sciences: Biology, Ecology*, **55**, 31–50.

Loman, J. (2006) Does nest site availability limit the density of hole nesting birds in small woodland patches? *Web Ecology*, **6**, 37–43.

MacArthur, R.H. & MacArthur, J.W. (1961) On bird species diversity. *Ecology*, **42**, 594–598.

MacArthur, R.H. & Wilson, E.O. (1967) *The Theory of Island Biogeography*. Princeton, NJ: Princeton University Press.

Mackenzie, J.M.D. (1951) Control of forest populations. *Quarterly Journal of Forestry*, (April), 1–8.

Marquis, R.J. & Whelan, C.J. (1994) Insectivorous birds increase growth of white oak through consumption of leaf-chewing insects. *Ecology*, **75**, 2007–2014.

Martin, J.-L., Drapeau, P., Fahrig, L. *et al.* (2012) Birds in cultural landscapes: Actual and perceived differences between northeastern North America and western Europe. In *Birds and Habitat: Relationships in Changing Landscapes*. Fuller, R.J. (ed.). Cambridge: Cambridge University Press, pp. 481–515.

Matthysen, E. (1999) Nuthatches (*Sitta europaea*: Aves) in forest fragments: Demography of a patchy population. *Oecologia*, **119**, 501–509.

Matthysen, E. (2005) Density-dependent dispersal in birds and mammals. *Ecography*, **28**, 403–416.

Matthysen, E. & Adriaensen, F. (1998) Forest size and isolation have no effect on reproductive success of Eurasian Nuthatches (*Sitta europaea*). *Auk*, **115**, 955–963.

Matthysen, E. & Currie, D. (1996) Habitat fragmentation reduces disperser success in juvenile nuthatches *Sitta europaea*: Evidence from patterns of territory establishment. *Ecography*, **19**, 67–72.

McDermott, M.E. & Wood, P.B. (2011) Post-breeding bird responses to canopy tree retention, stand size, and edge in regenerating Appalachian hardwood stands. *Forest Ecology and Management*, **262**, 547–554.

McShea, W.J. & Rappole, J.H. (2000) Managing the abundance and diversity of breeding bird populations through manipulation of deer populations. *Conservation Biology*, **14**, 1161–1170.

Mikusiński, G. (1995) Population trends in black woodpecker in relation to changes and characteristics of European forests. *Ecography*, **18**, 363–369

Mills, G.S., Dunning, J.B. & Bates, J.M. (1991) The relationship between breeding bird density and vegetation volume. *Wilson Bulletin*, **103**, 468–479.

Mitrus, C. (2003) A comparison of the breeding ecology of collared flycatchers nesting in boxes and natural cavities. *Journal of Field Ornithology*, **74**, 293–299.

Møller, A.P. (1989) Parasites, predators and nest boxes: Facts and artefacts in nest box studies of birds? *Oikos*, **56**, 421–423.

Møller, A.P., Adriaensen, F., Artemyev, A. *et al.* (2014) Clutch size variation in Western Palearctic secondary hole-nesting birds in relation to nest box design. *Methods in Ecology and Evolution*, **5**, 353–362.

Mönkkönen, M., Helle, P. & Soppela, K. (1990) Numerical and behavioural responses of migrant passerines to experimental manipulation of resident tits (*Parus* spp.): Heterospecific attraction in northern breeding bird communities? *Oecologia*, **85**, 218–225.

Moorman, C.E. & Guynn, D.C. (2001) Effects of group-selection opening size on breeding bird habitat use in a bottomland forest. *Ecological Applications*, **11**, 1680–1691.

Morrison, E.B. & Lindell, C.A. (2012) Birds and bats reduce insect biomass and leaf damage in tropical forest restoration sites. *Ecological Applications*, **22**, 1526–1534.

Nilsson, K., Sangster, M., Gallis, C. *et al.* (eds.) (2011) *Forests, Trees and Human Health*. New York: Springer.

Nilsson, S.G. (1979) Density and species richness of some forest bird communities in South Sweden. *Oikos*, **33**, 392–401.

Nilsson, S.G. (1987) Limitation and regulation of population density in the Nuthatch *Sitta europaea* (Aves) breeding in natural cavities. *Journal of Animal Ecology*, **56**, 921–937.

Noss, R.F. & Daly, K.M. (2006) Incorporating connectivity into broad-scale conservation planning. In *Connectivity Conservation*. Crooks, K.R. & Sanjayan, M. (eds.). Cambridge: Cambridge University Press, pp. 587–619.

Olsson, O., Wiktander, U., Malmqvist, A. & Nilsson, S.G. (2001) Variability of patch type preferences in relation to resource availability and breeding success in a bird. *Oecologia*, **127**, 435–443.

Otto, C.R.V. & Roloff, G.J. (2012) Songbird response to green-tree retention prescriptions in clearcut forests. *Forest Ecology and Management*, **284**, 241–250.

Palang, H., Printsmann, A., Gyuro, E.K., Urbanc, M., Skowronek, E. & Woloszyn, W. (2006) The forgotten rural landscapes of Central and Eastern Europe. *Landscape Ecology*, **21**, 347–357.

Palomo, I., Montes, C., Martín-López, B. *et al.* (2014) Incorporating the social-ecological approach in protected areas in the Anthropocene. *BioScience*, **64**, 181–191.

Parviainen, J. (2005) Virgin and natural forests in the temperate zone of Europe. *Forest Snow and Landscape Research*, **79**, 9–18.

Parviainen, J., Bücking, W., Vandekerkhove, K., Schuck, A. & Päivinen, R. (2000) Strict forest reserves in Europe: Efforts to enhance biodiversity and research on forests left for free development in Europe (EU-COST-Action E4). *Forestry*, **73**, 107–118.

Parviainen, J. & Schuck, A. (2011) Maintenance, conservation and appropriate enhancement of biological diversity in forest ecosystems. In: *State of Europe's Forests 2011: Status and Trends in Sustainable Forest Management in Europe*. Oslo: FOREST EUROPE, UNECE and FAO, pp. 65–97.

Penteriani, V., Ferrer, M. & Delgado, M.M. (2011) Floater strategies and dynamics in birds, and their importance in conservation biology: Towards an understanding of nonbreeders in avian populations. *Animal Conservation*, **14**, 233–241.

Penteriani, V., Otalora F. & Ferrer, M. (2008) Floater mortality within settlement areas can explain the Allee effect in breeding populations. *Ecological Modelling*, **213**, 98–104.

Peterken, G.F. (1993) *Woodland Conservation and Management* (2nd ed.). London: Chapman & Hall.

Petit, D.R., Petit, K.E., Grubb, T.C. & Reichhardt, L.J. (1985) Habitat and snag selection by woodpeckers in a clear-cut: An analysis using artificial snags. *Wilson Bulletin*, **97**, 525–533.

Pietzarka, U. & Roloff, A. (1993). Forest edge management in consideration of natural vegetation dynamics. *Forstarchiv*, **64**, 107–113.

Porneluzi, P.A., Brito-Aguilar, R., Clawson, R.L. & Faaborg, J. (2014) Long-term dynamics of bird use of clearcuts in post-fledging period. *Wilson Journal of Ornithology*, **126**, 623–832.

Porneluzi, P.A. & Faaborg, J. (1999) Season-long fecundity, survival, and viability of ovenbirds in fragmented and unfragmented landscapes. *Conservation Biology*, **13**, 1151–1161.

Poulsen, B.O. (2002) Avian richness and abundance in temperate Danish forests: Tree variables important to birds and their conservation. *Biodiversity and Conservation*, **11**, 1551–1566.

Pöysä, H. & Pöysä, S. (2002) Nest-site limitation and density dependence of reproductive output in the common goldeneye *Bucephala clangula*: Implications for the management of cavity-nesting birds. *Journal of Applied Ecology*, **39**, 502–510.

Quine, C.P., Fuller, R.J., Smith, K.W. & Grice, P.V. (2007) Stand management: A threat or opportunity for birds in British woodland? *Ibis* (Suppl. 2), **149**, 161–174.

Remm, J., Lõhmus A. & Remm, K. (2006) Tree cavities in riverine forests: What determines their occurrence and use by hole-nesting passerines? *Forest Ecology and Management*, **221**, 267–277.

Revilla, E., Wiegand, T., Palomares, F., Ferreras, P. & Delibes, M. (2004) Effects of matrix heterogeneity on animal dispersal: From individual behavior to metapopulation-level parameters. *American Naturalist*, **164**, E130–E153.

Richard, Y. & Armstrong, D.P. (2010) Cost distance modelling of landscape connectivity and gap-crossing ability using radio-tracking data. *Journal of Applied Ecology*, **47**, 603–610.

Roberge, J.-M., Laudon, H., Björkman, C. *et al.* (2016) Socio-ecological implications of modifying rotation lengths in forestry. *Ambio*, **45**, 109–123.

Robles, H. & Ciudad, C. (2012) Influence of habitat quality, population size, patch size, and connectivity on patch-occupancy dynamics of the middle spotted woodpecker. *Conservation Biology*, **26**, 284–293.

Robles, H. & Ciudad, C. (2017) Floaters may buffer the extinction risk of small populations: An empirical assessment. *Proceedings of the Royal Society B*, **284**, 20170074. http://dx.doi.org/10.1098/rspb.2017.0074.

Robles, H., Ciudad, C. & Matthysen, E. (2011) Tree-cavity occurrence, cavity occupation and reproductive performance of secondary cavity-nesting birds in oak forests: The role of traditional management practices. *Forest Ecology and Management*, **261**, 1428–1435.

Robles, H., Ciudad, C. & Matthysen, E. (2012) Responses to experimental reduction and increase of cavities by a secondary cavity-nesting bird community in cavity-rich Pyrenean oak forests. *Forest Ecology and Management*, **277**, 46–53.

Robles, H., Ciudad, C., Vera, R. & Baglione, V. (2007b) No effect of habitat fragmentation on post-fledging, first-year and adult survival in the middle spotted woodpecker. *Ecography*, **30**, 685–694.

Robles, H., Ciudad, C., Vera, R., Olea P.P. & Matthysen, E. (2008) Demographic responses of middle spotted woodpeckers (*Dendrocopos medius*) to habitat fragmentation. *Auk*, **125**, 131–139.

Robles, H., Ciudad, C., Vera, R., Olea P.P., Purroy, F.J. & Matthysen, E. (2007a) Sylvopastoral management and conservation of the middle spotted woodpecker at the south-western edge of its distribution range. *Forest Ecology and Management*, **242**, 343–352.

Robles, H. & Martin, K. (2013) Resource abundance and quality determine the inter-specific associations between ecosystem engineers and resource users in a cavity-nest web. *PLoS ONE*, **8** (9), e74694.

Robles, H. & Martin, K. (2014) Habitat-mediated variation in the importance of ecosystem engineers for secondary cavity nesters in a nest web. *PLoS ONE*, **9** (2), e90071.

Robles, H. & Olea, P.P. (2003) Distribution and abundance of Middle Spotted Woodpecker *Dendrocopos medius* in a southern population of the Cantabrian Mountains. *Ardeola*, **50**, 275–280.

Robles, H. & Pasinelli, G. (2014) Woodpeckers as model organisms in a changing world – Foreword to the 7th International Woodpecker Conference Proceedings. *Acta Ornithologica*, **49**, 203–206.

Root, R.B. (1973) Organization of a plant–arthropod association in simple and diverse habitats: The fauna of collards (*Brassica oleracea*). *Ecological Monographs*, **43**, 95–124.

Rosenvald, R. & Lõhmus, A. (2008) For what, when and where is green-tree retention better than clear-cutting? A review of the biodiversity aspects. *Forest Ecology and Management*, **255**, 1–15.

Rost, J., Hutto, R.L., Brotons, L. & Pons, P. (2013) Comparing the effect of salvage logging on birds in the Mediterranean Basin and the Rocky Mountains: Common patterns, different conservation implications. *Biological Conservation*, **158**, 7-13.

Sandom, C.J., Ejrnæs, R., Hansen, M.D.D. & Svenning, J.-C. (2014) High herbivore density associated with vegetation diversity in interglacial ecosystems. *Proceedings of the National Academy of Sciences*, **111**, 4162–4167.

Schütz, J.-P. (1999) Close-to-nature silviculture: Is this concept compatible with species diversity? *Forestry*, **72**, 359–366.

Seymour, R.S. & Hunter, M.L. (1999) Principles of ecological forestry. In *Maintaining Biodiversity in Forest Ecosystems*. Hunter, M.L. (ed.). Cambridge: Cambridge University Press, pp. 22–61.

Söderström, B. (2009) Effects of different levels of green- and dead-tree retention on hemi-boreal forest bird communities in Sweden. *Forest Ecology and Management*, **257**, 215–222.

Smith, K.W. (2007) The utilization of dead wood resources by woodpeckers in Britain. *Ibis*, **149** (Suppl. 2), 183–192.

Smith, K.W. & Smith, L. (2013) The effect of supplementary feeding in early spring on the breeding performance of the great spotted woodpecker *Dendrocopos major*. *Bird Study*, **60**, 169–175.

Sunde, P. (2005) Predators control post-fledging survival in tawny owls, *Strix aluco*. *Oikos*, **110**, 461–472.

Swift, T.L. & Hannon, S.J. (2010) Critical thresholds associated with habitat loss: A review of the concepts, evidence, and applications. *Biological Reviews*, **85**, 35–53.

Thompson, F.R. & Burhans, D.E. (2004) Differences in predators of artificial and real songbird nests: Evidence of bias in artificial nest studies. *Conservation Biology*, **18**, 373–380.

Thompson, F.R. & DeGraaf, R.M. (2001) Conservation approaches for woody, early successional communities in the eastern United States. *Wildlife Society Bulletin*, **29**, 483–494.

Vega Rivera, J.H., Rappole, J.H., McShea, W.J. & Haas, C.A. (1998) Wood thrush postfledging movements and habitat use in northern Virginia. *Condor*, **100**, 69–78.

Vera, F.W.M. (2000) *Grazing Ecology and Forest History*. Wallingford, UK: CABI.

Verner, J. & Larson, T.A. (1989) Richness of breeding bird species in mixed-conifer forests of the Sierra Nevada, California. *Auk*, **106**, 447–463.

Verschuyl, J., Riffell, S., Miller, D. & Wigley, T.B. (2011) Biodiversity response to intensive biomass production from forest thinning in North American forests – A meta-analysis. *Forest Ecology and Management*, **261**, 221–232.

Villard, M.-A., Martin, P.R. & Drummond, C.G. (1993) Habitat fragmentation and pairing success in the Ovenbird (*Seiurus aurocapillus*). *Auk*, **110**, 759–768.

Ward, M.C. & Schlossberg, S. (2004) Conspecific attraction and the conservation of territorial birds. *Conservation Biology*, **18**, 519–525.

Warren, M.S. & Fuller, R.J. (1993) *Woodland Rides and Glades: Their Management for Wildlife* (2nd ed.). Peterborough, UK: Joint Nature Conservation Committee.

Wesołowski, T. (2002) Antipredator adaptations in nesting Marsh Tits *Parus palustris*: The role of nest site security. *Ibis*, **144**, 593–601.

Wesołowski, T. (2005) Virtual conservation: How the European Union is turning a blind eye to its vanishing primeval forests. *Conservation Biology*, **19**, 1349–1358.

Wesołowski, T. & Fuller, R.J. (2012) Spatial variation and temporal shifts in habitat use by birds at the European scale. In *Birds and Habitat: Relationships in Changing Landscapes*. Fuller, R.J. (ed.). Cambridge: Cambridge University Press, pp. 63–92.

Wilson, M.W., Gittings, T., Kelly, T.C. & O'Halloran, J. (2010) The importance of non-crop vegetation for bird diversity in Sitka spruce plantations in Ireland. *Bird Study*, **57**, 116–120.

Zahner, V., Sikora, L. & Pasinelli, G. (2012) Heart rot as a key factor for cavity tree selection in the black woodpecker. *Forest Ecology and Management*, **271**, 98–103.

Zanette, L., Doyle, P. & Trémont, S.M. (2000) Food shortage in small fragments: evidence from an area-sensitive passerine. *Ecology*, **81**, 1654–1666.

14 · Future Forests: Avian Implications and Research Priorities

GRZEGORZ MIKUSIŃSKI, JEAN-MICHEL ROBERGE AND ROBERT J. FULLER

Forest ecosystems are subject to continuous changes, partly linked to temporal dynamics and natural disturbances, and partly to direct and indirect influences of anthropogenic origin. These alterations have clear effects on forest biodiversity at all spatial and temporal scales (Fischer *et al.* 2013). Birds are not immune to these changes, although many species are able to adapt to and even take advantage of these alterations (e.g., Maklakov *et al.* 2011). On the other hand, many habitat specialists have great difficulty coping with loss and degradation of their critical forest habitats. For example, specialist forest birds are now relatively scarce in western Europe and the Mediterranean, where historically forests have been severely fragmented by human activity. By comparison, strong populations of specialist species persist in eastern Europe and Fennoscandia, where human impacts have been lower (see Chapters 6 and 8). The effects of different disturbances on forest-bird communities and particular species have been extensively studied, as illustrated by several chapters in this book. It is now possible to forecast, with growing confidence, which types of species would be broadly affected (negatively or positively) by the changes that are expected to occur over the coming decades in forest ecosystems at global, regional and local scales. In this closing chapter, we consider future prospects for forest birds. Although we present some global patterns and outlooks, we put particular emphasis on the non-tropical parts of the Northern Hemisphere, which form the focus of this book (see Chapter 1). We briefly synthesise the main environmental changes that are likely to shape populations and communities of forest birds in the future; research on all these areas would help in developing mitigation and management strategies for dealing with undesirable changes from an avian perspective. Here, we have attempted to draw together themes that have arisen in the previous chapters and point to the likely future drivers of forest-bird communities.

14.1 Forests in the Future

For a long time, forest loss and fragmentation have been the most important factors affecting forest biodiversity in general and birds in particular, especially in the tropics (Brooks *et al.* 2002; Tracewski *et al.* 2015). However, the pattern of forest loss, measured by change in forest area, has been gradually shifting. According to the FAO Global Forest Resources Assessment, the global rate of forest loss has decreased since 2010 to 0.08% annually, half the rate in the 1990s (FAO 2015). This change is not equally distributed in space: forest cover is stable or expanding most in temperate and some boreal regions, while the overall rate of deforestation in the tropics is slowing but still high (Keenan *et al.* 2015). Moreover, trends differ among regions within biomes. For example, Brazil's well-documented reduction in deforestation has been offset by increasing forest loss in Indonesia, Malaysia, Paraguay, Bolivia, Zambia and Angola (Hansen *et al.* 2013). The regional gains in forest area are largely explained by the increase of planted forest (Sloan & Sayer 2015).

When assessing the potential ecological consequences of these anthropogenic dynamics, it is important to recognise that forest cover is a very crude measure of the availability of forest habitat for wildlife; changes in tree-species composition and the physical structure of the forest will be the primary determinants of habitat quality for many forest species (see Chapter 13; Lazdinis *et al.* 2005). Along with loss and fragmentation of forests, many human-driven processes have degraded these ecosystems through different forms of management or exploitation (Heywood & Watson 1995; Wenhua 2004; Hosonuma *et al.* 2012). In the Northern Hemisphere, the temperate and Mediterranean forests have been widely exploited and altered throughout a long history of human use, whereas the boreal zone holds a relatively large proportion of less-impacted forest (Potapov *et al.* 2008; Gauthier *et al.* 2015).

Forests managed for production purposes may, to some extent, function as habitat for a variety of forest organisms (Hartley 2002; Carnus *et al.* 2006). However, the simplification of managed forests (sometimes to the level of planted even-aged monocultures), the use of short forestry rotations and the replacement of native species by introduced tree species are examples of actions that create ecosystems quite unlike natural forests. These production forests are of limited value for species dependent on features such as decaying wood and large trees (Danielsen *et al.* 2009; Paillet *et al.* 2010; Demarais *et al.* 2017; Chapter 10). Even if there are successful attempts to diversify managed and plantation forests for biodiversity conservation reasons (e.g., Lindenmayer *et al.* 2006, Brockerhoff *et al.* 2008; Chapter 13), we can expect that the rising demand for forest products, including biofuels, is likely to generate a trend towards simplified forest ecosystems in many regions, with limited capacity to serve as habitat for diverse biotic communities (Weih 2004; Koh & Ghazoul 2008; Walmsley & Godbold 2010). The degradation of forests may also occur in formally protected areas as a consequence of climate change, discontinued natural processes, human disturbance and illegal forest resource extraction (e.g., Tang *et al.* 2010; Hamann & Aitken 2013).

Some changes may affect forest biodiversity outside the forest itself. Scattered trees in natural and cultural landscapes, old rural parks and wood-pasture can provide important habitat features for many species that otherwise depend on forests (Manning *et al.* 2006; Lõhmus & Liira 2013; Hartel *et al.* 2014). Especially in landscapes where forest is highly fragmented, scattered trees may assist dispersal between forest patches. In England, there has been a very large reduction in the numbers of trees on farmland over the last century and a half (Barnes *et al.* 2016). Changes in farming practices, tree diseases and urbanisation are processes that may lead to loss of trees and consequent biodiversity loss (Elmqvist *et al.* 2004; Plieninger 2012).

As well as providing crucial habitats for large parts of the world's terrestrial biodiversity, forests deliver a wide range of essential provisioning and regulating ecosystem services for humanity (Millennium Ecosystem Assessment 2005). Without doubt, forests and their associated biodiversity will continue to be altered through land-use change, resource extraction and shifting management methods (Rudel *et al.* 2005; Agrawal *et al.* 2008; Chazdon 2008; Pereira *et al.* 2010). Enhanced conservation and restoration measures will be required if the aim is to deliver both ecosystem services *and* habitat for specialised forest species. This huge challenge for biodiversity conservation will be exacerbated by changing climate conditions at a global scale.

The direct and indirect effects of climate change are generating pervasive and far-reaching consequences for forests (Millar *et al.* 2007; Trumbore *et al.* 2015). The resilience of forest ecosystems to climatic changes is chiefly determined by the phenotypic plasticity of species, or their ability to migrate to suitable sites, but in all cases there are limits to adaptability (Visser 2008; Berg *et al.* 2010). The responses of trees – the main biotic structural component of forests – to climate change are particularly critical. Drought and heat stress have been shown to result in elevated tree mortality in forests worldwide (Allen *et al.* 2010). Several studies in the Northern Hemisphere predict that the number, extent and intensity of forest fires will increase (Stocks *et al.* 1998; Wotton *et al.* 2010; Bedia *et al.* 2014). Warming of the climate and predicted elevated seasonal humidity related to higher winter precipitation will affect trees not only directly, but also indirectly, through effects on insect outbreaks, pathogens, invasive plants and increased herbivore populations (e.g., La Porta *et al.* 2008; Dukes *et al.* 2009).

Through a range of mechanisms, climate change will cause contractions, expansions and shifts of geographic ranges of particular tree species (Cheaib *et al.* 2012; Zhu *et al.* 2012), with subsequent alterations of ecological interactions (e.g., Gómez-Aparicio 2011) that will reshape the characteristics of future forests. For example, Hamann and Wang (2006) predicted that the northern range limit of several conifer tree species in British Columbia, Canada, will gain potential habitat at a pace of at least 100 km per decade by shifting northwards, whereas common hardwood species will be generally unaffected by climate change, and some of the most important conifer species are expected to lose a large portion of their suitable habitat. Such changes will likely lead to the appearance of 'no-analogue communities' (Williams *et al.* 2007) with altered capacity to provide habitat for different organisms, including birds.

The effects of climate change on forest ecosystems often interact with other past and future human environmental impacts. Past degradation and fragmentation of forests are likely to exacerbate some of the negative effects of climate change by, for example, reducing the ability of species to disperse across landscapes and reach environments that have become suitable (Noss 2001; Krosby *et al.* 2010). Expanding international trade has facilitated invasions of numerous insects and pathogens into new regions, causing substantial damage (e.g., Pautasso 2013; Pautasso *et al.* 2013), and the cumulative effects of these processes interacting with climate change are predicted to aggravate impacts on forest ecosystems (Ramsfield *et al.* 2016). Overall, we can expect some shift in the future management of forest resources to deal with the challenges of high uncertainty. This will encompass diverse mitigation strategies aimed at improving the long-term resilience of forest ecosystems (Millar *et al.* 2007). However, we are likely to witness a general intensification of forest biomass production, with generally negative consequences for biodiversity (e.g., Felton *et al.* 2016b) over large parts of the Northern Hemisphere, given current political trends for increased use of non-fossil energy sources (Smeets & Faaij 2007). In parallel, the quest for more environmentally sustainable forest management strategies (e.g., continuous cover forestry, greater use of native tree species in silviculture and increasing the area of protected forest to meet international targets) is likely to continue. The big questions are how widely these measures will be adopted and what their effects will be.

14.2 Future Changes in Forest Environments: Implications for Bird Populations

14.2.1 Shifts in Forest Management Systems

Future management of forest resources will inevitably have critical and rapid effects on forest bird communities through the alteration of habitat structures and key resources. Many of the chapters in this book illustrate how human-driven forest dynamics affect birds at multiple temporal and spatial scales (e.g., Chapters 2, 6 and 8). One can hypothesise that, for a given magnitude of future anthropogenic impact, future species loss may be relatively large in regions which today support populations of many specialised forest-bird species. Regions where forests have been highly fragmented for centuries, such as parts of western Europe, tend to have a more depauperate avifauna (see Chapter 5), mainly composed of habitat generalists, which may be more resilient to intensified management.

Despite the multiple pressures on forests, there are some reasons to be optimistic. Increased environmental awareness in different parts of the world (partly as a result of increased prosperity) may lead to actions that improve the conservation status of forest birds. Future trends in environmental awareness and action will be dictated by complex socio-political processes at multiple scales and are therefore not predictable as such. Nonetheless, based on recent international agreements (e.g., the Aichi Biodiversity Targets 2010 and the European Natura 2000 initiative), it can be assumed that areas of protected forest will increase in many parts of the world. Another positive trend is the increasing use of 'ecological forestry' principles which can embrace green-tree and deadwood retention, two alternatives to clearcutting, thereby diversifying the age structure of trees and mimicking natural dynamics (see Chapter 13; Table 14.1).

Table 14.1 Processes expected to alter temperate and boreal forests in the coming decades and potential implications for bird communities. For each process, the main likely drivers are identified: 1. Biophysical changes: changes to properties of the environment (e.g., climate). 2. Climate change mitigation: measures aiming to limit future climate change (e.g., carbon sequestration). 3. Climate adaptation: measures aiming to adapt to a changed future climate (e.g., improving forest resilience). 4. Demand for wood products: increased demand for wood products (e.g., saw timber, biofuel). 5. Biodiversity conservation: actions to conserve or restore biodiversity. 6. Land-use changes: changes in land use and rural economies. 7. Social values: increased importance of the social values of forest environments (e.g., aesthetics, recreation). 8. Ethics: ethical aspects related to forests and forest-dwelling species. Areas and topics where we consider current knowledge needs to be greatly improved are indicated as a PRIORITY RESEARCH AREA. Chapters that are particularly relevant to each process are listed in the first column.

Process or change	1. Biophysical changes	2. Climate change mitigation	3. Climate adaptation	4. Demand for wood products	5. Biodiversity conservation	6. Land-use changes	7. Social values	8. Ethics	Potential implications for birds
Altered ecosystem properties as a result of climate change [Chapters 6, 7, 14]	X								Habitat alteration and mismatches in timing of phenological events. Possible regional loss of keystone tree species.
Increased forest damage from pest and pathogen outbreaks as well as abiotic processes (fire, windthrow, flooding) [Chapter 8, 9]	X								Habitat loss for some forest specialists; temporary habitat improvement for deadwood specialists, species benefiting from tree uprooting, and species preferring open or early successional forest. PRIORITY RESEARCH AREA: Impacts of tree diseases on tree species composition and habitat quality for birds.

(cont.)

Table 14.1 (*cont.*)

Process or change	1. Biophysical changes	2. Climate change mitigation	3. Climate adaptation	4. Demand for wood products	5. Biodiversity conservation	6. Land-use changes	7. Social values	8. Ethics	Potential implications for birds
Increased biomass extraction for biofuel production purposes (e.g., slash and stump extraction) [Chapters 6, 13]		X		X					Loss of deadwood substrates used for foraging and nesting. Decreased habitat complexity in early phases of forest growth.
Increased use of fertilisation in forestry [Chapter 6]		X		X					Shortened rotation time (see below). Changed bird community composition, possibly involving an increase in songbird density if the productivity of the system was raised.
Increased use of fast-growing non-native tree species and hybrids [Chapter 10]		X	X	X					Decreased habitat suitability compared to more natural forest ecosystems, but potentially improved conditions compared to agricultural crops. Loss of late-seral habitat.
Shortened rotations (possibly following techniques to increase forest productivity) [Chapters 6, 8, 13]		X	X	X					Decreased total area, connectivity and temporal persistence of late-seral habitats, but increase in area of clearcuts and early successional forest.

Management action					Likely consequences for birds
Increased establishment of mixed-species stands with broadleaves and conifers, as well as novel mixtures of broadleaved trees [Chapter 8, 13]		X	X		Increased habitat quality for bird species requiring mixed tree composition or broadleaved trees in regions dominated by conifer plantations. PRIORITY RESEARCH AREA: understanding the effects of different tree species mixtures on habitat quality for birds.
Prolonged rotations [Chapters 3, 4, 6, 8, 13]	X	X		X	Increase in amounts and connectivity of late-seral habitats. Reduction in area of early successional forest.
Continuous cover forestry (as an alternative to clearcutting systems) [Chapters 10, 13]	X	X		X	Increase in amounts and connectivity of late-seral habitats. Reduction in area of early successional forest and, depending on exact system of continuous cover, fewer forest gaps. PRIORITY RESEARCH AREA: Understanding the effects of different continuous cover forestry systems on habitat quality for birds.
Continued or increased use of tree retentions	X	X		X	Habitat improvement for some species (e.g., nest

(cont.)

Table 14.1 (*cont.*)

Process or change	1. Biophysical changes	2. Climate change mitigation	3. Climate adaptation	4. Demand for wood products	5. Biodiversity conservation	6. Land-use changes	7. Social values	8. Ethics	Potential implications for birds
in clearcutting forestry [Chapters 6, 13]									trees, feeding sites, improved connectivity). PRIORITY RESEARCH AREA: Understanding the large-scale and long-term effects of green-tree retention on forest bird populations in managed landscapes.
Increased use of ecological forest restoration methods in existing forest (e.g., active deadwood creation) [Chapter 13]					X				Habitat improvement for some species (e.g., woodpeckers feeding on dead trees).
Setting aside forest for free development (i.e., no management) [Chapters 6, 13]		X			X		X	X	Increase in late-seral habitats and structurally complex forest.
Afforestation [Chapters 8, 10]		X		X		X			Habitat improvement for some species, depending on the characteristics of the planted forest. Initial massive increase in early growth forest. Negative impacts on farmland specialists.

Pressure/Driver		Consequences for birds
Abandonment of traditional grazing land or cultivation on marginal land [Chapter 9]	X	Less habitat for forest birds depending on semi-open forest ecosystems including tree-line habitats. Negative impacts on farmland specialists. Gradual increase in large areas of old forest.
Expansion of recreation activities, especially snow sports in the mountains [Chapter 7]	X	Habitat degradation due to direct disturbance by humans. Habitat loss due to expanding infrastructure. New opportunities for species associated with human settlements (e.g., some Corvidae).
Increasing non-productive use of urban/suburban forests [Chapter 14]	X	Habitat improvements for birds linked to older seral stages of forests (only those species that will tolerate an urban environment) as well as for users of fine scale habitat mosaic. PRIORITY RESEARCH AREA: Develop better understanding of the tolerance of different species to urban contexts and of the dynamics of urban bird populations.

(cont.)

Table 14.1 (cont.)

Process or change	1. Biophysical changes	2. Climate change mitigation	3. Climate adaptation	4. Demand for wood products	5. Biodiversity conservation	6. Land-use changes	7. Social values	8. Ethics	Potential implications for birds
Cessation of predator hunting and persecution [Chapter 12]							X	X	Further increase in generalist predators (Corvidae, foxes, etc.) affecting breeding success and habitat quality by increased predation pressure.
Gradual disappearance of trapping and hunting of migratory birds (e.g., in Mediterranean areas) [Chapter 12]							X	X	Increased survival of migrating forest birds.
Increasing ungulate populations in forests [Chapter 13]	X						X	X	Removal of woodland understorey and reduced recruitment of trees. Negative effects on bird species requiring complex vegetation structures and special tree species (e.g., aspen as a preferred substrate for hole excavation, rowan as a source of berries).

In many northern countries, the past decades have been characterised by increased consideration of biodiversity conservation within industrial forestry, mainly by retaining trees at clearcutting and establishing 'set-aside' areas where harvesting is not done (see, for example, Angelstam *et al.* 2011; Simonsson *et al.* 2015; Chapter 6). Considering that these conservation measures have a relatively short history of implementation, it is still too early to observe their full-scale, long-term effects on habitat availability (Roberge *et al.* 2015). Nevertheless, recent changes in the characteristics of Swedish forests linked to environmental considerations (increases in areas of old forest, retention trees and deadwood) have coincided with positive population trends for several forest bird species, both generalists and specialists (Ram *et al.* 2017). We call for future research evaluating the long-term and large-scale effects of these recently adopted conservation measures on birds, for example through landscape-scale modelling studies (e.g., Mönkkönen *et al.* 2014). In addition to more passive tree retention and forest protection approaches, a number of active measures for actual re-creation or restoration of key forest habitats are also being introduced on a larger scale (e.g., mechanical deadwood creation, prescribed burning), with positive short-term effects on birds of conservation concern (e.g., Kalies *et al.* 2010; Versluijs *et al.* 2017). Even within plantation forests there are opportunities to improve habitat quality and create new kinds of wildlife habitat (Chapter 10). Moreover, in both Europe and North America, there is increased recognition of the mechanisms by which burgeoning deer numbers can affect habitat quality for birds (e.g., Newson *et al.* 2012; Holt *et al.* 2013a, b; Chollet & Martin 2013; Table 14.1) and of the need to develop integrated deer and forest management approaches (Fuller 2013; Eichhorn *et al.* 2017).

One of the main shifts in forest management outside the boreal zone is the increasing use of continuous cover systems. These systems, sometimes termed 'irregular forestry', are highly variable in that they range from single tree harvesting to small-scale patch felling. Whilst there are several studies in North America, the implications for birds and other wildlife of the diverse forms of continuous cover management have scarcely been explored in Europe (Chapter 13; Table 14.1).

A limited number of modelling studies have addressed how future shifts in forest management could affect bird communities. Mitchell *et al.* (2008) modelled how different management alternatives (limiting the size of clearcuts, setting aside older stands, no active management) would affect forest birds over a 40-year time span at four locations in the southeastern US. Among the different management scenarios tested, in addition to 'no active management', the alternative with the lowest size of clearcuts (24 ha) secured a stable and positive outcome for the forest bird community in the studied landscape. Nixon *et al.* (2014) evaluated the effects on five target bird species of four management scenarios (current management, no conservation action, forest conservation easement and ecological forestry) for Michigan's Upper Peninsula, modelled 100 years into the future. Collectively, the ecological forestry scenario with the smallest total area of even-aged early seral management (i.e., least harvesting) was ranked as the best. In northern Japan, Toyoshima *et al.* (2013) demonstrated possible effects of different management strategies in larch *Larix kaempferi* plantations, Todo fir *Abies sachalinensis* plantations and natural forests over the next 100 years on three different guilds of forest birds: hole-nesters, early successional species and species linked to mature coniferous forests. The scenario that involved a decreased intensity of forest management clearly promoted hole-nesters and species linked to mature coniferous forest, while high replanting rates after clearcutting would support early successional species.

For the production forest landscapes of central Finland, Mönkkönen *et al.* (2014) explored biodiversity and economic outcomes of different forest management strategies using, amongst other biodiversity indicators, five bird species specialised on different habitats. Over a 50-year planning horizon, setting aside the whole landscape from forest management was the most beneficial strategy for three-toed woodpecker *Picoides tridactylus*, lesser spotted woodpecker *Dryobates minor* and long-tailed tit *Aegithalos caudatus*. Extending the rotations by 30 years was the best strategy for capercaillie *Tetrao urogallus*, and enhanced green-tree retention proved best for hazel grouse *Tetrastes bonasia*. Even though we can expect species-specific responses to future shifts in forest management systems, it seems that increased areas of set-asides (with low or no human intervention) as well as less intensive forestry methods, such as prolonged rotations and increased green-tree retention, would be beneficial for forest specialist species. However, these all imply economic costs, meaning that future management planning will require exploring and finding acceptable trade-offs.

14.2.2 Effects of Climate Change and Potential Mitigation through Management

Nearly three decades ago, in the introduction to the book *Biogeography and Ecology of Forest Bird Communities*, Keast (1990) focused mostly on forest loss and degradation – logging of tropical forests, slash-and-burn agriculture, forestry intensification – and their negative effects on biodiversity and avifauna. Such habitat changes have largely persisted over the intervening decades, and in many regions they have become more severe. When Keast's book was written nearly 30 years ago, climate change was not considered as the profoundly pressing issue it has become today. In one of the first publications warning about negative effects of climate change on forests and birds, Schneider (1992) simply pointed to the fact that the more rapid the climatic change, the higher the probability of disruption and 'surprise' in the ecosystems affected. Since then, hundreds of relevant studies have been conducted, predicting future developments under different climate change scenarios. Birds in general are predicted to be dramatically affected by climate warming (see review by Pearce-Higgins & Green 2014); every degree Celsius increase in temperature could cause the extinction of 100–500 species (Sekercioglu et al. 2008). Below we present some examples of studies that address the future responses of forest birds to a changed climate.

Matthews et al. (2011) related the spatial redistribution of 39 tree species in the eastern United States to future availability of habitat for birds. They predicted that, due to climate change, the mean 'habitat centres' for 147 studied bird species are projected to move, on average, between 98 and 203 km to the north-northeast by the end of the 21st century. They also suggested that under increased temperatures, residents would be more likely to see their ranges expand due to strong positive relationships between their northern boundary limits and winter temperatures, while migratory species may be at greater risk of losing considerable areas of their current habitats (see also Root 1988; Lemoine & Böhning-Gaese 2003). Relatively more species that have forests as their primary habitat (53 species) were predicted to experience a decline of habitat availability in comparison to non-forest species, which were more often predicted to gain habitat.

Birds are obviously tracking the warming climate, but apparently not always fast enough, resulting in substantial spatial and temporal lags in relation to projected habitat suitability (e.g., Both et al. 2006; Devictor et al. 2008). Predicted northern shifts in habitat distribution for 10 boreal forest bird species in Finland are associated with an expected loss of suitable habitat area resulting from climate change, on average 54% by 2021–2050 and 81% by 2051–2080 (Virkkala et al. 2008). A complete loss of suitable habitat was predicted for two species, two-barred crossbill *Loxia leucoptera* and pine grosbeak *Pinicola enucleator*.

The effects of climate change need to be considered simultaneously with those of direct anthropogenic impacts on forest ecosystems. Results from the Leech and Crick (2007) review of (observed and potential) impacts of climate change on birds breeding in temperate woodlands of the western Palearctic pointed to direct and indirect effects on the survival rates and productivity of bird species. These authors claimed that unless active management is undertaken, the relatively low dispersal rates of tree species could lead to a decrease in the total area of some forest habitat types, because losses at the southern edge of the range are likely to occur much quicker than expansion at the northern edge. The question is, how likely is it that active forest management will be effective in counteracting the expected negative effects of the changing climate? Using a modelling approach, Gottschalk and Reiners (2015) explored the effects of different scenarios of forest conversion (from coniferous to deciduous) as a mitigation measure on 25 common forest bird species in Germany. Climate change alone predicted the decline of 19 species out of the 25 (6 species increased). However, forest conversion to deciduous modulated climate change effects in such a way that it amplified (15 species) and weakened (10 species) the predicted gains and losses of the species' population sizes due to climate change. The strongest positive mitigation effects were predicted for marsh tit *Poecile palustris*, hawfinch *Coccothraustes coccothraustes*, blue tit *Cyanistes caeruleus* and robin *Erithacus rubecula*, with forest conversion completely compensating for climate-driven population losses in these species.

In North America, LeBrun *et al.* (2017) compared predicted effects of future climate change and different management scenarios on five species of birds linked to different forest successional phases (worm-eating warbler *Helmitheros vermivorum*, pine warbler *Setophaga pinus*, prairie warbler *S. discolor*, northern bobwhite *Colinus virginianus*, blue-winged warbler *Vermivora cyanoptera*). The models forecasted that management had a greater impact on their abundance (almost 50% change under some scenarios) than climate (<3% change). In contrast, simulation of climate change effects on a Neotropical migrant (ovenbird *Seiurus aurocapilla*) in forests of New Brunswick, Canada, under different forest management scenarios predicted a much larger impact of climate change on the local population of this species over the coming 80 years due to expected negative changes in habitat quality (Haché *et al.* 2016).

It appears that even if some general recommendations can be devised for climate change mitigation on biodiversity (Heller & Zavaleta 2009), the life history of particular species and the local and regional characteristics of forest environments are going to be crucial in determining outcomes. In subalpine forests, for example, Braunisch *et al.* (2014) found that adaptive habitat management (e.g., increasing numbers of snags, creating gaps, increasing bilberry *Vaccinium* spp. cover) can, to some extent, buffer the negative effects of climate change on forest-dwelling bird species (see also Chapter 7). However, it partly requires working against the natural dynamics (e.g., increasing the length of 'unnatural' edges or changing the tree-species composition). Moreover, such management may be inconsistent with adaptive forestry practices implemented to cope with the economic risks of climate change, such as shortening of harvesting periods (Roberge *et al.* 2016) or changes in the tree-species composition (Felton *et al.* 2016a).

Where the increasing woodfuel market leads to more intensive management of forest, it can potentially improve conditions for young-growth species (Fuller *et al.* 2007a; Fuller 2013). Nevertheless, the associated shortening of rotations that may be expected would reduce quantities of deadwood and thereby be detrimental to many forest specialists. Grodsky *et al.* (2016a, b) examined the importance of forest-harvest residues for early successional birds in the south-eastern United States and the effect of removing these residues on increasing bioenergy production. They found that harvest residues were of rather limited importance for birds. In Europe, however, several breeding and wintering bird species appear to use downed wood in addition to vegetation, and harvest residues may initially provide food and cover for early-successional birds in regenerating stands prior to vegetation regrowth. Also, an increasing interest in harvesting stumps to produce bioenergy is feared to have wider negative consequences on forest biodiversity (Walmsley & Godbold 2010). Even if there is no available empirical evidence of negative effects on forest birds, one can expect detrimental effects of such practices on black woodpecker *Dryocopus martius*, since cut stumps form a major foraging substrate for this large bird specialised on a carpenter ant *Camponotus* spp. diet (Mikusiński 1997; Rolstad *et al.* 1998). Recently, Tarr *et al.* (2017) predicted gains and losses of wildlife habitat (including habitat of seven forest bird species) originating from projected bioenergy-induced landscape changes in the south-eastern United States under a 'business as usual' scenario. For several mature forest species, including prothonotary *Protonotaria citrea*, Swainson's *Limnothlypis swainsonii* and cerulean *Setophaga cerulea* warblers, an increased area of conventional forestry due to bioenergy demands resulted in additional habitat losses.

Overall, some of the future changes to forest management expected as a response to climate change may have negative impacts on forest biodiversity, while others may prove beneficial (Felton *et al.* 2016b).

Examples of measures with potentially negative impacts on specialised forest birds include shortened rotation lengths to decrease the risk of windthrow damage, logging residue extraction and the planting of introduced tree species for biofuel production. On the other hand, some climate change adaptation or mitigation measures may have positive implications for declining bird species, e.g., the planting of more broad-leaved trees to decrease windthrow risks, the use of continuous cover forestry and the adoption of prolonged rotations for carbon sequestration (Felton *et al.* 2016b).

14.2.3 Forests in an Urbanising World

The proportion of the world's population living in urban areas has increased rapidly in the past decades. Today, more than half of the people on the planet live in cities and towns, and this urbanisation process is expected to continue in the future (UPPF 2017). Urbanisation is widely regarded as one of the major threats to biodiversity, with a homogenising effect on physical environments, usually replacing natural or semi-natural ecosystems with extremely simplified systems supporting filtered remnants of native species (McKinney 2006). Furthermore, the movement of people from the countryside to cities (i.e., rural exodus; Sanz *et al.* 2013) may have large consequences for the development of forest environments in the gradually depopulated countryside (see below).

Bird communities of urban environments are quite different from those of rural landscapes; urbanisation tends to favour omnivorous, granivorous and hole-nesting species and typically leads to an increase in avian biomass but a reduction in richness (Chace & Walsh 2006). High levels of fragmentation, the typically small size of urban woodlots, various direct human-induced disturbances (e.g., free ranging pets, noise and direct encounters with humans and vehicles), the presence of bird feeders and other food sources, the large areas covered by artificial surfaces, the availability of artificial nesting sites, and modified predation pressure all shape forest bird communities in urban areas (Melles *et al.* 2003; Sandström *et al.* 2006; Rodewald & Shustack 2008; Hedblom & Söderström 2010; Minor & Urban 2010; Marzluff *et al.* 2016). However, many forest birds, including some specialised species, are able to adapt to urban environments, particularly if these provide structurally complex woody vegetation (Rutz 2008; Evans *et al.* 2009; Minor & Urban 2010; Chapter 6). For some species, urban forests may constitute sink habitats, while others may never colonise urban forests.

Although both regional and local factors are important in structuring urban bird communities, several studies point to a greater importance of the latter. Evans *et al.* (2009) suggested that urban bird communities respond positively to increasing structural complexity, species richness of woody vegetation and supplementary feeding, and negatively to human disturbance. In a meta-analysis of 18 studies, Clergeau *et al.* (2001) concluded that urban bird communities are independent of the bird diversity of adjacent landscapes, and that local features are more important than surrounding landscapes in determining species richness. Therefore, careful planning of existing or new green urban areas obviously has the potential to deliver positive conservation outcomes for forest avifaunas in urban settings (Mörtberg & Wallentinus 2000; Fernández-Juricic 2004; Fontana *et al.* 2011).

Urban forestry that has biodiversity conservation and recreation as the main management goals has great potential to create forests attractive to both humans and wildlife (Alvey 2006; Heyman *et al.* 2011). With an increasing interest in securing green infrastructure in cities (already established in many countries), many urban and suburban environments could support an increasing proportion of forest biodiversity, potentially creating new opportunities for forest birds. The role of forest birds in providing cultural ecosystem services (e.g., amenity values through birdsong and the visual presence of birds in otherwise largely human-dominated landscapes) might be expected to feature more strongly in the planning of future urban environments (Hedblom *et al.* 2017). There may be health benefits, too (Fuller *et al.* 2007b; Luck *et al.* 2011). The future ultimately depends, however, on the values that society places on such green infrastructure; exactly what type of biodiversity develops will depend to a large degree on the vision for these habitat patches and how they are managed.

The other key question is what will happen with forest environments in those areas where rural exodus (i.e., resettlement of people from rural to urban areas) leads to decreased human populations. Where forest cover increases through land abandonment or afforestation, new opportunities are created for habitat restoration which may improve the situation for many forest birds (e.g., Preiss *et al.* 1997; Santos *et al.* 2006; Twedt *et al.* 2006; Wilson *et al.* 2012). However, it is not necessarily positive for all forest bird species (Carrascal *et al.* 2014; Chapter 9). From a broader bird conservation perspective, there is a need to take into account the former land use (Graham *et al.* 2017) and possible losses of non-forest species of conservation interest. In some parts of Europe, much forest biodiversity has been locally sustained through traditional land-use systems, such as wood-pasture. These systems are clearly threatened by land abandonment and afforestation (Hartel *et al.* 2014; Chapter 13). Finally, the existence of vibrant human communities in rural landscapes may even sometimes create a check on highly industrialised forestry due to an appreciation of the amenities and cultural value of forests. In largely abandoned landscapes, one can expect greater opportunities for implementing very intensive forestry based on plantations of non-native, fast-growing species and the use of fertilisers, herbicides and short rotations. Summarising, the fate of forests and forest birds in an urbanising world is a very complex issue with implications both for future urban and rural areas.

14.3 Conclusions – Key Issues for Forest Bird Conservation

Knowledge concerning forest birds has been accumulating at a fast pace in recent decades. Nonetheless, many areas remain where knowledge is weak. In Table 14.1, we summarise key processes likely to affect future forests in the Northern Hemisphere as well as their expected effects on the bird fauna. We have identified areas where, in our opinion, knowledge is relatively weak and research is a priority. This list of processes, and the implications for birds, will need to be kept under constant review. With complex systems such as forests, and with many stochastic processes acting at multiple scales, predictions are never very accurate. Moreover, it is often difficult to distinguish the effects of anthropogenic and natural drivers of change. The great challenge is to consider simultaneously multi-scale factors of environmental change while accounting for phenotypic plasticity and the ability of birds to adapt (see Chapter 3).

Conservation priorities and the trajectory and traditions of research on forest birds can differ across regions, so the processes listed in Table 14.1 will not apply universally. This was well illustrated by Martin *et al.* (2012), who compared perceived conservation issues and research approaches in North America and Europe. In the case of boreal forests, there was strong convergence in issues and approaches on the two continents, with substantial intercontinental collaboration amongst ecologists. However, in the case of temperate broadleaved forest, there were more differences. Regarding forest fragmentation, for example, in North America there has been a stronger focus on the effect of nest predation, whereas in Europe attention has been mainly on individuals, populations and dispersal. Long-term studies of focal species are more common in Europe, and there has been a strong focus on species that use nest boxes.

Population dynamics of migratory species may be driven by factors operating outside the breeding season, i.e., during migration or in wintering grounds (Holmes 2007; Ockendon et al. 2012; Chapters 11, 12). Where populations are declining, it is crucial to identify at what stage of the annual cycle limiting factors are operating. There is generally a dearth of information about the requirements of forest birds outside the breeding season. This includes (i) habitat use and resource needs in the immediate post-breeding season (better information exists for North American than European birds) and (ii) habitat use in winter. The latter point applies to all species, whether residents, short-distance migrants or long-distance migrants.

In Table 14.1, we focus on processes that are expected to result in present and future conservation challenges. Whilst there is great scope to advocate for more basic research on the behaviour and ecology of forest birds, we have refrained from making recommendations as it would have required a formal horizon scanning exercise involving a multitude of leading scientists representing a range of ornithological research fields. Nonetheless, we believe that knowledge of the behaviour and ecology of birds must underpin effective conservation, hence sharp distinctions between basic and applied research are rather unhelpful.

The future of forest bird communities, and especially of species for which only forests can provide habitat, relies partially on natural processes that we do not fully understand and have limited ability to harness, and also on a complex of human-driven factors that potentially are more amenable to management. In most cases, the successful management and conservation of forest bird communities will need transdisciplinary approaches, where strong ecological knowledge works in tandem with deep understanding of human actions at multiple spatial and temporal scales (e.g., Alberti et al. 2011). Nowhere is this integrated approach more relevant than in European forests, which have such a long history of profound modification by humans and are now required to deliver multiple functions. Finding solutions to protect and restore forests in ways that are tailored to diverse regional, cultural and historical contexts is the challenge that lies ahead.

Acknowledgements

We thank Kathy Martin and Martin Green for their constructive comments.

References

Agrawal, A., Chhatre, A. & Hardin, R. (2008) Changing governance of the world's forests. *Science*, **320**, 1460–1462.

Alberti, M., Asbjornsen, H., Baker, L.A. *et al.* (2011) Research on coupled human and natural systems (CHANS): Approach, challenges, and strategies. *The Bulletin of the Ecological Society of America*, **92**, 218–228.

Allen, C.D., Macalady, A.K., Chenchouni, H. *et al.* (2010) A global overview of drought and heat-induced tree mortality reveals emerging climate change risks for forests. *Forest Ecology and Management*, **259**, 660–684.

Alvey, A.A. (2006) Promoting and preserving biodiversity in the urban forest. *Urban Forestry and Urban Greening*, **5**, 195–201.

Angelstam, P., Andersson, K., Axelsson, R., Elbakidze, M., Jonsson, B.G. & Roberge, J.-M. (2011) Protecting forest areas for biodiversity in Sweden 1991–2010: The policy implementation process and outcomes on the ground. *Silva Fennica*, **45**, 1111–1133.

Barnes, G., Pillatt, T. & Williamson, T. (2016) Rural tree populations in England: Historic character and future planting policy. *British Wildlife*, **27**, 392–401.

Bedia, J., Herrera, S., Camia, A., Moreno, J.M. & Gutierrez J.M. (2014) Forest fire danger projections in the Mediterranean using ENSEMBLES regional climate change scenarios. *Climatic Change*, **122**, 185–199.

Berg, M.P., Kiers T.E., Driessen, G. *et al.* (2010) Adapt or disperse: Understanding species persistence in a changing world. *Global Change Biology*, **16**, 587–598.

Both, C., Bouwhuis, S., Lessells, C.M. & Visser, M.E. (2006) Climate change and population declines in a long-distance migratory bird. *Nature*, **441**, 81–83.

Braunisch, V., Coppes, J., Arlettaz, R., Suchant, R., Zellweger, F. & Bollmann, K. (2014) Temperate mountain forest biodiversity under climate change: Compensating negative effects by increasing structural complexity. *PLoS ONE*, **9** (**5**): e97718.

Brockerhoff, E.G., Jactel, H., Parrotta, J.A., Quine, C.P. & Sayer J. (2008) Plantation forests and biodiversity: Oxymoron or opportunity? *Biodiversity and Conservation*, **17**, 925–951.

Brooks, T.M., Mittermeier, R.A., Mittermeier, C.G. *et al.* (2002) Habitat loss and extinction in the hotspots of biodiversity. *Conservation Biology*, **16**, 909–923.

Carnus, J.-M., Parrotta, J., Brockerhoff, E. *et al.* (2006) Planted forests and biodiversity. *Journal of Forestry*, **104**, 65–77.

Carrascal, L.M., Galvan, I., Sanchez-Oliver, J.S. & Rey Benayas J.M. (2014) Regional distribution patterns predict bird occurrence in Mediterranean cropland afforestations. *Ecological Research*, **29**, 203–211.

Chace, J.F. & Walsh, J.J. (2006) Urban effects on native avifauna: A review. *Landscape and Urban Planning*, **74**, 46–69.

Chazdon, R.L. (2008) Beyond deforestation: Restoring forests and ecosystem services on degraded lands. *Science*, **320**, 1458–1460.

Cheaib, A., Badeau, V., Boe, J. *et al.* (2012) Climate change impacts on tree ranges: Model intercomparison facilitates understanding and quantification of uncertainty. *Ecology Letters*, **15**, 533–544.

Chollet, S. & Martin, J.-L. (2013) Declining woodland birds in North America: Should we blame Bambi? *Diversity and Distributions*, **19**, 481–483.

Clergeau, P., Jokimäki, J. & Savard, J.-P.L. (2001) Are urban bird communities influenced by the bird diversity of adjacent landscapes? *Journal of Applied Ecology*, **38**, 1122–1134.

Danielsen, F., Beukema, H., Burgess, N. *et al.* (2009) Biofuel plantations on forested lands: Double jeopardy for biodiversity and climate. *Conservation Biology*, **23**, 348–358.

Demarais, S., Verschuyl, J.P., Roloff, G.J., Miller, D.A. & Wigley, T.B. (2017) Tamm review: Terrestrial vertebrate biodiversity and intensive forest management in the U.S. *Forest Ecology and Management*, **385**, 308–330.

Devictor, V., Julliard, R., Couvet, D. & Jiguet, F. (2008) Birds are tracking climate warming, but not fast enough. *Proceedings of the Royal Society B*, **275**, 2743–2748.

Dukes, J.S., Pontius, J., Orwig, D. *et al.* (2009) Responses of insect pests, pathogens, and invasive plant species to climate change in the forests of northeastern North America: What can we predict? *Canadian Journal of Forest Research*, **39**, 231–248.

Eichhorn, M.P., Ryding, J., Smith, M.J., Gill, R.M.A., Siriwardena, G.M. & Fuller, R.J. (2017) Effects of deer on woodland structure revealed through terrestrial laser scanning. *Journal of Applied Ecology*, **54**, 1615–1626.

Elmqvist, T., Colding, J., Barthel, S. *et al.* (2004) The dynamics of social-ecological systems in urban landscapes: Stockholm and the National Urban Park, Sweden. *Annals of the New York Academy of Sciences*, **1023**, 308–322.

Evans, K.L., Newson, S.E. & Gaston, K.J. (2009) Habitat influences on urban avian assemblages. *Ibis*, **151**, 19–39.

FAO (2015) *Global Forest Resources Assessment 2015*. Rome: UN Food and Agriculture Organization.

Felton, A., Gustafsson, L., Roberge, J.-M. *et al.* (2016b) How climate change adaptation and mitigation strategies can threaten or enhance the biodiversity of production forests: Insights from Sweden. *Biological Conservation*, **194**, 11–20.

Felton, A., Nilsson, U., Sonesson, J. *et al.* (2016a) Replacing monocultures with mixed-species stands: Ecosystem service implications of two production forest alternatives in Sweden. *Ambio*, **45** (Suppl. 2), 124–139.

Fernández-Juricic, E. (2004) Spatial and temporal analysis of the distribution of forest specialists in an urban-fragmented landscape (Madrid, Spain): Implications for local and regional bird conservation. *Landscape and Urban Planning*, **69**, 17–32.

Fischer, A., Marshall, P. & Camp, A. (2013) Disturbances in deciduous temperate forest ecosystems of the northern hemisphere: Their effects on both recent and future forest development. *Biodiversity and Conservation*, **22**, 1863–1893.

Fontana, S., Sattler, T., Bontadina, F. & Moretti, M. (2011) How to manage the urban green to improve bird diversity and community structure. *Landscape and Urban Planning*, **101**, 278–285.

Fuller, R.A., Irvine, K.N., Devine-Wright, P., Warren, P.H. & Gaston, K.J. (2007b) Psychological benefits of greenspace increase with biodiversity. *Biology Letters*, **3**, 390–394.

Fuller, R.J. (2013) Searching for biodiversity gains through woodfuel and forest management. *Journal of Applied Ecology*, **50**, 1295–1300.

Fuller, R.J., Smith, K.W., Grice, P.V., Currie, F.A. & Quine, C.P. (2007a) Habitat change and woodland birds in Britain: Implications for management and future research. *Ibis*, **149** (Suppl. 2), 261–268.

Gauthier, S., Bernier, P., Kuuluvainen, T., Shvidenko, A.Z. & Schepaschenko, D.G. (2015) Boreal forest health and global change. *Science*, **349**, 819–822.

Gómez-Aparicio, L., García-Valdés, R., Ruíz-Benito, P. & Zavala, M.A. (2011) Disentangling the relative importance of climate, size and competition on tree growth in Iberian forests: Implications for forest management under global change. *Global Change Biology*, **17**, 2400–2414.

Gottschalk, T.K. & Reiners, T.E. (2015) Forest conversion can help to mitigate impacts of climate change on common forest birds. *Annals of Forest Science*, **72**, 335–348.

Graham, C.T., Wilson, M.W., Gittings, T. *et al.* (2017) Implications of afforestation for bird communities: The importance of preceding land-use type. *Biodiversity and Conservation*, **26**, 3051–3071.

Grodsky, S.M., Moorman, C.E., Fritts, S.R. *et al.* (2016b) Winter bird use of harvest residues in clearcuts and the implications of forest bioenergy harvest in the southeastern United States. *Forest Ecology and Management*, **379**, 91–101.

Grodsky, S.M., Moorman, C.E., Fritts, S.R., Castleberry, S.B. & Wigley, T.B. (2016a) Breeding, early-successional bird response to forest harvests for bioenergy. *PLoS ONE*, **11**, e0165070.

Haché, S., Cameron, R., Villard, M.-A., Bayne, E.M. & MacLean, D.A. (2016) Demographic response of a neotropical migrant songbird to forest management and climate change scenarios. *Forest Ecology and Management*, **359**, 309–320.

Hamann, A. & Aitken, S.N. (2013) Conservation planning under climate change: Accounting for adaptive potential and migration capacity in species distribution models. *Diversity and Distributions*, **19**, 268–280.

Hamann, A. & Wang, T. (2006) Potential effects of climate change on ecosystem and tree species distribution in British Columbia. *Ecology*, **87**, 2773–2786.

Hansen, M.C., Potapov, P.V., Moore, R. *et al.* (2013) High-resolution global maps of 21st-century forest cover change. *Science*, **342**, 850–853.

Hartel, T., Hanspach, J., Abson, D.J., Mathe, O., Moga, C.I. & Fischer, J. (2014) Bird communities in traditional wood-pastures with changing management in Eastern Europe. *Basic and Applied Ecology*, **15**, 385–395.

Hartley, M.J. (2002) Rationale and methods for conserving biodiversity in plantation forests. *Forest Ecology and Management*, **155**, 81–95.

Hedblom, M., Knez, I., Ode Sang, Å. & Gunnarsson, B. (2017) Evaluation of natural sounds in urban greenery: Potential impact for urban nature preservation. *Royal Society Open Science*, **4**, Article no. 170037.

Hedblom, M. & Söderström, B. (2010) Landscape effects on birds in urban woodlands: An analysis of 34 Swedish cities. *Journal of Biogeography*, **37**, 1302–1316.

Heller, N.E. & Zavaleta, E.S. (2009) Biodiversity management in the face of climate change: A review of 22 years of recommendations. *Biological Conservation*, **142**, 14–32.

Heyman, E., Gunnarsson, B., Stenseke, M., Henningsson, S. & Tim, G. (2011) Openness as a key-variable for analysis of management trade-offs in urban woodlands. *Urban Forestry and Urban Greening*, **10**, 281–293.

Heywood, V.H. & Watson, R.T. (1995) *Global Biodiversity Assessment*. Cambridge: Cambridge University Press.

Holmes, R.T. (2007) Understanding population change in migratory songbirds: Long-term and experimental studies of Neotropical migrants in breeding and wintering areas. *Ibis*, **149** (Suppl. 2), 2–13.

Holt, C.A., Fuller, R.J. & Dolman, P.M. (2013a) Deer reduce habitat quality for a woodland songbird: Evidence from settlement patterns, demographic parameters, and body condition. *Auk*, **130**, 13–20.

Holt, C.A., Fuller, R.J. & Dolman, P.M. (2013b) Exclusion of deer affects responses of birds to woodland regeneration in winter and summer. *Ibis*, **156**, 116–131.

Hosonuma, N., Herold, M., De Sy, V. *et al.* (2012) An assessment of deforestation and forest degradation drivers in developing countries. *Environmental Research Letters*, **7**, Article no. 044009.

Kalies, E.L., Chambers, C.L. & Covington, W.W. (2010) Wildlife responses to thinning and burning treatments in southwestern conifer forests: A meta-analysis. *Forest Ecology and Management*, **259**, 333–342.

Keast, A. (1990) *Biogeography and Ecology of Forest Bird Communities*. The Hague: SPB Academic Publishing.

Keenan, R.J., Reams, G.A., Achard, F., de Freitas, J., Grainger, A. & Lindquist, E. (2015) Dynamics of global forest area: Results from the FAO Global Forest Resources Assessment 2015. *Forest Ecology and Management*, **352**, 9–20.

Koh, L.P. & Ghazoul, J. (2008) Biofuels, biodiversity, and people: Understanding the conflicts and finding opportunities. *Biological Conservation*, **141**, 2450–2460.

Krosby, M., Tewksbury, J., Haddad, N.M. & Hoekstra, J. (2010) Ecological connectivity for a changing climate. *Conservation Biology*, **24**, 1686–1689.

La Porta, N., Capretti, P., Thomsen, I.M., Kasanen, R., Hietala, A.M. & Von Weissenberg, K. (2008) Forest pathogens with higher damage potential due to climate change in Europe. *Canadian Journal of Plant Pathology*, **30**, 177–195.

Lazdinis, M., Roberge, J.-M., Kurlavičius, P., Mozgeris, G. & Angelstam, P. (2005) Afforestation planning and biodiversity conservation: Predicting effects on habitat functionality in Lithuania. *Journal of Environmental Planning and Management*, **48**, 331–348.

LeBrun, J.J., Schneiderman, J.E., Thompson, F.R. *et al.* (2017) Bird response to future climate and forest management focused on mitigating climate change. *Landscape Ecology*, **32**, 1433–1446.

Leech, D.I. & Crick, H.Q.P. (2007) Influence of climate change on the abundance, distribution and phenology of woodland bird species in temperate regions. *Ibis*, **149** (Suppl. 2), 128–145.

Lemoine N. & Böhning-Gaese, K. (2003) Potential impact of global climate change on species richness of long-distance migrants. *Conservation Biology*, **17**, 577–586.

Lindenmayer, D.B., Franklin, J.F. & Fischer, J. (2006) General management principles and a checklist of strategies to guide forest biodiversity conservation. *Biological Conservation*, **131**, 433–445.

Lõhmus, K. & Liira, J. (2013) Old rural parks support higher biodiversity than forest remnants. *Basic and Applied Ecology*, **14**, 165–173.

Luck, G.W., Davidson, P., Boxall, D. & Smallbone, L. (2011) Relations between urban bird and plant communities and human well-being and connection to nature. *Conservation Biology*, **25**, 816–826.

Maklakov, A.A., Immler, S., Gonzalez-Voyer, A., Ronn, J. & Kolm, N. (2011) Brains and the city: Big-brained passerine birds succeed in urban environments. *Biology Letters*, **7**, 730–732.

Manning, A.D., Fischer, J. & Lindenmayer D.B. (2006) Scattered trees are keystone structures: Implications for conservation. *Biological Conservation*, **132**, 311–321.

Martin, J.-L., Drapeau, P., Fahrig, L. *et al.* (2012) Birds in cultural landscapes: Actual and perceived differences between northeastern North America and western Europe. In *Birds and Habitat: Relationships in Changing Landscapes*. Fuller, R.J. (ed.). Cambridge: Cambridge University Press, pp. 481–515.

Marzluff, J.M., Clucas, B., Oleyar, M.D. & DeLap, J. (2016) The causal response of avian communities to suburban development: A quasi-experimental, longitudinal study. *Urban Ecosystems*, **19**, 1597–1621.

Matthews, S.N., Iverson, L.R., Prasad, A.M. & Peters, M.P. (2011) Changes in potential habitat of 147 North American breeding bird species in response to redistribution of trees and climate following predicted climate change. *Ecography*, **34**, 933–945.

McKinney, M.L. (2006) Urbanization as a major cause of biotic homogenization. *Biological Conservation*, **127**, 247–260.

Melles, S., Glenn, S. & Martin, K. (2003) Urban bird diversity and landscape complexity: Species-environment associations along a multiscale habitat gradient. *Ecology and Society*, **7** (**1**), 5.

Mikusiński, G. (1997) Winter foraging of the black woodpecker *Dryocopus martius* in managed forest in south-central Sweden. *Ornis Fennica*, **74**, 161–166.

Millar, C.I., Stephenson, N.L. & Stephens, S.L. (2007) Climate change and forests of the future: Managing in the face of uncertainty. *Ecological Applications*, **17**, 2145–2151.

Millennium Ecosystem Assessment (2005) *Ecosystems and Human Well-being: Synthesis.* Washington, DC: Island Press.

Minor, E. & Urban, D. (2010) Forest bird communities across a gradient of urban development. *Urban Ecosystems*, **13**, 51–71.

Mitchell, M.S., Reynolds-Hogland, M.J., Smith, M.L. *et al.* (2008) Projected long-term response of Southeastern birds to forest management. *Forest Ecology and Management*, **256**, 1884–1896.

Mönkkönen, M., Juutinen, A., Mazziotta, A. *et al.* (2014) Spatially dynamic forest management to sustain biodiversity and economic returns. *Journal of Environmental Management*, **134**, 80–89.

Mörtberg, U. & Wallentinus, H.-G. (2000) Red-listed forest bird species in an urban environment – Assessment of green space corridors. *Landscape and Urban Planning*, **50**, 215–226.

Newson, S.E., Johnston, A., Renwick, A.R., Baillie, S.R. & Fuller, R.J. (2012) Modelling large-scale relationships between changes in woodland deer and bird populations. *Journal of Applied Ecology*, **49**, 278–286.

Nixon, K., Silbernagel, J., Price, J., Miller, N. & Swaty, R. (2014) Habitat availability for multiple avian species under modeled alternative conservation scenarios in the Two Hearted River watershed in Michigan, USA. *Journal for Nature Conservation*, **22**, 302–317.

Noss, R.F. (2001) Beyond Kyoto: Forest management in a time of rapid climate change. *Conservation Biology*, **15**, 578–590.

Ockendon, N., Hewson, C.M., Johnston, A. & Atkinson, P.W. (2012) Declines in British-breeding populations of Afro-Palaearctic migrant birds are linked to bioclimatic wintering zone in Africa, possibly via constraints on arrival time advancement. *Bird Study*, **59**, 111–125.

Paillet, Y., Bergès, L., Hjältén, J. *et al.* (2010) Biodiversity differences between managed and unmanaged forests: Meta-analysis of species richness in Europe. *Conservation Biology*, **24**, 101–112.

Pautasso, M. (2013) *Phytophthora ramorum* – A pathogen linking network epidemiology, landscape pathology and conservation biogeography. *CAB Reviews*, **8**, no. 024.

Pautasso, M., Aas, G., Queloz, V. & Holdenrieder, O. (2013) European ash (*Fraxinus excelsior*) dieback – A conservation biology challenge. *Biological Conservation*, **158**, 37–49.

Pearce-Higgins, J.W. & Green, R.E. (2014) *Birds and Climate Change: Impacts and Conservation Responses.* Cambridge: Cambridge University Press.

Pereira, H.M., Leadley, P.W., Proença, V. *et al.* (2010) Scenarios for global biodiversity in the 21st century. *Science*, **330**, 1496–1501.

Plieninger, T. (2012) Monitoring directions and rates of change in trees outside forests through multitemporal analysis of map sequences. *Applied Geography*, **32**, 566–576.

Potapov, P., Yaroshenko, A., Turubanova, S. *et al.* (2008) Mapping the world's intact forest landscapes by remote sensing. *Ecology and Society*, **13**, Article no. 51.

Preiss, E., Martin, J.-L. & Debussche, M. (1997) Rural depopulation and recent landscape changes in a Mediterranean region: Consequences to the breeding avifauna. *Landscape Ecology*, **12**, 51–61.

Ram, D., Axelsson, A.-L., Green, M., Smith, H.G. & Lindström, Å. (2017) What drives current population trends in forest birds – Forest quantity, quality or climate? A large-scale analysis from northern Europe. *Forest Ecology and Management*, **385**, 177–188.

Ramsfield, T.D., Bentz, B.J., Faccoli, M., Jactel, H. & Brockerhoff, E.G. (2016) Forest health in a changing world: Effects of globalization and climate change on forest insect and pathogen impacts. *Forestry*, **89**, 245–252.

Roberge, J.-M., Lämås, T., Lundmark, T., Ranius, T., Felton, A. & Nordin, A. (2015) Relative contributions of set-asides and tree retention to the long-term availability of key forest biodiversity structures at the landscape scale. *Journal of Environmental Management*, **154**, 284–292.

Roberge, J-M., Laudon, H., Björkman, C. *et al.* (2016) Socio-ecological implications of modifying rotation lengths in forestry. *Ambio*, **45** (Suppl. 2), 109–123.

Rodewald, A.D. & Shustack, D.P. (2008) Urban flight: Understanding individual and population-level responses of Nearctic-Neotropical migratory birds to urbanization. *Journal of Animal Ecology*, **77**, 83–91.

Rolstad, J., Majewski, P. & Rolstad E. (1998) Black woodpecker use of habitats and feeding substrates in a managed Scandinavian forest. *Journal of Wildlife Management*, **62**, 11–23.

Root, T. 1988. Environmental factors associated with avian distributional boundaries. *Journal of Biogeography*, **15**, 489–505.

Rudel, T.K., Coomes, O.T., Moran, E. *et al.* (2005) Forest transitions: Towards a global understanding of land use change. *Global Environmental Change*, **15**, 23–31.

Rutz, C. (2008) The establishment of an urban bird population. *Journal of Animal Ecology*, **77**, 1008–1019.

Sandström, U.G., Angelstam, P. & Mikusiński, G. (2006) Ecological diversity of birds in relation to the structure of urban green space. *Landscape and Urban Planning*, **77**, 39–53.

Santos, T., Telleria, J.L., Diaz, M. & Carbonell, R. (2006) Evaluating the benefits of CAP reforms: Can afforestations restore bird diversity in Mediterranean Spain? *Basic and Applied Ecology*, **7**, 483–495.

Sanz, A.S.R., Fernandez, C., Mouillot, F., Ferrat, L., Istria, D. & Pasqualini, V. (2013) Long-term forest dynamics and land-use abandonment in the Mediterranean Mountains, Corsica, France. *Ecology and Society*, **18** (2), Article no. 38.

Schneider, S.H. (1992) Global climate change: Ecosystems effects. *Interdisciplinary Science Reviews*, **17**, 142–148.

Sekercioglu, C.H., Schneider, S.H., Fay, J.P. & Loarie, S.R. (2008) Climate change, elevational range shifts, and bird extinctions. *Conservation Biology*, **22**, 140–150.

Simonsson, P., Gustafsson, L. & Ostlund, L. (2015) Retention forestry in Sweden: Driving forces, debate and implementation 1968–2003. *Scandinavian Journal of Forest Research*, **30**, 154–173.

Sloan, S. & Sayer, J.A. (2015) Forest Resources Assessment of 2015 shows positive global trends but forest loss and degradation persist in poor tropical countries. *Forest Ecology and Management*, **352**, 134–145.

Smeets, E.M.W. & Faaij, A.P.C. (2007) Bioenergy potentials from forestry in 2050: An assessment of the drivers that determine the potentials. *Climatic Change*, **81**, 353–390.

Stocks, B.J., Fosberg, M.A., Lynham, T.J. *et al.* (1998) Climate change and forest fire potential in Russian and Canadian boreal forests. *Climatic Change*, **38**, 1–13.

Tang, L., Shao, G., Piao, Z. *et al.* (2010) Forest degradation deepens around and within protected areas in East Asia. *Biological Conservation*, **143**, 1295–1298.

Tarr, N.M., Rubino, M.J., Costanza, J.K., McKerrow, A.J., Collazo, J.A. & Abt, R.C. (2017) Projected gains and losses of wildlife habitat from bioenergy-induced landscape change. *GCB Bioenergy*, **9**, 909–923.

Toyoshima, Y., Yamaura, Y., Mitsuda, Y., Yabuhara, Y. & Nakamura, F. (2013) Reconciling wood production with bird conservation: A regional analysis using bird distribution models and forestry scenarios in Tokachi district, northern Japan. *Forest Ecology and Management*, **307**, 54–62.

Tracewski, L., Butchart, S.H.M., Donald, P.F., Evans, M., Fishpool, L.D.C. & Buchanan, G.M. (2016) Patterns of twenty-first century forest loss across a global network of important sites for biodiversity. *Remote Sensing in Ecology and Conservation*, **2** (1), 37–44.

Trumbore, S., Brando, P. & Hartmann, H. (2015) Forest health and global change. *Science*, **349**, 814–818.

Twedt, D.J., Uihlein, W.B. III & Blaine, E.A. (2006) A spatially explicit decision support model for restoration of forest bird habitat. *Conservation Biology*, **20**, 100–110.

UPPF (2017) United Nations Population Fund. www.unfpa.org/urbanization.

Versluijs, M., Eggers, S., Hjältén, J., Löfroth, T. & Roberge, J.-M. (2017) Ecological restoration in boreal forest modifies the structure of bird assemblages. *Forest Ecology and Management*, **401**, 75–88.

Virkkala, R., Heikkinen, R.K., Leikola, N. & Luoto, M. (2008) Projected large-scale range reductions of northern-boreal land bird species due to climate change. *Biological Conservation*, **141**, 1343–1353.

Visser, M.E. (2008) Keeping up with a warming world: Assessing the rate of adaptation to climate change. *Proceedings of the Royal Society B*, **275**, 649–659.

Walmsley, J.D. & Godbold, D.L. (2010) Stump harvesting for bioenergy: A review of the environmental impacts. *Forestry*, **83**, 17–38.

Weih, M. (2004) Intensive short rotation forestry in boreal climates: Present and future perspectives. *Canadian Journal of Forest Research*, **34**, 1369–1378.

Wenhua, L. (2004) Degradation and restoration of forest ecosystems in China. *Forest Ecology and Management*, **201**, 33–41.

Williams, J.W. & Jackson, S.T. (2007) Novel climates, no-analog communities, and ecological surprises. *Frontiers in Ecology and the Environment*, **5**, 475–482.

Wilson, M.W., Gittings, T., Pithon, J., Kelly, T.C., Irwin, S. & O'Halloran J. (2012) Bird diversity of afforestation habitats in Ireland: Current trends and likely impacts. *Biology and Environment: Proceedings of the Royal Irish Academy*, **112B**, 55–68.

Wotton, B.M., Nock, C.A. & Flannigan, M.D. (2010) Forest fire occurrence and climate change in Canada. *International Journal of Wildland Fire*, **19**, 253–271.

Zhu, K., Woodall, C.W. & Clark, J.S. (2012) Failure to migrate: Lack of tree range expansion in response to climate change. *Global Change Biology*, **18**, 1042–1052.

Species Index

Subject Index